B395 .H47 2007

Herrmann, Fritz-Gregor.

Words & ideas : the
roots of Plato's
2007.

DISCARD

2009 01 19

D1478399

Humber College Library
3199 Lakeshore Blvd. West
Toronto, ON M8V 1K8

WORDS AND IDEAS

1651-01

WORDS & IDEAS

The Roots of Plato's Philosophy

Fritz-Gregor Herrmann

The Classical Press of Wales

First published in 2007 by
The Classical Press of Wales
15 Rosehill Terrace, Swansea SA1 6JN
Tel: +44 (0)1792 458397
Fax: +44 (0)1792 464067
www.classicalpressofwales.co.uk

Distributor
Oxbow Books,
10 Hythe Bridge Street,
Oxford OX1 2EW
Tel: +44 (0)1865 241249
Fax: +44 (0)1865 794449

Distributor in the United States of America
The David Brown Book Co.
PO Box 511, Oakville, CT 06779
Tel: +1 (860) 945–9329
Fax: +1 (860) 945–9468

© 2007 The author

All rights reserved. No part of this publication may be reproduced, stored in a retrieval system, or transmitted, in any form or by any means, electronic, mechanical, photocopying, recording or otherwise, without the prior permission of the publisher.

ISBN 978–1-905125–20–3

A catalogue record for this book is available from the British Library

Typeset by Ernest Buckley, Clunton, Shropshire
Printed and bound in the UK by Gomer Press, Llandysul, Ceredigion, Wales

---

The Classical Press of Wales, an independent venture, was founded in 1993, initially to support the work of classicists and ancient historians in Wales and their collaborators from further afield. More recently it has published work initiated by scholars internationally. While retaining a special loyalty to Wales and the Celtic countries, the Press welcomes scholarly contributions from all parts of the world.

The symbol of the Press is the Red Kite. This bird, once widespread in Britain, was reduced by 1905 to some five individuals confined to a small area known as 'The Desert of Wales' – the upper Tywi valley. Geneticists report that the stock was saved from terminal inbreeding by the arrival of one stray female bird from Germany. After much careful protection, the Red Kite now thrives – in Wales and beyond.

parentibus. magistro.

caris, propter quos hanc lucem semper amatam
aspexi, hoc donum laetitiam pariat.
olim qui iuvenes in ludo nos docuisti,
serius hoc munus nunc tibi iusta ferat.

CONTENTS

Contents

PREFACE

μάλα γὰρ φιλοσόφου τοῦτο τὸ πάθος, τὸ θαυμάζειν· οὐ γὰρ ἄλλη ἀρχὴ φιλοσοφίας ἢ αὕτη.

This is indeed very much the predicament of the philosopher: to wonder. Indeed, there is no beginning of philosophy other than that.

My interest in Plato's words and ideas has a history of which I shall give an outline at the beginning. In order to do that, I must talk about Plato first. Socrates' words at *Theaetetus* 155d2–4, quoted above, are addressed to, and are about, the youth Theaetetus. But they could also be seen as Plato's re-interpretation of what Socrates himself had been doing, perhaps in life, certainly in Plato's own earlier dialogues. Socrates' philosophy consists not least in asking questions: 'What is justice?', 'What is courage?', 'What is modesty?', 'What is goodness?'.

These questions arise out of puzzlement. They often end in ἀπορία, a situation from which there is 'no way out'. But they also reflect the other side of wondering: admiration, respect and awe. For justice, courage, modesty and goodness are the traditional virtues of Greek culture and Greek consciousness. Socrates wonders about the values which are at the core of the society of which he is a part. Socrates, according to tradition, did not have answers to these questions. Plato did not have all the answers either. But he did have a preliminary answer: the reason why there are no answers of the traditional sort to these questions is precisely that there are some things that cannot be reduced further. When thinking about 'the good' and 'the beautiful', there is no 'definition'. This circumstance, however, does not stop Plato from asking 'what it is'. For Plato, there is an answer even if there is no 'definition'. There can be knowledge of what the good is, or what the beautiful is, without an 'account', a λόγος, that could be given. To mark this insight, Plato turned the Socratic question of 'what it is', τί ἔστιν, into a noun: 'what something is' is the 'being' of that thing, its οὐσία.[1] But when one has arrived at this point and contemplates the οὐσία of something, there is then no further questioning of the accustomed sort. Plato's answer is designed to provide an end point to the question of 'what something is', so that this end point can be the beginning of a new sort of question. These questions of a different sort increasingly occupy Plato in the dialogues which come after the *Republic*. They will not be the subject of *this* investigation.

However, the Socratic questions of 'what is justice?', 'what is courage?', 'what is modesty?' and 'what is goodness?' also lie largely outside the compass of this book. It is the middle period, the transition from Socratic asking about traditional values and traditional concepts to a different type of philosophy in Plato's later dialogues that I shall be concerned with. This middle ground is occupied by the *Phaedo*, the *Symposium* and the *Republic*. The *Republic* constitutes the summation and consummation of Plato's wrestling with Socratic questions. The *Symposium* portrays Socrates in the context of all the intellectual currents present in the urbane gatherings of Athens' cultural elite. The *Phaedo*, by contrast, links Socratic questioning with Presocratic thought. In the *Phaedo*, more than in any other dialogue before the *Republic*, Plato demarcates his own position against the positions of his philosophical predecessors.

This claim concerning the *Phaedo* is the answer to the question from which this investigation took its departure. The point of departure was the *Phaedo*, which I read in Cambridge in the academic year 1990–1. When I had to answer the question whether Plato, in the *Phaedo*, argues for the existence of Forms or, by contrast, assumes the existence of Forms in his proofs of the immortality of the soul without argument, I realized that the words for Forms which I had learned as a schoolboy, εἶδος and ἰδέα, did not appear in the *Phaedo* until just before the final argument on page 102. This was a surprise.

Having read at school chapters from Xenophon's *Memorabilia*, Plato's *Apology*, large parts of the *Crito* and the *Phaedo*, the *Symposium*, large parts of the *Republic*, and *Metaphysics* A 6.987a29–988a17, and M 4–5, 1078b7–1080a11, Aristotle's criticism of Plato's 'Theory of Forms', and in my first years at university in Munich, Heidelberg and Edinburgh the *Gorgias*, *Parmenides*, *Theaetetus* and *Ion*, I had, through no fault of my teachers, formed an altogether dogmatic view of Plato's philosophy. In studying the *Euthydemus*, the *Symposium* and the *Phaedo* between 1989 and 1991 at Cambridge, I came to see what I did *not* know. Among the many things I did not know and did not understand was why Plato did not throughout use the words for Forms, εἶδος and ἰδέα, in the dialogue that seemed to be *about* forms almost from the beginning. More fundamentally, in reading the *Phaedo* on that occasion, I realized that, once I had become aware of all the various expressions Plato employed in talking about the Forms, the two I did not understand were just those which I had learned many years before, εἶδος and ἰδέα. I realized that I did not know what these words meant. And because of that, I could not translate them any more in any meaningful way.

'What was it in the terms εἶδος and ἰδέα that made Plato choose them *at the end* of the *Phaedo*?' I did not have an answer to that question, and all the answers I could obtain from the people I asked and the books I read at the time seemed, to some extent, coloured by post-Platonic traditions. It seemed as if those Platonist traditions, whether originating with Aristotle and his successors or the Neoplatonists and their successors, did not leave room for such a question. My project – and I was aware that I was not the first to adopt this approach – was therefore to understand Plato from Plato, through Plato, and out of Plato. 'By studying the words εἶδος and ἰδέα in all of Plato, and in particular in those dialogues up to and including the *Republic*,' I thought, 'I shall find the true meaning of the words εἶδος and ἰδέα. And once I have understood the meaning of the words, I may be able to understand Plato's philosophy.'

This approach was misconceived in at least two fundamental respects: it operated with an implicit notion of 'meaning' that was inadequate, and it worked on the premise that Plato – his language and his thought – could be understood without consideration of the traditions that lay behind his philosophy. But it is impossible to understand Plato's words and ideas without an understanding of the roots of Plato's philosophy. This book is the result of an attempt to understand Plato's early philosophy against the background of what came before. The basis of this investigation is the corpus of pre-Platonic texts that have survived, in whole or in part. Its focus is the *Phaedo*. Its method is a mixture of diachronic and synchronic semantics, traditional philological commentary and philosophical analysis. Its result is a revised picture of what precisely the main philosophical influences were at a formative stage of Plato's own philosophy.

What of εἶδος and ἰδέα? It will become apparent that these two words, which were synonymous in almost all contexts in the common Greek language of the fifth century, did each have *one* philosophical domain which was entirely its own. It was a philosophical consideration that led Plato to bring them together again and make them part of his own answer to the Socratic question of 'what something is'.

This book is based on work originally undertaken for my Edinburgh PhD. In David Robinson and Christopher Strachan I had two supervisors who were prepared to meet every Wednesday afternoon to read and discuss Plato, and to extend these discussions late into the evening. One cannot wish for better supervision. I must acknowledge in particular the help of David Robinson, who 'did not believe a word of it', but who spent years to set me right in matters of Greek language and thought from Homer to Aristotle and beyond. He also read and commented on parts of the final draft of this book. To Richard Stalley and Michael Stokes, my examiners, I owe numerous important suggestions. Over the years, I have had many enjoyable conversations with Daniel Ogden; the title of this book was forged on his anvil. Graham Hogg read the penultimate draft of the whole and commented on matters of style and presentation. Antony Hatzistavrou has likewise read the penultimate draft; his questions have led me to present many points more succinctly and with greater clarity. His comments and those I received from Duncan Large and Konrad Herrmann forced me to re-write large sections of the introduction and conclusion.

I should also like to thank Paolo Crivelli, Ceri Davies, the late Michael Frede, Alan Lloyd, Ulrike Hogg, Byron Harries, Gordon Howie, Ariel Meirav, Sergio Neri, Susanna Neri, Roy Pinkerton, Ian Repath, Dory Scaltsas, the members of the Scottish Ancient Philosophy Reading Group, and colleagues at Edinburgh and Swansea. I benefited greatly from comments on material that was presented at seminars in Dublin, Edinburgh, Glasgow, Lampeter and London, and at a meeting of the Northern Association for Ancient Philosophy at Nottingham.

I have received help of a different kind from John Coxon, the eldest son of the late Allan Coxon (1909–2000), the editor of Parmenides and commentator on Plato's *Parmenides*. John Coxon presented the substantial collection of classical texts and commentaries of his father as a gift to scholars in Edinburgh. The books are now in constant use in various projects, and I am sincerely grateful to John Coxon and to Carolyn, the widow of Allan Coxon.

I should like to acknowledge the generous financial support I received from the Scottish Office in the form of a Major Scottish Studentship from 1992 to 1995, and from the Arts and Humanities Research Board in the form of a Study Leave Award in the spring of 2002. I am grateful for a term's study leave in 2002 to the University of Edinburgh, and to Swansea University for a sabbatical semester in the autumn of 2006.

Four sections of this book are developed from articles and chapters which have previously appeared elsewhere: parts of the chapter on μετέχειν in Part I in *Philosophical Inquiry* 25 (Herrmann 2003a); the chapter on οὐσία in Part III in *New Essays on Plato* (Herrmann 2006b); some material of the chapters on εἶδος in Parts II and III in *Archiv für Begriffsgeschichte* 48 (Herrmann 2006a); parts of the chapter on ἰδέα in Part III in *La catena delle cause*, edited by Carlo Natali and Stefano Maso (Herrmann 2005) – I am grateful to the editors.

Anton Powell has commented on a draft of the whole book and is thus behind both 'that-it-is' and 'what-it-is'. I am grateful to him and to the anonymous referee who recommended inclusion of the book in the CPW series. Ernest Buckley, typesetter to the press, is much more than that, as all who have had the benefit of his expertise and support agree. I should like to thank him for all his help and advice. My research students Simon Trafford and Jeremy Welch have helped with reading the proofs, which I gratefully record.

Lastly, I should like to thank my parents who never questioned my decisions and have supported me throughout, and my wife who questions all my decisions and supports me no less. This book is dedicated to my parents and to the memory of Siegfried Lohse (1932–89), who, over nine happy years at school, taught me to think Greek.

INTRODUCTION

As a philosopher and as an author of literary dialogues, Plato is unsurpassed. He is the first and, before imperial Roman times, the only Greek philosopher all of whose published works have come down to us intact. He was recognized already in antiquity as a master of literary composition, a circumstance that contributed to the survival of his works. One approach to Plato's dialogues is to discuss their content as philosophy. Another approach is to consider first the language Plato used in writing these dialogues. For, both as a philosopher and as a writer, Plato is part of a long tradition. Through explicit discussions, literary allusions and verbal echoes, Plato indicates to the readers of his dialogues how his own philosophy is intended to be understood in the context of these literary and philosophical traditions.

To the modern student of Plato, however, not all allusions to and verbal echoes of earlier writers will be obvious. This is true in particular as regards Plato's philosophical terminology. In considering his philosophical language, one can distinguish the following cases. (1) Plato himself coins a technical term to convey a new philosophical concept. (2) Plato adopts a philosophical term from one (or more) of his predecessors, either (a) adopting the philosophical concept to which the term referred or (b) adapting and adopting the term to convey a new philosophical concept. (3) Plato, in introducing a philosophical concept, mentions a philosophical term one of his predecessors had used, not in order to adopt and to employ it subsequently, but only at the point of introducing a new thought.[2]

Approaching Plato's writings through a study of his philosophical language is a preliminary step towards a study of his philosophy. An understanding of Plato's language is indispensable for an interpretation of his philosophy. But since Plato's own aim was primarily a philosophical one, we are entitled to ask how much importance Plato would have attached to the terms he adopts to express his thoughts. We can ask if there are instances of what appear to be key philosophical terms in Plato's own philosophy that in reality owe their presence in Plato's dialogues solely or primarily to their previous occurrence in the writings of earlier thinkers. Some terms may have acquired their own momentum and thus have their own history within Plato's thought by having become fruitful in his thinking and philosophy. But others may have their function exclusively or predominantly at the stage of Plato's formulating

1

a thought for the first time: once the thought is introduced, the reference to earlier philosophical thinking is no longer needed and the inherited terminology may be discarded. In investigating a set of terms deemed central to the philosophy of Plato's middle dialogues and in unearthing the roots of Plato's language and thought, one aim of this book is thus to allow the modern reader of Plato's dialogues to see what is old and what is new, what is inherited and what is distinctive in his philosophy.

The language of Plato's *Phaedo*

The range of the terms selected and of the text passages studied is closely confined: while other works of Plato's early and middle period will on occasion be adduced to sketch the intellectual and semantic context, the dialogue which forms the starting point of this investigation is the *Phaedo*. The dialogue occupies pages 57 to 118, less than a fifth of the first volume of the five-volume Oxford Classical Texts edition. Yet, in this dialogue, and more specifically on pages 95e to 107b, we have Plato's ontology in a nutshell, together with the terminology of Plato's so-called Theory of Forms or Theory of Ideas. In this one passage, we find: Plato's search for αἰτία or 'explanation'; the method of ὑπόθεσις or 'assumption'; καλόν and ἀγαθόν, 'beautiful' and 'good', as central topics of Plato's concern, singled out by the phrase αὐτὸ καθ' αὑτό, 'itself by itself'; in addition, the relationship which the many beautiful things have with 'that beautiful' is referred to as μετέχειν, 'having of' or 'sharing'; the relationship 'the beautiful' has with the many beautiful things in the perceptible realm is that its παρουσία, its 'presence', or its κοινωνία, its 'communion', makes them beautiful; through 'the beautiful', beautiful things come to be beautiful. Then, the discussion widens to include things big and small as well as mathematical numbers. At 101c2 ff., not only is the verb μετέχειν, 'having of' or 'sharing', repeated, but a noun μετάσχεσις, 'a sharing', is coined to highlight this important relationship; and in addition, δυάς and μονάς, the 'dyad' and the 'monad', are referred to as that whose ἰδία οὐσία, whose 'own being' or 'nature', 'things which are two' or 'which are one' respectively 'have of' or 'share'. Eventually, the terms εἶδος, 'type', and ἰδέα, 'figure', the two words which used to be translated as 'idea' and which are now more commonly translated as 'form', are introduced at 102b1 and 104b9 respectively. The former, εἶδος, is introduced together with the notion that 'the things coming to have a share' in any one of the εἴδη, τὰ μεταλαμβάνοντα, have their 'designation' and their 'name', their 'benaming'[3] or ἐπωνυμία, from those 'types'. μορφή, 'form', occurs twice. In addition, things like μέγεθος, 'bigness', are repeatedly said 'to be in', ἐνεῖναι and εἶναι ἐν, the many things around us, or in this specific case in a person who is big. Thus we have, as the vocabulary of Plato's ontology in the *Phaedo*, μετέχειν, 'having of' or 'sharing'; μεταλαμβάνειν, 'coming to share'; μετάσχεσις, 'a sharing (in something)'; αὐτὸ καθ᾽ αὑτό, 'itself by itself'; εἶδος and ἰδέα, 'idea'; μορφή, 'shape' or 'form'; οὐσία, 'being'; ἐπωνυμία, 'designation' or 'benaming'; παρουσία, 'being there' or 'presence'; κοινωνία, 'communion'; ἐνεῖναι and εἶναι ἐν, 'being in'; ὑπόθεσις, 'assumption'; and αἰτία, 'cause-and-reason'. The object of this investigation is to explore the meaning and the usage of some of these words and a few of their close congeners[4] in Plato's dialogues, and the historical conditions which led Plato to adopt these terms.[5] The philosophers who will turn out to be most relevant in connection with one or more of the technical terms listed are the Pythagoreans, and in particular Philolaus of Croton; the atomists, and in particular Democritus of Abdera; and Anaxagoras of Clazomenae and Diogenes of Apollonia.

No special pleading is required to make claims concerning a connection of one sort or another particularly between what Plato says in the *Phaedo* and on the one hand the Pythagoreans, on the other Anaxagoras and Diogenes; indeed, both Anaxagoras and the Pythagorean Philolaus are named in the dialogue. The originality of this study lies rather in the precise way in which connections are claimed to have obtained between the various philosophical systems. Working out the details of the premises on which such specific claims can be made will occupy the bulk of the main chapters of the book. This will involve discussion of significant occurrences of the terms selected, from their earliest attested instances to the time of Plato, in the various genres and types of Greek literature. Often, the first contexts considered will be from the Homeric epics, but what is probably the first instance of ἰδέα, for example, is found in a poem by Theognis, i.e. dating, if the poem is genuinely by Theognis, most probably to some time in the sixth century BC. The inclusion of non-philosophical texts in our discussion serves a double purpose. It allows to determine whether philosophical usage is in tune with common language or constitutes technical usage; and, as importantly, it helps in determining not only what a particular term could mean and how it was used, but also what a particular term did not mean and how, to the best of our knowledge, it was not used.

Approaches to Plato

In translating passages of Greek, notably from Plato's dialogues, I shall often in my own usage diverge from the terms traditionally found in translations of Plato's dialogues and discussions of his philosophy. The intention in this is to avoid the often unconscious adoption of concepts which were developed in the course of centuries of post-Platonic tradition. One corollary of this tradition is that of doing Ancient Philosophy 'in Latin'. This may be illustrated with the following example:

> For Plato posited that forms which are in corporeal matter are derived from forms subsisting without matter, by way of a certain participation. For he went on to posit a certain man, subsisting non-materially, and similarly a horse, and accordingly also concerning the other things out of which these particular sensibles here are constituted, in that there remains in corporeal matter a certain impression from these separate forms, by way of a certain assimilation which he called participation. And according to the order of forms Platonists went on to posit an order of separate substances; say, there is one separate substance which is horse, which is the cause of all horses; above it is a certain separate life, which they call life per se, and cause of all life; and beyond there is a certain \<substance\> which they name being itself, and cause of all being.

While one may not agree that all of this was held in just this way by Plato, there is probably little in the terminology itself that would be deemed terminologically offensive by the majority of philosophically trained twenty-first-century readers. But how close this terminology is to that of mediaeval scholasticism, a glance at the Latin will teach:

> Plato enim posuit formas quae sunt in materia corporali, derivari a formis sine materia subsistentibus, per modum participationis cuiusdam. Ponebat enim hominem quemdam immaterialiter subsistentem, et similiter equum, et sic de aliis, ex quibus constituuntur haec singularia sensibilia, secundum quod in materia corporali remanet quaedam impressio ab illis formis separatis, per modum assimiliationis cuiusdam, quam participationem vocabat. Et secundum ordinem formarum ponebant platonici ordinem substantiarum separatarum; puta quod una substantia separata est quae est equus, quae est causa omnium equorum; supra quam est quaedam vita separata, quam dicebant per se vitam, et causam omnis vitae; et ulterius quamdam, quam nominabant ipsum esse, et causam omnis esse. Thomas Aquinas, *Summa Theologica*, 1.65.4

It is not difficult to find Greek equivalents for most of the terms underlined:

assimiliatio	ὁμοίωσις	causa	αἰτία
constituo	συνίστημι	corporalis, -e	σωματοειδής, -ές
forma	εἶδος	immaterialis	ἀυλός
impressio	ἀποτύπωμα	materia	ὕλη
ordo	τάξις	participatio	μέθεξις
per se	καθ' αὑτό, καθ' αὑτά	pono, posui	τίθημι, ἔθηκα
sensibilia	αἰσθητά	separatus	χωριστός
subsistere	ὑφίστασθαι	substantia	οὐσία

But a glance at the Greek words shows two things: first, more than a third of the terms listed here are not actually Plato's; and secondly, of those which can be found in Plato, perhaps the two most significant ones, εἶδος and οὐσία, have as Latin equivalents in the passage of Aquinas words which may be suited to a translation of some Aristotelian contexts, but which could not be used in a literal translation of a dialogue of Plato's. This last claim, potentially controversial, will be substantiated in the course of the discussion of Plato's usage below.

In discussing Plato's usage, I shall often use language suggestive of Plato's possessing a high degree of reflection, not only on the world around him, but also on his own activity. I shall speak in terms of Plato's addressing, accepting or rejecting a certain view; of Plato's being aware of who among his predecessors and contemporaries held what view; and of being aware in what respect or respects views held by others differed from views held by himself, or views being developed by himself. In the same way, I shall describe Plato's attitude to the common Greek language in which he was brought up, and the particular terminologies which he encountered in the writings of others. I am aware that this is open to criticism. We cannot, in the strictest sense of the word, *know* what Plato thought or what his intentions were, regardless of whether a character in a dialogue pronounces on a matter which is the topic of our discussion or not. But there are degrees of probability. Presumably, we know more about Plato's thoughts concerning geometry than we know about his culinary tastes, both because of the content of the dialogues and because of our knowledge of philosophical and literary conventions. We can see, for example, how fifth-century Athenian tragedians reacted to one another in composing their tragedies.[6] Moreover, we can make deductions from Aristotle's writings: leaving aside his explicit statements concerning the history of philosophy, which are always coloured in one way or another in accordance with his own philosophical purposes, we can reconstruct from the very way in which he transformed and distorted views of his predecessors – be it deliberately or otherwise – at least some of the ways in which philosophical speculation was pursued.[7] Thus, to say that in this or that point of content or turn of phrase Plato is consciously reacting to Anaxagoras is not an outrageous statement. On the other hand, were one to leave out the qualification 'consciously', this weaker claim might still contribute to our understanding of what Plato was doing, and might thus still be worth considering. I shall sometimes make claims of this weaker and safer sort, sometimes of the stronger, more controversial and less demonstrable sort. For – to echo Socrates' words in the *Phaedo* – while it will always be safer to make a claim of the safer sort, it may sometimes be more illuminating to entertain the stronger claim as a possibility. Ultimately, though, it often matters more to see where the roots of Plato's philosophy lie than to determine the extent to which Plato was aware of all the influences on his own thinking at each stage.

As regards stages of Plato's thinking, I should briefly state my position regarding authenticity and chronology. I cannot here add positive arguments to the ones with which the scholarly discussion abounds.[8] I do, though, hold the following as incontrovertible: first, Plato, whether he was born in 429, 428, 427 or in 424 BC,[9] did not write all the dialogues, epigrams and letters handed down to us under his name simultaneously or in one and the same year, but whatever he did write he wrote over a period of many decades; secondly, there were contexts in antiquity in which authors of literary creations attributed their creations, for one reason or another, to the authorship of a well-known historical (or, for that matter, mythological) figure, rather than claiming them for their own. However, between these assertions and any definitive statement concerning the authenticity of a particular Platonic dialogue and its relative chronological position to one and all of the other dialogues, there lie many steps which require detailed argumentation, and one must avoid adopting the rash attitude of jumping to conclusions which is castigated by Socrates in the *Philebus* (16c–17a). All the same, for present purposes it is fair to state the relative chronological order of some of the dialogues which I think most probable. Much of my own reasoning behind this order is without doubt impressionistic, but some arguments will emerge in the course of subsequent discussion to support aspects at least of this arrangement.

> *Ion*
> *Laches*
> *Charmides, Protagoras*
> *Gorgias*
> *Meno*
> *Euthyphro*
> *Phaedo, Symposium*
> *Republic*
> *Parmenides, Theaetetus*
> *Sophist*
> *Politicus, Cratylus*
> *Phaedrus, Timaeus*
> *Philebus*

Where two dialogues appear on one line, I am not certain about their chronological order relative to each other. I do not know where to place the *Lysis* and *Euthydemus*, other than that they both seem to me to come after the *Gorgias* and before the *Parmenides*, and I do not regard the *Hippias Major* as authentic.

Not much depends on the actual historical order of composition for my argument, but my impressionistic beliefs may on occasion explain the order in which parts of the subsequent discussion proceed. By way of clarification, though, a word regarding the *Parmenides* and, in connection with that, the order in which arguments from different dialogues must be discussed: the discussion between Socrates and Parmenides in the first part of the dialogue is clearly a critique of something. Moreover, it is, to my mind, clearly a critique which can be understood only against the arguments of the *Phaedo* in particular, but also of some of the other dialogues besides. This fact has a corollary. Regardless of whether the critique of the *Parmenides* is interpreted as self-criticism on Plato's part, as philosophical development, as warning against a mis-reading, e.g. by taking things *au pied de la lettre*: as a critique, this passage can be understood and evaluated only against an understanding and evaluation of the earlier passages and contexts there criticized; and for as long as it is not decided whether, and if so to what extent, Plato is serious in his critique in the *Parmenides*, one must not confuse the issues discussed in the earlier dialogues by importing in a haphazard fashion bits and pieces from that later dialogue. The old rule is in principle correct, that each dialogue must first be read as a piece of argumentation in its own right. This, though, is true only in a qualified way of individual arguments within dialogues. Of course, one must, here as well, first understand each argument. But what Plato wants to achieve with an argument, whether he is committed to it or otherwise, what function he thinks it can perform: all that can only be seen in the context of the dialogue in which it is embedded. But if this is true for a particular dialogue, it cannot be denied that, with a view to Plato's œuvre as a whole, on occasion something may be learnt from a later dialogue for the understanding of an earlier work. No generalizing prescript will be fully satisfactory.[10]

Plato's response to his predecessors: two examples
It may be asked with a view to the undertaking as a whole: What is the benefit of such a study? What do we gain for an understanding of Plato's *philosophy* from a knowledge of the history of certain words which form part of Plato's *language*? Is it not sufficient to read the dialogues of Plato and the treatises of Aristotle to arrive at a correct picture of their shared beliefs as well as their differences, and does not that enable us sufficiently to interpret these two authors? Two simple examples may illustrate the limitations, but also the possibilities, of what can be achieved by a study of words and phrases of the sort here undertaken.

i. Zeno
A much-discussed problem in Plato's *Phaedo* is that of the first sustained discussion in that dialogue of something's being introduced with the tag 'itself', where the Greek for 'itself', αὐτό, which is added to a phrase, signifies somehow that – in contrast with (the) many things of the perceptible world

around us which are such-and-such – what is such-and-such 'itself' is not the same as those many things.[11] The first occurrence of αὐτό, 'itself', in this technical sense is at *Phaedo* 65d, when Socrates first introduces what for Plato is his main concern throughout the early and middle dialogues. Socrates asks Simmias (65d4–8):

φαμέν τι εἶναι δίκαιον αὐτὸ ἢ οὐδέν;
φαμὲν μέντοι νὴ Δία.
καὶ αὖ καλόν γέ τι καὶ ἀγαθόν;
πῶς δ' οὔ;

Do we say that 'just itself' is something or nothing?
By Zeus, we certainly do say <that it is something>.
And again beautiful <is> certainly something, and also good <is something>?
But how not?

The tag αὐτό then recurs nine pages later, at *Phaedo* 74a. The overt context of 74a is that of ἀνάμνησις or 'remembering', the word often translated as 'recollection'. But, as Plato indicates clearly by the way he lets Socrates comment on his arguments, there is no commitment on the author's part to either this notion of ἀνάμνησις specifically or indeed to a belief in the immortality of the soul of the individual in general.[12] The purpose of *Phaedo* 74a–75d is rather to discuss one aspect of what is at 102b being referred to by Phaedo, the character of the dialogue, as τὰ εἴδη, 'the ideas', 'the types', i.e. the things themselves, things like the beautiful itself, the good, the just, and so on. Here, at 74a, the issue is introduced abruptly by Socrates' question (74a9–12):

σκόπει δή, ἦ δ' ὅς, εἰ ταῦτα οὕτως ἔχει. φαμέν πού τι εἶναι ἴσον, οὐ ξύλον λέγω ξύλῳ οὐδὲ λίθον λίθῳ οὐδ' ἄλλο τῶν τοιούτων οὐδέν, ἀλλὰ παρὰ ταῦτα πάντα ἕτερόν τι, αὐτὸ τὸ ἴσον· φῶμέν τι εἶναι ἢ μηδέν;

Thus look, said he, if that is so. We say somehow that equal is something,[13] not wood, I mean, to wood, nor stone to stone, nor another <one> of such things, but beside all those something other, the equal itself: should we say that that is something or nothing?

The abruptness of this question is to an extent mitigated by the fact that this pattern of thinking had briefly been introduced at 65d, and of course by the circumstance that body (and subsequently also soul)[14] has been talked about as being 'itself by itself', αὐτὸ καθ' αὑτό, since 64c. The terminology of 'αὐτὸ τό', followed by a noun or nominalized expression, on the other hand, is familiar to readers from Plato's earlier dialogues. This usage is not frequent, but it does occur in a relevant way to isolate and single out a topic under discussion as stripped of all attending circumstances, i.e. without the other things that habitually co-occur with what is under investigation, be that co-occurrence in the world accessible to the senses or in one's thought. A good example is *Protagoras* 354c. Socrates interrogates an imagined group of people and seeks to obtain agreement on their reactions from Protagoras (354c3–e2):

οὐκοῦν τὴν μὲν ἡδονὴν διώκετε ὡς ἀγαθὸν ὄν, τὴν δὲ λύπην φεύγετε ὡς κακόν;
συνεδόκει.
τοῦτ᾽ ἄρα ἡγεῖσθ᾽ εἶναι κακόν, τὴν λύπην, καὶ ἀγαθὸν τὴν ἡδονήν, ἐπεὶ καὶ αὐτὸ τὸ χαίρειν τότε λέγετε κακὸν εἶναι, ὅταν μειζόνων ἡδονῶν ἀποστερῇ ἢ ὅσας αὐτὸ ἔχει, ἢ λύπας μείζους παρασκευάζῃ τῶν ἐν αὐτῷ ἡδονῶν· ἐπεὶ εἰ κατ᾽ ἄλλο τι αὐτὸ τὸ χαίρειν κακὸν καλεῖτε καὶ εἰς ἄλλο τι τέλος ἀποβλέψαντες, ἔχοιτε ἂν καὶ ἡμῖν εἰπεῖν· ἀλλ᾽ οὐχ ἕξετε.
οὐδ᾽ ἐμοὶ δοκοῦσιν, ἔφη ὁ Πρωταγόρας.
ἄλλο τι οὖν πάλιν καὶ περὶ αὐτοῦ τοῦ λυπεῖσθαι ὁ αὐτὸς τρόπος; τότε καλεῖτε αὐτὸ τὸ λυπεῖσθαι ἀγαθόν, ὅταν ἢ μείζους λύπας τῶν ἐν αὐτῷ οὐσῶν ἀπαλλάττῃ ἢ μείζους ἡδονὰς τῶν λυπῶν παρασκευάζῃ; ἐπεὶ εἰ πρὸς ἄλλο τι τέλος ἀποβλέπετε, ὅταν καλῆτε αὐτὸ τὸ λυπεῖσθαι ἀγαθόν, ἢ πρὸς ὃ ἐγὼ λέγω, ἔχετε ἡμῖν εἰπεῖν· ἀλλ᾽ οὐχ ἕξετε.
ἀληθῆ, ἔφη, λέγεις, ὁ Πρωταγόρας.

Now, do you pursue pleasure as being something good, but flee pain as something bad?
It seemed to him, too <, that they did>.
So you think that thing to be something bad, pain, and pleasure something good, as you also call 'enjoying' itself then to be something bad when it deprives of pleasures greater than the ones which it holds, or when it affords pains greater than the pleasures <entailed> in it. Because if you call 'enjoying' itself bad according to something other <than that>, and with a view to some other end, you would also be able to tell us <what it is>: but you will not be able <to do so>.
Nor do they seem to me <to be able to do so>, said Protagoras.
So again in turn is it the same thing with 'feeling pain' itself? Do you then call 'feeling pain' itself good, whenever it either rids of greater pains than the ones which are <entailed> in it, or when it affords pleasures greater than the pains it affords? Because if you have in view some other end, when you call 'feeling pain' itself good, some end other than that with a view to which I say <you call these things>, you can tell us <what it is>; but you cannot.
What you say is true, said Protagoras.

'Enjoying' itself and 'feeling pain' itself are processes or states or affections or passions of human beings, and are in that not on a par with 'just', 'good' and 'beautiful'. But as far as usage of the tag 'itself' is concerned, the passage from the *Protagoras* is comparable to that in the *Phaedo*.[15] In Socrates' singling out in the *Phaedo* the just, the good, the beautiful and then, at 74a, the equal with the tag αὐτό, there is thus nothing new in terms of the language or terminology employed.

9

The next step in Socrates' argument, at *Phaedo* 74b, is to ask for the origin of our knowledge and understanding of what is equal. The phrase λαβόντες…ἐπιστήμην at 74b4 refers to the process of acquisition of conscious awareness of the equal in this life.[16] In seeing equal objects, equal sticks and stones, we arrive at knowledge of the equal as being different from the many equal things; for equal stones and sticks sometimes 'appear equal to one, but not to another'. Leaving aside the vexed issue of how the datives in τῷ μὲν…τῷ δὲ… are to be construed at 74b8,[17] on any reading the many equal objects are contrasted with the equal itself which does not appear equal and unequal. But instead of saying αὐτὸ τὸ ἴσον ἔστιν ὅτε ἄνισόν σοι ἐφάνη, '<with regard to> the equal itself, is it <the case> that it has ever appeared unequal to you', Socrates says (74c1–2):

τί δέ; αὐτὰ τὰ ἴσα ἔστιν ὅτε ἄνισά σοι ἐφάνη, ἢ ἡ ἰσότης ἀνισότης;

But what about this: <with regard to> the equal(s) themselves, is it <the case> that they have ever appeared unequal(s) to you, or equality inequality?

The sense of the passage 74a–75d as a whole is clear, but there is, starting with Olympiodorus (*In Phaedonem* 159.11.12–15), widespread disagreement over, on the one hand, both meaning and reference of the phrase αὐτὰ τὰ ἴσα, on the other Plato's motivation for using here, as at *Parmenides* 129b, but not elsewhere in the *Phaedo*, nor anywhere else in the other middle dialogues, a nominalized articulated neuter adjective in the plural rather than the singular.[18] Does αὐτὰ τὰ ἴσα refer to the multiple instantiations of the notion of 'the equal itself' in the minds of many human beings, as Olympiodorus suggests? Does it refer to what is equal in nature as logically being more than one thing, because equality expresses a relation? Does the plural expression refer to perfect instantiations of equality, for example in the realm of mathematics?[19]

Regardless of which of these solutions one were to adopt, a two-fold difficulty remains: first, why would Plato use a different expression without making use of it subsequently, either by showing in what way it has a different point of reference or by exploiting the fact that he had at his disposal this linguistic variant; and secondly, in connection with the latter, why is there an apparent plural phrase αὐτὰ τὰ ὅμοια, 'the similar(s) itself', at *Parmenides* 129b, and only there?

A possible answer to the question why Plato uses the plural phrase at *Phaedo* 74b may indeed lie hidden in the *Parmenides*. There, Socrates had asked Zeno to repeat the opening argument of his treatise. Socrates then summarizes (127e1–4):

πῶς, φάναι, ὦ Ζήνων, τοῦτο λέγεις; εἰ πολλά ἐστι τὰ ὄντα, ὡς ἄρα δεῖ αὐτὰ ὅμοιά τε εἶναι καὶ ἀνόμοια, τοῦτο δὲ δὴ ἀδύνατον· οὔτε γὰρ τὰ ἀνόμοια ὅμοια οὔτε τὰ ὅμοια ἀνόμοια οἷόν τε εἶναι; οὐχ οὕτω λέγεις;

How, he said, Zeno, do you mean that? If the things-that-are are many, that thus it is necessary that they are similar and also dissimilar, but that this surely is impossible: for neither are the dissimilar(s) capable of being similar(s), nor the similar(s) dissimilar(s)? Don't you say (and mean it) so?

It has been pointed out that all of Socrates' summary must be Zeno's first argument, i.e. that the example of 'many cannot *be* because they would be similar and dissimilar at once' is Zeno's first example.[20] This is confirmed by three passages in Proclus' *Commentary on Plato's* Parmenides, 619.30–620.1, 632.6–15 and 788.29–31. The first reads:

ὁ δὴ τοῦ Παρμενίδου μαθητὴς Ζήνων…γράφει τι βιβλίον, ἐν ᾧ δαιμονίως ἐδείκνυεν οὐκ ἐλάττω ἑπόμενα δυσχερῆ τοῖς πολλὰ τὰ ὄντα τιθεμένοις ἢ ὅσα τοῖς ἓν τὸ ὂν εἰρηκόσιν ἔδοξεν ἀπαντᾶν· καὶ γὰρ ὅμοιον καὶ ἀνόμοιον ταὐτὸν ἐδείκνυ καὶ ἴσον καὶ ἄνισον ἐσόμενον…

Thus Zeno, the pupil of Parmenides…writes a book, in which he showed in miraculous manner that there follow difficulties no less severe for those who posit that there are many things than those encounter who have said that what *is* is one: for he also showed that the same thing will be similar and dissimilar and equal and unequal…

The second passage, 632.6–15, says about Plato' Parmenides:

δεικνύντα τὸν ὅμοιον τρόπον ἐκείνῳ τὰ ἀντικείμενα περὶ ταὐτόν· καὶ ὡς ἐκεῖνος ἤλεγχε τὰ πολλὰ δεικνὺς αὐτὰ καὶ ὅμοια καὶ ἀνόμοια καὶ ταὐτὰ καὶ ἕτερα καὶ ἴσα ὄντα καὶ ἄνισα, κατὰ τὰ αὐτὰ δὴ καὶ αὐτὸν ἀποφαίνειν τὸ ἓν ὅμοιον καὶ ἀνόμοιον, καὶ οὐχ ὅμοιον καὶ οὐκ ἀνόμοιον, ταὐτὸν, οὐ ταὐτὸν, ἕτερον, οὐχ ἕτερον, καὶ ἐπὶ πάντων ὡσαύτως, καὶ τιθέντα καὶ ἀναιροῦντα τὰ μαχόμενα, καὶ οὐχ ὡς ἐκεῖνος τιθέντα μόνον…

showing in a manner similar to him [Zeno] the opposites concerning the same thing: as that man [Zeno] made his proof in showing that the many things are themselves both similar and dissimilar and the same and other and being equal also unequal, so he [Plato's Parmenides] also thus showed in the same way that the one is similar and dissimilar, and not similar and not dissimilar, the same, not the same, other, not other, and for each proposition in that same manner, both positing and abolishing the contested items, and not just positing, as that man [Zeno] had done…

Finally, we find at 788.29–31:

δεύτερον τοίνυν ἐκεῖνον παραλάβωμεν τὸν λόγον, ὅς φησιν αὐτὰ μὲν τὰ φαινόμενα καὶ ἴσα καὶ ἄνισα, καὶ ὅμοια καὶ ἀνόμοια…

Secondly, let us now take up that argument which says that the phenomena themselves are equal and unequal, and similar and dissimilar…

As has been noted by Hoffmann and Dillon, this is evidence on the one hand for the presence of the argument concerning the many as similar and dissimilar discussed by Socrates at *Parmenides* 129b, but on the other also for the presence of the pair 'equal – unequal' in Zeno's treatise, and that not at a random place, but in second position right after 'similar – dissimilar'. The context in Zeno, as is stated in the *Parmenides* and confirmed by Proclus, is that of reaching a paradox concerning the things that *are* by making deductions from the premise 'if there are many (things)' or 'if many (things) *are*'. The second consequence is that '[if there are many] they are both equal and unequal', which may have been presented by Zeno as a refutation of the assumption that 'there are many'. That is to say, the constituents of Zeno's hypothetical world would be the many which are equal and unequal. Zeno constructs the paradox that τὰ ἴσα are ἄνισα. This statement, the second in Zeno's book, must have been a famous sophism, together with the one that τὰ ὅμοια are ἀνόμοια. This is why Socrates can say (*Phaedo* 74b7–c2):

ἆρ' οὐ λίθοι μὲν ἴσοι καὶ ξύλα ἐνίοτε ταὐτὰ ὄντα τῷ μὲν ἴσα φαίνεται, τῷ δ' οὔ;
πάνυ μὲν οὖν.
τί δέ; αὐτὰ τὰ ἴσα ἔστιν ὅτε ἄνισά σοι ἐφάνη, ἢ ἡ ἰσότης ἀνισότης;

Do not stones which are equal, and also sticks, sometimes, while being the same, seem equal to one, but to another not?
Very much so.
But what about this: Have the equals themselves ever seemed to you unequal, or equality inequality?

In speaking of 'equal', he uses a famous Zenonian example. In introducing the notion of φαίνεται, 'appears', i.e. what elsewhere in Plato is the opposition of 'appearance' and 'being', itself an opposition of Presocratic origin, he removes the sting from Zeno's argument, since now the fact that something 'appears equal and unequal' to someone does not entail that there is something that 'is equal and unequal'. And by using, at this one point, the expression αὐτὰ τὰ ἴσα, Plato is not so much abstracting from the examples of stones and sticks, which indeed contained the plural form of the adjective, as quoting a Zenonian 'τὰ ἴσα...ἄνισα' by the *ad hoc* creation of 'αὐτὰ τὰ ἴσα...ἄνισα...;'. And since this is indeed not in concord with either common usage or Plato's own usage in this passage, before or after, he immediately adds the nouns, 'ἢ ἡ ἰσότης ἀνισότης;', so that the quotation can stand as a quotation, but cannot give rise to confusion; confusion is avoided by the immediate reformulation; the connective ἢ, 'or', is effectively epexegetic, or explanatory, rather than disjunctive, or introducing an alternative.[21]

What difference does pointing to Zeno as one specific source for a discussion of the issue of τὰ ἴσα make to an interpretation of *Phaedo* 74a–75d? The question of philosophical doctrine, i.e. does αὐτὰ τὰ ἴσα refer to a unity or a plurality, is certainly not resolved simply by naming an earlier philosopher who talked about a plurality of objects as being ἴσα καὶ ἄνισα; the consequent question of where these multiple objects would have to be located ontologically is *a fortiori* not answered by such a reference. The grammatical-*cum*-linguistic issue of whether an articulated neuter plural adjective could, and whether it would, be taken by a fourth-century Greek readership to refer to a plurality or otherwise is even less affected. (All that can be said is that if, as argued by Dale 1987, the 'neuter plural adjective' expression need not imply plural reference at all, Plato *can* use this expression without introducing a new item in addition to αὐτὸ τὸ ἴσον.) But while the linguistic issue is barely touched and the point of philosophical doctrine as such not affected, a decision on whether or not to see an implied reference or allusion to Zeno will make a difference in the following way: *if* the phrase αὐτὰ τὰ ἴσα brings to mind Zeno on any level, that may be its sole function. The reader may not be entitled, and is certainly nowhere in the text encouraged, to ask for the philosophical implications of the plural at this point. The phrase is not introduced 'as a plural-phrase', but 'as a Zeno-quotation'. The function of the clause αὐτὰ τὰ ἴσα ἔστιν ὅτε ἄνισά σοι ἐφάνη would thus be to contrast what Socrates is doing with what Zeno was doing.[22] Zeno, or so it is perceived and presented, thought that he could deduce from 'there are many things' the contradictory 'the equal(s) are unequal' as detrimental to the assumption of plurality in some way. Socrates contrasts 'the equal (are) unequal', which is harmless if interpreted as 'equal sticks and stones sometimes are (or appear) *in some way* unequal', with 'the equal(s) themselves (are) never unequal' and 'equality never inequality', which guarantees the logical structure of the world and explains contradictory appearances. There is at least the possibility that Plato did indeed use the puzzling phrase αὐτὰ τὰ ἴσα, and that this phrase would be puzzling to the ancient Greek reader if he had time to reflect on it, but that at the same time its function was exhausted once Zeno had been brought to mind, for which reason it could be discarded, not to be used again.[23] Only when Zeno became the subject of discussion in the *Parmenides* would Plato reactivate this device, on that occasion with the very first rather than the second example of the famous Eleatic treatise, viz. 'the similar'.

We have here an example of a phrase, a formulation, which Plato uses at two points in his dialogues because it recalls a specific argument of one of his predecessors. In the *Phaedo*, this phrase, which constitutes a modified adaptation of a Zenonian example, is integrated into Plato's new ontological model, in which the many equal things, the many equals, are contrasted with 'the equals themselves', that is to say 'equality', 'the equal itself'. The concept of such a thing as the equal itself, or indeed the beautiful itself and the good itself, etc., will continue to be fundamental to Plato's thought. The plural phrases 'the equals themselves' and 'the similars themselves', by contrast, are used only where Zeno's thought is evoked.

ii. Parmenides

The second example concerns Plato's response to Parmenides at *Symposium* 210e–211e as discussed by Friedrich Solmsen.[24] In his article 'Parmenides and the description of perfect beauty in Plato's *Symposium*', Solmsen demonstrates two things. On the one hand, he shows that Plato's conception of what that is which he calls 'that which *is* beautiful', αὐτὸ ὃ ἔστι καλόν, owes something specific to Parmenides. On the other hand, he plausibly traces some of the *terms* Plato uses at *Symposium* 210e–211e back to Parmenides, but explains with regard to other terms Plato uses in what way that, while being not the same as those of Parmenides, they are equivalents to terms used by Parmenides. Of particular significance is Solmsen's discussion of 211a8–b2:[25]

οὐδέ που ὂν ἐν ἑτέρῳ τινι, οἷον ἐν ζώῳ ἢ ἐν γῇ ἢ ἐν οὐρανῷ ἢ ἔν τῳ ἄλλῳ, ἀλλ' αὐτὸ καθ' αὑτὸ μεθ' αὑτοῦ μονοειδὲς ἀεὶ ὄν ['nor in any way being in another, as in a living being or on land or in the sky or in anything else, but being uniform, eternally, itself by itself with itself']. The former half of the description continues to cut off the true καλόν from its individual manifestations. [Note 17: Cf. 211b7–d1, where after the separation of αὐτὸ τὸ καλόν from its individual manifestations the latter are again treated as way stations leading to the former.] With the second part we may compare ταὐτόν τ' ἐν ταὐτῶι τε μένον καθ' ἑαυτό τε κεῖται [Parmenides B8, 29; 'it lies, the same, and remaining in the same, and by itself'], notwithstanding the fact that Parmenides employs the reflexive pronoun only once, in καθ' ἑαυτό ['by itself'] (cf. Plato's καθ' αὐτό), while in the two other instances he stresses sameness. Elsewhere Plato does know sameness as the opposite of otherness – cf. *Parm.*, ibid. 57 f. – e.g. when he points out that a Form μονοειδὲς ὂν αὐτὸ καθ' αὑτό, ὡσαύτως κατὰ ταὐτὰ ἔχει [*Phaedo* 78d5–7; 'being uniform, itself by itself, it is in the same manner according to the same']. By such a description he asserts at one and the same time self-identity and the 'by itself' (i.e. separateness). [Note 18: Besides *Phaedo*, 78d5–7 (here quoted) note also d1–5 and similar characteristics combined in the description of the soul, which is συγγενής ['akin'] to the Forms, *Phaedo*, 79d1–6. The ταὐτόν ['the same'] vested in the one Form is emphasized as early as *Meno*, 72c2 (cf. 74a9, 75a4).)] In the present context [*Symposium* 211a–b] αὐτὸ καθ' αὑτό ['itself by itself'] suits his purpose because it brings out the contrast to ἐν ἑτέρῳ τινί ['in some other'] (a8) as effectively as does Parmenides' own τῷ δ' ἑτέρῳ μὴ ταὐτόν ['but not the same as another'] (58 in the section on δόξαι ['opinions']), and Parmenides too as soon as he had introduced distinction and duality uses – in the same line as μὴ ταὐτόν ['not the same'] – a κατ' αὐτό ['by itself'], which Plato (like some contemporary interpreters) may have understood as reflexive, although it is not certain that it was meant thus by Parmenides.

14

This suggests strongly that Plato not only, as one would expect, operates broadly speaking within the Eleatic tradition, but that he makes specific and conscious reference, adopting the phrase καθ' ἑαυτό, 'by itself', and standardizing it in his own terminology as αὐτὸ καθ' αὐτό, 'itself by itself', an expression he frequently employs to isolate things like the beautiful itself, but which in dialogues after the *Republic* gains wider currency in his philosophy.

It is worth exploring the implications of Solmsen's observations. His claim is not that, before Plato, it was only Parmenides who used the phrase καθ' ἑαυτό, 'by itself', or that Plato was the first to combine it with the pronoun αὐτός, 'self'. For illustrative purposes, one may consider the following examples of related expressions. In his *History*, Thucydides refers to Syracuse as (7.28.3):

πόλιν οὐδὲν ἐλάσσω αὐτήν γε καθ' αὑτὴν τῆς τῶν Ἀθηναίων,

a city in no way smaller, itself by itself, than that of the Athenians.

Among the dramatists, Sophocles lets Oedipus address the chorus at the beginning of *Oedipus Rex* (62–4):

τὸ μὲν γὰρ ὑμῶν ἄλγος εἰς ἕν' ἔρχεται
μόνον καθ' αὑτόν, κοὐδέν' ἄλλον, ἡ δ' ἐμὴ
ψυχὴ πόλιν τε κἀμὲ καὶ σ' ὁμοῦ στένει.

For your affliction is directed to one thing
alone by itself, and nothing else, while my
soul moans for the city and for me and for you at once.

In Euripides' *Ion*, Ion addresses Xuthus, king of Athens, who has just been identified as his father. He is reluctant to move with him to Athens, thinking of the childless wife who would be his step-mother (607–11):[26]

ἐλθὼν δ' ἐς οἶκον ἀλλότριον ἔπηλυς ὢν
γυναῖκά θ' ὡς ἄτεκνον, ἣ κοινουμένη
τὰς συμφοράς σοι πρόσθεν, ἀπολαχοῦσα νῦν
αὐτὴ καθ' αὑτὴν τὴν τύχην οἴσει πικρῶς,
πῶς οὐχ ὑπ' αὐτῆς εἰκότως μισήσομαι...

But given that I shall come to the house as to a foreign house, being a stranger,
and to your wife as to someone who is childless, having had in common
those afflictions with you, previously, but who will now, left destitute,
herself by herself bear this fate bitterly,
how will I not – quite properly – be hated by her...

In Aristophanes' *Clouds*, the simple Strepsiades is led through the *phrontisterion* of Socrates by one of the students, who explains the various tasks pursued in this establishment (187–94):

STREPSIADES: ἀτὰρ τί ποτ' εἰς τὴν γῆν βλέπουσιν οὑτοί;

15

STUDENT:	ζητοῦσιν οὗτοι τὰ κατὰ γῆς.
STREPSIADES:	βολβοὺς ἄρα
	ζητοῦσι...
	τί γὰρ οἴδε δρῶσιν οἱ σφόδρ' ἐγκεκυφότες;
STUDENT:	οὗτοι δ' ἐρεβοδιφῶσιν ὑπὸ τὸν Τάρταρον.
STREPSIADES:	τί δῆθ' ὁ πρωκτὸς εἰς τὸν οὐρανὸν βλέπει;
STUDENT:	αὐτὸς καθ' αὑτὸν ἀστρονομεῖν διδάσκεται.

STREPSIADES:	But why ever do they look into the earth?
STUDENT:	They are searching for what is under the earth...
STREPSIADES:	Truffles it is thus
	they are searching...
	But what are those doing, stooping to the ground so much?
STUDENT:	Those are scrutinizing Erebus under Tartarus.
STREPSIADES:	But why does their anus look at the sky?
STUDENT:	Itself by itself it is being taught to do astronomy.

In Book 3 of the *Memorabilia*, Xenophon has Socrates observe a fellow symposiast (3.14.2):

καταμαθὼν δέ ποτε τῶν συνδειπνούντων τινὰ τοῦ μὲν σίτου πεπαυμένον, τὸ δὲ ὄψον αὐτὸ καθ' αὑτὸ ἐσθίοντα...

but when at some stage he perceived one of the fellow symposiasts leaving aside the bread, but eating the meat itself by itself...

The phrase 'itself by itself' is thus part of the common Attic language, used to single out a person or thing for consideration by itself, in isolation from its context. And while the passage from Aristophanes may be meant to reflect 'Socratic' usage, and while Xenophon may have written this part of the *Memorabilia* after some of Plato's middle dialogues had become publicly available, both passages look all the same as if they were reflecting common usage rather than specialized philosophical terminology. Nor does Plato use the tag καθ' αὑτ- exclusively in the context of 'Forms'. In the *Meno*, Socrates says (88c4–d1):

εἰ ἄρα ἀρετὴ τῶν ἐν τῇ ψυχῇ τί ἐστιν καὶ ἀναγκαῖον αὐτῷ ὠφελίμῳ εἶναι, φρόνησιν αὐτὸ δεῖ εἶναι, ἐπειδήπερ πάντα τὰ κατὰ τὴν ψυχὴν αὐτὰ μὲν καθ' αὑτὰ οὔτε ὠφέλιμα οὔτε βλαβερά ἐστιν, προσγενομένης δὲ φρονήσεως ἢ ἀφροσύνης βλαβερά τε καὶ ὠφέλιμα γίγνεται.

So if excellence is one of the things in the soul and if it is also necessary for it to be something beneficial, then it must be understanding, since indeed all the things to do with the soul are themselves by themselves neither beneficial nor harmful, but when understanding or lack of understanding enter in addition, then they become harmful or beneficial.

At the end of the dialogue, Socrates sums up what has been achieved in the following words (100b2–6):

ἐκ μὲν τοίνυν τούτου τοῦ λογισμοῦ, ὦ Μένων, θείᾳ μοίρᾳ ἡμῖν φαίνεται
παραγιγνομένη ἡ ἀρετὴ οἷς ἂν παραγίγνηται· τὸ δὲ σαφὲς περὶ αὐτοῦ εἰσόμεθα
τότε, ὅταν πρὶν ᾧτινι τρόπῳ τοῖς ἀνθρώποις παραγίγνεται ἀρετή, πρότερον
ἐπιχειρήσωμεν αὐτὸ καθ' αὑτὸ ζητεῖν τί ποτ' ἔστιν ἀρετή.

So, from this calculation, Meno, excellence reveals itself to us as something
that comes to be with those with whom it comes to be by divine dispensation:
but we shall know clearly about that when, before attempting to search for the
manner in which excellence comes to be with people, we attempt to search for
whatever excellence is, itself by itself.

At *Meno* 100b, the phrase αὐτὸ καθ' αὑτό, 'itself by itself', which is neuter,
may, grammatically, qualify the indirect question, 'whatever excellence is',
or it may qualify ἀρετή, 'excellence', which is feminine, because the object of
a search or definition, as the thing looked for, is often referred to by neuter
pronouns. At *Meno* 88c, it is unspecified 'things in the soul' which are said
to be neither good nor bad if looked at in isolation. In neither case are we
dealing with 'Forms' in the sense of the *Phaedo*, though the nouns εἶδος,
'type', and οὐσία, 'being', had been introduced by Socrates in his search for
what excellence is at *Meno* 72a–73a.[27]

If all of that is taken into account, what Solmsen's analysis does show is
that after having used the phrase αὐτὸ καθ' αὑτό, which is part of common
Attic idiom in the second half of the fifth century, in contexts that anticipate
'Forms', and after having used it in the *Phaedo* in a semi-technical way to
refer to the things themselves which are at the centre of Socrates' investigations, Plato creates in the *Symposium* a context in which there are so many
explicit and implicit allusions to and echoes of the poem of Parmenides that
he effectively tells the reader that some of what Parmenides has said about
his 'being' in some significant ways applies to 'the beautiful', which has now
been revealed as the highest object of human desire and striving. At the same
time, as Solmsen emphasizes, the differences between Parmenides and Plato
are as obvious as what is shared.

Plato has thus, after having used the phrase αὐτὸ καθ' αὑτό on previous
occasions, used this passage in the *Symposium* to reveal his philosophical
roots which manifest themselves in this case in his adaptation of a particular
phrase that has become an integral part of Plato's own philosophical terminology. It is interesting to note, as does Solmsen, that at least in the extant
fragments of Parmenides the phrase with the reflexive pronoun occurs only
once. This does not in any way invalidate either Plato's exercise or Solmsen's
interpretation. It must be observed that this interpretation itself does, of
course, not hang on this one phrase; rather, by comparing the one passage,

as a whole, with the other, as a whole, and by then looking for individual parallels, a dependency can be demonstrated beyond reasonable doubt. Once this has been done in the case of *Symposium* 211a–b, and once a connection between Plato's use of αὐτὸ καθ' αὑτό and the thought of the Presocratic Parmenides has been established, the reader of Plato is then entitled to ask to what extent earlier occurrences of the same phrase in Plato are also already evidence for an acquaintance with and a conscious echo of the Presocratic. Indeed, one may conclude that it is unreasonable to assume that use of the phrase αὐτὸ καθ' αὑτό in the *Phaedo* at least could be thought of as independent of Parmenides.

Before leaving this example, a final consideration. While the phrase καθ' αὑτό is otherwise not found in the extant fragments of the Presocratics, two fragments of Anaxagoras contain the phrase ἐφ' ἑαυτοῦ, 'unto itself', which seems to express either the same as Parmenides' καθ' ἑαυτό, or, if not that, so at least a closely related notion (B6,1–9; B12, 4–11):[28]

καὶ ὅτε δὲ ἴσαι μοῖραί εἰσι τοῦ τε μεγάλου καὶ τοῦ σμικροῦ πλῆθος, καὶ οὕτως ἂν εἴη ἐν παντὶ πάντα· οὐδὲ χωρὶς ἔστιν εἶναι, ἀλλὰ πάντα παντὸς μοῖραν μετέχει. ὅτε τοὐλάχιστον μὴ ἔστιν εἶναι, οὐκ ἂν δύναιτο χωρισθῆναι, οὐδ' ἂν ἐφ' ἑαυτοῦ γενέσθαι, ἀλλ' ὅπωσπερ ἀρχὴν εἶναι καὶ νῦν πάντα ὁμοῦ. ἐν πᾶσι δὲ πολλὰ ἔνεστι καὶ τῶν ἀποκρινομένων ἴσα πλῆθος ἐν τοῖς μείζοσί τε καὶ ἐλάσσοσι.

And when there are shares of the big and the small equal in amount, also in that way would there be everything in everything: nor is there 'being separate', but everything has a share of everything. And when there is no 'being the smallest <thing>', it would not be possible to be separated-and-apart, nor to come-to-be unto itself, but just as with respect to its beginning, so also now, everything is together. But in all <things> there are many <things>, and equal as regards their number of what is discrete in the larger and the smaller <things>.

τὰ μὲν ἄλλα παντὸς μοῖραν μετέχει, νοῦς δέ ἐστιν ἄπειρον καὶ αὐτοκρατὲς καὶ μέμεικται οὐδενὶ χρήματι, ἀλλὰ μόνος αὐτὸς ἐπ' ἐωυτοῦ ἐστιν. εἰ μὴ γὰρ ἐφ' ἑαυτοῦ ἦν, ἀλλά τεωι ἐμέμεικτο ἄλλωι, μετεῖχεν ἂν ἁπάντων χρημάτων, εἰ ἐμέμεικτό τεωι· ἐν παντὶ γὰρ παντὸς μοῖρα ἔνεστιν, ὥσπερ ἐν τοῖς πρόσθεν μοι λέλεκται· καὶ ἂν ἐκώλυεν αὐτὸν τὰ συμμεμειγμένα, ὥστε μηδενὸς χρήματος κρατεῖν ὁμοίως ὡς καὶ μόνον ἐόντα ἐφ' ἑαυτοῦ.

Now as for the other <things>, they have a share of everything, but mind is unlimited and self-governing and is mixed with no thing, but alone is itself unto itself. For if it were not unto itself, but mixed with any other <thing>, it would have of all things, if it were mixed with any: for in everything there is a share of everything, as was said by me in the foregoing: and the <things> mixed with it would have prevented it, so that it would not have ruled any thing in the same way as it <now> does, being itself unto itself.

Clearly, the way in which Mind in Anaxagoras is 'by itself' or 'unto itself' owes something to Parmenides' description of his 'being'. Anaxagoras' dialect, albeit much affected by corrections in the course of transmission, has strong Ionic traces, and ἐπί with the genitive of the reflexive may well have been used by him not as a conscious alternative chosen to express something different, but as an idiomatic phrase synonymous with Parmenides καθ' ἑαυτό. This seems to be supported by fifth- and early fourth-century usage. The phrase αὐτὸ ἐφ' ἑωυτοῦ is frequent in the Hippocratic corpus; Herodotus has αὐτὸν ἐφ' ἑωυτοῦ at 5.106.17 and 7.10.9 of an individual, and more often ἐφ' ἑωυτῶν in the plural, of citizens of a city. But the expression is not restricted to the Ionic dialect. Thucydides puts αὐτὴ δ' ἐφ' ἑαυτῆς, said of a city, in the mouth of the Syracusan Athenagoras at 6.40.2; the same phrase is used by Xenophon, *Hellenica* 5.1.34; Plato himself uses αὐτὸ δ' ἐφ' αὐτοῦ at *Theaetetus* 160b10.

That is to say, while καθ' αὐτό is certainly overall more frequent than ἐφ' αὐτοῦ to express that someone or something is 'by itself', both expressions are in use and, so far as we can see, are synonymous. Plato could, had he so wished, have adopted Anaxagoras' ἐφ' αὐτοῦ, given his acquaintance with Anaxagoras' writings and in particular given his use of Anaxagoras B6 and B12.[29] It is Plato's conscious decision to use καθ' αὐτό, and *Symposium* 211a–b shows that, *inter alia* by using this phrase, Plato set what he said about the beautiful itself in relation to what Parmenides had said. Moreover, given the frequency of the phrase in the *Phaedo* and its occurrence in the *Meno*, Plato's decision to use καθ' αὐτό is not bound up with the context in the *Symposium*. Already with a view to the dialogues of his middle period as a whole, one must think in terms of Plato's reception of Parmenides' poem itself, not of an indirect reception of Parmenides' thought through later Eleatics and other Presocratic philosophers.[30]

These two examples[31] illustrate in different ways how an investigation into Plato's usage in conjunction with and in the context of interpretation of his philosophical thought may lead to pre-Platonic philosophical contexts an awareness of which enriches our understanding of Plato, because it allows us to ask for the specific differences between Plato's thought and that of his respective predecessors. These differences often point most clearly to what Plato's own philosophical contribution is at any given place. In the case of the first example, αὐτὰ τὰ ἴσα, we were dealing with a phrase which itself did not become part of Plato's technical vocabulary. In the case of (αὐτὸ) καθ' αὐτό, the phrase did establish itself as part of Plato's technical terminology and was as such received and adapted by Aristotle and subsequent philosophers. Both are examples of *phrases* rather than technical *terms*.[32] And both examples have

19

here been dealt with largely within the context of fifth- and fourth-century philosophy. This was possible because, while Plato's philosophical affiliations needed elucidation, there was no controversy over what the words under scrutiny meant themselves. That is, to some extent, different with the terms which form the subject of the subsequent investigation.

In the case of the verbs μετέχειν and μεταλαμβάνειν, ἐνεῖναι and παρεῖναι, and of the nouns παρουσία, εἶδος, ἰδέα and μορφή, it is important to see who among Plato's predecessors used which term in what context. But it is as important to establish in the first place what these terms meant.[33] Especially where there is controversy, this is not possible from within the corpus of sixth- to fourth-century philosophical texts alone. In establishing the semantics of μετέχειν, μεταλαμβάνειν, ἐνεῖναι, παρεῖναι, παρουσία, εἶδος, ἰδέα and their congeners, Part I and Part II are thus concerned with the histories of these words in Greek literature before the *Phaedo*, as in matters of usage and application only extensive diachronic discussion will allow certainty. The focus of Part III is on the usage of the *Phaedo*. It opens with a discussion of οὐσία, as Plato's own philosophical coinage, and in the subsequent chapters attempts an application of the results of the findings of Part I and II to a reading of *Phaedo* 95e–107b.

PART I

Chapter 1

μετέχειν

Socrates' first dialectical encounter in Plato's *Parmenides* is with Zeno, the younger companion and 'pupil' of Parmenides. Having listened to an exposition by Zeno, Socrates asks him to read out again the first ὑπόθεσις or 'supposition' of the first λόγος or 'argument' of his συγγράμματα or 'treatise' which had then for the first time been brought to Athens, by Zeno and Parmenides themselves (127a7–d7). Socrates then summarizes this first ὑπόθεσις (127e1–4):[34]

εἰ πολλά ἐστι τὰ ὄντα, ὡς ἄρα δεῖ αὐτὰ ὅμοιά τε εἶναι καὶ ἀνόμοια, τοῦτο δὲ δὴ ἀδύνατον· οὔτε γὰρ τὰ ἀνόμοια ὅμοια οὔτε τὰ ὅμοια ἀνόμοια οἷόν τε εἶναι;

[You say, Zeno:] If things are many (Or: If there are many things), it is then necessary for them to be similar and also dissimilar, but that is impossible; for neither can dissimilar be similar nor similar be dissimilar.

Socrates objects to this way of reasoning (128e6–129b6):

οὐ νομίζεις εἶναι αὐτὸ καθ᾽ αὑτὸ εἶδός τι ὁμοιότητος, καὶ τῷ τοιούτῳ αὖ ἄλλο τι ἐναντίον, ὃ ἔστιν ἀνόμοιον· τούτοιν δὲ δυοῖν ὄντοιν καὶ ἐμὲ καὶ σὲ καὶ τἆλλα ἃ δὴ πολλὰ καλοῦμεν μεταλαμβάνειν; καὶ τὰ μὲν τῆς ὁμοιότητος μεταλαμβάνοντα ὅμοια γίγνεσθαι ταύτῃ τε καὶ κατὰ τοσοῦτον ὅσον ἂν μεταλαμβάνῃ, τὰ δὲ τῆς ἀνομοιότητος ἀνόμοια, τὰ δὲ ἀμφοτέρων ἀμφότερα; εἰ δὲ καὶ πάντα ἐναντίων ὄντων ἀμφοτέρων μεταλαμβάνει, καὶ ἔστι τῷ μετέχειν ἀμφοῖν ὅμοιά τε καὶ ἀνόμοια αὐτὰ αὑτοῖς, τί θαυμαστόν; εἰ μὲν γὰρ αὐτὰ τὰ ὅμοιά τις ἀπέφαινεν ἀνόμοια γιγνόμενα ἢ τὰ ἀνόμοια ὅμοια, τέρας ἂν οἶμαι ἦν· εἰ δὲ τὰ τούτων μετέχοντα ἀμφοτέρων ἀμφότερα ἀποφαίνει πεπονθότα, οὐδὲν ἔμοιγε, ὦ Ζήνων, ἄτοπον δοκεῖ, οὐδέ γε εἰ ἓν ἅπαντα ἀποφαίνει τις τῷ μετέχειν τοῦ ἑνὸς καὶ ταὐτὰ ταῦτα πολλὰ τῷ πλήθους αὖ μετέχειν.

Do you not believe there to be, itself by itself, a certain 'type' that is similarity,[35] and to such a thing again some other thing opposite, which is: dissimilar? <And do you not believe that> while these two things *are* [Or: while these

21

are two], I and you and the other things which we call many come to share in them? And those which come to share in similarity come to be similar both in the way, and to the extent, in which they come to share <in similarity>, but those <which come to share> in dissimilarity <come to be> dissimilar, and those <which come to share in> both <come to be> both? But even if all things come to share in both, which are opposite, and if <all things>, through sharing in both, are similar and dissimilar, themselves from themselves, why is that surprising? Certainly, if someone were to show the similars themselves becoming dissimilar, or the dissimilar similar, that would be alarming, I think: but if he shows that those which share in both have this double fate, that, Zeno, does not seem to be anything extraordinary, nor yet if someone shows all things as one through sharing in one, and in turn these same things as many through sharing in multitude.

In response to Socrates' criticism, Parmenides commends his zeal and seeks further clarification concerning the sorts of εἴδη, 'ideas' or 'types', which Socrates supposes there are. In his subsequent discussion of Socrates' views (131a–134e), Parmenides employs the same dialectical mode of argumentation as Zeno had used in his ὑπόθεσις, and as Parmenides himself will use again in the ὑποθέσεις of the second half of the dialogue:

If things share in or partake of an εἶδος, an 'idea' or 'type', like similarity and dissimilarity, one and many, just, beautiful, good, etc., then they partake of either a part of it or of the whole. But they cannot partake of the whole. Therefore they must partake of a part. But if they partake of a part, then what they partake of must be divisible into parts. However, assuming the divisibility of εἴδη leads to absurdities. Therefore, things cannot partake either of the whole or of parts of εἴδη. Again, if there is an εἶδος whenever there seems to be one ἰδέα 'on', 'at' or 'with' (ἐπί) all of a set of many things – what is traditionally referred to as the 'one-over-many' argument – then there will be an infinite number of εἴδη for each set of many things. But this, too, is absurd. And so forth with the ὑποθέσεις that εἴδη are thoughts, that they are paradigms, and that they are separate. One would perhaps expect that the conclusion, in each case, is that therefore one should not posit or assume there to be participation in εἴδη in the first place. This, however, is not what Parmenides actually concludes; he rather suggests that a different sort of training is necessary if one wants to undertake a defence of the view that those εἴδη exist and are something, but that, at the same time, this view of Socrates', that there *are* εἴδη, is necessary for intelligent discourse (134e–135d). Despite this insistence on the part of Parmenides, though, many readers ancient and modern have seen Plato's arguments here as detrimental to the assumption of the existence of what is referred to as 'εἴδη' by Socrates and Parmenides.[36] One of the aims of the investigation in this chapter will be to uncover some of the underlying assumptions of

Parmenides' first attack on Socrates' suggestion that there are certain εἴδη besides the many things there are, and to investigate in what ways Plato could have responded to these assumptions. The point of departure in this investigation is the observation that when Parmenides summarizes Socrates' position, just as Socrates had summarized Zeno's before beginning with his criticisms, Parmenides adopts Socrates' own usage of 128e6–130a2 and characterizes the relationship between the many things in this world and the εἴδη (130e5, 131a4, 8, b5, c5, 9, e3) as μετέχειν or 'sharing' (131c6); the particular things in this world, which stand in such a relation to these εἴδη, are referred to as μετέχοντα or 'what is sharing' (131c6); and the process of a thing's getting into such a relationship is designated as μεταλαμβάνειν or 'coming-to-share' (130e6, 131a1, 4, 5, e4, 5; μετάληψις, 'a coming-to-share', 131a5). This usage is familiar from earlier dialogues, notably the *Phaedo*.[37] Accordingly, the criticisms Parmenides advances against Socrates' suggestions, which resemble suggestions made in the *Phaedo*, have, in some respect, been seen as criticisms advanced against what is maintained in the *Phaedo*. This applies in particular to the notion of μετέχειν or 'sharing' as introduced in that dialogue. However, before one can attempt to discover what, if anything, has changed in Plato's mind between his writing the *Phaedo* and his writing the *Parmenides*, one must ask what motivated Plato in the first place to use the language of μετέχειν in the *Phaedo*.

Looking at pre-Platonic occurrences of the verb μετέχειν, μεταλαμβάνειν and their cognates will enable us to see both what Plato meant when he introduced the term μετέχειν in the *Phaedo* and, in the event, to whom among his predecessors he was responding in doing so. This, in turn, may shed light on the question of stages of development in Plato's philosophy.

1. ἔχειν and μετέχειν: the syntax and semantics of 'having' and 'sharing'

The Greek verb μετέχειν denotes a state or event of 'sharing', μεταλαμβάνειν the process of 'coming to share'.[38] The two words are often translated as 'partake', 'participate', and this is certainly a correct rendering in many contexts; but unlike the Latin *parti-cipio*, derived from *pars*, 'part', and *capio*, 'take', neither μεταλαμβάνειν nor μετέχειν is inherently or necessarily connected with μέρος or any other Greek word for 'part'.[39] This is, of course, not meant to suggest that in English all instances of 'participate' refer to the having of a part of something.[40] However, only if it were the case that the Greek words μετέχειν and μεταλαμβάνειν necessarily entailed just that, would a question like that by Parmenides at 131a4–5 be inevitable:

οὐκοῦν ἤτοι ὅλου τοῦ εἴδους ἢ μέρους ἕκαστον τὸ μεταλαμβάνον μεταλαμβάνει;

Now, obviously, each thing that comes to share comes to share in the whole type or in a part?[41]

A focus of this and the following sections will therefore be the question of how something is 'shared in' in pre-Platonic and early Platonic texts, and to what extent it is true that 'sharing in something' amounts to 'having a part of something'.

The semantics of μετέχειν can only be understood against the background of the semantics of ἔχειν. As is common with prefixed verbs in Greek,[42] the derived word μετέχειν, as far as one can judge from the words it can meaningfully connect syntactically, seems to have retained a closeness to the simplex ἔχειν. From the point of view of classical Greek, the basic meaning of ἔχειν, is 'have'. There was, however, no single verb for 'having' in Indo-European. The notion would be expressed with the verb 'to be' and the dative of the person to or for whom something is.[43] In terms of etymology, the Greek verb ἔχειν goes back to an Indo-European root *segʰ-, found *inter alia* also in German *Sieg, siegen, besiegen*: 'victory', 'be victorious', 'defeat'; the original meaning of the root may have been something like 'hold down, subdue', then 'hold (as a possession)', then 'have'.[44] The root *segʰ- would have yielded proto-Greek *hekʰ- and, with dissimilation of aspirates according to Grassmann's Law, ἐχ-.[45] In our earliest text, the *Iliad*, ἔχειν can mean 'to have, hold, possess, keep' with reference to both physical objects and, on the other hand, habits, states and conditions, bodily and mental.[46] Its application is by no means restricted to the 'having' of physical spatio-temporal objects. The extension, or range of applicability, of the word ἔχειν, the number and nature of subjects and objects it can meaningfully connect from the *Iliad* onward, is larger even than that of its English counterpart 'have'.

The concept of ἔχειν, as that of English 'have', is so general as just to signify that there is a relation between two parties,[47] a relation in which the subject refers to the superior or governing, the object to the inferior or governed party. But what is superior and what inferior in any given case depends solely on the emphasis given by the speaker of the language as the author of an utterance.[48] In fifth-century Greek, one can say, 'this man has a fever'; but it is as common to say, 'a fever has this man', where 'the fever' is the grammatical subject and 'this man' the object, and that not only in the context of medical treatises.

As regards the syntax of ἔχειν, in most cases the verb in its transitive use connects a subject with a direct object which is in the accusative. As is the case also with e.g. λαμβάνειν, 'take', the direct object may on occasion also be a noun in the genitive rather than the accusative. This genitive has traditionally, but potentially misleadingly, been called partitive.[49] Because this genitive is the case commonly found with μετέχειν, I shall here first

24

discuss a number of instances of the simplex ἔχειν in which ἔχειν, without a prefix μετά-, governs the genitive: In Book 16 of the *Iliad*, Patroclus has slain Hector's companion Cebriones. They fight over the body of the fallen warrior, Hector on one side, Patroclus on the other (759–64):

ὣς περὶ Κεβριόναο δύω μήστωρες ἀϋτῆς
Πάτροκλός τε Μενοιτιάδης καὶ φαίδιμος Ἕκτωρ
ἵεντ' ἀλλήλων ταμέειν χρόα νηλέϊ χαλκῷ.
Ἕκτωρ μὲν κεφαλῆφιν ἐπεὶ λάβεν οὐχὶ μεθίει·
Πάτροκλος δ' ἑτέρωθεν ἔχεν ποδός· οἳ δὲ δὴ ἄλλοι
Τρῶες καὶ Δαναοὶ σύναγον κρατερὴν ὑσμίνην.

So, around Cebriones, the two, eager for battle,
Patroclus, son of Menoetius, and shining Hector,
went to cut each other's skin with the pitiless spear.
Now Hector, when he had taken hold from the side of the head, did not let go;
but Patroclus from (or: on) the other side, held the foot. But the others in turn,
Trojans and Danaans, drove together their strong force.

Hector took, or got hold of, the body at or from the side where the head was; Patroclus, from or on the other side, 'had him by the foot', ἔχεν ποδός. The genitive is here used to denote that what it is about the foot that is affected by the verbal action is not clearly specified or quantified: Patroclus did not take the whole foot or all of the foot, he 'got hold of' and 'had of' the foot.

A parallel case, relevant in the light of Plato's use of μεταλαμβάνειν, is that of λαμβάνειν with genitive at *Odyssey* 18.100–2. Odysseus, in disguise, has beaten the insolent beggar Irus in a boxing contest. The suitors laugh:

αὐτὰρ Ὀδυσσεὺς | ἕλκε διὲκ προθύροιο λαβὼν ποδός, ὄφρ' ἵκετ' αὐλὴν | αἰθούσης τε θύρας...

But Odysseus | dragged him out into the open, taking (or: having taken) him by the foot, until he reached the court-yard | and the gates of the porch...

Lest it be objected that, since the phrases ἔχεν ποδός and λαβὼν ποδός are in the same position in the verse, one place is copied from the other and, therefore, does not constitute independent evidence, one may also compare *Odyssey* 5.428.[50] Odysseus attempts to get ashore in treacherous waters; when a wave throws him against the coastal rocks, he follows the advice of Athena:

ἀμφοτέρῃσι δὲ χερσὶν ἐπεσσύμενος λάβε πέτρης,
τῆς ἔχετο[51] στενάχων, εἷος μέγα κῦμα παρῆλθε.

But with both hands he quickly took hold of the rock,
to which he was clinging, groaning, until the large wave had gone by.

The rock is large, and Odysseus does not envelop it with his hands, or 'take it' in that sense; he 'takes hold of it', λάβε πέτρης. The case of 'taking' perhaps illustrates the point at issue even more clearly than that of 'having'. In the case of material objects, the construction of the verbs for taking or having may indeed amount to 'taking or having a part of something' as opposed to 'taking or having all of it'. In fact, however, no actual part is specified. The fact that 'a part', in a wide sense of that word, rather than 'the whole' is affected is grounded in the status of the object as a material thing; there is nothing in the genitive case governed by the verb which of itself suggests 'partitivity'.

The following instance of ἔχειν with the genitive illustrates that. In Sophocles' *Oedipus Rex*, Jocasta addresses her son and husband Oedipus (707–10):

σύ νυν ἀφεὶς σεαυτὸν ὧν λέγεις πέρι
ἐμοῦ 'πάκουσον καὶ μάθ' οὕνεκ' ἐστί σοι
βρότειον οὐδὲν μαντικῆς ἔχον τέχνης·
φανῶ δέ σοι σημεῖα τῶνδε σύντομα.

Now you, release yourself from the things you talk about
and listen to me and learn why you should assume that[52]
there is nothing mortal 'having of' the mantic skill:
and I shall show you succinct proofs of this.

While in the case of a material object the view that a part was 'had' could be maintained, in the case of something non-material like a skill that is less feasible. There is no suggestion here at least that anyone, mortal or immortal, who 'has of' the mantic skill should have only part of it on the grounds that there could be others who also 'have of' it. When both Zeus and Apollo 'have of' the mantic skill, that does not mean that Zeus knows what will happen next month and Apollo knows what will happen in the month after that. Applying the categories of parts and wholes to the issue of 'having of' or 'being in possession of' a skill would here introduce an alien notion. It is certainly possible that there are degrees of mastery with any given skill; but if this is so, the notion of 'degree' is not implied in, and cannot without further qualification be expressed by, ἔχειν, or for that matter μετέχειν, with the genitive.

2. μετέχειν in early Greek literature
The main difference in meaning between the simplex ἔχειν and the prefixed μετέχειν[53] lies in the notion that there is somebody 'with whom' one 'has' or 'has of' something. In this sense, 'share' or 'participate' can often be appropriate translations for μετέχειν, the 'having of something with somebody'. The following pre-Platonic and early Platonic instances of

μετέχειν have been selected to illustrate the range of usage and connotations of the word.

The prologue of Euripides' *Heraclidae* is spoken by Heracles' long-standing friend and companion, Iolaus. After a gnomic opening about the predicament of the man who stands by those close to him, Iolaus introduces himself as an actual example of this general statement (6–9):

ἐγὼ γὰρ αἰδοῖ καὶ τὸ συγγενὲς σέβων,
ἐξὸν κατ' Ἄργος ἡσύχως ναίειν, πόνων
πλείστων μετέσχον εἷς ἀνὴρ Ἡρακλέει,
ὅτ' ἦν μεθ' ἡμῶν...

For I, honouring decorously my kin,
while it would have been possible for me to live in peace at Argos,
being one man, I 'had of' very many toils indeed 'with' Hercules,
when he was with us...

Iolaus 'had of' very many toils which are not specified. 'Toils' as such are not material objects, even if they involve physical labour. The grammatical subject, the personal name 'Iolaus', refers to a single person; the one with whom he worked is given in a sociative dative.[54] This sentence of Euripides reflects the original syntactical situation. A parallel example is provided by Pindar. After an illustration of the vain deceitfulness of a dishonest person, Pindar contrasts himself with that man and his practices (*Pythian* 2.83):

οὔ οἱ μετέχω θράσεος·

I do not share with him his boldness.

Here, it is more obvious than with the previous example that the dative (οἱ, 'with him') is a sociative. One may further compare Xenophon, *Historia Graeca* 2.4.20–1. The context is that of the defeat in battle of the 'three thousand' hoplites who support the oligarchy of the 'thirty' in 404 BC. They are addressed by Cleocritus, a herald, who is part of the democratic party of exiles who hold the fortress of Phyle under the leadership of Thrasybulus. Cleocritus says:

τί ἀποκτεῖναι βούλεσθε; ἡμεῖς γὰρ ὑμᾶς κακὸν μὲν οὐδὲν πώποτε ἐποιήσαμεν,
μετεσχήκαμεν δὲ ὑμῖν καὶ ἱερῶν τῶν σεμνοτάτων καὶ θυσιῶν καὶ ἑορτῶν τῶν
καλλίστων, καὶ συγχορευταὶ καὶ συμφοιτηταὶ γεγενήμεθα καὶ συστρατιῶται,
καὶ πολλὰ μεθ' ὑμῶν κεκινδυνεύκαμεν καὶ κατὰ γῆν καὶ κατὰ θάλατταν ὑπὲρ
τῆς κοινῆς ἀμφοτέρων ἡμῶν σωτηρίας τε καὶ ἐλευθερίας. πρὸς θεῶν πατρῴων
καὶ μητρῴων καὶ συγγενείας καὶ κηδεστίας καὶ ἑταιρίας, πάντων γὰρ τούτων
πολλοὶ κοινωνοῦμεν ἀλλήλοις, αἰδούμενοι καὶ θεοὺς καὶ ἀνθρώπους παύσασθε
ἁμαρτάνοντες εἰς τὴν πατρίδα, καὶ μὴ πείθεσθε τοῖς ἀνοσιωτάτοις τριάκοντα,
οἳ ἰδίων κερδέων ἕνεκα ὀλίγου δεῖν πλείους ἀπεκτόνασιν Ἀθηναίων ἐν ὀκτὼ
μησὶν ἢ πάντες Πελοποννήσιοι δέκα ἔτη πολεμοῦντες.

27

Why do you want to kill us? Indeed, we have not ever done you any harm, but we share with you the most reverend holy acts and sacrifices and the most beautiful feasts, we were fellow-dancers in the chorus, fellow-students, fellow-soldiers, and we have faced many dangers with you, both on land and by sea, for the sake of common salvation and freedom of both our parties. By the gods of our fathers and mothers and by our kinship and connection and fellowship – indeed, we, many of us, have in common with each other all those things – in honouring and revering gods and men, cease from transgressing against the fatherland, and do not obey those most unholy thirty, who for their own private gain have killed very nearly more of the Athenians in eight months than all the Peloponnesians in ten years of war.

In this case, it is obvious that the shared sacrifices are occasions or events participated in by all present: there is no question of division or distribution, parts or wholes.[55] The passage has been quoted at length because Xenophon lets the herald begin his exhortation with a reference to their sharing of sacrifices and feasts and go on to talk about the resulting 'having things in common', κοινωνοῦμεν ἀλλήλοις; it may be important with a view to *Phaedo* 100 that the verbs μετέχειν and κοινωνεῖν can naturally co-occur, apparently as synonyms, regardless of the precise relationships and dependencies expressed or intended in either context. As regards Xenophon's use of μετέχειν at this place, however, one should note that Xenophon the author lets Cleocritus the herald use the same term for sharing which had previously been used by Critias, the uncle of Plato, who was leader of the thirty tyrants; by letting the two speakers employ the same terminology for similar purposes, attention is drawn to the different activities in which the addressees (have) allegedly participate(d), the difference in the things shared. After treacherously capturing the male citizens of Eleusis and bringing them in front of an Athenian 'court', Critias as spokesman of the thirty had, in order to implicate them in his crimes, addressed the three thousand thus (2.4.9):

ἡμεῖς, ἔφη, ὦ ἄνδρες, οὐδὲν ἧττον ὑμῖν κατασκευάζομεν τὴν πολιτείαν ἢ ἡμῖν αὐτοῖς. δεῖ οὖν ὑμᾶς, ὥσπερ καὶ τιμῶν μεθέξετε, οὕτω καὶ τῶν κινδύνων μετέχειν. τῶν οὖν συνειλημμένων Ἐλευσινίων καταψηφιστέον ἐστίν, ἵνα ταὐτὰ ἡμῖν καὶ θαρρῆτε καὶ φοβῆσθε.

We, he said, men, establish and arrange the constitution in no way less for you than for us ourselves. So it is necessary, as you will also share in <our> honours, that in the same way you share in <our> dangers too. So the captured Eleusinians are to be condemned, in order that you dare and you fear the same things as we do.

While in this passage there is no dative with μετέχειν, the dative ἡμῖν in the last clause quoted depends on the pronoun ταὐτὰ as a sociative dative in the requisite way.[56]

28

A development of the bare sociative dative can be seen at Sophocles, *Electra* 1168, where the force of the case is boosted by the addition of a preposition. At the news of Orestes' death, Electra addresses the urn in which she supposes the ashes of her brother to be contained (1165–9):

τοίγαρ σὺ δέξαι μ' ἐς τὸ σὸν τόδε στέγος,
τὴν μηδὲν ἐς τὸ μηδέν, ὡς σὺν σοὶ κάτω
ναίω τὸ λοιπόν. καὶ γὰρ ἡνίκ' ἦσθ' ἄνω,
ξὺν σοὶ μετεῖχον τῶν ἴσων· καὶ νῦν ποθῶ
τοῦ σοῦ θανοῦσα μὴ ἀπολείπεσθαι τάφου.

Receive me now in this your house,
me who is nothing receive in what is nothing, so that I live with you below
for the rest of time; for both when you were above,
I had with you a share of equal things: and now I yearn
in dying not to leave your grave.

The things which are equal in this case are not, and cannot be, quantified; as with the previous examples, there is no sharing in the sense of distribution involved. In this instance, the sociative force of the dative has been emphasized by addition of the preposition ξύν, 'with'.

A variant to the dative – in terms of the history of the language likewise later in origin – is μετά with the genitive. An example is found in a Theognidean epigram. 'Poverty, why don't you visit our neighbour?' (353 f.):

μηδὲ μεθ' ἡμέων | αἰεὶ δυστήνου τοῦδε βίου μέτεχε.

And do not with us always share this wretched life.

Here, the preposition μετά, 'with', not only emphasizes the community of Poverty with those who address her, it is also less ambiguous than a bare dative would be; in that way, the prepositional phrase can be near the beginning of the line.[57] In most cases, however, the point of reference of the sociative dative or the genitive with μετά, respectively, would unambiguously be known from the content of the clause itself or from its context; that is why the complement can frequently be omitted altogether, as at Herodotus 3.80:

εἴδετε μὲν γὰρ τὴν Καμβύσεω ὕβριν ἐπ' ὅσον ἐπεξῆλθε, μετεσχήκατε δὲ καὶ τῆς τοῦ μάγου ὕβριος.

For you know which point the hybris of Cambyses had reached; and you as well have had your share of the hybris of the Magus.

The Persians who are addressed here had first been ruled by the king Cambyses and then by two brothers from the tribe of the Magi. The Persians had experienced together with each other, and each 'had with the others of', the hybris displayed by the tyrants. A parallel case is Herodotus 1.127; most of the army of the Medes has been persuaded to side with the Persians in an act of treason; only a few do not know of the plan:

ὡς δὲ οἱ Μῆδοι στρατευσάμενοι τοῖσι Πέρσῃσι συνέμισγον, οἱ μέν τινες αὐτῶν ἐμάχοντο, ὅσοι μὴ τοῦ λόγου μετέσχον, οἱ δὲ αὐτομόλεον πρὸς τοὺς Πέρσας, οἱ δὲ πλεῖστοι ἐθελοκάκεόν τε καὶ ἔφευγον.

But as the Medes going into battle encountered the Persians, some of them fought, as many as did not share in the plan, but others defected to the Persians, and most were mean and took flight.

Those who 'are in the secret' are contrasted with those who are not; some 'have of' or 'share in' the word, together with each other, others do not 'have it together with those who do'. Those who share in the word or plan or secret, however, do not each have part of it but rather know, each of them, the plan which consists in siding with the Persians.[58]

One final example of this application of μετέχειν gives rise to a further consideration. Sappho fr. 54 (LP) is quoted by Stobaeus (*Florilegium* 4.12):

κατθάνοισα δὲ κείσῃι οὐδέ ποτα
μναμοσύνα σέθεν
ἔσσετ' οὐδὲ πόθα <εἰς> ὔστερον· οὐ
γὰρ πεδέχῃις βρόδων
τῶν ἐκ Πιερίας, ἀλλ' ἀφάνης
κἠν Ἀίδα δόμωι
φοιτάσεις πὲδ ἀμαύρων νεκύων
ἐκπεποταμένα.[59]

When you die it is over:
later on no memory,
no longing will ask for you,
for you did not 'have of' the roses,
those of Pieria; but inconspicuously
to the house of Hades
you will go, with the feeble dead,
already flown away.

In this case, those who have those roses of Pieria are, by way of contrast, tacitly implied in the description of the one addressed who does not have them. This, like the example of Herodotus 1.127, is of importance in the following respect: One would naturally assume that when some are said not to 'have of' the flowers of the Muses or not to be in the secret, there are others who do share in inspiration or in the secret, respectively. With a negative statement, though, one could imagine a situation in which nobody actually does share in inspiration or in the secret, or in whatever else is at issue. If a situation of

30

someone's having of something together with someone else is negated for an individual, there are the three possible cases of (a) a number of others' having the object, (b) another single individual's having the object, and (c) no-one else's having the object. This trichotomy can then be extended to positive statements in the following way. If someone has something together with someone else, 'someone else' may refer to more than one person or just one person. The next step is to think of a situation in which many people *could* have something together with others. For each individual, one would say that once he has acquired something he 'has of' it together with all those who also have acquired it. To say that, however, does not presuppose that anyone else actually has acquired it or 'has of it'. If the qualification 'together with those who have acquired it' is left unexpressed, as in the instances quoted, it would seem a natural extension for the application of the verb μετέχειν to be applied to cases of only one person's actually 'having of' something, if the nature and extent of that 'having' is left unspecified, and if there *could* be others who also have of it.

3. μετέχειν μέρος τινός: 'having a part of something' and related issues

In cases of 'having of' something in which that which one 'has of' something is not precisely specified, there can nevertheless be some kind of adverbial complement, as in e.g. Xenophon, *Hiero* 2.6:

τῶν μεγίστων ἀγαθῶν ἐλάχιστα μετέχουσιν.

They share least in the greatest goods.

Here ἐλάχιστα is clearly adverbial,[60] indicating some sort of degree, though it would be difficult to measure and quantify the μέγιστα ἀγαθά precisely. By contrast, when that which is had with others is either quantified or precisely defined otherwise, μετέχειν governs a direct accusative object. This usage is confined to a few cases and generally rare. An example is Aristophanes, *Plutus* 1144:

οὐ γὰρ μετεῖχες τὰς ἴσας πληγὰς ἐμοί.

For you don't share with me the same [number of] blows.

The adjective ἴσος characterizes the object as something definite and quanti-fiable, in this case 'the same blows' the speaker receives or, alternatively, 'the same number of blows'. In a parallel way, adjectival αὐτός is employed by Demosthenes (Lexic. ad Philemon. gramm. p. 253 Osann.):

μετέχοντες τὴν αὐτὴν δόξαν τοῖς Λακεδαιμονίοις.

They shared with the Spartans the same opinion.

As with the simplex ἔχειν, a direct object which is concrete and clearly defined is in the accusative. Additionally, one should note that with the last two examples also those together with whom one has something are explicitly given in the sentence.[61]

A related type of extension of μετέχειν plus genitive is that with indefinite or interrogative τί. Herodotus recounts a speech by Artabanus to his nephew Xerxes, who had a nightly vision whose divine origin Artabanus doubts. He summarizes (7.16.3):

> εἰ δὲ ἄρα μή ἐστι τοῦτο τοιοῦτο οἷον ἐγὼ διαιρέω, ἀλλά τι τοῦ θείου μετέχον, σὺ πᾶν αὐτὸ συλλαβὼν εἴρηκας· φανήτω γὰρ δὴ καὶ ἐμοί, ὡς καὶ σοί, διακελευόμενον.

> But if this is not something of the sort I analyse it as, but has something of the divine, you will have correctly summed it all up: indeed, let it thus appear to me, too, as it appeared to you, being summoned.

'But if it has something [or: in some respect] of the divine' is an extension of the simple ἀλλὰ τοῦ θείου μετέχον, 'but if it had of the divine'. τι, 'something', in this context comes close to indefinite που, 'somehow, in some way', or to other similar adverbial complements which underline rather than delimit the vagueness of the reference of object and verb; that is all the more so if one construes τι as an accusative of respect.

Finally, one case of μετέχειν with direct accusative object is that of μετέχειν μέρος or μοῖραν τινός, where μετέχειν is employed to denote the having of something quantified, together with someone else or, in fact, more frequently, together with many others. Herodotus describes the land of the Massagetae whom Cyrus wants to subdue after his conquest of Babylon. Having mentioned some peculiarities of other regions and peoples bordering the Caspian sea, he continues with an account of the great plain extending to the east as far as the eye can see (1.204):

> τοῦ ὦν δὴ πεδίου <τούτου> τοῦ μεγάλου οὐκ ἐλαχίστην μοῖραν μετέχουσι οἱ Μασσαγέται.

> Now, the Massagetae had not the least part of this plain.

Here, the 'part had' is in the accusative of the direct object, that of which the part is a part, that is to say that which is shared, is in the genitive, as with the previous example.[62] This usage, common enough with material objects, could be extended to cases which do not, or not exclusively, involve material objects. At Thucydides 1.73, representatives of the Athenians summarize their efforts in the Persian wars:[63]

> καὶ γὰρ ὅτε ἐδρῶμεν, ἐπ᾽ ὠφελίᾳ ἐκινδυνεύετο, ἧς τοῦ μὲν ἔργου μέρος μετέσχετε, τοῦ δὲ λόγου μὴ παντός, εἴ τι ὠφέλει, στερισκώμεθα.

For when we acted, we took a risk for a benefit of whose effect you have a share <with us>, but of whose glory, if it is of benefit, <we ask you> not to deprive us altogether.

The clause ἧς τοῦ μὲν ἔργου μέρος μετέσχετε refers to part of the gain of the Athenian efforts which now the Spartans and the other Greeks have together with the Athenians; μέρος does here not solely refer to a physical part of a physical object.[64]

4. The syntax of μετέχειν: a summary

The phrase μετέχειν μέρος τινός is thus established in pre-Platonic prose. It means 'having a share of something', where the share and the thing shared in can, but need not exclusively, be material, physical objects. One should, though, note a peculiarity inherent in the expression μετέχειν μέρος τινός: If someone 'has of' something and someone else also 'has of' it in the requisite way, they 'have of' it together. Alternatively one may say: someone has something together with someone else. If, however, someone has a part of something and someone else also has a part of it, neither of them has his part together with the other party unless they both happen to have the same part. That, though, is clearly not the case in Herodotus' description of the land in which the Massagetae dwell. When Herodotus says that 'they have not the smallest part of the plain', and uses μετέχειν to express that relation of possession, it is implied that there are others who live in and possess other parts and not the same part of the same plain.[65]

This difficulty, inherent in the logic of the expression μετέχειν μέρος τινός, suggests that μέρος is an addition, in some ways redundant, to the original expression μετέχειν τινός. That in itself, as we have seen, is an extension of the simple ἔχειν τινός. The addition of the prefix μετα- originally had the purpose of making explicit that there are many[66] who 'have of' the same thing together. μετέχειν governs the genitive, for the same reason ἔχειν sometimes governs the genitive, when the object, or the relation between subject and object expressed by the verb, is in some way undefined or undefinable, lacking specification, qualification or quantification. On the other hand, μετέχειν, like ἔχειν on most occasions, governs the accusative when the object referred to is something concrete, known and defined, or a particular instantiation of something. If the thing shared in is a material, physical, quantifiable object and if the phrase μετέχειν μέρος τινός is employed, the issue of parts and wholes arises, and one can legitimately ask for the size or quantity of the share.

Of the examples discussed above, however, some at least do by their content not qualify for an interpretation in terms of parts and wholes. Even if Pindar, *Pythian* 2.83 – οὔ οἱ μετέχω θράσεος, 'I do not share that boldness

with him', and Theognis' address to Poverty (353 f.) – ...μηδὲ μεθ᾽ ἡμέων |
αἰεὶ δυστήνου τοῦδε βίου μέτεχε, 'do not with us have always of this wretched
life' – are left aside because the clauses are negative so that it is both inde-
terminable and irrelevant if part or whole of the object is had, at Herodotus
3.80 (εἴδετε μὲν γὰρ τὴν Καμβύσεω ὕβριν ἐπ᾽ ὅσον ἐπεξῆλθε, μετεσχήκατε δὲ
καὶ τῆς τοῦ μάγου ὕβριος, 'for you know which point the hybris of Cambyses
had reached; and you as well have had your share of the hybris of the Magus'),
no-one would assume that Otanes addresses his audience μετεσχήκατε (plus
genitive) because he meant to imply that they had (or had experienced) one
part of the tyrant's insolence, while there was another part they did not have
or 'have of'. As we have seen, the same is true of Herodotus 1.127: οἱ μέν
τινες αὐτῶν ἐμάχοντο, ὅσοι μὴ τοῦ λόγου μετέσχον, 'the one part of them
fought, all those who did not share in the secret': this does not suggest that
those who were in the secret had heard only part of the words or part of the
plan, speech or story; those who shared the secret all knew the full story.

It should be added at this point, though, that while the language-historical
considerations given above (on why and how both ἔχειν and μετέχειν govern
either the accusative or the genitive, depending on context) can explain
patterns of early usage, there are no prescriptive rules and regulations.
Language changes. In fifth- and fourth-century Greek, transitive ἔχειν
governs a direct accusative object, with very few exceptions; μετέχειν governs
a direct genitive object, with the exception of a few set phrases like μετέχειν
μέρος τινός. That is to say, it is not possible to analyse each and every instance
of the simplex with the accusative as an example of a subject's having a particular, well-specified object, or, conversely, each and every instance of μετέχειν
with the genitive as an example of the sharing of an unspecified object. The
distinction seems to hold true for the most part. It is, however, on the one
hand the nature of the object shared, on the other the overall context and the
intentions of the author that determine whether μετέχειν with the genitive
expresses the sharing or participating in something by having a part of it or,
contrariwise, by having of a thing in the same way in which others who share
also have of that thing. Each instance must be interpreted in its own right.

5. μετέχειν in Plato's *Laches*

Instances of the verbs μετέχειν and μεταλαμβάνειν in Plato's early dialogues
are in line with pre-Platonic usage. The *Laches* starts off as a conversation
on the right education of the young, held in Athens some time between the
battle at Delium in 424 BC (*Laches* 181b) and that of Mantinea in which
Laches fell in 418 BC.[67] The initial question – whether it is useful for boys
to learn how to fight in full armour from someone who practises that as an
art-form – is turned into an enquiry into the nature of ἀνδρεία, 'courage',

when Socrates enters the discussion. He does so on the recommendation of Laches, a renowned general, who praises Socrates for his prowess in battle. Laches' opinion that justice is some sort of perseverance is questioned by Socrates when conclusions drawn from the original statement and additional premises held by Laches start to contradict each other (193e3):

ἔργῳ μὲν γάρ, ὡς ἔοικε, φαίη ἄν τις ἡμᾶς ἀνδρείας μετέχειν, λόγῳ δ', ὡς ἐγῷμαι, οὐκ ἄν, εἰ νῦν ἡμῶν ἀκούσειε διαλεγομένων.

For, as it seems, someone overhearing our conversation now may say that in our deeds we share in bravery, but not, as I believe, in our words.

The point of that remark clearly is that while both Laches and Socrates are brave in battle, in contrast with others (cf. 181b), they are not able to sustain an argument in conversation. In conversation, they have no share in bravery at all, it seems. With regard to their deeds, however, Socrates simply states that they have displayed courage, not that they are in partial but not full possession of it. In fact, any suggestion that they are not really or fully courageous would almost defeat the purpose of the argument at this point. It seems unlikely that the author Plato or his character Socrates had the notion of 'part' in mind at all when employing the 'partitive' genitive ἀνδρείας here.[68]

Towards the end of the dialogue *Laches*, Nicias proposes his view of justice as some sort of ἐπιστήμη or understanding. Laches, who is in mocking, if not hostile, opposition after having been refuted by Socrates, tries to ridicule Nicias for his semantic distinction between 'daring' and 'courageous' and hopes to gain Socrates' approval when he brands it as vain sophistry, not worthy of one entrusted with a leading role in the city. To that Socrates replies (197e2):

πρέπει μέν που, ὦ μακάριε, τῶν μεγίστων προστατοῦντι μεγίστης φρονήσεως μετέχειν· δοκεῖ δέ μοι Νικίας ἄξιος εἶναι ἐπισκέψεως, ὅποι ποτὲ βλέπων τοὔνομα τοῦτο τίθησι τὴν ἀνδρείαν.

It is somehow fitting, dear friend, for the one who commands to 'have of' the greatest insight: and Nicias seems to me worthy of consideration, and it is worth seeing what he was envisaging when he posited that term 'courage'.

Socrates makes a general observation, introduced with πρέπει, 'it is fitting or beseeming'. What is fitting or beseeming may at times be different from what is actually achieved. But Socrates does not talk about that here. He describes in the abstract what is to be expected and what is aimed at. One should expect that a great man of action shares in the greatest insight – together with other great men who may also be sharing this insight. If Prodicus, Damon and Nicias all have insight into the distinction between θρασύς and ἀνδρεῖος, 'daring' and 'courageous', one can say μετέχουσι ταύτης τῆς ἐπιστήμης, 'they

share this insight', and the meaning of that is that they have all understood
that distinction, not that each one of them has understood part of it, let
alone each one a different part. There is no differentiation as regards degrees
of courage. From 196d1 onwards, the moment when Socrates starts inter-
rogating Nicias, he treats that ἐπιστήμη which is ἀνδρεῖα as something which
is either present or absent. Not everybody has it (196d4); a physician or
prophet – who each have their own specific ἐπιστήμη – will not be brave ἐὰν
μὴ αὐτὴν ταύτην τὴν ἐπιστήμην προσλάβῃ, 'unless he grasps this knowledge
in addition'; all animals, which are called ἄλογα at *Protagoras* 321c1, do not
have it. Laches and Lamachus, however, are brave and in that respect wise.
The question whether they are brave in one respect but not in another, or
brave but not fully so, is not raised.

6. μετέχειν in Plato's *Charmides*
Charmides 158c4 seems, at first sight, to present a slightly different case.
Socrates asks Charmides:

> αὐτὸς οὖν μοι εἰπὲ πότερον ὁμολογεῖς τῷδε καὶ φῂς ἱκανῶς ἤδη σωφροσύνης
> μετέχειν ἢ ἐνδεὴς εἶναι;

> Please, therefore, to inform me whether you admit the truth of what Critias has
> been saying; have you or have you not this quality of temperance? (tr. Jowett)

This translation by Jowett is not literal, but it is correct as regards the exclu-
siveness of choice. However, there is the possibility that Socrates does not
doubt that Charmides was a moderate boy on the whole, but that he asks
here specifically if Charmides is already sufficiently in possession of temperance and moderation. There may be degrees of σωφροσύνη, although these
putative degrees are at no stage the topic of the dialogue. If, however, there
are here degrees of σωφροσύνη, that would be implied by the adverb ἱκανῶς,
'sufficiently', and not by the verb μετέχειν. After all, if there were degrees of
moderation, ἱκανῶς σωφροσύνης μετέχειν would mean 'to be sufficiently in
possession of moderation' and therefore 'to be moderate'. Instructive in that
respect is the conclusion of the dialogue. After the failure of Charmides,
Critias and Socrates to see what σωφροσύνη is, and after Socrates has
suspected that it, σωφροσύνη, may be altogether useless, he takes back this
last verdict, turning to Charmides (175e5):

> ταῦτ' οὖν πάνυ μὲν οὐκ οἴομαι οὕτως ἔχειν, ἀλλ' ἐμὲ φαῦλον εἶναι ζητητήν· ἐπεὶ
> τήν γε σωφροσύνην μέγα τι ἀγαθὸν εἶναι, καὶ εἴπερ γε ἔχεις αὐτό, μακάριον
> εἶναί σε. ἀλλ' ὅρα εἰ ἔχεις τε καὶ μηδὲν δέῃ τῆς ἐπῳδῆς· εἰ γὰρ ἔχεις…

> This, now, I do not at all believe to be so, but I believe rather that I am a poor
> searcher: because I do believe that σωφροσύνη is certainly some great good, and

36

if you have it, you are happy and blessed. But see if you have it and if you do not need the incantation: for if you have it...

At the beginning of the dialogue – when Charmides was compared with the other youths of his age, and before a discussion of what σωφροσύνη is had been entered into – Socrates had asked if Charmides sufficiently 'had of' moderation and health of soul. At the end of the conversation which centred first on Charmides and then on σωφροσύνη, Socrates refers to the virtue as μέγα τι ἀγαθὸν, 'a great good', and can then address Charmides as an individual who has, or does not have, something which is at that moment treated as a single, well-specified thing. Socrates three times uses the simplex ἔχειν with accusative to denote the relation of 'having the virtue of moderation'. The choice of μετέχειν with genitive or ἔχειν with accusative seems to be a matter of perspective and emphasis. The choice does not seem to be determined by considerations of quantitative or qualitative gradation or partial participation *versus* perfection and full possession.

7. ἔχειν and μετέχειν in Plato's *Protagoras*

In Plato's *Protagoras*, Socrates asks Protagoras in what way anyone associating with the sophist would benefit. To justify his claim that he can make people better and therefore convey a certain ἀρετή, 'excellence', Protagoras tells a myth to illustrate the distribution among human beings of crafts and skills on the one hand and things like δικαιοσύνη, 'justice', and σωφροσύνη, 'prudent moderation', on the other. In the myth, the Titan Epimetheus equips all the animals with attributes and abilities necessary for survival, but through his lack of prudence leaves men unequipped. To make up for that omission, his brother Prometheus steals a certain wisdom, skill, or knowledge from the gods Hephaestus and Athena and gives it to man (321d3–5):

τὴν μὲν οὖν περὶ τὸν βίον σοφίαν ἄνθρωπος ταύτῃ ἔσχεν, τὴν δὲ πολιτικὴν οὐκ εἶχεν.

So man had the wisdom, skill, or knowledge about life, but the political, social or communal wisdom or skill he had not.

ἄνθρωπος, or 'man', is here in the collective singular; mankind is considered in isolation; their 'having' or 'possessing a skill' is expressed by ἔχειν with the accusative.[69]

Shortly after that, Plato lets Protagoras summarize: ὁ ἄνθρωπος θείας μέτεσχε μοίρας (322a3), 'man shared the divine lot, portion, share or condition'.[70] Here, mankind is seen as one group, the gods as another. Both groups have something in common. Together with the other, each of them 'has of' or shares the same condition of possessing a certain wisdom or knowledge. This 'having together with' someone else is expressed by μετέχειν.[71] This distinction between the simplex and the prefixed verb is maintained subsequently. Because, recounts Protagoras, 'men did not yet have social skills' – πολιτικὴν γὰρ τέχνην οὔπω εἶχον (322b5) – they were neither able to wage war against the animals nor to live together without doing each other wrong. Zeus fears for the extinction of the race and sends Hermes to bring αἰδώς and δίκη, 'awe'[72] and 'right', to mankind, 'so that there be order and chains of friendship bringing them together' (322c2). Protagoras continues (322c3–323d2):

ἐρωτᾷ οὖν Ἑρμῆς Δία τίνα οὖν τρόπον δοίη δίκην καὶ αἰδῶ ἀνθρώποις·
'πότερον ὡς αἱ τέχναι νενέμηνται, οὕτω καὶ ταύτας νείμω; νενέμηνται δὲ
ὧδε· εἷς ἔχων ἰατρικὴν πολλοῖς ἱκανὸς ἰδιώταις, καὶ οἱ ἄλλοι δημιουργοί·
καὶ δίκην δὴ καὶ αἰδῶ οὕτω θῶ ἐν τοῖς ἀνθρώποις, ἢ ἐπὶ πάντας νείμω;'
– 'ἐπὶ πάντας,' ἔφη ὁ Ζεύς, 'καὶ πάντες μετεχόντων· οὐ γὰρ ἂν γένοιντο
πόλεις, εἰ ὀλίγοι αὐτῶν μετέχοιεν ὥσπερ ἄλλων τεχνῶν· καὶ νόμον γε θὲς
παρ' ἐμοῦ τὸν μὴ δυνάμενον αἰδοῦς καὶ δίκης μετέχειν κτείνειν ὡς νόσον
πόλεως.' οὕτω δή, ὦ Σώκρατες, καὶ διὰ ταῦτα οἵ τε ἄλλοι καὶ Ἀθηναῖοι,
ὅταν μὲν περὶ ἀρετῆς τεκτονικῆς ᾖ λόγος ἢ ἄλλης τινὸς δημιουργικῆς,
ὀλίγοις οἴονται μετεῖναι συμβουλῆς, καὶ ἐάν τις ἐκτὸς ὢν τῶν ὀλίγων
συμβουλεύῃ, οὐκ ἀνέχονται, ὡς σὺ φῄς – εἰκότως, ὡς ἐγώ φημι – ὅταν δὲ εἰς
συμβουλὴν πολιτικῆς ἀρετῆς ἴωσιν, ἣν δεῖ διὰ δικαιοσύνης πᾶσαν ἰέναι καὶ
σωφροσύνης, εἰκότως ἅπαντος ἀνδρὸς ἀνέχονται, ὡς παντὶ προσῆκον ταύτης
γε μετέχειν τῆς ἀρετῆς ἢ μὴ εἶναι πόλεις. αὕτη, ὦ Σώκρατες, τούτου αἰτία.
  ἵνα δὲ μὴ οἴῃ ἀπατᾶσθαι ὡς τῷ ὄντι ἡγοῦνται πάντες ἄνθρωποι πάντα ἄνδρα
μετέχειν δικαιοσύνης τε καὶ τῆς ἄλλης πολιτικῆς ἀρετῆς, τόδε αὖ λαβὲ τεκμήριον.
ἐν γὰρ ταῖς ἄλλαις ἀρεταῖς, ὥσπερ σὺ λέγεις, ἐάν τις φῇ ἀγαθὸς αὐλητὴς εἶναι,
ἢ ἄλλην ἡντινοῦν τέχνην ἣν μὴ ἔστιν, ἢ καταγελῶσιν ἢ χαλεπαίνουσιν, καὶ οἱ
οἰκεῖοι προσιόντες νουθετοῦσιν ὡς μαινόμενον· ἐν δὲ δικαιοσύνῃ καὶ ἐν τῇ ἄλλῃ
πολιτικῇ ἀρετῇ, ἐάν τινα καὶ εἰδῶσιν ὅτι ἄδικός ἐστιν, ἐὰν οὗτος αὐτὸς καθ'
αὑτοῦ τἀληθῆ λέγῃ ἐναντίον πολλῶν, ὃ ἐκεῖ σωφροσύνην ἡγοῦντο εἶναι, τἀληθῆ
λέγειν, ἐνταῦθα μανίαν, καί φασιν πάντας δεῖν φάναι εἶναι δικαίους, ἐάντε ὦσιν
ἐάντε μή, ἢ μαίνεσθαι τὸν μὴ προσποιούμενον δικαιοσύνην·[73] ὡς ἀναγκαῖον
οὐδένα ὅντιν' οὐχὶ ἁμῶς γέ πως μετέχειν αὐτῆς, ἢ μὴ εἶναι ἐν ἀνθρώποις.
  ὅτι μὲν οὖν πάντ' ἄνδρα εἰκότως ἀποδέχονται περὶ ταύτης τῆς ἀρετῆς
σύμβουλον διὰ τὸ ἡγεῖσθαι παντὶ μετεῖναι αὐτῆς, ταῦτα λέγω· ὅτι δὲ αὐτὴν
οὐ φύσει ἡγοῦνται εἶναι οὐδ' ἀπὸ τοῦ αὐτομάτου, ἀλλὰ διδακτόν τε καὶ
ἐξ ἐπιμελείας παραγίγνεσθαι ᾧ ἂν παραγίγνηται, τοῦτό σοι μετὰ τοῦτο
πειράσομαι ἀποδεῖξαι. ὅσα γὰρ ἡγοῦνται ἀλλήλους κακὰ ἔχειν ἄνθρωποι φύσει
ἢ τύχῃ, οὐδεὶς θυμοῦται οὐδὲ νουθετεῖ οὐδὲ διδάσκει οὐδὲ κολάζει τοὺς ταῦτα
ἔχοντας...

Now, Hermes asked Zeus in which way he should give right and awe to men:
'Should they be distributed like the crafts and skills, and should I distribute
them, too, in that way? But they are distributed in the following way: One
<man>, having medical skill, is sufficient for many laymen; and the other
craftsmen, too <are in the same way each sufficient for many laymen>: should

I therefore set right and awe, too, in that way among men, or should I distribute them over all?' – 'Over all,' said Zeus, 'and let all share: indeed, there would not be cities, if <only> few of them shared as <is the case> with the other skills and crafts; and set it even as a law from me: to kill anyone who is not capable of sharing in right and awe, as a disease of the city.' Thus, Socrates, therefore and because of that the other <cities> and the Athenians believe, whenever there is a debate about the excellence that is architectural skill, or any other skill of a craftsman, that deliberation and the giving of advice is <a matter> for few <men only>; and whenever anybody from outside these few gives advice, they do not allow it, as you say; naturally, as I say; but whenever they go into deliberation about the excellence that is political skill, which, as a whole, necessarily goes through justice and prudent moderation, they allow every man <to speak>, in the belief that it befits everybody to share in this excellence at least, and that otherwise there would not be states. This, Socrates, is the explanation of that.

But lest you believe that you will be deceived <when you assume> that really all men hold that each and everybody shares in justice and the rest of that excellence which is political skill, take also this evidence: indeed, with all the other skill and excellence, as you say, if anyone claims to be a good flute-player, or <good> in respect of any other craft with regard to which he is not <good>, they either laugh at him or abuse him, and his relatives approach him and admonish him as a madman. In the case of justice and the rest of the excellence that is political skill, even if they know that somebody is unjust, if he himself says the truth about himself in front of others, which they would have held to be prudent and moderate behaviour in the previous case, to speak the truth, here they hold it to be madness, and say that it is necessary that all say that they are just, whether they are or not, or else that the one who does not pretend to be just is mad: just as if it were necessary that without exception everybody should in one way or another share in it, or not be among men <at all>.

Now, with regard to the fact that they naturally accept each and everybody as adviser about that skill and excellence because they hold that everybody shares in it, I say that. But with regard to their holding that it is not by nature, nor by itself, but that it comes to be with whomever it comes to be as something taught and from practice and care, this I shall try to show you in what follows. For, as regards all the bad things men mutually hold that other <men> have by nature or by chance, nobody gets angry or admonishes or teaches or punishes those who have them...

Hermes asks first if he should distribute αἰδῶς and δίκη, 'awe' and 'right', in the same way the τέχναι, the 'skills', are distributed. He then explains to Zeus that with regard to each of the τέχναι it is sufficient for a large number of people, if one person 'has' that skill.[74] But Zeus insists that αἰδῶς and δίκη be given to all men, and that everybody should 'have of' them together with everybody else. For there would not be cities if few <men> 'have of' them as with the other skills.[75]

While in the sentences with ἔχειν as predicate discussed so far the subject was looked at and considered in isolation, here the emphasis is on individuals as members of a group. When Zeus says that all should 'have of' αἰδώς and δίκη, he means that distributively and not collectively: each member of the class of human beings should be endowed with αἰδώς and δίκη, so that all men 'have of' them together. Likewise, in the second sentence (322d2), where ὀλίγοι, 'few', are the subject, these 'few' are treated severally: each of the few would 'have of' right and awe together with the rest of that group; what they would have, however, is not quantified or qualified. It is only much later (327a5, e2; 328a8) that Protagoras introduces even the thought of gradation of virtue or excellence to make the particular point that it would be sensible to hire him as a teacher. Without that interested standpoint of Protagoras' which is introduced at a later point, the story told in the myth would in itself, if anything, run counter to differentiation of degrees of ἀρετή. That is, of course, not to say that, since αἰδώς and δίκη are the object of μετέχειν, one has to think of αἰδώς as a whole and δίκη as a whole, which would both be had or possessed by someone as wholes; it is rather the case that the very notion of part and whole, completeness and defectiveness, of amount, gradation or gradability as such, is absent from this context.

The myth is finished now and Protagoras has begun with its application. Starting, by way of contrast, with the example of deliberation in matters of arts and crafts, as an instance of which he quotes ἀρετὴ τεκτονική, 'the craft of the master builder-*cum*-architect', he moves on to deliberation of political matters which he does not call συμβουλὴ τῶν πολιτικῶν but συμβουλὴ πολιτικῆς ἀρετῆς, and says that it is fitting for everyone ταύτης γε μετέχειν τῆς ἀρετῆς, 'to share in *this* skill at least'. Everybody together with everybody else should 'have of' it. Finally, at 323c2 ff., Protagoras infers that everybody is admitted to public counsels as all think that 'to everybody, there is of this ἀρετή,' and he continues to prove its teachability by contrasting the behaviour and attitude of men towards those bad qualities or attributes of which they think that one has them by nature. Here he describes a concrete example of men's criticizing particular faults they perceive among themselves and with each other. These faults are quantified and denoted as countable with the neuter plural relative ὅσα...κακὰ ἔχειν, 'as many bad things as they have' or 'all the bad things they have'. The simple verb governs the direct object in the accusative since Protagoras is here talking about individual possessions or properties of human beings viewed as individuals, not, as was the case with excellence, about the unspecifiable 'having of' or sharing in something together with somebody else.

8. μετέχειν in Plato's *Gorgias*
There are three contexts containing the verbs μετέχειν and μεταλαμβάνειν in the *Gorgias*. Near the beginning of the dialogue, Socrates' friend Chaerepho

and Gorgias' pupil Polus have a short exchange of words before Socrates and Gorgias continue to pursue the argument. In Socratic manner, Chaerepho asks Polus for the profession of Gorgias, and what one should call him accordingly. Polus answers eloquently (448c5):

ὦ Χαιρεφῶν, πόλλαι τέχναι ἐν ἀνθρώποις εἰσὶν ἐκ τῶν ἐμπειριῶν ἐμπείρως ηὑρημέναι· ἐμπειρία μὲν γὰρ ποιεῖ τὸν αἰῶνα ἡμῶν πορεύεσθαι κατὰ τέχνην, ἀπειρία δὲ κατὰ τύχην. ἑκάστων δὲ τούτων μεταλαμβάνουσιν ἄλλοι ἄλλων ἄλλως, τῶν δὲ ἀρίστων οἱ ἄριστοι· ὧν καὶ Γοργίας ἐστὶν ὅδε, καὶ μετέχει τῆς καλλίστης τῶν τεχνῶν.

Chaerepho, there are many skills and crafts among men, found expertly from experience: for experience makes our life go according to plan and skill, but lack of experience according to chance. Of each of these, some get in some manner of one, some of another, but the best <get> of the best: and to those belongs also Gorgias here, and he 'has of' and possesses the finest of the skills and crafts.

Of course, the phrasing of the statement is highly rhetorical, and perhaps not much emphasis should be put on any individual word. If one takes the words seriously, though, μεταλαμβάνουσιν ἄλλοι ἄλλων ἄλλως says both that different people take up different arts and crafts and that they do so in different ways. It is likely that Polus does not mean to imply that in any society any one occupation is pursued by one individual only; ἄλλως, however, could very well imply that each and every one take up their respective professions in their own way. This would allow for degrees of mastery and degrees of perfection. Imperfect participation, however, the having of part of a skill rather than all of it, would then be indicated by the qualification contained in ἄλλως. Imperfection is not inherent in the verbs denoting the sharing in and having of something. For it is far from Polus to suggest that Gorgias possesses (only) a part of rhetoric when he says about him καὶ μετέχει τῆς καλλίστης τῶν τεχνῶν.

Later on in the dialogue, Callicles enters the discussion and delivers a long speech on the appropriate place of philosophy and practical pursuit of political matters in the life of an individual. At one point, he summarizes (485a3):

ἀλλ' οἶμαι τὸ ὀρθότατόν ἐστιν ἀμφοτέρων μετασχεῖν. φιλοσοφίας μὲν ὅσον παιδείας χάριν καλὸν μετέχειν, καὶ οὐκ αἰσχρὸν μειρακίῳ ὄντι φιλοσοφεῖν· ἐπειδὰν δὲ ἤδη πρεσβύτερος ὢν ἄνθρωπος ἔτι φιλοσοφῇ, καταγέλαστον, ὦ Σώκρατες, τὸ χρῆμα γίγνεται...

But I believe it is most proper to 'have of' both of them.[76] As much as is fine for education <one should> 'have of' and share in philosophy, and it is not unseemly for a man to philosophize while young: but when someone already

41

older still philosophizes as a man, the matter becomes ridiculous, Socrates…

Syntactically, φιλοσοφία is here treated like τέχνη in the previous example. Callicles' suggestion is not that a youth may philosophize a little, but not perfectly. When one is young, one may do philosophy; no degrees are envisaged. The phrase ὅσον παιδείας χάριν refers, in this case, to the education of the young. If Callicles had meant to suggest anything else, that would have damaged his case, as the corollary would have been that as an adult one should engage in politics in an imperfect way; that is not what he means when he says τὸ ὀρθότατόν ἐστιν ἀμφοτέρων μετασχεῖν, 'it is most proper to have of both of them'. The limit set to the study of philosophy is one of age, and time in that sense; 'one should not overdo something' does not here imply that, while one is in the process of doing something, one should not do it properly and exhaustively.

Gorgias 467e is a slightly different case. A distinction has been drawn between 'what we do' on the one hand, and on the other 'what we do it for'. What we want is the end, not the means to that end. A further distinction is that everything is good or bad or between the two, neither-good-nor-bad. Socrates continues (467e6–468a3):

οὐκοῦν λέγεις εἶναι ἀγαθὸν μὲν σοφίαν τε καὶ ὑγίειαν καὶ πλοῦτον καὶ τἆλλα τὰ τοιαῦτα, κακὰ δὲ τἀναντία τούτων; – ἔγωγε. – τὰ δὲ μήτε ἀγαθὰ μήτε κακὰ ἆρα τοιάδε λέγεις, ἃ ἐνίοτε μὲν μετέχει τοῦ ἀγαθοῦ, ἐνίοτε δὲ τοῦ κακοῦ, ἐνίοτε δὲ οὐδετέρου, οἷον καθῆσθαι καὶ βαδίζειν καὶ τρέχειν καὶ πλεῖν, καὶ οἷον αὖ λίθους καὶ ξύλα καὶ τἆλλα τὰ τοιαῦτα;

Now, do you say that wisdom, health and riches and the other things of that sort are something good, but that their opposites are bad? – I do. – And do you say that neither good nor bad are such things which sometimes 'have of' the good, but sometimes of the bad, and sometimes of neither, such as sitting and walking and running and sailing, and again such as stones and sticks and the other things of that sort?

In contrast with the examples discussed so far, the subject of μετέχειν in the last sentence is not a human being. Something is said to share at times in one, at times in another of two opposites, good and bad. But for as long as something shares in what is good, there is no suggestion that it does so only partially. When, for example, 'walking' is bad because one would catch the boat only when running, and if the point is to catch rather than to miss the boat, walking is then not to some degree good, to some degree bad; in this context, 'walking' is bad and 'running' is good. This is also indicated by the addition that the activity and the things listed sometimes are neither good nor bad.[77]

9. Recapitulation

μετέχειν is thus employed with a wide range of objects, but in Plato particularly with non-physical objects from the domain of psychology or character-description. The verb denotes a 'having of' something together with somebody else; no specific qualitative or quantitative portion is specified. μετέχειν by itself does not necessarily mean 'having a part' (of something); if that meaning is intended, it must be clearly expressed in the context, for example by the addition, in the accusative, of a noun for 'part' like μέρος. Pre-Platonic and early Platonic usage are in concord as regards meaning and applicability of the verb.

CHAPTER 2

παρουσία, παρεῖναι, παραγίγνεσθαι

An investigation into the usage of παρουσία and παρεῖναι is prompted by Socrates' use of the word παρουσία at *Phaedo* 100d. There, Socrates declares that something is καλόν, 'beautiful', through the presence of the beautiful itself, αὐτὸ τὸ καλόν. He says that his explanation for any thing's being beautiful is (100d5):

> ...ὅτι οὐκ ἄλλο τι ποιεῖ αὐτὸ καλὸν ἢ ἡ ἐκείνου τοῦ καλοῦ εἴτε παρουσία εἴτε κοινωνία εἴτε ὅπη δὴ καὶ ὅπως προσαγορευομένη.[78]

> ...that not any other thing makes it beautiful than the presence or community – or however and in whatever way it be addressed – of *that* beautiful.

Whatever the precise meaning of Socrates' qualification (here in parenthesis), the statement as a whole seems to suggest that the relation that holds between, on the one side, τὸ καλόν, 'the beautiful', and, on the other, any particular thing which is καλόν, 'beautiful', may be described, at least among other things, as παρουσία, 'presence'. It should be noted that, were it not for this occurrence at *Phaedo* 100d, the term παρουσία would probably not have attracted much attention from those interested in the philosophical terminology of the 'theory of forms'. Of the two contexts in which the noun παρουσία appears in the manuscripts after the *Phaedo*, *Republic* 4.437e3–6 and *Sophist* 247a5, the first does not refer to the presence of forms 'to', 'at', 'with' or 'by' particulars, and the second has been suspected on good grounds.[79] It can thus be concluded that *if* παρουσία is a technical term in the context of a 'theory of forms', that must be so in or before the *Phaedo*. Before looking at the two contexts in which the noun παρουσία occurs in dialogues earlier than the *Phaedo*, I will briefly consider instances in earlier Greek literature, not only of the noun παρουσία, but also of the much commoner verbs παρεῖναι and παραγίγνεσθαι, in order to establish their application and the contexts in which they are used in pre-Platonic usage. It should be noted, though, that this exercise is not so much concerned with establishing the meaning of the noun or of either verb as with the contexts in which they occur; in particular, sections 1 to 3 list occurrences of παρά, πάρα, παρεῖναι and παραγίγνεσθαι with a view to the range of grammatical subjects that are commonly said 'to be there' or 'to be present'.[80]

45

1. The semantics of παρεῖναι and 'being there' in Homer

A number of distinct uses of παρεῖναι can, I think, sensibly be regarded as distinct.[81] First, παρεῖναι, 'being there', is used of people who are present at an occasion or in particular with other people. This usage is found from the *Iliad* onwards throughout Greek literature.[82] It is so frequent that I will refrain from giving examples. It is found throughout Plato's dialogues, e.g. *Gorgias* 447b6; 457b6; 458b6, 7; 461c7, d1; 474a1; 482b1; 518d3. Secondly, there is an occasional use of impersonal πάρεστι where it could be said to come close in meaning to ἔξεστι, 'it is possible',[83] e.g. *Gorgias* 448a5 where it could be attributed to Gorgias' high-flown or poetical style. Thirdly, παρεῖναι is used of 'the present time',[84] with Plato notably in the phrase ἐν τῷ (νῦν) παρόντι, 'at present'.[85] Fourthly, παρεῖναι can be used of 'things', in the widest sense of that word, present to someone.[86] This usage, again, is found from Homer onwards.

As mentioned in the previous chapter, there was, to our knowledge, no single verb for 'having' in Indo-European.[87] Instead, forms of the verb 'to be' were used, with the dative of the person 'to whom' something 'was' or belonged, or at whose disposal it was. This usage is well preserved in Archaic and Classical Greek down to Plato's times, as may, *exempli gratia*, be seen in the following sentence in the *Gorgias* (486c8–d1):

…ζηλῶν οὐκ ἐλέγχοντας ἄνδρας τὰ μικρὰ ταῦτα, ἀλλ' οἷς ἔστιν καὶ βίος καὶ δόξα καὶ ἄλλα πολλὰ ἀγαθά.

…not emulating men who scrutinize these small matters, but those 'to whom there is' a life and a reputation and many other goods (good things).

When this rather general notion of 'being to' or 'for someone' was felt not to express specifically enough the relation holding between the thing 'had' and the 'haver', the person having, it could be delimited by the addition of certain adverbs which over time became preverbs.[88] The general meaning of the preverb παρα- is 'close by', 'next to'. The emphasis is often on the immediate closeness and proximity of the object or person.[89]

An example of πάρα in that sense is *Odyssey* 4.559. Menelaus relates to Telemachus what Proteus has told him about Odysseus (4.555–60):

υἱὸς Λαέρτεω, Ἰθάκῃ ἔνι οἰκία ναίων·
τὸν δ' ἴδον ἐν νήσῳ θαλερὸν κατὰ δάκρυ χέοντα,
νύμφης ἐν μεγάροισι Καλυψοῦς, ἥ μιν ἀνάγκῃ
ἴσχει· ὁ δ' οὐ δύναται ἣν πατρίδα γαῖαν ἱκέσθαι·
οὐ γάρ οἱ πάρα νῆες ἐπήρετμοι καὶ ἑταῖροι,
οἵ κέν μιν πέμποιεν ἐπ' εὐρέα νῶτα θαλάσσης.

The son of Laertes, living in his home in Ithaca:
but him I saw on an island, shedding a thick tear,

in the palace of the nymph Calypso, who holds him by force;
but he is unable to return to his fatherland.
Indeed, ships with oars are not there for him, and comrades,
who might send him along the broad backs of the sea.

Odyssey 4.558 constitutes a good example of ἔχειν with its old, original force of 'holding subdued' an adversary.[90] Line 559 is a nominal clause without copula.[91] The sentence οὐ γάρ οἱ νῆες ἐπήρετμοι καὶ ἑταῖροι would have been complete and well-formed by itself. The subject of the sentence is complex, with an inanimate and an animate component; the addition of πάρα serves to specify that he did not have anything or anybody 'with' him or 'at' him or 'by' his side. With *Odyssey* 4.555–60, one can compare 14.80. Eumaeus, the swine-herd, invites the stranger, Odysseus:

ἔσθιε νῦν, ὦ ξεῖνε, τά τε δμώεσσι πάρεστιν…

Eat now, stranger, what is there [what there is] for servants…

The difference between this and the previous example is that, in the clause τά τε δμώεσσι πάρεστιν, there is a copula, and πάρα is bound as a preverb, no longer free as an adverb. The two previous examples had physical or material objects for grammatical subjects. But already in Homer, non-physical, immaterial things can function as subjects as well. At *Odyssey* 17.345 ff., Telemachus advises the swineherd, Eumaeus, to tell the beggar, Odysseus, not to be too shy to ask the suitors for alms. He finishes with the sententious remark (17.347):

αἰδὼς δ' οὐκ ἀγαθὴ κεχρημένῳ ἀνδρὶ παρεῖναι.

Bashfulness is not good for a needy man, to be with him.

In the particular case of αἰδώς, it is to be noted that this sort of construction, and the consequent αἰδὼς πάρεστι, may well be older than any verbal form like αἴδομαι to express the presence of awe, reverence, fear or shame.[92]

That is different with the following Iliadic example. Apollo, the god, has deceived Achilles, the best and strongest of the Greeks, in the guise of Agenor. When the god removes the delusion and mocks Achilles, Achilles replies in angry tones. He could have taken the life of many Trojans (22.18–20):

νῦν δ' ἐμὲ μὲν μέγα κῦδος ἀφείλεο, τοὺς δὲ σάωσας
ῥηϊδίως, ἐπεὶ οὔ τι τίσιν γ' ἔδεισας ὀπίσσω.
ἦ σ' ἂν τεισαίμην, εἴ μοι δύναμίς γε παρείη.

But now you have deprived me of great fame, in saving those
easily, because you do not in any way fear vengeance afterward.
Certainly, I should take vengeance on you, if indeed there were the power
with me.

The word δύναμις, 'power', 'ability', is a verbal noun, both semantically and by its actual derivation. A conditional like *Iliad* 1.393, ἀλλὰ σύ, εἰ δύνασαί γε, περίσχεο παιδὸς ἑῆος, 'but you, if, certainly, you can, protect your son', shows that it was the speaker's choice to give a verbal or a nominal form to his statement.

While in the case of αἰδώς it could be argued that Ἀιδώς, 'Awe', was a goddess like Φόβος, 'Fear', Ἔρις, 'Quarrel', Ἀλκή, 'Strength', and Ἰωκή, 'Rout', at *Iliad* 5.739 f., or like Κράτος and Βία, 'Force' and 'Violence', in Pseudo-Aeschylus' *Prometheus Bound*, and that therefore the instances of αἰδώς mentioned above should be counted with the personal use of παρεῖναι, the same could not as easily be claimed for δύναμις. And even if at *Iliad* 22.20 one could imagine Δύναμις standing by Achilles as did Athena at *Iliad* 1.193–222 – a picture, I think, not intended by the poet – the same could not be said of *Odyssey* 2.62, where the half-line *Iliad* 22.18b is repeated. There, Telemachus complains to the people of Ithaca about his situation; the suitors are consuming his father's property and make a general nuisance of themselves; Telemachus declares (2.60–2):

> ἡμεῖς δ᾽ οὔ νύ τι τοῖοι ἀμυνέμεν· ἦ καὶ ἔπειτα
> λευγαλέοι τ᾽ ἐσόμεσθα καὶ οὐ δεδαηκότες ἀλκήν.
> ἦ τ᾽ ἂν ἀμυναίμην, εἴ μοι δύναμίς γε παρείη.

> But we, now, are somehow not of the sort to defend ourselves at all; and surely also later
> we shall be miserable and not experienced in strength.
> Surely, I would defend myself, if only power and ability were there for me.

With these words, spoken at the height of desperation, one can compare what Telemachus says to his father Odysseus when the suitors are slain. After the complete reversal of circumstances and of mood, Homer lets him use the same words in a statement indicating his newly gained confidence, with the main verb-forms in the indicative rather than the potential optative (23.127):

> ἡμεῖς δ᾽ ἐμμεμαῶτες ἅμ᾽ ἑψόμεθ᾽, οὐδέ τι φημὶ
> ἀλκῆς δευήσεσθαι, ὅση δύναμίς γε πάρεστι.

> But we shall follow eagerly at the same time, nor do I in any way say
> that we lack strength, as much as power and ability are there.

In these two passages, both ἀλκή, which is something taught and known at 2.60, and δύναμις are practical abilities or properties of human beings. That is already true of δύναμις at *Iliad* 8.294, from which the last half-line of the previous example is quoted. Teucer, praised for his skill by Agamemnon, replies (8.292–4):

> Ἀτρείδη κύδιστε, τί με σπεύδοντα καὶ αὐτὸν

ὀτρύνεις; οὐ μέν τοι ὅση δύναμίς γε πάρεστι
παύομαι.

Most famous Atreides, why do you spur me on, as I am already eager myself?
I certainly do not stop, as much as power and ability are there.

In this instance, the person 'to whom' the subject *'is'* is not expressed in the subordinate clause, as it is understood from the main clause; in traditional terminology, (πάρ)εστι has its full existential force. Power is *there* because power *is*. The last five examples demonstrate that πάρεστι as a predicate, with the dative of the person expressed or implied, is employed with non-material things as grammatical subjects, which from a later point of view pertain to the sphere of the mind, the soul or the emotions, in the same way as it is employed with material things like ships or food. It is not possible to determine which use was prior, or indeed whether a speaker of the language would have drawn such a distinction.

2. παρεῖναι in early Greek lyric poetry and tragedy
In lyric poetry and tragedy, a wider range of subjects to παρεῖναι is found. In the seventh century, Mimnermus says in an elegiac couplet (8 West):

...ἀληθείη δὲ παρέστω
σοὶ καὶ ἐμοί, πάντων χρῆμα δικαιότατον.

...but truth be there
with you and me, of all <things> the justest thing.

A little later, Theognis declares at the imagined occasion of someone's stealing his verses (21 West):

οὐδέ τις ἀλλάξει κάκιον τοὐσθλοῦ παρεόντος.

Nor will anyone switch to something worse from something noble that is there <already>.

In one of his political elegies, Solon says about unjust statesmen (4.9 f. West):

οὐ γὰρ ἐπίστανται κατέχειν κόρον οὐδὲ παρούσας
εὐφροσύνας κοσμεῖν δαιτὸς ἐν ἡσυχίῃ.

Indeed, they do not understand <how> to master satiety nor, when cheerfulness is present, to be decorous in the quiet of a feast.

It is Solon, too, who states that death will take away rich and poor alike (24.1–4 West):

ἶσόν τοι πλουτέουσιν, ὅτῳ πολὺς ἄργυρός ἐστι
καὶ χρυσὸς καὶ γῆς πυροφόρου πεδία

49

ἵπποί θ' ἡμίονοί τε, καὶ ᾧ μόνα ταῦτα πάρεστι,
γαστρί τε καὶ πλευραῖς καὶ ποσὶν ἁβρὰ παθεῖν,

…

Surely, an equal measure is there for the rich, to whom much silver is
and gold and plains of fertile soil
and horses and mules, and again for the one to whom only this is there:
for his stomach and loins and feet to experience soft things,

…

This is a good example both of how ἔστιν can be used in parallel with
πάρεστιν plus dative, and of how physical or material objects can function
as grammatical subjects side by side with immaterial ones. The grammatical
subject to πάρεστι is the infinitival noun phrase ἁβρὰ παθεῖν, 'experiencing
soft things'.

Also in the sixth century, Anacreon gives his version of man's fear of old
age and death (50 Page):

πολιοὶ μὲν ἡμῖν ἤδη
κρόταφοι κάρη τε λευκόν,
χαρίεσσα δ' οὐκέτ' ἤβη
πάρα, γηραλέοι δ' ὀδόντες,
γλυκεροῦ δ' οὐκέτι πολλὸς
βιότου χρόνος λέλειπται.

Grey indeed for us already
are our temples, and the head is white,
and gracious youth is no longer
with us; old are our teeth;
no longer is there much time
of sweet life left.

A generation later, Simonides writes in an elegy, part of which Stobaeus
quotes under the heading 'About life, that it is short and cheap and full of
concern' (8.4 West):

…πάρεστι γὰρ ἐλπὶς ἑκάστῳ
ἀνδρῶν, ἥ τε νέων στήθεσιν ἐμφύεται.

…indeed, there is hope for everyone
of <all> men, and it grows in the breasts of the young.

Theognis has a variation of the old adage μέτρον ἄριστον, 'measure is best'
(693 f.):

πολλούς τοι κόρος ἄνδρας ἀπώλεσεν ἀφραίνοντας·
γνῶναι γὰρ χαλεπὸν μέτρον, ὅτ' ἐσθλὰ παρῇ.

Surely, greed has destroyed many foolish men:

indeed, difficult it is to recognize measure, when good things are there.

Turning to fifth-century Athenian tragedy, in Aeschylus' *Persians* (353–432) three instances of the verb occur in one messenger-speech alone:

…φόβος δὲ πᾶσι βαρβάροις παρῆν | γνώμης ἀποσφαλεῖσιν· (391 f.)

…but fear was there with all <of us> barbarians | having failed in our plan;

…καὶ παρῆν ὁμοῦ κλύειν | πολλὴν βοήν· (401 f.)

…and there was at once the hearing of many a shout;

…ὡς δὲ πλῆθος ἐν στενῷ νεῶν
ἤθροιστ᾽, ἀρωγὴ δ᾽ οὔτις ἀλλήλοις παρῆν | … (413 f.)

…but as the multitude of ships was gathered in the strait
no help was there for each other.

In each case, the subject is non-tangible. 'Fear' and 'hearing shouts' were present; 'help' was not present; the sense of this last example may well be, by implication, that help was not possible; but that is implicit rather than explicit in the same way in which 'there was no escape' implies, but does not say explicitly, that escape was not possible.

In Sophocles' *Antigone*, the guard who must inform Creon of the attempt to perform burial rites for the outlawed Polynices explains that he does not know who has done the deed and reports how he himself learnt of the event (253 f.):

ὅπως δ᾽ ὁ πρῶτος ἡμῖν ἡμεροσκόπος
δείκνυσι, πᾶσι θαῦμα δυσχερὲς παρῆν.

But as the first guard of the day
showed it to us, to all there was a wonder hard to handle.

And in Sophocles' late play *Electra*, Electra admits in a speech to her sister, which began with the statement that no friends are present[93] and that they must act themselves (958–62):

ποῖ γὰρ μενεῖς ῥᾴθυμος, ἐς τίν᾽ ἐλπίδων
βλέψασ᾽ ἔτ᾽ ὀρθήν; ᾗ πάρεστι μὲν στένειν
πλούτου πατρῴου κτῆσιν ἐστερημένη,
πάρεστι δ᾽ ἀλγεῖν ἐς τοσόνδε τοῦ χρόνου
ἄλεκτρα γηράσκουσαν ἀνυμέναιά τε.

Indeed, for how long will you wait inert, looking to which
of all hopes as still standing upright? You, to whom there is sorrowing,
as you are bereft of possession of fatherly wealth;

51

but hurting is there that to this point in time
you have grown older without marital bed and wedding song.

A little later, the two sisters Electra and Chrysothemis exchange the following
lines (1031 f.):

ἄπελθε· σοὶ γὰρ ὠφέλησις οὐκ ἔνι.
ἔνεστιν· ἀλλὰ σοὶ μάθησις οὐ πάρα.

Go away! Indeed, no profit is there in you.
There is! But with you there is no understanding.

Euripides' Hecuba says in reply to the lament of the chorus leader (*Hecuba*
585–8):

ὦ θύγατερ, οὐκ οἶδ᾽ εἰς ὅ τι βλέψω κακῶν,
πολλῶν παρόντων· ἢν γὰρ ἅψωμαί τινος,
τόδ᾽ οὐκ ἐᾷ με, παρακαλεῖ δ᾽ ἐκεῖθεν αὖ
λύπη τις ἄλλη διάδοχος κακῶν κακοῖς.

Daughter, I do not know to which of the evils I shall look,
with so many there: indeed, whichever I shall touch,
it does not let me go, but invites from over there again
another sorrow, successor of evils for evils.

In the last two lines, 'the bad <things>' are grammatical subjects to predicates
which otherwise have animate subjects. That personification was invited
by the apposition πολλῶν παρόντων, in which the verb – while perfectly
natural with inanimate things for subjects – could be seen, or re-interpreted,
as denoting the presence of an active agent. Whereas the one bad <thing>
touched upon is still neuter, the grief or pain in its wake is feminine. This
type of expression occurs in a natural way in this poetic context; but we shall
see in section 7 how, in Plato's *Gorgias*, such language can be exploited for
philosophical ends.

In the *Orestes*, the following words are exchanged between Electra and her
brother (1177–80):

ἐγώ, κασίγνητ᾽, αὐτὸ τοῦτ᾽ ἔχειν δοκῶ,
σωτηρίαν σοὶ τῷδέ τ᾽ ἐκ τρίτων τ᾽ ἐμοί.
θεοῦ λέγεις πρόνοιαν. ἀλλὰ ποῦ τόδε;
ἐπεὶ τὸ συνετόν γ᾽ οἶδα σῇ ψυχῇ παρόν.

I, brother, seem to have just that,
salvation for you and him and in third place also for myself.
Providence of god is what you say. But where is that thing?
Because I know that understanding is there with your soul.

Electra 'has' salvation, and Orestes knows that 'the intelligent is present to her soul'. With comparable words, Cadmus addresses Agaue in the *Bacchae* (1268):

τὸ δὲ πτοηθὲν τόδ' ἔτι σῇ ψυχῇ πάρα;

But is this dreaded thing still with your soul?

In both instances, it is somebody's soul to which something, intelligence and excitement respectively, is present.

3. πάρα and παρεῖναι in Empedocles and Democritus

Empedocles has the following apostrophe (DK31B114, 1–2):

ὦ φίλοι, οἶδα μὲν οὕνεκ' ἀληθείη πάρα μύθοις,
οὓς ἐγὼ ἐξερέω…

Friends, I know that truth is by the words
which I shall speak…[94]

In the context of his physics of mixture and separation, with the ontological premise that nothing will come out of nothing, Empedocles remarks about fire, water, earth and air, with strife apart from them and love in amongst them (DK31B17, 36–8):

ταῦτα γὰρ ἰσά τε πάντα καὶ ἥλικα γένναν ἔασι,
τιμῆς δ' ἄλλης ἄλλο μέδει, πάρα δ' ἦθος ἑκάστῳ,
ἐν δὲ μέρει κρατέουσι περιπλομένοιο χρόνοιο.

Indeed, these are all equal and of the same age as to their birth,
but one commands one honour, another another, and by each there is
a character, but in their turn they rule when the time is fulfilled.

It is fairly safe to assume that this usage of πάρα δ' ἦθος ἑκάστῳ, 'and by each there is a (i.e. 'its own') character', is transferred from the human to the elemental sphere. At a different point in the same book, Empedocles draws the conclusion that – as a result of those insights into the physics of the world – no wise man will hold (DK31B15, 4–7):

οὐκ ἂν ἀνὴρ τοιαῦτα σοφὸς φρεσὶ μαντεύσαιτο,
ὡς ὄφρα μέν τε βιῶσι, τὸ δὴ βίοτον καλέουσι,
τόφρα μὲν οὖν εἰσίν, καί σφιν πάρα δειλὰ καὶ ἐσθλά,
πρὶν δὲ πάγεν τε βροτοὶ καὶ <ἐπεὶ> λύθεν, οὐδὲν ἄρ' εἰσίν.

Indeed, a man wise in his mind would not foretell this:
that as long as they live – what they call life –
so long they *are*, and mean things and noble are to them,
but before mortals are congealed and when they are dissolved, they are thus nothing.

It would be rash to restrict the reference of the archaic polar expression for 'good and bad', δειλὰ καὶ ἐσθλά, to material goods as if Empedocles referred just to poverty and wealth, to the exclusion of pain and pleasure.[95]

If we can trust our source (Stobaeus 3.18.35), Democritus declared (DK68B235):

ὅσοι ἀπὸ γαστρὸς τὰς ἡδονὰς ποιέονται ὑπερβεβληκότες τὸν καιρὸν ἐπὶ βρώσεσιν ἢ πόσεσιν ἢ ἀφροδισίοισιν, τοῖσι πᾶσιν αἱ μὲν ἡδοναὶ βραχεῖαί τε καὶ δι' ὀλίγου γίνονται, αἱ δὲ λῦπαι πολλαί. τοῦτο μὲν γὰρ τὸ ἐπιθυμεῖν ἀεὶ τῶν αὐτῶν πάρεστι καὶ ὁκόταν γένηται ὁκοίων ἐπιθυμέουσι, διὰ ταχέος τε ἡ ἡδονὴ παροίχεται, καὶ οὐδὲν ἐν αὐτοῖσι χρηστόν ἐστιν ἀλλ' ἢ τέρψις βραχεῖα, καὶ αὖθις τῶν αὐτῶν δεῖ.

Those who get their pleasures from their stomach in exceeding the measure in eating and drinking and love-making, to all those, pleasures come to be brief and for a short time, but griefs many. Indeed, that desiring of those things is always there for them, and even at the point when they get what they desire, pleasure passes by swiftly, and nothing in those things is valuable other than a quick enjoyment, and already there is a lack of and need for those things again.

That, if genuinely Democritean, is interesting, not least because it constitutes such a close parallel to some of the arguments in the *Gorgias*. The phrase ἡ ἡδονὴ παροίχεται may reflect terminological usage; in Presocratic contexts, παροίχεσθαι is used as the first member of a temporal sequence παροιχόμενον, παρόν, μέλλον, 'past', 'present' and 'future'.[96] If that is relevant, ἡδονὴ παροίχεται could mean that even at the moment of fulfilment 'pleasure has already passed by', as opposed to ἡδονὴ πάρεστι, 'pleasure is present'.

4. παρεῖναι in pre-Platonic literature: a summary
To recapitulate, in pre-Platonic literature, the following non-material things are said to be 'by', 'to', 'with' or 'at' someone:

αἰδώς, δύναμις, ἀλήθεια, τὸ ἔσθλον, εὐφροσύνη, ἀβρὰ παθεῖν, ὥρα, ἥβη, ἐλπίς, ἐσθλά, φόβος, κλύειν πολλὴν βοήν, ἀρωγή, θαῦμα, μάθησις, στένειν and ἀλγεῖν, κακὰ πολλά; τὸ συνετὸν and τὸ πτοηθὲν τῇ ψυχῇ; ἦθος, δειλὰ καὶ ἐσθλά, τὸ ἐπιθυμεῖν.

awe, power and ability, truth, the noble, cheerfulness, experiencing pleasant things, young age, youth, hope, noble things, fear, hearing many a shout, help, wonder, understanding, groaning and hurting, many bad things; to the soul, understanding and that which has been dreaded; character, mean things and noble things, desiring.

Furthermore, it is implied at two places that λύπη, 'pain' (Euripides,

Hecuba 585 ff.), and ἡδονή, 'pleasure' (Democritus 235), are present. While it is possible that many of those words denoted at some point in time, or else in certain contexts, gods or divine powers, namely αἰδώς, δύναμις (?), ἀλήθεια, εὐφροσύνη, ὥρα, ἥβη, ἐλπίς, φόβος, θαῦμα, ἦθος, it is evident from the passages quoted that there were many contexts in which that was clearly not the case. Moreover, in terms of word class, some of the grammatical subjects to παρεῖναι are gerunds, i.e. substantivized infinitives, or substantivized adjectives; this establishes that παρεῖναι did not exclusively or necessarily convey the notion of a person's or a material object's presence. A whole range of concrete and abstract things figure as subjects: forces, emotions, 'states of mind', experiences, qualities, properties, actions and passions.[97] They are said to be present with people, or in some cases (Euripides, *Orestes* 1177 ff.; *Bacchae* 1268) with their souls. It is difficult to decide what exact status can be assigned to things like εὐφροσύνη or ἐλπίς, whether the words denote emotions or events or states of the mind or of the soul or of the whole person. Likewise, what is a man's ἥβη? Is μάθησις an action or a faculty or a quality? Is φόβος, if present to a crowd of people, something external to the individual or internal in each of them? It would be even more difficult to say what this 'presence' which is signified by παρεῖναι amounted to. Or perhaps, it is too much already to claim that there is anything 'signified'. What can be claimed with certainty is that, in a broadly-speaking psychological context, παρεῖναι is employed to connect non-material things with animate subjects. In addition, Empedocles at least can ascribe an ἦθος, a 'character' or 'characteristic', to either his forces νεῖκος and φιλότης, or even to them and the elements together.

5. παρουσία in pre-Platonic literature

As opposed to the verb παρεῖναι, the noun παρουσία is absent from Homer, Hesiod, and the early poets. As far as our sources are concerned, it seems to be an altogether Attic word.[98] With the tragedians, it usually denotes the presence of a person with others or at a particular event. As such, it is not very frequent. Its occurrence in that sense at Sophocles *Electra* 948 deserves particular attention. In the second line of the long speech addressed to her sister, Electra declares:

παρουσίαν μὲν οἶσθα καὶ σύ που φίλων
ὡς οὔτις ἡμῖν ἐστιν...

Presence of friends – you surely know also yourself –
that there is none for us...

It is one thing to speak of the presence of friends when friends are present. It is potentially quite another thing to declare *about* presence of friends that none is present. Instead of saying: φίλον μὲν οἶσθα καὶ σύ ὡς οὔτις ἡμῖν ἐστιν, 'you know also yourself that no friend is present with us', thus making the friend the object of knowledge, it is their presence of which Chrysothemis is said to have knowledge. It seems as if a consequence of the nominalization of παρεῖναι is that this 'presence' has become something in its own right, something one can talk about. Its status approximates that of ἀρωγή, 'help', in Aeschylus' *Persians* where the messenger reports (402): ἀρωγὴ δ' οὔτις ἀλλήλοις παρῆν, 'but there was no help present for them from one another'. Nevertheless, it is not necessary to postulate a new meaning, 'help, support', for παρουσία here. παρουσία φίλων, 'presence of friends', is the state of affairs obtaining when φίλοι πάρεισιν, 'friends are present'. Sophocles' sentence, παρουσίαν μὲν οἶσθα καὶ σύ που φίλων ὡς οὔτις ἡμῖν ἐστιν, potentially invites the question: 'What is this παρουσία which is not but could be there, and what is its status?' One need not suppose that Sophocles himself thought about that question. Poetical usage serves as preparation for philosophical speculation without entailing it.

There are only a few cases of παρουσία where the noun does not refer to the presence of a person at some place or occasion, but the presence of an object, be it material or non-material, to either a person or an inanimate object.[99] They can be regarded as straightforward nominalizations of clauses or phrases containing the verb παρεῖναι. One instance is Euripides *Hecuba* 227 f.:

γίγνωσκε δ' ἀλκὴν καὶ παρουσίαν κακῶν
τῶν σῶν.

But recognize strength and presence of the evils which are yours.

Here, Odysseus advises Hecuba to acknowledge and accept her own situation: the power of the victor and her own helplessness, her κακά which are with her. A similar case is Aristophanes, *Thesmophoriazusae* 1048 f. Mnesilochus, attendant to Euripides, bewails his fate:

ὦ κατάρατος ἐγώ· τίς ἐμὸν οὐκ ἐπόψεται
πάθος ἀμέγαρτον ἐπὶ κακῶν παρουσίᾳ;

O cursed me! Who will not consider
what I suffer as unenviable, with the presence of evils?

In Aristophanes' comedy, Mnesilochus' style is the tragic style of Euripides.

παρουσία before Plato is thus a poetical word, used by the tragedians in contexts which require a heightened mode of expression. The noun which is comparatively rare does not betray any semantic development beyond the nominalization of the verb παρεῖναι. With the noun, however, the temporal aspect, always present with παρεῖναι, is more pronounced.

6. παραγίγνεσθαι in fifth-century Greek prose

As opposed to παρεῖναι, παραγίγνεσθαι seems to be much less frequently used with subjects other than human beings, individuals or groups.[100] Stobaeus, notoriously unreliable as regards the wording of his quotations, reports as a saying of Democrates (Stobaeus 4.3.39; Democritus (?) DK68B108):

διζημένοισι τἀγαθὰ μόλις παραγίνεται, τὰ δὲ κακὰ καὶ μὴ διζημένοισιν.

To those who search for the good things, they come with difficulty; but the bad things come even to those who do not search.

A little earlier, Stobaeus quotes a long passage from Antiphon the Sophist πέρι ὁμονοίας (Stobaeus 4.22, 2.66; DK87B49):[101]

ἐν τῷ αὐτῷ δέ γε τούτῳ, ἔνθα τὸ ἡδύ, ἔνεστι πλησίον που καὶ τὸ λυπερόν· αἱ γὰρ ἡδοναὶ οὐκ ἐπὶ σφῶν αὐτῶν ἐμπορεύονται, ἀλλ᾽ ἀκολουθοῦσιν αὐταῖς λῦπαι καὶ πόνοι. ἐπεὶ καὶ ὀλυμπιονῖκαι καὶ πυθιονῖκαι καὶ οἱ τοιοῦτοι ἀγῶνες καὶ σοφίαι καὶ πᾶσαι ἡδοναὶ ἐκ μεγάλων λυπημάτων ἐθέλουσι παραγίνεσθαι· τιμαὶ γάρ, ἆθλα, δελέατα, ἃ ὁ θεὸς ἔδωκεν ἀνθρώποις, μεγάλων πόνων καὶ ἱδρώτων εἰς ἀνάγκας καθιστᾶσιν.

But certainly in that same thing in which there is the pleasant, therein is also somehow close by the painful: indeed, pleasures do not enter by themselves, but pains follow them and toils. Just as the victories at Olympia and Delphi, and such contests, and skills and all pleasures are in the habit of coming to be with <men> from great exertions; indeed, honours, prizes, delights, things that god gives to men, lead to the necessities of great toils and much sweat.

In the clause ἐπεὶ…παραγίνεσθαι, when taken on its own, παραγίνεσθαι is as good as synonymous with γίγνεσθαι. The complement ἀνθρώποις, however, should be understood from the context as object to the verb. If this text belongs in the fifth century, it is the closest extant pre-Platonic parallel to the usage of *Gorgias* 506, which will be discussed in due course.[102]

One doubtful example of παραγίγνεσθαι with inanimate subject is Thucydides 1.15:

κατὰ γῆν δὲ πόλεμος, ὅθεν τις καὶ δύναμις παρεγένετο, οὐδεὶς ξυνέστη.

Wars by land there were none, none at least by which power was acquired.
(tr. Crawley and Feetham)

If the text of the manuscripts is to be kept, an alternative translation is that offered by Warner 1954: 'There was no warfare by land which resulted in the acquisition of an empire.' Here, δύναμις παρεγένετο is to be taken as absolute, 'power arose' or 'power came into being' or even 'there was power'.[103]

Another possible instance of παραγίνεται is Archytas 47B1 which, if the textual tradition is sound, would be of particular importance owing to the celebrated influence of the Tarentine on Plato. In a treatise on Harmonics,

Archytas discusses the generation of sound by way of things hitting each other. Some of those sounds we cannot perceive at all. He continues (DK I, 433, 13):

τὰ μὲν οὖν ποτιπίπτοντα ποτὶ τὰν αἴσθασιν ἃ μὲν ἀπὸ τᾶν πλαγᾶν ταχὺ παραγίνεται καὶ <ἰσχυρῶς>, ὄξεα φαίνεται, τὰ δὲ βραδέως καὶ ἀσθενῶς, βαρέα δοκοῦντι ἦμεν.

Now, concerning what falls to perception, what comes to be there from a blow fast and strongly, that appears high-pitched, but what comes to be there from a blow slowly and weakly, that seems to be low-pitched.

The context, however, suggests that the correct reading may well be παρα-κινεῖται for παραγίνεται.[104]

With or without *dativus commodi*, παραγίγνεσθαι with inanimate subject is not in frequent use before Plato. Although one would suppose this usage to be natural enough, it is difficult to say if many occurrences of the sort of Isocrates *Philippus* (5.34) were around at the time.[105] In a pathetic attempt to endear himself and the city of Athens to Philip of Macedon, Isocrates claims for Athens a share in Heracles' becoming immortal and reports how Athens has also helped the children of Heracles against the evil-doer Eurystheus:

[ἡ πόλις ἡ ἡμετέρα] μόνη...τοὺς παῖδας τῶν φόβων τῶν ἀεὶ παραγιγνομένων αὐτοῖς ἀπήλλαξεν.

[Our city] alone freed his children from the fears that were always arising for them.

The phrase τῶν ἀεὶ παραγιγνομένων is potentially ambiguous; as a matter of idiom, it should mean: 'whenever there were any', 'on those occasions that there were any'. For that, one may usefully compare Thucydides 1.22.1:[106]

ὡς δ' ἂν ἐδόκουν ἐμοὶ ἕκαστοι περὶ τῶν αἰεὶ παρόντων τὰ δέοντα μάλιστ' εἰπεῖν, ἐχομένῳ ὅτι ἐγγύτατα τῆς ξυμπάσης γνώμης τῶν ἀληθῶς λεχθέντων, οὕτως εἴρηται.

But as much as possible <things are reported as follows>: as it seemed to me that each said what was necessary about what was there at any given time, while staying as close as possible to the overall sentiment of what was actually said, so things are said <here>.

With this last example, τὰ παρόντα refers to 'things', 'events', 'situations', as a verbal noun, without a depending dative indicating 'to' or 'for' whom these events occurred. This shows a higher degree of abstraction than could be observed in the passage from Isocrates, in which the participle in predicative position depended on a noun; the fears that arose were there for a specific group of people who were named.

7. 'Being present' in the *Gorgias* and other early dialogues of Plato

In Plato's early dialogues, the verb παρεῖναι is most often used in the context of someone's 'being present'. Also frequent is the use of the present participle to denote 'present time', both in the phrase ἐν τῷ (νῦν) παρόντι (*passim*) and in phrases like 'the present situation', ἡ παροῦσα τύχη and ἡ παροῦσα συμφορά (*Crito* 43c3; 47a1), with overtones of 'chance' and 'affliction' respectively. In the early dialogue *Ion*, Socrates once refers to those οἷς νοῦς μὴ πάρεστιν, 'to whom mind is not present', 'for whom there is no understanding' (*Ion* 534d3). That is comparable to both Sophocles *Electra* 1032: ἀλλὰ σοὶ μάθησις οὐ πάρα, 'but understanding is not there for you', and to Euripides *Orestes* 1180: ἐπεὶ τὸ συνετόν γ' οἶδα σῇ ψυχῇ παρόν, 'because I know that comprehension is present with your soul'.

There is a precedent also for an occurrence of παρεῖναι in the *Meno*. The context is that of the famous Socratic tenet that no-one *wants* what is bad; one aspect of this is that it may happen that someone *desires* something that is bad; Meno thinks that this could be the case regardless of whether that person knows that what they desire is actually bad and not good. Socrates insists and asks whether anyone would actually want something bad 'to come to be for him' (which is, as has been discussed, one way of saying: would anyone want to come to have, or to get, something which they think is bad). Meno still thinks that this is a possibility. Socrates then asks (*Meno* 77d3):

πότερον ἡγούμενος τὰ κακὰ ὠφελεῖν ἐκεῖνον ᾧ ἂν γένηται, ἢ γιγνώσκων τὰ κακὰ ὅτι βλάπτει ᾧ ἂν παρῇ;

(Does that person want to get what he thinks is bad) believing that the bad things would benefit the one to whom they come to be, or knowing that bad things harm the one to whom they are present?

This usage of παρεῖναι is paralleled by that of Hecuba (Euripides *Hecuba* 585 f.): ὦ θύγατερ, οὐκ οἶδ' εἰς ὅ τι βλέψω κακῶν, | πολλῶν παρόντων, 'daughter, I do not know to which of the evils I shall look, | with so many there'. The nominalized neuter plural forms of adjectives which were so frequently employed as abstract nouns in fifth-century Greek[107] can function as grammatical subjects of παρεῖναι, with or without the dative of the person or people 'to whom something is'. In the cases discussed so far, Plato's usage does not differ from common Greek usage as far as those applications of the word are concerned.

That may be slightly different with the noun παρουσία and with the verbs παρεῖναι and παραγίγνεσθαι when they are used in connection with the noun. We shall therefore now discuss in turn the two contexts in which παρουσία occurs in Plato's dialogues before the *Phaedo*, namely *Gorgias* 497e–498e and *Lysis* 217 f. By *Gorgias* 461, rhetoric, the topic of discussion between Gorgias and Socrates, has been linked with the issue of justice and injustice. As Gorgias appears to contradict himself, Polus, the younger friend and follower of Gorgias, takes over and gets involved in an argument over whether it is better to suffer or to do wrong. After a hint at 463, Socrates introduces the categories of beautiful and ugly in connection with good and bad and pleasure and pain at 474. Socrates manages to obtain Polus' agreement that it is worse to do than to suffer wrong on the grounds that doing wrong is 'uglier', and concludes, a little abruptly, that the just man has no real use for the practice of rhetoric. At that point, at 481b, Callicles, the Athenian host of Gorgias and – except for 447, the very beginning of the dialogue, and a brief remark at 458 – up to now a passive bystander to the conversation, enters angrily into the discussion. He introduces the distinction 'by nature' and 'by law' or 'custom' and maintains that by 'nature' suffering wrong is both worse and 'uglier' than doing wrong. His second distinction is that between the weak people who constitute the largest part of the population and are responsible for law and custom, and those who are capable of having more, the stronger, more able, better and worthier (483). In his search for who these 'better' people are, Socrates makes Callicles concur that they are those who are more 'sensible and knowledge-able' (489e). Callicles then is forced to specify that he means those who are more 'sensible and knowledgeable' in matters concerning state and society, and who are 'courageous' enough to enforce their views; and further, those who rule and know no bounds to their rule, be it over others or themselves (491). Callicles' position is that 'pleasurable' and 'good' is one and the same, 'understanding' and 'courage', however, different from each other and from 'the good' (495d). Socrates first proves this wrong by showing that while one cannot live well and badly at once, it is possible to experience pleasure and displeasure at once, and while the latter two may cease to exist simulta-neously, that is not the case with the former two (497). Socrates then begins a new argument to the same effect with the following words (497e1–3):

τοὺς ἀγαθοὺς οὐχὶ ἀγαθῶν παρουσίᾳ ἀγαθοὺς καλεῖς, ὥσπερ [τοὺς] καλοὺς οἷς ἂν κάλλος παρῇ;

Do you not call the good (people) good through and by presence of good(s), just as beautiful those to whom beauty is present?

He continues by reminding Callicles of his calling the brave and sensible good, the cowardly and senseless bad, and showing that these two groups of people experience pleasure and pain to the same extent. Are then both the good and the bad both good and bad to the same extent? He resumes (498d2–e2):

οὐκ οἶσθ' ὅτι τοὺς ἀγαθοὺς ἀγαθῶν φῂς παρουσίᾳ εἶναι ἀγαθούς, καὶ κακοὺς δὲ κακῶν; τὰ δὲ ἀγαθὰ εἶναι τὰς ἡδονάς, κακὰ δὲ τὰς ἀνίας; – ἔγωγε. – οὐκοῦν τοῖς χαίρουσιν πάρεστιν τἀγαθά, αἱ ἡδοναί, εἴπερ χαίρουσιν; – πῶς γὰρ οὔ; – οὐκοῦν ἀγαθῶν παρόντων ἀγαθοί εἰσιν οἱ χαίροντες; – ναί. – τί δέ; τοῖς ἀνιωμένοις οὐ πάρεστιν τὰ κακά, αἱ λῦπαι; – πάρεστιν. – κακῶν δέ γε παρουσίᾳ φῂς σὺ εἶναι κακοὺς τοὺς κακούς· ἢ οὐκέτι φῂς; – ἔγωγε.

Do you not know that you say that the good (people) are good through and by presence of good(s), and bad (people) <through and by presence> of bad(s)?[108] But the good things <you say> are the pleasures, but <the> bad <things>, the pains? – I certainly do. – Now, to those who are cheerful, the good things are present, the pleasures, if really they are cheerful? – Indeed, how not? – Now, good things being present, those who are cheerful are good? – Yes. – What then: are not the bad things, the pains, present to those who feel pain? – They are present. – But through and by presence of bad things, certainly, you at least say that the bad are bad: or do you no longer say that? – I certainly do.

The same thought recurs seven pages later in the dialogue. After Callicles has introduced the distinction 'good pleasures' and 'bad pleasures', Socrates restates what he established with Polus at 467c–468e, that everything else is done for the sake of the good (499e). That includes pleasant things, so that we do 'the pleasant for the sake of the good', τὸ ἡδὺ ἕνεκα τοῦ ἀγαθοῦ (506c9; cf. 500a2). Socrates continues, asking the questions and answering himself on behalf of Callicles and himself (506c9–d7):

ἡδὺ δέ ἐστιν τοῦτο οὗ παραγενομένου ἡδόμεθα, ἀγαθὸν δὲ οὗ παρόντος ἀγαθοί ἐσμεν; – πάνυ γε. – ἀλλὰ μὴν ἀγαθοί γέ ἐσμεν καὶ ἡμεῖς καὶ τἆλλα πάντα ὅσ' ἀγαθά ἐστιν, ἀρετῆς τινος παραγενομένης; – ἔμοιγε δοκεῖ ἀναγκαῖον εἶναι, ὦ Καλλίκλεις. – ἀλλὰ μὲν δὴ ἥ γε ἀρετὴ ἑκάστου, καὶ σκεύους καὶ σώματος καὶ ψυχῆς αὖ καὶ ζῴου παντός, οὐ τῷ εἰκῇ κάλλιστα παραγίγνεται…;

But 'pleasant' is this: when it comes to be present, we are pleased and enjoy and feel pleasure. And 'good' is this: when it is present, we are good? – Very much so. – But yet, certainly both we are good, and all else that is good <is good>, when some goodness and excellence has come to be present? – That seems to me to be necessary, Callicles. – But yet, the goodness of each <thing>, be that an implement or a body or a soul, and again in the case of all living beings: the goodness of each does not come to be present most beautifully in random manner…?

This last passage, as can be seen from the presence of παραγίγνεσθαι besides παρεῖναι, deals with the process of becoming in addition to the state of being good.

παρουσία at *Gorgias* 497 f. thus occurs in the context of psychology, in a broad sense of that term. At its first occurrence, a case parallel to that of the presence of good things is added by way of explanation: 'Do you not call the good <people> good through the presence of good <things>, just as <you

call> beautiful <those> to whom beauty is present?' When the statement is repeated a page later, it is expanded; different types of people, people with differing qualities are characterized. The reason for their difference is seen in the presence of something or, respectively, the presence of its opposite. What is present in the one case are ἀγαθά, 'good things', and these good things are then said to be αἱ ἡδοναί, 'the pleasures'; in the other case κακά, 'bad things', are present, and these bad things are αἱ ἀνίαι or αἱ λῦπαι, 'the distresses and griefs or displeasures'. Before one can begin to explore philosophical implications of this repeated statement, and draw inferences for the rest of Socrates' argument, it is necessary to see what exactly Socrates is proposing at this point. Callicles is asked to agree that he call τοὺς ἀγαθοὺς ἀγαθῶν παρουσίᾳ ἀγαθούς, ὥσπερ καλοὺς οἷς ἂν κάλλος παρῇ, 'the good (people) good through and by presence of good(s), just as beautiful those to whom beauty is present'. Callicles does agree to that. That is at a stage where Callicles still speaks his mind and does as yet not simply reply 'if it please you', with only little variation in his choice of words. So, whatever we as modern readers may feel, the addressee of Socrates' statement takes no offence at the words in their present form. Plato thus presents them as acceptable. Nevertheless, there is an indication that something is slightly unusual with the first part of the sentence: that one calls 'good people good "through" (or: "by", or: "because of") the presence of good <things>'. If it did not have anything peculiar about it, the additional clause – 'just as <one calls> beautiful <those> "to" (or: "with", or: "at") whom beauty is <present>' – would not be necessary. Or, conversely, as there is an additional clause, its presence must be explained, and it may be best understood as a necessary explanation of what is said in the first clause, necessary because something is not clear in terms of content, or of language, or of both language and content.

It seems, at least, as if Socrates thought that Callicles would find it easier to understand or to accept the statement καλὸς ᾧ κάλλος πάρεστι, 'he is beautiful to whom beauty is present', or the generalizing and therefore perhaps slightly stronger one καλὸς ᾧ ἂν κάλλος παρῇ, 'he is beautiful to whomever beauty be present', than the other, οἱ ἀγαθοὶ ἀγαθῶν παρουσίᾳ ἀγαθοί, 'the good are good through the presence of good(s)'. If we suppose for the moment that this latter statement is a semantically and pragmatically fully equivalent linguistic alternative to ἀγαθὸς ᾧ ἀγαθά πάρεστι, the difference between that and καλὸς ᾧ κάλλος πάρεστι is twofold. On the one hand there is the lexical difference of the predicate adjective of the main clause, ἀγαθός *versus* καλός, on the other the lexical and grammatical difference of the subject of the relative clause that functions as subject of the main clause, ἀγαθά versus κάλλος. Apparently, Socrates considers the statement that 'beautiful is someone to whom beauty is present', with the noun κάλλος in the singular, as more readily intelligible or at least more acceptable than that 'good is someone to whom good <things> are present'. That could be so either because there is a relevant difference in content, in point of reference, between 'good' and 'beautiful', or between the subject's being a noun in the singular and, respectively, a neuter adjective in the plural. Perhaps it is best, however, to start by looking at how Callicles could understand the sentence in a way which enabled him to agree without question. Callicles says to Socrates in his first long speech at 484c–d that those who concern themselves with philosophy for too long a time will be unacquainted (ἄπειρος) with all those things with which to be acquainted (ἔμπειρος) is necessary for 'a man who wants to be καλὸν κἀγαθὸν καὶ εὐδόκιμον', 'beautiful-and-good and reputable'; that is to say, to the formulaic aristocratic ideal of perfection, 'being beautiful-and-good', that of social acceptance and belonging to a peer-group is added. Callicles then provides a number of examples of what one should have experience of: 'the laws of the state, the language used in private and public negotiations, the human pleasures and desires, and altogether the customs'. After a lengthy exposition on the evils of philosophy when practised excessively, he finishes his speech by quoting and interpreting some Euripidean lines (486b):

καίτοι πῶς σοφὸν τοῦτό ἐστιν, ὦ Σώκρατες, ἥτις εὐφυῆ λαβοῦσα τέχνη φῶτ' ἔθηκε χείρονα...; ἀλλ', ὠγαθέ, ἐμοὶ πείθου, παῦσαι δὲ ἐλέγχων, πραγμάτων δ' εὐμουσίαν ἄσκει, καὶ ἄσκει ὁπόθεν δόξεις φρονεῖν...· ζηλῶν οὐκ ἐλέγχοντας ἄνδρας τὰ μικρὰ ταῦτα, ἀλλ' οἷς ἔστιν καὶ βίος καὶ δόξα καὶ ἄλλα πόλλα ἀγαθά.

For how is this <a> wise <thing>, Socrates, an art which taking a well-endowed man renders him worse...? But, my good man, trust me, stop scrutinizing words, exercise the soundness of practical pursuits, and exercise what will make you seem sensible...: do not imitate men scrutinizing such small matters, but those 'to whom is' [i.e.: who have] a life, a reputation, and many other good <things>.

In his last clause, Callicles presumably refers to those men who would fit his earlier description of being καλοὶ κἀγαθοὶ καὶ εὐδόκιμοι, but here he paraphrases οἷς ἔστιν καὶ βίος καὶ δόξα καὶ ἄλλα πόλλα ἀγαθά. As βίος καὶ δόξα, 'a life and a reputation', are themselves good things, Callicles' usage suggests indeed that he calls καλοὺς κἀγαθούς, 'beautiful-and-good', those οἷς ἔστιν πόλλα ἀγαθά, 'to whom there are many good things'. That is not at all far away from Socrates' question at 497e1–3:

τοὺς ἀγαθοὺς οὐχὶ ἀγαθῶν παρουσίᾳ ἀγαθοὺς καλεῖς, ὥσπερ καλοὺς οἷς ἂν κάλλος παρῇ;

Do you not call the good (people) good through and by presence of good(s), just as beautiful those to whom beauty is present?

One therefore need not suppose that Callicles had reason to interfere at this point on grounds of the content of Socrates' question; a question which in terms of the dramatics of the dialogue may even contain a deliberate verbal allusion on Socrates' part to the closing sentence of Callicles'; just as Socrates deliberately echoes and transforms Callicles' language at 490e5–8 when he says:

ἀλλ' εἰ μὴ τὰ τοιαῦτα λέγεις, ἴσως τὰ τοιάδε· οἷον γεωργικὸν ἄνδρα περὶ γῆν φρόνιμόν τε καὶ καλὸν καὶ ἀγαθόν, τοῦτον δὴ ἴσως πλεονεκτεῖν τῶν σπερμάτων καὶ ὡς πλείστῳ σπέρματι χρῆσθαι εἰς τὴν αὑτοῦ γῆν.

But if you do not say things of this sort, perhaps of the following: such as that a soil-tilling man, knowledgeable about the earth and beautiful-and-good, that he thus should perhaps have more seed than others, and should use as much seed as possible on his own land.

This part as well of Socrates' examination begins with an address in the second person singular and is thus phrased in a way which suggests that 'what Callicles says' is of interest to Socrates. In his search for what Callicles meant by declaring that 'the better men' had by nature a right 'to have more', πλεονεκτεῖν or πλέον ἔχειν, he modifies Callicles' phrase καλὸν κἀγαθὸν καὶ εὐδόκιμον by saying φρόνιμόν τε καὶ καλὸν καὶ ἀγαθόν. It is to be noted, though, that this modification is not distorting, and that although it was Socrates who at 489e introduced the term φρόνιμος by asking (489e7–8): ... τοὺς βελτίους καὶ κρείττους πότερον τοὺς φρονιμωτέρους λέγεις ἢ ἄλλους τινάς, 'is it that you call the better and stronger those who have more sense and are more knowledgeable than any others', Callicles had used φρονεῖν, 'having sense; being right-minded; having knowledge', in his final exhortation at 486c, and he readily picks up Socrates' suggestion when he confirms (490a6–8):

ἀλλὰ ταῦτ' ἔστιν ἃ λέγω. τοῦτο γὰρ οἶμαι ἐγὼ τὸ δίκαιον εἶναι φύσει, τὸ βελτίω ὄντα καὶ φρονιμώτερον καὶ ἄρχειν καὶ πλέον ἔχειν τῶν φαυλοτέρων.

But this is what I say. Indeed, this I believe to be the just by nature, that the one who is better and has more sense and knowledge also rules and has more than those who are lower and meaner.

More importantly, if Socrates is in accordance with Callicles' usage and sentiments in asking (497e1–3): τοὺς ἀγαθοὺς οὐχὶ ἀγαθῶν παρουσίᾳ ἀγαθοὺς καλεῖς, ὥσπερ καλοὺς οἷς ἂν κάλλος παρῇ, 'Do you not call the good (people) good through and by presence of good(s), just as beautiful those to whom beauty is present?', one need not speculate at this point what Socrates could have meant by ἀγαθά, or what he wanted Callicles to understand, or how Callicles understood it. The content of ἀγαθά need not be specified for Callicles, since he cannot be expected to find fault at this point with an expression he himself had used.[109] This is not to deny that Socrates knew where he wanted the argument to go. It is, however, to forestall attacks on Socrates by modern readers of the dialogue who suggest that Socrates' question is both misconceived and unfair in suggesting that Callicles calls τοὺς ἀγαθοὺς ἀγαθῶν παρουσίᾳ ἀγαθούς.[110]

When Socrates asks Callicles (497e): τοὺς ἀγαθοὺς οὐχὶ ἀγαθῶν παρουσίᾳ ἀγαθοὺς καλεῖς, ὥσπερ καλοὺς οἷς ἂν κάλλος παρῇ, 'Do you not call the good (people) good through and by presence of good(s), just as beautiful those to whom beauty is present?', he uses ἀγαθῶν παρουσία in just the same way Euripides had used κακῶν παρουσία, 'the presence of bad <things>' (*Hecuba* 227 f.). κάλλος πάρεστι, 'beauty is present', has its parallel in Anacreon's ἥβη πάρα, 'youth is present'. Likewise with Socrates' and Callicles' exchange at 498d2, quoted above.[111] As we have seen, the use of ἀγαθά, κακά, ἡδονή, and λύπη as subjects to παρεῖναι has its precedents in poetical and philosophical usage. The same was true with Socrates' second dealing with that topic (*Gorgias* 506c–508c). Again, ἡδύ and ἀγαθόν were present. ἀρετῆς τινος παραγενομένης and ἀρετὴ παραγίγνεται, however, are expressions introduced at 506c ff. for the first time in the dialogue. The expression ἀρετὴ παραγίγνεται, 'goodness comes to be present', and the notion connected with it is found elsewhere in Plato's early dialogues. The opening question of the dialogue *Meno*, composed not long after the *Gorgias*, is (70a1–4):

> ἔχεις μοι εἰπεῖν, ὦ Σώκρατες, ἆρα διδακτὸν ἡ ἀρετή; ἢ οὐ διδακτὸν ἀλλ' ἀσκητόν; ἢ οὔτε ἀσκητὸν οὔτε μαθητόν, ἀλλὰ φύσει παραγίγνεται τοῖς ἀνθρώποις ἢ ἄλλῳ τινὶ τρόπῳ;

> Can you tell me, Socrates, whether goodness is something teachable and taught? Or is it not teachable but can be got through practice? Or neither through practice nor learning, but it comes to be there for people by nature? Or in some other manner?

The opening sentence is an elaborate Gorgianic period, and we learn presently that Meno, who asks Socrates this question, is himself a pupil of Gorgias. Socrates explains that before deciding on Meno's questions one has to know what ἀρετή is. When Socrates poses this question for the fifth or sixth time after various unsuccessful attempts at an answer by Meno, Meno repeats his original request (*Meno* 86c7–d2):

> ἀλλ' ἔγωγε ἐκεῖνο ἂν ἥδιστα, ὅπερ ἠρόμην τὸ πρῶτον, καὶ σκεψαίμην καὶ ἀκούσαιμι, πότερον ὡς διδακτῷ ὄντι αὐτῷ δεῖ ἐπιχειρεῖν, ἢ ὡς φύσει ἢ ὡς τίνι ποτὲ τρόπῳ παραγιγνομένης τοῖς ἀνθρώποις τῆς ἀρετῆς.

> But I certainly should most gladly investigate what I asked first, and hear about that, whether it is necessary to attempt it as something teachable and taught, or that it is by nature, or in what other way, that goodness comes to be with men.

65

Eventually, it is Socrates who summarizes their efforts at the end of the dialogue. He says to Meno (99e4–100a2):

εἰ δὲ νῦν ἡμεῖς ἐν παντὶ τῷ λόγῳ τούτῳ καλῶς ἐζητήσαμέν τε καὶ ἐλέγομεν, ἀρετὴ ἂν εἴη οὔτε φύσει οὔτε διδακτόν, ἀλλὰ θείᾳ μοίρᾳ παραγιγνομένη ἄνευ νοῦ οἷς ἂν παραγίγνηται, εἰ μή τις εἴη τοιοῦτος τῶν πολιτικῶν ἀνδρῶν οἷος καὶ ἄλλον ποιῆσαι πολιτικόν.

But now, if we have investigated and spoken well throughout this conversation, goodness may well be neither by nature nor something teachable, but come to be there through divine lot without mind for whomever it comes to, if it is the case that there is no-one among politicians such that he can also make another person versed in political matters.

The repetition of the words, not only the thought, of ἀρετή παραγίγνεται, suggests that they were a sort of set phrase, perhaps a stock topic of Gorgias' own teaching.[112] Earlier than the *Gorgias*, in the *Protagoras*, Protagoras declares in the explanation following his myth (323c4–8):

ὅτι μὲν οὖν πάντ' ἄνδρα εἰκότως ἀποδέχονται περὶ ταύτης τῆς ἀρετῆς σύμβουλον διὰ τὸ ἡγεῖσθαι παντὶ μετεῖναι αὐτῆς, ταῦτα λέγω· ὅτι δὲ αὐτὴν οὐ φύσει ἡγοῦνται εἶναι οὐδ' ἀπὸ τοῦ αὐτομάτου, ἀλλὰ διδακτόν τε καὶ ἐξ ἐπιμελείας παραγίγνεσθαι ᾧ ἂν παραγίγνηται, τοῦτό σοι μετὰ τοῦτο πειράσομαι ἀποδεῖξαι.

Now, that it is reasonable that they accept each and every man as an adviser where excellence is concerned because of their believing that 'there is of it to everyone', I say those things [i.e., what has just been said]; but that they believe that goodness is not by nature, nor of its own accord, but taught and teachable and from exercising and practising comes to be with whomever it comes to be, this I shall try to show you after those things.

That in saying οὐ φύσει Protagoras at this point in the dialogue means 'not by nature *alone*' is evident from 327b–c where he admits differences in skill, and analogously in ἀρετή, according to an individual's being εὐφυής or ἀφυής, 'well-endowed' or 'un-endowed', respectively.[113] But apart from concerns that may be specific to either the dialectic of the dialogue or to Protagoras the sophist, diction and argumentation show marked similarities with the passages of the *Meno* discussed above.

While the *Protagoras* contains constructive doctrines proposed by the master, the *Euthydemus* is full of destructive arguing by two of his adherents.[114] In their manner of speaking and, most of all, their usage,[115] they follow Protagoras. Their programme as well is modelled on his. In the beginning of the dialogue, the younger brother Euthydemus declares (273d8–9):

ἀρετήν, ἔφη, ὦ Σώκρατες, οἰόμεθα οἵω τε εἶναι παραδοῦναι κάλλιστ' ἀνθρώπων καὶ τάχιστα.

We two, Socrates, believe that we are capable of giving <to people> excellence and goodness most beautifully and fastest among men.

Here παραδοῦναι is the *causative* or *factitive* to παραγίγνεσθαι; by their action of ἀρετήν παραδοῦναι, 'giving and providing goodness', they effect ἀρετήν παραγίγνεσθαι, 'that goodness comes to be there' for those whom they teach. The common prefix παρα- is suggestive of the semantic relation. While in many respects the *Euthydemus* is connected with the sophist Protagoras, Euthydemus' statement a few lines later (274a10), ἐπ᾽ αὐτό γε τοῦτο πάρεσμεν, ὦ Σώκρατες, 'certainly, for this very thing, Socrates, we are there', is strongly reminiscent of the opening paragraphs of the *Gorgias* where Chaerepho uses the same words in response to Callicles when he says (447b6): ἐπ᾽ αὐτό γέ τοι τοῦτο πάρεσμεν, even if the context of the remark is a different one. The following passage from the *Euthydemus* is reminiscent of the dialogue *Gorgias* as well, both in usage and in content (280b1–8):

συνωμολογησάμεθα τελευτῶντες οὐκ οἶδ᾽ ὅπως ἐν κεφαλαίῳ οὕτω τοῦτο ἔχειν, σοφίας παρούσης, ᾧ ἂν παρῇ,[116] μηδὲν προσδεῖσθαι εὐτυχίας· ἐπειδὴ δὲ τοῦτο συνωμολογησάμεθα, πάλιν ἐπυνθανόμην αὐτοῦ τὰ πρότερον ὡμολογημένα πῶς ἂν ἡμῖν ἔχοι. ὡμολογήσαμεν γάρ, ἔφην, εἰ ἡμῖν ἀγαθὰ πολλὰ παρείη, εὐδαιμονεῖν ἂν καὶ εὖ πράττειν. – συνέφη. – ἆρ᾽ οὖν εὐδαιμονοῖμεν ἂν διὰ τὰ παρόντα ἀγαθά, εἰ μηδὲν ἡμᾶς ὠφελοῖ ἢ εἰ ὠφελοῖ;

We agreed, eventually, I don't know how, that the matter was principally thus that, wisdom being present, for whomever it is present, for him nothing is required in addition for happiness: but when we had agreed on that, I enquired again from him – concerning the things previously agreed upon – how they might be for us <now>. Indeed we had agreed, said I, that in case much good were to be there for us, we would be happy and fare well. – He agreed. – So is it the case that we would be happy because of the present goods[117] if they were to benefit us in no way, or if they were to benefit us?

The substitution of σοφία for ἀρετή had been effected by Socrates at 277d–e where he moves from ἀρετή, the term used by Euthydemus, first to ἐπιστήμη, and then to σοφία. Otherwise, the affinity of this passage to *Gorgias* 497e–498e and 506c–d is remarkable. Incidentally, the statement that εἰ ἡμῖν ἀγαθὰ πολλὰ παρείη, εὐδαιμονεῖν ἂν καὶ εὖ πράττειν <ἡμᾶς>, 'if many good things were to be present with and for us, we might well be happy and fare well', which is readily agreed upon here can serve as external confirmation for the conclusion reached above for reasons internal to the *Gorgias*, that the similar statement there could be readily understood by all present.[118]

While that passage of the *Euthydemus* pointed to its connection with the *Gorgias*, a related passage two pages later suggests the theme of the 'Gorgianic' dialogue *Meno* and of the *Protagoras*[119] (*Euthydemus* 282b7–c3):

πάνυ μὲν οὖν εὖ μοι δοκεῖς λέγειν, ἦ δ' ὅς. – εἰ ἔστι γε, ὦ Κλεινία, ἦν δ' ἐγώ, ἡ σοφία διδακτόν, ἀλλὰ μὴ ἀπὸ ταὐτομάτου παραγίγνεται τοῖς ἀνθρώποις...

So now you seem to me to speak very well, said he. – If, certainly, Clinias, wisdom is teachable, said I, but does not come to be there for human beings of its own accord...

The thought of ἀρετὴ παραγίγνεται is thus present in the context of Plato's dialogues with both the Sophist Protagoras and his followers, and the rhetor Gorgias and his pupils. It is clearly connected with education, and even if in what is preserved in the extant fragments of either Protagoras or Gorgias they do not use those words, it can be deduced with a fair degree of certainty from the four dialogues *Gorgias*, *Protagoras*, *Meno* and *Euthydemus* that the phrase ἀρετὴ παραγίγνεται itself was part of common educated Greek idiom.

8. 'Being present' in Plato's *Charmides*

If Plato's usage at *Gorgias* 497e–498e and 506c–d is thus likely to have its precedents with regard to both the semantic and the syntactic conventions of παρεῖναι, παρουσία, and παραγίγνεσθαι, is that to say that there is nothing unusual or new at all with Socrates' question (497e1–3): τοὺς ἀγαθοὺς οὐχὶ ἀγαθῶν παρουσίᾳ ἀγαθοὺς καλεῖς, ὥσπερ καλοὺς οἷς ἂν κάλλος παρῇ; 'Do you not call the good (people) good through and by presence of good(s), just as beautiful those to whom beauty is present?' Is it correct unqualifiedly to adduce as a similar and comparable case *Charmides* 158e7–8, δῆλον γὰρ ὅτι εἴ σοι πάρεστιν σωφροσύνη, ἔχεις τι περὶ αὐτῆς δοξάζειν, 'for it is clear that if moderation is with you, you can have an opinion about it', and to assume that this is common Greek from Homer onwards?[120]

In one point *Gorgias* 497e1–3 does differ from both the pre-Platonic examples discussed above and the early Platonic examples collected in the previous section, though that may not be a matter of usage. When Homer says εἴ μοι δύναμίς γε παρείη (*Iliad* 22.20), that is virtually the same as εἰ δυναίμην γε (cf. *Iliad* 1.393). A sentence like *Odyssey* 17.347, αἰδὼς δ' οὐκ ἀγαθὴ κεχρημένῳ ἀνδρὶ παρεῖναι, virtually amounts to saying either αἰδεῖσθαι οὐκ ἀγαθὸν κεχρημένῳ ἀνδρὶ or κεχρημένῳ ἀνδρὶ οὐκ ἀγαθὸν αἰδοίῳ εἶναι. In these and most of the other cases cited in the previous sections, the phrase containing the verb παρεῖναι could be replaced by a phrase containing an adjective or a verb which expressed the notion denoted by the respective subjects to the verb παρεῖναι. In each case it would be difficult to say wherein the exact difference between the two corresponding clauses lies.

A good example of this apparent semantic equivalence of different ways of phrasing the same thought is *Charmides* 158b5–c4:

εἰ μέν σοι ἤδη πάρεστιν, ὡς λέγει Κριτίας ὅδε, σωφροσύνη καὶ εἰ σώφρων
ἱκανῶς, οὐδὲν ἔτι σοι ἔδει... εἰ δ' ἔτι τούτων ἐπιδεὴς εἶναι δοκεῖς, ἐπαστέον
πρὸ τῆς τοῦ φαρμάκου δόσεως. αὐτὸς οὖν μοι εἰπὲ πότερον ὁμολογεῖς τῷδε καὶ
φῂς ἱκανῶς ἤδη σωφροσύνης μετέχειν ἢ ἐνδεὴς εἶναι;

So, if, as Critias here says, moderation is already there for you and present with
you, and you are sufficiently moderate, nothing further is missing for you...
But if you still seem to be lacking in these things, an incantation must be made
before administering the drug. So tell me yourself whether you agree with him
and say yourself that you already have sufficiently of moderation, or whether
you are lacking?

Here it seems as if to the native Greek speaker, σώφρων εἶ, σωφροσύνη
πάρεστιν σοί, and σωφροσύνης μετέχεις were not only describing the
same state of affairs, but were also otherwise fully equivalent.[121] All three
phrases say something about the person they are predicated of. They say of
Charmides that he is moderate. In the fifth century at least, that does not
presuppose anything about the status of what is predicated. It does not imply
anything about σωφροσύνη. If σωφροσύνη πάρεστιν σοί and σώφρων εἶ are
equivalent, σωφροσύνη need not be anything in itself.[122] Charmides exists,
and he is moderate. But does *moderation* exist?

A native speaker employing the phrase σωφροσύνη πάρεστιν need not
have thought about σωφροσύνη as something in its own right at all. That is
different with *Charmides* 158e7: δῆλον γὰρ ὅτι εἴ σοι πάρεστιν σωφροσύνη,
ἔχεις τι περὶ αὐτῆς δοξάζειν, 'for it is clear that if moderation is with you, you
can have an opinion about it'. Instead of declaring that 'if moderation "is to"
Charmides, one can say something about Charmides', Socrates postulates
that 'if moderation "is to" Charmides, one can say something about moderation'. That may be Socrates' new and original assumption. The question τί
ἐστι ἀρετή, 'what is goodness', can be, and in Platonic dialogues frequently is,
understood as a question about people. It is understood in that way notably
by Socrates' interlocutors. As such, it is not Socrates' question but a question
which belongs to his times and circumstances. Only if and when τί ἐστι
ἀρετή, or τί ἐστι σωφροσύνη, is understood as a question about ἀρετή and
about σωφροσύνη, and not about people's being good and people's being
moderate, ἀρετή and σωφροσύνη respectively can be regarded as something
in their own right. That, of course, does as yet not tell us anything about the
status assigned to them, it does not even imply that they were thought of
as having any particular status. Asking for ἀρετή and σωφροσύνη, however,
rather than for a person's being good or moderate, is a step towards asking
what status ἀρετή and σωφροσύνη have. *Charmides* 158e7, δῆλον γὰρ ὅτι εἴ
σοι πάρεστιν σωφροσύνη, ἔχεις τι περὶ αὐτῆς δοξάζειν, 'for it is clear that
if moderation is with you, you can have an opinion about it', implies that

σωφροσύνη is something – at least an object of thought. In the same way, *Gorgias* 497e1–3, τοὺς ἀγαθοὺς οὐχὶ ἀγαθῶν παρουσίᾳ ἀγαθοὺς καλεῖς, ὥσπερ καλοὺς οἷς ἂν κάλλος παρῇ: 'Do you not call the good (people) good through and by presence of good(s), just as beautiful those to whom beauty is present?', implies that both ἀγαθά and κάλλος *are something*. Just as at *Charmides* 158e7 Socrates assumes that if one has moderation, one can pronounce an opinion about moderation, so at *Gorgias* 497e1–3 he postulates a relation between good people and something good, between beautiful people and beauty. Regardless of how that relation is conceived (the instrumental dative παρουσίᾳ may suggest a causal relation),[123] for there to be a relation there have to be *relata*.

The ἀγαθά through whose presence good men are called good are something distinct from those good men. Likewise with the second clause. While κάλλος πάρεστιν αὐτῷ can be said to equal καλός ἐστιν, in which case nothing is implied concerning what κάλλος may be, saying that that person is beautiful 'to whom there is beauty'[124] may imply that that beauty is something distinct from that person. As we have seen,[125] in the case of the ἀγαθά it need not be surprising either to find that they are something distinct,[126] or that it is their presence by which people are said to be good. What is surprising is that κάλλος, beauty, is apparently said to be something distinct in the same way.

9. 'Being present' in Plato's *Gorgias*: unresolved issues
498d2, the passage first looked at in section 7 above, does not offer anything more specific on the relation between ἀγαθά and ἀγαθοί either. It is not only stated there that the good are good by the presence of good things, but also that 'to those who are cheerful (or: experience pleasure) there are the good things, the pleasures, if only they are cheerful'. That is on the premise that all that is good is pleasure. But on that assumption, it seems, the two statements that 'someone is good or experiences pleasure' and 'good things or pleasures "are to" someone' are materially equivalent: 'those who experience pleasure experience pleasure if and only if good things or pleasures "are to" them'. Neither this nor the related passage at *Gorgias* 506–8, however, specifies the precise nature of the relation which underlies this concomitance of 'good things being present' and 'people being good'. Instead, *Gorgias* 506c–d presents further difficulties. On the newly granted assumptions that good is not the same as pleasant, and that we do what we do for the sake of the good, Socrates had declared (506c9–d7):

ἡδὺ δέ ἐστιν τοῦτο οὗ παραγενομένου ἡδόμεθα, ἀγαθὸν δὲ οὗ παρόντος ἀγαθοί ἐσμεν; – πάνυ γε. – ἀλλὰ μὴν ἀγαθοί γέ ἐσμεν καὶ ἡμεῖς καὶ τἆλλα πάντα ὅσ' ἀγαθά ἐστιν, ἀρετῆς τινος παραγενομένης; – ἔμοιγε δοκεῖ ἀναγκαῖον εἶναι, ὦ

Καλλίκλεις. – ἀλλὰ μὲν δὴ ἥ γε ἀρετὴ ἑκάστου, καὶ σκεύους καὶ σώματος καὶ ψυχῆς αὖ καὶ ζῴου παντός, οὐ τῷ εἰκῇ κάλλιστα παραγίγνεται…;

But 'pleasant' is this: when it comes to be present, we are pleased and enjoy and feel pleasure. And 'good' is this: when it is present, we are good? – Very much so. – But yet, certainly both we are good, and all else that is good <is good>, when some goodness and excellence has come to be present? – That seems to me to be necessary, Callicles. – But yet, the goodness of each <thing>, be that an implement or a body or a soul, and again in the case of all living beings: the goodness of each does not come to be present most beautifully in random manner…?

The passage gives rise to a number of questions without providing the answers. First, as noted above, παραγίγνεται refers to a process, not to a state of affairs. Something comes to be present. Does what comes to be present exist before it comes to be present, or does it not? Secondly, while at 497e–498e Socrates spoke of ἀγαθά which are present, at 506c–d it is ἀγαθόν. This term, the adjective in the neuter singular, was introduced in a natural way in the context of discussion of the goal of and motivation for our actions. Does replacing ἀγαθά by ἀγαθόν make a difference to the content of the statement at 506c–d? Does the introduction of the term ἀρετή make a difference to the argument? And fourthly, is it the same relation which holds between the ἀγαθά and the ἀγαθοί at 497e–498e, and at 506c–d between the ἀγαθόν on the one hand, the ἀγαθοί and all that is ἀγαθά on the other? Answers to at least some of these questions are suggested by points raised in the dialogues from the *Meno* onwards; that is not to suggest, though, that Plato had either formulated the questions or could have provided an answer at the time of composition of the *Gorgias*.

10. παρουσία in Plato's *Lysis*
The question raised by Socrates half way through the short dialogue *Lysis* is (212a8–b2):

ἐπειδάν τίς τινα φιλῇ, πότερος ποτέρου φίλος γίγνεται, ὁ φιλῶν τοῦ φιλουμένου ἢ ὁ φιλούμενος τοῦ φιλοῦντος.

When somebody loves somebody else, which one of the two becomes friend of which one of the two: the loving one of the loved one, or the loved one of the loving one, or is there no difference?

In the course of answering this initial question, the investigation is extended to cover the meaning or meanings of φίλος in all its applications. In a conversation with Menexenus, Socrates explores the uses of the word φίλος as an active, a passive, and a reciprocal term. Next, in a conversation with Lysis, he propounds 'the poets' saying' that τὸ ὅμοιον τῷ ὁμοίῳ ἀνάγκη ἀεὶ φίλον εἶναι, that 'it is necessary that the similar is friends with the similar' (214b3). This is then modified, since the bad person or thing cannot be friend of or friends with anything at all; the good one, on the other hand, seems to be self-sufficient, and therefore not to be in need of anything or anyone. So, again with a poet's support, the opposite opinion is reached, τὸ ἐναντίον τῷ ἐναντίῳ μάλιστα φίλον εἶναι, 'that the opposite is most friends with the opposite' (216a4). The implications of that appear to make nonsense. So, at 216c, Socrates has a new suggestion: that the neither-good-nor-bad is friend of the good. This is elaborated by way of a medical example (217a–b): the diseased person's body, being neither good nor bad as a body, longs for and is friend of medicine 'because of illness', διὰ νόσον. From there, Socrates continues (217b4–218c3):

τὸ μήτε κακὸν ἄρα μήτ' ἀγαθὸν φίλον γίγνεται τοῦ ἀγαθοῦ διὰ κακοῦ παρουσίαν. – ἔοικεν. – δῆλον δέ γε ὅτι πρὶν γενέσθαι αὐτὸ κακὸν ὑπὸ τοῦ κακοῦ οὗ ἔχει. οὐ γὰρ δή γε κακὸν γεγονὸς ἔτι ἄν τι τοῦ ἀγαθοῦ ἐπιθυμοῖ καὶ φίλον εἴη· ἀδύνατον γὰρ ἔφαμεν κακὸν ἀγαθῷ φίλον εἶναι. – ἀδύνατον γάρ. – σκέψασθε δὴ ὃ λέγω. λέγω γὰρ ὅτι ἔνια μέν, οἷον ἂν ᾖ τὸ παρόν, τοιαῦτά ἐστι καὶ αὐτά, ἔνια δὲ οὔ. ὥσπερ εἰ ἐθέλοι τις χρώματί τῳ ὁτιοῦν ἀλεῖψαι, πάρεστίν που τῷ ἀλειφθέντι τὸ ἐπαλειφθέν. – πάνυ γε. – ἆρ' οὖν καὶ ἔστιν τότε τοιοῦτον τὴν χρόαν τὸ ἀλειφθέν, οἷον τὸ ἐπόν; – οὐ μανθάνω, ἦ δ' ὅς. – ἀλλ' ὧδε, ἦν δ' ἐγώ. εἴ τίς σου ξανθὰς οὔσας τὰς τρίχας ψιμυθίῳ ἀλείψειεν, πότερον τότε λευκαὶ εἶεν ἢ φαίνοιντ' ἄν; – φαίνοιντ' ἄν, ἦ δ' ὅς. – καὶ μὴν παρείη γ' ἂν αὐταῖς λευκότης. – ναί. – ἀλλ' ὅμως οὐδέν τι μᾶλλον ἂν εἶεν λευκαί πω, ἀλλὰ παρούσης λευκότητος οὔτε τι λευκαὶ οὔτε μέλαιναί εἰσιν. – ἀληθῆ. – ἀλλ' ὅταν δή, ὦ φίλε, τὸ γῆρας αὐταῖς ταὐτὸν τοῦτο χρῶμα ἐπαγάγῃ, τότε ἐγένοντο οἷόνπερ τὸ παρόν, λευκοῦ παρουσίᾳ λευκαί. – πῶς γὰρ οὔ; – τοῦτο τοίνυν ἐρωτῶ νῦν δή, εἰ ᾧ ἄν τι παρῇ, τοιοῦτον ἔσται τὸ ἔχον οἷον τὸ παρόν· ἢ ἐὰν μὲν κατά τινα τρόπον παρῇ, ἔσται, ἐὰν δὲ μή, οὔ; – οὕτω μᾶλλον, ἔφη. – καὶ τὸ μήτε κακὸν ἄρα μήτ' ἀγαθὸν ἐνίοτε κακοῦ παρόντος οὔπω κακόν ἐστιν, ἔστιν δ' ὅτε ἤδη τὸ τοιοῦτον γέγονεν. – πάνυ γε. – οὐκοῦν ὅταν μήπω κακὸν ᾖ κακοῦ παρόντος, αὕτη μὲν ἡ παρουσία ἀγαθοῦ αὐτὸ ποιεῖ ἐπιθυμεῖν· ἡ δὲ κακὸν ποιοῦσα ἀποστερεῖ αὐτὸ τῆς τε ἐπιθυμίας ἅμα καὶ τῆς φιλίας τοῦ ἀγαθοῦ. οὐ γὰρ ἔτι ἐστὶν οὔτε κακὸν οὔτε ἀγαθόν, ἀλλὰ κακόν· φίλον δὲ ἀγαθῷ κακὸν οὐκ ἦν. (Having obtained consent on that last point, Socrates resumes the argument after a brief digression; 218b6.) νῦν ἄρα, ἦν δ' ἐγώ, ὦ Λύσι καὶ Μενέξενε, παντὸς μᾶλλον ἐξευρήκαμεν ὃ ἔστιν τὸ φίλον καὶ οὔ. φαμὲν γὰρ αὐτό, καὶ κατὰ τὴν ψυχὴν καὶ κατὰ τὸ σῶμα καὶ πανταχοῦ, τὸ μήτε κακὸν μήτε ἀγαθὸν διὰ κακοῦ παρουσίαν τοῦ ἀγαθοῦ φίλον εἶναι. – παντάπασιν ἐφάτην τε καὶ συνεχωρείτην οὕτω τοῦτ' ἔχειν.

So the neither-bad-nor-good becomes a friend of the good because of the presence of the bad. – It seems so. – But that is clear, certainly: before it itself becomes bad from the bad it has. For certainly, anything that has become bad would no longer desire the good or be its friend: for it is impossible, we said, that the bad becomes friends with the good. – Impossible indeed. – Consider thus what I say. Indeed, I say that some things are such as that which is present with them also themselves, but others are not. Just as when someone wanted to dye something with a certain colour, the dye applied is somehow present to the thing dyed. – Most certainly. – Now, is it then also the case that the thing dyed is – with regard to its colour – such as that which is on it? – I do not understand, said he. – But <I mean it> in the following way, said I. If someone were to dye your hair – which is auburn – with white lead, would it then *be* white, or would it *appear* white? – Appear, he said. – Yet also in that case would whiteness certainly be present to it. – Yes. – But all the same, it still would not be white any the more; but, with whiteness present, it is neither white in any way nor is it black. – True. – But when, friend, old age had brought on this same colour to your hair, then it would have become like that which was present to it: with the presence of the white, <they would *be*> white. – Indeed, how not. – It is this, then, I thus ask now: Is it the case that – if something is present to something else – that which has it will be such as that which is present? Or is it the case that if it is present in a certain way, it will be, but if not, not? – Rather the latter, he said. – And the neither-good-nor-bad is sometimes not yet bad while the bad is present, at other times it already has become such. – Most certainly. – Now, whenever it is not yet bad while the bad is present, this presence it is which makes it desire the good. But the presence which makes bad deprives it at once of the desire of and the friendship with the good; indeed, it no longer is neither-bad-nor-good, but bad. And the bad was not friends with the good! [Having obtained consent on that last point, Socrates resumes the argument after a brief digression; 218b6.] So now, said I, Lysis and Menexenus, we have found out what being friends is, and what not. For we say it is, both as regards soul and as regards body, and everywhere, that the neither-bad-nor-good is friend of the good because of the presence of the bad. – In every way, both of them said, and concurred that this was so.

On the basis of what has been said in the previous sections, this passage can be dealt with briefly. The κακόν which is present could be something external or internal. It is distinct from that 'to which it is'. It affects that 'to which it is' just as if it were something active (…γίγνεται…διὰ κακοῦ παρουσίαν. … γενέσθαι…ὑπὸ τοῦ κακοῦ οὗ ἔχει). As a result, that 'to which it is' may or may not become οἷον ἂν ᾖ τὸ παρόν, 'of whatever sort that which is present is'. In the example of something which by being present does not turn that 'to which it is' into something which is such as itself, what is present is something external. That its presence is of an external nature is emphasized by the phrase οἷον τὸ ἐπόν, 'of the sort of that which is on it', in which τὸ παρόν, 'what is there; what is present', has been replaced with τὸ ἐπόν, 'what is on (something)'. In the example of something which by being present does turn that 'to which it is' into something which is such as itself (ἐγένοντο οἷόνπερ τὸ παρόν, λευκοῦ παρουσίᾳ λευκαί), what is present is something internal. The distinction between the two cases is being introduced to answer the question:

εἰ ᾧ ἄν τι παρῇ, τοιοῦτον ἔσται τὸ ἔχον οἷον τὸ παρόν· ἢ ἐὰν μὲν κατά τινα τρόπον παρῇ, ἔσται, ἐὰν δὲ μή, οὔ;

Is it the case that – if something is present to something else – that which has it will be such as that which is present? Or is it the case that if it is present in a certain way, it will be, but if not, not?

The same thing can be present in different ways.[127] It is one thing to ask how successful the example, in the *Lysis*, of 'white' or 'whiteness' is in the context of real and true *versus* merely perceived colour of hair; and it may be argued that, because colour is something so inextricably linked with sense-perception, it is not a good example after all. It is quite a different matter to claim that Plato was not aware of the implications of the term παρουσία when composing the early dialogues. In the *Gorgias*, the word is used with apparent unconcern, but nevertheless in a fully conscious way, as analysis of 497 f. has shown;[128] what is present there is not a physical, corporeal object; whether what is present there exists at all is a question not raised. Grammatically, though, παρουσία is treated identically in the *Gorgias* and in the *Lysis*. That is to say, the ox, whose presence meant so much danger to the integrity of Socrates' character at *Euthydemus* 301a, would not have threatened Lysis and Menexenus after their conversation with Socrates.

11. Recapitulation
From Homer to Plato, usage of παρεῖναι is altogether uniform. Leaving aside impersonal use – a large number of composites in '-εστιν' may be used to denote 'it is possible' – the verb can refer to the presence of people, at a place, an event, a conversation; the present or contemporary time; and finally the presence of things, in the widest sense of that word. The things present may be material objects, but – from Homer onwards – they may just as well be incorporeal entities, even though the conceptual framework to express this observation had, of course, not yet been developed. Present in that way are not only potentially divine powers, but a whole range of concrete and abstract things: forces, emotions, states of mind, qualities, properties, actions, passions. The noun παρουσία is narrower in its application than the verb; it can denote the presence of the same sorts of thing that the verb παρεῖναι denotes; it belongs to a different register, though, and when used in prose may well have had connotations of poetic style and gravity. παραγίγνεσθαι, 'come to be present', on the other hand, tends to be used mostly with *people* in early texts. The rise of sophistic teaching and education, however, made it necessary to stress the advantages of acquisition of positive characteristics

and abilities; consequently, the application of the verb was extended in that context so as to cover all those qualities which were said to 'be present' with someone. Sophistic education, influence of Gorgias and also Protagoras, is also the context in which that potentially ontologically significant sentence is pronounced at *Gorgias* 497e1–3:

> τοὺς ἀγαθοὺς οὐχὶ ἀγαθῶν παρουσίᾳ ἀγαθοὺς καλεῖς, ὥσπερ καλοὺς οἷς ἂν κάλλος παρῇ;

> Do you not call the good <people> good through presence of good(s), just as < those people> beautiful to whom beauty is present?

It cannot be determined with certainty, however, how abstract a thing either the ἀγαθά or κάλλος were thought to be by Plato. And, whether genuinely Platonic or spurious, the *Hippias Major* should serve as a warning to the reader not to assume too readily that either ἀγαθά or κάλλος in the *Gorgias* was thought of as even potentially abstract. An advance towards that distinction is made, though, when the noun παρουσία is employed and its meaning and implications discussed at *Lysis* 217a–b, where it is established, at least partly explicitly, that things can be present in different ways with different consequences, and that the consequence of the presence of a thing to another thing or to a person depends also on what sort of thing it is. All this must be borne in mind when it comes to an assessment of *Phaedo* 100d.[129]

CHAPTER 3

ἐνεῖναι, ἐγγίγνεσθαι

In the discussion between Socrates, Cebes, and Simmias at *Phaedo* 100b–105e, it looks as if much of Socrates' final proof that the soul is immortal hinges on the fact that certain things like the beautiful itself, the good itself, and the large itself are in us and the other objects of this world, and determine what anything is, and what it is called, by being in them. ἐνεῖναι and ἐγγίγνεσθαι are terms used to denote that relation at 103b and 105b–c, but εἶναι ἐν is found much more frequently, with reference to the same sort of relation.

That has led students of Plato to postulate that 'forms are in particulars'. At least, when 'forms', or 'ideas' are mentioned, *one* of the ways in which they are talked about suggests that they are *in* particulars. Ross, representative of the *communis opinio*, comments on *Phaedo* 102d7 that 'Socrates proceeds to point out that not only cannot an Idea itself be characterized by its opposite, but also the particularization of one Idea in a particular thing cannot be characterized by the opposite Idea.' He later lists ἐν, εἶναι ἐν, ἐνεῖναι, ἐγγίγνεσθαι, κεῖσθαι ἐν, as the first sub-group of that 'group of words implying or suggesting the immanence of the Forms'.[130] A study of ἐνεῖναι and related terms seems thus justified both because of the issue of immanence, interesting in its own right and because the relationship which ἐνεῖναι is intended to express has been seen, at various times, as the same as, complementary to or, by contrast, in competition with that described by μετέχειν.

1. ἐνεῖναι, εἶναι ἐν, and ἐγγίγνεσθαι in early Greek literature

In parallel with the treatment of μετέχειν and παρεῖναι, we shall begin with an investigation into the uses of the words ἐνεῖναι, εἶναι ἐν, and ἐγγίγνεσθαι in early Greek literature, in order to establish what sorts of subject and object they could connect, and what sort of relation the verbs were used to denote. Then, instances of the verbs in early dialogues of Plato will be discussed with a view to whether there is anything in their employment in those texts that is suggestive of a semantic development.

First, the purely spatial usage of the words will very briefly be considered. Spatial usage is primary in the sense that it furnishes the model compared with which all other usages seem metaphorical. An early instance of the verb ἐνεῖναι[131] in that spatial application is *Odyssey* 10.45. On their way home from the island of Aeolus, Odysseus has fallen asleep. Since he had given strict orders not to touch the wine-skin entrusted to him by their host, his comrades expect it to contain a wealthy gift, and their leader addresses them (10.45–6):

ἀλλ' ἄγε θᾶσσον ἰδώμεθα, ὅττι τάδ' ἐστίν,
ὅσσος τις χρυσός τε καὶ ἄργυρος ἀσκῷ ἔνεστιν.

Come, let us see quickly, what that is, how much gold and silver there is in the wineskin.

Similarly, out of the eight occurrences of the word in Herodotus' *Histories*, five denote spatial 'being in'. People, animals, treasures are in houses or ships, the ring of Polycrates is in the belly of the fish. And Hecataeus, in many ways Herodotus' predecessor, says in a description of a foreign country (292 J.):

ἐν τοῖσιν οὔρεσι δένδρεα ἔνι ἄγρια,

there are wild trees in those mountains.

There are trees in the mountains. Should one say that this spatial use of ἐνεῖναι already is metaphorical? Perhaps not, but it is worth noting that there are potentially two distinct concepts of spatial 'being in'. Two different sorts of situation can be thought of and described in the same terms of 'being in'; for those trees are certainly not in the same way in the mountains as pieces of gold are in a wineskin, or a man in a house, or a ring in the belly of a fish.

Earlier than that, however, earlier even than the first attested usage of the verb connecting two material things, is an instance of a different kind of extension. In Book 24 of the *Iliad*, Priam scolds the Trojans who have gathered in his palace and sends them away with the words (24.239–40):

ἔρρετε λωβητῆρες ἐλεγχέες· οὔ νυ καὶ ὑμῖν
οἴκοι ἔνεστι γόος, ὅτι μ' ἤλθετε κηδήσοντες;

Go, worthless cowards: Is not there now wailing in the house also for you, that you come distressing me?

There is wailing in the house. Of course, one could say one of two things; either: what is meant is that there are people wailing in the house, and in that sense wailing is in the house; or: Γόος was a god or *daimon*, like Ἀιδώς at *Odyssey* 17.347, or like Φόβος, Ἔρις, Ἀλκή and Ἰωκή at *Iliad* 5.739 f., or like Κράτος and Βία in the *Prometheus Bound*, and that therefore the example is just one of a person being in a house.[132] If the need of explanation is felt at all, however, if the clause 'there is wailing in the house for you as well' is felt to require interpretation, a different kind of metonymy seems to be closer at hand: 'there is cause for wailing in your houses, too'.[133] That would be more abstract a notion. Irrespective of what γόος signifies in this particular case, introducing an abstract noun of the class of words which can denote actions, processes or states of the mind of individuals, expressions or personal characteristics or qualities, paves the way for use of the same sort of thing as subject of the verb in other situations too.

While it is not inconceivable that someone may want to argue that γόος with Homer is a *daimon* or spirit, such an interpretation could not easily be upheld with the following example. Early in the sixth century BC, Solon wrote in one of his elegies, in a tone of scornful exhortation, that men must not blame the gods for grief they suffer by their own fault, in this case tyrannical government. 'Each one of you', says Solon, 'looks for his own individual advantage' (11.6):

σύμπασιν δ' ὑμῖν χαῦνος ἔνεστι νόος,

in all of you together, however, there is a porous, empty mind.

Here 'mind', whatever else it may be, is neither a person nor a physical object, as might be argued for e.g. φρήν, but it is not a *daimon* either. And mind is said to be in a person or in a group of people. This usage of such a thing as mind being *in* someone is common with the tragedians of the fifth century.[134] On one occasion, Aeschylus has material and non-material things as subjects to ἐνεῖναι side by side (*Sisyphus* fr. 229):

καὶ <γὰρ> θανόντων ἰσὶν οὐκ ἔνεστ' ἰκμάς,
σοὶ δ' οὐκ ἔνεστι κῖκυς οὐδ' αἱμόρρυτοι
φλέβες.

For in the sinews of the dead there is no moisture, and in you there is no vigour, nor veins flowing with blood.

It is difficult to say if the range of subjects to ἐνεῖναι was extended first to a person's qualities or characteristics, like κῖκυς, 'vigour', or to temporary states or actions of a person, like γόος, 'wailing'. In some cases, it is hard to attribute that which is in someone to one of these categories at all. When Orestes says (Sophocles, *Electra* 1243–4):

ὅρα γε μὲν δὴ κἀν γυναιξὶν ὡς Ἄρης
ἔνεστιν·

Watch out and see that, indeed, Ares is in women as well...

What is Ares? A general characteristic? A passing state? A set of thoughts or actions? Or, as could be claimed with some justification in this case, a god? This last possibility must be taken seriously, though it would lead too far to exploit it fully. With Sophocles, at any rate, actions are prevailing as points of reference of the subjects of ἐνεῖναι. When Deianeira and her attendants hear of Heracles' imminent return at the beginning of Sophocles' *Trachiniae*, they rejoice. Deianeira, however, qualifies cautiously (296–7):

> ὅμως δ' ἔνεστι τοῖσιν εὖ σκοπουμένοις
> ταρβεῖν τὸν εὖ πράσσοντα μὴ σφαλῇ ποτε.

> Yet there is 'fearing' in those who consider well the one who does well: lest he fall one day.

And she continues (298):

> ἐμοὶ γὰρ οἶκτος δεινὸς εἰσέβη, φίλαι,

> For powerful pity comes upon me, friends.

That seems to imply that pity, having entered her, is now in her. But as we have seen with Solon's νοῦς, it is not only emotions which are in human beings. So, a few scenes later in the same play, Deianeira declares before carrying out her plan to win back Heracles (590–1):

> οὕτως ἔχει γ' ἡ πίστις, ὡς τὸ μὲν δοκεῖν
> ἔνεστι, πείρᾳ δ' οὐ προσωμίλησά πω.

> Such is <my> trust <in what has been done> that there is 'believing' in <me>, yet so far I have not engaged with experience.

Alternatively, one may construe this last sentence as saying that 'there is cause and reason for believing and trust' in the situation or the circumstances, rather than 'an inclination or a willingness to believe' in the person, Deianeira.

Use of ἔνεστι in the sense of 'it is possible' will be passed over. There are cases where it seems as if – like ἔστιν, ἔξεστι, and sometimes πάρεστι – ἔνεστι could be employed in that way. This, though, is not necessarily so with *Antigone* 213–14:

> νόμῳ δὲ χρῆσθαι παντὶ πού γ' ἔνεστί σοι
> καὶ τῶν θανόντων χὡπόσοι ζῶμεν πέρι.

> In you [Creon] it is to use every law, both about the dead and about us who live.

It would be difficult to assert that the force of ἔνεστί σοι is just to denote possibility, 'it is possible for you to use every law'. A translation 'using every law is in you' would bring out the parallel to the foregoing examples. Then one could compare the grammatical subjects of ἔνεστι and say that while in the previous passage δοκεῖν, as denoting an action, can be seen as referring to something, a process or a state, internal to a person, the last example shows an extension of the potential point of reference of the subject of ἐνεῖναι to action of whatever sort. 'The using of the law' which is in Creon potentially refers to an externally manifested action.

A further example is from Sophocles' late play *Electra*, a play also otherwise rich in constructions with both ἐνεῖναι and παρεῖναι. In this case, a characteristic whose effects are external is found side by side with one whose effects are internal. When Electra understands her sister to refuse help, she reproaches her (1031):

ἄπελθε· σοὶ γὰρ ὠφέλησις οὐκ ἔνι.

Away, for in you there is no aiding.

To this, Chrysothemis replies (1032):

ἔνεστιν· ἀλλὰ σοὶ μάθησις οὐ πάρα.

There is in <me>. But with you there is no learning.

It should be noted that in this particular context, in the realm of personal qualities, ἔνεστιν and πάρεστιν seem to be interchangeable. Before we leave Sophocles, one last case, which may become important in a later context, should briefly be mentioned. With it, we leave the sphere of human beings as 'things' in which something else *is*. The sort of characteristics encountered as being in men can also be said to be in λόγοι, in 'words', or 'sentences', or 'speeches', or perhaps 'thoughts'. Again it is the late play *Electra* from which the first example is drawn. After a heated exchange between the two sisters, the chorus of attendants admonishes them to refrain from anger (368–9):

ὡς τοῖς λόγοις | ἔνεστιν ἀμφοῖν κέρδος...

As in your thoughts there is profit for both of <you>...

Likewise, we read in a fragment the general advice (fr. 259.1 Radt):

ἔνεστι γάρ τις καὶ λόγοισιν ἡδονή,
λήθην ὅταν ποιῶσι τῶν ὄντων κακῶν...

For there is pleasure even in words, when they make you forget what is bad...

κέρδος, 'profit', and ἡδονή, 'pleasure', are said to be in (the) words. In both cases, it is not a consideration of or thought about 'profit' or 'pleasure' mentioned in the speeches, but the words 'have it in them' to be profitable or pleasurable. To say that profit or pleasure are in the words, of course, may just be a manner of speaking; just as the λόγοι in the fragment are said to 'make' or 'produce' something, namely forgetfulness – the λόγοι are 'personified' – and just as in the *Euthydemus* Socrates is, semi-seriously, criticized[135] for saying that 'a sentence wants to say something'. In the absence of expressions like 'words can afford consolation', though, one must reckon with the possibility that in saying 'pleasure is in the words' the speaker thinks of 'pleasure in the words' literally, and not of 'words referring to' or 'reflecting' or 'causing pleasure', just as one must not exclude the possibility that Orestes refers to a god when he says that 'Ares is in women, too'.[136]

2. ἐνεῖναι, εἶναι ἐν, and ἐγγίγνεσθαι in the Presocratics and the Hippocratic Corpus

There are two further significant contexts of ἐνεῖναι and related words in pre-Platonic literature. Among the Presocratics it is notably Anaxagoras who says that the elements he posits are in something, or something is in the elements. Simplicius reports (*Physica* 155.23; DK59B1):

ὅτι δὲ Ἀναξαγόρας ἐξ ἑνὸς μίγματος ἄπειρα τῷ πλήθει ὁμοιομερῆ ἀποκρίνεσθαί φησιν πάντων μὲν ἐν παντὶ ἐνόντων, ἑκάστου δὲ κατὰ τὸ ἐπικρατοῦν χαρακτηριζομένου, δηλοῖ διὰ τοῦ πρώτου τῶν φυσικῶν λέγων ἀπ' ἀρχῆς· ‘ὁμοῦ πάντα χρήματα ἦν, ἄπειρα καὶ πλῆθος καὶ σμικρότητα· καὶ γὰρ τὸ σμικρὸν ἄπειρον ἦν. καὶ πάντων ὁμοῦ ἐόντων οὐδὲν ἔνδηλον ἦν ὑπὸ σμικρότητος· πάντα γὰρ ἀήρ τε καὶ αἰθὴρ κατεῖχεν, ἀμφότερα ἄπειρα ἐόντα· ταῦτα γὰρ μέγιστα ἔνεστιν ἐν τοῖς σύμπασι καὶ πλήθει καὶ μεγέθει.’

Anaxagoras says that 'homoeomera', indefinite in amount, separate themselves out of one mixture, while all things are in everything, that each of them is characterized by what is prevailing <in it>, may become clear from what he says at the beginning of his first book of Physics where he says: 'Together were all things, indefinite both as regards their amount and their smallness: for also the small was indefinite. And while all things were together, nothing was clear<ly discernible> through their smallness: for mist and aether held everything down, both of them being indefinite: for those are the biggest and most in all the things together, both as regards their amount and as regards their largeness.'

If the identification of the last lines as genuine words of Anaxagoras is correct, he himself used the word ἔνεστιν to describe the relation he supposed to hold between individual elements and the whole of his κόσμος. Considering what else is reported of him, this seems to be altogether likely. ἐνεῖναι also occurs in two other passages in Simplicius that are commonly recognized as genuine Anaxagorean fragments (*Physica* 34.28; DK59B4):

τούτων δὲ οὕτως ἐχόντων χρὴ δοκεῖν ἐνεῖναι πολλά τε καὶ παντοῖα ἐν πᾶσι τοῖς συγκρινομένοις καὶ σπέρματα πάντων χρημάτων καὶ ἰδέας παντοίας ἔχοντα καὶ χροιὰς καὶ ἡδονάς... πρὶν δὲ ἀποκριθῆναι ταῦτα πάντων ὁμοῦ ἐόντων οὐδὲ χροιὴ ἔνδηλος ἦν οὐδεμία· ἀπεκώλυε γὰρ ἡ σύμμιξις πάντων χρημάτων, τοῦ τε διεροῦ καὶ τοῦ ξηροῦ καὶ τοῦ θερμοῦ καὶ τοῦ ψυχροῦ καὶ τοῦ λαμπροῦ καὶ τοῦ ζοφεροῦ, καὶ γῆς πολλῆς ἐνεούσης καὶ σπερμάτων ἀπείρων πλῆθος οὐδὲν ἐοικότων ἀλλήλοις. οὐδὲ γὰρ τῶν ἄλλων οὐδὲν ἔοικε τὸ ἕτερον τῷ ἑτέρῳ. τούτων δὲ οὕτως ἐχόντων ἐν τῷ σύμπαντι χρὴ δοκεῖν ἐνεῖναι πάντα χρήματα.

If that be so, it is necessary to believe that in everything combined there are many and varied <things>, namely seeds of all objects, having varied guises and colours and tastes… But before those were separated off, while everything was together, not a single colour was apparent: for the mixture of all things forbade that, of the moist and the dry, the warm and the cold, the bright and the sombre; and much earth was therein, and seeds unlimited in number, alike in nothing. For neither was any of the other things in anything like any other. If that be so, it is necessary to believe that in the all, all objects are in.

With that, one can compare the following (Simplicius *Physica* 164.25; DK59B6):

καὶ ὅτε δὲ ἴσαι μοῖραί εἰσι τοῦ τε μεγάλου καὶ τοῦ σμικροῦ πλῆθος, καὶ οὕτως ἂν εἴη ἐν παντὶ πάντα· οὐδὲ χωρὶς ἔστιν εἶναι, ἀλλὰ πάντα παντὸς μοῖραν μετέχει. ὅτε τοὐλάχιστον μὴ ἔστιν εἶναι, οὐκ ἂν δύναιτο χωρισθῆναι, οὐδ' ἂν ἐφ' ἑαυτοῦ γενέσθαι, ἀλλ' ὅπωσπερ ἀρχὴν εἶναι καὶ νῦν πάντα ὁμοῦ. ἐν πᾶσι δὲ πολλὰ ἔνεστι καὶ τῶν ἀποκρινομένων ἴσα πλῆθος ἐν τοῖς μείζοσί τε καὶ ἐλάσσοσι.

And when there are equal parts of the big and the small, as regards their amount, also in that way everything would be in everything: nor is there being apart, but everything has a part of everything <together with everything else>. When there is nothing which is the smallest, no 'being parted' is possible, nor coming to be by itself, but as it was in the beginning, so now everything is together. And in everything there are many things of those separated off, equal in amount in the bigger and the smaller <things>.

The same use of ἐνεῖναι in the context of physics is found with Diogenes of Apollonia, as with Anaxagoras both in the doxography and in what is recognized as his genuine words. (Aristotle, *De Respiratione* 471a3 ff.; DK64A31):

Διογένης δ' ὅταν ἀφῶσι [οἱ ἰχθύες] τὸ ὕδωρ διὰ τῶν βραγχίων ἐκ τοῦ περὶ τὸ στόμα περιεστῶτος ὕδατος ἕλκειν τῷ κενῷ τῷ ἐν τῷ στόματι τὸν ἀέρα ὡς ἐνόντος ἐν τῷ ὕδατι ἀέρος…

But Diogenes says that, whenever [fish] let water go through their gills, they draw from the water that is standing about their mouth – by means of the empty [void] in their mouth – air, as air is in the water.

Again, it is Simplicius who preserves extensive extracts, among which we find the following (*Physica* 152.22–153.4; DK64B5):

καί μοι δοκεῖ τὸ τὴν νόησιν ἔχον εἶναι ὁ ἀὴρ καλούμενος ὑπὸ τῶν ἀνθρώπων, καὶ ὑπὸ τούτου πάντας καὶ κυβερνᾶσθαι καὶ πάντων κρατεῖν· αὐτὸ γάρ μοι τοῦτο θεὸς δοκεῖ εἶναι καὶ ἐπὶ πᾶν ἀφῖχθαι καὶ πάντα διατιθέναι καὶ ἐν παντὶ ἐνεῖναι. καὶ ἔστιν οὐδὲ ἕν ὅ τι μὴ μετέχει τούτου· μετέχει δὲ οὐδὲ ἕν ὁμοίως τὸ ἕτερον τῷ ἑτέρῳ, ἀλλὰ πολλοὶ τρόποι καὶ αὐτοῦ τοῦ ἀέρος καὶ τῆς νοήσιός εἰσιν. ἔστι γὰρ πολύτροπος, καὶ θερμότερος καὶ ψυχρότερος καὶ ξηρότερος καὶ ὑγρότερος καὶ σταῦιμόι+ρ̣ο̣ς καὶ ὀξυτέρην κίνησιν ἔχων, κ̣αὶ ἄ̣λ̣λ̣α̣ι̣ πολλαὶ ἑτεροιώσιες ἔνεισι καὶ ἡδονῆς καὶ χροιῆς ἄπειροι.

And to me it seems that that which has understanding is what is called air by men, and that by it everything is governed, and that it has power over everything: and even that seems to me to be god who has got to everything, who orders all things, and who is in everything; and there is not one thing that does not 'have of' it: but not one thing has <of it> in like wise with a single other one, but there are many ways both of air and of understanding. For it is manifold: warmer and colder, drier and moister, stiller and having quicker motion, and there are many alterations of taste and colour in it, unlimited.

We see that as Anaxagoras had his many elements in everything, and νοῦς in some, so Diogenes has his one ἀήρ in everything. Diogenes here seems to be dependent on Anaxagoras. If there are many things it makes more sense to say that everything is in everything, since while it is not nonsensical to say that the one thing which in its undifferentiated form underlies everything is in all the differentiated things, this manner of speaking is more easily understood as transferred from a model of explanation of the world where there are many different things which can be said to be in the various things there are.

The other area abundant in ἐνεῖναι, and moreover ἐγγίγνεσθαι, is medicine. A brief glance at the entries of the two verbs in the *Index Hippocraticus* will suffice.[137] About the general usage the editors comment: '*saepe de signis, velut* ὀδύνη, δίψα, ἀψυχίη, βήξ, ὕπνος, καῦμα', ('pain', 'thirst', 'fainting', 'cough', 'sleep', 'fever').

In *Airs, Waters, and Places*, for example, the author declares about cities exposed to cold winds (4):

τοῖσι δὲ παιδίοισιν ὕδρωπες ἐγγίγνονται ἐν τοῖσιν ὄρχεσιν, ἕως σμικρὰ ᾖ· ἔπειτα, προϊούσης τῆς ἡλικίης, ἀφανίζονται.

Children suffer from dropsies in the testicles while they are little, which disappear as they grow older.   (tr. Jones)

But since the various authors of the treatises were physicists as well as physicians, we also find physical elements being in the body as in e.g. the *Nature of Man* (1.5):

οὔτε γὰρ τὸ πάμπαν ἠέρα λέγω τὸν ἄνθρωπον εἶναι, οὔτε πῦρ, οὔτε ὕδωρ, οὔτε γῆν, οὔτ᾽ ἄλλο οὐδέν, ὅ τι μὴ φανερόν ἐστιν ἐνεὸν ἐν τῷ ἀνθρώπῳ.

For I do not say that man is wholly air, nor fire, nor water, nor earth, nor anything else which is not apparent as being in man.

The author continues a little later (2.13): πολλὰ γάρ ἐστιν ἐν τῷ σώματι ἐνεόντα, 'for many things are in the body'. Countless examples from the Hippocratic Corpus could be added for those uses.

3. ἐνεῖναι, εἶναι ἐν, and ἐγγίγνεσθαι in early dialogues of Plato

As is to be expected, ἐγγίγνεσθαι and ἐνεῖναι occur in Plato's early dialogues in connection with subjects and objects taken from all the different groups of words mentioned. There are 42 instances in the early dialogues up to and including the *Symposium*. Not relevant to our investigation is, first, occasional purely spatial use without consequences of any sort to the argument; secondly, occurrences in quotations from poetry, if the clauses containing the words are not subsequently discussed; thirdly, casual occurrences of common expressions like νοῦς ἔνεστιν, if Socrates does not pun on such expressions or draws attention to what would follow if they were taken 'literally'.

Common expressions like νοῦς ἔνεστιν, though, are regularly analysed and on that basis reinterpreted by Plato. *Ion* 534b is a case in point. Socrates declares at 533d that, in explaining Homer, people like Ion do not exercise a skill, but that a godly, divine power moves them, or that a power, δύναμις, is 'put into' them (ἐντίθησι, 533d). In 534a, the state of being ἔνθεος, 'enthused', is contrasted with the normal one of being ἔμφρων, 'mindful', or 'in one's right mind'. In that latter state a poet is unable to make poetry; and Socrates continues (534b4–7):

> καὶ οὐ πρότερον οἷός τε ποιεῖν πρὶν ἂν ἔνθεός τε γένηται καὶ ἔκφρων καὶ ὁ νοῦς μηκέτι ἐν αὐτῷ ἐνῇ· ἕως δ' ἂν τουτὶ ἔχῃ τὸ κτῆμα, ἀδύνατος πᾶς ποιεῖν ἄνθρωπός ἐστιν καὶ χρησμῳδεῖν.

> And he will not be able to compose until he becomes enthused and 'out of his mind' and until the mind is no longer in him: but so long as he has this possession, a man is incapable of composing or foretelling.

This, of course, is an interpretation of the words ἔνθεος, 'enthused', or 'in whom god is', ἔκφρων, 'mindless', or 'out of one's mind', and νοῦς ἔνεστιν ἔν τινι, 'mind is in someone', 'someone is mindful' or 'in his right mind'. The phrases are taken literally and reinterpreted. Mind becomes something in itself. As governing one's thoughts, it is here in opposition to the god. Both mind and god seem to be something separate in principle, something other than the particular human being they relate to at any given moment. This is apparent a short while later in the text (534c–d) when Socrates declares ὁ θεὸς ἐξαιρούμενος τούτων τὸν νοῦν, that 'the god takes the mind out of' the poets, and that it is not the poets who speak, οἷς νοῦς μὴ πάρεστιν, ἀλλ' ὁ θεὸς αὐτός ἐστιν ὁ λέγων, 'to whom there is no mind, but that it is the god himself who speaks'. νοῦς πάρεστιν, rather than ἔνεστιν, is the marginally commoner phrase, employed here after the pun on the alternative expression. Plato does not develop that thought in the *Ion* in terms of a theory of mind. The example demonstrates, however, that Plato is capable of consciously playing with common language and idiom. It is this sort of serious pun which often makes it difficult to assess the full implications of certain phrases or colloquial expressions, or again of analogies adduced from other spheres of life, as for example the sciences. As a consequence, it is on occasion difficult to determine whether a term is part of a fixed philosophical terminology of Plato's, or used on the spur of the moment to illustrate a particular point.

4. ἐνεῖναι and ἐγγίγνεσθαι in Plato's *Gorgias*

In view of that, a few passages in the *Gorgias*, the *Charmides*, and the *Phaedo*, dialogues also otherwise of importance in an assessment of Plato's ontology, shall now be considered.[138] For readers of Plato familiar with the *Phaedo*, Plato's usage at *Gorgias* 497 ff. is reminiscent of the 'Theory of Forms or Ideas', and scholarly opinion is divided regarding the significance of that phenomenon. It is notably the use of παρουσία and παρεῖναι there that gives rise to differing interpretations.[139] In this environment, towards the end of the dialogue *Gorgias*, we find four occurrences of ἐγγίγνεσθαι in close proximity. Is their occurrence there connected with that of the other words suggestive of Plato's later ontological statements? Socrates and Callicles have just returned to the original question of what rhetoric is, and then if it aims at the good or at the pleasant; and Socrates had tried to persuade Callicles that the two are distinct. Callicles holds that there were rhetors in the past in possession of what Socrates requires: their aim was 'that the souls of the audience be as good as possible.' Socrates remains sceptical. Then, at 503e, he makes some remarks concerning the method of finding out if one of those named really had the soul of his audience in mind. He maintains that a good man, one who says what is best, does not speak at random, ἀλλ' ἀποβλέπων πρός τι, 'but looking at something', just as all the other craftsmen look each at his own work or task, not randomly, 'but so that what they produce have a certain form'.

In his usual fashion, Socrates then lists a number of other professions: the painters, the builders, the shipwrights, whomsoever you like, and he continues that one can see that each of them εἰς τάξιν τινα…τίθησιν ὃ ἂν τιθῇ, 'sets what he sets in a certain arrangement', and fits one thing together with the other, ἕως ἂν τὸ ἅπαν συστήσηται τεταγμένον τε καὶ κεκοσμένον πρᾶγμα, 'until each one thing stays together as one well-arranged and ordered object' (504a1). Likewise, the craftsmen concerned with the body, sports coaches and physicians, κοσμοῦσι τὸ σῶμα καὶ συντάττουσιν, 'order and arrange the body'. τάξις and κόσμος, declares Socrates, is their aim. He obtains Callicles' consent that this is true for the soul as well as the body. Then he asks for the name of that order and good arrangement in the body (504b7–c2):

τί οὖν ὄνομά ἐστιν ἐν τῷ σώματι τῷ ἐκ τῆς τάξεώς τε καὶ τοῦ κόσμου γιγνομένῳ;[140]

ὑγίειαν καὶ ἰσχὺν ἴσως λέγεις.
ἔγωγε. τί δὲ αὖ τῷ ἐν τῇ ψυχῇ ἐγγιγνομένῳ ἐκ τῆς τάξεως καὶ τοῦ κόσμου;

What, then, is the name in the case of the body for that which results from the arrangement and order?
Perhaps you mean health and strength.
Yes. And what <is the name> for that which comes into, or comes into being in the soul from arrangement and order?

When Callicles does not answer, and Socrates has to explain (504c7–e3):

ἐμοὶ γὰρ δοκεῖ ταῖς μὲν τοῦ σώματος τάξεσιν ὄνομα εἶναι ὑγιεινόν, ἐξ οὗ ἐν
αὐτῷ ἡ ὑγίεια γίγνεται καὶ ἡ ἄλλη ἀρετὴ τοῦ σώματος... ταῖς δέ γε τῆς ψυχῆς
τάξεσι καὶ κοσμήσεσιν νομιμόν τε καὶ νόμος, ὅθεν καὶ νόμιμοι γίγνονται καὶ
κόσμιοι· ταῦτα δ' ἔστιν δικαιοσύνη τε καὶ σωφροσύνη... οὐκοῦν πρὸς ταῦτα
βλέπων ὁ ῥήτωρ ἐκεῖνος, ὁ τεχνικός τε καὶ ἀγαθός...<ἐρεῖ>... πρὸς τοῦτο ἀεὶ
τὸν νοῦν ἔχων, ὅπως ἂν αὐτῷ τοῖς πολίταις
    δικαιοσύνη μὲν ἐν ταῖς ψυχαῖς γίγνηται,
    ἀδικία δὲ ἀπαλλάττηται,
    καὶ σωφροσύνη μὲν ἐγγίγνηται,
    ἀκολασία δὲ ἀπαλλάττηται,
    καὶ ἡ ἄλλη ἀρετὴ ἐγγίγνηται,
    κακία δὲ ἀπίῃ.

For it seems to me that 'healthy' is the name for those arrangements of the body from which health comes to be in it and the other goodness and excellence of the body... But 'lawful' and 'law' <are the names> for those arrangements and that order of the soul from which <people> become 'lawful' and 'orderly': but that is justice and moderation... Now, looking towards these things, the rhetor <we were speaking of>, the one who is skilled and good, will speak, always having in mind that for the citizens whom he is addressing
    justice may come to be in their souls,
    but injustice may depart,
    and moderation may come to be there
    but licentiousness may depart,
    and what else there is of goodness may come to be there
    but badness may go away.

It is impossible not to perceive the Gorgianic antithetical phrases at the end of Socrates' exposition.[141] But not only the last paragraph of that section is imitation of Gorgias; and it is not only the style that is Gorgianic. For, while it is correct to state that Plato has Socrates also elsewhere draw parallels between the health of the body and the health of the soul, and while one is justified to point to *Gorgias* 447e–9e where Socrates had already spoken of 'medicine and justice' as bad states of body and soul respectively, there are elements in the discussion of *Gorgias* 503e–7c which seem to go beyond anything Plato has previously suggested. 504d in particular has seemed so striking to commentators that is has been marked as a watershed in Plato's development.[142] But while it may be true that Socrates argues in an un-Socratic manner here, what is perceived as un-Socratic in the *Gorgias* often points to conscious discussion of Gorgianic tenets rather than unprecedented innovations on the part of Plato. It is, for example, not often that Plato adduces 'the painter' as primary example of a craftsmen who looks, not at the physical objects surrounding him, but at a certain order so that his work has a certain form.[143] Starting a list of δημιουργοί with painters, however, makes good sense as a reaction to Gorgias' own picture of the methods of γραφεῖς, 'painters', in his *Encomium to Helen*, where painters are characterized as follows (18):

ἀλλὰ μὴν οἱ γραφεῖς ὅταν ἐκ πολλῶν χρωμάτων καὶ σωμάτων ἓν σῶμα καὶ σχῆμα τελείως ἀπεργάσονται τέρπουσι τὴν ὄψιν.

But painters please the eye when in a finished manner they construct, from many colours and bodies, one body and shape.

This is in a speech which commences with the words (1):

κόσμος πόλει μὲν εὐανδρία, σώματι δὲ κάλλος, ψυχῇ δὲ σοφία, πράγματι δὲ ἀρετή, λόγῳ δὲ ἀλήθεια· τὰ δὲ ἐνάντια τούτων ἀκοσμία.

Order for a city is 'having good men', for a body it is 'beauty', for a soul 'wisdom', for an object 'goodness', for a speech 'truth': but the opposites of these are disorder.

Here κόσμος, 'order', is what makes something, anything, good and praiseworthy. The order of the body is found side by side with the order of the soul. And later on in the same speech, Gorgias declares (14):

τὸν αὐτὸν δὲ λόγον ἔχει ἥ τε τοῦ λόγου δύναμις πρὸς τὴν τῆς ψυχῆς τάξιν ἥ τε τῶν φαρμάκων τάξις πρὸς τὴν τῶν σωμάτων φύσιν.

The power of a speech has the same ratio to the arrangement (τάξις) of the soul as prescription (τάξις) of medicine has to the nature of the body.

Here we see that Gorgias not only drew a parallel between the order of the body and the order of the soul, he also compared the influence of speech on soul with the influence of medicine on body. Seen with that perspective, it appears natural for Plato – in a passage in which Socrates implicitly criticizes and attacks Gorgias in general and in matters of detail, using the very examples Gorgias had advanced – to elaborate on those examples, to take over the language of Gorgias, and to take Gorgias' comparisons further. Having adopted the Gorgianic – though not necessarily exclusively Gorgianic – notion of the κόσμος and τάξις of body and soul, Socrates proceeds to talk of health coming to be in a body, and subsequently moderation and justice coming to be in a soul, using the medical terminology of ἐγγίγνομαι. ἀπαλλάσσω as well is regularly used of the disappearing of diseases or symptoms in the *Hippocratic Corpus*.[144] The same language is used in the summary of the present passage at *Gorgias* 506d5–e4.

Consequently, what can be observed is that the medical usage of ἐγγίγνεσθαι with health and diseases as order and disorder coming to be in the body gave rise to the use of the word with moderation and justice and their opposites as order or disorder coming to be in the soul. Plato is in that way developing imagery and patterns of comparison used previously by Gorgias whose views he attempts to disprove, using the opponent's own language and methods. The language of medicine, by the way, is also the explanation of the repeated occurrence of 'something's' being in something else, e.g. health and strength being in man and women,' at the beginning of the *Meno* (72 f.); Meno, we recall, is presented as a pupil of Gorgias.

5. ἐνεῖναι and ἐγγίγνεσθαι in Plato's *Charmides*

In the *Charmides*, the situation is not altogether dissimilar from that in the *Gorgias*. Again it is a context of approximately three pages, this time near the beginning of the dialogue, where ἐγγίγνεσθαι, and subsequently ἐνεῖναι, are employed repeatedly.

Socrates, returning from a military campaign, is eager to get to know young men of philosophical disposition, and he asks his friends if there are any. In an attempt to enter unobtrusively into a conversation with the youth Charmides, he uses his uncle Critias' advice to pretend to be a medical man in possession of a cure for Charmides' headache. For a moment it looks as if Socrates would not get far at all with his plan, since Charmides knows who Socrates is. But Socrates can proceed despite that. He knows a magic spell, he says, but just as – as the doctors rightly say – one cannot cure a part of the body, for example the head, by itself, so one cannot cure the body without the soul. At 156c, the phrase used of 'the head by itself', αὐτὴν ἐφ' ἑαυτῆς, is used by Anaxagoras and can thus be associated with scientific terminology. After it has been stated that it would be wrong to treat the head αὐτὴν ἐφ' ἑαυτῆς, Socrates repeats that his teacher Zalmoxis emphasizes that it would be wrong to try and treat the body alone (157a3–b1):

θεραπεύεσθαι δὲ τὴν ψυχὴν ἔφη, ὦ μακάριε, ἐπῳδαῖς τισιν, τὰς δ' ἐπῳδὰς ταύτας τοὺς λόγους εἶναι τοὺς καλούς· ἐκ δὲ τῶν τοιούτων λόγων ἐν ταῖς ψυχαῖς σωφροσύνην ἐγγίγνεσθαι, ἧς ἐγγενομένης καὶ παρούσης ῥᾴδιον ἤδη εἶναι τὴν ὑγίειαν καὶ τῇ κεφαλῇ καὶ τῷ ἄλλῳ σώματι πορίζειν.

He said that <it is necessary> to treat the soul with spells, but that those spells are the speeches, namely the beautiful ones: from speeches of that sort, moderation would come into being in the soul: when it has got there and is close by, it is easier already to procure health both for the head and for the rest of the body.

Up to that point, there is nothing unusual with Plato's usage. Following the same pattern as in the *Gorgias*, Plato has Socrates use ἐγγίγνεσθαι, the common word for diseases' being in the body, for σωφροσύνη being in the soul. It is only two pages later, when the matter is taken up again, that we can see Plato making a distinct point while apparently simply repeating what he has stated already. At first, Socrates simply restates at 158b5–8:

εἰ μέν σοι ἤδη πάρεστιν, ὡς λέγει Κριτίας ὅδε, σωφροσύνη καὶ εἶ σώφρων ἱκανῶς, οὐδὲν ἔτι σοι ἔδει οὔτε τῶν Ζαλμόξιδος οὔτε τῶνἈβάριδος τοῦ Ὑπερβορέου ἐπῳδῶν...

If moderation is already with you, as Critias here says, and if you are moderate, you are no longer in need of spells, be it of Zalmoxis or of Abaris the Hyperborean.

This is again ordinary Greek usage. σωφροσύνη πάρεστί σοι and εἶ σώφρων can be two different ways of saying the same thing. The picture changes slightly a few lines later. Charmides is hesitant about praising himself, and Socrates proposes to conduct an investigation. He says at 158e6–9a10:

τῇδε τοίνυν, ἔφην ἐγώ, δοκεῖ μοι βελτίστη εἶναι ἡ σκέψις περὶ αὐτοῦ. δῆλον γὰρ ὅτι εἰ σοι πάρεστιν σωφροσύνη, ἔχεις τι περὶ αὐτῆς δοξάζειν. ἀνάγκη γάρ που ἐνοῦσαν αὐτήν, εἴπερ ἔνεστιν, αἴσθησίν τινα παρέχειν, ἐξ ἧς δόξα ἄν τίς σοι περὶ αὐτῆς εἴη ὅτι ἐστὶν καὶ ὁποῖόν τι ἡ σωφροσύνη· ἢ οὐκ οἴει; ... ἵνα τοίνυν τοπάσωμεν εἴτε σοι ἔνεστιν εἴτε μή, εἰπέ, ἦν δ' ἐγώ, τί φῂς εἶναι σωφροσύνην κατὰ τὴν σὴν δόξαν.

In this way, I said, an investigation into that seems to me to be best. For it is clear that if moderation is with you, you can give an opinion about it. For it is necessary that being in, if it is in, it affords some perception, from which there would be an opinion at your disposal, what and how (= of what sort) moderation is. ... Therefore, so that we can consider now if it is in you or not, tell me, I said, what you say moderation is according to your own opinion.

In the same way as in the passage from the *Ion* quoted above, Socrates moves from a natural expression to an unfounded conclusion, this time mediated by an additional step. Between 'moderation is with you' and 'therefore you must know what it is', Socrates inserts: 'so it must yield some perception'. 'Perception', it may be noted, leads to 'opinion', not to 'knowledge'. (That distinction, again, goes back at least to Gorgias, in this case to the *Palamedes*.) In each case, one could say, a compound verb-phrase representing a monadic, one-place or monovalent predicate is interpreted as a dyadic, two-place, or bivalent predicate, stating a relation between two *relata*. The soul, or the particular human being, on the one hand, and moderation on the other. The significance this has for subsequent discussion in the *Charmides* cannot be considered here.

Finally, whereas the being 'in' someone of δικαιοσύνη and σωφροσύνη in the *Gorgias* and *Charmides* is introduced by way of medical examples, where in both cases the process of reaching a state is described with ἐγγίγνεσθαι, there are places in both the *Protagoras* (352b) and the *Meno* (85c, 86a) at which ἐπιστήμαι or ἀληθεῖς δόξαι are said to be in people, without further ado. It is conceivable that those latter expressions were close enough in content to νοῦς or φρονεῖν ἔνεστιν to pass unheeded, while, by contrast, few people besides Socrates would accept without explanation an expression in which one of the traditional virtues has taken the place of knowledge or thought, and that therefore an introduction is needed in those cases. More importantly, it could be observed that, in the *Charmides* and more pointedly in the *Gorgias*, Plato uses the language of those whose views he discusses or attacks. That, however, is not to say that he makes that language part of his own terminology henceforth; nor even that he is committed to it at the time he employs it.

6. Recapitulation

Of all the composite verbs derived from εἶναι and γίγνεσθαι, ἐνεῖναι and ἐγγίγνεσθαι are the widest and most general in their application, due to the nature of the semantic vagueness of ἐν-, 'in'. The two verbs can connect things in a purely physical, spatial way, but can also refer to a mind's or a thought's being in a person, or to certain qualities' being in words. Because the relation expressed by the two verbs lacks specificity, they were found suitable in particular in physical theory and speculation such as that of Anaxagoras, as well as in medicine, where ἐγγίγνεσθαι and ἐνεῖναι (with the dative of the person affected) became the standard terms for 'contracting' and 'having' a disease respectively. In this latter context, the verbs are encountered on more than one occasion in early Platonic usage.

PART II

Form. Plato's words for his Forms or Ideas (*eidos, idea*, roughly synonymous) meant both visible form and nature, kind or species.[145]

In its succinctness, this statement sums up well the *communis opinio* of the past two centuries, not to say millennia. There are few dissenting voices concerning synonymity, and there are fewer still concerning the semantics of the two words. As regards synonymity or otherwise of εἶδος and ἰδέα in the *Euthyphro* and at *Phaedo* 95e–107b, and in the *Republic*, discussion must be postponed to Part III. But as regards the semantic development of the two words from their respective earliest occurrences down to the time of Plato, the only way to determine meaning, or meanings, and subsequently to judge the issue of synonymity, is to trace the histories of the two words εἶδος and ἰδέα separately. The next two chapters will be devoted to that task, with only a minor amount of cross-referencing and thus, as is inevitable, with some repetition. More so than with the verbs discussed previously, it will on occasion be necessary to discuss the context of an individual instance at some length. As stated above, the purpose of this is twofold. The aim is both to establish what εἶδος and ἰδέα *could* mean and also what εἶδος and ἰδέα did not mean and, to the best of our knowledge, could not have meant.

CHAPTER 4

εἶδος

1. εἶδος in Homer

The earliest occurrence of the noun εἶδος in extant Greek literature is at *Iliad* 2.58.[146] Zeus has sent a pernicious Dream to Agamemnon. About this Dream it is said (20–2):

στῆ δ᾽ ἄρ᾽ ὑπὲρ κεφαλῆς Νηληΐῳ υἷι ἐοικώς,
Νέστορι, τόν ῥα μάλιστα γερόντων τῖ᾽ Ἀγαμέμνων·
τῷ μιν ἐεισάμενος προσεφώνεε θεῖος Ὄνειρος…

He stood above <Agamemnon's> head, being like the son of Neleus,
Nestor, whom Agamemnon esteemed most highly of all elder men;
looking like him, godly Dream addressed him…

The speech follows. This is reported to the council of kings by Agamemnon the following morning (56–8):

κλῦτε, φίλοι· θεῖός μοι ἐνύπνιον ἦλθεν Ὄνειρος
ἀμβροσίην διὰ νύκτα· μάλιστα δὲ Νέστορι δίῳ
εἶδός τε μέγεθός τε φυήν τ᾽ ἄγχιστα ἐῴκει…

Listen, friends: godly Dream came to me as a sleep-vision
during the ambrosial night: being most like divine Nestor
in guise and size and growth.

And Agamemnon goes on to report what this Dream, standing by his head, told him. This Dream was like Nestor in εἶδος, μέγεθος, φυή. The verbs used to express this likeness are ἔοικα and εἴδομαι, 'to *be* like'. Both verbs have strong visual connotations. ἔοικα seems to be a more general word for '*being* like'; but 'that which *is* like', the εἰκών, is in the first place something visual, an 'image' or 'picture', i.e. what '*appears* like' something (else). And though the verb εἴδομαί τινι, and in particular perhaps the aorist participle εἰσάμενος, could be '*being* like' or '*appearing* like' in other respects as well – e.g. in respect of voice, designated by φθογγή at *Iliad* 2.791 and 13.216, and by φωνή at 20.81 – it is originally the visual aspect which is the point of comparison. Examples are *Odyssey* 1.105, where the verb occurs after the description of the visible attributes of Athena's disguise, and

95

Chapter 1

Odyssey 2.267 f.:

> ...σχεδόθεν δέ οἱ ἦλθεν Ἀθήνη,
> Μέντορι εἰδομένη ἠμὲν δέμας ἠδὲ καὶ αὐδήν,

> ...to him came Athena,
> appearing like Mentor in build and also in voice.

With *Odyssey* 2.267 f. may also be compared *Iliad* 13.45, where it is said of Poseidon: εἰσάμενος Κάλχαντι δέμας καὶ ἀτειρέα φωνήν, 'appearing like Calchas in build and unwearied voice'. In both instances, the phrase 'and in voice' is added because in each case the god in question is about to *say* something presently; even where that is the case, though, εἰσάμενος suggests the likeness in 'appearance', in 'guise', in 'looks', in the first place.

εἶδος is derived from the same root ⁎u̯/ớid-, 'see', as εἴδομαι, 'appear, seem, give oneself the appearance, appear like', and as ἰδεῖν, εἶδον, 'see'; the latter two are used in suppletion as aorist forms to ὁράω, 'see'. εἶδος is 'that which looks at' and 'that which is seen'. With Homer, however, it is always the εἶδος *of* someone 'which looks at' or 'which is seen' by someone else; 'that which looks at' in the sense of 'that which is facing' the spectator.

At *Iliad* 2.58 quoted above, the εἶδος of Nestor is set side by side with, and thereby distinguished from, his μέγεθος and his φυή.[147] Those two aspects of Nestor were, of course, visible and seen as well. εἶδος may therefore be more specific than just 'that which is seen by someone else'. μέγεθος is 'bigness, size' straightforwardly. φυή is something like 'growth' in that old sense of the word which encompasses 'stature'. At *Iliad* 20.370, it is again found side by side with εἶδος. After Achilles has slain Hector, the other Greeks rush forward:

> οἳ καὶ θηήσαντο φυὴν καὶ εἶδος ἀγητὸν | Ἕκτορος.

And they looked at the admirable stature and appearance of Hector.

At *Iliad* 1.115, Agamemnon is furious about Calchas' proposal to hand Chryseïs back to her father, her, whom he wants to take home since she is in no respect inferior to his wife Clytaemnestra, οὐ δέμας οὐδὲ φυήν, οὔτ' ἂρ φρένας οὔτε τι ἔργα, 'not in build nor in growth, nor yet in wits nor in any of her works'. δέμας, the noun to δέμω, 'build', is 'build'. It is, for the present task, not necessary to determine with precision what exactly φυή, 'growth' or 'stature', means when it is contrasted with 'size', 'guise' and 'build'. δέμας, in turn, which we have seen in opposition to φυή, is on occasion juxtaposed with εἶδος as well. In *Iliad* 24, Priam has set off from Troy to ransom the body of Hector at night when other men are asleep; he meets Hermes, who has been sent by Zeus; Hermes, disguised as a young Achaean warrior, declares that he will give Priam safe conduct (24.371): φίλῳ δέ σε πατρὶ ἐίσκω, 'for

I liken you to my father'. To him replies godlike Priam, Πρίαμος θεοειδής, that a benevolent god must have sent such a guard and leader (376 f.):

οἷος δὴ σὺ δέμας καὶ εἶδος ἀγητός, | πέπνυσαί τε νόῳ...

You, how admirable in build and guise, you are endowed with mind...

It may be noted that, here already, one can observe an opposition that will become significant later, that between attributes of the body, the visible, the external, like δέμας and εἶδος, with the mind or thought or intelligence of what we would call a person.[148]

From the *Odyssey*, one may adduce Calypso's words when in a last attempt she tries to persuade Odysseus to stay with her. She knows that he is 'longing to see his wife', ἱμειρόμενός περ ἰδέσθαι | σὴν ἄλοχον (*Odyssey* 5.209–10). But she, Calypso, is in no respect inferior to her (212–13):

οὐ δέμας οὐδὲ φυήν, ἐπεὶ οὔ πως οὐδὲ ἔοικε
θνητὰς ἀθανάτῃσι δέμας καὶ εἶδος ἐρίζειν.

Neither in build nor in growth, since it is not fitting in any way
that mortal women strive with immortals as regards build and guise.

To that, Odysseus replies (215–17):

οἶδα καὶ αὐτὸς
πάντα μάλ', οὕνεκα σεῖο περίφρων Πηνελόπεια
εἶδος ἀκιδνοτέρη μέγεθός τ' εἰσάντα ἰδέσθαι.

I know full well myself
that against you, thoughtful Penelope
is weaker to look at in guise and in size.

In this passage of a dozen lines, ἰδέσθαι and εἶδος are the two terms repeated in the comparison of the two women. There cannot be any doubt that in line 217, εἶδος ἀκιδνοτέρη μέγεθός τ' εἰσάντα ἰδέσθαι, the poet relies on the reader's realizing the etymological connection of the first and last words of that verse.[149]

The potential differences between external appearance and other characteristics of a person, underlying the debate with Calypso, are dealt with more explicitly later on in the *Odyssey*.[150] When, on the island of Scheria, Odysseus is taunted by Euryalus (8.164): οὐδ' ἀθλητῆρι ἔοικας, *you are not like a fighter*, Odysseus retorts (167–77):

οὕτως οὐ πάντεσσι θεοὶ χαρίεντα διδοῦσιν
ἀνδράσιν, οὔτε φυὴν οὔτ' ἄρ' φρένας οὔτ' ἀγορητύν.
ἄλλος μὲν γὰρ εἶδος ἀκιδνότερος πέλει ἀνήρ,
ἀλλὰ θεὸς μορφὴν ἔπεσι στέφει, οἱ δέ τ' ἐς αὐτὸν
τερπόμενοι λεύσσουσιν· ὁ δ' ἀσφαλέως ἀγορεύει

αἰδοῖ μειλιχίῃ, μετὰ δὲ πρέπει ἀγρομένοισιν,
ἐρχόμενον δ᾽ ἀνὰ ἄστυ θεὸν ὣς εἰσορόωσιν.
ἄλλος δ᾽ αὖ εἶδος μὲν ἀλίγκιος ἀθανάτοισιν,
ἀλλ᾽ οὔ οἱ χάρις ἀμφιπεριστέφεται ἐπέεσσιν,
ὣς καὶ σοὶ εἶδος μὲν ἀριπρεπές, οὐδέ κεν ἄλλως
οὐδὲ θεὸς τεύξειε, νόον δ᾽ ἀποφώλιός ἐσσι.

Not in one way do the gods give pleasing things to all
men, neither as regards growth nor yet mind nor eloquence.
One man, indeed, is rather weak of appearance,
but god wreathes shape around his words, and the other men look at him,
delighted; but he speaks unfailingly
with soothing reverence; he finds favour with those who are gathered,
just as if they looked at a god walking through the city.
Again, another man resembles the gods as regards his guise,
but for him, no grace is wreathed around his words,
just as you are very stately as regards your 'look',
a god could not fit it otherwise; as to mind, however, you are useless.

Odysseus names three characteristics of a man, φυή, 'growth', φρένες, 'wits', ἀγορητύς, 'speaking-in-public'. The first one of these, 'growth', seems to contribute to how one looks, one's 'look' or 'appearance' or 'guise', εἶδος. It is difficult to say whether the positive qualities of the eloquent man are to be attributed exclusively to his ἀγορητύς, his 'ability to speak well', or if that is somehow subordinated to his φρένες, his 'wits', which in that way contribute to his speaking 'with soothing reverence'. Regardless of how that matter is decided, however, these two inner qualities or characteristics are strictly separated from the external appearance; and if, with regard to both the *Iliad* and the *Odyssey*, commentators have felt inclined to postulate a relation in Homer's mind between the good look of a hero and other positive and valuable attributes, this passage clearly shows that while beautiful appearance is something positive in itself, the poet was capable of separating and isolating that characteristic of looks or appearance as something external, and he probably expected his audience to do so, too.

As we have seen already, it is not only the poet of the *Odyssey* who so distinguishes between the external and the inner characteristics of a person. One may also compare that passage from the *Iliad* on which *Odyssey* 8.164, and the related passage in *Odyssey* 11, are clearly modelled: in Book 3 of the *Iliad*, Helen is on the tower of the Scaean gate, overlooking the battlefield, together with the old men of Troy. Priam asks her to identify various Greek leaders. First he sees Agamemnon and inquires who he is. Next, he asks for Odysseus, whom he describes as shorter but broader than Agamemnon. Helen replies that this is Odysseus, εἰδὼς παντοίους τε δόλους καὶ μήδεα πυκνά, 'who knows various crafts and dense cunning' (202). This is confirmed by Antenor who once was host to Odysseus and Menelaus when the two came on an embassy to negotiate terms for a return of Helen without armed conflict. Antenor declares (208): ἀμφοτέρων δὲ φυὴν ἐδάην καὶ μήδεα πυκνά. 'Of both, I then learned their growth and dense cunning.' Standing up, Menelaus made the stronger impression, sitting down it was Odysseus, and Antenor continues (212–24):

ἀλλ᾽ ὅτε δὴ μύθους καὶ μήδεα πᾶσιν ὕφαινον,
ἤτοι μὲν Μενέλαος ἐπιτροχάδην ἀγόρευε,
παῦρα μέν, ἀλλὰ μάλα λιγέως, ἐπεὶ οὐ πολύμυθος
οὐδ᾽ ἀφαμαρτοεπής· ἦ καὶ γένει ὕστερος ἦεν.
ἀλλ᾽ ὅτε δὴ πολύμητις ἀναΐξειεν Ὀδυσσεύς·
στάσκεν, ὑπαὶ δὲ ἴδεσκε κατὰ χθονὸς ὄμματα πήξας,
…
φαίης κε ζάκοτόν τέ τιν᾽ ἔμμεναι ἄφρονά τ᾽ αὔτως.
ἀλλ᾽ ὅτε δὴ ὄπα τε μεγάλην ἐκ στήθεος εἵη
καὶ ἔπεα νιφάδεσσιν ἐοικότα χειμερίῃσιν,
οὐκ ἂν ἔπειτ᾽ Ὀδυσῆΐ γ᾽ ἐρίσσειε βροτὸς ἄλλος·
οὐ τότε γ᾽ ὧδ᾽ Ὀδυσῆος ἀγασσάμεθ᾽ εἶδος ἰδόντες.[151]

But when they wove their words and cunning for all of us,
verily, Menelaus spoke fluently;
little, but very clearly; a man neither wordy
nor missing the point; and that while he was later by birth.
But when Odysseus, of much cunning, got up:
he stood there; he looked down, fixing his eyes to the ground,
…
You would have said that he was full of ill-will, and witless, too;
but when he sent forth his big voice from his chest,
and words like snow-bearing winter-storms,
then no other man would have rivalled Odysseus:
and we did not admire him in that way when we first saw his guise.

There cannot be any doubt that both Menelaus and Odysseus are of kingly appearance. Odysseus is broader than Agamemnon, and Menelaus broader still. Yet, Odysseus is more awe-inspiring when sitting. The description of the two is positive throughout. It is against this background that the closing remark of Antenor is to be seen. The Trojans were amazed when they saw the two kings. But their amazement when they heard Odysseus speak was not in any way related to, or rivalled by, that previous amazement which had resulted merely from the impression created by his 'look', his εἶδος, which for the poet of the *Iliad* was just as much something purely external that did not tell the spectator anything about what is inside a person, as it was for the poet of the *Odyssey*. One could explicate line 224 as: 'and <though we had admired him already when he had been sitting there in silence>, when

99

we first saw his guise we did not admire him <to the extent we subsequently did when he made his speech>.' It should also be noted that the εἶδος, the 'look', or 'guise', of a person, is not the same as his habits or gestures either; Agamemnon could recognize the figure of the god-sent Dream as that of Nestor in the first place because it was alike in look, not because of the way Dream walked or talked.

εἶδος is thus derived from a root meaning 'see'. It was felt by Homer to be thus connected. It is always the 'εἶδος of a person' which is talked of. Of the visible characteristics of human beings, εἶδος is contrasted with μέγεθος, 'size', φυή, 'growth' or 'stature', and δέμας, 'build'; as a physical, external attribute, it is also contrasted with non-physical attributes like φρένες, 'wits', and νοῦς, 'mind'. It can safely be rendered 'guise', 'look', 'looks', 'appearance', but, contrary to common belief, there is no evidence to suggest that εἶδος should at any given place be reduced to 'the appearance or complexion of the face'. Nor again is there any indication that εἶδος has come to mean 'body' with Homer.

2. -ειδης in Homer

These general words of summary and explanation must be modified in two ways. First, there is one, and in Homeric epic only one,[152] case in which εἶδος is applied not to a human being but to an animal. In *Odyssey* 17, Odysseus returns to his palace after having been absent for twenty years. He is disguised as a beggar. When he arrives in the company of the swineherd Eumaeus, Argus, his dog, whom he had left when he went to Troy, recognizes him, but is too weak to leave his position on the dung-hill where the negligence of the house-maids has banished him. Odysseus hides a tear and asks the swineherd (17.306–8):

Εὔμαι᾽, ἦ μάλα θαῦμα κύων ὅδε κεῖτ᾽ ἐνὶ κόπρῳ.
καλὸς μὲν δέμας ἐστιν, ἀτὰρ τόδε γ᾽ οὐ σάφα οἶδα,
ἢ δὴ καὶ ταχὺς ἔσκε θέειν ἐπὶ εἴδεϊ τῷδε |...;

Eumaeus, what a wondrous thing that this dog lies in the dung.
Surely, he is beautiful in build, though this I do not know for sure:
if he has speed to run, on top of this appearance |...?[153]

Considering that the term εἶδος has its own, special application in the context of description of animals in later Greek literature, this passage has attracted particular attention. The whole characterization of the dog Argus, however, portrays him as, if anything, more human than the other human beings.[154] If the passage thus cannot be used with a view to the semantics of εἶδος in the context of description of animals, it nevertheless serves as confirmation that the poet of the *Odyssey* in particular draws a sharp line between outward appearance and other qualities. As at *Odyssey* 8.167 ff., quoted above, it is φυή, 'growth', which contributes to the εἶδος of a person, here it is καλὸν δέμας, 'beautiful build', to which in the first place τόδε εἶδος refers. Perhaps it is necessary to stress that though, undoubtedly, the whole description of the dog is meant to be positive, it is not the word εἶδος on its own which – as it were as a term which is somehow endowed with positive connotations by itself – picks up the expression καλὸς μὲν δέμας ἐστίν, but rather the phrase εἶδος τόδε, 'this particular εἶδος', which refers to something positive just because the point of reference of the demonstrative phrase is something positive.[155]

But while this occurrence of εἶδος can probably not be counted as a proper exception to the general observation that εἶδος in Homer is always 'the εἶδος of a person', there is another, quite different context that may compel one to postulate a semantic extension of the noun beyond 'the guise', 'the look (of somebody)': there is a group of adjectives in -ειδης, which element is derived from the noun εἶδος. In *Iliad* and *Odyssey* it is represented by εὐειδής, ἠεροειδής, θεοειδής, ἰοειδής, and μυλοειδής. If what has been said about εἶδος above is correct without qualification, one would expect these words to mean 'of beautiful or handsome guise', 'of good look' or 'of good looks', 'of the guise, or look, of ἀήρ', 'of the guise, or look, of a god', 'of the guise, or look, of violets' and 'of the guise, or look, of a mill-stone', respectively. To determine if this is so, the adjectives will now be discussed in turn.

The one instance of εὐειδής in the Homeric epics seems to conform with expectations. At *Iliad* 3.48, Hector says to Paris: γυναῖκ' εὐειδέ' ἀνῆγες, 'you abducted a good-looking woman.' He had begun his speech with the famous words (39): Δύσπαρι, εἶδος ἄριστε, 'wretched Paris, best of look,' and had added that the Greeks now laugh at him, whilst previously (44–5),

φάντες ἀριστῆα πρόμον ἔμμεναι, οὕνεκα καλὸν
εἶδος ἔπ', ἀλλ' οὐκ ἔστι βίη φρεσὶ οὐδέ τις ἀλκή,

thinking of you as a champion of the foremost rank, because 'to you, there is'[156] a beautiful guise, but there is no force to your wits, nor any strength.

And a little later, he pictures a fight of Paris with Menelaus (54–5):

οὐκ ἄν τοι χραίσμῃ κίθαρις τά τε δῶρ' Ἀφροδίτης,
ἥ τε κόμη τό τε εἶδος, ὅτ' ἐν κονίῃσι μιγείης.

Then the cithara and the gifts of Aphrodite, your hair and guise, would hardly be of any use to you, when you were mixed with the dust.

This reference to Paris' good looks is taken up two lines later in the formulaic line of reply (58):

τὸν δ' αὖτε προσέειπεν Ἀλέξανδρος θεοειδής.

To him, again, replied Alexander of the guise of a god.

Since physical beauty is one of the topics of this passage, and, in particular, physical beauty in contrast with other characteristics which are not positive in the same way, it seems appropriate to take εὐειδής and θεοειδής as referring just to 'look', or 'guise', here. The other occurrences of θεοειδής in *Iliad* and *Odyssey* may all likewise refer to 'the guise or look of a god' only, as opposed to any other of the god's characteristics; one may think of the adjectives ἀντίθεος or θεοείκελος as comprising those other characteristics as well; but that need not be determined here.

The adjective ἰοειδής, for which LSJ suggest 'like the flower ἴον; purple' is used as an epithet to πόντος at *Iliad* 11.298 and *Odyssey* 5.56 and 11.107. ἠεροειδής, 'misty, cloudy, dark', occurs much more frequently; sometimes likewise with πόντος, as for example at *Iliad* 23.744 and *Odyssey* 12.285;[157] but it is also epithet to the cave and rock of Scylla at *Odyssey* 12.80 and 233, and to a lovely grotto, sacred to the nymphs, on Ithaca at *Odyssey* 13.103. These two adjectives will be discussed in due course.

The only instance of μυλοειδής, derived from μύλη, *millstone*, is at *Iliad* 7.270. The scene is the duel between Hector and Ajax. Both send forth their spears and run atilt at each other. Hector, though wounded, then lifts a stone (7.264–70):

ἀλλ' ἀναχασσάμενος λίθον εἵλετο χειρὶ παχείῃ
κείμενον ἐν πεδίῳ μέλανα τρηχύν τε μέγαν τε·
τῷ βάλεν Αἴαντος δεινὸν σάκος ἑπταβόειον
μέσσον ἐπομφάλιον, περιήχησεν δ' ἄρα χαλκός.
δεύτερος αὖτ' Αἴας πολὺ μείζονα λᾶαν ἀείρας
ἧκ' ἐπιδινήσας, ἐπέρεισε δὲ ἶν' ἀπέλεθρον,
εἴσω δ' ἀσπίδ' ἔαξε βαλὼν μυλοειδέι πέτρῳ | ...

But, driven back, he lifted, with his broad hand, a stone
which lay on the ground, black and rough and big.
With it, he hit the mighty seven-hided shield of Ajax
right on the boss, and loud echoed the bronze-frame.
Second came Ajax, lifting a much bigger rock
and whirling it about, and he applied vast strength to it:
in he broke the shield, hitting it with a boulder 'of the guise of a mill-stone'...

There is a fundamental difference on the one hand between εὐειδής and all the other compounds in -ειδης, and on the other hand between the pair εὐειδής and θεοειδής and the remaining three, ἠερο-, ἰο-, and μυλοειδής. The first element of the compound adjective εὐειδής is derived from an adverb, not, as with all the other adjectives in -ειδης, from a noun. As a corollary, εὐειδής in itself does not provide any information pertaining to the semantics, or more specifically to a potential semantic development, of εἶδος; whatever εἶδος may be, anyone or anything εὐειδής or εὐειδές has a good εἶδος.[158] At its one and only occurrence, εὐειδής is applied to a person, who is thus characterized as 'of good εἶδος'. Likewise, θεοειδής is always used with reference to an individual human being. Now, if anybody looks like somebody else, there is in principle no restriction to the degree of resemblance in look. It is conceivable that two distinct human beings look perfectly alike. It is also certainly implied in the tale of the Dream appearing to Agamemnon that the Dream looked quite like Nestor. That is not to say that Homer or his audience had a notion of 'degree of resemblance' at all. If, on the other hand, θεοειδής is 'of the guise of a god', it is not necessary to know what a god looks like, and while perfect resemblance should be possible in theory, all that the epithet specifies is that the person to whom it is applied has, somehow, the εἶδος of a god. At any rate, as was the case with εὐειδής, usage of θεοειδής does not provide new information concerning the meaning of the noun εἶδος.

'Perfect resemblance' is clearly not intended in the case of ἰοειδής. If the sea is 'of the look of a violet', that must refer to colour or shading or brightness, somehow; for however different from ours the Greek concept of colour may have been, the sea does and did not have the shape or size of a violet, and does not otherwise look like the flower in those respects.[159] That is, of course, understood whenever the word is used. It does not require explanation. The adjective ἰοειδής thus clearly points to a possible extension in meaning, in the first place of the suffix -ειδής.

μυλοειδής is a less transparent case. Any stone of approximately adequate composition may perfectly resemble a mill-stone in look. But is that what is intended? Colour is probably irrelevant; mill-stones would have come in different shades. Shape is a more likely criterion; but while a boulder washed down over centuries may be perfectly circular, one wonders if the stone Ajax lifted and threw had a hole equivalent to the one of the nether stone into which the mill-rind would have been fitted. Perfect resemblance in look or guise is thus certainly not excluded, but it is much more likely that the stone only partly resembled a mill-stone, namely first and foremost in size; further, given that the stone Hector had lifted is described as λίθον μέλανα τρηχύν τε μέγαν τε, 'a stone, black and rough and big', there may have been a resemblance in surface structure. And while it is possible that the poet also thought of resemblance in shape and in the non-visible quality of weight, that cannot be determined with certainty. But these speculations concerning the precise reference of μυλοειδής should not without necessity influence translation. μυλοειδής is 'of the guise' or 'of the look of a mill-stone'. 'Of the size of a mill-stone', 'large as a mill-stone', or 'of the shape of a mill-stone', are not translations of the word μυλοειδής, but interpretations of the whole context. In a poetic translation of a text any one of these alternative translations may be acceptable; a dictionary, or a philological commentary, should be more precise.[160] The translation 'like a mill-stone', on the other hand, implies that a semantic shift, beyond the specific reference to the εἶδος of a person or thing, has already taken place in Homer, which is more than can be proved with certainty.[161] In the same way, something is imported into the text if εὐειδής is rendered 'well-shaped or comely' rather than straightforwardly 'good-looking',[162] and also when θεοειδής is rendered 'godlike' rather than just 'looking like a god'; one would at least have to argue the case for the more general 'godlike' anywhere in Homer.[163]

Thus, in order to render μυλοειδής with 'like a mill-stone' one has to postulate that -ειδης as a means of deriving adjectives from nouns has, in Homer already, lost its original force, the reference to the 'guise' or 'look' of the thing. That could have happened under the influence of the verb derived from εἶδος, εἴδομαι, which, as we have seen, could refer to 'resemblance in voice' as well as 'look'. But in order to postulate this semantic development for Homer, one would want positive, compelling evidence of some sort. That, however, is not provided by the instances of words in -ειδης adduced and discussed above.

It is possible to construct an argument for ἠεροειδής parallel to that of μυλοειδής above. ἀήρ is 'haze' or 'mist'.[164] In order to see in what way or ways objects are called 'of the look of haze' or 'of the look of mist', it is necessary to see what it is in the look of *haze* that is paralleled in the look or appearance of the object which is labelled ἠεροειδής. This requires a comparison of the occurrences of ἠεροειδής in their respective contexts, especially given the notorious uncertainty concerning the precise reference of the noun ἀήρ. At *Odyssey* 12.260, Odysseus and most of his comrades have just escaped Scylla and Charybdis. Although they are all tired, Odysseus intends to avoid the island of Helius with his cattle, and wants to sail all through the night. Eurylochus scolds him and says that he should let his tired comrades rest; and he continues (284–90):

ἀλλ' αὕτως διὰ νύκτα θοὴν ἀλάλησθαι ἄνωγας
νήσου ἀποπλαγχθέντας ἐν ἠεροειδέι πόντῳ.
ἐκ νυκτῶν δ' ἄνεμοι χαλεποί, δηλήματα νηῶν,
γίγνονται· πῇ κέν τις ὑπεκφύγοι αἰπὺν ὄλεθρον,
ἤν πως ἐξαπίνης ἔλθῃ ἀνέμοιο θύελλα,
ἢ Νότου ἢ Ζεφύροιο δυσαέος, οἵτε μάλιστα
νῆα διαρραίουσι θεῶν ἀέκητι ἀνάκτων....

But you order us all the same to steer away from the island
and err through the fast-setting night, on the sea looking like haze.
But from the nights, harsh winds come into being, the banes of ships:
how could anyone escape utter destruction,

if in some way suddenly there came a burst of wind,
either of Notus or stormy Zephyrus, which – above all –
rip apart ships against the will of the gods, the lords.

ἠεροειδής is here epithet to the sea; the situation envisaged, though, is that of an imagined *storm* at sea: is there a relation between the storm at sea and the sea's quality of 'looking like haze'?[165] In that case, it may also be relevant to decide whether, as an attribute, ἠεροειδής denotes a permanent or a transitory characteristic. ἠεροειδής is an epithet to πόντος on most of its occurrences. πόντος, the 'sea', has other epithets as well; we find, for example, ἐνὶ οἴνοπι πόντῳ, 'in/on the sea looking like wine', at *Iliad* 23.316; (ἔνθορε) μείλανι πόντῳ, '(she threw herself into) the black sea', at *Iliad* 24.79. These are two cases of colour-terms[166] serving as epithets to πόντος. The noun does, of course, also occur on its own; as, for example, at *Iliad* 8.478 f.: τὰ νείατα πείρατα...γαίης καὶ πόντοιο, 'the lowest bounds of land and sea'. But while there cannot be any doubt that πόντος meant 'sea' for Homer as for the Greeks of later days, it is relevant that having lost the Indo-European word cognate to Latin *mare*, 'sea', the Greeks employed a great number of different terms of different provenance to refer to the sea; and the etymological origins of these terms may be relevant as well, in particular in cases in which a word denoting 'sea', or a cognate form, was otherwise still in active use. An obvious case in point is κέλευθος and the neuter plural/collective-generic κέλευθα, 'track'. Since the word is also otherwise in use in the general sense of 'track', it is necessary to distinguish its application to the sea by the addition of epithets. ὑγρὰ κέλευθα, 'the wet tracks', and ἰχθυόεντα κέλευθα, 'the fishy tracks', denote the sea, while λιγέων ἀνέμων λαιψηρὰ κέλευθα, 'the swift tracks of loud winds', are situated in a different region. Likewise with πόντος. πόντος, derived from a root *pṇth-, is an old word for a 'path'.[167] The phrase πόντος ἁλὸς πολιῆς, 'of the path of the grey sea', at *Iliad* 21.59, serves as an indication that πόντος meant a 'path' even at a time when ἅλς had already come to mean 'sea'; for, on the one hand, even in poetry it would not make sense to say 'of the sea of the grey sea', on the other, ἅλς does show a qualification not only in having the attribute 'grey' but also in being feminine here, while ἅλς meaning 'salt' is, where that can be determined, always masculine; that is how the Homeric dialect can connect the two words allegedly both denoting 'sea' in the one phrase 'the path of the grey salt-water'.[168] πόντος, like κέλευθα, needs some qualification by an adjective if it is meant to refer to the sea. Only after having been in use in that way for a long time, and of course in particular if the word is no longer used with a different application, can that sort of qualification be dropped, as at *Iliad* 8.479.[169] Accordingly, we find ἀπείριτος πόντος, 'the path without boundary', at *Odyssey* 10.195; or μεγακήτης πόντος, 'the mighty-monstered path', at *Odyssey* 3.158; and also phrases like 'the black path', 'the wine-looking path', 'the path of the look of violets', πόντος ἰοειδής, or 'the path of the look of haze', πόντος ἠεροειδής. When one walks on land, the path is solid and non-transparent. When one travels at sea, the path is not solid and nearly transparent, depending on the grade of perturbation; in the same way mist or haze are not solid and nearly transparent. But is it the look of haze which distinguishes the sea as a path from other paths? Or is it the quality of being penetrable like mist or haze? If it is the former, ἠεροειδής could be classed alongside other colour-terms, like ἰοειδής; if the latter, alongside other qualitative adjectives like ἀπείριτος, 'without boundary', or μεγακήτης, 'mighty-monstered'. Is the epithet ἠεροειδής given to a cave or a grotto because of the look of their openings which, especially at the seaside, is likely to be 'misty'?[170]

It may not be possible to decide if, in any given case, the intention of the application of μυλοειδής or ἠεροειδής, 'of the guise of a mill-stone' and 'of the look of haze', is to denote that the objects to which the words refer have the visual appearance of a mill-stone or haze, respectively, or rather have some other quality or function of the objects denoted by the nouns the adjectives are derived from, or both. More important, perhaps, than to decide this question, is to note that unlike εὐειδής and θεοειδής, the other three Homeric adjectives in -ειδης, viz. ἰοειδής, ἠεροειδής and μυλοειδής, serve as attributes to nouns denoting objects, not people. Once -ειδης is employed in the derivation of adjectives from nouns denoting objects in that sense, and used in contexts in which these adjectives are then applied to objects, too, it is no longer perfect resemblance in look, but partial resemblance of some sort, which is referred to. When adjectives in -ειδης are applied where there is partial resemblance between the look of one thing and the look of another thing, but also partial resemblance in some other quality or function, as for example the lack of solidity or the purpose of crushing and grinding, it is only a short step from using those adjectives in -ειδης exclusively as signifying 'of the look of' and 'looking like', to employing them also in the more general sense of 'being like'. In a way, this extension, at least prefigured in Homer, is parallel to that of the verb εἴδομαι: 'appearing like' first must have referred to visual appearance only, but then could encompass other aspects of the appearance of a person, too. With Homer, there always seems to be a visual element in the 'likeness' referred to by the verb or one of the adjectives. These words, however, show in which way the reference of the noun εἶδος will change from 'look and visual appearance' to 'appearance' in a more general sense. This semantic development of the noun εἶδος, however, does not set in immediately.

3. εἶδος in Hesiod

While for the most part in concord with Homeric usage as concerns the noun εἶδος, the works of Hesiod show the first stages of a different semantic development of the noun. Of the four instances of the word in Hesiod's *Theogony*, the first can be directly compared with the description of Odysseus' dog Argus at *Odyssey* 17.306–8: after an enumeration of the attributes of the hundred-handed Giants, it is said (153):

ἰσχὺς δ' ἄπλητος κρατερὴ μεγάλῳ ἐπὶ εἴδει.

Immense mighty strength on top of big appearance.

That topic is resumed in the description of the Titanomachy, when the three Hundred-Handers are mentioned again at 617 ff. Their father had imprisoned them (619–20):

ἠνορέην ὑπέροπλον ἀγώμενος ἠδὲ καὶ εἶδος | καὶ μέγεθος,

in awe of their overweening manliness, as well as their guise and size.[171]

Not unprecedented either is the use of εἶδος in a passage of the *Works and Days*: at 714, Hesiod concludes a paragraph of admonition to his brother with the words:

...σὲ δὲ μή τι νόον κατελεγχέτω εἶδος.

...let *your* disposition not disgrace your appearance.[172]

This opposition of external and internal characteristics, εἶδος and νόος, is parallel to that of *Odyssey* 8.164 ff., or *Iliad* 3.212 ff., discussed above.

At *Theogony* 259, in the middle of the catalogue of sea-nymphs, one of them[173] is introduced thus:

Εὐάρνη τε φυήν τ' ἐρατὴ καὶ εἶδος ἄμωμος.

Euarne, of lovely growth as well as blameless guise.

While there is nothing new in this usage, it should be noted again that εἶδος can refer to the look of a woman just as well as to the look of a man; naturally, due to their subject matter, that is frequently the case in the Hesiodic fragments known as Ἠοῖαι. One principal context in that work is that of comparison of mortal and immortal females, of which Calypso's comparison of herself and Penelope at *Odyssey* 5.212 ff., quoted above, is both example and model. A standard phrase is: ...ἣ εἶδος ἐρήριστ' ἀθανάτῃσι, '...who competed with the immortals as to guise' (e.g. frs. 23a.16; 180.14 Merkelbach–West). Another oft-repeated half-line, applicable to any female character, is: ...ἐπήρατον εἶδος ἔχουσαν, 'having loveable look' (e.g. fr. 25.39 M.–W.); a metrically slightly different variant thereof is: ...πολυήρατον εἶδος ἔχουσαν (e.g. *Theogony* 908). Just because εἶδος can refer to the guise of a woman as well as to that of a man, though, one must not be led to render it 'beauty' instead of 'guise', 'look', or 'appearance'. That also applies to cases like Ibicus, fr. 1a (Page). The poet sings of the Greeks who destroyed Troy (5–6):

[ξα]νθᾶς Ἑλένας περὶ εἴδει | [δῆ]ριν πολύυμνον ἔχοντες,

having a much-sung struggle about the looks of auburn-haired Helen.

The war was about Helen. The poet can say that it was about the looks of Helen. Of course, Helen was good-looking; everybody knew that; so Ibicus can talk of her 'looks' and need not explicitly mention her 'beauty', which may, though, also be suggested by the epithet 'auburn'.[174]

Related to the type of comparison of divine and human females discussed above is also the first of the two occurrences of εἶδος in Hesiod's *Works and Days*. Pandora is created and equipped by the gods. Zeus orders Hephaestus (62–3):

...ἀθανάτης δὲ θεῆς εἰς ὦπα ἐΐσκεν | παρθενικῆς καλὸν εἶδος ἐπήρατον·

...that, regarding her face, he liken the beautiful loveable appearance of the maiden to the immortal goddesses.

This sentence serves as a confirmation that εἶδος denotes 'appearance', 'look', in general; by the phrase εἰς ὦπα it is specified which part of the body should be like that of goddesses in appearance; the attribute καλόν indicates in a similar way that εἶδος in and by itself does not mean beauty. In one respect, however, *Works and Days* 63 is different from the other Hesiodic comparisons of mortals with immortals. εἶδος is here direct accusative object, not accusative of respect. That is significant since an extension of the ways in which a word can be employed syntactically regularly precedes, and often implies, a change in the semantics of that word. The noun εἶδος occurred otherwise almost exclusively as an accusative of respect,[175] as a modal complement to a clause; here it appears as the direct object. That is why one can think of translating the whole clause '...that he liken her to immortal goddesses as regards her face, the beautiful loveable appearance of a maiden',[176] which would give 'appearance' a status different from that of a mere attribute.

Finally, at Hesiod *fr.* 43a (M-W), 70 ff., εἶδος is the subject. The context there is in a way similar to that of *Works and Days* 60 ff. Athena teaches her skills to a maiden, perhaps Eurynome.[177] Hesiod continues (72–4):

...νόεσκε γὰρ ἶσα θεῆσι
[τῆς καὶ ἀπὸ χρ]οϊῆς ἠδ' εἵματος ἀργυφέοιο
[λάμφ' οἷόν τε] θεοῦ χαρίεν τ' ἀπὸ εἶδος ἄητο...

> She equalled goddesses in thought,
> and brightness beamed from her skin and silver clothes
> as of a god, and graceful appearance breathed from her.

Here εἶδος, like κάλλος in the probably related passage in the *Hymn to Demeter*,[178] is active subject of a clause. This new syntactical position of εἶδος will play a role in fifth-century usage.

4. εἶδος in early Greek lyric and tragedy

In non-epic archaic poetry, the noun εἶδος generally denotes guise or outward appearance.[179] In Attic tragedy, there are two occurrences of εἶδος in the extant works of Aeschylus; in both cases the word refers to the external appearance or guise.[180] Of the two instances in Sophocles' extant tragedies, the first one, in the relatively early play *Trachiniae*, refers straightforwardly to Heracles' disfigured guise (1069); the second one is found in the late play *Electra*. Orestes returns in disguise and asks Electra, who has received the urn which allegedly contains his ashes (1177):

ἦ σὸν τὸ κλεινὸν εἶδος Ἠλέκτρας τόδε;

Is yours here Electra's renowned appearance?

As with *Works and Days* 62 f.,[181] it is difficult to decide if εἶδος is here just the external appearance of a named individual, or rather the whole person, metonymically. The genitive in the sentence 'Is yours here Electra's renowned appearance?' seems to be a descriptive genitive, comparable to the 'of-phrase' in expressions like 'a fine figure of a man', where the 'figure' *is* the 'man';[182] τὸ κλεινὸν εἶδος *is* Electra, perhaps with *enallage* of the attribute.[183]

5. εἶδος in Herodotus

With Herodotus, the semantic range of εἶδος widens and becomes more differentiated.[184] Of course, there are many cases where εἶδος is used of a person to denote guise, appearance, looks.[185] That is also the case when εἶδος is in the plural, as at 2.53: In 2.52, Herodotus declares that the Pelasgians did not have names for their gods (…ἐπωνυμίην δὲ οὐδ' οὔνομα ἐποιεῦντο οὐδενὶ αὐτῶν); later on, they adopted foreign names for their gods; those names were then taken over by the Greeks; Herodotus continues:

ὅθεν δὲ ἐγένοντο ἕκαστος τῶν θεῶν, εἴτε αἰεὶ ἦσαν πάντες, ὁκοῖοί τε τίνες τὰ εἴδεα, οὐκ ἠπιστέατο μέχρι οὗ πρώην τε καὶ χθὲς ὡς εἰπεῖν λόγῳ.… ['Ησίοδος γὰρ καὶ Ὅμηρός] εἰσι οἱ ποιήσαντες θεογονίην Ἕλλησι καὶ τοῖσι θεοῖσι τὰς ἐπωνυμίας δόντες καὶ τιμάς τε καὶ τέχνας διελόντες καὶ εἴδεα αὐτῶν σημήναντες.

But whence each of the gods stems, or if they were always there, and how they were with regard to their looks, <all that> was not known until yesterday or the day before, so to speak.... [Hesiod, indeed, and Homer] were the ones who made a theogony for the Greeks, gave the gods their designations,[186] divided the honours and skills for each of them, and gave notice what should be their looks.

At 8.113, likewise, εἶδος is used in its original sense of 'looks', 'appearance', 'guise'. Once he has reached Thessaly, Mardonius employs the entire armies of some of the nations following the Persians:

ἐκ δὲ τῶν ἄλλων συμμάχων ἐξελέγετο κατ᾽ ὀλίγους, τοῖσι εἴδεά τε ὑπῆρχε διαλέγων καὶ εἰ τέοισί τι χρηστὸν συνῄδεε πεποιημένον...

From the other allies he selected few, choosing those who had the looks, or those he knew to have done something worthy.

Here, it is a matter of pragmatics, not semantics, to observe that any evaluatively neutral word may adopt positive or negative connotations when it is in a certain position in the sentence, or when it has the appropriate emphasis, or when it is marked with other specific devices, or when it occurs in a certain context – in many a language.[187]

Appearance, guise, look, is also denoted by εἶδος in the context of animal description.[188] Herodotus states, in writing about Egyptian animals (2.69):

κροκοδείλους δὲ Ἴωνες ὠνόμασιν, εἰκάζοντες αὐτῶν τὰ εἴδεα τοῖσι παρὰ σφίσι γιγνομένοισι κροκοδείλοισι.

The Ionians called them crocodiles, however, in likening their appearances to the crocodiles which occur in their country.

In a description of Arabia, we read (3.107):

τὰ γὰρ δένδρεα ταῦτα τὰ λιβανωτοφόρα ὄφιες ὑπόπτεροι, σμικροὶ τὰ μεγάθεα, ποικίλοι τὰ εἴδεα, φυλάσσουσι πλήθεϊ πολλοὶ περὶ δένδρον ἕκαστον...

Winged snakes, small in size, varicoloured in look, guard these frankincense-bearing trees, many in number about each tree.

That last translation differs in one point of grammar from the original. As with all the examples so far quoted from Herodotus, here as well εἶδος is in the plural. Homer used εἶδος in descriptions of named individuals; in Homer's works, the noun occurred, naturally, in the singular. As we observed, the usage of Hesiod and the early lyric poets does not differ from Homer's in that respect. That Herodotus has εἶδος in the plural when it comes to animal description may be taken as an indication that the noun still denotes the look, the guise, the appearance of the individual animal, not of a species of animal. 'The winged snakes have varicoloured appearances' does not show the same degree of abstraction as 'the winged snake has a varicoloured appearance' when this sentence refers to a type or, as we would say, species of snake, not an individual animal.

However, sentences of this general type, too, are frequent with Herodotus. In comparing them to the ants of Greece, he says about a gigantic breed of Indian ants 'which are not as large as dogs' (μεγάθεα [plural!] ἔχοντες κυνῶν μὲν ἐλάσσονα) but larger than foxes (3.102):

> οὗτοι ὦν οἱ μύρμηκες ποιεύμενοι οἴκησιν, ὑπὸ γῆν ἀναφορέουσι τὴν ψάμμον κατά περ οἱ ἐν τοῖσι Ἕλλησι μύρμηκες κατὰ τὸν αὐτὸν τρόπον, εἰσὶ δὲ καὶ τὸ εἶδος ὁμοιότατοι.

> Now, these ants, in building their habitation, carry up sand from under the earth, just as the ants with the Greeks; they are, after all, most similar also as far as their look is concerned.

Here εἶδος may still refer just to the outward appearance. The statement, however, that the gigantic ants look like the normal ants in Greece is made after a remark about their activities. The clause εἰσὶ δὲ καὶ τὸ εἶδος ὁμοιότατοι has explanatory force, δὲ καὶ almost causal function. And although it is not an individual animal, and though in talking about their size Herodotus employs the plural μεγάθεα, the εἶδος, which is the *tertium comparationis* of the Greek and the Indian ants, is in the singular. The Greek ants have one εἶδος, and the Indian ants have one εἶδος; with regard to that εἶδος the members of the one group are most similar to those of the other group; the functions all these ants perform are identical, too; the only difference mentioned is the difference in size.

Does Herodotus mean to say that as far as their 'type' or 'species' is concerned, the two groups of ants are most similar? – The context allows for this interpretation but does not require it. When Herodotus has in mind this biological distinction, he uses γένος, as at 3.113, where he talks about the wonders of Arabia:

> δύο δὲ γένεα ὀίων σφι ἔστι θώματος ἄξια...

> They have two kinds of sheep worth marvelling at.

Against that, the statement about the ants, εἰσὶ δὲ καὶ τὸ εἶδος ὁμοιότατοι, seems to refer to the look of the animals, even if a connection between look and activities performed by the animals is implied in the description. The same use of εἶδος as at 3.102 recurs in the subsequent section (3.103):

> τὸ μὲν δὴ εἶδος ὁκοῖόν τι ἔχει ἡ κάμηλος, ἐπισταμένοισι τοῖσι Ἕλλησι οὐ συγγράφω· τὸ δὲ μὴ ἐπιστέαται αὐτῆς, τοῦτο φράσω. κάμηλος ἐν τοῖσι ὀπισθίοισι σκέλεσι ἔχει τέσσερας μηροὺς καὶ γούνατα τέσσερα, τά τε αἰδοῖα διὰ τῶν ὀπισθίων σκελέων πρὸς τὴν οὐρὴν τετραμμένα.

Now, what appearance the camel has I will not write down for the Greeks who know; but as regards what is not known of it [i.e. the camel], let me say this: at its hind legs, the camel has four thighs and four knees, and its genitals are stretched out between the hind legs towards the tail.

Here again, the singular, this time of both the animal and its εἶδος, is used in the description, not of an individual animal, but of a type, or of a species. As regards the meaning of εἶδος, however, there cannot be any doubt that the word refers to external appearance or guise or look: non-apparent features, common to the whole species, are contrasted with the visible εἶδος.

We observe that in the context of animal description, Herodotus can talk about members[189] of one species, of one γένος, in his terminology, and use the plural form both of the name of the animal and of εἶδος; or he can talk about the appearance of an animal, having both εἶδος and the name of the animal in the singular, while referring to the species and specific, not individual, characteristics. The latter implies a higher degree of abstraction, not necessarily conscious on Herodotus' part, and represents at the same time a semantic extension, in that the 'look', 'guise', or 'appearance' is no longer bound to be 'the look of an individual'.

That use is also found once in the context of description of human beings. Various peoples, ἔθνεα, follow the Persians against the Greeks. Among them are the Aethiopians. Of them, there are two different sections.[190] In comparing the Aethiopians in the East with those in the West, Herodotus (7.70) says:

διαλλάσσοντες εἶδος μὲν οὐδὲν τοῖσι ἑτέροισι, φωνὴν δὲ καὶ τρίχωμα μοῦνον.

They differ in no way from the others in appearance, only in voice [language] and hair.

Here, the people compared with each other, belonging to two groups, are many; the appearance of any one member of one group does not differ from that of any one member of the other group. They all have one appearance. Ethnography is thus the other, closely related, area besides zoology where reference to an εἶδος need not be reference to the εἶδος of an individual person.

The third such context in Herodotus is one in which neither human nor other animate beings are described. It is necessary to consider separately how the word is employed in that sphere. To talk of the εἶδος of a *thing* is a new development. An example is Herodotus 4.185, a description of salt production in western Libya:

ὁ δὲ ἅλς αὐτόθι καὶ λευκὸς καὶ πορφυρέος τὸ εἶδος ὀρύσσεται.

The salt dug there is white as well as purple in look.

Of worked up minerals, the main visible distinguishing mark is colour. So, for someone whose emphasis is clearly on relating and *depicting* things at home and abroad, it is natural to mention the colour of a mineral while describing its appearance.[191]

The other instance of εἶδος where the word is not referring to the εἶδος of something animate carries far wider implications. At 1.94, Herodotus relates that the Lydians have more or less the same habits and customs as the Greeks. They were, however, the first to coin gold and silver, the first to become merchants; and, he relates, the Lydians say that also the games, παιγνίαι, now common in their place and with the Greeks, were their invention. Once, at a time of dearth, they had to find a way to pass their time without thinking of food:

ἐξευρεθῆναι δὴ ὧν τότε καὶ τῶν κύβων καὶ τῶν ἀστραγάλων καὶ τῆς σφαίρης καὶ τῶν ἀλλέων πασέων παιγνιέων τὰ εἴδεα, πλὴν πεσσῶν· τούτων γὰρ ὧν τὴν ἐξεύρεσιν οὐκ οἰκηοῦνται Λυδοί.

Then 'the appearances' of cubes and ankle-bones[192] and of the ball and of all other games were invented,[193] except for draughts; indeed, now, the invention of those, the Lydians do not appropriate.

If Herodotus were speaking of the toys, the playthings, which the Lydians invented, τὰ εἴδεα could be the 'looks' or 'appearances' of these implements. But while it is true that, in the case at hand, the games played bear the names of the objects they are played with, in what way, one may ask, could τῶν παιγνιέων τὰ εἴδεα refer to 'the appearances of the games'? – If it is 'appearance over time', i.e. either what is responsible for creating an impression in the mind of someone who is watching the games being played, or the impression thus created, that would be a decidedly different application of εἶδος: The noun would refer to a process or action. Since, however, Herodotus speaks of the *invention* of games, it is unlikely that he is thinking of 'appearance' at all. What is invented is, on the one hand, the implements, the toys or objects; on the other hand, the rules which determine the 'ways' the games are played. εἶδος in the sense of 'the way' something happens or is done, a sense in which the noun will be encountered in other contexts in due course, may have arisen as a consequence of a transfer from 'the appearance of an individual', person or thing, to 'the appearance of an action'. The alternative is to suppose that the meaning 'type', well-attested for the late fifth century, had been firmly established for εἶδος at the time of Herodotus' writing 1.94, and that Herodotus could employ the noun in that sense without further comment. In that case, one should note that Herodotus, in concord with Greek usage otherwise, is speaking of the invention of 'the types of other games' rather than 'the other types of game(s)'. This 'new' sense of εἶδος as 'type' will be discussed in due course. However, regardless of which of these alternatives one opts for, τὰ εἴδεα at Herodotus 1.94 cannot idiomatically be translated as 'the appearances'.

There are thus two distinct, though not necessarily strictly separate, developments in the semantics of εἶδος which can be traced in the text of Herodotus. In Book 1, the plural εἶδος may, on one occasion, refer to 'the ways' things happen or develop or come about or are done. Secondly, in various places in Books 2 and 3, in the context of animal description, εἶδος refers collectively to the appearance all members of one species have in common. In that context, comparisons of animals contain phrases like 'most similar in εἶδος', and it is implied that identity in εἶδος is somehow connected with identity in γένος – that, though, is not made explicit.[194]

6. εἶδος in the Hippocratic Corpus

For all we know, some Hippocratic writings antedate, if not Herodotus, at least Thucydides, and we shall thus discuss εἶδος in early Hippocratic literature before turning to Thucydides.[195] Discussion of the Hippocratics will also precede the brief section on the use of εἶδος by Presocratic philosophers, some of whom are certainly earlier than anything in the Hippocratic writings, and earlier than the two historians; this order of proceeding is adopted because the Hippocratic writings form a corpus large enough to allow us to draw definite conclusions about semantic developments, which is not always possible on the basis of the scanty fragments of the Presocratics.[196]

There seems to be no general agreement on when exactly any one of the Hippocratic treatises was written.[197] But while any selection of writings of the Corpus as pre-Platonic will retain some degree of arbitrariness, the following works at least are generally agreed to be of an early date: περὶ ἀέρων, ὑδάτων, τόπων, *On Airs, Waters, and Places*; προγνωστικόν, *Prognostic*; ἐπιδημιῶν α᾽, γ᾽, *Epidemics* I + III; κατ᾽ ἰητρεῖον, *In the Surgery*; περὶ ἀγμῶν, *On Fractures*; περὶ ἄρθρων (ἐμβολῆς), *On Joints*; μοχλικόν, *Instruments of Reduction*; περὶ χυμῶν, *Humours*; περὶ φύσιος ἀνθρώπου, *Nature of Man*; and περὶ ἱερῆς νόσου, *The Sacred Disease*.[198] The *Nature of Man* will be discussed in section 5 of the chapter on ἰδέα. I do not think it safe to regard either περὶ φυσῶν, *Breaths*,[199] or the potentially highly important, but actually highly controversial, περὶ ἀρχαίης ἰητρικῆς, *On Ancient Medicine*,[200] as pre-Platonic, and will therefore not discuss its usage here.

7. εἶδος in *Airs, Waters, and Places*

Turning to *Airs, Waters, and Places*, the first point to be noticed is the relative frequency with which the noun εἶδος occurs in this treatise.[201] Since εἶδος, from Homer onwards, denotes 'appearance', 'guise', 'look', that high frequency would seem natural, as the author's task is to describe what sort of environment has what sort of influence on people in different regions, and for him that includes a description of the people he has met in those regions. One of the first things, however, even a layman notes when coming to an inhabited foreign country is whether the people there look different from the ones at home. It is also natural that, while Homer predicates a man's appearance as excellent, godlike, or most seemly, a medical man would draw attention to different distinctions. An example syntactically in parallel with Homer – in that εἶδος, or rather the plural εἴδεα, is accusative of respect – and conceptually at least compatible with Homer's world of thought, occurs in section 12. There is a mild region in Asia Minor:

τούς τε ἀνθρώπους εὐτραφέας εἶναι καὶ τὰ εἴδεα καλλίστους καὶ μεγέθει μεγίστους καὶ ἥκιστα διαφόρους ἐς τά τε εἴδεα αὐτῶν καὶ τὰ μεγέθεα...

The people are well-nourished, most beautiful as to their looks, very tall of size, very little different <from one another> with a view to their looks as well as their size.

It is interesting to observe how in the phrase καὶ τὰ εἴδεα καλλίστους καὶ μεγέθει μεγίστους an accusative of respect and an instrumental dative occur side by side and in parallel; awareness of these constructions and of the grammatically equivalent variants in the following examples will also be important in connection with Plato's syntax and usage. A case of the plural εἴδεα as a direct accusative object of a verb of having can be found in section 15. There is much fog in Phasis, the author reports, and he continues:

διὰ ταύτας δὴ τὰς προφάσιας τὰ εἴδεα ἀπηλλαγμένα τῶν λοιπῶν ἀνθρώπων ἔχουσιν οἱ Φασιηνοί· τά τε γὰρ μεγέθεα μεγάλοι, τὰ πάχεα δ' ὑπερπάχητες, ἄρθρον τε κατάδηλον οὐδὲν οὐδὲ φλέψ· τήν τε χροιὴν ὠχρὴν ἔχουσιν ὥσπερ ὑπὸ ἰκτέρου ἐχόμενοι· φθέγγονταί τε βαρύτατον ἀνθρώπων, τῷ ἠέρι χρεώμενοι οὐ λαμπρῷ, ἀλλὰ νοτώδει καὶ θολερῷ· πρός τε ταλαιπωρεῖν τὸ σῶμα ἀργότεροι πεφύκασιν.

Due to those causes, then, the Phasians have looks different from all other people. As to their 'sizes', they are tall; as to being fat, they are obese, and neither vein nor joint is visible. They have a pale colour, as though they were affected by jaundice; they sound deepest of <all> men, since the air they use is not clear, but moist and thick. They are rather idle as regards straining their bodies.

While εἴδεα here is the direct accusative object of ἔχουσιν, one would not feel the need to emend if the text read τὰ εἴδεα ἀπηλλαγμένοι τῶν λοιπῶν ἀνθρώπων (εἰσὶν) οἱ Φασιηνοί, 'as regards their looks, the Phasians are different from all other people'; one can regard the grammatical construction of this example as syntactically close to an accusative of respect. Another accusative of respect is encountered in section 20 of the treatise, where it is said that the Scythians are of moist constitution:

> ...τὰ δὲ θήλεα θαυμαστὸν οἷον ῥοϊκά ἐστί τε καὶ βλαδέα[202] τὰ εἴδεα.

...as regards the female children, it is astonishing how crooked and soft they are as to looks.

But throughout the treatise, the noun εἶδος is also found in a different grammatical construction. We read about men living in cities exposed to hot winds in winter in section 3:[203]

> τά τε εἴδεα ἐπὶ τὸ πλῆθος αὐτῶν ἀτονώτερα εἶναι...

Their appearances are, for the most part, rather slack.

In English, one would expect the generic singular in such a context ('their appearance is...'), and one would naturally employ the possessive pronoun as qualifying the noun; in Greek, εἴδεα is plural, and the genitive of the pronoun αὐτῶν, 'of theirs, of them', depends on and thus qualifies the noun. The example is thus parallel to the one found two sections later, in section 5. We learn about those in eastward-facing cities with hot winds in summer:

> τά τε εἴδεα τῶν ἀνθρώπων εὔχροά τε καὶ ἀνθηρά ἐστι μᾶλλον ἢ ἄλλη ἢν μή τις νοῦσος κωλύῃ.

The appearances of the people are of good colour and flowering more than elsewhere, unless some disease prevents this.

A further example of this usage occurs in the last section but one. By way of summary, the author states in section 23 that, as against Asia, in Europe except for Scythia, there are violent seasonal changes, different in different regions. He continues:

> διότι τὰ εἴδεα διηλλάχθαι νομίζω τῶν Εὐρωπαίων μᾶλλον ἢ τῶν Ἀσιηνῶν καὶ τὰ μεγέθεα διαφορώτατα αὐτὰ ἑωυτοῖς εἶναι κατὰ πόλιν ἑκάστην.

Therefore, I believe, differ the appearances of Europeans more than those of the Asians, and their 'sizes' are most different from one another according to each city.

To take stock: thus far, as with Homer, εἶδος in *Airs, Waters, and Places* co-occurs with, or is employed in the vicinity of, μέγεθος; people are predicated κάλλιστοι τὰ εἴδεα; the εἶδος itself is εὔχρων or ἀνθηρόν which, while not attested for, would be feasible with Homer. Predicates like ἄτονον, 'slack', ῥοϊκόν, 'crooked', βλαδύ, 'soft', on the other hand, point to the particular interests of the physician. Yet, those latter adjectives, too, all belong to the visible sphere and can thus denote what is part of someone's appearance.[204] When, in section 15 of *Airs, Waters and Places*, it is said of the Phasians that they have an εἶδος different from that of the rest of mankind, and when that statement is followed by a reference first to their size, their volume, their colour, and then their 'sounding deep', it need not be inferred from this that the author thought of someone's εἶδος as also comprising voice; starting from his usual point of departure, he lists a number of factors which contribute to the difference in guise or appearance, and then names an additional distinction, that concerning voice. It is to be noted that, in all the examples quoted, εἶδος is in the plural. Many people of one ἔθνος, one 'race' or 'nation', or at least one φῦλον, one 'tribe', are described, and so the author refers to their εἴδεα, just as the Ionian Herodotus talks of the εἴδεα of animals of one species.

It is, however, not always the case that the noun εἶδος in *Airs, Waters, and Places*, is accusative of respect, or a direct object accusative to a verb of having, or has a genitive of a noun denoting a human being depending on it. The following are examples of an absolute use of εἶδος. Section 13 concludes with a generalizing statement. Land is affected by the changes of the seasons, and so, in the same way, are human beings, too:

> εἰσὶ γὰρ φύσιες αἱ μὲν ὄρεσιν ἐοικυῖαι δενδρώδεσί τε καὶ ἐφύδροισιν, αἱ δὲ λεπτοῖσί τε καὶ ἀνύδροις, αἱ δὲ λειμακεστέροις τε καὶ ἑλώδεσι, αἱ δὲ πεδίῳ τε [καὶ]²⁰⁵ ψιλῇ καὶ ξηρῇ γῇ. αἱ γὰρ ὧραι αἱ μεταλλάσσουσαι τῆς μορφῆς τὴν φύσιν εἰσὶ διάφοροι. ἢν δὲ διάφοροι ἔωσι μέγα σφέων αὐτέων, διαφοραὶ καὶ πλείονες γίνονται τοῖς εἴδεσι.

There are, indeed, natures²⁰⁶ which are like mountains, the ones wooded and well-watered, others light and un-watered, others rather meadowy and marshy, then again those which are like a bare plain and dry land. The seasons, indeed, which change the nature of the shape are different; but whenever they are very different from one another, the differences will also become larger for the appearances.

εἶδος here is apparently a term more general than μορφή, which latter refers to the 'shape' of 'form' of the body alone. It could be argued, though, that rather than dealing with an absolute use of εἶδος here, one should assume that the qualifying genitive 'of people' is implied and has been left unexpressed. This interpretation, however, is not available in the following case. In section 10, it is reported that in years with dry winters and rainy spring, various diseases are likely to occur.

> καὶ δυσεντερίας εἰκός ἐστι γίνεσθαι καὶ τῇσι γυναιξὶ καὶ τοῖς εἴδεσι τοῖς ὑγροτάτοισι.

It is also probable that dysenteries occur, both with the women and with the moistest 'appearances'.

This usage recalls Hesiod's *Works and Days* 62 f.[207] The context was that of Zeus' giving Hephaestus orders for the creation of Pandora. As an alternative to ἀθανάτῃς δὲ θεῇς εἰς ὦπα ἐίσκεν | παρθενικῆς καλὸν εἶδος ἐπήρατον, 'that he liken the beautiful lovable appearance | of the maiden to the immortal goddesses as to face,' it was suggested to punctuate differently, and to read and translate ἀθανάτῃς δὲ θεῇς εἰς ὦπα ἐίσκεν, | παρθενικῆς καλὸν εἶδος ἐπήρατον, 'that he liken her to immortal goddesses as to her face, | the beautiful lovable appearance of a maiden.' This suggestion, while perhaps leading to an anachronistic result in the case of Hesiod, was possible in the light of usage like that of the Hippocratic author. In the case of *Airs, Waters and Places* 10, it seems obvious from the grammar of the sentence that εἶδος does not refer to 'the appearance of a person' but rather, metonymically, to 'a person'. εἶδος is used in an absolute way, a shift in use and application similar to the one which took place with the English word 'appearance' in the context of inanimate objects, when, for example, E. King writes in *Philosophical Transactions of the Royal Society* II, 1667: 'White and clean appearances…all figur'd like the lesser sort of Birds Eggs.'[208] There, the objects themselves, not the impressions they make, or the perceptions they provoke, are called 'appearances', and it is in that way that τὰ εἴδεα τὰ ὑγρότατα, 'the wettest', or perhaps 'softest', 'appearances', can be seen as co-ordinate with αἱ γυναῖκες, 'the women'.

Looking at the treatise as a whole, though, it is not obvious what conclusions can be drawn on the basis of this absolute use of εἶδος. The final section of the treatise, *Airs, Waters, and Places* 24, contains six instances of the plural εἶδος in different grammatical contexts, and it is difficult, if not impossible, to decide whether – in those cases in which the word neither is accusative of respect nor has a possessive genitive depending on it – one must supply 'of the people' with εἴδεα, or what the word is supposed to mean when standing on its own. In section 24, the author has finished his description of Europe and Asia. He states:

ἔνεισι δὲ καὶ ἐν τῇ Εὐρώπῃ φῦλα διάφορα ἕτερα ἑτέροισι καὶ τὰ μεγέθεα καὶ τὰς μορφὰς καὶ τὰς ἀνδρείας. τὰ δὲ διαλλάσσοντα ταῦτά ἐστιν, ἃ καὶ ἐπὶ τῶν πρότερον εἴρηται. ἔτι δὲ σαφέστερον φράσω. ὁκόσοι μὲν χώρην ὀρεινήν τε οἰκέουσι καὶ τρηχεῖαν καὶ ὑψηλὴν καὶ ἔνυδρον, καὶ αἱ μεταβολαὶ αὐτοῖσι γίνονται τῶν ὡρέων μέγα διάφοροι, ἐνταῦθα εἰκὸς εἴδεα μεγάλα εἶναι καὶ πρὸς τὸ ταλαίπωρον καὶ τὸ ἀνδρεῖον εὖ πεφυκότα, καὶ τό τε ἄγριον καὶ τὸ θηριῶδες αἱ τοιαῦται φύσιες οὐχ ἥκιστα ἔχουσιν. …(κοῖλα χωρία)… εἰ μέντοι ποταμοὶ μὲν μὴ εἴησαν, τὰ δὲ ὕδατα λιμναῖά τε καὶ στάσιμα πίνοιεν καὶ ἐλώδεα, ἀνάγκη τὰ τοιαῦτα εἴδεα προγαστρότερα καὶ σπληνώδεα εἶναι. ὁκόσοι δὲ ὑψηλήν τε οἰκέουσι χώρην καὶ λείην καὶ ἀνεμώδεα καὶ ἔνυδρον, εἶεν ἂν εἴδεα μεγάλοι καὶ ἑωυτοῖσι παραπλήσιοι· ἀνανδρότεραι δὲ καὶ ἡμερότεραι αἱ γνῶμαι. ὁκόσοι δὲ λεπτά τε καὶ ἄνυδρα καὶ ψιλά, τῇσι μεταβολῇσι τῶν ὡρέων οὐκ εὔκρητα, ἐν ταύτῃ τῇ χώρῃ τὰ εἴδεα εἰκὸς σκληρά τε εἶναι καὶ ἔντονα καὶ ξανθότερα ἢ

μελάντερα καὶ τὰ ἤθεα καὶ τὰς ὀργὰς αὐθάδεάς τε καὶ ἰδιογνώμονας. ὅκου γὰρ
αἱ μεταβολαί εἰσι πυκνόταται τῶν ὡρέων καὶ πλεῖστον διάφοροι αὐταὶ ἑωυτῇσιν,
ἐκεῖ καὶ τὰ εἴδεα καὶ τὰ ἤθεα καὶ τὰς φύσιας εὑρήσεις πλεῖστον διαφερούσας.

μέγισται μὲν οὖν εἰσιν αὗται τῆς φύσιος αἱ διαλλαγαί, ἔπειτα δὲ καὶ ἡ χώρη,
ἐν ᾗ ἄν τις τρέφηται καὶ τὰ ὕδατα. εὑρήσεις γὰρ ἐπὶ τὸ πλῆθος τῆς χώρης τῇ
φύσει ἀκολουθέοντα καὶ τὰ εἴδεα τῶν ἀνθρώπων καὶ τοὺς τρόπους.

In translating this passage, it may be helpful to discuss its language paragraph
by paragraph, as the author's style is as rough and rugged as some of the
regions he describes. Numerous inconcinnities and anacoluthous constructions in a text laconic and terse make it difficult to determine whether
a particular occurrence of εἶδος marks a semantic development or is just an
instance of an elliptical or merely careless construction.

> In Europe as well, there are tribes different from one another as to size, as to
> shape, and as to manliness. The points of difference are just those which I have
> indicated above. I will, however, describe them yet more clearly. All those who
> inhabit a mountainous, rough, high, and well-watered country – and if the
> changes of the seasons are great with them – there it is probable that 'appear-
> ances' are tall and by nature tending to 'the hard-working' and 'the manly', and
> such 'natures' do not least have 'the wild' and 'the brutish'.[209]

It seems as though at least in this one instance, the phrase 'εἴδεα μεγάλα εἶναι
καὶ πρὸς τὸ ταλαίπωρον καὶ τὸ ἀνδρεῖον εὖ πεφυκότα', εἶδος is to be taken
as absolute in the above-stated sense. This, one could argue, is most telling
due to the way the sentence is continued, again by way of change of grammatical construction: καὶ τό τε ἄγριον καὶ τὸ θηριῶδες αἱ τοιαῦται φύσιες
οὐχ ἥκιστα ἔχουσιν; in that latter clause, φύσιες, 'natures', is the subject. It
seems as if just as a person of a certain φύσις, or 'nature', can be referred to
as a certain φύσις, so a person of a certain εἶδος, 'appearance', can be referred
to as a certain εἶδος. But whereas in English that semantic shift has taken
place in the case of 'nature', perhaps furthered by authors with a classical
education, it has not done so in the case of 'appearance'. There is thus
a difficulty facing the translator in such a context. 'Appearance' would be
a possible translation of εἶδος in the case of things, inanimate objects; but it
is not commonly considered suitable as a word that covers in its application
both things and people.

There is, though, a different way to construe the same phrase. One could
see the clause in question, 'there it is probable that "appearances" are tall
and by nature tending to "the hard-working" and "the manly"', as parallel to
a hypothetical 'there it is probable that eyeballs are shortened and by nature
tending to "the short-sighted"', or some such clause referring to the make-up
of any particular part of the body. εἴδεα and φύσιες would then simply refer
to the 'appearances' and 'natures' 'of the people' described. εἶδος would not

be 'an appearance' in the sense of 'a person appearing', but simply 'appearance', namely 'of a person', in the accustomed way. For our purposes, it is not necessary to choose between the two ways of translating the sentence; it is sufficient to see that semantically potentially ambivalent contexts such as this one have played their part in the rise of an absolute use of εἶδος as 'an appearance'.

To resume translation: after a few general remarks about the influence which hollow regions have on their inhabitants, regions where rivers render the water healthy,[210] the author continues:

> Certainly, though, if there are no rivers and thus they[211] drink waters which are swampy, stagnant and marshy, it is necessary that such 'appearances' are pot-bellied and with enlarged spleen.

Though at first this sentence seems to resolve the issue just discussed in favour of an absolute use, because in the phrase τοιαῦτα εἴδεα the determining 'such' is apparently anaphoric in a way which prevents 'such appearances' from referring to anything else but the people just implicitly referred to by the main verb of the second part of the protasis, it can again not be excluded that 'such appearances' is simply a shorthand for 'the appearances of such people', a case parallel to what was suggested for τοιαῦται φύσιες above. Taking the phrase that way may be supported by the next occurrence of εἶδος:

> People, however, who inhabit land high, light, windy, and well-watered, are tall as to <their> appearances, and very much like one another: their minds rather unmanly and tame.

In this instance, εἶδος is clearly accusative of respect. The very next sentence, though, another case of an anacoluthous construction, presents the same ambiguities as those encountered above, though the grammatical context is a little more complicated.

> People <who inhabit land> thin, unwatered, bare, and not well-balanced as regards the changes of the seasons – in that land it is probable that the 'appearances' are hard and intense, fair rather than dark, and the characters and tempers wilful and independent. Indeed, where the changes of the seasons are most frequent, and <the seasons> most different from one another, there you will also find the appearances and the characters and the natures as differing most widely.

Here, it is impossible to decide if in the sentence ὁκόσοι δὲ λεπτά τε καὶ ἄνυδρα καὶ ψιλά, τῇσι μεταβολῇσι τῶν ὡρέων οὐκ εὔκρητα, ἐν ταύτῃ τῇ χώρῃ τὰ εἴδεα εἰκὸς σκληρά τε εἶναι καὶ ἔντονα καὶ χαντότερα ἢ μελάντερα καὶ τὰ ἤθεα καὶ τὰς ὀργὰς αὐθάδεάς τε καὶ ἰδιογνώμονας, there is to be a caesura after εὔκρητα so that τὰ εἴδεα…καὶ τὰ ἤθεα καὶ τὰς ὀργὰς were to be the subjects of the *accusative-and-infinitive phrase*, or if τοσούτους or τούτους or the like is to be supplied so that τὰ εἴδεα...καὶ τὰ ἤθεα καὶ τὰς ὀργὰς would be accusatives of respect,[212] as is clearly the case in the subsequent sentence:

> These, now, are the greatest differences in nature, then also the land in which someone is reared, and the waters. You will find, indeed, that for the most part the appearances and the ways of the people follow the nature of the land.

In that concluding sentence, τὰ εἴδεα τῶν ἀνθρώπων, the expression 'the appearances of the people', is unambiguous again, due to the presence of the possessive genitive. It is, thus, *possible* that the plural εἴδεα repeatedly refers to persons as 'appearances' in *Airs, Waters, and Places* 24; not least due to the author's obscure style, though, a decision on this point is difficult; a new absolute use may point to an emerging new sense of the words εἶδος, but more often than not the syntax is ambiguous – just as one would expect at the point of semantic enlargement.[213]

8. εἶδος in *Airs, Waters, and Places* 11

Once in *Airs, Waters, and Places*, εἶδος is in the singular. In section 11 of the treatise, it is stated that changes of season especially, but also other 'astronomical' events, have serious consequences for the diseased:

> τά τε γὰρ νοσεύματα μάλιστα ἐν ταύτῃσι τῇσιν ἡμέρῃσιν κρίνεται. καὶ τὰ μὲν ἀποφθίνει, τὰ δὲ λήγει, τὰ δὲ ἄλλα πάντα μεθίσταται ἐς ἕτερον εἶδος καὶ ἑτέρην κατάστασιν.

> And mostly, indeed, the diseases are decided in those days. And some die away, others calm down, all the others change to another appearance and another condition.

The sentence containing εἶδος seems to admit of several interpretations.[214] One is to say that, here, εἶδος is not the 'εἶδος of a person' but 'the εἶδος of a disease'. A disease, one could infer, has at any stage of its occurrence an εἶδος, an 'appearance' or 'guise', in the old sense of that word found e.g. in the eighteenth-century treatise *Health and Long Life* by Sir William Temple: 'Both [diseases] were thought to appear in many various Guises.'[215] In view of general Hippocratic tenets, on the other hand, one could take the sentence καὶ τὰ μὲν ἀποφθίνει, τὰ δὲ λήγει, τὰ δὲ ἄλλα πάντα μεθίσταται ἐς ἕτερον εἶδος καὶ ἑτέρην κατάστασιν to mean that the disease in question gives way to another disease altogether.[216] For this use of μεθίστασθαι, one could adduce, e.g., *Diseases* 1.29. Overheating of the upper cavity is given as a cause for vomiting; then there is added:

> διὰ τοῦτο δ' αὐτὸ καὶ ἐς περιπλευμονίην ἐκ καύσου τε καὶ πλευρίτιδος μάλιστα μεθίσταται τὰ νοσήματα...

> For that same reason, too, diseases often change from fever and pleurisy to pneumonia.[217]

For the question of the meaning of εἶδος in the sentence from *Airs, Waters, and Places* 11, καὶ τὰ μὲν ἀποφθίνει, τὰ δὲ λήγει, τὰ δὲ ἄλλα πάντα μεθίσταται ἐς ἕτερον εἶδος καὶ ἑτέρην κατάστασιν, one has to decide between the two possibilities outlined above. A clue may lie in the proper understanding of what is signified by κατάστασις.[218]

In this context, and as the question of different seasons of the year is relevant at this point in *Airs, Waters, and Places*, it should be noted that, in the Hippocratic Corpus, the noun κατάστασις has its applications both in the context of seasons of the year and in the context of conditions of specific diseases. As for the use of κατάστασις as applied to the seasons, one may compare *Prognostic* 25. First, some general medical advice is given to those who want to forecast accurately; then there is added:

χρὴ δὲ καὶ τὰς φορὰς τῶν νοσημάτων τῶν αἰεὶ ἐπιδημεόντων ταχέως ἐνθυμεῖσθαι καὶ μὴ λανθάνειν τὴν τῆς ὥρης κατάστασιν.

But it is also necessary quickly to give thought to attacks of diseases which are at any given time epidemic, and not to forget the constitution of the season.

But this context can be excluded from consideration. At *Airs, Waters, and Places* 11, κατάστασις cannot apply to the seasons, since on the one hand the point of talking about change of season at all seems to be to draw attention to the change of weather conditions that goes with it; on the other hand, it would be awkward to have two different points of reference, the diseases for εἶδος, and the astronomico-meteorological situation for κατάστασις.

As for the use of κατάστασις as applied to a disease, one may compare *Prognostic* 20. There, it is declared that there are certain critical days for fevers. They are not always easy to make out.

ἀλλὰ χρὴ ἀπὸ τῆς πρώτης ἡμέρης ἐνθυμεῖσθαι καὶ καθ' ἑκάστην τετράδα προστιθεμένην σκέπτεσθαι καὶ οὐ λήσει, ὅπῃ τρέψεται. γίνεται δὲ καὶ τῶν τεταρταίων ἡ κατάστασις ἐκ τούτου τοῦ κόσμου.

But it is necessary to give thought to <the matter> from the first day and at each additional fourth day – and you will not fail to see where things turn. The constitution also of quartan fevers develops out of this order.

The author of *Airs, Waters, and Places* does not always write in the clearest style. His grammar is not always coherent. Yet, if each and every disease of which it is not correct to say either ἀποφθίνει or λήγει, whatever the exact meaning of those two words may be, turns to a different condition, and that condition is a different 'constitution of disease', then – though the words τὰ δὲ ἄλλα πάντα μεθίσταται ἐς ἕτερον εἶδος καὶ ἑτέρην κατάστασιν *need* not imply anything about the disease's being the same or not – one could argue in terms of pragmatics, in the sense that in any given context an author would aim to provide the reader with what is relevant: a different disease implies a different constitution anyway; therefore, if it is stressed that the disease passes into a different constitution with change of astronomical season, it must be the same disease. But that is not an altogether cogent line of argumentation. The context of *Airs, Waters, and Places* 11 is ambiguous. Neither the point of reference of εἶδος nor the meaning of the word there can be determined with any degree of certainty.[219] But probability seems to be on the side of thinking, as did Gillespie (1912, 187) in terms of changing into a different 'type' of disease; i.e. this treatise as well has one instance of the noun εἶδος at the threshold to this new sense of the word.

9. εἶδος in *Epidemics* Books 1 and 3

There are five instances of εἶδος in *Epidemics* 1 and 3; in all of them, the word seems to be employed in the same way, marking the transition in meaning from 'appearance' to 'type'. *Epidemics* 1, section 19:

πλῆθος μὲν οὖν τῶν νοσημάτων ἐγένετο. ἐκ δὲ τῶν καμνόντων ἀπέθνῃσκον μάλιστα μειράκια, νέοι, ἀκμάζοντες, λεῖοι, ὑπολευκόχρωτες, ἰθύτριχες, μελανότριχες, μελανόφθαλμοι, οἱ εἰκῇ καὶ ἐπὶ τὸ ῥάθυμον βεβιωκότες, ἰσχνόφωνοι, τρηχύφωνοι, τραυλοί, ὀργίλοι. καὶ γυναῖκες πλεῖσται ἐκ τούτου τοῦ εἴδεος ἀπέθνῃσκον.

Now the number of illnesses was great. And, of the patients, there died chiefly striplings, young people, people in their prime, the smooth, the fair-skinned, the straight-haired, the black-haired, the black-eyed, those who had lived recklessly and carelessly, the thin-voiced, the rough-voiced, the lispers, the passionate.[220] Very many women, too, of this *type* died.

The list of 'types' of people includes some 'types' which are mutually exclusive, such as the age groups and, probably, some of the types of voice. It is therefore people who displayed one or more, not all, of the said characteristics, who were most likely to die. 'And not only the male', the author adds; this is not because the adjectives used for the description of the diseased are of masculine gender; the author also elsewhere remarks separately on how women were affected by diseases occurring 'in a given constitution'.[221] When he declares καὶ γυναῖκες πλεῖσται ἐκ τούτου τοῦ εἴδεος ἀπέθνῃσκον, he does not seem to draw a line between the age classes and the other characteristics either; among the characteristics, moreover, 'those who had lived recklessly and carelessly' does refer to a style of life rather than to any personal features, appearance, or guise. The author, therefore, does not seem to say: 'women of that *appearance* died', but more likely something like 'women of that *type*'.

In *Epidemics* I 20, εἶδος does not refer to the type of a *person*:

οἱ μὲν οὖν πλεῖστοι τῶν νοσησάντων ἐν τῇ καταστάσει ταύτῃ τούτῳ τῷ τρόπῳ διενόσησαν, καὶ οὐδένα οἶδα τῶν περιγενομένων, ᾧτινι οὐχ ὑπέστρεψαν αἱ

123

κατὰ λόγον ὑποστροφαὶ γενόμεναι, καὶ διεσῴζοντο πάντες, οὓς κἀγὼ οἶδα, οἷσιν αἱ ὑποστροφαὶ διὰ τοῦ εἴδεος τούτου γενοίατο. οὐδὲ τῶν διανοσησάντων διὰ τούτου τοῦ τρόπου οὐδενὶ οἶδα ὑποστροφὴν γενομένην πάλιν.

Now, most of the diseased in this 'constitution' went through their disease in that way, and I do not know any one, of those who recovered, whom the relapses did not affect according to the list I have set out; and all were saved, of whom I know, whom relapses affected of this type. And I do not know of anyone living through their disease in that way whom relapse would have affected again.

If there is, in this passage, a difference in sense between τούτῳ τῷ τρόπῳ, an instrumental dative, and the modal-*cum*-instrumental prepositional phrase διὰ τούτου τοῦ τρόπου, it is a very slight one.[222] The force of the phrase διὰ τοῦ εἴδεος τούτου should be modal-*cum*-instrumental in the same way.[223] It may well be that εἶδος is chosen mainly for the sake of variation, since otherwise τρόπος would occur three times in succession in a context which appears to be redundant anyway. This is not meant to suggest that εἶδος and τρόπος are synonymous here. τρόπος is the turn something takes, the way something goes.[224] εἶδος is here 'appearance', or 'guise' in Temple's sense, in the sense of how a thing – object, person, or event – habitually or typically appears: 'all those I know were saved when the relapses affected them in that guise'. Examples of this sort, 'relapses coming about in one guise were fatal, relapses coming about in a different guise were not fatal', pave the way to the use of εἶδος in the sense of 'type'.

The three instances of εἶδος in *Epidemics* 3 are again in the 'constitution', not in one of the 'cases'. Several diseases are named which occurred in this period. Then it is stated (3.3):

τὰ μὲν ἐπιδημήσαντα νοσήματα ταῦτα. ἑκάστου δὲ τῶν ὑπογεγραμμένων εἰδέων ἦσαν οἱ κάμνοντες καὶ ἔθνησκον πολλοί. συνέπιπτε δ' ἐφ' ἑκάστοισι τούτων ὧδε...

Now, those were the epidemic diseases <in this constitution>. And of each of the above-said types there were patients and there died many. As symptoms occurred with each of those the following: ... [an enumeration of the symptoms follows].

After a description of other diseases, including ardent fevers, in the preceding sections, section 12 begins:

πολλὰ δὲ καὶ ἄλλα πυρετῶν ἐπεδήμησεν εἴδεα, τριταίων, τεταρταίων, νυκτερινῶν, συνεχέων, μακρῶν, πεπλανημένων, ἀσωδέων, ἀκαταστάτων.

But also many other types of fevers were epidemic, tertians, quartans, night fevers, fevers continuous, protracted, irregular, fevers attended by nausea, fevers of no definite character.[225]

Here, πολλὰ καὶ ἄλλα πυρετῶν εἴδεα refers to 'many other *types* of fever'. Finally, in section 13, we learn that 'consumption' was the worst and most widespread disease of that constitution. Its symptoms and development are described in detail. Then section 14 commences:

> εἶδος δὲ τῶν φθινωδέων ἦν τὸ λεῖον, τὸ ὑπόλευκον, τὸ φακῶδες, τὸ ὑπέρυθρον, τὸ χαροπόν, λευκοφλεγματίαι, πτερυγώδεες· καὶ γυναῖκες οὕτω.

> But the type of the consumptive people was: the smooth, the whitish, the lentil-coloured, the reddish, the bright-eyed; leuco-phlegmatous people, those with shoulder-blades projecting like wings. And the women likewise.

It is impossible to say whether εἶδος here is meant to refer just to the external 'appearance' of the people affected by consumption, or whether it is the 'type' of those affected which is characterized.[226] The fact that all the characterizations happen to be externally visible may suggest that 'appearance' is intended. Against this, it could be objected that since among the characteristics are found λευκοφλεγματίαι and πτερυγώδεες, both denoting people,[227] the author must mean a 'type' or 'types', not 'appearance' or 'appearances'. To that objection it could be replied that this inference is not safe since these two types of people come last; it is possible that the two terms denoting further characteristics were added to the list of 'appearances' with slight inconcinnity.

While this last case may be left undecided, the extension which took place with the application of the noun εἶδος cannot be called into question. In *Epidemics* 1 and 3, there are instances of εἶδος where translating the word as 'appearance' or 'guise' would be unidiomatic or even misleading, while translating εἶδος as 'type' seems to convey the sense of the passages in question. One must bear in mind, however, that to the Greek ear it was still the same word εἶδος which was employed in each case; and *Epidemics* 1 and 3 shows that, at least in some cases, the same clause seems to admit of two alternative renderings, with 'guise' or 'appearance', or with 'type'. While the two English words 'guise' and 'type' stand quite apart, it is not clear that the question whether the author had meant 'guise' or 'type' would have been meaningful to the author himself or a reader at the time when the treatise was written.

10. εἶδος in Herodotus and the Hippocratic Corpus: a retrospect
Accumulating more instances would not add anything new, but merely confirm these observations. In the cases not discussed here, there is no conflicting evidence; nor is there anything that would indicate a further semantic development. 'Type' seems to be firmly established as a meaning of εἶδος separate from, and co-existing with, 'guise, appearance'. With all the instances of εἶδος in the treatises *In the Surgery, On Fractures, On Joints,*

Instruments of Reduction, *Humours*, and *The Sacred Disease*,[228] the word seems to denote either 'guise, appearance' or 'type', in the ways outlined above.[229]

The final instance of εἶδος in the *Histories* of Herodotus discussed in section 5 above was that of 1.94:

ἐξευρεθῆναι δὴ ὦν τότε καὶ τῶν κύβων καὶ τῶν ἀστραγάλων καὶ τῆς σφαίρης καὶ τῶν ἀλλέων πασέων παιγνιέων τὰ εἴδεα, πλὴν πεσσῶν· τούτων γὰρ ὦν τὴν ἐξεύρεσιν οὐκ οἰκηιοῦνται Λυδοί.

εἶδος there appeared to be applied to how the games were played: i.e. either to the process, something not static but dynamic, or to the rules; but definitely not to the respective material object used. A clue to what εἶδος could mean is now furnished by the use of the word in some of the early Hippocratic treatises. There, εἶδος is applied to things characterized by any set of characteristics, visible or not visible. Commonly, the noun εἶδος would appear in a genitive phrase of the type 'a person of that εἶδος', 'a disease of that εἶδος'. In these cases, 'type' suggested itself as a translation of εἶδος. The inverted phrase is also found: 'these and other types of disease', 'two types of something'.[230] But there is also a possibility of referring to diseases or patients characterized as to 'the above-said εἴδεα', or again by declaring: 'the εἶδος of them was this or that'. In those cases, neither 'type' nor 'guise, appearance' would be fully idiomatic; it is not that either word would necessarily be incorrect as a translation of εἶδος, but in each case the context shows that the connotations of εἶδος are slightly different from those of either English term; the difference becomes apparent in the differing syntactical relations εἶδος can enter. Bearing that in mind, 'of all other games the *types*' may be acceptable as a translation of 'τῶν ἀλλέων πασέων παιγνιέων τὰ εἴδεα'.

The passage discussed at the end of section 8 above could be explained in the same way. At *Airs, Waters, and Places* 11, it is stated: καὶ τὰ μὲν ἀποφθίνει, τὰ δὲ λήγει, τὰ δὲ ἄλλα πάντα μεθίσταται ἐς ἕτερον εἶδος καὶ ἑτέρην κατάστασιν. That could indeed be understood as meaning: 'And the ones die away, others calm down, all the others change to another type and another condition'. Considering the usage of *Epidemics* 1 and 3, and also, it seems, of Herodotus, this translation in itself would not presuppose a decision on whether the author has in mind the same disease or a different, new one.

In the Hippocratic corpus, εἶδος is used with a high degree of abstraction. What determines an εἶδος and what is referred to by εἶδος need not have a visual component at all; the noun in either singular or plural can be applied to something – person, object, state or event – marked by one or more than one characteristic. Syntactically, εἶδος appears to be more versatile than either 'guise, appearance' or 'type', in that in all its senses it seems to be employable with any one of the constructions possible with one or other of the English words.

11. εἶδος in Empedocles

Among the Presocratic philosophers, it is, so far as we can make out, only Empedocles who employs εἶδος with any frequency or significance.[231] If Plutarch, *De facie quae in orbe lunae apparet* 926d (DK31B27), quotes accurately, a line by Empedocles contains the formulaic ἠελίοιο…ἀγλαὸν εἶδος, 'the bright appearance of the sun'. It is impossible to determine if the genitive ἠελίοιο is a possessive or a descriptive genitive. [232] εἶδος as the 'appearance (of something)' is found once more, though with slightly different emphasis. In 31B71 (4 ff.), the εἴδη of mortals are opposed to their χροῖα:

εἰ δέ τί σοι περὶ τῶνδε λιπόξυλος ἔπλετο πίστις,
πῶς ὕδατος γαίης τε καὶ αἰθέρος ἠελίου τε
κιρναμένων εἴδη τε γενοίατο χροῖά τε θνητῶν
τόσσ', ὅσα νῦν γεγάασι συναρμοσθέντ' Ἀφροδίτῃ…

But if trust concerning those things be in any way deficient for you:
how from water and earth and aether and sun,
when they are mixed, appearances and colours of mortal beings come about,
whichever have come about now, fitted by and through Aphrodite…

Translating χροῖα as 'colour' suggests itself, especially as it is found side by side with εἶδος which could then be 'shape' or 'form'.[233] It may, however, be worth bearing in mind that – though admittedly more than half a century later and in a predominantly Attic context – an opposition of colour and shape was expressed by contrasting χρώμα or χρόα with σχῆμα, not with εἶδος. That is all the more significant as in that text, *Meno* 73e–76e, Socrates states that Meno as a follower of Gorgias accepts and adheres to the views of Empedocles (76c). But elsewhere in Presocratic philosophy as well, σχῆμα, rather than εἶδος, seems to be the term firmly established to denote physical 'shape' or 'form'.[234] It is, therefore, rash to see an opposition of form versus colour in Empedocles 31B71. εἶδος, 'appearance', as a term for the more general concept may be followed in any description of a thing by any term for a concept which strictly speaking forms part of it; the connective τε…τε, as elsewhere καί, 'and', is here epexegetic, explanatory-*cum*-specifying; colour does belong to appearance, as well as to 'an appearance'; appearance, as well as 'an appearance', comprises colour: the wording of 'appearances and colours of mortal beings come into being' is thus slightly redundant, but it is so in a manner perfectly common in both verse and prose.[235]

In 31B22, as most other extant lines of Empedocles preserved by Simplicius, the world we live in is described as containing on the one hand things in concord with their parts, namely the sun, the earth, the sky, and the sea; then those mixed well and fittingly, likewise in concord; and, he concludes:

ἐχθρὰ <δ' ἃ> πλεῖστον ἀπ' ἀλλήλων διέχουσι μάλιστα

127

γέννῃ τε κρήσει τε καὶ εἴδεσιν ἐκμάκτοισι,
πάντῃ συγγίνεσθαι ἀήθεα…

But those which stand furthest apart from one another are most hostile
to birth and mixture and moulded appearances,
wholly unaccustomed to getting together…[236]

Here, εἶδος is used absolutely; 'an appearance' in the sense of 'a thing that
appears'. The same usage is found in two more fragments. 31B73 as well
belongs to a physical or cosmological context (4 f.):

…
ὡς δὲ τότε χθόνα Κύπρις, ἐπεί τ’ ἐδίηνεν ἐν ὄμβρῳ,
εἴδεα ποιπνύουσα θοῷ πυρὶ δῶκε κρατῦναι.

…

and how at that time Cypris, when she had moistened earth in rainstorms,
eagerly attending to appearances, gave them to swift fire to strengthen them.

As with 31B22, the product of a process of γένεσις, of becoming and coming
into being, that which as a result appears as distinct, is called 'an appearance'.
Such a distinct result of a process is also the picture a painter produces; the
work and craftsmanship of painters is described in 31B23, 3–7:

οἵτ’ ἐπεὶ οὖν μάρψωσι πολύχροα φάρμακα χερσίν,
ἁρμονίῃ μείξαντε τὰ μὲν πλέω, ἄλλα δ’ ἐλάσσω,
ἐκ τῶν εἴδεα πᾶσιν ἀλίγκια πορσύνουσι,
δένδρεά τε κτίζοντε καὶ ἀνέρας ἠδὲ γυναῖκας
θῆράς τ’ οἰωνούς τε καὶ ὑδατοθρέμμονας ἰχθῦς.

Now, when they grasp with their hands drugs of varied colour,
mixing with fitting measure more of the one, less of the other,
they prepare from them appearances similar to all the things,
creating trees and men and women,
animals and birds and fish which are nourished by water.

It may be noted in this context that painters do not just create shapes or
forms, but indeed reproduce the whole appearance, and the appearance as
a whole, of the thing they set out to represent.[237]

The case is different with the three remaining instances of εἶδος, different
in the same way that some of the instances of εἶδος in the medical writers
discussed above were different. And it may not be irrelevant that at least one
of the three contexts, 31B98 (11–15), while certainly part of a cosmological
discussion, is distinctly physiological or medical:[238]

ἡ δὲ χθὼν τούτοισιν ἴση συνέκυρσε μάλιστα,
Ἡφαίστῳ τ’ ὄμβρῳ τε καὶ αἰθέρι παμφανόωντι
Κύπριδος ὁρμισθεῖσα τελείοις ἐν λιμένεσσιν,

εἴτ' ὀλίγον μείζων εἴτε πλεόνεσσιν ἐλάσσων·
ἐκ τῶν αἷμά τε γέντο καὶ ἄλλης εἴδεα σαρκός.

But earth, most equal with and to them, met them:
Hephaestus and rain and all-shining aether,
anchoring in the perfect harbours of Cypris;
be there a little more or a little more less:
from those, blood came into being, and also the types of other flesh.

The various 'types of flesh', whatever they are,[239] would 'appear' differently;
in that sense they could be said to be different, distinct 'appearances'. But the
grammatical construction of εἴδεα in the plural, with a dependent genitive,
indicates the transition to the separate new sense of εἶδος as 'type' discussed
above. It is likely, though, that the semantic development outlined took
place in a non-poetic context and was only afterwards employed in Empedocles' verse. The irreducibly ambiguous transitional occurrences of the
word found in the professedly medical writers are absent from Empedocles.
There may of course be varying degrees of abstraction in Empedocles as well;
in 31B98 εἴδη clearly refers to types of things visibly different, and so does
31B115 (53 f.):

φυομένους παντοῖα διὰ χρόνου εἴδεα θνητῶν
ἀργαλέας βιότοιο μεταλλάσσοντα κελεύθους.

[It is an old law that daimones who have committed a crime
must wander about a long time,]
growing [living/being born] through time as manifold types of mortal beings,
taking on toilsome ways of life.

A case more difficult to determine is presented by 31B125 (2 f.); in the
line preserved fully, the appearances of the two types of things in question
are different. Though the context is too uncertain for any firm conclusions
concerning usage, here perhaps for the first time, εἶδος is used absolutely,
that is to say without the qualification of e.g. a genitive, with the meaning
of 'type':

ἐκ μὲν γὰρ ζωῶν ἐτίθει νεκρὰ εἴδε' ἀμείβων,
<ἐκ δὲ νεκρῶν ζώοντα>.

Indeed, from living things he made dead ones, exchanging the types,
<and from dead living>.

It may be much safer, though, to assume that, while indeed used in an
absolute way, εἶδος is here, too, used in the sense of 'appearance':

Indeed, exchanging them, he made dead appearances from living ones,
<and from dead living>.[240]

But even if 31B125 is left aside altogether, it cannot be doubted that Empedocles employed εἶδος in the sense of 'type' without comment, explanation, or the suggestion that this use reflects innovative usage or a recent semantic development. The observations made on the occasion of the discussion of the Hippocratic writings above are thus to be seen as systematic rather than narrowly chronological; both the authors of the extant Hippocratic writings and Empedocles used material which had been used before, describing and setting it out in a language which had gradually evolved in a way suited to that material. It is not surprising that all stages of linguistic development should coexist in one and the same text, or collection of texts, especially where the text in question conservatively preserves traditional diction, as can be assumed for the Hippocratic corpus. Oral traditions of the craft of medicine contain layers of old or antiquated diction side by side with linguistic innovations, in the same way as legal or religious texts do. Thus, when one traces a supposed development of εἶδος within selected Hippocratic writings, it is not implied that this development took place for the first time in those chance survivals under scrutiny; it is rather the case that what has been reconstructed as a potential semantic development is reflected or survives in the passages discussed. The usage of the Hippocratic texts considered reflects a development which seems to have taken place, and in a sense come to a conclusion, by the time Empedocles composed his poem or poems.[241]

12. εἶδος in Thucydides

In all of Thucydides, there are six instances of the word εἶδος. His usage does not seem to be markedly different from what has been observed so far. There is, however, a slight development. On occasion, εἶδος refers to the appearance, not of an object but of an action or event.[242] Towards the end of his account of the fifth year of the war, in relating the events of the summer of 427 BC, Thucydides comments on how στάσις, 'civil strife', had become more common in communities all over Greece after Athens and Sparta had gone to war, since the opposing parties in the cities, democrats and oligarchs, could rely on help from those two cities respectively, as both of them were in need of allies. Thucydides continues (3.82.2):

καὶ ἐπέπεσε πολλὰ καὶ χαλεπὰ κατὰ στάσιν ταῖς πόλεσι, γιγνόμενα μὲν καὶ αἰεὶ ἐσόμενα, ἕως ἂν ἡ αὐτὴ φύσις ἀνθρώπων ᾖ, μᾶλλον δὲ καὶ ἡσυχαίτερα καὶ τοῖς εἴδεσι διηλλαγμένα, ὡς ἂν ἕκασται αἱ μεταβολαὶ τῶν ξυντυχιῶν ἐφιστῶνται. ἐν μὲν γὰρ εἰρήνῃ καὶ ἀγαθοῖς πράγμασιν αἵ τε πόλεις καὶ οἱ ἰδιῶται ἀμείνους τὰς γνώμας ἔχουσι διὰ τὸ μὴ ἐς ἀκουσίους ἀνάγκας πίπτειν· ὁ δὲ πόλεμος ὑφελὼν τὴν εὐπορίαν τοῦ καθ᾽ ἡμέραν βίαιος διδάσκαλος καὶ πρὸς τὰ παρόντα τὰς ὀργὰς τῶν πολλῶν ὁμοιοῖ.

And many hardships befell the cities in civil strife, as always come about and will always be, as long as the nature of men remains the same, yet more so, or less severe, or changed in their appearances, according to how all the several changes of fortune occur. Indeed, in peace and when things are well, both cities and individuals have better judgement because they do not fall into involuntary need; but war that takes away well-being of everyday life is a violent teacher and assimilates to current circumstances the emotions of the many.

The way in which circumstances, events that occur, appear as different, according to fortune, are the εἴδη, 'the appearances', of those events which are said to have changed.

This usage is in some ways parallel to Euripides, *Iphigenia in Tauris* 817. Orestes has just disclosed his identity to Iphigenia. In disbelief, she demands proof of identity. Orestes reports what, he says, he has been told by Electra: Iphigenia once wove a garment depicting the quarrel of their ancestors Atreus and Thyestes. Iphigenia agrees, and Orestes continues (816 f.):

ORESTES: εἰκώ τ' ἐν ἱστοῖς ἡλίου μετάστασιν.
IPHIGENIA: ὕφηνα καὶ τόδ' εἶδος εὐμίτοις πλοκαῖς.

ORESTES: And you depicted on the loom the sun's reversal.
IPHIGENIA: I wove also that 'appearance' with fine-threaded twinings.

Once εἶδος has been established with its absolute sense of 'an appearance', the word can be employed to refer to any thing thus denoted, the point of reference need not be a single object or a single living being; with Euripides, it is the appearance of an action, a snapshot of an event, which is referred to.[243]

While there is, I believe, no principal difference in usage with the Thucydidean example, it is nevertheless worth observing that in the case of Thucydides on the one hand what is referred to as being capable of different *appearances* has previously, at the beginning of the sentence, been denoted by a neuter plural adjective, i.e. the diction of the passage as a whole is in itself inherently more abstract; on the other hand, and more importantly, the 'events', γιγνόμενα, are many, and the syntax is undecided as to whether each and every event is different according to circumstances, or whether there are several types of events, a possibility which may be suggested by the way the next sentence continues that thought. Use of εἶδος as 'the appearance (of an action)'[244] is not far from that of εἶδος as 'the type (of an action)' and thus 'the way (something happens)'. Accordingly, one could translate as follows:

καὶ ἐπέπεσε πολλὰ καὶ χαλεπὰ κατὰ στάσιν ταῖς πόλεσι,…μᾶλλον δὲ καὶ ἡσυχαίτερα καὶ τοῖς εἴδεσι διηλλαγμένα, ὡς ἂν ἕκασται αἱ μεταβολαὶ τῶν ξυντυχιῶν ἐφιστῶνται.

And many hardships befell the cities in civil strife…yet more so, or less severe, or changed in their 'ways', according to how all the several changes of fortune occur.

It should be noted also that the phrasing of τοῖς εἴδεσι διηλλαγμένα is familiar from the medical writers. In *Airs, Waters and Places* 15, we encountered the phrase τὰ εἴδεα ἀπηλλαγμένα, and in 23 τὰ εἴδεα διηλλάχθαι; since the phrase φύσις ἀνθρώπων, too, is potentially reflecting medical usage, one can assume that 'with changed appearance(s)' or 'with changed type(s)' or 'changed in (respect of) their appearance(s)/type(s)' is also medical terminology.

What may appear as a further extension of the semantics of εἶδος, 'way' in addition to 'appearance' and 'type', is thus much less an innovation than may be suggested by the use of an altogether different term in English. The innovation in usage is application of the word εἶδος to an action or event, something dynamic, rather than to a static physical or corporeal body, object or thing. This move has not to the same extent taken place in English, so that in the majority of cases 'appearance' or 'appearances' would not serve as an idiomatic translation.[245]

It is, on the other hand, not surprising that clear cases of this new application occur at a time when εἶδος as 'type' is firmly established; in speaking of 'types' of things, one need not exclusively, or indeed not at all, refer to visual features of the things discussed. When εἶδος is used to denote 'the way' things happen, there may be a visual element to the action, event or scene referred to, as was the case with Euripides, *Iphigenia in Tauris*, 817; that, however, need not be so, and in the case of Thucydides 3.82.2 the difference in εἴδη of the hardships occurring is probably not primarily one of visual appearance. In that, application of εἶδος to events is more abstract and less concrete than the original application of the word to physical objects. This is in principle parallel to the degree of abstraction found with the use of εἶδος as referring to a 'type' of thing. Extension of applicability from things to events may have been prompted, but was definitely facilitated, by the more abstract meaning εἶδος had acquired in denoting 'type'.

The next instance of εἶδος to be considered, Thucydides 3.62, has in philological scholarship and practice been taken as evidence for a peculiar, separate meaning of the word. This appears to have been the result of an attempt to interpret too small a passage of text in isolation. In order to understand the force of the argument at 3.62, however, the wider context of the passage must be taken into account. The scene is that of the confrontation of Theban and Plataean opinion after the defeat of Plataea at the hands of the Spartans and their Theban allies. The Thebans plead for harsh punishment, rejecting the historical account given by the Plataeans to justify their allegiances. Having summarized events before the Persian wars, the Thebans continue:

ἐπειδὴ δὲ καὶ ὁ βάρβαρος ἦλθεν ἐπὶ τὴν Ἑλλάδα, φασὶ μόνοι Βοιωτῶν οὐ μηδίσαι, καὶ τούτῳ μάλιστα αὐτοί τε ἀγάλλονται καὶ ἡμᾶς λοιδοροῦσιν. ἡμεῖς δὲ μηδίσαι μὲν αὐτοὺς οὔ φαμεν διότι οὐδ' Ἀθηναίους, τῇ μέντοι αὐτῇ ἰδέα ὕστερον ἰόντων Ἀθηναίων ἐπὶ τοὺς Ἕλληνας μόνους αὖ Βοιωτῶν ἀττικίσαι.

καίτοι σκέψασθε ἐν οἵῳ εἴδει ἑκάτεροι ἡμῶν τοῦτο ἔπραξαν. ἡμῖν μὲν γὰρ ἡ πόλις τότε ἐτύγχανεν οὔτε κατ' ὀλιγαρχίαν ἰσόνομον πολιτεύουσα οὔτε κατὰ δημοκρατίαν· ὅπερ δέ ἐστι νόμοις μὲν καὶ τῷ σωφρονεστάτῳ ἐναντιώτατον, ἐγγυτάτω δὲ τυράννου, δυναστεία ὀλίγων ἀνδρῶν εἶχε τὰ πράγματα.

Subsequently, during the foreign invasion of Hellas, they say that they were the only state in Boeotia which did not collaborate with the Persians. This is the point which they use most frequently for their self-glorification and for deriding us. We say that the only reason why they did not collaborate was that the Athenians did not do so either, and, following up the same principle, we shall find that when the Athenians began to attack the liberties of Hellas, Plataea was the only state in Boeotia which collaborated with Athens.

Consider, too, what type of government we each had at the time of these events. Our constitution then was not an oligarchy, giving all men equal rights before the law, nor was it a democracy: power was in the hands of a small group of powerful men, and this is the form of government nearest to dictatorship and farthest removed from law and the virtues of moderation.   (tr. Warner)

I quote Warner's translation because it seems to me to represent a majority opinion on the meaning of εἶδος in this passage. The Greek sentence in question, καίτοι σκέψασθε ἐν οἵῳ εἴδει ἑκάτεροι ἡμῶν τοῦτο ἔπραξαν, is rendered on the basis of the immediately following statement as: 'Consider, too, what type of government we each had at the time of these events.' A reasoning behind this translation may run along the following lines. The Thebans, in giving their version of events, try to justify their actions during the Persian wars two generations before, contrasting their own situation with that of the Plataeans who, they say, were 'atticizing' then as they are now. They, the Thebans, however, had hard times. καίτοι σκέψασθε ἐν οἵῳ εἴδει ἑκάτεροι ἡμῶν τοῦτο ἔπραξαν. 'Yet, see also in what sort of εἶδος each of us [two states] acted.' This announcement, the argument runs, is followed by an account of constitutional matters at Thebes at the time, and therefore εἶδος here must mean something like 'type of government', 'constitution'.[246]

If that were so, we would be justified in our expectation to find next a contrasting description of the 'constitution' of the Plataeans at the time, since the Thebans had announced that they would show in what εἶδος each of the two parties acted. As we read on, however, we find nothing of the sort, apart, perhaps, from the one phrase not central to the Theban argumentation, that the Plataeans acted ἔχοντες…τοὺς νόμους οὕσπερ μέχρι τοῦ δεῦρο, 'having just those laws which you have to this day' (64.3). While, I maintain, this phrase is not central to their argumentation, its context provides the point the Thebans want to stress, the point to which they have led up from 62.3 onwards. In 64.3, the Thebans criticize the involvement on the part of the Plataeans in action against Aegina, where they supported the Athenians instead of preventing the campaign: καὶ ταῦτα οὔτε ἄκοντες ἔχοντές τε τοὺς νόμους οὔσπερ μέχρι τοῦ δεῦρο καὶ οὐδενὸς ὑμᾶς βιασαμένου ὥσπερ ἡμᾶς. 'And that [you did] not unwillingly, and having just those laws which you have to this day, and while there was nobody forcing you as was the case with us.' The double opposition central to this part of the Thebans' speech is that of ἑκόντες – ἄκοντες and οὐ βιαζόμενοι – βιαζόμενοι, 'willingly – unwillingly' and 'not-forced – forced'. It culminates in the sentence concluding this section of the argument (64.5): τὰ μὲν οὖν ἐς τὸν ἡμέτερόν τε ἀκούσιον μηδισμὸν καὶ τὸν ὑμέτερον ἑκούσιον ἀττικισμὸν τοιαῦτα ἀποφαίνομεν. 'Such are the things we advance as regards our unwilling Medizing and your willing Atticizing.' This point has been carefully prepared in the intervening section of the text. At 62.4, the Thebans claim with regard to their own city: ...καὶ ἡ ξύμπασα πόλις οὐκ αὐτοκράτωρ οὖσα ἑαυτῆς τοῦτ' ἔπραξεν, '...and that the city did while as a whole not exercising power over its own affairs'. In this sentence, οὐκ αὐτοκράτωρ οὖσα ἑαυτῆς is equivalent to ἄκοντες καὶ βιαζόμενοι. The word ἄκοντες itself occurs a few paragraphs later, when the Plataeans are accused of collaboration; had they entered into an alliance with the Athenians solely for purposes of defence against Thebes, they could have refrained from joining aggressive Athenian ventures and could have counted on Spartan help since they had been allies of the Spartans from the time of the Persian wars; the Thebans allege the Plataeans would have done so (63.2): εἴ τι καὶ ἄκοντες προσήγεσθε ὑπ' Ἀθηναίων – 'if in any way you were brought forward by the Athenians against your will.' And in the next sentence that is reinforced by: ἀλλ' ἑκόντες καὶ οὐ βιαζόμενοι ἔτι εἵλεσθε μᾶλλον τὰ Ἀθηναίων, 'but willingly and not forced you eagerly chose the side of Athens.'

This, then, is the context in which the statement καίτοι σκέψασθε ἐν οἵῳ εἴδει ἑκάτεροι ἡμῶν τοῦτο ἔπραξαν must be read. The argument of the Thebans is: where they themselves acted against Greece, that happened involuntarily and when they were forced to do so; where the Plataeans acted together with the Athenians against Greece, that happened voluntarily and without anybody forcing them to do so.[247] Thus, the Thebans' introductory advice to the Spartans is: 'Yet, consider in which "way" each one of us did that.' Constitutional considerations play only a subordinate role in an argument that serves to establish that one party acted in a voluntary manner, the other forced by one thing or another. Use of εἶδος as 'the way' in which something happens or is done is the same as that observed at 3.82.2. εἶδος at 3.62.3 neither refers to the 'situation' of the two parties involved in general, nor to their 'type of government' or 'constitution' in particular.

We have seen that Thucydides on occasion uses εἶδος in the sense of 'manner' or 'way (in which something is done)', and how this usage may have developed on the one hand by extension of application from 'appearance (of a thing)' to 'appearance (of an action)', prompted on the other hand by the use of εἶδος meaning 'type (of person)', 'type (of thing)' from which could be derived, again by way of extension of application, 'type (of action)', 'manner or way (of acting)'.

On that basis, the two instances of εἶδος in Book 2 present no difficulties, bearing in mind that what in translation may suggest two, three, or more different meanings of the one word εἶδος need not have been viewed as such by Thucydides and his original readership. By 2.50.1 Thucydides has given a detailed account of the way the epidemic of 430 BC affected people, giving both the symptoms of the disease and in particular the order in which they occurred. Those who survived an attack did so only with loss of limbs or of eye-sight or of memory. He continues:

γενόμενον γὰρ κρεῖσσον λόγου τὸ εἶδος τῆς νόσου, τά τε ἄλλα χαλεπωτέρως ἢ κατὰ τὴν ἀνθρωπείαν φύσιν προσέπιπτεν ἑκάστῳ καὶ ἐν τῷδε ἐδήλωσε μάλιστα ἄλλο τι ὂν ἢ τῶν ξυντρόφων τι…

Indeed, the way of the disease having become greater than an account <could tell>, it also otherwise befell everybody harder than is fit for human nature, but in the following <respect> it was most clear that it was something other than any of the indigenous <diseases>…

I take γενόμενον γὰρ κρεῖσσον λόγου τὸ εἶδος τῆς νόσου as a free nominative preceding the main clause whose implied subject is νόσος, with προσέπιπτεν as predicate; that is to say, the *disease* befell the people, not the εἶδος of the disease. The εἶδος of the disease is here on the one hand the 'way' it took, on the other hand its 'appearance' in the sense of its manifestation in the various symptoms so vividly and visually described by Thucydides in the preceding paragraphs.[248] It would perhaps not be altogether incorrect to translate τὸ εἶδος τῆς νόσου as 'the type of the disease'; one would have to bear in mind, though, that, as discussed previously, 'type' on the whole is a much more abstract term in English than εἶδος is here. 2.50.1 is a particularly good example of how and why translation is impossible; 'way', 'manner', 'appearance', 'type', all capture aspects of what εἶδος entails, and it can be demonstrated with a fair degree of precision how the word came to denote all those things; nevertheless, not one of the English terms has remotely the same range of connotations as the Greek word has.

The next occurrence of εἶδος to be considered, preceding the previous instance by a few chapters, may at first seem slightly less straightforward. Half way through his funeral oration (2.35–46), Pericles captures what is to him the essence of Athenian nature and culture (2.41.1):

ξυνελών τε λέγω τήν τε πᾶσαν πόλιν τῆς Ἑλλάδος παίδευσιν εἶναι καὶ καθ᾽

ἕκαστον δοκεῖν ἄν μοι τὸν αὐτὸν ἄνδρα παρ' ἡμῶν ἐπὶ πλεῖστ' ἂν εἴδη καὶ μετὰ χαρίτων μάλιστ' ἂν εὐτραπέλως τὸ σῶμα αὔταρκες παρέχεσθαι.

And, in summary, I declare that the whole city is an education to Greece, and that it seems to me that with us, in each and every case, the same man possesses a body in <the> most ways <possible>[249] and, with grace, most seemingly[250] self-sufficient.

In this sentence, ἐπὶ πλεῖστ' ἂν εἴδη...αὔταρκες could, I believe, either mean 'in the most ways possible...self-sufficient' or, construing the preposition more strictly, 'self-sufficient for the most εἴδη'; if the latter were a possible way of construing the sentence, one would have to posit absolute use of εἶδος, or at least of the plural εἴδη; the word would have acquired a meaning like 'type(s) of action' or 'way(s) of acting', or else 'type(s) of task' or 'type(s) of situation', i.e. what was supplied in the text with the examples discussed above has here become part of the meaning of the word itself. But since there is no necessity of construing the sentence this way, one should, in the absence of unambiguous instances of this usage elsewhere, be wary of adopting this explanation, which would require the positing of a major semantic development.

That stage of semantic development may have been reached, however, towards the end of Thucydides' work, assuming that, roughly speaking, composition of the account of the war proceeded on the whole from the first to the last book. The same, apparently idiomatic, expression containing εἶδος is found at 6.77.2 and then at 8.56.2. At 6.77.2 Hermocrates from Syracuse declares in a speech at Camarina that all Sicilians should oppose Athens together; he presents the alternative in the form of a question:

ἢ μένομεν ἕως ἂν ἕκαστοι κατὰ πόλεις ληφθῶμεν, εἰδότες ὅτι ταύτῃ μόνον ἁλωτοί ἐσμεν καὶ ὁρῶντες αὐτοὺς ἐπὶ τοῦτο τὸ εἶδος τρεπομένους ὥστε τοὺς μὲν λόγοις ἡμῶν διιστάναι, τοὺς δὲ ξυμμάχων ἐλπίδι ἐκπολεμοῦν πρὸς ἀλλήλους, τοῖς δὲ ὡς ἑκάστοις τι προσηνὲς λέγοντες δύνανται κακουργεῖν;

Or should we wait until all of us are defeated, city by city, knowing that in such a way alone are we conquerable and seeing them turning to just that εἶδος, <namely> that some of us they make oppose each other with the help of words, some they make fight each other creating the expectation of military support, some they manage to harm by saying something soothing to each of them <severally>.

At 8.56.2 the Athenian general Pisander arrives at the camp of the Persian satrap Tissaphernes after Athenian victory over Chios; Alcibiades, who is with Tissaphernes, wants to return to Athens, but sees that his time has not come yet since Tissaphernes is likely not to take sides against Sparta as yet:

Ἀλκιβιάδης δέ - οὐ γὰρ αὐτῷ πάνυ τὰ ἀπὸ Τισσαφέρνους βέβαια ἦν, φοβουμένου τοὺς Πελοποννησίους μᾶλλον καὶ ἔτι βουλομένου, καθάπερ καὶ ὑπ’ ἐκείνου ἐδιδάσκετο, τρίβειν ἀμφοτέρους – τρέπεται ἐπὶ τοιόνδε εἶδος ὥστε τὸν Τισσαφέρνην ὡς μέγιστα αἰτοῦντα παρὰ τῶν Ἀθηναίων μὴ ξυμβῆναι.

But Alcibiades – indeed, things from Tissaphernes’ side did not seem quite decided to him, also according to what he himself had taught <Tissaphernes>: to let them [Athens and Sparta] extirpate each other – Alcibiades turned to such an εἶδος, <namely> that Tissaphernes would not get together with the Athenians by demanding too much from them.

Obviously, translating εἶδος with ‘way’ here is not wholly satisfactory; ‘way of action’ or ‘way of acting’ would probably make the meaning clearer. A planned, considered ‘way of acting’, a sequence of actions in that sense, may be called a ‘scheme’, and perhaps ‘scheme’ is acceptable as translation for εἶδος in these two cases where a phrase ἐπὶ τοῦτο τὸ εἶδος τρεπομένους or τρέπεται ἐπὶ τοιόνδε εἶδος is followed by ὥστε, rendered above as ‘namely that’; in both cases the subordinate clause is factitive rather than consecutive, the ὥστε clause states the content of the εἶδος to which people turn, which is the content of their intentions and actions, rather than giving the consequence or resulting event or state of affairs which comes about after people have turned to a certain εἶδος.

In a sense, it does not matter whether one settles for ‘way of acting’ or ‘way of action’, or rather for ‘scheme’; the latter, however, has the advantage of being one word rather than a phrase, and therefore, if it could be shown that εἶδος had in some contexts the connotations of ‘scheme’, that word might be preferable as a translation which could help preserving not only the general meaning, but also the tone of a passage. Confirmation that the meaning of εἶδος could indeed approximate ‘scheme’ is provided by the remaining instance of εἶδος in Thucydides. In his account of the events of the summer of 411, Thucydides outlines the various considerations different factions of the Four Hundred held when it looked as if Alcibiades’ return to Athens was imminent. Many tried to dissociate themselves from the radical regime, so that, although being part of the oligarchic government, they would be considered as reformers and would, by introducing a real rule of the Five Thousand, be immune from punishment. But, so says Thucydides, most of them proposed that course of action for the sake of their own political advancement alone, as is typical with oligarchies; looking at Alcibiades, they wanted to achieve the position of sole ruler for themselves. There were others who wanted to uphold the current system. Over against the reform party and their plans, these others are characterized by Thucydides in the following words (8.90.1):

οἱ δὲ τῶν τετρακοσίων μάλιστα ἐναντίοι ὄντες τῷ τοιούτῳ εἴδει καὶ προεστῶτες…

But those of the Forty who were most opposed to such a way of acting, and
their leaders...

And he continues by relating that this faction sent for help to Sparta, and
that they fortified portions of the city walls.[251] Here εἶδος refers to a whole
course of action retrospectively. The reason why this passage may support
a rendering of εἶδος with 'scheme' here is that before Thucydides brands the
proposals of the reformers as born out of self-interest alone, he refers to them
by saying (89.3):

ἦν δὲ τοῦτο τὸ σχῆμα πολιτικὸν τοῦ λόγου αὐτοῖς...

That was the political (or: constitutional) scheme of their proposal [252]...

'Scheme', of course, is here used without any intended connotations of
deviousness.[253]

The connections of Thucydides' method and diction with those of the
Hippocratic writings have been stated repeatedly; the particular use of
εἶδος as 'way of acting' or 'scheme', however, seems to have been general
Attic rather than a specialized usage adopted by Thucydides for his own
reasons. A passage in Aristophanes' *Plutus* which, though undoubtedly later
in composition than the last Book of Thucydides' history, is free from any
medical or otherwise specialized vocabulary, confirms this: Chremylus has
invited Plutus into his house and has sent off Cario to fetch the old men
from the fields; Cario summons them, and there is an entertaining interlude
in which the chorus of old men assume different roles from mythology: they
and Cario mockingly threaten each other with punishments associated with
those mythical characters; they are acting as if they were a chorus, in one
case at least a chorus in a Satyr play; this goes on to mutual amusement until
Cario puts an end to it by saying (316–18)

ἀλλ' εἶα νῦν τῶν σκωμμάτων ἀπαλλαγέντες ἤδη
ὑμεῖς ἐπ' ἄλλ' εἶδος τρέπεσθ',
ἐγὼ δ' ἰὼν...

But well now, stopping those jests right now,
turn to another way (of behaving and acting),
but I will go and...

Cario tells the chorus to behave differently, to 'turn to another εἶδος'. Given
that Thucydides can use the phrase in the same way, I see no need to look for
any connections that εἶδος in that sense could have with 'acting a part' in the
passage quoted from Aristophanes. We do not know how common a phrase
ἐπὶ ἄλλο/τοῦτο/τοιοῦτον εἶδος τρέπεσθαι was, but it seems to have been part
of common Attic usage.[254]

With Thucydides, the first Attic prose author to have been considered here, εἶδος is thus fairly consistently applied to actions, often qualified as 'this' or 'that' or 'another'; it seems to denote a 'type (of action)', a 'way (of acting)', and then a 'scheme' or 'way or type of action or acting'; that this usage may be colloquial Attic is confirmed by Aristophanes. As we have seen, this development is a natural extension of application of εἶδος to an action instead of to a thing, facilitated by use of the word as denoting 'type' in addition to 'appearance'.

13. εἶδος in early dialogues of Plato

Turning to Plato's own use of the word εἶδος,[255] it is not surprising to find almost all the shades of meaning, or all the various senses which εἶδος had acquired over the centuries, given that the dialogues vary so widely in tone, subject matter, and most of all in interlocutors. On the whole, though, εἶδος is as frequent or as rare a word in Plato's early dialogues as it is, on average, with Herodotus, Thucydides or the orators.

What has been identified above as the earliest usage, εἶδος as referring to a person's appearance, found in particular in contexts of praise of a person, occurs naturally in the aristocratic Athenian circles in which most of the early conversations of Socrates are set. Praise of a youth's pleasing appearance is found at the beginning of more than one dialogue. Thus, when Socrates enquires at the beginning of the *Lysis* with whom Hippothales, an acquaintance of his, is enamoured, and when thereupon Ctesippus – instead of his unexpectedly bashful friend – in answer supplies the name of Lysis, and Socrates confesses not to have heard of a youth answering to that name, Ctesippus declares (204e3–6):

οὐ γὰρ πάνυ, ἔφη, τὶ αὐτοῦ τοὔνομα λέγουσιν, ἀλλ᾽ ἔτι πατρόθεν ἐπονομάζεται διὰ τὸ σφόδρα τὸν πατέρα γιγνώσκεσθαι αὐτοῦ. ἐπεὶ εὖ οἶδ᾽ ὅτι πολλοῦ δεῖς τὸ εἶδος ἀγνοεῖν τοῦ παιδός· ἱκανὸς γὰρ καὶ ἀπὸ μόνου τούτου γιγνώσκεσθαι.

Not very much indeed, he said, do they use his name, but he is still named[256] after his father, due to his father's being so well known. For I know well that you are far from not knowing the boy's appearance; he is capable indeed of being recognized even from that alone.

A parallel instance of εἶδος denoting guise or appearance is Charmides 154d5. The setting is again a palaestra; this time Socrates, having just returned from a military campaign, had asked more generally whether there was any youth distinguished in intelligence or beauty or both; when Charmides was announced and had entered, so Socrates reports, he seemed to him wondrous as to size and beauty, ἐκεῖνος ἐμοὶ θαυμαστὸς ἐφάνη τό τε μέγεθος καὶ τὸ κάλλος (c1). When all, old and young, were overwhelmed,

Chaerepho addressed Socrates (d1–2):

> τί σοι φαίνεται ὁ νεανίσκος…ὦ Σώκρατες; οὐκ εὐπρόσωπος;

> How does the youth seem to you, Socrates? … Not handsome of face?

And when Socrates agrees strongly, Chaerepho continues (d4–5):

> οὗτος μέντοι…εἰ ἐθέλοι ἀποδῦναι, δόξει σοι ἀπρόσωπος εἶναι· οὕτως τὸ εἶδος πάγκαλός ἐστιν.

> Yet, were he willing to undress, he would seem to you to be without face: so all-beautiful of appearance is he.

To that, all agree. Charmides is τὸ εἶδος πάγκαλος, 'all-beautiful of appearance or guise'; or maybe 'beautiful as to his whole appearance', not only as to his face.[257] Socrates gives a twist to that answer by exclaiming that Charmides would be well-nigh invincible if only he were in addition τὴν ψυχὴν…εὖ πεφυκώς, 'by nature well endowed as to his soul' (e1). Critias, aristocrat and uncle to Charmides, eagerly asserts with aristocratic terminology that this is the case (e4): ἀλλ᾽…πάνυ καλὸς καὶ ἀγαθός ἐστιν καὶ ταῦτα. 'But…he is very 'beautiful and good' as to that as well.' Thereupon Socrates suggests (e5–6):

> τί οὖν…οὐκ ἀπεδύσαμεν αὐτοῦ αὐτὸ τοῦτο καὶ ἐθεασάμεθα πρότερον τοῦ εἴδους;

> What then…wouldn't we rather undress of him just that <element> and look at it before looking at his appearance.

Just as in the case of this last example a person's appearance is contrasted with his soul, so, on one occasion in the *Protagoras*, Socrates – in providing a model for how he would like his discussion with Protagoras to proceed – sets a person's appearance against τὰ τοῦ σώματος ἔργα, 'functions of the body', which are not necessarily purely visible or physical (352a1–6):

> ἆρ᾽ οὖν, ἦν δ᾽ ἐγώ, τῇδέ πῃ καταφανὲς ἂν ἡμῖν γένοιτο; ὥσπερ εἴ τις ἄνθρωπον σκοπῶν ἐκ τοῦ εἴδους ἢ πρὸς ὑγίειαν ἢ πρὸς ἄλλο τι τῶν τοῦ σώματος ἔργων, ἰδὼν τὸ πρόσωπον καὶ τὰς χεῖρας ἄκρας εἴποι· 'ἴθι δή μοι ἀποκαλύψας καὶ τὰ στήθη καὶ τὸ μετάφρενον ἐπίδειξον, ἵνα ἐπισκέψωμαι σαφέστερον,' καὶ ἐγὼ τοιοῦτόν τι ποθῶ πρὸς τὴν σκέψιν…

> Now, could things perhaps, said I, somehow become clear in the following way? Just as somebody examining a man from his appearance with a view either to health or to another one of the functions of the body, seeing his face and his hands,[258] may say: 'Come on, then, undress and show me also your chest and your midriff, so that I may examine you more clearly', so I, too, long for some such thing for <our> examination…

This is an important example of εἶδος clearly denoting 'appearance' of a person as a whole, comprising appearance of the face and the hands as well as appearance of chest and midriff. A person is, in respect of his εἶδος, compared to an animal in Meno's famous comparison of Socrates with the torpedo fish or electric ray whose Greek name is 'numbness' (*Meno* 80a4–7):

καὶ δοκεῖς μοι παντελῶς, εἰ δεῖ τι καὶ σκῶψαι, ὁμοιότατος εἶναι τό τε εἶδος καὶ τἆλλα ταύτῃ τῇ πλατείᾳ νάρκῃ τῇ θαλαττίᾳ· καὶ γὰρ αὕτη τὸν ἀεὶ πλησιάζοντα καὶ ἁπτόμενον ναρκᾶν ποιεῖ...

And you seem to me in everything – if mocking, too, is in order at times – to be, both in appearance and otherwise, most similar to that flat ray, the sea fish: indeed, that too makes numb whoever comes close and touches.

There is one instance of εἶδος as applied to the appearance of an object. In that section of the *Gorgias* in which Socrates fervently discusses with Callicles what rhetoric really is, he draws at one point a comparison between what the orator does and what craftsmen do (503d6–e7):[259]

φέρε γάρ, ὁ ἀγαθὸς ἀνὴρ καὶ ἐπὶ τὸ βέλτιστον λέγων, ἃ ἂν λέγῃ ἄλλο τι οὐκ εἰκῇ ἐρεῖ, ἀλλ᾽ ἀποβλέπων πρός τι·[260] ὥσπερ καὶ οἱ ἄλλοι πάντες δημιουργοὶ βλέποντες πρὸς τὸ αὑτῶν ἔργον ἕκαστος οὐκ εἰκῇ ἐκλεγόμενος προσφέρει <ἃ προσφέρει>, ἀλλ᾽ ὅπως ἂν εἶδός τι αὐτῷ σχῇ τοῦτο ὃ ἐργάζεται. οἷον εἰ βούλει ἰδεῖν τοὺς ζωγράφους, τοὺς οἰκοδόμους, τοὺς ναυπηγούς, τοὺς ἄλλους πάντας δημιουργούς, ὅντινα βούλει αὐτῶν, ὡς εἰς τάξιν τινὰ ἕκαστος ἕκαστον τίθησιν ὃ ἂν τιθῇ...

Come, now, the good man and the one who speaks to the best <end>, will, of course, say whatever he says not at random, but looking at something: just as all the other craftsmen as well,[261] looking at their own work, produce, each of them, what they produce not selecting <things> at random, but so that <the things> they are working at have a certain appearance. For example, if you want to see the painters, the builders, the shipwrights, all the other craftsmen, whomsoever of them you want, how each one of them puts whatever he deals with into a certain order...

The craftsmen listed subsequently do all produce something, some object that can be seen. This object is to have 'a certain appearance', εἶδός τι, and that appearance which is to be achieved is to be envisaged and aimed at in the process of production. The knowledgeable craftsman knows what the finished product will look like, he knows its εἶδος, its 'looks' or 'appearance'.[262]

There are, likewise, examples of εἶδος as 'type' or 'way'. In his conversation with Gorgias about Gorgias' profession, a conversation in which nothing is taken for granted, Socrates had obtained a preliminary answer (454b5–7):

ταύτης τοίνυν τῆς πειθοῦς λέγω [τὴν ῥητορικὴν εἶναι τέχνην], ὦ Σώκρατες, τῆς ἐν τοῖς δικαστηρίοις καὶ ἐν τοῖς ἄλλοις ὄχλοις, ὥσπερ καὶ ἄρτι ἔλεγον, καὶ περὶ τούτων ἅ ἐστι δίκαιά τε καὶ ἄδικα.

I say, now, Socrates, that [rhetoric is the art] of that persuasion which <has its place> in the law-courts and in other crowds, such as I have just mentioned, and which is about the things that are just and unjust.

Upon that, Socrates draws a distinction between μεμαθηκέναι and πεπιστευκέναι, 'having understood' something and 'having gained trust in' something,[263] and when Gorgias agrees he continues (454e1–5):

ἀλλὰ μὴν οἵ τέ γε[264] μεμαθηκότες πεπεισμένοι εἰσὶν καὶ οἱ πεπιστευκότες. – ἔστι ταῦτα. – βούλει οὖν δύο εἴδη θῶμεν πειθοῦς, τὸ μὲν πίστιν παρεχόμενον ἄνευ τοῦ εἰδέναι, τὸ δ' ἐπιστήμην; – πάνυ γε.

But yet, persuaded <of something> are certainly both those who have understood <something> and those who have gained trust <in something>. – That is so. – Now, do you want us to posit two types of persuasion, the one conveying trust without knowledge, the other <conveying> understanding?[265] – Most certainly.

Later on in the same dialogue, Socrates alludes in irony to that differentiation in dealing with Gorgias' pupil Polus, whose manners are much less dignified and refined than those of his master. When Polus – after previously laying down the law on how to lead a discussion – laughs off one of Socrates' representations, Socrates replies (473e2–3):

ἄλλο αὖ τοῦτο εἶδος ἐλέγχου ἐστίν, ἐπειδάν τίς τι εἴπῃ, καταγελᾶν, ἐλέγχειν δὲ μή;

Is that another type of proof[266] again, when somebody says something, to laugh it off, but not to disprove it?

This seems indeed to be an allusion and not just a chance repetition of εἶδος in a vaguely similar context; for although there is nothing surprising about the use of εἶδος as meaning 'type' with either Plato or, if one is inclined to believe that Plato's Socrates is using Gorgianic diction, Gorgias himself towards the end of the fifth century BC, to speak of δύο εἴδη πειθοῦς or of an εἶδος ἐλέγχου has something technical about it.

Less confirmation than could be expected is found in the diction of that great follower of Gorgias, Isocrates.[267] In his speech *Against the Sophists*, written about 390 BC and at least implicitly alluded to elsewhere in the *Gorgias*,[268] Isocrates explains in detail how to compose speeches; learning the various elements by heart is not difficult (16), but choosing from them and arranging them appropriately requires a good teacher and good natural abilities (17),

...καὶ δεῖν τὸν μὲν μαθητὴν πρὸς τῷ τὴν φύσιν ἔχειν οἵαν χρὴ τὰ μὲν εἴδη τὰ τῶν λόγων μαθεῖν...

...and it is necessary that the learner in addition to having the requisite nature learns the types of speeches.

This, however, refers to different types of speeches delivered for different purposes and on different occasions. A context similar to that is found in the *Protagoras* at that point where Socrates feels he has to cut short his discussion with Protagoras because they cannot agree on how to proceed with question and answer; in particular, Socrates proclaims that he cannot cope with long speeches, and he requests that since Protagoras claims to be able to lead any kind of conversation, Protagoras should comply. Callias, Alcibiades and Critias intervene, then Prodicus and Hippias, the other two famous sophists present, each give a brief address to convince Socrates and Protagoras to continue. Hippias argues for a compromise (337e2–338a5):

ἐγὼ μὲν οὖν καὶ δέομαι καὶ συμβουλεύω, ὦ Πρωταγόρα τε καὶ Σώκρατες, συμβῆναι ὑμᾶς ὥσπερ ὑπὸ διαιτητῶν ἡμῶν συμβιβαζόντων εἰς τὸ μέσον, καὶ μήτε σὲ τὸ ἀκριβὲς τοῦτο εἶδος τῶν διαλόγων ζητεῖν τὸ κατὰ βραχὺ λίαν, εἰ μὴ ἡδὺ Πρωταγόρᾳ, ἀλλ' ἐφεῖναι καὶ χαλάσαι τὰς ἡνίας τοῖς λόγοις, ἵνα μεγαλοπρεπέστεροι καὶ εὐσχημονέστεροι ἡμῖν φαίνωνται, μήτ' αὖ Πρωταγόραν πάντα κάλων ἐκτείναντα, οὐρίᾳ ἐφέντα, φεύγειν εἰς τὸ πέλαγος τῶν λόγων ἀποκρύψαντα γῆν, ἀλλὰ μέσον τι ἀμφοτέρους τεμεῖν.

Now, I for one ask and advise, Protagoras and Socrates, that you come together in front of us, who gather as arbiters, and that neither you seek that extreme type of conversation with very short <questions and answers>, if that is not pleasant to Protagoras, but to let loose and relax the reins for your words, so that they seem to us grander and in better shape, nor again, I call upon Protagoras, may he, stretching out everything, letting loose with a fair wind, flee to the sea of words, hiding from sight the land, but that both somehow cut <through the sea of words>[269] in the middle.

τὸ ἀκριβὲς τοῦτο εἶδος τῶν διαλόγων, 'that extreme type of conversation', is set against a stretched-out way of speaking, for ἐκτείνειν, the hinge on which Hippias' metaphor hangs, can be used for drawing out one's speech. Since both λόγος and διάλογος are nouns closely connected to the verbs λέγειν and διαλέγεσθαι which express the actions of 'speaking' and 'conversing', those εἴδη τῶν διαλόγων are 'types of conversation' and 'ways of conversing'; but whereas in translation the one pays more attention to the nominal, static quality of a διάλογος as an event, the other more to its verbal, dynamic quality as a process, there is no such differentiation in the Greek.

The next occurrence of εἶδος to be considered may just be another instance of εἶδος meaning 'type', but there are difficulties which oppose that neat solution. The *Laches* is a report of a discussion about education between the two Athenian generals Nicias and Laches; the two have been consulted by Lysimachus, son of Aristides, and Melesias, son of Thucydides, who are uncertain how to educate their own two sons. When Socrates is drawn into that conversation by Laches, he shifts the focus from particular pieces and devices of education to why education takes place in the first place, and what it is concerned with. They agree that education is concerned with the soul, with excellence in the soul. And since the conversation arose from watching a display in arms, Socrates suggests that they first look at ἀνδρεία, 'courage'. When Laches replies that 'courage is fighting in battle without leaving one's rank', Socrates agrees but asks if there is not courage in flight as well, as in the fighting techniques of the Scythians, or as Homer reports of Aeneas in the *Iliad*. To that, Laches replies (191b4–7):

καὶ καλῶς γε, ὦ Σώκρατες· περὶ ἁρμάτων γὰρ ἔλεγε. καὶ σὺ τὸ τῶν Σκύθων ἱππέων πέρι λέγεις· τὸ μὲν γὰρ ἱππικὸν [τὸ ἐκείνων] οὕτω μάχεται, τὸ δὲ ὁπλιτικὸν [τό γε τῶν Ἑλλήνων], ὡς ἐγὼ λέγω.

And rightly so, Socrates: indeed, he spoke about chariots. And what you mention of the Scythians is about horsemen. Indeed, cavalry fights in that manner, but infantry as I said.

After a brief modification of that statement by Laches, Socrates resumes (191c7–e2):

τοῦτο τοίνυν ὃ ἄρτι ἔλεγον, ὅτι ἐγὼ αἴτιος μὴ καλῶς σε ἀποκρίνασθαι, ὅτι οὐ καλῶς ἠρόμην – βουλόμενος γάρ σου πυθέσθαι μὴ μόνον τοὺς ἐν τῷ ὁπλιτικῷ ἀνδρείους, ἀλλὰ καὶ τοὺς ἐν τῷ ἱππικῷ καὶ ἐν σύμπαντι τῷ πολεμικῷ εἴδει, καὶ μὴ μόνον τοὺς ἐν τῷ πολέμῳ, ἀλλὰ καὶ τοὺς ἐν τοῖς πρὸς τὴν θάλατταν κινδύνοις ἀνδρείους ὄντας, καὶ ὅσοι γε πρὸς νόσους καὶ ὅσοι πρὸς πενίας ἢ καὶ πρὸς τὰ πολιτικὰ ἀνδρεῖοί εἰσιν, καὶ ἔτι αὖ μὴ μόνον ὅσοι πρὸς λύπας ἀνδρεῖοί εἰσιν ἢ φόβους, ἀλλὰ καὶ πρὸς ἐπιθυμίας ἢ ἡδονὰς δεινοὶ μάχεσθαι καὶ μένοντες καὶ ἀναστρέφοντες – εἰσὶ γάρ πού τινες, ὦ Λάχης, καὶ ἐν τοῖς τοιούτοις ἀνδρεῖοι.

Now, that is what I said just now, that it is my fault that you do not answer well, because I did not put the question well – indeed, I meant to learn from you not only who is courageous in infantry fighting, but also who is courageous in cavalry fighting and in the whole type of fighting in war, and not only those courageous in war, but also those courageous in the face of dangers at sea, and those who are courageous in the face of diseases, and poverty, and politics, and moreover again not only those who are courageous in the face of griefs and fears, but also in the face of desires and pleasures, strong in fighting them, both keeping in rank and turning around against them – indeed, there are somehow those, Laches, courageous in such things, too.

One could interpret this explanation by Socrates as containing a classificatory scheme not too dissimilar in nature from those in the *Sophist* and the *Politicus*. This is suggested in particular by the repeated use of nominalized neuter adjectives in -ικον. Now, in both those late dialogues, the nouns εἶδος and γένος are used with reference to items at various levels of such classificatory schemes.[270] Therefore encountering εἶδος in the phrase ἐν σύμπαντι τῷ πολεμικῷ εἴδει does not surprise; τὸ πολεμικὸν εἶδος or τὸ εἶδος τοῦ πολεμικοῦ is one type of pursuit or situation, here opposed to being faced with danger at sea, illness, poverty, politics. In all those different types of situation men can be courageous or otherwise. Courage in battle is thus only one type of courage, and – as we learn subsequently – only one type of courage-in-the-face-of-hardships, as opposed to courage-in-the-face-of-pleasures. In view of that, it could be argued that showing courage ἐν τῷ ὁπλιτικῷ, 'in infantry-fighting', ἐν τῷ ἱππικῷ, 'in cavalry-fighting', ἐν τῷ περὶ ἁρμάτων, 'in chariot-fighting', are three different types, three different εἴδη of courage in three different types or εἴδη of fighting in war.

If that were so, there would be some slight oddities in the structure of Socrates' picture of where we find courageous men. The nominalized neuter adjectives are in themselves not uncommon in late fifth- early fourth-century philosophical discourse.[271] So there is nothing unusual about Laches', not Socrates', introducing τὸ ἱππικόν and τὸ ὁπλιτικόν, nor in Socrates' picking up those terms. But Socrates does not speak about courage ἐν τῷ ὁπλιτικῷ καὶ ἐν τῷ ἱππικῷ καὶ ἐν ἄλλῳ τινὶ πολεμικῷ εἴδει (or: ...ἐν ἄλλῳ τινὶ εἴδει τοῦ πολεμικοῦ), 'in infantry-fighting and cavalry-fighting and any other type of fighting in war'. Instead, he calls τὸ πολεμικόν an εἶδος before naming any other εἶδος of that of which τὸ πολεμικόν is an εἶδος; he does not at all state explicitly what fighting in war is supposed to be a type or way of; nor is the term εἶδος used again subsequently. A translation of ἐν σύμπαντι τῷ πολεμικῷ εἴδει as 'in the whole type (or: 'way') of fighting in war' is thus potentially problematic. It is not only difficult to translate εἶδος, it is difficult to see why εἶδος is introduced here at all. The most obvious parallel to our passage in an early dialogue is *Gorgias* 465 f., an extended classification,[272] abounding in words terminating in -ικος.[273] Yet the only word which could be regarded as even a semi-technical term in that discussion is μόριον, 'part' (463a3 and *passim*); no mention is made of εἶδος or γένος. That is to say, classificatory analyses of pursuits and activities like those in the *Gorgias* and the *Laches* do not require the terminology of γένος and εἶδος. If that is accepted – and since on the basis of what can be known about εἶδος at the time of composition of the *Laches* no satisfactory translation can be provided, no sense be made of the phrase ἐν σύμπαντι τῷ πολεμικῷ εἴδει – I do not see an alternative to athetizing εἴδει; a radical cure, but one which leaves a text consistent in itself in terms of sense and diction. My suggestion is that a reader of the dialogue, possibly at an early stage, detected the classificatory scheme, connected it with what he knew from the *Sophist* and *Politicus*, or from reading Aristotle, or from an oral tradition which had its origin in the Academy or the Lyceum, made a note that here we have a process of division; in that note the word εἶδος was used; subsequently, it was incorporated in the text in an all–too plausible way.[274]

There is one other instance of εἶδος in the early dialogues which seems to diverge from usage of the word discussed so far. Towards the end of the *Lysis*, Socrates proposes to Lysis and Menexenus the following conclusion to their investigation of φιλία, 'friendship', and in particular of who loves whom and who is loved by whom when two men are φίλοι, 'dear friends' (221e7–222a3):

> καὶ εἰ ἄρα τις ἕτερος ἑτέρου ἐπιθυμεῖ, ἦν δ' ἐγώ, ὦ παῖδες, ἢ ἐρᾷ, οὐκ ἄν ποτε
> ἐπεθύμει οὐδὲ ἤρα οὐδὲ ἐφίλει, εἰ μὴ οἰκεῖός πῃ τῷ ἐρωμένῳ ἐτύγχανεν ὢν ἢ
> κατὰ τὴν ψυχὴν ἢ κατά τι τῆς ψυχῆς ἦθος ἢ τρόπους ἢ εἶδος.

This has been rendered as:

> 'And boys,' I said, 'if one man desires another or adores him, he'd never desire
> or adore or love him, if he weren't in some way in fact akin to the man adored,
> either in his soul, or in some disposition of his soul, or in his conduct, or in his
> looks.'
> (tr. Watt)

This translation takes the genitive τῆς ψυχῆς in the phrase τῆς ψυχῆς ἦθος ἢ τρόπους ἢ εἶδος as depending on and thereby qualifying only ἦθος and not τρόπους and εἶδος as well. One could point to *Symposium* 209b–c as a parallel for the sentiment thus expressed. In the *Symposium*, it is indeed the case that the one who loves and desires, and therefore wants to beget in what is beautiful, first looks at beautiful bodies, σώματα, and then at beautiful souls; this is subsequently repeated and extended. On this reading of the *Lysis*, the same thought is presented at 221e–222a in reverse order.

There is, however, an alternative way of understanding the *Lysis* passage. Socrates says: 'And so, children, if anybody desired anybody else, said I, or were enamoured, he would not ever desire or be enamoured or love, if he did not somehow happen to be familiar to and with the beloved, either as to soul or any habit of the soul or wonts or ways.' This way of construing the syntax could be supported by a comparison with *Symposium* 207e, where Plato speaks of τρόποι and ἤθη of the soul. In parallel, at *Lysis* 222a, where the one who loves is said to be familiar to and with the one who is loved ἢ κατὰ τὴν ψυχὴν ἢ κατά τι τῆς ψυχῆς ἦθος ἢ τρόπους ἢ εἶδος, one could understand: 'either regarding the soul, or some habit of the soul, or wonts of the soul, or some way of the soul'. What is 'a way of the soul'? In the absence of a developed theory of a soul that has distinct parts, one may nevertheless distinguish between different activities, thoughts and patterns of behaviour by speaking of habits, ways and wonts of a soul. The *Lysis* and the *Symposium* do not provide enough detail to allow us even to assert that the passages cited reflect a developed theory of the soul, but the use of εἶδος here encountered has parallels in the *Republic*, there as well in connection with ἦθος (cf. e.g. 400d–402c), and may thus reflect specialized usage in the context of psychology, potentially drawn from a pre-Platonic source now lost to us.[275]

14. εἶδος: etymology and semantics

The history, meaning and usage of εἶδος in pre-Platonic literature and Plato's early dialogues can be sketched as follows. εἶδος can denote 'appearance; guise; type; way(s); scheme'. The etymological root which εἶδος shares on the one hand with ἰδέα, 'appearance', and ἰδεῖν, 'see', on the other with εἰδέναι, οἶδα, 'know', is *u̯/oid-. Derivations from this root are preserved in many Indo-European languages, some of which provide examples of parallel semantic developments. It may be of particular interest to consider three English examples:[276]

> **wise**[1] waiz (arch.) manner, fashion. OE. *wīse* (rarely *wīs*) mode, condition, thing, cause, occas. song, corr. to OFris. *wīs*, OS. *wīsa* (Du. *wijze*), OHG. *wīsa*, *wīs* manner, custom, tune (G. *weise*), ON. *vísa* stanza, * *vīs* in *ǫðruvís* otherwise: – CGerm. (exc. Goth.) *wīsōn*, *wīsō*, f. **wit* wit[2]; for the sense-development cf. rel. Gr. *eîdos* form, shape, kind, state of things, course of action. See -WISE.

> **-wise** waiz terminal el. (suffix) descending from OE. *wīse* WISE[1] as used (like cogn. forms in other Germ. langs.) in various adverb. expressions meaning 'in such-and-such a manner, way, or respect' and containing an adj. or an attrib. sb. with or without a governing prep., e.g. OE. *(on) ōþre wīsan* in another fashion, OTHERWISE, *on scípwīsan* after the manner of a ship, like a ship. Several of these have become permanent, as *anywise*, *likewise*, *nowise*. Sense-contact with -WAYS, denoting direction, appears in late ME., and *lengthways*, *longways*, *sideways* are contemp. in XVI with *lengthwise*, *longwise*, *sidewise*.

> **guise** gaiz style, fashion. XIII (La3.). – (O)F. *guise* = Pr. *guiza*, Sp., It. *guisa*: – Rom. * *wīsa* – Germ. * *wīsōn* WISE[1]. Cf. DISGUISE.

There are two English words which are, like εἶδος, s-stem derivatives: 'wise' and 'guise', which both go back to a proto-Germanic *wīsa. Of the two, 'guise' has in some of its applications visual connotations. English 'wise' in the sense of 'manner' has not survived as part of common usage as a noun in its own right; it is found, however, as the second part of compounds such as 'otherwise', 'likewise' or 'clockwise'. The reason why 'wise' and '-wise' are no longer in active use is that in certain contexts there was a semantic overlap with the similar-sounding 'ways' and '-ways'. As a result, some of the uses of English 'way, ways' go back to some of the uses of the noun 'wise' which has been replaced by 'way(s)', and we found that 'way, ways', was sometimes suitable as a translation for εἶδος. OE. *wīse* to some extent seems to have covered both states and events, actions or processes, just as in fifth-century Greek usage εἶδος in the sense 'type' covers both 'type (of thing)' and 'type (of acting)'.

Something should be said on the choice of the English word 'type' in preference to words which can in certain contexts be counted as near-synonyms in English. The disadvantage of 'type' as a term chosen to render εἶδος in this context is that it is in origin a loan-word, ultimately going back to a Greek word other than the one it is used to translate: τύπος, a 'blow, strike; impression (as a result of a blow or strike)', does in itself not bear any visual connotations. The semantic development, however, which led to a meaning 'type', a development which can be traced back to the second half of the fifth century and which came to completion in Hellenistic times,[277] relies on the visual impact of the physical impression that was, originally, the result of a physical blow or strike. At any rate, in common English usage – specialized vocabulary of printing and numismatics apart – 'type' is first and foremost an abstract term, denoting 'the general form, structure, or character distinguishing a particular kind, group, or class of beings or objects',[278] or something characterized by that distinguishing mark.

This last lexical definition provides a sound basis for demonstrating the advantages which 'type' has over other possible English translations of εἶδος. Three reasons in particular speak against using 'form': on the one hand, the word 'form' has strong connotations of 'bodily form' and 'shape'.[279] But as has been shown, εἶδος does mean 'looks, appearance, guise', it does not mean 'bodily form', 'shape', 'body', just as it does not mean 'beauty'. Of course, physical objects do have 'shape' and 'bodily form'; those two concepts may even be subsumed under the concept of 'appearance'; but just as 'appearance' in English is not simply synonymous with 'form' or 'shape', εἶδος in Greek does not mean the same as either μορφή, 'form', or σχῆμα, 'shape'.[280]

The second reason for using 'type' to translate εἶδος where εἶδος does not mean 'appearance' is a negative one and, like the third, is bound up with scholarly tradition. It is, of course, true that the English word 'form' in some of its senses can refer to what the Greek word εἶδος can refer to in some of its senses. Therein, however, lies a danger. If εἶδος is translated 'form', one would always have to qualify immediately in what sense that word is to be understood, and which senses of 'form' are *not* intended. It is not wrong in principle to translate the Greek word εἶδος into Latin *forma* or English 'form' in some contexts, but it would be wrong to do so always and regardless of context. But while this, *mutatis mutandis*, could also be said of 'type' – as indeed of any set of two words which do not cover an identical range of meaning – there is less of a temptation to read all the potential connotations of 'type' back into εἶδος than there is in the case of 'form', not least because there is not the same semantic overlap between 'type' and 'appearance' as there is with 'form' and 'appearance' in English.

This is closely related to the third reason for preferring 'type' to 'form' as a translation of εἶδος. 'Form' has been used as a translation of the word εἶδος in Plato so universally that – for the Ancient Philosopher – it has become wholly devoid of meaning, and there is a danger that this process is irreversible even if one is aware of this circumstance; using the word 'form' to translate εἶδος prevents one from asking what is meant by the term.

But this must be asked if one wants to know why Plato introduced the noun εἶδος to refer to 'the beautiful itself' and 'the good itself', because the question 'why did Plato adopt the term εἶδος' is intimately bound up with the question 'in what sense did Plato employ the term εἶδος when he adopted it' in the context of 'the beautiful itself' and 'the good itself'. But while looking at contexts in which the term εἶδος is employed in pre-Platonic Greek literature allowed us to some extent to see what the word could mean and what it could not mean before Plato, the questions why Plato decided to adopt it and in what sense he used it in the *Phaedo* have not received an answer yet. These questions will be addressed in Part III.

CHAPTER 5

ἰδέα

ἰδέα may be as ancient a formation as εἶδος, but its first occurrence in extant Greek literature is late. ἰδέα is not part of the Homeric dialect, and that not for metrical reasons, as is shown by the first occurrence of a form of the word in a Theognidean elegiac poem. On etymological grounds, one would expect ἰδέα, an *a*-stem derived from the zero grade of the root *u̯ᶜ/₀id-, to refer to the totality of a visual impression as given or perceived in an instant.[281] As for English words that capture the notion of 'the totality of a visual impression as given or perceived in an instant', one could think of 'look', 'looks', 'appearance', 'guise'. For that reason, and because there is indeed a considerable overlap in meaning, εἶδος and ἰδέα are often treated as, or explicitly stated to be, synonyms, and this must certainly be appropriate in many contexts. Wherever it is obviously the case that εἶδος and ἰδέα are synonymous in that way, it is thus not necessary to repeat all the arguments stated already in the preceding chapter.[282]

1. ἰδέα in early Greek poetry

The first instance of ἰδέα to be considered is found at the end of a poem by Theognis, which may be complete and which is, by scholarly consent, genuine (119–28):

> χρυσοῦ κιβδήλοιο καὶ ἀργύρου ἀνσχετὸς ἄτη
> Κύρνε, καὶ ἐξευρεῖν ῥάδιον ἀνδρὶ σοφῷ   120
> εἰ δὲ φίλου νόος ἀνδρὸς ἐνὶ στήθεσσι λελήθῃ
> ψυδρὸς ἐών, δόλιον δ' ἐν φρεσὶν ἦτορ ἔχῃ,
> τοῦτο θεὸς κιβδηλότατον ποίησε βροτοῖσιν,
> καὶ γνῶναι πάντων τοῦτ' ἀνιηρότατον.
> οὐδὲ γὰρ εἰδείης ἀνδρὸς νόον οὔτε γυναικός,   125
> πρὶν πειρηθείης ὥσπερ ὑποζυγίου,
> οὐδέ κεν εἰκάσσαις †ὥσπερ ποτ' ἐς ὥριον ἐλθών·†
> πολλάκι γὰρ γνώμην ἐξαπατῶσ' ἰδέαι.

> False gold or silver is a threat that can be checked,
> Cyrnus; an expert quickly finds it out;   120
> but if a comrade's secret disposition's false

151

and in his breast he has an untrue heart,
this is the basest counterfeit that God has put
before us, and it costs most pain to test.
You cannot know a man's or woman's character 125
until you've tried if it will bear a load,
nor can you judge as if inspecting merchandise:
so often the appearances deceive.[283] (tr. West)

The first appearance of ἰδέα thus marks another case of contrasting a person's external 'looks' or 'appearance' with his mind or thoughts of the sort familiar from Homer onwards.[284] Cyrnus is warned to beware of a man's or woman's νόος, 'mind', 'character', 'disposition', where that νόος is not known. What can be seen, and therefore known,[285] is only the looks, the external appearance of a person. Aristophanes' *Plutus* offers a close parallel for the contrast of visible and non-visible characteristics of a person; Penia, Poverty, claims that she produces better men than Plutus, Wealth, is capable of producing (557–61):

σκώπτειν πειρᾷ καὶ κωμῳδεῖν τοῦ σπουδάζειν ἀμελήσας,
οὐ γιγνώσκων ὅτι τοῦ Πλούτου παρέχω βελτίονας ἄνδρας
καὶ τὴν γνώμην καὶ τὴν ἰδέαν. παρὰ τῷ μὲν γὰρ ποδαγρῶντες
καὶ γαστρώδεις καὶ παχύκνημοι καὶ πίονές εἰσιν ἀσελγῶς,
παρ' ἐμοὶ δ' ἰσχνοὶ καὶ σφηκώδεις καὶ τοῖς ἐχθροῖς ἀνιαροί.

You try to mock and ridicule, not concerned with being serious,
not realizing that I produce men better than Plutus can do,
as regards their minds and their appearance. With him, indeed, there are
<men> gouty,
with bellies, broad-legged, licentiously fat,
with me <there are men> thin and wasp-like, grievous to their enemies.

γνώμη and ἰδέα are here contrasted in a slightly different fashion, but the same opposition of internal and external is presupposed by the argument. The same opposition of 'mind' and 'appearance' seems to be present in Aristophanes and Theognis. However, especially if line 128 is supposed to be the end of Theognis' poem, it could contain a gnomic statement, a conclusion in form of a proverb:

πολλάκι γὰρ γνώμην ἐξαπατῶσ' ἰδέαι.

Often indeed appearances deceive the mind.

If that be so, the ἰδέαι need no more be the appearances of the individuals just mentioned than they are in the standing phrase 'appearances deceive'; ἰδέα would, as early as Theognis' poem, be used for 'appearance' in an absolute sense. ἰδέα would not refer to 'the appearance (of somebody)';

rather, 'appearance', syntactically the subject of an active predicate, abstractly denotes anything or anybody that appears. Reading the line in this way would cover the particular interpretation that the people concerning whom Theognis warns Cyrnus give the appearance of reliability without being reliable. That is to say, ἰδέαι may refer to 'the individuals' appearing other than they are' in a non-physical sense. From the context in Theognis alone one cannot say if, in the sixth century BC, ἰδέα meant just 'looks (of a person)' or rather 'appearance' in an absolute sense, with all the connotations either of εἶδος or of the English word 'appearance'.

Early fifth-century instances of the word may indicate that ἰδέα at that stage indeed just meant 'looks, appearance, guise (of a person)'; Pindar concludes *Olympian* 10 by stating that he has praised Archestratus for his boxing victory some time ago as a youth at Olympia (103 f.):

ἰδέᾳ τε καλόν | ὥρᾳ τε κεκραμένον...

beautiful in (with/through/by) his appearance, 'mixed' with youth...

The form of ἰδέα is in the instrumental dative rather than the accusative of respect frequently encountered with εἶδος in similar contexts.[286] This construction, ἰδέα in the instrumental dative depending on a passive participle, is also found in a fragment of the doctor-*cum*-mystic Empedocles. In his cosmological system, at one of the extreme points in the struggle of friendship and quarrel, quarrel is at the depth of the whirling rotation, friendship in the middle; from there she begins with her work of composition, putting together what is unmixed. At first, quarrel is still within the whirl and within some of the members and parts of everything, but he is retreating to the outer edges, and friendship is spreading (Simplicius *Physica* 32.11 = DK31B35.14–17):

αἶψα δὲ θνῆτ' ἐφύοντο· τὰ πρὶν μάθον ἀθάνατ' εἶναι,
†ζωρά τε τὰ πρὶν ἄκρητα†[287] διαλλάξαντα κελεύθους,
τῶν δέ τε μισγομένων χεῖτ' ἔθνεα μυρία θνητῶν,
παντοίαις ἰδέῃσιν ἀρηρότα, θαῦμα ἰδέσθαι.

But forthwith there grew mortal beings! what (had) previously learned to be immortal; ...changing their ways; but of the mixed things, there poured forth innumerable races of mortal beings, fitted together, with all sorts of appearances, a marvel to behold.

Usage of παντοίαις ἰδέῃσιν ἀρηρότα is parallel to that of ἰδέα...κεκραμένον in the Pindaric poem. All that seems to be intended here is 'appearance', 'look'. Although it is not the grammatical object to the infinitive, Empedocles connects, through their respective positions in the line, the noun ἰδέῃσιν with the infinitive ἰδέσθαι, 'look, see'.

Close in time to Pindar, and probably antedating Empedocles only by
a little, are the following lines by Xenophanes (Clemens Alexandrinus,
Stromata 5.109.3 = DK21B15):

ἀλλ' εἰ χεῖρας ἔχον βόες <ἵπποι τ'>[288] ἠὲ λέοντες
ἢ γράψαι χείρεσσι καὶ ἔργα τελεῖν ἅπερ ἄνδρες,
ἵπποι μέν θ' ἵπποισι βόες δέ τε βουσὶν ὁμοίας
καί <κε> θεῶν ἰδέας ἔγραφον καὶ σώματ' ἐποίουν
τοιαῦθ' οἷόν περ καὐτοὶ δέμας εἶχον <ἕκαστοι>.

But if oxen and horses or lions had hands
or could draw with hands and accomplish works men can accomplish,
horses would draw the appearances of their gods similar to horses
and oxen to oxen, and would make the [gods'] bodies
such as they also themselves each have their build.

σῶμα and δέμας, it could be argued, are variants, for metrical reasons,
expressing the same concept.[289] Is ἰδέα yet another variant? Or is it significant
that, in accordance with their chosen medium of production, the animals
make σώματα or 'bodies' of statues in three dimensions, but ἰδέαι, 'appearances' or 'figures' in drawings and paintings of two dimensions? On the basis
of the few early passages, it is impossible to prove or exclude either possibility.
As in the case of εἶδος, 'appearance, look(s), guise' represent safe translations of ἰδέαι. It may be noted, though, that, with the potential exception of
Theognis 128, 'figure' suggests itself as a translation in all cases considered
so far, and as a translation would bring out a specific nuance of what seems
to be intended.

2. ἰδέα as 'appearance' in fifth-century Greek literature
This picture is confirmed by a large number of fifth-century texts. Close in
context to Xenophanes is Protagoras, if Diogenes Laertius can be relied upon
to quote verbatim (D.L. 9.51 = DK80B4):

περὶ μὲν θεῶν οὐκ ἔχω εἰδέναι, οὔθ' ὡς εἰσὶν οὔθ' ὡς οὐκ εἰσὶν οὔθ' ὁποῖοί
τινες ἰδέαν.

About the gods, I cannot know, either that they are or that they are not, or
again how they are as regards their appearance.

With that may be compared the final lines of the choral ode which the chorus
of eponymous Clouds sing at their entry in Aristophanes' play. Having
described to the audience their ascent from the sea to the sky in adhortative
subjunctives, they conclude, still out of view (288–90):

ἀλλ' ἀποσεισάμεναι νέφος ὄμβριον
ἀθανάτας ἰδέας ἐπιδώμεθα

τηλεσκόπῳ ὄμματι γαῖαν.

But having shaken the rainy mist
off our immortal appearance, let us look,
with far-seeing eye, upon the earth.[290]

Aristophanes' Clouds, as they appear on stage, are anthropomorphous – as
Greek gods were in general in literature and art. It is against that background
that Xenophanes and Protagoras can speak, in an absolute sense, of the
'appearance' or the 'figure' of a god or gods. The human 'figure', asserted,
doubted or denied, is in the background of their arguments. This usage is
probably also found in the Hippocratic treatise *Airs, Waters, and Places*.
After a detailed discussion on different environments and the differences in
inhabitants which result, the concluding lines of this work as we have it read
(24.49):

αἱ μὲν ἐναντιώταται φύσιές τε καὶ ἰδέαι ἔχουσιν οὕτως· ἀπὸ δὲ τουτέων
τεκμαιρόμενος τὰ λοιπὰ ἐνθυμέεσθαι, καὶ οὐχ ἁμαρτήσῃ.

Such are the natures and appearances most opposed to each other: judging from
those infer the rest, and you will not go wrong.

From the context, it is difficult to say if φύσιες refers to the different types of
environment and nature in that sense, or if – as may seem more natural at first
sight – it refers to the different natures of man or men there are;[291] in either
case, but in the latter in particular, ἰδέα refers to the totality of what is, on
inspection, perceived of a person, a person's 'appearance' or 'figure'.[292]

3. ἰδέα in Anaxagoras and Diogenes of Apollonia

Not long after Xenophanes,[293] Anaxagoras uses the word ἰδέα in a way significant for subsequent Greek philosophy. Simplicius reports (*Physica* 34.28 =
DK59B4):

λέγει γὰρ μετ' ὀλίγα τῆς ἀρχῆς τοῦ πρώτου 'περὶ φύσεως' Ἀναξαγόρας οὕτως·
'τούτων δὲ οὕτως ἐχόντων χρὴ δοκεῖν ἐνεῖναι πολλά τε καὶ παντοῖα ἐν πᾶσι
τοῖς συγκρινομένοις καὶ σπέρματα πάντων χρημάτων καὶ ἰδέας παντοίας
ἔχοντα καὶ χροιὰς καὶ ἡδονάς.'

Indeed, Anaxagoras, close to the beginning of Book 1 of *On Nature*, speaks
thus: 'These things being so, it is right to think that there were, in all the things
that were being put together, many things, of all kinds, and seeds of all things –
[seeds] having figures and colours and savours of every kind.'[294]

Leaving aside the details of what little we have of the context of this
statement, it sets out one of the principles of the ontology and physics of
Anaxagoras. The sentence was found close to the beginning of his work

about which Simplicius, giving his interpretation of the Presocratic, declares (*Physica* 155.23):

...δηλοῖ διὰ τοῦ πρώτου τῶν 'φυσικῶν' λέγων ἀπ' ἀρχῆς· 'ὁμοῦ χρήματα πάντα ἦν, ἄπειρα καὶ πλῆθος καὶ σμικρότητα.'

[That Anaxagoras says what has just been summarized] is clear from Book 1 of the Physics where he says: 'All things were together, infinite as to amount and as to smallness.'

If one gives a temporal interpretation to those fragments, one arrives at the following picture: there was a state when nothing was distinct, when none of the composite bodies which constitute our world had come into being, when all the seeds were in one mixture from which nothing had separated off. Later, in our world, where there are συγκρινόμενα, 'composite bodies', which somehow have separated off, they contain those seeds which are the seeds of all things. These smallest and ultimate constituents are said to have καὶ ἰδέας παντοίας καὶ χροιὰς καὶ ἡδονάς, 'appearances, and colours, and tastes and smells of all sorts'. It is not impossible, as we have seen in the opening sections of the chapter on εἶδος, that ἰδέαι are in general the 'appearances' things can have, that one aspect of appearance is highlighted by way of grammatical co-ordination, and that ἡδοναί, 'tastes and smells', are then added, as if by way of an afterthought. It is, however, likewise possible, and indeed with a view to the nature of the co-ordination of the three nouns more probable, that the three words refer to three distinctive properties or qualities of the seeds. In that case, ἰδέαι refers to a characteristic, in principle accessible to perception by the senses, as are colours and tastes, but distinct from either; if this is so and if what has been said above about potential connotations of ἰδέα is correct, Anaxagoras may indeed have meant that the seeds differ in their 'figures, colours and tastes'.[295]

A slightly different context, but nevertheless one in many ways dependent on Anaxagoras, is that of the physics of Diogenes of Apollonia as quoted and summarized by Simplicius (*Physica* 151.28 = DK64B2–B5).[296] Diogenes attempts to prove first that everything is one, as can be seen from the interaction of things; secondly, that all things are ordered by some sort of mind or understanding, for otherwise they would not have the measures we see them having; lastly, that for all living beings it is air that is life and soul and understanding. Therefore (B5), τὸ τὴν νόησιν ἔχον, 'that which has understanding', is what men call air. Everything has a share in it, and air displays as many variations as understanding does. Air is at times warmer, at times colder, drier, wetter, calmer, more agile, and changing as regards taste and smell and colour in infinite ways. Yet, differences are not complete, nor are similarities, for complete similarity amounts to being the same. And Diogenes continues

156

(64B5.18–21 = fr. 9.17–20 Laks):

ἅτε οὖν πολυτρόπου ἐούσης τῆς ἑτεροιώσιος πολύτροπα καὶ τὰ ζῷα, καὶ πολλὰ καὶ οὔτε ἰδέαν ἀλλήλοις ἐοικότα οὔτε δίαιταν οὔτε νόησιν ὑπὸ τοῦ πλήθεος τῶν ἑτεροιώσεων.

Now, because alteration is manifold, the animals are also manifold;[297] many, and like one another neither in appearance nor in diet nor in understanding, through the multitude of the alterations.

Speaking of the ἰδέα, the 'appearance' or 'figure' of an animal, is, as will be seen, common in Herodotus and therefore presumably in common usage generally; in the case of Diogenes, however, this is linked with physical theory, and since he is arguing here from physics to biology, one may be justified in seeing changes in the states of air – as regards all the qualities mentioned, as regards smell and taste, colour, and (one may add) as regards figure – behind the differences in diet, understanding and appearance or figure of living beings.

Concerning the question, though, of whether one is entitled to posit specific connotations of 'figure' rather than the general connotations of 'appearance' for ἰδέα at this stage, it is worth returning to the passage of Aristophanes' *Clouds* discussed in section 2 above. In the *Clouds*, the issue of which gods there are is first raised by the character Socrates in 247 f., when he reveals to Strepsiades that the common gods do not have currency with them; rather, it is the Clouds who are their *daimones* (253). At the beginning of the *parodos*, Socrates calls for reverent silence and then begins his invocation of the gods of the *phrontistērion* (264–6):

ὦ δέσποτ' ἄναξ, ἀμέτρητ' Ἀήρ, ὃς ἔχεις τὴν γῆν μετέωρον,
λαμπρός τ' Αἰθήρ, σεμναί τε θεαὶ Νεφέλαι βροντησικέραυνοι,
ἄρθητε, φάνητ', ὦ δέσποιναι, τῷ φροντιστῇ μετέωροι.

O lord master, unmeasured Air, who holds the earth aloft,
and shining Aether, and solemn goddesses, Clouds thunder-lightening,
arise, appear to the thinker, o ladies aloft.

Air had of course been mentioned before (*Clouds* 227 ff.), in what has been identified as a passage full of allusions to Diogenes of Apollonia.[298] Now Air, Aether and most of all the Clouds are invoked, and it is the eponymous clouds who appear, closing their opening song with the words quoted above (288–90):

ἀλλ' ἀποσεισάμεναι νέφος ὄμβριον
ἀθανάτας ἰδέας ἐπιδώμεθα
τηλεσκόπῳ ὄμματι γαῖαν.

157

> But having shaken the rainy mist
> off our immortal appearance, let us look,
> with far-seeing eye, upon the earth.

This strophe and, after a comic exchange between Socrates and Strepsiades, the corresponding antistrophe are sung before the Clouds become visible. In awe after his initial doubt, Strepsiades then asks Socrates whether the women who sing these solemn things are heroines. 'No, but the heavenly Clouds,' answers Socrates, describing their powers in a way which is, again, compatible with mock-reception of Diogenes (316–18). Strepsiades then wants to see them revealed; forms of ἰδεῖν and ὁρᾶν are prominent over the next lines (322–7). At this point of their first appearance at the entrance to the *orchêstra*, Socrates asks Strepsiades whether he did not believe the Clouds to be goddesses (329). In the ensuing discussion of their works and their godhead, the following amusing altercation takes place (340–55):

STREPSIADES: λέξον δή μοι, τί παθοῦσαι,
          εἴπερ νεφέλαι γ᾽ εἰσὶν ἀληθῶς, θνηταῖς εἴξασι γυναιξίν;
          οὐ γὰρ ἐκεῖναί γ᾽ εἰσὶ τοιαῦται.
SOCRATES: φέρε, ποῖαι γάρ τινές εἰσιν;
STREPSIADES: οὐκ οἶδα σαφῶς· εἴξασιν δ᾽ οὖν ἐρίοισιν πεπταμένοισιν,
          κοὐχὶ γυναιξίν, μὰ Δί᾽, οὐδ᾽ ὁτιοῦν· αὗται δὲ ῥῖνας ἔχουσιν.
SOCRATES: ἀπόκριναί νυν ἅττ᾽ ἂν ἔρωμαι.
STREPSIADES: λέγε νυν ταχέως ὅτι βούλει.
SOCRATES: ἤδη ποτ᾽ ἀναβλέψας εἶδες νεφέλην κενταύρῳ ὁμοίαν
          ἢ παρδάλει ἢ λύκῳ ἢ ταύρῳ;
STREPSIADES: νὴ Δί᾽ ἔγωγ᾽. εἶτα τί τοῦτο;
SOCRATES: γίγνονται πάνθ᾽ ὅτι βούλονται· κᾆτ᾽ ἢν μὲν ἴδωσι κομήτην
          ἄγριόν τινα τῶν λασίων τούτων, οἷόνπερ τὸν Ξενοφάντου,
          σκώπτουσαι τὴν μανίαν αὐτοῦ κενταύροις ᾔκασαν αὐτάς.
STREPSIADES: τί γὰρ ἢν ἅρπαγα τῶν δημοσίων κατίδωσι Σίμωνα, τί δρῶσιν;
SOCRATES: ἀποφαίνουσαι τὴν φύσιν αὐτοῦ λύκοι ἐξαίφνης ἐγένοντο.
STREPSIADES: ταῦτ᾽ ἄρα, ταῦτα Κλεώνυμον αὗται τὸν ῥίψασπιν χθὲς
          ἰδοῦσαι, ὅτι δειλότατον τοῦτον ἑώρων, ἔλαφοι διὰ τοῦτ᾽
          ἐγένοντο.
SOCRATES: καὶ νῦν γ᾽ ὅτι Κλεισθένη εἶδον, ὁρᾷς, διὰ τοῦτ᾽ ἐγένοντο
          γυναῖκες.

STREPSIADES: Thus tell me this, what has affected them,
          if they really are *clouds*, that they are like women?
          For those [STREPSIADES *points to the sky*] certainly are not of
          that sort.
SOCRATES: Come, of what sort then are they?
STREPSIADES: I don't know clearly. But they are, now, like tufts of wool
          spread out,

and not like women, by Zeus, not in any way: but these here
have noses.

SOCRATES: Answer now, what I ask!

STREPSIADES: Say, now, quickly what you want.

SOCRATES: Looking up, have you ever yet seen a cloud similar to
a centaur, or a leopard or a wolf or an ox?

STREPSIADES: By Zeus, I have! But what of it?

SOCRATES: They become whatever they want: and so when they see
a hairy boorish one of these shaggy folks there, like the son of
Xenophantus, they mock his mania and liken themselves to
centaurs.

STREPSIADES: What indeed if they see the robber of public funds Simon,
what do they do?

SOCRATES: Letting appear his nature, they suddenly become wolves.

STREPSIADES: So that's what it is. Just so on seeing Cleonymus the shield-
dropper yesterday, because they saw him being a great coward,
because of that they became deer.

SOCRATES: And now because they have seen Clisthenes, you see, because
of that they have become women.

The clouds 'are like women'; the verb employed is εἴξασι (341), a form
of ἐοικέναι, the verb first encountered at *Iliad* 2.58, the very first passage
discussed in the Chapter on εἶδος;[299] later on in the passage, we find the
cognate εἰκάζω (350). The notion introduced in this comic context is that of
a correspondence between 'nature', φύσις (352), and appearance, the same
correspondence that was seen at *Airs, Waters, and Places* 24.49 discussed in
section 2 above,[300] where a correlation was established between φύσιες and
ἰδέαι. The exchange of Socrates and Strepsiades can thus now be linked back
to the words of the clouds in their opening stanza. The clouds cast off their
immortal ἰδέα. On stage, they are like mortal women. But when Socrates
then describes how the clouds can appear in the sky, what is distinctive in
his description is not colour or material, it is the figures in which the Clouds
cast themselves. His usage concerning the 'figures' which the clouds take on
is parallel to that of Diogenes of Apollonia who states that animals are not
alike as regards their figure, οὔτε ἰδέαν ἀλλήλοις ἐοικότα (64B5). It should be
noted that the Clouds, who are in Aristophanes' play the visual manifestation
of Air, can turn into anything they like, just as the Air of Diogenes can turn
into anything (64B2–B5). Reception of Diogenes in Aristophanes' *Clouds*,
as has been noticed, goes far beyond the passages presented in DK64C1.
That, though, implies that it is legitimate in principle to adduce Aristoph-
anic usage in interpreting Diogenes. As regards ἰδέα, the combined evidence
of the natural philosopher and the comic playwright point to a meaning of
'figure', a more specific notion than general 'appearance'. The specific type of
reception of the works and the words of a natural philosopher in a comedy

like the *Clouds* may also suggest that certain words would in an appropriate context have been perceived and recognized 'technical usage'.

4. ἰδέα in Democritus

A feature shared by Anaxagoras, Empedocles, and Leucippus and Democritus is what they variously call περιχώρησις or δῖνος or δίνη; this whirling rotation, vortex or cosmic swirl has a central role in their cosmology. It is set off by νοῦς, 'mind', with Anaxagoras (cf. Simplicius, *Physica* 300.27 = DK59B13); it is either just there, or set off by friendship and quarrel, with Empedocles (e.g. B35); and it is coming about by chance, and developing by necessity, with Leucippus and Democritus (Diogenes Laertius 9.31–3 on Leucippus = DK67A1). In all three cosmological systems, there are things smaller than, and prior to, what we perceive around us. Democritus allegedly declared (Simplicius *Physica* 327.24 = DK68B167):

δῖνον ἀπὸ τοῦ παντὸς ἀποκριθῆναι παντοίων ἰδεῶν.

A whirling of appearances of all sorts was separated off from the all.

What those 'appearances' are, is impossible to say from this fragment alone, whether or not one is prepared to accept Gomperz's emendation of εἰδέων to ἰδέων. They could be the smallest particles which were floating about in the emptiness and are now separated off, in ordered or as yet in unordered form (cf. Sextus Empiricus, *Adversus Mathematicos* 7.116 f. = DK68B164). On the other hand, they could just as well be what results from this process of separation, comparable with Empedocles' ἔθνεα μυρία θνητῶν, παντοίαις ἰδέῃσιν ἀρηρότα of DK31B35 quoted in section 1 above;[301] they could be the product of that whirling separation. There is, though, evidence favouring the former interpretation, gathered by Diels and Kranz under the heading of 68A57:

SCHOL. BASILII [ed. Pasquali Gött. Nachr. 1910, 196] Δ. ἰδέας. [CLEM.] Recogn. VIII 15 [DOX. 250 de principiis] D. ideas. PLUT. adv. Colot. 8 p. 1110F τί γὰρ λέγει Δ.; οὐσίας ἀπείρους τὸ πλῆθος ἀτόμους τε κἀδιαφόρους, ἔτι δ' ἀποίους καὶ ἀπαθεῖς ἐν τῷ κενῷ φέρεσθαι διεσπαρμένας· ὅταν δὲ πελάσωσιν ἀλλήλαις ἢ συμπέσωσιν ἢ περιπλακῶσι, φαίνεσθαι τῶν ἀθροιζομένων τὸ μὲν ὕδωρ τὸ δὲ πῦρ τὸ δὲ φυτὸν τὸ δ' ἄνθρωπον· εἶναι δὲ πάντα τὰς ἀτόμους ἰδέας ὑπ' αὐτοῦ καλουμένας, ἕτερον δὲ μηδέν· ἐκ μὲν γὰρ τοῦ μὴ ὄντος οὐκ εἶναι γένεσιν, ἐκ δὲ τῶν ὄντων μηδὲν ἂν γενέσθαι τῷ μήτε πάσχειν μήτε μεταβάλλειν τὰς ἀτόμους ὑπὸ στερρότητος· ὅθεν οὔτε χρόαν ἐξ ἀχρώστων οὔτε φύσιν ἢ ψυχὴν ἐξ ἀποίων καὶ <ἀπαθῶν> ὑπάρχειν…

One should note that this represents three potentially independent sources for Democritus' use of the word ἰδέα, two in Greek and one in Latin. Of course, the fact that Clemens Romanus, in writing in Latin, uses the Greek loan-word '*idea*' is not incontrovertible proof; but it is difficult to see why Clemens should have used *idea* in this specific context for any word other than ἰδέα; the Greek scholion is, of course, not open to this potential objection. As regards Plutarch, part of the passage is translated by R.D. McKirahan (1994, 323):

> What does Democritus say? That substances unlimited in multitude, atomic and not different in kind, and moreover incapable of acting or being acted upon, are in motion, scattered in the void. When they approach one another or collide or become entangled, the compounds appear as water or fire or as a plant or a human, but all things are atoms, which he calls forms; there is nothing else. For from what is not there is no coming to be, and nothing could come to be from things that are because on account of their hardness the atoms are not acted upon and do not change. (Plutarch, *Against Colotes* 8.1110F–1111A)

C.C.W. Taylor (1999, 142) translates:

> For what does Democritus say? That an infinite number of atomic, undifferenti-ated substances, incapable of affecting or being affected, travel about, scattered in the void. And whenever they approach one another, these collections appear as water, fire, a plant or a man. Everything consists of the atoms, which he calls 'forms', and there is nothing else. For there is no coming to be from what is not, and nothing could come to be from what is, since, because of their solidity, the atoms neither are affected nor change. Hence no colour comes into being from colourless things, nor any nature or soul from things which can neither affect nor be affected.

In their translations, both Taylor and McKirahan follow those who punctuate differently: εἶναι δὲ πάντα τὰς ἀτόμους, ἰδέας ὑπ' αὐτοῦ καλουμένας.[302] This makes for smoother syntax; as has been pointed out, though, the feminine gender of τὰς ἀτόμους here and a few lines below in the same passage requires an explanation which a phrase ἄτομοι ἰδέαι would provide.[303] But whatever else the passages collected by Diels under DK68A57 may entail, they seem to indicate that ἰδέα was a word of some significance for Democritus; and it is possible that Hesychius did think of Democritus when he glossed (68B141):

ἰδέα· ἡ ὁμοιότης, μορφή, εἶδος. καὶ τὸ ἐλάχιστον σῶμα.[304]

But it should be added that while this is generally accepted as referring to Democritus,[305] he is not mentioned by name. So, while direct, incontro-vertible evidence for ἰδέα as a technical term for the atoms in Democritus' philosophy is not strong,[306] it is difficult to see why anybody should have introduced ἰδέα into discussions of Democritus' philosophy had the word not occurred in his writings, and moreover in those sections which are

161

concerned with atoms. After all, in his description of atoms, there are plenty of other terms Democritus has either coined himself, or at least used in his own peculiar way.[307] So it is safe to assume that the word ἰδέα was indeed one of the terms Democritus himself used to denote the smallest indivisible particles he posited.[308] Should he have used it in that way, he would have done so presumably because ἰδέα as 'appearance' or 'figure' in an absolute sense can be used in reference to any body that has extension and certain physical characteristics;[309] at the same time, ἰδέα was not a common word that would have been in frequent use in colloquial Greek, and Democritus, as far as we can judge, paid attention to language, style and unusual turn of phrase; in addition, ἰδέα had figured, albeit in a less specialized sense, in Anaxagoras and in Empedocles. Democritus' atoms did not differ in solidity; they may have differed in weight; but they definitely did differ in their 'figures'; they differed as 'figures'; they were different 'figures'. Otherwise, Democritus' whole system of conglomerates would no longer cohere: the difference in 'figure' was the reason atoms stuck together.[310]

5. ἰδέα in Herodotus

In Herodotus, ἰδέα can refer to the figure of a human being, an animal, or even a plant. In Book 4, he describes the countries and people neighbouring Scythia (100 ff.); the Tauri, Agathyrsi, Neuri, Man-eaters, Black-cloaks, Geloni, Budini, and Sauromatae (102). Talking about the Budini and the Geloni (108), Herodotus gives a description strongly resembling descriptions in the Hippocratic *Airs, Waters, and Places*.

Βουδῖνοι δὲ ἔθνος ἐὸν μέγα καὶ πολλὸν γλαυκόν τε πᾶν ἰσχυρῶς ἐστι καὶ πυρρόν.

The Budini, being a people great and numerous, are all very bright-eyed and ruddy.

The Geloni are of Greek origin and speak a language mixed from Greek and Scythian elements.

Βουδῖνοι δὲ οὐ τῇ αὐτῇ γλώσσῃ χρέωνται καὶ Γελωνοί, οὐδὲ δίαιτα ἡ αὐτή. (109) οἱ μὲν γὰρ Βουδῖνοι ἐόντες αὐτόχθονες νομάδες τέ εἰσι καὶ φθειροτραγέουσι μοῦνοι τῶν ταύτῃ, Γελωνοὶ δὲ γῆς τε ἐργάται καὶ σιτοφάγοι καὶ κήπους ἐκτημένοι, οὐδὲν τὴν ἰδέην ὅμοιοι οὐδὲ τὸ χρῶμα. ὑπὸ μέντοι Ἑλλήνων καλέονται καὶ οἱ Βουδῖνοι Γελωνοί, οὐκ ὀρθῶς καλεόμενοι.

But the Budini do not speak the same language as the Geloni, nor do they have the same diet. Indeed, the Budini, being autochthonous people, are nomads and, alone of all the people there, eaters of pine-seed, but the Geloni work the soil and eat grain and have gardens, being in no respect similar as regards their appearance, nor as regards their colour. Yet the Budini, too, are called Geloni by the Greeks – incorrectly.

And Herodotus goes on to describe the land they inhabit. It is possible that Herodotus points to a difference in 'appearance' generally, and then proceeds by stressing one aspect of appearance, namely colour. The text, however, allows for a reading that makes Herodotus state a difference between the two people in 'figure' and in colour. The argument for this would be in parallel with that concerning the usage of Anaxagoras DK59B4, discussed in section 3 above.[311]

Just as Herodotus speaks of the εἶδος, the 'appearance', of an animal in the course of his descriptions of foreign countries,[312] so he also speaks of an animal's ἰδέα. When the Persian army is arranged for the decisive battle against the Lydians, Harpagus the Mede advises Cyrus to set up an ad hoc 'camel cavalry' in front of his army to disable the cavalry of Croesus (1.80):

ταῦτα μὲν παραίνεσε, τὰς δὲ καμήλους ἔταξε ἀντία τῆς ἵππου τῶνδε εἵνεκεν· κάμηλον ἵππος φοβέεται καὶ οὐκ ἀνέχεται οὔτε τὴν ἰδέην αὐτῆς ὁρέων οὔτε τὴν ὀδμὴν ὀσφραινόμενος.

Thus, he recommended those things; but he positioned the camels opposite the cavalry for the following reasons: the horse fears the camel, and it can stand neither seeing its appearance nor smelling its odour.

This passage does not provide any additional evidence. One could argue: what the horse sees is, of course, the camel's appearance, everything there is to see about the camel, the totality of its visual impact. But what it perceives first is the camel's figure, not any particular attribute, as the eyes, or the colour, or the hair. And even if the horse is near enough to smell the camel, what is most impressive in terms of its appearance is its figure. But none of this would compel us to posit a meaning 'figure' in addition to 'appearance' or 'looks', had we not previously decided on 'figure' on independent grounds.[313] The same is true of the next instance. In Herodotus' description of Egypt, we read the following about hippopotami (2.71):

οἱ δὲ ἵπποι οἱ ποτάμιοι <ἐν> νομῷ μὲν τῷ Παπρημίτῃ ἱροί εἰσι, τοῖσι δὲ ἄλλοισι Αἰγυπτίοισι οὐκ ἱροί. φύσιν δὲ παρέχονται ἰδέης τοιήνδε· τετράπουν ἐστὶ δίχηλον, ὁπλαὶ βοός, σιμόν, λοφιὴν ἔχον ἵππου, χαυλιόδοντας φαῖνον, οὐρὴν ἵππου καὶ φωνήν, μέγαθος ὅσον τε βοῦς ὁ μέγιστος.

The hippopotami, however, are sacred in the Papremitian region, but not sacred to the other Egyptians. And as regards the nature of their figure, they present the following: it is a cloven-hoofed quadruped, hooves of an ox, flat-nosed, having the mane of a horse, visible tusks, the tail and voice of a horse, and as regards size it is like the biggest ox.

Apart from voice – which is added as being like that of a horse after it is stated that the tail is that of a horse – all features enumerated are both visible and distinctive in terms of outline and contour. That would agree with a meaning 'figure' for ἰδέα, but the context does not require this special meaning. So also with 2.92. Herodotus describes two types of lilies which grow in Egypt. One grows in the water and is called Lotus by the Egyptians. He continues:

ἔστι δὲ καὶ ἄλλα κρίνεα ῥόδοισι ἐμφερέα, ἐν τῷ ποταμῷ γινόμενα καὶ ταῦτα, ἐξ ὧν ὁ καρπὸς ἐν ἄλλη κάλυκι παραφυομένη ἐκ τῆς ῥίζης γίνεται, κηρίῳ σφηκῶν ἰδέην ὁμοιότατον· ἐν τούτῳ τρωκτὰ ὅσον τε πυρὴν ἐλαίης ἐγγίνεται συχνά, τρώγεται δὲ καὶ ἁπαλὰ ταῦτα καὶ αὖα.

Other lilies also grow in the river, which are like roses; the fruit of these is found in a calyx springing from the root by a separate stalk, and is most like to a comb made by wasps; this produces many eatable seeds as big as an olive-stone, which are eaten both fresh and dried.[314]

The phrase κηρίῳ σφηκῶν ἰδέην ὁμοιότατον, 'most similar to a comb of wasps in appearance' or 'figure', displays the accusative of respect so commonly found in constructions with εἶδος.

At first sight, 2.76 is just another instance of ἰδέα in that sense:

εἶδος δὲ τῆς ἴβιος τόδε· μέλαινα δεινῶς πᾶσα, σκέλεα δὲ φορέει γεράνου, πρόσωπον δὲ ἐς τὰ μάλιστα ἐπίγρυπον, μέγαθος ὅσον κρέξ. τῶν μὲν δὴ μελαινέων τῶν μαχομένων πρὸς τοὺς ὄφις ἥδε ἰδέη.[315] τῶν δ' ἐν ποσὶ μᾶλλον εἰλεομένων τοῖσι ἀνθρώποισι – διξαὶ γὰρ δή εἰσι ἴβιες – ἥδε· ψιλὴ τὴν κεφαλὴν καὶ τὴν δειρὴν πᾶσαν, λευκόπτερος πλὴν κεφαλῆς καὶ αὐχένος καὶ ἀκρέων τῶν πτερύγων καὶ τοῦ πυγαίου ἄκρου – ταῦτα δὲ τὰ εἶπον πάντα μέλανά ἐστι δεινῶς – σκέλεα δὲ καὶ πρόσωπον ἐμφερὴς τῇ ἑτέρῃ. τοῦ δὲ ὄφιος ἡ μορφὴ οἵη περ τῶν ὕδρων, πτίλα δὲ οὐ πτερωτὰ φορέει ἀλλὰ τοῖσι τῆς νυκτερίδος πτεροῖσι μάλιστά κη ἐμφερέστατα.

Now this is the appearance of the ibis. It is all deep black, with legs like a crane's, and a beak strongly hooked; its size is that of a landrail. Such is the figure of the ibis which fights the serpents. Those that most consort with men (for the ibis is of two kinds) have all the head and neck bare of feathers; their plumage is white, save the head and neck and the tips of wings and tail (these being deep black); the legs and beak are like those of the other ibis. The serpents are like water-snakes. Their wings are not feathered but most like the wings of a bat.[316]

It is tempting to see Herodotus' style as governed by the principle of *variatio*. He talks first of the appearance of a bird, then of that of a snake. First he uses the term εἶδος, then, referring to the description he has just given, by way of variation the term ἰδέα; finally, and only a few lines later, he employs μορφή, 'form', to refer to the appearance of serpent and water-snake. Without entering into a discussion of the meaning of μορφή here, it may be noted that in the case of serpent and water-snake, it is specifically the form of the bodies of those animals which is said to be alike; by contrast, the description of the appearance of the ibis contains a number of features *besides* bodily form. As for εἶδος, the word does indeed mean 'appearance', as is the case with many similar examples of animal descriptions in Herodotus.[317] However, regardless of the perceived textual difficulty, does ἰδέα just summarize what is said in the three preceding lines? While that is perfectly possible, since there is indeed a sufficient semantic overlap between εἶδος and ἰδέα, it is to my mind likewise possible that Herodotus introduces a new thought in the sentence in question and does not just summarize what went before. The sentence τῶν μὲν δὴ μελαινέων τῶν μαχομένων πρὸς τοὺς ὄφις ἥδε ἰδέη could mean: 'Now, that is the type of the black <ibises> which fight against the serpents.' That is to say, what is expressed in the parenthetical clause διξαὶ γὰρ δή εἰσι ἴβιες, 'indeed, twofold are the ibises', may have been anticipated in the clause which points out that the description hitherto has been that of one type of the bird.[318] While it is impossible to come to a firm conclusion on the basis of one instance, a meaning 'type' for ἰδέα in Herodotus does not depend on 2.76. Towards the end of Book 1, on the occasion of the narration of Cyrus' expansion to the north, Herodotus describes a number of Asian regions and peoples with their customs. The Caspian sea, Herodotus reports, is a sea by itself, not connected with the Mediterranean, the Atlantic and the Red Sea, which are all one. To the west of the Caspian, there is the Caucasus mountain range. And he continues (1.203):

ἔθνεα δὲ ἀνθρώπων πολλὰ καὶ παντοῖα ἐν ἑωυτῷ ἔχει ὁ Καύκασος, τὰ πολλὰ πάντα ἀπ' ὕλης ἀγρίης ζώοντα. ἐν τοῖσι καὶ δένδρεα φύλλα τοιῆσδε ἰδέης παρεχόμενα εἶναι λέγεται, τὰ τρίβοντάς τε καὶ παραμίσγοντας ὕδωρ ζῷα ἑωυτοῖσι ἐς τὴν ἐσθῆτα ἐγγράφειν· τὰ δὲ ζῷα οὐκ ἐκπλύνεσθαι...

The Caucasus has within it many and varied tribes of men, all of them living for the most part from the wild forest. In the <forest>, there are said to be trees having leaves of the following type: those who grind them, and mix them with water, paint pictures with them on their clothing: and the pictures cannot be washed out...

There is no question here of ἰδέα's meaning 'appearance', since there is no reference at all to the leaves' actual appearance. Leaving the slight grammatical inconcinnity aside, what is referred to in the following clause is the leaves' property and function. They are leaves of an unusual sort. Like εἶδος, ἰδέα, originally denoting 'appearance, guise', thus came to mean 'type'.

The next instance of ἰδέα in Herodotus is more difficult to assess. When his satraps had defeated and enslaved the rebellious Eretrians, Darius decided not to punish them but instead to let them settle in a place called Ardericca of which we are told (6.119.9–12):

...ἀπὸ μὲν Σούσων δέκα καὶ διηκοσίους σταδίους ἀπέχοντι, τεσσεράκοντα δὲ ἀπὸ τοῦ φρέατος τὸ παρέχεται τριφασίας ἰδέας. καὶ γὰρ ἄσφαλτον καὶ ἅλας καὶ ἔλαιον ἀρύσσονται ἐξ αὐτοῦ τρόπῳ τοιῷδε...

...its distance from Susa was two hundred and ten stadia, and forty <stadia its distance> from the well which provides three ἰδέαι. And indeed, asphalt and salt and oil are brought up from it in the following way...

It is indeed the case that three types *of stuff* are produced from this well; but there is no qualifying genitive: we are not told three types *of what*. In that respect, the absolute use of ἰδέα here comes close to that of Democritus when he asserts (Simplicius *Physica* 327.24 = DK68B167):

δῖνον ἀπὸ τοῦ παντὸς ἀποκριθῆναι παντοίων ἰδεῶν,

that a whirling of all sorts of appearances was separated off from the all.

If anything, Herodotus' usage is more definitely abstract, since with Democritus the possibility remains that παντοίων ἰδέων is a descriptive genitive: 'a whirl of many appearances' could be 'a whirl that manifests itself as many appearances', 'a whirl that appears now in one way, now in another'. That is not possible with Herodotus, and so taking ἰδέα as a term referring to a material object with Democritus, too, becomes inherently more likely. The well in Herodotus' report produces three distinct 'appearances' or 'figures' or 'types': but none of these English terms can easily be stretched so as to accommodate reference to just any sort of physical object.

The one remaining occurrence of ἰδέα in Herodotus is interesting in a different respect. At the outset of the campaign of the Persians against Eretria, the Eretrians ask Athens for help. Nevertheless, Herodotus relates, the city was divided (6.100):

τῶν δὲ Ἐρετριέων ἦν ἄρα οὐδὲν ὑγιὲς βούλευμα, οἳ μετεπέμποντο μὲν Ἀθηναίους, ἐφρόνεον δὲ διφασίας ἰδέας· οἱ μὲν γὰρ αὐτῶν ἐβουλεύοντο ἐκλιπεῖν τὴν πόλιν ἐς τὰ ἄκρα τῆς Εὐβοίης, ἄλλοι δὲ αὐτῶν ἴδια κέρδεα προσδεκόμενοι παρὰ τοῦ Πέρσεω οἴσεσθαι προδοσίην ἐσκευάζοντο.

Yet, the counsel of the Eretrians was not healthy, for on the one hand they sent for help to Athens, on the other they had in mind two schemes: indeed, part of the citizens had decided to leave the city for the mountains of Euboia, but others, thinking of the profit for themselves from the Persian prepared to carry out treason.

How a word like ἰδέα could have come to mean 'scheme' has been discussed in connection with Thucydides 6.77.2 and at 8.56.2 in section 12 of the chapter on εἶδος above.[319] One should note that ἰδέα here at Herodotus 6.100 refers to what is in somebody's mind; in the clause ἐφρόνεον δὲ διφασίας ἰδέας, the word ἰδέας is the direct object of a verb of thinking. But it would, of course, be an anachronism and incorrect to translate 'they had two *ideas*'; the clause rather means something like 'they contemplated two ways of acting'; those two 'ways' are then narrated.

6. ἰδέα in the Hippocratic Corpus

ἰδέα is not a term frequently encountered in early Hippocratic treatises.[320] The one instance in *Airs, Waters, and Places* has already been discussed.[321] The other treatise to be considered is *The Nature of Man*. Close to the beginning of that work there is a reference to Melissus; in thought and terminology, there seem to be repercussions of Anaxagoras; and as far as the subject matter set out in the opening paragraphs is concerned, there appears to be a reaction to Diogenes of Apollonia.[322] In all probability, therefore, this Hippocratic treatise is also later than most or all of what we have of Herodotus.

In chapter 1 of *Nature of Man*, the author, who professes to write about medicine only, rejects the ideas of those writers on nature who claim that everything is one, and that this one thing is everything; the one point they cannot agree on, though, is what this one thing is: air, fire, water or earth. They overthrow themselves with their arguments, and this ἑαυτὸν καταβάλλειν is here attributed to Melissus rather than Protagoras, perhaps because of Melissus' closer connection with the argument that everything is one.[323] In chapter 2, the author turns to the physicians, some of whom, he claims, say that man is blood, others that he is bile, yet others that he is phlegm. And comparing these medical men with those writing on nature, he continues (2.4–28):

> ἐπίλογον δὲ ποιέονται καὶ οὗτοι πάντες τὸν αὐτόν· ἓν γὰρ εἶναί φασιν, ὅ τι ἕκαστος αὐτῶν βούλεται ὀνομάσας, καὶ τοῦτο μεταλλάσσειν τὴν ἰδέην καὶ τὴν δύναμιν, ἀναγκαζόμενον ὑπό τε τοῦ θερμοῦ καὶ τοῦ ψυχροῦ, καὶ γίνεσθαι γλυκὺ καὶ πικρὸν καὶ λευκὸν καὶ μέλαν καὶ παντοῖον. ἐμοὶ δὲ οὐδὲ ταῦτα δοκεῖ ὧδε ἔχειν... πολλὰ γάρ ἐστιν ἐν τῷ σώματι ἐνεόντα, ἅ, ὅταν ὑπ᾽ ἀλλήλων παρὰ φύσιν θερμαίνεταί τε καὶ ψύχηται, καὶ ξηραίνεται καὶ ὑγραίνεται, νούσους τίκτει· ὥστε πολλαὶ μὲν ἰδέαι τῶν νουσημάτων, πολλὴ δὲ καὶ ἡ ἴησις ἐστίν. ἀξιῶ δὲ ἔγωγε τὸν φάσκοντα αἷμα εἶναι μοῦνον τὸν ἄνθρωπον, καὶ ἄλλο μηδέν, δεικνύειν αὐτὸν μὴ μεταλλάσσοντα τὴν ἰδέην μηδὲ γίνεσθαι παντοῖον, ἀλλ᾽ ἢ ὥρην τινὰ τοῦ ἐνιαυτοῦ ἢ τῆς ἡλικίης τῆς τοῦ ἀνθρώπου, ἐν ᾗ αἷμα ἐνεὸν φαίνεται μοῦνον ἐν τῷ ἀνθρώπῳ· εἰκὸς γὰρ εἶναι μίαν τινὰ ὥρην, ἐν ᾗ φαίνεται αὐτὸ ἐφ᾽ ἑαυτοῦ ἐνεόν...

But those as well all make the same postscript: indeed, they say there is one <thing>, whatever each one of them wants to call it, and this, they say, changes its appearance and its force, compelled by the warm and the cold, it becomes sweet and bitter and white and black and of all sorts. But to me, it does not seem to be so... Indeed, there are many <things> in the body, which, when against nature they are warmed or cooled or dried or wetted by each other, engender diseases: so that there are many appearances of illnesses, but there is also many a healing. I ask the one who says that man is blood alone, and nothing else, to show me someone who does not change his appearance and does not become of all sorts, but show me either a certain season of the year or a certain age of a man<'s life> when there seems to be only blood in a man: indeed it is plausible that there be one such season in which it appears being in itself by itself...

And summarizing that part of his work, he declares in chapter 5 (5–19):

φημὶ δὴ εἶναι καὶ φλέγμα καὶ χολὴν ξανθήν τε καὶ μέλαιναν. καὶ τουτέων πρῶτον μὲν κατὰ νόμον τὰ οὐνόματα διωρίσθαι φημὶ καὶ οὐδενὶ αὐτέων τωὐτὸ οὔνομα εἶναι, ἔπειτα κατὰ φύσιν τὰς ἰδέας κεχωρίσθαι, καὶ οὔτε τὸ φλέγμα οὐδὲν ἐοικέναι τῷ αἵματι, οὔτε τὸ αἷμα τῇ χολῇ, οὔτε τὴν χολὴν τῷ φλέγματι. πῶς γὰρ ἂν ἐοικότα εἴη ταῦτα ἀλλήλοισιν, ὧν οὔτε τὰ χρώματα ὅμοια φαίνεται προσορώμενα, οὔτε τῇ χειρὶ ψαύοντι ὅμοια δοκέει εἶναι; οὔτε γὰρ θερμὰ ὁμοίως ἐστίν, οὔτε ψυχρά, οὔτε ξηρά, οὔτε ὑγρά. ἀνάγκη τοίνυν, ὅτε τοσοῦτον διήλλακται ἀλλήλων τὴν ἰδέην τε καὶ τὴν δύναμιν, μὴ ἓν αὐτὰ εἶναι, εἴπερ μὴ πῦρ τε καὶ ὕδωρ ἕν τε καὶ ταὐτόν ἐστι. γνοίης δ᾽ ἂν τοῖσδε, ὅτι οὐχ ἓν ταῦτα πάντα ἐστίν, ἀλλ᾽ ἕκαστον αὐτέων ἔχει δύναμίν τε καὶ φύσιν τὴν ἑωυτοῦ...

Therefore I say that there also is phlegm and yellow and black bile. And of those I first claim that their names are defined by custom and that to none of them there is the same name [viz. as to another one of them], then that the appearances are separate by nature, and neither is phlegm in anything like to blood, nor blood to bile, nor bile to phlegm. Indeed, how should those <things> be like each other of which neither the colours appear similar to look at, nor do they seem to be like to the hand when touching? Indeed, neither are they alike warm nor alike cold nor alike dry nor alike wet. Now surely there is a necessity, when they differ so much from each other in appearance and force, that they are not one, if really fire and water are not one and the same. So you may know with that, that those are not all one, but that each one of them has its own force and nature...

The first occurrence of ἰδέα in chapter 2 of *The Nature of Man* refers indisputably to the appearance of whatever is posited as the one stuff of which man consists.[324] With the second occurrence in that chapter, πολλαὶ ἰδέαι τῶν νουσημάτων, there is a good case for arguing in favour of 'many types of diseases'; yet, since the actual appearances of the diseases are different, there is at least a possibility that the transition from one meaning to the other, from straightforward 'appearance' to 'type' in the sense defined in the preceding chapter, has as yet not taken place; not much rests on this for our purposes, but the qualifying indefinite πολλαί may point to a meaning 'type'. In chapter 5, the author states that of the things which are in the body, not only the names are different by convention, but also κατὰ φύσιν τὰς ἰδέας κεχωρίσθαι. From the emphasis on lack of ἐοικέναι or 'being like' in the following clauses, it is clear that it is again the appearances of the things which are distinct: 'that their appearances are separate by nature'. Then colour is named as an obvious element of appearance, warm, cold, dry and wet, what is sensed by the hand when touching, as primary δυνάμεις, 'forces' or 'powers'.

While the word ἰδέα, meaning 'appearance' and perhaps, on one occasion, 'type', is confined to those two places in the first half of the work, there are three occurrences of εἶδος towards the end. In chapter 9, the author states that diseases must be cured with a treatment which is the opposite of their causes.[325]

τὸ δὲ σύμπαν γνῶναι, δεῖ τὸν ἰητρὸν ἐναντίον ἵστασθαι τοῖσι καθεστεῶσι καὶ νοσήμασι καὶ εἴδεσι καὶ ὥρῃσι καὶ ἡλικίῃσι, καὶ τὰ συντείνοντα λύειν, καὶ τὰ λελυμένα συντείνειν...

But to know all, it is necessary that the physician positions himself opposite the prevailing diseases, types, seasons and ages, and must loosen what is tight and tighten what is loose...

There seems to me a measure of rhetoric in this prescription: the disease is the general object of concern for the physician, to an extent independent of the patient; the patient's appearance and type are what the physician sees himself with any given case: the time of year is again independent of and external to the patient, the age is internal. The theory of treatment by opposite is consistent: one can loosen what is tight. But how does one treat a young person or a ruddy person on that principle? A little later in the same chapter, it is repeated that, for those diseases which depend on regimen, treatment should be preceded by examining

τοῦ ἀνθρώπου τὴν φύσιν τὴν τε ἡλικίην καὶ τὸ εἶδος καὶ τὴν ὥρην τοῦ ἔτεος καὶ τῆς νούσου τὸν τρόπον,

a man's nature and age and type and the time of year and the way of the disease.

Here the order of things to consider is different in that everything pertaining to the person is enumerated first. Age, season, type and disease, in that order, are mentioned again two lines later. Finally, in chapter 15, the last section of the treatise, we learn:

οἱ πλεῖστοι τῶν πυρετῶν γίνονται ἀπὸ χολῆς· εἴδεα δὲ σφέων ἐστὶ τέσσαρα...

Most fevers come from bile: there are four types of them.

We then learn that those types are 'the continued', 'the quotidian', 'the tertian' and 'the quartan'. A possible inference concerning factors that influenced the author's choice of ἰδέα and εἶδος in *Nature of Man* will be drawn in section 10 below.[326]

7. ἰδέα in Thucydides
In all, there are 14 instances of the word ἰδέα in Thucydides. The word appears in all the various senses discussed so far. On one occasion, it denotes

'appearance' or 'figure'. The context of 6.4.5 is an excursus on the history and geography of Sicily. In fair detail, the foundations and affiliations of the various colonies are listed. Among others, we learn about the foundation of Zankle from Cyme, itself a Chalcidian town in Opician territory; this settlement was later called Messene, but, we are told:

ὄνομα δὲ τὸ μὲν πρῶτον Ζάγκλη ἦν ὑπὸ τῶν Σικελῶν κληθεῖσα, ὅτι δρεπανοειδὲς τὴν ἰδέαν τὸ χωρίον ἐστί – τὸ δὲ δρέπανον οἱ Σικελοὶ ζάγκλον καλοῦσιν...

At first, the name was Zankle, <the city> being called so by the Sicilians, because as regards its figure the place is like a sickle[327] – and the sickle the Sicilians call 'zanklon'...

ἰδέα does refer to the 'appearance' of the land, and perhaps more specifically to its 'figure'. More frequent in Thucydides, however, are instances of ἰδέα in the sense of 'type'; an example of the transitional stage between 'appearance' and 'type' can be seen at 2.51.1. At the end of his description of the epidemic which befell Athens in the summer of 430 BC, a description in the style of professional medical treatises of his time, Thucydides has this concluding sentence:[328]

τὸ μὲν οὖν νόσημα, πολλὰ καὶ ἄλλα παραλιπόντι ἀτοπίας, ὡς ἑκάστῳ ἐτύγχανέ τι διαφερόντως ἑτέρῳ πρὸς ἕτερον γιγνόμενον, τοιοῦτον ἦν ἐπὶ πᾶν τὴν ἰδέαν.

Now – leaving out a number of peculiarities as would befall any one person in a way different from any other – such was the disease on the whole with regard to its appearance.

With ἰδέα, Thucydides refers to the totality of the appearance or appearances the disease had with all the people it had befallen; that does involve appearance over time, but most of all ἰδέα refers to the appearance of the disease collectively. This collective use of ἰδέα may be seen as an intermediate stage between 'appearance (of a single object)' and 'type', since it does contain, at least implicitly, an abstraction from the particular instance whose appearance can be observed as such.

To be considered next is a number of passages where ἰδέα means 'type' either as 'type (of an event)' or as 'type (of an action)'. On five occasions, the word is part of a phrase πᾶσα ἰδέα κατέστη/πολλαὶ ἰδέαι κατέστησαν (with genitive), 'there obtained every type/many types (of something)'. Not found in that constellation before Thucydides, it seems to be a standing phrase with him. Its first occurrence is at 1.109.2.[329] There, Thucydides describes the situation of the Athenian contingent in Egypt towards the end of the Egyptian Expedition of 454 BC:

οἱ δ᾽ ἐν τῇ Αἰγύπτῳ Ἀθηναῖοι καὶ οἱ ξύμμαχοι ἐπέμενον, καὶ αὐτοῖς πολλαὶ ἰδέαι πολέμων κατέστησαν.

But those Athenians who were in Egypt, and their allies, stayed, and they were involved in many types of warfare.

It is to be noted that the verb κατέστησαν is employed like εἶναι, viz. verb in a finite form plus nominative of the thing 'had' plus *dativus commodi* of the person/people 'having', or a transformation of this construction. Here, the noun in the genitive, πολέμων, is in the plural; this is indicative of the early, pre-rationalized stage of semantic development discussed above. What was experienced were many different situations of the sort one experiences in war, and that plurality is expressed – in what could be called a *constructio ad sensum* of a sort common, at a colloquial level, with words denoting 'type' or 'sort' or 'kind' in many a language – through use of the plural of both the noun denoting 'type' and the dependent noun in the genitive that designates what there are types of; a purely logical construction would demand the singular for the latter. On the four occasions later on in his account, the phrase has – disregarding the tense of the verb – the form πᾶσα ἰδέα κατέστη, with ἰδέα in the singular, so that the question does not arise in the same way. The phrase πᾶσα ἰδέα κατέστη just discussed is employed with nouns like θανάτου, 'of death', ὀλέθρου, 'of disaster'; on one occasion, we read (3.98.3):

πᾶσά τε ἰδέα κατέστη τῆς φυγῆς καὶ τοῦ ὀλέθρου τῷ στρατοπέδῳ τῶν Ἀθηναίων.

There was every type of flight and disaster for the army of the Athenians.

Shortly afterwards, and still as part of the description of events of 426, the sixth year of the war, that is to say, in all probability written at more or less the same time, Thucydides relates of the defeated forces of the Ampraciots (3.112.6):

προκατειλημμένων δὲ τῶν ὁδῶν, καὶ ἅμα τῶν μὲν Ἀμφιλόχων ἐμπείρων ὄντων τῆς ἑαυτῶν γῆς καὶ ψιλῶν πρὸς ὁπλίτας, τῶν δὲ ἀπείρων καὶ ἀνεπιστημόνων ὅπη τράπωνται, ἐσπίπτοντες ἔς τε χαράδρας καὶ τὰς προλελοχισμένας ἐνέδρας διεφθείροντο. καὶ ἐς πᾶσαν ἰδέαν χωρήσαντες τῆς φυγῆς ἐτράποντό τινες καὶ ἐς τὴν θάλασσαν οὐ πολὺ ἀπέχουσαν.

With the roads taken in advance and, at the same time, the Antilochians being acquainted with their own land and fighting in light armour against hoplites, whereas the others (= the Ampraciots) being unacquainted and not knowing whither they should turn, the latter perished, falling into gullies and prepared ambushes. And giving way to any type of flight some even turned to the sea which lay not far off.

The phrase ἐς πᾶσαν ἰδέαν χωρήσαντες τῆς φυγῆς[330] should, to my mind, not be looked at in isolation, even if one were to agree that ἐς πᾶσαν ἰδέαν τῆς φυγῆς depended solely on χωρήσαντες and not somehow also on ἐτράποντο.

Behind the phrase there are common expressions like ἐς φυγὴν τρέπεσθαι, 'turn to flight';[331] a hypothetical and, I think, plausible line of development moves from 'turn/rush/give way to flight' to 'turn/rush/give way to any type of flight'; from there it is but a short step to isolating the phrase 'turn to any type of'; that may be at the origin of the phrase ἐπὶ ἄλλο/τοῦτο τὸ εἶδος τρέπεσθαι.[332] There is, of course, the alternative possibility that a collocation of the noun εἶδος and the verb τρέπεσθαι arose from the closeness in meaning of the noun εἶδος in the sense of 'way, manner' and the noun τρόπος. Returning to Thucydides' use of ἰδέα, the word can be translated as 'way' or 'ways' on four occasions,[333] including 3.62.2, where the Thebans accuse the Plataeans of 'atticizing', demonstrating that they have behaved like that on one occasion, namely when they alone of all the Boeotians did not medize solely because the Athenians did not – while the Thebans did:

> ...τῇ μέντοι αὐτῇ ἰδέᾳ ὕστερον ἰόντων Ἀθηναίων ἐπὶ τοὺς Ἕλληνας μόνους αὖ Βοιωτῶν ἀττικίσαι. καίτοι σκέψασθε ἐν οἵῳ εἴδει ἑκάτεροι ἡμῶν τοῦτο ἔπραξαν.

> ...in the same way, though, they later atticized again alone of all Boeotians when the Athenians went against the Greeks. Yet look in what way each of us did that.

And there follows the distinction between acting voluntarily and acting against one's will forced by circumstances. Seeing Thucydides as guided by the principle of *variatio* seems preferable to attempting to detect differences in connotations between ἰδέα and εἶδος here.

In the two remaining passages to be considered, ἰδέα seems to mean something like 'a way of acting' or 'scheme' in more or less the same way εἶδος does at 6.77.2, 8.56.2 and 8.90.1, and at Aristophanes' *Plutus* 317.[334] At 2.19.1 Thucydides describes the devastation of Attica at the hands of the Peloponnesian forces. Before destroying the crops, they tried to take the garrison Oenoë:

> ἐπειδὴ μέντοι προσβαλόντες τῇ Οἰνόῃ καὶ πᾶσαν ἰδέαν πειράσαντες οὐκ ἐδύναντο ἑλεῖν...ἐσέβαλον ἐς τὴν Ἀττικήν.

> But when in attacking Oenoë and trying every scheme they were not able to take it...they invaded Attica.

πᾶσα ἰδέα is either 'every way', namely of προσβαλεῖν, of 'attacking', or it is – in absolute use of the phrase – 'scheme', that is to say 'device', 'plan', 'way of action' as such, without reference to the preceding phrase.

The second context of ἰδέα in the sense of scheme is very similar indeed. The Peloponnesians are attacking Plataea; their efforts fail and they think of encircling the whole city with a wall (2.77.2):

πρότερον δὲ πυρὶ ἔδοξεν αὐτοῖς πειρᾶσαι εἰ δύναιντο πνεύματος γενομένου
ἐπιφλέξαι τὴν πόλιν οὖσαν οὐ μεγάλην· πᾶσαν γὰρ δὴ ἰδέαν ἐπενόουν, εἴ πως
σφίσιν ἄνευ δαπάνης καὶ πολιορκίας προσαχθείη.

But before <resorting to> that, it seemed <good> to them to try it with fire, if,
with a breeze setting in, they could set alight the city, which wasn't a big one:
indeed, they thought of every scheme – if only the city could be taken by them
without <having to resort to> expenditure and siege.

In both cases, the attacking forces try in every way to take the place they
attack. A shift in meaning, if there is a shift, is effected by the fact that the
action under consideration is not actually carried out and completed but
attempted and thought of only. A 'way of acting' which has its existence only
in somebody's mind is a scheme or plan. Whether a Greek native speaker
would have perceived that application as semantic extension cannot be
answered with confidence.

8. ἰδέα in Aristophanes

With Aristophanes, the word ἰδέα has the same semantic range as with
Thucydides.[335] Besides denoting 'appearance' and 'figure', it can also mean
'type', as at *Frogs* 383 f., an 'exhortation to invoke Demeter',[336] preceding the
actual hymn to the goddess by the chorus:

ἄγε νυν ἑτέραν ὕμνων ἰδέαν τὴν καρποφόρον βασίλειαν,
Δήμητρα θεάν, ἐπικοσμοῦντες ζαθέαις μολπαῖς κελαδεῖτε.

Come now, sound another type of hymn, exalting the fruit-bearing queen,
the goddess Demeter, with reverend dancing-songs.

ἰδέα means 'type' once, and once 'figure', at *Birds* 992–1003, where a pun
may be intended:

METON:	ἥκω παρ' ὑμᾶς...
PISTHETAERUS:	ἕτερον αὖ τουτὶ κακόν.
	τί δαὶ σὺ δράσων; τίς ἰδέα βουλεύματος;
	τίς ἡπίνοια, τίς ὁ κόθορνος τῆς ὁδοῦ;
METON:	γεωμετρῆσαι βούλομαι τὸν ἀέρα
	ὑμῖν, διελεῖν τε κατὰ γύας.
PISTHETAERUS:	πρὸς τῶν θεῶν,
	σὺ δ' εἶ τίς ἀνδρῶν;
METON:	ὅστις εἴμ' ἐγώ; Μέτων,
	ὃν οἶδεν Ἑλλὰς χὠ Κολωνός.
PISTHETAERUS:	εἶπέ μοι,
	ταυτὶ δέ σοι τί ἐστι;
METON:	κανόνες ἀέρος.
	αὐτίκα γὰρ ἀήρ ἐστι τὴν ἰδέαν ὅλος
	κατὰ πνιγέα μάλιστα. προσθεὶς οὖν ἐγώ

τὸν κανόν᾽ ἄνωθεν τουτονὶ τὸν καμπύλον,
ἐνθεὶς διαβήτην – μανθάνεις;

PISTHETAERUS: οὐ μανθάνω.

METON: I come to you...
PISTHETAERUS: This is yet another evil.
                    So, what are you doing? What type of plan?
                    What is the thought? What is the buskin of your way?
METON: I mean to measure the air for you,
                    dividing according to land-measures.
PISTHETAERUS: By the gods.
                    And who of all men are you?
METON: Who I am? Meton,
                    whom all Hellas knows and Colonus.
PISTHETAERUS: Tell me,
                    what is it you have there?
METON: Measures of the air.
                    First, indeed, air, as regards its figure, is as a whole
                    most like a baking-oven. Now, attaching
                    from above this curved measure, I,
                    setting in this compass – do you understand?
PISTHETAERUS: I don't understand.

There cannot be any doubt that in this quick stichomythic, and sometimes even semi-stichomythic exchange, repetition of ἰδέα would have been intentional, and noted as such by the audience. It is more difficult to say what significance that repetition had, and in particular whether there was an implied joke relying on two different senses of the word.

A 'way' of doing something is denoted by ἰδέα at *Thesmophoriazusae* 434–9, where the chorus of women praises Mikka, the woman who has just finished her speech:

οὔπω ταύτης ἤκουσα | πολυπλοκωτέρας γυναικὸς | οὐδὲ δεινότερον λεγούσης. | πάντα γὰρ λέγει δίκαια· | πάσας δ᾽ ἰδέας ἐξήτασεν, | πάντα δ᾽ ἐβάστασε φρενὶ πυκνῶς τε | ποικίλους λόγους ἀνηῦρεν | εὖ διεζητημένους.

Not ever have I heard a woman more versatile or more able to speak than that one. Indeed, everything she says is right: she has tried out all figures and ways <of speaking>, and she has put to proof everything in her mind and shrewdly found out varied expressions, well searched out.

It seems as if ἰδέα, used in a rhetorical context, but by laymen, could either just denote the various ways of speaking which were open to the orator, a usage which need not presuppose any specialization in vocabulary, or conversely ἰδέα could be a semi-technical term of rhetoric theory, a rhetorical 'figure', as it will be in the fourth century. However that may be, the word

174

appears to come to the speaker's mind naturally, and the very circumstance that it must remain uncertain whether technical usage is intended or not indicates how technical terminology could naturally arise from, or in turn enter, common usage.

A slightly more complicated context is that of *Clouds* 545–8. In this part of the *parabasis*, the chorus as the poet's mouthpiece mildly scold the audience for not awarding the first version of the *Clouds* first prize despite his innovative and inventive way of writing. He does not bother the audience with vulgar common-place jokes, and he does not reproduce over and over again a joke which was successful once:

κἀγὼ μὲν τοιοῦτος ἀνὴρ ὢν ποιητὴς οὐ κομῶ,
οὐδ' ὑμᾶς ζητῶ 'ξαπατᾶν δὶς καὶ τρὶς ταῦτ' εἰσάγων,
ἀλλ' αἰεὶ καινὰς ἰδέας εἰσφέρων σοφίζομαι
οὐδὲν ἀλλήλαισιν ὁμοίας καὶ πάσας δεξιάς…

And being such a poet, I nevertheless don't think too highly of myself, nor do I try to deceive you by producing the same things twice and thrice, but I, always introducing new schemes, devise them in no way similar to each other and all alike clever.

There are, I think, two possible ways of reading this passage. As an alternative to the translation just given, one could take καινὰς ἰδέας as referring to what Aristophanes provides in the lines immediately following, namely an assembly of personages he introduced and treated or mistreated, but only until his purpose was served, not in the endlessly repetitious and tedious manner of his colleagues. The named individuals Aristophanes then enumerates can be regarded as the 'new figures' he introduces on stage. In favour, however, of the translation proposed above, adhering to the traditional way of interpreting this passage, one could adduce the first fragment of Eupolis' *Autolycus*, in which one character accuses the other:

ἐπὶ καινοτέρας ἰδέας ἀσεβῶν βίον, ὦ μοχθηρός, ἔτριβες.

Worthless one, being impious, you wasted your life on newish schemes.

Here καινότερος, 'rather new', means 'new and therefore bad', as does νεώτερος elsewhere; nevertheless, although this connotation is clearly absent from Aristophanes, it is not impossible that καιναὶ ἰδέαι, 'new schemes', was something like a standing phrase, with positive or negative overtones according to context.[337]

9. ἰδέα in early dialogues of Plato

ἰδέα in early Plato is as rare a word as it is in the fifth-century authors discussed so far. There are two dialogues in which the word is used in an

175

aristocratic context with reference to the figure of a beautiful youth. The three instances in the *Charmides* all occur in the context of first Critias' and then Socrates' referring to Charmides' ἰδέα, his 'appearance' or 'figure'. At the beginning of the conversation, Critias is full of praise for his nephew and assures Socrates (157d1–4):

λέγω μέντοι σοι ὅτι Χαρμίδης τῶν ἡλικιωτῶν οὐ μόνον τῇ ἰδέᾳ δοκεῖ διαφέρειν, ἀλλὰ καὶ αὐτῷ τούτῳ, οὗ σὺ φῂς τὴν ἐπῳδὴν ἔχειν· φῂς δὲ σωφροσύνης· ἢ γάρ;

For sure, I tell you that Charmides appears to differ from the youths of his age not only in his figure, but also in that very thing concerning which you say you have an incantation: and you mean temperance, don't you?

As at its earliest occurrence in Theognis, ἰδέα or 'figure' is in some way contrasted with qualities of the mind. Taking up this praise by an uncle for his nephew, Socrates begins a conversation with the youth by praising his descent, and states (158a7–b4):

...τὰ μὲν οὖν ὁρώμενα τῆς ἰδέας, ὦ φίλε παῖ Γλαύκωνος, δοκεῖς μοι οὐδένα τῶν πρὸ σοῦ ἐν οὐδενὶ ὑποβεβηκέναι· εἰ δὲ δὴ καὶ πρὸς σωφροσύνην καὶ πρὸς τἆλλα κατὰ τὸν τοῦδε λόγον ἱκανῶς πέφυκας, μακάριόν σε, ἦν δ' ἐγώ, ὦ φίλε Χαρμίδη, ἡ μήτηρ ἔτικτεν.

As far as what is visible of your appearance is concerned, dear son of Glaucon, you seem to me not to lag behind any of your forbears in anything: thus, if, as this man says, you are also naturally fit as regards temperance and the other things <mentioned>, I said, your mother has born you a lucky person.

Both reference and context are virtually identical. Finally, at a point in their discussion when Socrates' arguments and concerns have produced an *aporia*, he scolds Charmides (175d6–e1):

...ὑπὲρ δὲ σοῦ, ἦν δ' ἐγώ, ὦ Χαρμίδη, πάνυ ἀγανακτῶ, εἰ σὺ τοιοῦτος ὢν τὴν ἰδέαν καὶ πρὸς τούτῳ τὴν ψυχὴν σωφρονέστατος, μηδὲν ὀνήσῃ ἀπὸ ταύτης τῆς σωφροσύνης...

...but on your behalf, I said, I am rather annoyed, Charmides, that you, being such <as you are> as regards appearance, and in addition to that very temperate as regards your soul, should not benefit at all from that temperance...

The context in the *Protagoras* is less elaborate, but otherwise similar. In describing the scene they encountered when they entered the house of the rich Callias, Socrates says while talking about those gathered around Prodicus (*Protagoras* 315d7–e1):

παρεκάθηντο δὲ αὐτῷ ἐπὶ ταῖς πλησίον κλίναις Παυσανίας τε ὁ ἐκ Κεραμέων καὶ μετὰ Παυσανίου νέον τι ἔτι μειράκιον, ὡς μὲν ἐγᾦμαι καλόν τε κἀγαθὸν τὴν φύσιν, τὴν δ' οὖν ἰδέαν πάνυ καλός.

By him, there sat on nearby benches Pausanias from Kerameus, and with Pausanias a young man, still a youth, as I think beautiful and good as regards his nature, but certainly very beautiful as regards his figure.

Without entering into a discussion as to whether ἰδέα in these four instances is supposed to refer to the 'appearance' of the two youths in general, or to their 'figure' in particular, we can see that Plato employs ἰδέα in his early dialogues to bestow 'heroic praise' in aristocratic circles; the term refers to the external, visible appearance or figure as opposed to the mind or nature of the young men described.

10. Recapitulation

At the end of the discussion of Thucydides' use of εἶδος it was stated that,[338] in Thucydides, εἶδος is fairly consistently applied to actions, often qualified as 'this' or 'that' or 'another'; it seems to denote a 'type of action', a 'way (of acting)', and then a 'scheme' or 'way or type of action or acting'; that this usage may be colloquial Attic is confirmed by Aristophanes. It could be shown that this development is a natural extension of application of εἶδος to an action instead of to a thing, facilitated by the use of the word as denoting 'type' in addition to appearance. That can now be supplemented and modified. We have seen that, with Herodotus, the word ἰδέα has a range of meanings and applications, beginning with what was, in all probability, the original meaning and application, the 'appearance' and 'guise' of a person, with connotations of a person's 'figure'; that the noun was then applied to animals, probably again with connotations of 'figure'; that there is an extension from that to 'type', applied to animals and plants. In a different direction, there is the same extension in Herodotus as was encountered in Democritus: a particular object or entity can be referred to as an ἰδέα. Lastly, there is an instance of ἰδέα referring to a 'way of acting' or 'way of action', where ἰδέα could be translated as 'scheme', since the way of action is presented as envisaged, as being present so far only in the mind.

If Herodotus had written at least part of his account by the mid-forties, a number of semantic extensions which ἰδέα apparently shares with εἶδος seem to have taken place with ἰδέα first. But it is difficult to assign certain dates to specific parts of the *Histories*. The relative chronology of the *Histories* and certain Hippocratic treatises, on which Thucydides is sometimes said to depend in his style, can therefore not be determined either. It is, of course, possible that the Ionian Herodotus of Halicarnassus was familiar with the parlance of the medical men from the neighbouring island of Cos, in which case he could have been influenced by their language in this respect; it is, however, likewise possible that the semantic extensions 'type', 'way of acting' and 'scheme', the last a sense of εἶδος found in Aristophanes, too,[339] were common fifth-century Greek rather than specialized vocabulary of one particular profession.[340] How these issues are decided, will have consequences for an evaluation of the conditions that underlie the semantic development of εἶδος. It is possible that the semantic development of εἶδος was influenced by a preceding parallel development of ἰδέα, or *vice versa*. Since there is an original semantic overlap between the two Greek words, there is always the possibility that subsequent extensions of connotations and extensions in application of one of the two terms will be transferred to the other. However, whether this potentiality is actualized in the case of any given sense, cannot be predicted; it can only be observed once it has occurred.

If a conclusion can be drawn from the one definitely early medical treatise in which ἰδέα and εἶδος co-occur, *The Nature of Man*,[341] it is perhaps the following: both Greek nouns can mean both 'appearance' and 'type'. The author speaks of πολλαὶ ἰδέαι νουσημάτων, 'many types of diseases', and of τέσσαρα εἴδεα πυρετῶν, 'four types of fevers'. However, as we have seen, the ἰδέαι in chapter 2 may refer more closely to visible manifestations.[342] Otherwise, the author uses ἰδέα when he talks about what we would call physics and chemistry, when he discusses Presocratic philosophical theories and their application to medicine. He employs εἶδος when he talks about the appearance of a person or the type of person the physician is dealing with. It is conceivable that this is not so by accident. It is possible that there was a large semantic overlap between εἶδος and ἰδέα, but that the latter word was more closely associated with physical theory.[343]

In the early dialogues of Plato, however, ἰδέα is rare. Where the word is used, it refers to the 'appearance' or 'figure' of a person; the people whose 'appearances' or 'figures' are mentioned are young and beautiful.

Chapter 6

μορφή

μορφή is a word of uncertain etymological origin. Its original meaning and subsequent early semantic development are not, and perhaps cannot be, sufficiently explained.[344] Where we encounter the word in fifth-century prose, it refers to the physical 'shape' of something or somebody.[345] μορφή occurs at *Phaedo* 103e and then once more, in the same context, at 104d. It need not at this stage be decided whether the word can lay claim to being a technical term in Plato's middle period, but both because of its role in Aristotle's philosophy and – for our purposes more importantly – because in the *Phaedo* the word appears, at first glance, to be synonymous with ἰδέα in one significant context, it may be worthwhile looking briefly at the usage of μορφή in early Greek literature. In what follows, I do not attempt to give a full history of the word, but rather to establish some features of its early usage.

1. μορφή in early Greek poetry

There are no occurrences of μορφή in the *Iliad* and in Hesiod; there are two instances in the *Odyssey*. Both occur in the frame of the Phaeacian books, not in one of the fabulous stories told by Odysseus; that is to say, they belong, on any theory of the composition of the poem, to the same stratum and the same poet. In both passages, μορφή is not used 'literally' with reference to the physical shape of something. The first of the two passages has been discussed in section 1 of the chapter on εἶδος above.[346] In Book 8 of the *Odyssey*, when in Scheria, Odysseus, guest of the Phaeacians, is taunted by Euryalus (164), οὐδ' ἀθλητῆρι ἔοικας, 'you are not like a fighter', Odysseus retorts (167–77):

οὕτως οὐ πάντεσσι θεοὶ χαρίεντα διδοῦσιν
ἀνδράσιν, οὔτε φυὴν οὔτ' ἄρ φρένας οὔτ' ἀγορητύν.
ἄλλος μὲν γὰρ εἶδος ἀκιδνότερος πέλει ἀνήρ,
ἀλλὰ θεὸς μορφὴν ἔπεσι στέφει, οἱ δέ τ' ἐς αὐτὸν
τερπόμενοι λεύσσουσιν· ὁ δ' ἀσφαλέως ἀγορεύει
αἰδοῖ μειλιχίῃ, μετὰ δὲ πρέπει ἀγρομένοισιν,
ἐρχόμενον δ' ἀνὰ ἄστυ θεὸν ὣς εἰσορόωσιν.
ἄλλος δ' αὖ εἶδος μὲν ἀλίγκιος ἀθανάτοισιν,

179

ἀλλ' οὖ οἱ χάρις ἀμφιπεριστέφεται ἐπέεσσιν,
ὡς καὶ σοὶ εἶδος μὲν ἀριπρεπές, οὐδέ κεν ἄλλως
οὐδὲ θεὸς τεύξειε, νόον δ' ἀποφώλιός ἐσσι.

Not in one way do the gods give pleasing things to all men, neither growth nor yet mind nor eloquence. One man, indeed, is weak in appearance, but god wreathes shape around his words, and the other men look at him, delighted; but he speaks unfailingly with soothing reverence; he finds favour with those who are gathered, just as if they looked at a god walking through the city. Again, another man resembles the gods as regards his look, but for him, no grace is wreathed around his words, just as you are very stately as to look, a god could not fit it otherwise, as to mind, however, you are useless.

The statement of θεὸς μορφὴν ἔπεσι στέφει, 'god wreathes shape around his words',[347] seems to be connected with ὁ δ' ἀσφαλέως ἀγορεύει, 'but he speaks unfailingly'; and it seems to be in contrast with νόον δ' ἀποφώλιός ἐσσι, 'as to mind, however, you are useless'. This is reminiscent of other passages in the *Odyssey* in which external appearance and mind are set into relation, as for example at 11.336 f., when Odysseus recounts his errands to the Phaeacians and, when he has finished, Arete, the queen, addresses her people (336–7):

Φαίηκες, πῶς ὕμμιν ἀνὴρ ὅδε φαίνεται εἶναι
εἶδός τε μέγεθός τε ἰδὲ φρένας ἔνδον ἐίσας;

Phaeacians, how does this man seem to be to you,
as regards look and size, and also equal wits within?

When Alcinous, the king, is asked to speak as well, he promises Odysseus gifts and a safe conduct home, provided he continues with his tale. Odysseus agrees to that request and does not fail to stress the need of copious gifts in order to establish his position as king on his return home. To that, Alcinous replies (11.363–8):

ὦ 'Οδυσεῦ, τὸ μὲν οὔ τί σ' ἐίσκομεν εἰσορόωντες
ἠπεροπῆά τ' ἔμεν καὶ ἐπίκλοπον, οἷά τε πολλοὺς
βόσκει γαῖα μέλαινα πολυσπερέας ἀνθρώπους
ψεύδεά τ' ἀρτύνοντας, ὅθεν κέ τις οὐδὲ ἴδοιτο·
σοὶ δ' ἔπι μὲν μορφὴ ἐπέων, ἔνι δὲ φρένες ἐσθλαί,
μῦθον δ' ὡς ὅτ' ἀοιδὸς ἐπισταμένως κατέλεξας...

Odysseus, looking at you, we do not liken you to a cheater and swindler, such as the black earth nourishes many men scattered all over the world who compose their deceits whence one would not see it: but with you, there is, surely, the shape of your words, and in you, there are noble wits, when you tell your tale with insight like a singer...

μορφὴ ἐπέων: 'the shape of your words' may not seem to be a satisfying translation; in order to make it look less paradoxical, 'shapeliness' and 'comeliness' have been suggested;[348] but that seems to evade rather than to further interpretation. μορφή here is not a distinguishing mark of Odysseus' words that implies truth. 'Shape' is a property also of the liar's words which deceive ὅθεν κέ τις οὐδὲ ἴδοιτο, 'whence one would not see it'. The external shape of Odysseus' words would not guarantee their truth; but 'to him', there also is understanding, insight like that of an ἀοιδός, a 'singer', whose office it is to tell the truth. What the queen praises in Odysseus is his own outward appearance and his wits within; that latter praise is taken up by the king who grants him 'shape of his words', but adds that he also has wits within – that is what makes himself and his story valuable rather than just deceptively pleasing. In this passage at least, μορφή, 'shape', seems to refer to something external, something from which one cannot see, and therefore cannot deduce, what the thing having this shape is like, i.e. in this case, if the words are, or are not, true.

In comparable fashion, in the first passage, *Odyssey* 8.167 ff., Odysseus starts off with 'what is pleasing'. That can be physical 'growth' or stature as external attributes or, as internal attributes, wits or, on this occasion, eloquence. ἀγορητύς is derived from the verb ἀγορεύω and signifies 'speaking-in-public'. Though 'speaking well in public' can be contrasted with 'looking good', it could also be contrasted with 'having understanding', just as 'having understanding' could be contrasted with 'looking good'. In Odysseus' statement, the *tertium comparationis* is 'pleasing', not 'good' or 'true'. At *Odyssey* 8.170, μορφή is that 'shape' which words must have if they are to be pleasing, so that Odysseus, in speaking about the man whose words do not have that shape, can declare in paraphrase (175):

ἀλλ' οὔ οἱ χάρις ἀμφιπεριστέφεται ἐπέεσσιν.

But for him, no grace is wreathed around his words.

That is not to be interpreted as if χάρις, 'grace', were a synonym of μορφή any more than εἶδος could be said to be a synonym of μορφή here. εἶδος is the 'look', the 'appearance' of a person, μορφή is the 'shape': and here it is the shape of the 'words', the ἔπη, which are present in the text as a necessary grammatical complement, just as ἀνήρ, the 'man', is that 'to which there is' (an) εἶδος. If the shape of words is pleasing, those words can be said to be pleasing, to have χάρις, and if the look of a man is pleasing, that man can be said to be pleasing: 'in that respect', as the dialectician Odysseus does not fail to emphasize.[349]

A poetic context may have contributed to the misapprehension that μορφή and εἶδος are synonyms in the sense of physical shape or form. In the prologue of Euripides' *Bacchae*, the god Dionysus explains his mission and the reasons behind his appearing in human form amongst mortals. Having told his story, he concludes (53–4):

ὧν οὕνεκ' εἶδος θνητὸν ἀλλάξας ἔχω
μορφήν τ' ἐμὴν μετέβαλον εἰς ἀνδρὸς φύσιν.

For those reasons, I have a mortal appearance [guise], having exchanged <my appearance>,
and I have changed my shape into the nature of a man.

Dionysus looks like a mortal man. His whole 'appearance', his εἶδος, is to that effect. He has achieved that by changing 'shape', μορφή. The result of his physical transformation is an altered appearance. 'Appearance' depends, in the realm of physical objects, *inter alia* on physical 'shape'. Euripides is precise in his choice of words.

In the same way, there obtains a relation between physical form and overall appearance in the Hippocratic *On the Sacred Disease*. Subject of section 16 are the contrary effects of the North- and the South-wind on nature, men and physical objects. All things feel the effects of the wind. The author continues (16.27–30):

ὁκόσα τε ἐν οἰκήμασι κεράμια ἢ κατὰ γῆς ἐστι μεστὰ οἴνου ἢ ἄλλου τινὸς ὑγροῦ, πάντα ταῦτα αἰσθάνεται τοῦ νότου καὶ διαλλάσσει τὴν μορφὴν ἐς ἕτερον εἶδος…

Also pots that are in houses or under the earth, full of wine or another liquid, all these things perceive the South-wind and change their shape into another appearance.

One could, of course, argue that in this last case the physical shape of a vessel is changed to another physical shape, that is to say another 'type' of physical shape. As we have seen in the chapter on εἶδος, the qualification, here 'of physical shape', can be omitted, and it is, by the end of the fifth century, idiomatic to say 'they change their shape (μορφὴν) into another type (εἶδος).' But this is not necessarily a natural reading.

Euripides, *Troades* 1265, shows a different semantic development of μορφή. Talthybius, the herald, arrives on stage with a set of orders; he instructs the junior officers to set fire to the city of Troy; the captured Trojans are to move from where they are at present; Hecuba is to follow him. His words are (1260–71):

αὐδῶ λοχαγοῖς, οἳ τέταχθ' ἐμπιμπράναι
Πριάμου τόδ' ἄστυ, μηκέτ' ἀργοῦσαν φλόγα
ἐν χειρὶ σῴζειν, ἀλλὰ πῦρ ἐνιέναι,
ὡς ἂν κατασκάψαντες Ἰλίου πόλιν
στελλώμεθ' οἴκαδ' ἄσμενοι Τροίας ἄπο.
ὑμεῖς δ', ἵν' αὑτὸς λόγος ἔχῃ μορφὰς δύο,

χωρεῖτε, Τρώων παῖδες, ὀρθίαν ὅταν
σάλπιγγος ἠχὼ δῶσιν ἀρχηγοὶ στρατοῦ,
πρὸς ναῦς Ἀχαιῶν, ὡς ἀποστέλλησθε γῆς.
σύ τ᾽, ὦ γεραιὰ δυστυχεστάτη γύναι,
ἕπου. μεθήκουσίν σ᾽ Ὀδυσσέως πάρα
οἵδ᾽, ᾧ σε δούλην κλῆρος ἐκπέμπει πάτρας.

I say to the lieutenants who are ordered to set alight this city of Priam, do not preserve the flame in your hand, where it is idle, but send the fire forth into the city, so that we may set off home, away from Troy, content, as we have burnt down the city of Troy.
But you – so that the same speech has two forms – as soon as the leaders of the army let their trumpets sound, go to the ships of the Achaeans, children of Troy, so as to leave your land.
And you, most wretched old woman, follow. Those come for you from Odysseus: the lot sends you out of your fatherland to him, as his slave.

Paley comments aptly:[350] ῾μορφὰς δύο, two indications or significations; that is, according to Matthiae, for the Trojan captives (the chorus) to depart at the sound of the trumpet, and for Hecuba to follow him immediately. But it might equally well refer to the command given above to the λοχαγοὶ, and to the further orders now communicated to the captives generally.᾽ The speech of the herald has two μορφαί. Does that mean ῾two indications or significations᾽, or does it mean ῾two parts᾽, or does it mean ῾two forms᾽ or ῾two aspects᾽, a happy one for his comrades and a sad one for the captives? If the last reading is possible, it would not be too remote from the ῾shape of words᾽ encountered above. But perhaps it is safer just to state that δύο μορφαί can be used abstractly to denote ῾two shapes, forms, categories, parts or divisions᾽ of something, whatever it is.

2. μορφή in Empedocles and Parmenides

A direct parallel to the passage from Euripides' *Bacchae* discussed in the previous section is furnished by Empedocles, who presupposes the same contrast between external shape or form and identity of being. Sextus Empiricus and Origen, in discussing Pythagorean abstinence from meat and metempsychosis, which by Origen (*Contra Celsum* 5.49) is termed τὸν περὶ τῆς ψυχῆς μετενσωματουμένης μῦθον, ῾the myth about the soul's being re-embodied᾽, adduce verses of Empedocles. Sextus quotes (*Adversus Mathematicos* 9.129 = DK31B137):

μορφὴν δ᾽ ἀλλάξαντα πατὴρ φίλον υἱὸν ἀείρας | σφάζει ἐπευχόμενος…

The father, lifting his dear son who has changed his shape, slaughters him praying.

183

The point of the thought expressed here is that the soul which is re-embodied remains the same; and that thereby the continuity of the person, in the modern sense of that word, is guaranteed. What changes, is only the outward shape, a shape which does not determine what, or who, somebody or something really is.

Empedocles uses μορφή in a way reminiscent of the usage of the *Odyssey* in another fragment, whose original context is not preserved (Simplicius *Physica* 159.13 = DK31B21):

ἀλλ᾽ ἄγε, τονδ᾽ ὀάρων προτέρων ἐπιμάρτυρα δέρκευ,
εἴ τι καὶ ἐν προτέροισι λιπόξυλον ἔπλετο μορφῇ,
...

Well then, look at this witness of my earlier words, if in them anything at all was incomplete in shape...[351]

We do not, of course, know what exactly had come before this passage, but for the present purpose this may not be relevant. Whatever it was, Empedocles presumably did not mean to say that his former words were incorrect or false; they were in some way insufficient. They were lacking in shape. This use of μορφή is the same as that of Alcinous who says that Odysseus' words have shape, or that of Odysseus who speaks more generally about someone who is capable of speaking pleasingly since his words have shape.[352]

An altogether different application of μορφή is found in Parmenides. Parmenides commences his exposition of this system with the words (B8.51–61):

...δόξας δ᾽ ἀπὸ τοῦδε βροτείας
μάνθανε κόσμον ἐμῶν ἐπέων ἀπατηλὸν ἀκούων.
μορφὰς γὰρ κατέθεντο δύο γνώμας ὀνομάζειν,
τῶν μίαν οὐ χρεών ἐστιν· ἐν ᾧ πεπλανημένοι εἰσίν.
ἀντία δ᾽ ἐκρίναντο δέμας καὶ σήματ᾽ ἔθεντο
χωρὶς ἀπ᾽ ἀλλήλων· τῇ μὲν φλογὸς αἰθέριον πῦρ,
ἤπιον ὄν, μέγ᾽ ἐλαφρόν, ἑωυτῷ πάντοσε τωυτόν,
τῷ δ᾽ ἑτέρῳ μὴ τωυτόν· ἀτὰρ κἀκεῖνο κατ᾽ αὐτὸ
τἀντία νύκτ᾽ ἀδαῆ, πυκινὸν δέμας ἐμβριθές τε.
τόν σοι ἐγὼ διάκοσμον ἐοικότα πάντα φατίζω,
ὡς οὐ μή ποτέ τίς σε βροτῶν γνώμῃ παρελάσσῃ.

... But from here on learn the human belief and opinions, listening to the deceptive order of my words. They made up their minds[353] to name two shapes, to name one of which is not right: in this they have gone astray. But they judged them [= the two shapes] to be opposite as regards their build; and they attributed to them signs separate from one another: To the one, the etherial fire of the flame, being mild, very light, in every way the same as itself, not the same as the other one; again also the other one for itself, as opposite, unknowing night, of dense and heavy build. I report to you the whole order as it is likely,[354] so that no 'insight' of mortals will ever overtake you.

Men decree to name two shapes, the one associated with etherial fire, the other with night, or, on a different reading, the one fire, the other night.[355] In Parmenides, we can observe that the same type of semantic shift – from denoting 'the shape (of something)' to denoting 'a shape' in an absolute sense – has taken place which had been observed in the case of both εἶδος and ἰδέα, which from having denoted 'an appearance (of something)' came to denote 'an appearance'. In Parmenides, the two μορφαί are two things.[356]

3. Recapitulation

μορφή is thus the physical 'shape' of something; the 'shape' or 'form' something has, be it a physical object or words of a certain shape or form; perhaps δύο μορφαί refers *abstractly* to a bipartite division; μορφή, however, can also be used absolutely with reference to a material entity that is labelled 'a shape'. The usage of Parmenides as well as the abstract use of δύο μορφαί in Euripides may be relevant in considering the occurrences of μορφή in the *Phaedo*.

PART III

In Part I and Part II, the terms μετέχειν, παρεῖναι, ἐνεῖναι, εἶδος, ἰδέα, μορφή and their congeners were investigated with a view to applying the results of this historico-semantic research to the *Phaedo*, and specifically to an interpretation of *Phaedo* 95e–107b. Part III will offer an interpretation of at least one important aspect of the dialogue, its philosophical ancestry among the Presocratics. With this end in mind, we shall examine, in the *Phaedo*, the occurrences of the terms whose histories we have traced in the previous chapters. But before we turn to those words whose historical development has been studied above, one term is to be considered which is, in many ways, Plato's own. The chapter on οὐσία, 'being', will elucidate the philosophical structure of Plato's thought in the *Phaedo* and in that way form the backdrop to the conclusions drawn in the subsequent chapters.

Chapter 7

οὐσία

1. οὐσία before Plato

οὐσία, one of the most fertile philosophical terms in post-Platonic philosophy, was, *qua* philosophical term, Plato's creation.[357] It is of course undisputed that the word existed in Attic Greek before Plato, but only with the meaning 'property' *vel sim.*, i.e. the collective noun that denotes ἅ τινι ἔστιν, 'what is (or 'is there') to (or 'for') somebody', 'someone's property or wealth'.[358] As such, the word is frequently found in the Attic dramatists and orators of the fifth and fourth centuries BC, and in Attic inscriptions.[359] But while the history of the word is well documented, it is necessary to ask again what it signifies in Plato's dialogues before the *Republic*. Only once that is established can it be decided whether the notion expressed had been anticipated by one of Plato's predecessors.

2. οὐσία in Plato's *Meno* and *Euthyphro*

When Plato for the first time introduces οὐσία with its new technical, philosophical meaning of 'being' in the *Meno* and the *Euthyphro*, he marks this new usage with definitional tags:

> SOCRATES: πολλῇ γέ τινι εὐτυχίᾳ ἔοικα κεχρῆσθαι, ὦ Μένων, εἰ μίαν ζητῶν ἀρετὴν σμῆνός τι ἀνηύρηκα ἀρετῶν παρὰ σοὶ κείμενον. ἀτάρ, ὦ Μένων, κατὰ ταύτην τὴν εἰκόνα τὴν περὶ τὰ σμήνη, εἴ μου ἐρομένου <u>μελίττης περὶ οὐσίας ὅτι ποτ' ἐστίν</u>, πολλὰς καὶ παντοδαπὰς ἔλεγες αὐτὰς εἶναι, τί ἂν ἀπεκρίνω μοι, εἴ σε ἠρόμην· 'ἆρα τούτῳ φῂς πολλὰς καὶ παντοδαπὰς εἶναι καὶ διαφερούσας ἀλλήλων, τῷ μελίττας εἶναι; ἢ τούτῳ μὲν οὐδὲν διαφέρουσιν, ἄλλῳ δέ τῳ, οἷον ἢ κάλλει ἢ μεγέθει ἢ ἄλλῳ τῳ τῶν τοιούτων; ' εἰπέ, τί ἂν ἀπεκρίνω οὕτως ἐρωτηθείς;
> MENO: τοῦτ' ἔγωγε, ὅτι οὐδὲν διαφέρουσιν, ᾗ μέλιτται εἰσίν, ἡ ἑτέρα τῆς ἑτέρας.

SOCRATES: I certainly seem to have good luck, Meno, if looking for one excellence I have found a swarm of excellences lying with you. But, Meno, according to the image, the one of the swarms, if when I asked you <u>about a bee, its being, what it is</u>,[360] you said that they are many and varied, what would you answer me if I asked you: 'Is it that through-and-in *this* you say they are many and varied and different from each other, through being bees? Or do they differ not at all through-and-in this, but through-and-in something else, such as through-

189

and in beauty or size or any other of such things?' Tell me, what would you answer thus asked?

MENO: This I would answer, that, in as much as they are bees, they differ not at all from one another. *Meno 72e3–73a5*

SOCRATES: καὶ κινδυνεύεις, ὦ Εὐθύφρων, ἐρωτώμενος <u>τὸ ὅσιον ὅτι ποτ' ἐστίν, τὴν μὲν οὐσίαν</u> μοι αὐτοῦ οὐ βούλεσθαι δηλῶσαι, πάθος δέ τι περὶ αὐτοῦ λέγειν, ὅτι πέπονθε τοῦτο τὸ ὅσιον, φιλεῖσθαι ὑπὸ πάντων θεῶν· ὅτι δὲ ὄν, οὔπω εἶπες. εἰ οὖν σοι φίλον, μή με ἀποκρύψῃ ἀλλὰ πάλιν εἰπὲ ἐξ ἀρχῆς τί ποτε ὂν τὸ ὅσιον εἴτε φιλεῖται ὑπὸ θεῶν εἴτε ὁτιδὴ πάσχει – οὐ γὰρ περὶ τούτου διοισόμεθα – ἀλλ' εἰπὲ προθύμως τί ἐστιν τό τε ὅσιον καὶ τὸ ἀνόσιον;

SOCRATES: And, Euthyphro, when asked about <u>the pious, what it is, its being</u> you seem not to be willing to reveal to me,[361] but just to give me 'something it has happen to it',[362] what happens to this 'pious', <namely> to be loved by all the gods: but *being what* [i.e., *what it is* while this happens to it], you have not yet said. So if that is fine by you, do not hide it from me, but say again from the beginning: *being what* is the pious loved by the gods or has happen to it whatever else may happen to it – for we do not disagree about that – but tell me freely: what *is* the pious and the impious? *Euthyphro 11a6–b5*

In both passages οὐσία comes to stand next to the phrase ὅτι ποτ' ἐστίν, 'what (ever) it is'. As direct questions, 'what (ever) is the pious?' and 'what (ever) is excellence?' have a form familiar from other early Platonic dialogues. The *context* in which the noun οὐσία is introduced is thus not new. By juxtaposing ὅτι ποτ' ἐστίν, as an indirect question, and οὐσία, Plato therefore defines sufficiently the sense in which he wants the noun οὐσία to be taken: οὐσία is 'what something is'. And from the *Meno* and *Euthyphro* alone one can also see that Plato's giving the meaning of 'what something is' to οὐσία is motivated partly by, or at least amounts to, an etymologizing of the noun by exploiting its similarity with the feminine singular participle οὖσα, 'being'.[363] At the same time it may be noted that, in the *Euthyphro*, οὐσία is contrasted with πάθος, just as at *Meno* 71b3–4, in the passage leading up to Socrates' introduction of the word οὐσία, 'what something is' is contrasted with 'what something is like': ὃ δὲ μὴ οἶδα <u>τί</u> ἐστιν, πῶς ἂν <u>ὁποῖόν</u> γέ τι εἰδείην; 'But in a case where I do not know <u>what</u> something is, how could I possibly know <u>of what sort</u> it is?'[364] It may be significant that therefore οὐσία here does not mean 'that something is'.

3. οὐσία in Plato's *Phaedo*: 65d–e, 76d–77a

This etymological interpretation of the word οὐσία – which otherwise meant 'possession, wealth, property' – as 'being' is also found in the *Phaedo*. The first of the five passages in the dialogue in which the term occurs is 65d9–e5:

ἤδη οὖν πώποτέ τι τῶν τοιούτων τοῖς ὀφθαλμοῖς εἶδες;

οὐδαμῶς, ἦ δ’ ὅς.

ἀλλ’ ἄλλῃ τινὶ αἰσθήσει τῶν διὰ τοῦ σώματος ἐφήψω αὐτῶν; λέγω δὲ περὶ
πάντων, οἷον μεγέθους πέρι, ὑγιείας, ἰσχύος, καὶ τῶν ἄλλων ἑνὶ λόγῳ ἁπάντων
τῆς οὐσίας ὃ τυγχάνει ἕκαστον ὄν· ἆρα διὰ τοῦ σώματος αὐτῶν τὸ ἀληθέστατον
θεωρεῖται, ἢ ὧδε ἔχει· ὃς ἂν μάλιστα ἡμῶν καὶ ἀκριβέστατα παρασκευάσηται
αὐτὸ ἕκαστον διανοηθῆναι περὶ οὗ σκοπεῖ, οὗτος ἂν ἐγγύτατα ἴοι τοῦ γνῶναι
ἕκαστον;

So have you ever yet seen any one of the things of that sort with your eyes?
Never, said he.
But have you touched them with any other sensation of those (we get) through
the body? But I am talking about everything, as for example about size, health,
strength, and, in a word, all other things' being,[365] what each happens to be: Is
it the case that what is truest of them is perceived through the body, or is it as
follows: whoever of us manages to the greatest extent and most accurately to
think through[366] each thing itself about which he speculates, this (person) may
well come closest to understanding each thing?

The definitional tag 'what each happens to be' echoes the similar phrases of
the *Meno* and the *Euthyphro*. What is new is the range of terms or notions or
concepts with whose 'being' Socrates is concerned, as well as the epistemological considerations which accompany the introduction of the term οὐσία
in the *Phaedo*. The phrase 'what each happens to be' defines the term οὐσία in
the same way as in the earlier two dialogues; together with the remainder of
the passage, it serves as a clear indication that οὐσία here, too, denotes 'being'
in the sense of 'what something is', not in the sense of 'that something is'.

The next two occurrences of οὐσία present a slightly different case
(76d7–77a5):

ἆρ’ οὖν οὕτως ἔχει, ἔφη, ἡμῖν, ὦ Σιμμία; εἰ μὲν ἔστιν ἃ θρυλοῦμεν ἀεί, καλόν τέ
τι καὶ ἀγαθὸν καὶ πᾶσα ἡ τοιαύτη οὐσία, καὶ ἐπὶ ταύτην τὰ ἐκ τῶν αἰσθήσεων
πάντα ἀναφέρομεν, ὑπάρχουσαν πρότερον ἀνευρίσκοντες ἡμετέραν οὖσαν, καὶ
ταῦτα ἐκείνῃ ἀπεικάζομεν, ἀναγκαῖον, οὕτως ὥσπερ καὶ ταῦτα ἔστιν, οὕτως καὶ
τὴν ἡμετέραν ψυχὴν εἶναι καὶ πρὶν γεγονέναι ἡμᾶς· εἰ δὲ μὴ ἔστι ταῦτα, ἄλλως
ἂν ὁ λόγος οὗτος εἰρημένος εἴη; ἆρ’ οὕτως ἔχει, καὶ ἴση ἀνάγκη ταῦτά τε εἶναι
καὶ τὰς ἡμετέρας ψυχὰς πρὶν καὶ ἡμᾶς γεγονέναι, καὶ εἰ μὴ ταῦτα, οὐδὲ τάδε;
ὑπερφυῶς, ὦ Σώκρατες, ἔφη ὁ Σιμμίας, δοκεῖ μοι ἡ αὐτὴ ἀνάγκη εἶναι, καὶ
εἰς καλόν γε καταφεύγει ὁ λόγος εἰς τὸ ὁμοίως εἶναι τήν τε ψυχὴν ἡμῶν πρὶν
γενέσθαι ἡμᾶς καὶ τὴν οὐσίαν ἣν σὺ νῦν λέγεις. οὐ γὰρ ἔχω ἔγωγε οὐδὲν οὕτω
μοι ἐναργὲς ὂν ὡς τοῦτο, τὸ πάντα τὰ τοιαῦτ’ εἶναι ὡς οἷόν τε μάλιστα, καλόν
τε καὶ ἀγαθὸν καὶ τἆλλα πάντα ἃ σὺ νυνδὴ ἔλεγες· καὶ ἔμοιγε δοκεῖ ἱκανῶς
ἀποδέδεικται.

So, Simmias, he said, is it not consequently like this: if what we always talk
about *is*,[367] a beautiful and a good and the whole being of this sort, and if to
this we refer everything <that we get> from our sensations, finding it again as
obtaining before, being ours, and if we liken those <things which we get from

our sensations> to it [i.e.: to the whole being of this sort], then it is necessary
that such as those things [i.e. the beautiful, the good and the whole being of this
sort], too, *are*, so also *is* our soul even before we were: but if those things [i.e. the
beautiful, the good and the whole being of this sort] are not, this account may
well have to be given in a different way? Is it like this, and there is equal necessity
that those things [i.e. the beautiful, the good and the whole being of this sort]
are and that our souls *are*, even before we were, and if not this, neither that?
Socrates, said Simmias, it seems to me that there is most obviously the same
necessity <for both>, and the account has certainly escaped to a beautiful
conclusion: that with equal necessity[368] *is* our soul before we have come to be
<u>and is the being which you now mention.</u> For I have nothing that is so clear to
me as this, that all such things *are* as much as possible, beautiful and good and
all the other things which you have just mentioned: and to me it seems that it
is demonstrated sufficiently.

The phrase πᾶσα ἡ τοιαύτη οὐσία must be rendered 'the whole being of this
sort': οὐσία here is the collective noun[369] for τὰ ὄντα, 'things'.[370] οὐσία thus
does not here refer to what a particular thing is; instead, it refers to the
totality of 'such' things, i.e. the totality of the things that are, the totality of
what is in the way the beautiful is and the good is; but οὐσία does not mean
'the existence' of things like the good and the beautiful. That is to say, there
is a semantic extension of the noun here; as is to be expected, this extension
is in line with possible application of forms of the verb εἶναι, 'to be'; but
the specific extension in this case is not in the direction of a so-called 'existential' εἶναι, but rather in the direction of the meaning of the plural of
the substantival neuter participle, τὰ ὄντα, which was a standard word in
common Greek parlance, simply denoting 'things'.[371] This helps to establish
the term οὐσία by linking it more firmly to its etymological connection with
εἶναι, and it may certainly help prepare further extension in meaning based
on different applications of the verb εἶναι; but this further extension itself
is not implied here.

4. οὐσία in Plato's *Phaedo*: 78c–d, 92c

The next occurrence of οὐσία, at *Phaedo* 78c6–d9, is best understood against
the usage in the previous context of 76d–77a:

οὐκοῦν ἅπερ ἀεὶ κατὰ ταὐτὰ καὶ ὡσαύτως ἔχει, ταῦτα μάλιστα εἰκὸς εἶναι τὰ
ἀσύνθετα, τὰ δὲ ἄλλοτ' ἄλλως καὶ μηδέποτε κατὰ ταὐτά, ταῦτα δὲ σύνθετα;
ἔμοιγε δοκεῖ οὕτως.
ἴωμεν δή, ἔφη, ἐπὶ ταὐτὰ ἐφ' ἅπερ ἐν τῷ ἔμπροσθεν λόγῳ. <u>αὐτὴ ἡ οὐσία ἧς</u>
<u>λόγον δίδομεν τοῦ εἶναι</u> καὶ ἐρωτῶντες καὶ ἀποκρινόμενοι, πότερον ὡσαύτως
ἀεὶ ἔχει κατὰ ταὐτὰ ἢ ἄλλοτ' ἄλλως; αὐτὸ τὸ ἴσον, αὐτὸ τὸ καλόν, <u>αὐτὸ ἕκαστον</u>
<u>ὃ ἔστιν, τὸ ὄν,</u> μή ποτε μεταβολὴν καὶ ἡντινοῦν ἐνδέχεται; ἢ ἀεὶ αὐτῶν <u>ἕκαστον</u>
<u>ὃ ἔστι,</u> μονοειδὲς ὂν αὐτὸ καθ' αὑτό, ὡσαύτως κατὰ ταὐτὰ ἔχει καὶ οὐδέποτε

οὐδαμῇ οὐδαμῶς ἀλλοίωσιν οὐδεμίαν ἐνδέχεται;
ὡσαύτως, ἔφη, ἀνάγκη, ὁ Κέβης, κατὰ ταὐτὰ ἔχειν, ὦ Σώκρατες.

What is always constant[372] and in the same way, is not this likely to be what is incomposite; but what is at one time in one way, at another in another, and never constant, this in turn composite?
To me, certainly, it seems so.
Let us therefore go, said he, to the same things to which we went in the previous account. This 'being' itself[373] of which we give as an account the 'it is' when we ask and answer, is it constant in the same way always, or at one time in one way, at another in another? Would the equal itself, the beautiful itself, each thing-that-is itself, 'what is',[374] ever admit change, even the slightest? Or <is it rather the case that> always, of those, each thing-that-is, being uniform, itself by itself, is constant in the same way and never in any way anyhow admits any alteration?
In the same way, said Cebes, it must be according to the same, Socrates.

Opinions on how to construe the Greek at 78d1 differ considerably.[375] Differences, though, concern mainly the syntactical and semantic analysis of the relative clause. That οὐσία here denotes what it denoted at its last occurrence is less controversial.[376] A further complication, however, is introduced by the phrase ἕκαστον ὃ ἔστιν, here translated 'each thing-that-is'. The Greek phrase ὃ ἔστιν is ambiguous. Depending on context, ὅ can either be interpreted as a relative or as an indirect interrogative pronoun; in the former case, the phrase ὃ ἔστιν may be translated 'which is' or 'which is there', in the latter, 'what it is' or 'what is'.[377] In the *Phaedo*, the phrase first occurs at 74b2, where ὅ is the indirect interrogative pronoun:

ἦ καὶ ἐπιστάμεθα αὐτὸ ὃ ἔστιν;[378]

'And certainly we also understand it, what it is?'

This is followed at 74d6 by αὐτὸ τὸ ὃ ἔστιν ἴσον,[379] 'the what-is-equal itself'. The phrase ὃ ἔστιν ἴσον may be part of a sentence 'we understand *what is equal*' or of a sentence 'we understand that which is equal'; but the definite article certainly favours the former analysis.[380] That ὃ ἔστιν at 74d6 is not a gloss is supported by 75b1–2, ἐκείνου τε ὀρέγεται τοῦ ὃ ἔστιν ἴσον, 'they are striving for that thing, the what-is-equal', to which may be added 75b5–6, εἰληφότας ἐπιστήμην αὐτοῦ τοῦ ἴσου ὅτι ἔστιν, 'having got understanding of the equal itself, what it is', where the indefinite pronoun rather than the relative functions as the indirect interrogative; that section of the dialogue is crowned by the memorable conclusion concerning recollection (75c10–d4):

οὐ γὰρ περὶ τοῦ ἴσου νῦν ὁ λόγος ἡμῖν μᾶλλόν τι ἢ καὶ περὶ αὐτοῦ τοῦ καλοῦ καὶ αὐτοῦ τοῦ ἀγαθοῦ καὶ δικαίου καὶ ὁσίου καί, ὅπερ λέγω, περὶ ἁπάντων οἷς ἐπισφραγιζόμεθα τοῦτο τὸ 'ὃ ἔστι' καὶ ἐν ταῖς ἐρωτήσεσιν ἐρωτῶντες καὶ ἐν ταῖς ἀποκρίσεσιν ἀποκρινόμενοι.[381]

193

For, consequently, now the account is no more about the equal than also about the beautiful itself and the good itself and the just and the pious and, as I say, about all those which we mark with that seal, the 'what-it-is', both in our questions when we ask and in our answers when we answer.

In all these cases, the phrase ὃ ἔστιν is thus best taken as an indirect question, 'what(-it-)is'. This poses a question for 78d3–5: should one understand Socrates' unusual usage of ὃ ἔστιν here in line with all the previous occurrences since 74b? One should then translate (78d3–5):

αὐτὸ τὸ ἴσον, αὐτὸ τὸ καλόν, αὐτὸ ἕκαστον ὃ ἔστιν, τὸ ὄν, μή ποτε μεταβολὴν καὶ ἡντινοῦν ἐνδέχεται;

as:

Would the equal itself, the beautiful itself, each what-it-is itself, that which *is* [τὸ ὄν], ever admit change, even the slightest?[382]

If this is so, it adds a dimension to *Phaedo* 78c6–d9 as an explicit reaction to Parmenides, who is the first to use τὸ ἐόν in the singular, as synonymous with εἶναι, to denote the totality of 'being'.[383] Plato's reaction, as has often been noted, is to ascribe all the attributes of Parmenides' one 'being' severally to each of the things themselves, the equal, the beautiful, etc. At 78d, οὐσία, 'being', is the collective of these 'beings'. And it is this usage that seems to be taken up at *Phaedo* 92c8: when Simmias is asked to choose between the two views 'that the soul is an attunement' and 'that learning is recollection', he decides against the former by recalling and summarizing what has been said about recollection. In conclusion, he declares (92d8–e2):

ἐρρήθη γάρ που οὕτως ἡμῶν εἶναι ἡ ψυχὴ καὶ πρὶν εἰς σῶμα ἀφικέσθαι, ὥσπερ αὐτῇ ἐστιν ἡ οὐσία ἔχουσα τὴν ἐπωνυμίαν τὴν τοῦ 'ὃ ἔστιν'· ἐγὼ δὲ ταύτην, ὡς ἐμαυτὸν πείθω, ἱκανῶς τε καὶ ὀρθῶς ἀποδέδεγμαι.

For it was somehow said that our soul *is* in that way also before having arrived in the body as is the 'being' (οὐσία) itself which has the designation of 'what-it-is': but I have accepted this <οὐσία>, as I persuade myself, sufficiently and correctly.

Here, it is Simmias rather than Socrates speaking. Simmias may be using ἡ οὐσία collectively, he may be using a generic singular; either way, οὐσία is defined again as 'what-it-is'. Simmias is shown to have adopted Socrates' usage, conscious that it is a neologism.

5. οὐσία in Plato's *Phaedo*: 101b–102a
The passage containing the last occurrence of οὐσία in the *Phaedo*, 101b10–102a2, presents difficulties of a different sort.

τί δέ; ἑνὶ ἑνὸς προστεθέντος τὴν πρόσθεσιν αἰτίαν εἶναι τοῦ δύο γενέσθαι ἢ
διασχισθέντος τὴν σχίσιν οὐκ εὐλαβοῖο ἂν λέγειν; καὶ μέγα ἂν βοῴης ὅτι οὐκ
οἶσθα ἄλλως πως ἕκαστον γιγνόμενον ἢ μετασχὸν τῆς ἰδίας οὐσίας ἑκάστου οὗ
ἂν μετάσχῃ, καὶ ἐν τούτοις οὐκ ἔχεις ἄλλην τινὰ αἰτίαν τοῦ δύο γενέσθαι ἀλλ᾽ ἢ
τὴν τῆς δυάδος μετάσχεσιν, καὶ δεῖν τούτου μετασχεῖν τὰ μέλλοντα δύο ἔσεσθαι,
καὶ μονάδος ὃ ἂν μέλλῃ ἓν ἔσεσθαι, τὰς δὲ σχίσεις ταύτας καὶ προσθέσεις καὶ
τὰς ἄλλας τὰς τοιαύτας κομψείας ἐῴης ἂν χαίρειν, παρεὶς ἀποκρίνασθαι τοῖς
σεαυτοῦ σοφωτέροις…

And again, wouldn't you beware of saying that when one is added to one, the
addition is reason for their coming to be two, or when one is divided, that
division is the reason? You'd shout loudly that you know no other way in which
each thing comes to be, except <u>by participating in the particular reality of any
given thing in which it does participate</u>; and in those cases you own no other
reason for their coming to be two, save participation in twoness: things that
are going to be two must participate in that, and whatever is going to be one
must participate in oneness. You'd dismiss those divisions and additions and
other such subtleties, leaving them as answers to be given by people wiser than
yourself…   (tr. Gallop)[384]

Before determining the meaning of οὐσία in this passage, an apparent
difficulty of syntax and semantics must be discussed. Translations and
commentaries habitually construe the clause ὅτι οὐκ οἶσθα ἄλλως πως
ἕκαστον γιγνόμενον ἢ μετασχὸν τῆς ἰδίας οὐσίας ἑκάστου οὗ ἂν μετάσχῃ
in the way Gallop does: i.e., concerning the expression οἶδα with accusative plus participle, 'I know that something does something', 'I know that
something is affected by something', ἕκαστον is considered to be the accusative subject and γιγνόμενον to be the participial predicate of the accusative-
plus-participle construction; the translation is thus something like 'you
know that each thing comes to be'. But, arguably, the phrase οἶσθα…ἕκαστον
γιγνόμενον can also be construed as follows: the accusative subject is omitted
and ἕκαστον γιγνόμενον represents the predicate, with ἕκαστον functioning
as complement to γιγνόμενον; in traditional terminology, ἕκαστον would
be the predicate adjective or predicate noun; a translation of the clause οὐκ
οἶσθα ἄλλως πως ἕκαστον γιγνόμενον ἢ μετασχὸν τῆς ἰδίας οὐσίας ἑκάστου
οὗ ἂν μετάσχῃ could then run 'you do not know of any other way of coming
to be each than by participating in the ἰδία οὐσία of each in which it happens
to participate.' The function of ἕκαστον and ἑκάστου in this sentence would
be similar to that of letters used as variables in general(izing) statements
since Aristotle: 'you do not know of any other way of coming to be x than
by participating in the ἰδία οὐσία of x in which it participates.' To give an
example, Socrates could have said: 'you do not know of any other way of
becoming *beautiful* than by participating in the ἰδία οὐσία of *beautiful*, in
which it participates.' This is in line with 100c–d, viz. that if anything is

beautiful, it is beautiful because it participates in the beautiful itself, and that the many beautiful things are beautiful because of the presence of that beautiful.

Additional support for this construal may derive from the context of 100e8–101c9. While from 100d6 to e6 Socrates was talking about the many *beautifuls*, the *bigs* and the *smalls*,[385] which are beautiful, big or small because they participate, respectively, in the beautiful, the big and the small itself, from 100e8 onwards he reverts to *someone's* or *something's* being larger or smaller or more. As he had said at 100c4–5 that if *something* else is beautiful other than the beautiful itself (εἴ τί ἐστιν ἄλλο καλὸν πλὴν αὐτὸ τὸ καλόν), it is so by participation, so at 100e8 he hypothesizes that 'if someone were to say that *some one person* is taller by a head than *some other person* (εἴ τίς τινα φαίη ἕτερον ἑτέρου τῇ κεφαλῇ μείζω εἶναι). Anachronistically speaking, Socrates is concerned, at least *inter alia*, with predication, with somebody's being tall, somebody's being small, something's being more, and not just with *beautifuls'* being beautiful, *bigs'* being big and *smalls'* being or becoming small.

It may be objected, though, that while all this may be so in the case of qualitative adjectives, 101b10 ff. presents a different case, as we are now dealing with numbers. The objection would be that as early as at 101b10–11, ἑνὶ ἑνὸς προστεθέντος τὴν πρόσθεσιν αἰτίαν εἶναι τοῦ δύο γενέσθαι should be translated with Hackforth 1955, 135: 'when one is added to one the addition is the cause of *there* coming to be two', not with Gallop as 'when one is added to one, the addition is the reason of *their* coming to be two'; i.e., we are now dealing with 'something's coming into being', not with 'something's becoming something'.[386] This thought is continued in 101c3, where the particular case of the coming into being of two is generalized to the coming into being of anything before Socrates returns at 101c4 to the specific case of two, when he says καὶ ἐν τούτοις οὐκ ἔχεις ἄλλην τινὰ αἰτίαν τοῦ δύο γενέσθαι ἀλλ' ἢ τὴν τῆς δυάδος μετάσχειν, which Hackforth (1955, 135) translates: 'and that in the case just mentioned you know of no other cause of there coming to be two save coming to participate in duality'.[387]

But this is unlikely. As part of the investigation 'into the cause-and-reason of generation and destruction', περὶ γένεσις καὶ φθορᾶς τὴν αἰτίαν (95e10), the issue of 'coming to be two' was first mentioned at 96e, which is also the place at which the other examples taken up at 100e ff. are first introduced (96e6–97b7):

πόρρω που, ἔφη, νὴ Δία ἐμὲ εἶναι τοῦ οἴεσθαι περὶ τούτων του τὴν αἰτίαν εἰδέναι, ὅς γε οὐκ ἀποδέχομαι ἐμαυτοῦ οὐδὲ ὡς ἐπειδὰν ἑνί τις προσθῇ ἕν, ἢ τὸ ἓν ᾧ προσετέθη δύο γέγονεν, <ἢ τὸ προστεθέν>, ἢ τὸ προστεθὲν καὶ ᾧ προσετέθη διὰ τὴν πρόσθεσιν τοῦ ἑτέρου τῷ ἑτέρῳ δύο ἐγένετο· θαυμάζω γὰρ εἰ ὅτε μὲν ἑκάτερον αὐτῶν χωρὶς ἀλλήλων ἦν, ἓν ἄρα ἑκάτερον ἦν καὶ οὐκ ἤστην

196

τότε δύο, ἐπεὶ δ᾽ ἐπλησίασαν ἀλλήλοις, αὕτη ἄρα αἰτία αὐτοῖς ἐγένετο τοῦ δύο γενέσθαι, ἡ σύνοδος τοῦ πλησίον ἀλλήλων τεθῆναι.

οὐδέ γε ὡς ἐάν τις ἓν διασχίσῃ, δύναμαι ἔτι πείθεσθαι ὡς αὕτη αὖ αἰτία γέγονεν, ἡ σχίσις, τοῦ δύο γεγονέναι· ἐναντία γὰρ γίγνεται ἢ τότε αἰτία τοῦ δύο γίγνεσθαι. τότε μὲν γὰρ ὅτι συνήγετο πλησίον ἀλλήλων καὶ προσετίθετο ἕτερον ἑτέρῳ, νῦν δ᾽ ὅτι ἀπάγεται καὶ χωρίζεται ἕτερον ἀφ᾽ ἑτέρου. οὐδέ γε δι᾽ ὅτι ἓν γίγνεται ὡς ἐπίσταμαι, ἔτι πείθω ἐμαυτόν, οὐδ᾽ ἄλλο οὐδὲν ἑνὶ λόγῳ δι᾽ ὅτι γίγνεται ἢ ἀπόλλυται ἢ ἔστι, κατὰ τοῦτον τὸν τρόπον τῆς μεθόδου, ἀλλά τιν᾽ ἄλλον τρόπον αὐτὸς εἰκῇ φύρω, τοῦτον δὲ οὐδαμῇ προσίεμαι.

I can assure you that I'm far from supposing I know the reason for any of those things, when I don't even accept from myself that when you add one to one, it's either the one to which the addition is made that's come to be two, or the one that's been added and the one to which it's been added, that have come to be two, because of the addition of one to the other. Because I wonder if, when they were apart from each other, each was one and they weren't two then; whereas when they came close to each other, this then became the reason for their coming to be two – the union in which they were juxtaposed.

Nor again can I any longer be persuaded, if you divide one, that this has now become a reason for its coming to be two; then it was their being brought close to each other and added, one to the other; whereas now it's their being drawn apart, and separated each from the other. Why, I can't even persuade myself any longer that I know why it is that one comes to be; nor, in short, why anything else comes to be, or perishes, or exists, following that method of inquiry. Instead I rashly adopt a different method, a jumble of my own, and in no way incline towards the other.   (tr. Gallop)[388]

In this passage, there is at least initially no ambiguity concerning the syntax of γίγνεσθαι: at 96e8–97a1, Socrates reports having wondered if either one or other (of two that have been added to each other) has come to be two, or again if both together have come to be two. Here, 'two' is complement to 'come to be', while 'the one', 'the other', or 'both the one and the other' are subjects. In what follows (97a3), Socrates states that part of his uncertainty and puzzlement relates to the fact that each of them was one, and they were not two then, while later they came to be two (97a4–5). That this is his way of perceiving the problem is unambiguously clear from the dative αὐτοῖς at the end of 97a4. Only after that (97a5–b7) does a potential ambiguity arise. When Socrates turns from addition to division, the expression τὸ δύο γίγνεσθαι, in different tenses and cases, is employed again. The sentence context alone does not allow one to decide whether Plato conceived of it as 'the fact that something comes to be two' or 'the fact that two come to be'. It should be noted, however, that on its previous occurrence the phrase did denote something's coming to be two, and that Plato has good reason to postpone the mentioning of a subject at 97a7: as becomes apparent at 97b2–3, he wants to present addition and division as parallel, the former as the coming-together of one of two with the other of the two, the latter as the being-led-apart and being-separated of one of two from the other of the two. In order to create this parallelism, he must talk of the one thing that is to be divided as if it already consisted of the two parts which are, at least in many cases of the division of one into two, only the result of that division: the apple, while whole, has no more two halves than it has three thirds. By avoiding the mention of a subject to δύο γίγνεσθαι from 97a7 onwards, Plato deflects from this potential awkwardness. The context of the passage, however, supports the view that there is no change of construction, and that Plato lets Socrates speak consistently of something's coming to be two. This seems to me to be so, regardless of the question of whether Plato would in the first place have recognized as relevant the distinction that results from translating the Greek phrase into English in the two different ways described.

In addition, it may be noted that, at 96e8–97a1, it is the one to which has been added, or the added one, or the added one together with the one added to, which has come to be two; at 97a3, it is *something* that 'is one'; in the phrase ἓν ἄρα ἑκάτερον ἦν, ἓν is predicated of ἑκάτερον. The subject of being one and becoming two is now, at least on the surface of the linguistic expression, something other than 'the one' and 'the two' of the previous sentence: this, however, does not seem to matter at all in this context; Plato lets Socrates move from one to the other without comment, as if the two ways of expressing himself were equivalent.

In applying the various observations derived from the preceding pages to 100c9–101c9, one may conclude that it may not matter whether Socrates is speaking of 'something's coming to be beautiful' or 'the beautifuls' coming to be beautiful': 'the beautifuls' are beautiful only once they have come to be beautiful, just as the two halves of an apple are 'the one and the other' only once the apple has been cut in two. But just as γίγνεσθαι καλά means 'coming to be beautiful', δύο γίγνεσθαι is best understood as 'coming to be two'; and this can then be generalized to ἕκαστον γίγνεσθαι, 'coming to be *each*', 'coming to be whatever each happens to come to be', 'coming to be x'. This ἕκαστον is the same here as ἕκαστον at 78d4 discussed above, in the phrase ἕκαστον ὃ ἔστιν, where ἕκαστον referred to each of the things which *are* in the same way in which the equal *is* and the beautiful *is*. To return to 101b9–101c9:

τί δέ; ἑνὶ ἑνὸς προστεθέντος τὴν πρόσθεσιν αἰτίαν εἶναι τοῦ δύο γενέσθαι ἢ διασχισθέντος τὴν σχίσιν οὐκ εὐλαβοῖο ἂν λέγειν; καὶ μέγα ἂν βοῷης ὅτι οὐκ οἶσθα ἄλλως πως ἕκαστον γιγνόμενον ἢ μετασχὸν τῆς ἰδίας οὐσίας ἑκάστου οὗ ἂν μετάσχῃ, καὶ ἐν τούτοις οὐκ ἔχεις ἄλλην τινὰ αἰτίαν τοῦ δύο γενέσθαι ἀλλ᾽ ἢ τὴν τῆς δυάδος μετάσχεσιν, καὶ δεῖν τούτου μετασχεῖν τὰ μέλλοντα δύο ἔσεσθαι, καὶ μονάδος ὃ ἂν μέλλῃ ἓν ἔσεσθαι, τὰς δὲ σχίσεις ταύτας καὶ προσθέσεις καὶ τὰς ἄλλας τὰς τοιαύτας κομψείας ἐῴης ἂν χαίρειν, παρεὶς ἀποκρίνασθαι τοῖς σεαυτοῦ σοφωτέροις…

This can now be translated as:

> What about this: would you not be on your guard when it came to stating that when one is added to one, the cause-and-reason of coming to be two is addition, or in the case of division the dividing? And shout out loud that you do not know of any other way of coming to be each than by sharing in the own proper being of each (whatever it is) in which it shares;[389] and in this specific case you do not have any other cause-and-reason of having come to be two than the sharing in twoness – and that it is necessary that whatever shall be two shares in that, and in unity whatever shall be one; but those dividings and additions and other such elaborate (causes-and-reasons) you would let go, leaving (them) to those more clever than you to answer (with)…

The consequences of this for an understanding of the concept of οὐσία are at least two: οὐσία at 101c3 still means the 'being' of something in the sense of 'what something is'. But οὐσία at 101c3 is made to refer to the being of that Two in which anything and everything that is or comes to be two participates. At this point in the *Phaedo*, οὐσία refers to the 'being' of what will shortly be referred to by the two words εἶδος and ἰδέα.[390] Perhaps that is why at this point the adjective ἰδία is added to οὐσία: the 'being' of a form is in a special sense 'its own' or 'its proper being'. The οὐσία of the beautiful itself is in a special way its 'own property'.

6. οὐσία in earlier dialogues of Plato

In the *Meno*, the *Euthyphro* and the *Phaedo*, οὐσία is thus in the first place 'what something is'. The noun can then also refer collectively to the totality of everything that *is* in the same way in which the beautiful itself *is*. And οὐσία can be the 'being', the 'what-it-is' of that beautiful itself. From here, there are two roads leading in different directions. One is to investigate if, and if so when, Plato took the step from the meaning 'what something is' to the meaning 'that something is': has this step been taken at e.g. *Republic* 525 or 585, or later at *Sophist* 219, etc.? I shall not go down that road now. The other line of investigation is to ask: What prompted Plato to adopt this term οὐσία in the first place? Was it his general interest in 'being' that led him to a noun which seemed to be, and in fact was, connected with the participle of the verb 'to be'? Or was οὐσία a technical philosophical term before Plato after all? And if so, in whose terminology? To answer these questions, it will now be necessary to look at the few instances of οὐσία in Plato's earlier dialogues where by common consent the noun does not simply mean 'property' in the sense of '(physical) possession'.

The three instances are *Charmides* 168c, *Gorgias* 472b and *Protagoras* 349b.[391] At all three places, explanation of the use of οὐσία must, I believe, start from the common Attic meaning 'possession, property'. There is no certainty concerning the order of composition of the three dialogues. I shall begin with the *Charmides*, a dialogue in which Socrates has a conversation about σωφροσύνη with the youth Charmides and subsequently his older relative Critias. In the course of their conversation, σωφροσύνη is defined as ἐπιστήμη, 'knowledge'; but it turns out not to be knowledge of any of the things of which the other arts, crafts and sciences are knowledge; so Socrates and the others arrive at a definition of σωφροσύνη as 'the knowledge of all other knowledge and of itself'. This is scrutinized by Socrates who starts in his criticism from the directedness of knowledge and builds his proof on analogy with other things which are directed towards something. At 168c4–168d7, he draws things together in a convoluted sentence of the sort which he himself sometimes mocks for being over-technical:

οὐκοῦν καὶ εἴ τι διπλάσιόν ἐστιν τῶν τε ἄλλων διπλασίων καὶ ἑαυτοῦ, ἡμίσεος δήπου ὄντος ἑαυτοῦ τε καὶ τῶν ἄλλων διπλάσιον ἂν εἴη· οὐ γάρ ἐστίν που ἄλλου διπλάσιον ἢ ἡμίσεος.

ἀληθῆ.

πλέον δὲ αὑτοῦ ὂν οὐ καὶ ἔλαττον ἔσται, καὶ βαρύτερον ὂν κουφότερον, καὶ πρεσβύτερον ὂν νεώτερον, καὶ τἆλλα πάντα ὡσαύτως, ὅτιπερ ἂν τὴν ἑαυτοῦ δύναμιν πρὸς ἑαυτὸ ἔχῃ, οὐ καὶ ἐκείνην ἕξει τὴν οὐσίαν, πρὸς ἣν ἡ δύναμις αὐτοῦ ἦν; λέγω δὲ τὸ τοιόνδε· οἷον ἡ ἀκοή, φαμέν, οὐκ ἄλλου τινὸς ἦν ἀκοὴ ἢ φωνῆς· ἦ γάρ;

ναί.

οὐκοῦν εἴπερ αὐτὴ αὑτῆς ἀκούσεται, φωνὴν ἐχούσης ἑαυτῆς ἀκούσεται· οὐ γὰρ ἂν ἄλλως ἀκούσειεν.

And if something is the double both of the other doubles and of itself, it would itself constitute a half, as would the others, if it were double, since there is not, I'm sure, a double of anything but a half.

True.

That which is the superior of itself will be the inferior of itself too, and what is heavier, lighter, and what is older, younger, and so on. Whatever relates its own faculty to itself will also have that essential nature to which its faculty was related, won't it? I mean something like this: hearing, for example, we say is the hearing of nothing other than sound, isn't it?

Yes.

If it is to hear itself, it will hear itself as possessing a *sound*, since it couldn't hear otherwise.[392]

Of the three passages, this is perhaps the one in which the sense of οὐσία is most difficult to explain.[393] It may be fruitful to begin by asking for the contexts and connotations of the other 'technical' term in the passage, δύναμις, which Watt translates as 'faculty'. The word occurs six times between 168b and 169a. It is introduced at 168b3 as the 'capacity', 'faculty', 'power' or 'capability' of something 'to be *of* something';[394] as such, it is an abstract concept, not unfamiliar in medical discussions of the faculties of the body, its organs and its senses, and of medicines; indeed, the one other context in which δύναμις occurs in the *Charmides* was Socrates' referring to the 'power' of the incantation with which he promised to cure the headache of Charmides at the beginning of their conversation (156b).

At 168d, Socrates generalizes that whatever has its *power* directed towards itself, must also have that οὐσία towards which the given *power* or *faculty* is directed otherwise: Hearing, for example, in order to be capable of hearing itself, would need that *possession* which hearing is directed towards otherwise, namely sound. That is to say, concerning the meaning of οὐσία in this context, it would be wrong to ask: 'What is the abstract noun that captures sound, sight, etc. as that which a faculty is directed towards?' This question would be misdirected because use of οὐσία here is determined by the notion of 'having something for oneself'.[395] Of course, if the *Charmides* were written after the *Republic*, one could speculate on a semantic development of the philosophical notion of 'being' via 'nature' to 'quality, property': but it should be noted that οὐσία here is not the οὐσία of something; the noun is used in an absolute way; οὐσία here is used in its everyday Attic sense of 'property, possession', not in the sense of 'the being *of* something', 'what something is'.

The *Protagoras* may present a case parallel in many ways. In discussing ἀρετή, 'goodness' or 'excellence', Socrates had asked Protagoras (329c3–d1):

καὶ αὖ πολλαχοῦ ἐν τοῖς λόγοις ἐλέγετο ὑπὸ σοῦ ἡ δικαιοσύνη καὶ σωφροσύνη καὶ ὁσιότης καὶ πάντα ταῦτα ὡς ἕν τι εἴη συλλήβδην, ἀρετή· ταῦτ' οὖν αὐτὰ δίελθέ μοι ἀκριβῶς τῷ λόγῳ, πότερον ἕν μέν τί ἐστιν ἡ ἀρετή, μόρια δὲ αὐτῆς ἐστιν ἡ δικαιοσύνη καὶ σωφροσύνη καὶ ὁσιότης, ἢ ταῦτ' ἐστιν ἃ νυνδὴ ἐγὼ ἔλεγον πάντα <u>ὀνόματα τοῦ αὐτοῦ ἑνὸς ὄντος</u>.

And then many times in your discourse you spoke of justice and soundness of mind and holiness and all the rest as all summed up as <u>the one thing</u>, excellence: Will you then explain precisely whether excellence is one thing, and justice and soundness of mind and holiness parts of it, or whether all these that I've just mentioned are <u>different names of one and the same thing</u>?[396]

After an inconclusive discussion, Socrates then begins a fresh attempt at agreement with a summarizing question at 349a8–c5:

ἦν δέ, ὡς ἐγῷμαι, τὸ ἐρώτημα τόδε· σοφία καὶ σωφροσύνη καὶ ἀνδρεία καὶ δικαιοσύνη καὶ ὁσιότης, πότερον ταῦτα, πέντε ὄντα ὀνόματα, ἐπὶ ἑνὶ πράγματί ἐστιν, ἢ <u>ἑκάστῳ τῶν ὀνομάτων τούτων ὑπόκειταί τις ἴδιος οὐσία καὶ πρᾶγμα ἔχον ἑαυτοῦ δύναμιν ἕκαστον</u>, οὐκ ὂν οἷον τὸ ἕτερον αὐτῶν τὸ ἕτερον; ἔφησθα οὖν σὺ οὐκ ὀνόματα ἐπὶ ἑνὶ εἶναι, ἀλλὰ ἕκαστον ἰδίῳ πράγματι τῶν ὀνομάτων τούτων ἐπικεῖσθαι, πάντα δὲ ταῦτα μόρια εἶναι ἀρετῆς, οὐχ ὡς τὰ τοῦ χρυσοῦ μόρια ὅμοιά ἐστιν ἀλλήλοις καὶ τῷ ὅλῳ οὗ μόριά ἐστιν, ἀλλ' ὡς τὰ τοῦ προσώπου μόρια καὶ τῷ ὅλῳ οὗ μόριά ἐστιν καὶ ἀλλήλοις ἀνόμοια, ἰδίαν ἕκαστα δύναμιν ἔχοντα.

The question, I think, was this: are 'wisdom', 'soundness of mind', 'courage', 'justice', and 'holiness' five names for the one thing, or <u>does there correspond to each of these names some separate thing or entity with its own particular power</u>, unlike any of the others? Now you said that they are not names for the one thing, but each is the name <u>of a separate thing</u>, and all of these are parts of excellence, not as the parts of gold are like one another and the whole of which they are parts, but as the parts of the face are unlike one another and the whole of which they are parts, each having <u>its own separate power</u>.[397]

The first difference that strikes the reader of these two obviously related passages is that Socrates, in asking for the status of the virtues, managed to express himself with minimal use of additional abstract nouns in the first passage, using in addition to ὄνομα, 'name', and μόριον, 'part', only pronouns and numerals. In the second passage, by contrast, he introduces as a counterpart to ὄνομα, 'name', πρᾶγμα, 'thing', where he had previously made do with ἕν τί, 'a certain one (thing)' (where 'thing' is supplied in the English translation only), and οὐσία, and he asks if this πρᾶγμα or each of the μόρια have their own δύναμις, 'power'. The second passage is therefore at least in this sense more technical. But do these nouns contribute anything to the content of Socrates' question? And in particular, what does οὐσία mean here?

The term δύναμις, 'power', which was also encountered in the *Charmides* passage above, had first been introduced in the *Protagoras* by Protagoras himself in the 'scientific' context of the myth of Epimetheus and Prometheus, where he said that Epimetheus gave to the various animals their various 'powers' or perhaps 'abilities' (320d5, e2, 321c1). But it was then reintroduced by Socrates at 330a4, to recur five more times.[398] Socrates speaks of an ἰδία δύναμις, an 'own, proper or specific power', of each of the virtues in direct analogy to the specific 'power' of each of the parts of the face, the eyes, the ears, the nose, etc. That is to say, in the context of the bodily senses, δύναμις was an established term, as at *Charmides* 168d. Immediately after introducing δύναμις in that way, Socrates then, at 330c1, asks if δικαιοσύνη, 'justice', is a πρᾶγμα, a 'thing',[399] and he uses that concession in his refutation of Protagoras' position. While both these terms have something technical about them, they are not so specialized that they would need definition; nor do the interlocutors comment on them otherwise. In the context of 349, the thing that corresponds to the name is *one* thing; as such, the thing is specific to the name. Just as Socrates speaks of an ἰδία δύναμις at 330a4, then here at 349c5, and once again at 359a7, so here at 349c1 he speaks of an ἴδιον πρᾶγμα, 'an own, proper, specific thing'; each of these things has its own power. And in this context Socrates adds a synonym: that underlying each name, there is its own οὐσία. The term is obviously redundant. What would the original audience have understood? That for each of these names, there lies by it 'its own property, that is (epexegetic καὶ), a thing having its own power' etc. It is not only οὐσία which is used metaphorically here,[400] but also the verb ὑπόκειται. 'Land' of some kind is a particularly common subject to the verb ὑπόκειμαι.[401] The metaphor serves to indicate the close connection of name and thing, which is as close as that of the old Attic landowner and his household to his land, his property. That such property is also static and stable, an aspect often seen as lying at the root of the metaphorical extension of οὐσία from a meaning of 'property' or 'real estate' to 'real being', a being which similarly is not subject to change: all this does not seem to be emphasized in the *Protagoras* passage.[402] Of course, if the *Protagoras* were written after the *Phaedo*, more would need saying.

The *Gorgias* passage, lastly, offers a different picture. In his conversation with Polus, Socrates makes a methodological point concerning the role of mutual agreement in discussion (472b3–c2):

ἀλλ᾽ ἐγώ σοι εἷς ὢν οὐχ ὁμολογῶ· οὐ γάρ με σὺ ἀναγκάζεις, ἀλλὰ ψευδομάρτυρας πολλοὺς κατ᾽ ἐμοῦ παρασχόμενος ἐπιχειρεῖς ἐκβάλλειν με ἐκ τῆς οὐσίας καὶ τοῦ ἀληθοῦς. ἐγὼ δὲ ἂν μὴ σὲ αὐτὸν ἕνα ὄντα μάρτυρα παράσχωμαι ὁμολογοῦντα περὶ ὧν λέγω, οὐδὲν οἶμαι ἄξιον λόγου μοι πεπεράνθαι περὶ ὧν ἂν ἡμῖν ὁ λόγος ᾖ· οἶμαι δὲ οὐδὲ σοί, ἐὰν μὴ ἐγώ σοι μαρτυρῶ εἷς ὢν μόνος, τοὺς δ᾽ ἄλλους πάντας τούτους χαίρειν ἐᾷς.

But I, though I am but a single individual, do not agree with you, for you produce no compelling reason why I should; instead you call numerous false witnesses against me in our attempt to evict me from my lawful property, the truth. I believe that nothing worth speaking of will have been accomplished in our discussion unless I can obtain your agreement, and yours alone, as a witness to the truth of what I say; and the same holds good for you, in my opinion; unless you can get just me, me only, on your side you can disregard what the rest of the world may say.[403]

The nature of the legal metaphor here employed has always been recognized by translators and commentators.[404] There is a temptation, though, to see more in this expression in a dialogue in which so much of the terminology of the theory of forms is employed. Of the terms we have so far discussed in this study, the *Gorgias* provides, in philosophically significant contexts, besides οὐσία at 472b6, the following: forms of μετέχειν and μεταλαμβάνειν, 'sharing and coming to share', at 448c and 467e7 (ἃ ἐνίοτε μὲν μετέχει τοῦ ἀγαθοῦ, 'what sometimes participates in the good'); παρουσία, 'presence', thrice between 497e–498e; εἶδος, 'form', at 503e4. By themselves, each of these passages allows for interpretation without reference to the theory of forms; but the cumulative weight of the philosophical terminology presents a temptation to see the dialogue as transitional. In this mode, Classen 1959a, 158, while stopping short of positing a new meaning for the word οὐσία, speaks of Socrates' 'concern for truth and in particular this aspect of οὐσία as reality'[405] which presupposes such a concept as 'reality' and also presupposes that 'reality' could have been part of the meaning of οὐσία in the first place; that this is so, though, has not been demonstrated.

Plato may, however, have played with his language in a different fashion. In common Attic usage, οὐσία meant 'property, possession'; but while the word was derived from the root for 'being', this was not felt, or at least it did not find expression in collocation with other forms of the same root.[406] In the *Meno*, *Euthyphro* and *Phaedo*, on the other hand, Plato made that connection by re-etymologizing the word as 'what something is'. It is conceivable that Plato may have made the connection between οὐσία and εἶναι in the *Gorgias*, but not necessarily in the way he will exploit it in later dialogues. As we have seen,[407] both the singular τὸ ὄν and the plural τὰ ὄντα could in common parlance mean 'the truth'. Plato may have made that connection: but he certainly does not dwell on it, and the context of *Gorgias* 472 does not require, or even strongly invite, such a pun.

7. ἐστώ in Philolaus

There is thus no clear indication in the early dialogues that Plato had etymologized οὐσία in the contexts of thought about 'being', a topic which had been central to philosophy since Parmenides. Does that mean that the coinage of οὐσία as 'being', 'what something is', is an *ad hoc* creation of Plato's, reflected in the *Phaedo* and the two dialogues which also otherwise presuppose large parts of the theory presented in the *Phaedo*, to wit, the *Meno* and the *Euthyphro*?[408]

There is one pre-Platonic context that may shed light on that question. It is that part of the report by Stobaeus (1.21.7d2–14) usually labelled as Philolaus Fragment 6:

περὶ δὲ φύσιος καὶ ἁρμονίας ὧδε ἔχει· ἁ μὲν ἐστὼ τῶν πραγμάτων, ἀΐδιος ἔσσα καὶ αὐτὰ μὰν ἁ φύσις θείαν τε καὶ οὐκ ἀνθρωπίνην ἐνδέχεται γνῶσιν, πλάν γα ἢ ὅτι οὐχ οἷόν τ' ἦν οὐθενὶ τῶν ἐόντων καὶ γιγνωσκομένων ὑφ' ἁμῶν γεγενῆσθαι μὴ ὑπαρχούσας τᾶς ἐστοῦς τῶν πραγμάτων, ἐξ ὧν συνέστα ὁ κόσμος, καὶ τῶν περαινόντων καὶ τῶν ἀπείρων. ἐπεὶ δὲ ταὶ ἀρχαὶ ὑπάρχον οὐχ ὁμοῖαι οὐδ' ὁμόφυλοι ἔσσαι, ἤδη ἀδύνατον ἦς κα αὐταῖς κοσμηθῆναι, εἰ μὴ ἁρμονία ἐπεγένετο, ᾡτινιῶν ἂν τρόπῳ ἐγένετο. τὰ μὲν ὦν ὁμοῖα καὶ ὁμόφυλα ἁρμονίας οὐδὲν ἐπεδέοντο, τὰ δὲ ἀνόμοια μηδὲ ὁμόφυλα μηδὲ † ἰσοταχῆ ἀνάγκα τὰ τοιαῦτα ἁρμονίᾳ συγκεκλεῖσθαι, εἰ μέλλοντι ἐν κόσμῳ κατέχεσθαι.

Concerning nature and harmony the situation is this: the being of things, which is eternal, and nature in itself admit of divine and not human knowledge, except that it was impossible for any of the things that are and are known by us to have come to be, if the being of the things from which the world-order came together, both the limiting things and the unlimited things, did not pre-exist. But since these beginnings preexisted and were neither alike or even related, it would have been impossible for them to have been ordered, if a harmony had not come upon them, in whatever way it came to be. Like things and related things did not in addition require any harmony, things that are unlike and not even related nor of [? the same speed], it is necessary that such things be bonded together by harmony, if they are going to be held in an order.

(tr. Huffman)[409]

Here, the phrases ἁ μὲν ἐστὼ τῶν πραγμάτων, which Huffman translates as 'the being of things', and μὴ ὑπαρχούσας τᾶς ἐστοῦς τῶν πραγμάτων, 'if the being of the things…did not pre-exist', contain a word ἐστώ which, like οὐσία, is formed from the Greek verbal root meaning 'to be', only that it is not derived from the participial stem *ont- but rather from *est-, the 'stem' of the third person singular present indicative active form ἔστι.[410] We shall turn shortly to the question whether the etymological connection was felt in fifth- and fourth-century Greece.

As far as Philolaus B6 is concerned, whether or not the 'context' created by Stobaeus is the original context in Philolaus' book, the content is in part epistemological: 'What can human beings know?' But Philolaus' epistemology, like Plato's, is inseparably linked to his ontology:

> ἁ μὲν ἐστὼ τῶν πραγμάτων ἀΐδιος ἔσσα καὶ αὐτὰ μὰν ἁ φύσις θείαν τε καὶ οὐκ ἀνθρωπίνην ἐνδέχεται γνῶσιν, πλάν γα ἢ ὅτι οὐχ οἷόν τ᾽ ἦν οὐθενὶ τῶν ἐόντων καὶ γιγνωσκομένων ὑφ᾽ ἁμῶν γεγενῆσθαι μὴ ὑπαρχούσας τᾶς ἐστοῦς τῶν πραγμάτων, ἐξ ὧν συνέστα ὁ κόσμος, καὶ τῶν περαινόντων καὶ τῶν ἀπείρων.

> The being of the things (ἁ…ἐστὼ τῶν πραγμάτων), being eternal, and nature itself, at least, accept divine and not human cognition, except, that is, for the fact that it would not be possible for any of the things-that-are and the things-that-are-known-by-us to be (as things that come-to-be: γεγενῆσθαι) if there had not been there (as-a-beginning: ὑπαρχούσας) the being of things (τᾶς ἐστοῦς τῶν πραγμάτων), both the limiting and the unlimiting (things), from which the world-order came together (συνέστα).

Huffman has a long note on the lemma ἁ μὲν ἐστώ (1993, 130–2), from which I quote the beginning:

> Except for this fragment ἐστώ is only found in the later Pythagorean tradition, although it is very rare even there… This might cast doubt on the authenticity of F6 but the situation is not as simple as it appears. First, although ἐστώ itself does not occur in the fifth century, a number of compounds of ἐστώ do occur, and thus suggest that ἐστώ itself is also a possibility for the fifth century. Democritus, Philolaus' contemporary, is said to have used εὐεστώ to refer to the tranquillity of mind which he regarded as the end of all human action (D.L. 9.45–6; see also DK F2c). Aeschylus uses the same compound several times where it seems to mean something like good fortune or well-being (*A*. 647, 929; *Th*. 187). Harpocration reports that Antiphon used the compound ἀειεστώ in

205

the sense of 'eternity' in the second book of his *Truth* (F22). Finally, Herodotus uses the compound ἀπεστώ to mean 'being away' or 'absence' (9.85).

In light of these parallels Burkert may be right to conclude that is 'obviously an Ionic formation' (1972, 256 n. 87). As he points out, Plato's *Cratylus* (401c2–4) suggests that the Doric form for οὐσία is ὠσία or ἐσσία. ἐστώ is obviously formed from the root *ἐσ-(εἰμί) [sic], and this, along with the compounds discussed above, indicates that it has the general meaning of οὐσία, 'being'. As in other uses of forms of the verb 'to be' in the Presocratics, it does not seem that it is used strictly to refer to either existence or essence, but rather represents a fused notion of existence and essence...

The fifth-century parallels of the compounds of -εστω are instructive not only with regard to the Ionic origin of the word first posited by Chantraine,[411] but because they have a parallel in the many -ουσία compounds common in Attic: συνουσία, 'a being together, a gathering', παρουσία, 'a being near, at or by; presence', ἀπουσία, 'a being away; absence', ἐξουσία, 'a being possible, possibility', etc.; the significance of these compounds in Attic is that they are all closely linked in meaning to the respective composite verbs; the -ουσία element in them means 'being' as a 'survival' from a time when the simplex must have had that meaning; the *composita* of οὐσία could therefore have served as an additional starting point for Plato's etymologizing, just as the -εστω compounds could serve as a model for the coinage of ἐστώ in the sense of 'being'.

The problem is: when Philolaus wrote, οὐσία did not mean 'being', as we have seen. Philolaus, however, is unlikely to have coined the simplex ἐστώ in the first place: because it was an Ionic word! Going by the presence of the Doric nominative singular feminine of the present active participle of the verb 'to be' in Philolaus B6, ἔσσα, Philolaus would indeed have said ἐσσία, i.e. he would have used one of the two forms suggested by Plato at *Cratylus* 401c.[412] One can thus only speculate about the real origin of ἐστώ; the source may indeed have been Democritus, who after all reportedly used one of the compounds of the word. But that is to some extent a separate question. Wherever Philolaus had got the word ἐστώ from, he used it in the sense of 'being', and applied it to the being of things in a way that comes very close indeed to Plato's usage in the *Phaedo*. And as the occurrence of the name of Philolaus early on in the dialogue in itself makes it plausible that Plato had read the book of Philolaus before writing the *Phaedo*, we may conclude that in the *Phaedo* the use of οὐσία as 'what something is' is not independent of Philolaus' use of ἐστώ, and indeed, Philolaus' use seems to some extent to have been the inspiration for Plato's new, etymologizing use of οὐσία. It must be noted, though, that Philolaus himself apparently had a different etymology of ἐστώ in mind: by glossing τᾶς ἐστοῦς τῶν πραγμάτων with the phrase ἐξ ὧν συνέστα ὁ κόσμος, he defines, in a manner of speaking, ἐστώ as that which 'stands' [and remains (?)] and as such is part and 'constituent' of the ever-changing composites of this world. What these firm constituents were in the ontology of Philolaus we shall explore in the next chapter.[413]

8. Recapitulation

In conclusion, let me summarize: οὐσία as 'being' is indeed Plato's coinage in the sense that the Attic word had not meant 'being' for centuries before Plato, and in the sense that there are no other writers before Plato who would have used the term with reference to 'the being of something'. There was metaphorical usage of οὐσία to the extent that what someone's property or wealth is, in a given context, need not always be the land, the physical possession, or the sum of one's countable, touchable wealth.[414] In the *Protagoras* and *Charmides*, Plato speaks of the οὐσία not of a person, but of abstract things: this may reflect usage of the word in discussions of 'meaning' by the Sophists, but we do not have the evidence to support this claim:[415] it seems, though, as if this metaphorical usage did not go back to the etymology of the word. In the *Gorgias*, Socrates may well etymologize when he refers to the truth as his patrimony; but that is not certain. In the *Meno*, the *Euthyphro* and the *Phaedo*, the picture is different: Plato clearly defines the new application of the word as 'the being' of something in the sense of 'what something is'. This seems to have been inspired by, or at least has an uncanny parallel in, the usage of Philolaus. Plato's innovation is thus partly at the level of language; but, as with other technical terms, as will be seen presently, his innovation lies mostly in what he applies the term to. For Plato, 'what is' is significantly different from 'what is' for Philolaus. And the central role of the 'being' of things in Plato's philosophy is a world apart from the 'being' of the Pythagorean. The discovery of the concept of the οὐσία of something as 'what something is' marks the true starting point of Plato's own explanation of the world. Against this background, we can now turn to those technical terms in the *Phaedo* whose histories in earlier literature we traced in Parts I and II.

CHAPTER 8

εἶδος in Plato's *Phaedo*

1. εἶδος in Plato's *Phaedo*: 57a–102a

The word εἶδος occurs with particular frequency in the *Phaedo*. This chimes well with Plato's general strategy in the dialogue of preparing the reader for philosophically significant passages by using early on in the dialogue the words that will form part of his technical terminology, often introducing them in a sense different from the one that will become relevant later. In the *Phaedo*, εἶδος occurs for the first time in connection with the argument from ἀνάμνησις, 'recollection' (72e–77d), in the mouth of the Theban Cebes. If learning is recollection, all that we remember now, we must first have got at an earlier time (73a1–2):

> τοῦτο δὲ ἀδύνατον, εἰ μὴ ἦν που ἡμῖν ἡ ψυχὴ πρὶν ἐν τῷδε τῷ ἀνθρωπίνῳ εἴδει γενέσθαι·

> But this would be impossible if the soul *were* not for us before having come to be in this human appearance.

We seem to be dealing here (73a1–2) with the concrete 'appearance' rather than the 'human way of existence and being'. This view is supported by the next occurrence of εἶδος (73d6–d10):

> οὐκοῦν οἶσθα ὅτι οἱ ἐρασταί, ὅταν ἴδωσιν λύραν ἢ ἱμάτιον ἢ ἄλλο τι οἷς τὰ παιδικὰ αὐτῶν εἴωθε χρῆσθαι, πάσχουσι τοῦτο· ἔγνωσάν τε τὴν λύραν καὶ ἐν τῇ διανοίᾳ ἔλαβον τὸ εἶδος τοῦ παιδὸς οὗ ἦν ἡ λύρα; τοῦτο δέ ἐστιν ἀνάμνησις.

> Now, do you know that lovers, whenever they see a lyre or a cloak or anything else that their beloved is wont to use, have the following happen to them: they recognize the lyre and grasp with their intellection the appearance of the boy whose lyre it is?! – But that is recollection.

Here it is τὸ εἶδος τοῦ παιδὸς, 'the appearance (or: the looks) of the boy', that impressed itself upon memory through visual perception. In a way similar to the first occurrence of εἶδος (73a1–2), the word is used again towards the end of the first argument, which Socrates summarizes for Simmias thus (76c11–12):

> ἦσαν ἄρα, ὦ Σιμμία, αἱ ψυχαὶ καὶ πρότερον, πρὶν εἶναι ἐν ἀνθρώπου εἴδει, χωρὶς σωμάτων, καὶ φρόνησιν εἶχον.

209

So, Simmias, the souls *were* also previously, before they were in man's appearance – without bodies, and having understanding.

In this brief section of the dialogue, there are twelve instances of forms of the word ἰδεῖν, 'see, behold'; this brings into view the visual element in the process of recollection. In this context, it is worth recalling that there are several stages in the syntactical development of εἶδος from Homer onwards: 'a man beautiful in appearance'; 'a man of beautiful appearance'; 'the beautiful appearance of a man'; 'a beautiful appearance' (as synecdoche said with reference to an individual human being); 'this human appearance' or 'man's appearance'. At 76c11–12, 'man's appearance' refers to the external visible appearance of the body; at the same time, the plural of 'souls' and of 'bodies' indicates that the singular of εἶδος is generic.

In the next section of the dialogue, 77d–84b, Socrates, in support of the thesis that our soul is immortal, points out that there are things constant and permanent as well as things changeable and transient. We see and perceive with our senses what is changeable; by contrast, we grasp with thought what is permanent; what is permanent is invisible, ἀιδῆ...καὶ οὐχ ὁρατά. Socrates continues (79a6–7):

Θῶμεν οὖν βούλει, ἔφη, δύο εἴδη τῶν ὄντων, τὸ μὲν ὁρατόν, τὸ δὲ ἀιδές;

Now, should we – do you want that? – he said, posit two types of things-that-are, the one visible, the other invisible?

As noted, this usage is also found with some medical writers.[416] And thus it is within common usage if one of these two types of things-that-are shortly afterwards becomes the topic of discussion (79b4–5):

ποτέρῳ οὖν ὁμοιότερον τῷ εἴδει φαμὲν ἂν εἶναι καὶ συγγενέστερον τὸ σῶμα;

Now, to which type of the two do we say that the body would be more similar and akin?

And with near identical phrasing Socrates asks immediately afterwards (79d10–e2) to which type of the two soul would be more similar and akin.

After that, εἶδος, next appears in the following section of the dialogue (84c–89c), which deals with 'the objections of the two men of Thebes and the reactions they elicit in Athens and Phlius'.[417] It is the Theban Cebes who employs again his earlier formula; before he advances his own objection to Socrates' previous conclusion, he clarifies that he does not intend to take back one point that had previously been agreed upon (87a1–2):

ὅτι μὲν γὰρ ἦν ἡμῶν ἡ ψυχὴ καὶ πρὶν εἰς τόδε τὸ εἶδος ἐλθεῖν,

that indeed our soul *was* even before entering this appearance.

While at first of similar appearance, the next occurrence of εἶδος in the *Phaedo* is of a different order. After a conversation about 'misology' with Phaedo (89c–91c), in the refutation of Simmias' objection in the next section but one (91c–95a), Socrates summarizes Simmias' position that the soul is comparable to the 'being-in-tune' of a lyre (91c8–d2):

> Σιμμίας μὲν γὰρ, ὡς ἐγᾦμαι, ἀπιστεῖ τε καὶ φοβεῖται μὴ ἡ ψυχὴ ὅμως καὶ θειότερον καὶ κάλλιον ὂν τοῦ σώματος προαπολλύηται ἐν ἁρμονίας εἴδει οὖσα·

> Indeed, Simmias, as I believe, mistrusts and fears that nevertheless the soul, though being something more divine and more beautiful than the body, would perish earlier than the latter, being 'in the way' of a harmony.

Here, the expression ἐν ἁρμονίας εἴδει οὖσα is unusual. Syntactically, the prepositional phrase displays the same structure as εἶναι ἐν ἀνθρώπου εἴδει (76c12). The sense, on the other hand, may be determined by a comparison with *Republic* 389b4, where it is said of deception that it could, perhaps, be beneficial for human beings ὡς ἐν φαρμάκου εἴδει, which is introduced as a variant to ὡς φάρμακον (382c10). A.D. Lindsay translates 'as a medicine', J.L. Davies and D.J. Vaughan 'in the way of a medicine', A. Bloom 'as a form of remedy'.[418] ἐν + genitive + εἴδει is certainly very rare before Aristotle; Aristotle frequently uses the expression ἐν ὕλης εἴδει, e.g. at *Metaphysics* A 3.983b7, where D. Ross translates 'of the nature of matter'.[419] The sense of 'in the way of a harmony' here in the *Phaedo* would then be that soul and harmony are, in the way explained by Simmias, comparable and similar. The formal and structural parallelism with ἐν ἀνθρώπου εἴδει is thus purely external, as in the phrase ἐν ἀνθρώπου εἴδει both the noun εἶδος is used in a different sense and, in connection with this, the preposition ἐν denotes a spatial relation. The expression ἐν ἀνθρώπου εἴδει is then used again in the same section of the dialogue. Socrates sums up his first refutation of Simmias: the view of the soul as harmony is incompatible with the interpretation of learning as 'remembering' or 'recollection', which entails (92b6–7):

> εἶναι τὴν ψυχὴν πρὶν καὶ εἰς ἀνθρώπου εἶδός τε καὶ σῶμα ἀφικέσθαι,

> that the soul *is* before arriving in man's appearance and the body.

Socrates could of course just as well have said 'before the soul arrives in the body'; but Socrates here quotes again Cebes' introductory remark; the addition 'and in the body' ensures that there is no ambiguity in reference.

After that, Socrates uses the word εἶδος twice in the account of the development of his views on natural science and the make-up of the world which culminates in the introduction of his own new method (95a–102a). Socrates recounts that he had expected from Anaxagoras a description of the world which would explain why and how everything is ordered for the best (98a1–2):

καὶ εἴ μοι ταῦτα ἀποφαίνοι, παρεσκευάσμην ὡς οὐκέτι ποθεσόμενος αἰτίας ἄλλο εἶδος.

And I had made up my mind that – were he to show me that – I would not long for another type of explanation.[420]

Socrates employs the same turn of phrase when he introduces his own way of explanation (100b3–9):

ἔρχομαι γὰρ δὴ ἐπιχειρῶν σοι ἐπιδείξασθαι τῆς αἰτίας τὸ εἶδος ὃ πεπραγμάτευμαι, καὶ εἶμι πάλιν ἐπ' ἐκεῖνα τὰ πολυθρύλητα καὶ ἄρχομαι ἀπ' ἐκείνων...

Indeed I thus continue in trying to show you the type of explanation with which I have concerned myself, and I am going again to those much-prattled <things> and beginning from them...

Socrates thus contrasts his own way of explanation, his way to posit reasons-and-causes, with that of Anaxagoras. His approach to the things-that-are is one among many.

Thus, up to this point of the discussion reported, εἶδος refers to the appearance of a human being in the sense of (a) man's appearance at 73a (A); to the looks and appearance of an individual boy at 73d (B); to the appearance of a human being at 76c (A); to the two types or ways of being of things-that-are at 79a–b and d–e (C); to the appearance of a human being at 87a (A); at 91d, ἐν ἁρμονίας εἴδει is 'in the way of a harmony' (D); at 92b, εἶδος refers to the appearance of a human being (A); at 98a and 100b, εἶδος is the type or way of explanation (E). The sequence is ABACCCADAEE. Among these expressions, (D) is not common, and (A) has a slightly unfamiliar ring. Notwithstanding, and while it is granted that alternative translations may on occasion be possible, the senses in which the noun εἶδος is employed up to this point in the *Phaedo* can be explained with reference to common fifth- and fourth-century Greek usage.[421]

2. εἶδος in Plato's *Phaedo*: 102a–b

At this point, Socrates has made a start with his new method. Simmias and Cebes are enthusiastic. So is Echecrates. He suddenly interrupts Phaedo's account, on this occasion not, as had been the case before at 88c, because he is afraid for the argument, but because he is excited in his agreement. Does this interruption make Phaedo lose his thread? One might almost think so. For when he continues, he takes up his story with the words (102a11): 'As I believe, when this was granted him...'

Phaedo first gives a summary of what had already been reported. This summary is strange on any reading. Phaedo says, speaking with his own voice (102a11–b3):

ὡς μὲν ἐγὼ οἶμαι, ἐπεὶ αὐτῷ ταῦτα συνεχωρήθη, καὶ ὡμολογεῖτο εἶναί τι ἕκαστον τῶν εἰδῶν καὶ τούτων τἆλλα μεταλαμβάνοντα αὐτῶν τούτων τὴν ἐπωνυμίαν ἴσχειν, τὸ δὴ μετὰ ταῦτα ἠρώτα,

As I believe, when this was granted him and it was agreed that each of the εἴδη is something, and that the other things get and have the designation of those [i.e. the εἴδη] themselves in taking part in them [i.e. in the εἴδη], after that, then he asked this...

What is meant here, anybody who has paid even slight attention to Phaedo's narrative will understand. Phaedo obviously refers to what Socrates recounted from 100b onwards. Following on from the last quotation in section 1 above, Socrates had continued (100b5–c7):

...ὑποθέμενος εἶναί τι καλὸν αὐτὸ καθ᾽ αὑτὸ καὶ ἀγαθὸν καὶ μέγα καὶ τἆλλα πάντα· ἃ εἴ μοι δίδως τε καὶ συγχωρεῖς εἶναι ταῦτα, ἐλπίζω σοι ἐκ τούτων τὴν αἰτίαν ἐπιδείξειν καὶ ἀνευρήσειν ὡς ἀθάνατον ἡ ψυχή.
ἀλλὰ μήν, ἔφη ὁ Κέβης, ὡς διδόντος σοι οὐκ ἂν φθάνοις περαίνων.
σκόπει δή, ἔφη, τὰ ἐξῆς ἐκείνοις ἐάν σοι συνδοκῇ ὥσπερ ἐμοί. φαίνεται γάρ μοι, εἴ τί ἐστιν ἄλλο καλὸν πλὴν αὐτὸ τὸ καλόν, οὐδὲ δι᾽ ἓν ἄλλο καλὸν εἶναι ἢ διότι μετέχει ἐκείνου τοῦ καλοῦ· καὶ πάντα δὴ οὕτως λέγω. τῇ τοιᾷδε αἰτίᾳ συγχωρεῖς;

...in that I assume that the beautiful itself is something, and the good and the big and all the others: if you grant me that and admit that these things *are*, I hope from those things to demonstrate to you the explanation and find that the soul is something immortal.
But certainly, said Cebes, as if I had granted it, continue with speed.
Consider, thus, said he, whether you think also like me when it comes to the following point. For it seems to me that, if anything else is beautiful apart from the beautiful itself, then it is beautiful through none other than that it participates in that 'beautiful': and I mean that with a view to each and everything. Do you concede to me that explanation?

So this, the Ideas and Participation in Ideas, is what Phaedo refers to at 102b. Only that the word 'idea' has not been used up to now. Socrates had spoken of the just itself, the beautiful and the good; then also of 'bigness', health and strength (65d). Next, the equal was introduced (74a–75c); that case gave rise to generalization 74c9–d4 and was resumed and confirmed at 76d–77a, the point to which 100b makes conscious verbal allusion. All that which always stays the same, which is constant and permanent, was the topic also of 78c–80b, summed up in one expression at 83b1 as 'that which is itself by itself'.

We are thus witnessing an odd spectacle. In an extended conversation between Socrates and his friends, we hear about the just itself, the beautiful, the good, 'bigness', strength, the equal and the pious that each of them is immutable. In parallel, and without any connection, there are instances of the noun εἶδος in virtually every section of the dialogue; the noun is employed in different senses and different constructions. Then, suddenly, the last – and for Socrates' friends and companions conclusive – proof of the immortality of the soul of the individual makes reference to and use of the εἴδη of the big and small, even and odd, warm and cold, etc.

From the context, it is clear that these εἴδη must be the same as what had been referred to in conversation previously. There cannot be any doubt over the point of reference of the word. But what does the word mean? How is one to understand εἴδη in this context? Is the 'εἶδος of the odd' the 'look', the 'appearance', the 'type' or the 'way' of the odd? Would it help, or would it have helped, if one had decided from the start to translate εἶδος, as is customary, as 'form'? But such a translation of εἶδος as 'form' would always and at each point have required the addition that at all places before *Phaedo* 102b, 'form' must be understood exclusively either as 'visible appearance' or 'type' or 'way', not as 'shape' or 'body' or 'configuration' or 'quality'. Nothing would thus have been gained for an understanding of the occurrence of εἶδος at *Phaedo* 102b. It is rather the case that 'form' is so often chosen as a translation of εἶδος in earlier literature, and by so many translators, precisely because the Latin tradition originating in Republican Rome has made 'form' the standard translation for εἶδος at *Phaedo* 102, in the *Republic* and more generally in Plato and most of all Aristotle. But that does not change the fact that 'those εἴδη' in the *Phaedo* are introduced unexpectedly to an unprepared reader. What εἶδος is meant to *mean* here nobody knows.

3. εἶδος in Philolaus
Of course, it is not quite like that. For *Phaedo* speaks – and continues to speak – as if he were not saying anything new or unaccustomed; he has not introduced anything unexpected or incomprehensible as far as his listeners are concerned. But those who are listening to him are the Pythagoreans at Phlius.[422] Phaedo uses the word εἴδη when he addresses directly, in his own voice, the Pythagoreans to whom he had previously reported 'verbatim' what Socrates and the others had said; in that report, different terms had been used. Socrates, Simmias, Cebes and the others could talk about the beautiful and the good without this terminology. What was Phaedo thinking? What was Plato thinking? Why does he change the terminology of 'itself', 'itself by itself', and even of the οὐσία of things, 'what something is', and suddenly talk about εἴδη?

214

One context in which the word εἶδος had appeared before Plato has as yet not been touched upon. It is one of the few fragments of Philolaus which are generally accepted as genuine.[423] We recall that Philolaus was the one Pythagorean named by Socrates earlier in the dialogue,[424] when he was invoked as an authority against suicide (61d–e). This excludes the possibility that Plato did not know about Philolaus.[425] Stobaeus quotes Philolaus (Eclogae 1.21.7c, 1.188.9 Wachsmuth; DK44B5):

ὅ γα μὰν ἀριθμὸς ἔχει δύο μὲν ἴδια εἴδη, περισσὸν καὶ ἄρτιον, τρίτον δὲ ἀπ' ἀμφοτέρων μειχθέντων ἀρτιοπέριττον· ἑκατέρω δὲ τῶ εἴδεος πολλαὶ μορφαί, ἃς ἕκαστον αὐτὸ σημαίνει.

Number certainly has two proper types (or: two types of its own), odd and even, but a third mixed of both of the two: even-odd:[426] but there are many forms of each type of the two, which [forms] each thing itself indicates.

In the first clause, the accusative plural εἴδη is direct object to ἔχει. Philolaus could, alternatively, have said τῷ γα μὰν ἀριθμῷ ἐστὶ δύο μὲν ἴδια εἴδη or ἔστι γα μὰν δύο μὲν ἴδια εἴδη τῶ ἀριθμῷ, in parallel with *Phaedo* (79a6–7), quoted above:[427]

θῶμεν οὖν βούλει, ἔφη, δύο εἴδη τῶν ὄντων, τὸ μὲν ὁρατόν, τὸ δὲ ἀιδές;

It is interesting that the subsequent expression ἑκατέρω δὲ τῶ εἴδεος on the one hand takes up what was said in the first clause, but that εἶδος, on the other hand, is used in an absolute way in the sense that only the context determines that 'each of the two types' refers to 'types of number'. In the context of arithmetic, the two types are the odd and the even. (It should be noted that in the last clause ἕκαστον, 'each', which refers here to each of the two things odd and even, has the tag αὐτό, 'itself'.) In Philolaus B5 there is thus prefigured an absolute use of εἶδος as technical term. The patchy state of preservation of the writings of Philolaus and those close to him prevents us from knowing how widespread this usage was. But *one* further inference may be possible.

One of the richest extant sources concerning Pythagoreanism in the late fifth and early fourth centuries is Aristotle, *Metaphysics* A 5.985b ff. It appears as if 986a15 contained a summary of Philolaus B5. Immediately afterwards, Aristotle adds (986a22):

ἕτεροι δὲ τῶν αὐτῶν τούτων τὰς ἀρχὰς δέκα λέγουσιν εἶναι τὰς κατὰ συστοιχίαν λεγομένας...

But others among those same people say that the 'beginnings', which are recounted in columns, are ten[428]...

πέρας	καὶ	ἄπειρον	limit	and	unlimited
περιττὸν	καὶ	ἄρτιον	odd	and	even
ἓν	καὶ	πλῆθος	one	and	multitude

δέξιον	καὶ	ἀριστερόν	right	and	left
ἄρρεν	καὶ	θῆλυ	male	and	female
ἠρεμοῦν	καὶ	κινούμενον	still	and	moving/moved
εὐθὺ	καὶ	καμπύλον	straight	and	curved
φῶς	καὶ	σκότος	light	and	dark
ἀγαθὸν	καὶ	κακόν	good	and	bad
τετράγωνον	καὶ	ἑτερόμηκες	square	and	oblong

It is not decisive here who these Pythagoreans are.[429] It is interesting, though, that for example the pair 'odd and even' appears with Philolaus, in the table of opposites and in the *Phaedo*. Against this background, the fact that in the *Phaedo* opposites figure prominently from the start gains in importance. Thinking in terms of opposites is, of course, a general feature of sixth- and fifth-century Greek speculation; the 'Ionians' and the examples of warm and cold and dry and moist are often adduced. And we have seen that Zeno's oppositions may have been in Plato's mind at *Phaedo* 74–5.[430] But opposites are also part of what we know about fifth-century 'Pythagorean' thought in the widest sense of this term. At any rate, with Philolaus and in the *Phaedo*, 'odd' and 'even' are εἴδη. And it is thus possible that the nameless Pythagoreans thought in these categories: there are two 'types' of 'things-that-are', good and bad, light and dark, male and female, etc. Phaedo can then summarize for the Pythagoreans at Phlius (102a11–b1):

ἐπεὶ αὐτῷ ταῦτα συνεχωρήθη, καὶ ὡμολογεῖτο εἶναί τι ἕκαστον τῶν εἰδῶν...

when this was granted him and it was agreed that each of the εἴδη is something...

Echecrates and *his* friends and companions will have immediately accepted and understood the thought thus phrased, since both thinking in opposites and the terminology was familiar. Many of the pairs of opposites which Socrates had adduced in the course of his conversation also played their part in Pythagorean views of the world.[431]

One may object that at *Metaphysics* A 5.986a22 ff., Aristotle does not call the opposites εἴδη, nor does he suggest that anybody else did. But while this is so, it cannot be decisive as an objection. Where Aristotle reports on positions of his predecessors, he does not as a rule consistently employ their terminology, unless it is important to him for his own constructive or polemical purposes. In that way, εἶδος, be it in the singular or in the plural, does not occur at 985a15 either, although Philolaus B5 is not implausible as a source for that section.[432]

The word εἶδος in the sense of 'type' could thus be used in an absolute way to denote one or other of two opposite *things*. That, of course, does not in any way presuppose a Platonic 'theory of forms'. On the contrary. If and when there was talk of εἴδη, there was the term; but what was important to Plato, the beautiful itself, the good and the just as the things which for him determined the 'being' of the world – these things as such, moreover without their corresponding opposites, were not at the centre of Pythagorean or otherwise Presocratic speculation. Plato, however, may have exploited the fact that 'good' appeared as a στοιχεῖον, 'an element', at all; and if there is any truth in the view that Pythagoreans before Plato assigned the number four to justice, one may add that 'justice' as well as 'good' figured in Pythagorean doctrine. There was thus a certain overlap in interest which Plato could draw on. Adopting Philolaus' terminology allows him then to replace individual elements in the explanation of the world of the Pythagorean with his own explanations. This, in turn, does not make Plato a Pythagorean. Rather, Plato says, addressing the Pythagoreans: if certain εἴδη are posited as fundamental constituting elements of the world, then these εἴδη must be the good, the beautiful and the just, and not pairs of opposites, which must appear random in the light of Socratic discussion. The word εἶδος can be taken over as a technical term provided one accepts what Plato has laid down as holding true of these fundamental constituents: the 'good', 'beautiful', 'just' is characterized as immutable, invisible, non-corporeal, uniform. Looking at the historical background of εἶδος has thus led to Philolaus, as had been the case with οὐσία.[433] But while Philolaus is undoubtedly one of the targets of Plato in the *Phaedo*, he is not the only one, as an investigation of ἰδέα will demonstrate. Before we turn to this other term for 'Form', let us briefly turn back to a passage in the *Meno*, a dialogue which is by common consent earlier than the *Phaedo* and which is implicitly alluded to in the *Phaedo* when the topic of *anamnēsis* or recollection is first raised (72e–73b).

4. εἶδος in Plato's *Meno*

Immediately after the *Meno* passage quoted in chapter 7 on οὐσία above,[434] in which Socrates, in his search for ἀρετή had asked Meno for the οὐσία of a bee, what a bee *is*, and after Meno has confirmed that he could tell him what all bees have in common *qua* bees, Socrates continues (72c5–73a5):

οὕτω δὴ καὶ περὶ τῶν ἀρετῶν· κἂν εἰ πολλαὶ καὶ παντοδαπαί εἰσιν, ἕν γέ τι εἶδος ταὐτὸν ἅπασαι ἔχουσιν δι' ὃ εἰσὶν ἀρεταί, εἰς ὃ καλῶς που ἔχει ἀποβλέψαντα τὸν ἀποκρινόμενον τῷ ἐρωτήσαντι ἐκεῖνο δηλῶσαι, ὃ τυγχάνει οὖσα ἀρετή· ἢ οὐ μανθάνεις ὅτι λέγω;
δοκῶ γέ μοι μανθάνειν· οὐ μέντοι ὡς βούλομαί γέ πω κατέχω τὸ ἐρωτώμενον.
πότερον δὲ περὶ ἀρετῆς μόνον σοι οὕτω δοκεῖ, ὦ Μένων, ἄλλη μὲν ἀνδρὸς εἶναι, ἄλλη δὲ γυναικὸς καὶ τῶν ἄλλων, ἢ καὶ περὶ ὑγιείας καὶ περὶ μεγέθους καὶ περὶ ἰσχύος ὡσαύτως; ἄλλη μὲν ἀνδρὸς δοκεῖ σοι εἶναι ὑγίεια, ἄλλη δὲ γυναικός; ἢ ταὐτὸν πανταχοῦ εἶδός ἐστιν, ἐάνπερ ὑγίεια ᾖ, ἐάντε ἐν ἀνδρὶ ἐάντε ἐν ἄλλῳ ὁτῳοῦν ᾖ;

217

ἡ αὐτή μοι δοκεῖ ὑγίειά γε εἶναι καὶ ἀνδρὸς καὶ γυναικός.

οὐκοῦν καὶ μέγεθος καὶ ἰσχύς; ἐάνπερ ἰσχυρὰ γυνὴ ᾖ, τῷ αὐτῷ εἴδει καὶ τῇ αὐτῇ ἰσχύϊ ἰσχυρὰ ἔσται; τὸ γὰρ τῇ αὐτῇ τοῦτο λέγω· οὐδὲν διαφέρει πρὸς τὸ ἰσχὺς εἶναι ἡ ἰσχύς, ἐάντε ἐν ἀνδρὶ ᾖ ἐάντε ἐν γυναικί. ἢ δοκεῖ τί σοι διαφέρειν; οὐκ ἔμοιγε.

ἡ δὲ ἀρετὴ πρὸς τὸ ἀρετὴ εἶναι διοίσει τι, ἐάντε ἐν παιδὶ ᾖ ἐάντε ἐν πρεσβύτῃ, ἐάντε ἐν γυναικὶ ἐάντε ἐν ἀνδρί;

ἔμοιγέ πως δοκεῖ, ὦ Σώκρατες, τοῦτο οὐκέτι ὅμοιον εἶναι τοῖς ἄλλοις τούτοις.

So also concerning virtues: even if they are many and varied, they certainly somehow have *one* εἶδος, the same, because of which they are virtues, looking at which it is easy for the one who answers to show clearly, to the one who asks, that which happens to be virtue: or don't you understand what I say?
I certainly seem to myself to understand: Yet I certainly have not yet got a hold of what is being asked to the extent that I should wish.
But does it seem to you to be like this only concerning virtue, or also concerning health and size and strength in the same way? Does it seem to you that there is *one* 'health of a man', *another* 'of a women', and <*another*> 'of the others'? Or is it the same εἶδος everywhere, if it really is a case of health, whether it is in a man or in anyone else?
Health of a man and of a woman certainly seems to me to be the same.
Well now, also size and strength? Whenever a woman is strong, will she be strong by the same εἶδος and by the same strength? But I mean the following with 'by the same': Strength does not differ at all with a view to 'being strength', whether it is in a man or in a woman. Or does it seem to you to differ?
It doesn't.
But will virtue with a view to 'being virtue' differ in any way, whether it is in a boy or in an old man, or in a woman or in a man?
It somehow seems to me, Socrates, that this is no longer similar to those other cases.

In quick succession, Socrates uses the term εἶδος thrice. As this happens just after the example of the bees, does he mean that bees and virtues and health and strength have the same 'type'? In the context of zoology, εἶδος had been used by, for example, Herodotus. But the point of comparing one type of bee with another was precisely that they were, or belonged to, different types. The term εἶδος is at home in, and familiar from, the context of zoology, but the meaning does not quite fit the context of the *Meno*. Likewise, while one could think of courage, modesty and piety as *types* of virtue, here Socrates asks whether virtue *qua* virtue has one type. He seems to use εἶδος in an absolute sense. The additional examples which Socrates provides are health and size and strength. Again, in the context of medicine, εἶδος was a term encountered in a variety of texts, notably in its application to types of people. But one could also speak of the 'type' of a particular disease. This, however, seemed to be against the background of there being various types of disease.

That is to say, as with zoology, the example of health, as invoking the context of medicine, allows for the term εἶδος, but the notion of health as one 'type' is unprecedented. The impression that the term εἶδος is out of place is yet stronger in the case of strength, where the innovative nature of Socrates' usage is highlighted by addition of the κύριον, the 'main term', after an epexegetic καί, 'and <that is to say>'; 'and <by that I mean>': τῷ αὐτῷ εἴδει καὶ τῇ αὐτῇ ἰσχύϊ, 'by the same *type* [?] and <by that I mean> by the same strength'. Socrates could not indicate more clearly that he is aware that he is operating outside common usage.

While *Meno* 72c–73a is thus not fully in tune with common usage, one may point to a passage in another dialogue of Plato which seems to contain the same phraseology. *Gorgias* 503d–e was adduced in Part II, chapter 4, section 13 as an example of the use of εἶδος as referring to the appearance of an object. Socrates says to Polus (503d6–e7):

φέρε γάρ, ὁ ἀγαθὸς ἀνὴρ καὶ ἐπὶ τὸ βέλτιστον λέγων, ἃ ἂν λέγῃ ἄλλο τι οὐκ εἰκῇ ἐρεῖ, ἀλλ᾽ ἀποβλέπων πρός τι· ὥσπερ καὶ οἱ ἄλλοι πάντες δημιουργοὶ βλέποντες πρὸς τὸ αὐτῶν ἔργον ἕκαστος οὐκ εἰκῇ ἐκλεγόμενος προσφέρει <ἃ προσφέρει>, ἀλλ᾽ ὅπως ἂν εἶδός τι αὐτῷ σχῇ τοῦτο ὃ ἐργάζεται. οἷον εἰ βούλει ἰδεῖν τοὺς ζωγράφους, τοὺς οἰκοδόμους, τοὺς ναυπηγούς, τοὺς ἄλλους πάντας δημιουργούς, ὅντινα βούλει αὐτῶν, ὡς εἰς τάξιν τινὰ ἕκαστος ἕκαστον τίθησιν ὃ ἂν τιθῇ...

Come, now, the good man and the one who speaks to the best <end>, will, of course, say whatever he says not at random, but looking at something: just as all the other craftsmen as well, looking at their own work, produce, each of them, what they produce not selecting <things> at random, but so that <the things> they are working at have a certain appearance. For example, if you want to see the painters, the builders, the shipwrights, all the other craftsmen, whomsoever of them you want, how each one of them puts whatever he deals with into a certain order...

It has been noted that Dodds (1959, 328) translates 503e1 ff. as 'just as all other craftsmen, with an eye to their own function, each of them applies the measures he applies, not at random but selecting them in order to get the thing he is making a particular form,' and that the passage in the *Gorgias* has by some been interpreted as one of the foreshadowings of the full-blown Theory of Forms. While I have translated εἶδος at 503e as 'appearance', it could be argued that the emphasis on a fixed order and arrangement suggests that Socrates is thinking of objects of a certain 'type' rather than just of a certain 'appearance'; while the example of the painter does not fit this interpretation neatly, it could probably be accommodated. One can then point in addition to the phrase ἀποβλέπων πρός τι/βλέποντες πρός..., 'looking towards something', a phrase also found at *Meno* 72c, and conclude that

Plato was indeed working within the same conceptual framework, employing the same technical terminology in both dialogues.

But this would be rash. The language and imagery of *Gorgias* 503d–e is fully within common Greek usage and self-explanatory in the sense that no reference to specific contexts from outside the dialogue is needed in order to translate and understand the passage. *Meno* 72c–73a, by contrast, is not self-explanatory in this sense. The expression ἀποβλέψαντα, 'looking at', at *Meno* 72c is best understood as a conscious quotation from or allusion to *Gorgias* 503d. Plato adds the context of arts and crafts to the range of contexts in which the term εἶδος is found. Socrates' suggestion is that in searching for the 'being' of ἀρετή one may think of the arts and crafts as one analogy; just as in the crafts the craftsman in producing a tool of a certain type looks in his mind at the function of a thing in order to give it one 'type' or 'appearance', so Meno should attempt to find that one 'type' that is common to all ἀρετή, 'virtue', so that he can then look for orientation to this 'type'. But it is not clear whether the craft-analogy, if it is that, will be helpful in the process of determining what virtue is. Nor is it clear that the term εἶδος fits this context as well as it fitted that of *Gorgias* 503d–e.

At *Meno* 72c–73a, the term εἶδος is introduced in the context of Socrates' asking for 'what something *is*', its οὐσία. The terminology of εἶδος is appropriate in this context from the point of view of the *Phaedo*. But, even though the sense of the *Meno* passage as a whole is readily accessible, it is not obvious from the passage whether the contemporary reader would or could have made sense of the *term* εἶδος. Socrates' way of phrasing his questions rather suggests that this was not the case, and that Plato thus here introduces new terminology in need of further explanation. The reader of the *Meno* who has not read the *Phaedo* will not be able fully to make sense of Socrates' usage.

This, at least, could be maintained without qualification unless εἶδος was a term already familiar from elsewhere in the sense in which it is encountered from *Phaedo* 102b onwards. That this should be so is not impossible. One could think of two scenarios, which are not mutually exclusive. One is, that discussion of philosophical issues and concepts in the Academy at least on occasion preceded Plato's introducing these concepts and notions to a wider audience in writing. If some of these discussions were open to the public, there is a possibility that Platonic terminology became familiar outside the narrow confines of the 'school'; at any rate, this usage would be familiar to those within the school, who may, for all we know, have been the primary readership.[435] The other scenario is that εἶδος was indeed a term that occurred in some Pythagorean contexts, as suggested above. In that case, both Pythagoreans and those who were, like Simmias and Cebes, to some degree familiar with Pythagoreanism, would have understood *something* when

Socrates uses εἶδος at *Meno* 73, even if the connection to Pythagorean εἴδη is less than obvious; the fact that *anamnēsis* is mentioned a few pages later in the dialogue is a clear enough indication that allusion to Pythagorean concepts cannot be excluded at this stage.

But be that as it may, I should maintain that the use of εἶδος in the passage in the *Meno* is not fully self-explanatory, and that we as modern readers would not be able to make adequate sense of it if we did not have the *Phaedo* and the *Republic*. At least in this respect, the *Meno* as a vehicle of Platonic philosophy is not self-contained. And given that εἶδος in the *Meno* occurs in the same context as οὐσία, another term that could be traced back to Philolaus, it may be best to see Plato in a continuous but as yet unfinished dialogue with the Pythagorean, a dialogue in which he lets the reader share. In that respect, the *Meno* contains the promise of 'resolution' in the *Phaedo*.

CHAPTER 9

ἰδέα in Plato's *Phaedo*

1. εἶδος and μορφή at *Phaedo* 103e

After the first introduction of the term εἶδος at 102b1, Phaedo reports the next phase of Socrates' argument, in which Socrates uses the examples of the comparatives μείζων, 'taller, bigger, larger', and ἐλάττων, 'shorter, smaller', together with the positives μέγας, 'big' and σμικρός, 'small', and the nouns μέγεθος, 'tallness, bigness, largeness', and σμικρότης, 'shortness, smallness'. In a relevant sense, 'taller and shorter' had been an example at 70e–71b, at 75c and among the 'physical' puzzles at 96d, and μέγα had been given as the third after καλόν and ἀγαθόν at 100b, before the addition of 'and all the others', clearly by way of preparation for the discussion of 102b–103a. Especially the distinction Socrates makes at 102d between αὐτὸ τὸ μέγεθος and τὸ ἐν ἡμῖν μέγεθος, an opposition taken up at 103b in the clause αὐτὸ τὸ ἐναντίον ἑαυτῷ ἐναντίον οὐκ ἄν ποτε γένοιτο, οὔτε τὸ ἐν ἡμῖν οὔτε τὸ ἐν τῇ φύσει, 'the opposite itself would never become opposite to itself, neither the one in us nor the one in nature', has exercised commentators, and we shall return to that issue below, in the discussion of ἐνεῖναι, 'being in', and 'immanence'. First, we shall proceed on the generally-accepted assumption that Socrates has here introduced a third thing, besides on the one hand the many people from time to time called tall and on the other hand tallness itself, leaving aside the issue of whether this third thing, or class of things, is 'the property tall(ness)', the 'form' as opposed to the 'Form', an 'immanent form', a 'form-copy', 'the character tall(ness)', or whatever else; Plato does not at this stage attach any such label to it.

Socrates appears to make this distinction, at least in the first place, in order to lead to the further observation that just as the warm itself will never admit the cold, so also fire, which always by necessity is warm, will never admit the cold, and just as the cold will never admit the warm, so snow, which always by necessity is cold, will never admit the warm. This is summarized in the generalizing statement of 103e3–7:

ἔστιν ἄρα, ἦ δ' ὅς, περὶ ἔνια τῶν τοιούτων, ὥστε μὴ μόνον αὐτὸ τὸ εἶδος ἀξιοῦσθαι τοῦ αὐτοῦ ὀνόματος εἰς τὸν ἀεὶ χρόνον, ἀλλὰ καὶ ἄλλο τι ὃ ἔστι μὲν οὐκ ἐκεῖνο, ἔχει δὲ τὴν ἐκείνου μορφὴν ἀεί, ὅτανπερ ᾖ. ἔτι δὲ ἐν τῷδε ἴσως

223

ἔσται σαφέστερον ὃ λέγω· τὸ γὰρ περιττὸν ἀεί που δεῖ τούτου τοῦ ὀνόματος
τυγχάνειν ὅπερ νῦν λέγομεν· ἢ οὔ;

So it is, he said, with some of the things of that sort, that not only the type itself
(αὐτὸ τὸ εἶδος) is worthy of its name into eternity, but also some other thing
which while it is not that (ἐκεῖνο = ἐκεῖνο τὸ εἶδος) nevertheless has the form of
that (τὴν ἐκείνου μορφὴν) always, whenever it *is*. But yet in what follows it will
be clearer what I mean: indeed, the odd must always somehow get that name
which we are now uttering; or is it not so?

And Socrates goes on to say that not only the odd will always be called odd,
but also any triad, or amount or set of three, and any pentad, or amount or
set of five, will always also be called odd. At 103e, in the sentence quoted, it
is now Socrates himself who, in Phaedo's report, uses the word εἶδος. Socrates
speaks like a Pythagorean. He refers to a thing like 'the warm' or 'the cold'
as αὐτὸ τὸ εἶδος, 'the type itself'. The type itself always has its own, proper
name. But something else, which is not the type itself, but has the form of
the type for as long as it *is*, also has the name of the type. This is illustrated by
Socrates with the examples of the odd and the even. The type itself, e.g. the
odd itself, has the 'name' 'odd', but also the triad and the pentad, which are
not the odd but have the 'form', the μορφή, of the odd, have the 'name' 'odd'.
This recalls again Philolaus B5:

ὃ γα μὰν ἀριθμὸς ἔχει δύο μὲν ἴδια εἴδη, περισσὸν καὶ ἄρτιον…ἑκατέρω δὲ τῶ
εἴδεος πολλαὶ μορφαί, ἃς ἕκαστον αὐτὸ σημαίνει.

Number certainly has two proper types (or: two types of its own), odd and
even…but there are many forms (μορφαί) of each type of the two, which
[forms] each thing itself indicates.

For Philolaus as well, 'odd' and 'even', in this order, were the types. Of each
type, there were 'many forms', πολλαὶ μορφαί. The most natural interpretation of that is that three, five, seven, etc., or all triads, pentads, heptads, etc.,
are the many 'forms' or 'formations' of the 'type' 'odd'. They are called, in
an absolute way, μορφαί τοῦ εἴδους, 'forms' or 'formations of the type', and
'they have the form of the type', ἔχουσι τὴν τοῦ εἴδους μορφήν. This last
step is speculative. We have too little context to allow us to say exactly what
Philolaus meant by πολλαὶ μορφαί, 'many forms', and it is impossible to say
whether Plato would have called a triad one 'form' or 'formation' of the odd,
μορφὴ τοῦ περιττοῦ, just because he let Socrates say of a triad, which is always
also odd, that it has 'the form of the type', τὴν τοῦ εἴδους μορφήν. But if there
is any connection between Philolaus B5 and this section of the *Phaedo* as far
as the term εἶδος is concerned, then Plato's use of μορφή in connection with
εἶδος at 103e cannot be accidental but should likewise point to Philolaus
in some way. That there is such a connection is as good as confirmed by the
example of the odd and the even following immediately.

224

As far, however, as the usage of μορφή is concerned, it may be worth revisiting Parmenides B8, 53: μορφὰς γὰρ κατέθεντο δύο γνώμας ὀνομάζειν, 'they laid down as their cognitions to name two shapes'. In one respect at least, Parmenidean usage may be relevant in considering Philolaus B5 as well as the occurrences of μορφή in the *Phaedo*. In Parmenides B8, we see an absolute usage of μορφή as referring to something. Moreover, the two things addressed as 'shapes' or 'forms' are opposites. One need not re-ignite the old question of Parmenides' alleged Pythagoreanism. It is sufficient to state that, regardless of the origin of Parmenidean usage, there is a certain overlap in the absolute application of μορφή between Parmenides B8, Philolaus B5 and *Phaedo* 103e.[436]

2. ἰδέα at *Phaedo* 104c

To return to the *Phaedo*: two separate distinctions are introduced between 102b and 103e. On the one hand, there is, in addition to the many big things, bigness itself and now also bigness in us. On the other hand, whatever is three, is also odd, without itself being the odd; the passage in itself does not allow to decide whether this is intended to apply to and hold true of any set of three things only, or also of the three itself.[437]

Next, Socrates announces that he will now show why he has introduced the latter of these distinctions (104b6–c1):

ὃ τοίνυν, ἔφη, βούλομαι δηλῶσαι, ἄθρει. ἔστιν δὲ τόδε, ὅτι φαίνεται οὐ μόνον ἐκεῖνα τὰ ἐναντία ἄλληλα οὐ δεχόμενα, ἀλλὰ καὶ ὅσα οὐκ ὄντ' ἀλλήλοις ἐναντία ἔχει ἀεὶ τἀναντία, οὐδὲ ταῦτα ἔοικε δεχομένοις ἐκείνην τὴν ἰδέαν ἢ ἂν τῇ ἐν αὐτοῖς οὔσῃ ἐναντία ᾖ, ἀλλ' ἐπιούσης αὐτῆς ἤτοι ἀπολλύμενα ἢ ὑπεκχωροῦντα.

Now, he said, note what I wanted to make clear. It is this: not only do those opposites show themselves as not accepting each other, but also whatever, not being opposite to each other, always has the opposites, these things, too, do not resemble those that accept whatever appearance is opposite to the one that is in them (=in 'these', i.e. the former), but when it advances, they either perish or retreat.

The military metaphors of advancing, retreating and perishing, first employed at 102d and repeated at 103d, will be discussed in due course. As regards the phrasing of the thought expressed, it is here that Socrates introduces the term ἰδέα into the discussion. And while εἶδος occurred in the *Phaedo* with particular frequency, this is the point at which ἰδέα makes its first appearance in the whole of the dialogue. There are subsequently four more instances of the noun in quick succession between 104b6 and 104e1, and a further occurrence in the same philosophical context at 105d13; the word is then

225

found twice more, in a non-technical sense in the context of the myth, at 108d9 and 109b5.

While some of the earlier modern commentators declared that, at this stage in the *Phaedo*, Plato uses εἶδος, μορφή and ἰδέα synonymously, the assumption has been prevalent for some time now that the latter two are synonyms in the *Phaedo*, but are different from and contrasted with εἶδος.[438] On either view, though, the syntax of 104b9 f. is unusual: an ἰδέα is said to be *in* something, as is implied in the phrase τῇ ἐν αὐτοῖς οὔσῃ. So far, this 'being in something' has neither been said of εἶδος nor of μορφή. But because, at 102b7 f., 'bigness in us' is contrasted with 'bigness itself', and because 'bigness itself' is the εἶδος, it could be concluded that the 'bigness in us' is the ἰδέα. If this is so, it is to be noted that while it would by a small stretch of the imagination be acceptable to say that in the case of the type (εἶδος) 'big', something that is big 'has' or 'accepts' the form (μορφή) of the type (εἶδος), or that is 'has' or 'accepts' the appearance (ἰδέα) of the type (εἶδος), it is hardly possible to say of the 'appearance of something' – or for that matter the 'type of something', in the ordinary, non-technical sense of 'type' – that 'it is in something' else. The sense of ἰδέα here cannot thus be said to be 'appearance' or 'type (of something)' in a straightforward way. The syntax of ἰδέα suggests that the noun refers rather to a *thing* by its nature such that it can be *in* something. This constitutes an absolute use of ἰδέα.

3. εἶδος, μορφή and ἰδέα in Plato's *Phaedo*: 104c–105b

After these preliminary remarks on ἰδέα, the following passage may best be considered in its entirety (104c7–105b4):

οὐκ ἄρα μόνον τὰ εἴδη τὰ ἐναντία οὐχ ὑπομένει ἐπιόντα ἄλληλα, ἀλλὰ καὶ ἄλλ' ἄττα τὰ ἐναντία οὐχ ὑπομένει ἐπιόντα.
ἀληθέστατα, ἔφη, λέγεις.
βούλει οὖν, ἦ δ' ὅς, ἐὰν οἷοί τ' ὦμεν, ὁρισώμεθα ὁποῖα ταῦτά ἐστιν;
πάνυ γε.
ἆρ' οὖν, ἔφη, ὦ Κέβης, τάδε εἴη ἄν, ἃ ὅτι ἂν κατάσχῃ μὴ μόνον ἀναγκάζει τὴν αὑτοῦ ἰδέαν αὐτὸ ἴσχειν, ἀλλὰ καὶ ἐναντίου αὐτῷ ἀεί τινος;
πῶς λέγεις;
ὥσπερ ἄρτι ἐλέγομεν. οἶσθα γὰρ δήπου ὅτι ἃ ἂν ἡ τῶν τριῶν ἰδέα κατάσχῃ, ἀνάγκη αὐτοῖς οὐ μόνον τρισὶν εἶναι ἀλλὰ καὶ περιττοῖς.
πάνυ γε.
ἐπὶ τὸ τοιοῦτον δή, φαμέν, ἡ ἐναντία ἰδέα ἐκείνῃ τῇ μορφῇ ἣ ἂν τοῦτο ἀπεργάζηται οὐδέποτ' ἂν ἔλθοι.
οὐ γάρ.
εἰργάζετο δέ γε ἡ περιττή;
ναί.
ἐναντία δὲ ταύτῃ ἡ τοῦ ἀρτίου;
ναί.

ἐπὶ τὰ τρία ἄρα ἡ τοῦ ἀρτίου ἰδέα οὐδέποτε ἥξει.
οὐ δῆτα.
ἄμοιρα δὴ τοῦ ἀρτίου τὰ τρία.
ἄμοιρα.
ἀνάρτιος ἄρα ἡ τριάς.
ναί.
ὃ τοίνυν ἔλεγον ὁρίσασθαι, ποῖα οὐκ ἐναντία τινὶ ὄντα ὅμως οὐ δέχεται αὐτό, τὸ ἐναντίον – οἷον νῦν ἡ τριὰς τῷ ἀρτίῳ οὐκ οὖσα ἐναντία οὐδέν τι μᾶλλον αὐτὸ δέχεται, τὸ γὰρ ἐναντίον ἀεὶ αὐτῷ ἐπιφέρει, καὶ ἡ δυὰς τῷ περιττῷ καὶ τὸ πῦρ τῷ ψυχρῷ καὶ ἄλλα πάμπολλα – ἀλλ᾽ ὅρα δὴ εἰ οὕτως ὁρίζῃ, μὴ μόνον τὸ ἐναντίον τὸ ἐναντίον μὴ δέχεσθαι, ἀλλὰ καὶ ἐκεῖνο, ὃ ἂν ἐπιφέρῃ τι ἐναντίον ἐκείνῳ, ἐφ᾽ ὅτι ἂν αὐτὸ ἴῃ, αὐτὸ τὸ ἐπιφέρον τὴν τοῦ ἐπιφερομένου ἐναντιότητα μηδέποτε δέξασθαι. πάλιν δὲ ἀναμιμνήσκου· οὐ γὰρ χεῖρον πολλάκις ἀκούειν. τὰ πέντε τὴν τοῦ ἀρτίου οὐ δέξεται, οὐδὲ τὰ δέκα τὴν τοῦ περιττοῦ, τὸ διπλάσιον (τοῦτο μὲν οὖν καὶ αὐτὸ ἄλλῳ ἐναντίον, ὅμως δὲ τὴν τοῦ περιττοῦ οὐ δέξεται)· οὐδὲ δὴ τὸ ἡμιόλιον οὐδὲ τἆλλα τὰ τοιαῦτα [τὸ ἥμισυ] τὴν τοῦ ὅλου, καὶ τριτημόριον αὖ καὶ πάντα τὰ τοιαῦτα, εἴπερ ἕπῃ τε καὶ συνδοκεῖ σοι οὕτως.
πάνυ σφόδρα καὶ συνδοκεῖ, ἔφη, καὶ ἕπομαι.

So not only the opposite types (εἴδη) do not stand firm when they go against each other, but also certain other opposite things do not stand firm when they [i.e. the opposite types] approach.

You speak most truly.

Do you now want us, said he, if we are capable of doing so, to determine of what sort those things are?

Very much so.

Would it not be these things, Cebes, said he, which that which possesses them not only forces to have its own ἰδέα, but also always of an opposite?

How do you mean?

As we said just now: for you certainly know that whatever things the ἰδέα of three possesses, that it is a necessity for those not only to be three, but also odd.

Very much so.

Upon such a thing, thus, we say the ἰδέα which is opposite to that form (μορφή) which brings that about would never come.

Indeed not.

But certainly, the odd <form> brings it about.

Yes.

But opposite to that is the <form> of the even?

Yes.

So, upon the three the ἰδέα of the even will never come?

Certainly not.

Thus the three do [or: three does] not have a share in the even?

They do not have a share.

So the triad is un-even.

Yes.

Thus, what I said <I wanted> to be determined, of what sort are the things which while not being opposite to something nevertheless do not admit the opposite itself – just as now the triad, while not being opposite to the even, accepted it in nothing more, for it (the triad) always carries along the opposite to it (the even), and the dyad (always carries along the opposite) to the odd, and fire (always carries along the opposite) to the cold and <in the same way behave> very many other things – but see, thus, if you determine in this way: not only does the opposite not admit the opposite, but also that which brings along an opposite to that thing, against which it goes, the <opposite->carrying itself never admits the opposition of the thing carried. But once again, recollect: indeed, it is not worse to hear it many times. The five will not admit the <ἰδέα> of the even, nor the ten the <ἰδέα> of the odd, <as> the double (Now that, in turn, is itself opposite to another, but it will all the same not admit the <ἰδέα> of the odd): nor <will> consequently the one-and-a-half and the other things of that sort <admit> the <ἰδέα> of the whole, and again <the> third and all things of that sort, if you follow and if it seems to you, too, to be so.

Indeed, it does seem to me, too, to be so, he said, and I do follow.

In this passage, *Phaedo* 104c7–105b4, there is one occurrence of the plural εἴδη, one of μορφή, and four of ἰδέα; but there are also six incomplete expressions with the feminine form of the definite article in the singular, either followed by an adjective in concord or by an articulated neuter adjective in the genitive singular: in the first two of these cases, the context suggests that μορφή be supplied as the feminine noun, in the last four ἰδέα.

The passage presents the following difficulty for the assumption that εἶδος refers to 'the thing itself', or 'in nature', as opposed to 'the thing in us', while ἰδέα is synonymous with μορφή and refers to 'the thing in us' as opposed to 'the thing in nature' or 'the thing itself'. On that assumption, the things themselves are usually supposed to be immutable and eternal, in concord with what is said elsewhere in the dialogue; but if that is so, the opening statement at 104c7 f. would appear nonsensical: τὰ εἴδη τὰ ἐναντία οὐχ ὑπομένει ἐπιόντα ἄλληλα, 'the opposite types (εἴδη) do not stand firm when they go against each other'. It is clearly stated that the opposite types go against each other. But if only 'the things in us' can do or suffer anything, τὰ εἴδη τὰ ἐναντία here must refer to the opposite types in us.[439]

Secondly, the passage presents the following difficulty for the assumption that Socrates uses εἶδος when he thinks of, anachronistically speaking, the generic term as opposed to μορφή and ἰδέα, which are used in the case of specific terms; on this view, if something is possessed or held down by the μορφή or the ἰδέα of three, this implies, by way of logical-*cum*-semantic entailment, that this thing also 'has of' the εἶδος oddness.[440] But at 104d Socrates speaks of the μορφή of the odd and the even, and at 105a–b, of the ἰδέα of, respectively, the odd, the even and the whole.

It is thus impossible to maintain consistently that Plato upheld terminological distinctions either along the 'in nature'-'in us' or along the 'entailed/carried along'-'entailing/carrying along' divide. At most, one could state that there is no unambiguous example of a use of μορφή or ἰδέα in which either noun *must* refer to a 'thing itself'.[441]

The fact, though, that it is not possible to provide unambiguous Platonic terms for 'Platonic Form' on the one hand and 'property' on the other need not mean that Plato does not introduce these distinctions here. We shall return to that issue shortly. First, however, we must turn once more to the issue of translation. It could be shown why Plato would have wanted to use the terms εἶδος and μορφή. But in what sense and why is ἰδέα introduced here as a technical term? What does ἰδέα mean? These questions are particularly pressing because it seems as if, whatever distinctions Plato meant to draw at 102b–105b, he could have labelled them with εἶδος and μορφή. In other words, whatever distinctions may be intended between εἶδος and μορφή, it is not obvious that ἰδέα is used to refer to anything other than what μορφή could refer to.[442]

It is thus safe to conclude that Plato had independent reasons for wishing to introduce the noun ἰδέα. But what were these reasons?

4. ἰδέα in the *Euthyphro*

It is against this background that, in order to illuminate the usage of *Phaedo* 104b–105b, the one context in an earlier dialogue is adduced which displays the noun ἰδέα and which at the same time is usually taken to contain the theory of forms *in nuce*, or an early stage of that theory, or at least to contain clear foreshadowings of that theory, *Euthyphro* 5c–6e.[443] The text reads (5c8–d5, 6c9–e7):

SOCRATES: ...νῦν οὖν πρὸς Διὸς λέγε μοι ὃ νυνδὴ σαφῶς εἰδέναι διισχυρίζου, ποῖόν τι τὸ εὐσεβὲς φῂς εἶναι καὶ τὸ ἀσεβὲς καὶ περὶ φόνου καὶ περὶ τῶν ἄλλων; ἢ οὐ ταὐτόν ἐστιν ἐν πάσῃ πράξει τὸ ὅσιον αὐτὸ αὑτῷ, καὶ τὸ ἀνόσιον αὖ τοῦ μὲν ὁσίου παντὸς ἐναντίον, αὐτὸ δὲ αὑτῷ ὅμοιον καὶ ἔχον μίαν τινὰ ἰδέαν κατὰ τὴν ἀνοσιότητα πᾶν ὅτιπερ ἂν μέλλῃ ἀνόσιον εἶναι;

...

νυνὶ δὲ ὅπερ ἄρτι σε ἠρόμην πειρῶ σαφέστερον εἰπεῖν. οὐ γάρ με, ὦ ἑταῖρε, τὸ πρότερον ἱκανῶς ἐδίδαξας ἐρωτήσαντα τὸ ὅσιον ὅτι ποτ' εἴη, ἀλλά μοι εἶπες ὅτι τοῦτο τυγχάνει ὅσιον ὂν ὃ σὺ νῦν ποιεῖς, φόνου ἐπεξιὼν τῷ πατρί.
EUTHYPHRO: καὶ ἀληθῆ γε ἔλεγον, ὦ Σώκρατες.
SOCRATES: ἴσως. ἀλλὰ γάρ, ὦ Εὐθύφρων, καὶ ἄλλα πολλὰ φῂς εἶναι ὅσια.
EUTHYPHRO: καὶ γὰρ ἔστιν.
SOCRATES: μέμνησαι οὖν ὅτι οὐ τοῦτό σοι διεκελευόμην, ἕν τι ἢ δύο με διδάξαι τῶν πολλῶν ὁσίων, ἀλλ' ἐκεῖνο αὐτὸ τὸ εἶδος ᾧ πάντα τὰ ὅσια ὅσιά ἐστιν; ἔφησθα γάρ που μιᾷ ἰδέᾳ τά τε ἀνόσια ἀνόσια εἶναι καὶ τὰ ὅσια ὅσια· ἢ οὐ μνημονεύεις;

EUTHYPHRO: ἔγωγε.

SOCRATES: ταύτην τοίνυν με αὐτὴν δίδαξον τὴν ἰδέαν τίς ποτέ ἐστιν, ἵνα εἰς ἐκείνην ἀποβλέπων καὶ χρώμενος αὐτῇ παραδείγματι, ὃ μὲν ἂν τοιοῦτον ᾖ ὧν ἂν ἢ σὺ ἢ ἄλλος τις πράττῃ φῶ ὅσιον εἶναι, ὃ δ' ἂν μὴ τοιοῦτον, μὴ φῶ.

I quote R.E. Allen's translation and comment:[444]

SOCRATES: ...So now in Zeus' name, tell me what you confidently claimed just now that you knew: what sort of thing do you say the pious and impious are, both with respect to murder and other things as well? Or is not the holy, itself by itself, the same in every action? And the unholy, in turn, the opposite of all the holy – is it not like itself, and does not everything which is to be unholy have a certain single character with respect to unholiness?

...

right now, try to answer more clearly the question I just asked. For, my friend, you did not sufficiently teach me before, when I asked you what the holy is: you said that the thing you are doing now is holy, prosecuting your father for murder.

EUTHYPHRO: Yes, and I told the truth, Socrates.

SOCRATES: Perhaps. But, Euthyphro, are there not many other things you say are holy too?

EUTHYPHRO: Of course there are.

SOCRATES: Do you recall that I did not ask you to teach me about some one or two of the many things which are holy, but about the characteristic itself by which all holy things are holy? For you agreed, I think, that it is by one character that unholy things are unholy and holy things holy. Or do you not recall?

EUTHYPHRO: I do.

SOCRATES: Then teach me what this same character is, so that I may look to it and use it as a standard, which, should those things which you or someone else may do be of that sort, I may affirm that they are holy, but should they not be of that sort, deny it.

Allen comments:

The words ἰδέα (5d, 6d, e) and εἶδος (6d), here rendered neutrally as 'character' and 'characteristic', are used in this context as synonyms, and their use is technical. Both derive from the root *Ϝιδ, which appears in common Greek verbs for seeing and knowing, in Latin *videre*, German *wissen*, and English 'wise' and 'wit'. Their meaning appears originally to have been associated with the 'look' of a thing, its *species* or outward appearance; they were used by pre-Platonic mathematicians to mean figure, shape, or pattern, and in a parallel use they meant the human figure, the human shape. (n. 1: And are so used by Plato at *Charmides*, 154d, 158a, *Protagoras*, 352a.) In the medical writers, εἶδος meant 'constitution', or the sort or kind of a disease. Thucydides speaks of death in every ἰδέα, every form, and a mask in Euripides uses the word to ask the nature of something, what sort of thing it is. (n. 2: For further discussion, see Burnet, [1924], on 5d, e; A.E. Taylor, *Varia Socratica*, pp. 178–267; C.M. Gillespie, *Classical Quarterly*, vi (1912), pp. 179–203. For Presocratic uses, see

Diels-Kranz, *Die Fragmente der Vorsokratiker*, vol. iii (8th edn.). R.S. Bluck, *Plato's* Meno, pp. 224–5, gives further references.)[445]

The ordinary meaning of 'sort' or 'kind' is a common one in Plato; but the words are here used in a special way. The εἶδος or ἰδέα is a universal, the same in all its instances and something the instances *have* (5d); it is in some sense a condition for the existence of holy things, that *by* which – the dative is instrumental – holy things are holy; and it is a standard or παράδειγμα for determining what things are holy and what are not. In short, the words εἶδος or ἰδέα carry freight they do not ordinarily bear, and for that reason commentators have often translated them as 'Idea' or 'Form'. The latter is preferable. 'Idea' has the advantage of closer relation to Greek; but Locke, who first introduced the word into English philosophy, also gave it a subjective and psychological connotation it has never since lost. Etymologically, this is perhaps in some ways commendable. As a translation of what is here meant, it is misleading.

Socrates' question, 'What is the holy?', then, is the question, 'What is the Form of holiness?' The notion of Form here involved will guide the dialectic throughout the remainder of the dialogue.

Allen's comment has been quoted at length because it sums up much that has been asserted and denied in the chapters on εἶδος or ἰδέα in Part II above. Allen is correct on etymology and the early meaning of 'look' and 'appearance', but, in our investigation, we have not found either noun in the sense of 'shape' or 'pattern', and it is the 'appearance' rather than the 'shape' of a human being that is referred to in the *Protagoras* and *Charmides*. There is no firm pre-Platonic evidence for the alleged mathematical usage. In particular, a meaning of 'character' or 'characteristic' is far from being 'neutral': there is, despite Gillespie (1912) and Baldry (1937), whom Allen should have mentioned in this connection, no sufficient evidence for such an abstract notion in pre-Platonic literature.

Before we turn to what ἰδέα does mean here in the *Euthyphro*, the manner in which the term εἶδος is introduced besides ἰδέα should be noted: while the latter occurs thrice and gives unity to the passage which it frames (5c–6e), εἶδος occurs once only, in Socrates' clarificatory question at the close of the passage, just before the second occurrence of ἰδέα (6d9–e2):

μέμνησαι οὖν ὅτι οὐ τοῦτό σοι διεκελευόμην, ἕν τι ἢ δύο με διδάξαι τῶν πολλῶν ὁσίων, ἀλλ' ἐκεῖνο αὐτὸ τὸ εἶδος ᾧ πάντα τὰ ὅσια ὅσιά ἐστιν; ἔφησθα γάρ που μιᾷ ἰδέᾳ τά τε ἀνόσια ἀνόσια εἶναι καὶ τὰ ὅσια ὅσια· ἢ οὐ μνημονεύεις;

Do you remember, now, that it was not this that I requested from you, that you teach me one or two of the many holy things, but that εἶδος itself through and by which all the holy things are holy? Indeed, you said somehow that through one ἰδέα the unholy things are unholy and the holy holy: or do you not remember?

A comparison with Plato's usage in the *Euthyphro* itself and elsewhere shows that τὸ εἶδος is here almost certainly a marginal gloss in origin, incorporated into the text possibly at an early stage.[446] In a manner similar to his talking about the πρῶτον φίλον in the *Lysis*, Socrates asks for ἐκεῖνο αὐτὸ ᾧ πάντα τὰ ὅσια ὅσιά ἐστιν, 'that itself through and by which all the holy things are holy'. The instrumental dative of the relative pronoun is then re-used in the subsequent clause, when Socrates paraphrases his own earlier suggestion which he now attributes to Euthyphro who at 5d had consented (6d11–e1): μιᾷ ἰδέᾳ τά τε ἀνόσια ἀνόσια εἶναι καὶ τὰ ὅσια ὅσια, 'through one ἰδέα are the unholy things unholy and the holy holy'. This syntactical device has implications for the semantics of ἰδέα. At 5d3–5, when Socrates asked with a view to the holy about that which is the same in each action and then moves to the unholy, he phrases his thought as follows: αὐτὸ δὲ αὑτῷ ὅμοιον καὶ ἔχον μίαν τινὰ ἰδέαν κατὰ τὴν ἀνοσιότητα πᾶν ὅτιπερ ἂν μέλλῃ ἀνόσιον εἶναι, 'itself similar with itself, and having one ἰδέα in accordance with its unholiness, everything that would want to be unholy'. At that point, 'having one ἰδέα' could mean 'having one appearance' or 'having one type'. The grammatical construction with the instrumental dative[447] at 6d11–e1, however, cannot easily be translated in either of these two ways. Holy things are not holy through or by one and the same 'appearance' or through or by one 'type'. But perhaps the dative is not instrumental in the causal sense, but rather comitative, in the way τούτῳ τῷ τρόπῳ, 'in that manner', denotes the way something is done.[448] Perhaps Socrates says at 5d that all impious or unholy actions have one appearance and at 6d–e that all unholy things are unholy in one way, to conclude at 6e4f. that Euthyphro should teach him that way or manner in which all holy things are holy and that way or manner in which all unholy things are unholy. On the other hand, one could read *Euthyphro* 5d–6e as implying that the one ἰδέα through which all things holy are holy is the holy itself. If we had only the *Euthyphro*, a decision on what ἰδέα means could not be reached on the basis of the pre-Platonic semantics of ἰδέα and the syntax of the three occurrences in the dialogue.

The *Euthyphro* has thus little to offer for an understanding of the usage of ἰδέα in the *Phaedo*. The syntax of the noun in the *Euthyphro* is, at least in part, different from that in the *Phaedo*, and the semantics are as open to dispute as is the case in the later dialogue.

5. What are ἰδέαι in Plato's *Phaedo*?

If there is no direct way of determining the meaning of ἰδέα in the *Phaedo*, it may be necessary to approach the question of meaning indirectly. We shall therefore begin anew and collect what has been said about the nature and the function of that which has now obtained the name of ἰδέα. In the context of the unreliability of sense perception (*Phaedo* 65b), Socrates introduced the examples of the just itself, the beautiful and the good (65d), to each of which itself by itself the soul would go itself by itself (66a). In this context, the philosopher who attempted this approach was described as θηρεύων τῶν ὄντων, 'hunting for the things that are'; this was a means of attaining truth, and the man who achieved this was designated τευξόμενος τοῦ ὄντος, 'the one who will attain that which is'[449] (cf. 65c). This was also the context in which the noun οὐσία, 'being', was first introduced. (The phrase τὴν τοῦ ὄντος θήραν, 'the hunt for that which is', is then found at 66c.)[450]

Next, at 74a, the equal itself was said never to be or seem anything other than equal, while everything else that is equal strives to be like the equal (75a and b), just as at 65c the soul, trying to be free from the body, was striving for that which is. At 75c–d, the label 'ὃ ἔστιν' was given to the equal, the bigger, the smaller, the beautiful itself, the good itself, the just, the holy, and to other things of that sort, which were left unnamed and unmentioned. These are the things of which there is knowledge from a point before the use of perception(s), αἰσθήσεις (75d), a thought repeated with slightly fewer examples at 76d–77a.

After that, in the so-called argument from affinity, especially at 78c–80b, Socrates emphasizes the difference between σύνθετα and ἀσύνθετα, 'things composed', or consisting of parts, and 'things un-composed'. The latter are likely to behave and be always the same and according to the same. Memorable is the summary of that thought at 78c6–d9, quoted in section 4 of the chapter on οὐσία above:

οὐκοῦν ἅπερ ἀεὶ κατὰ ταὐτὰ καὶ ὡσαύτως ἔχει, ταῦτα μάλιστα εἰκὸς εἶναι τὰ ἀσύνθετα, τὰ δὲ ἄλλοτ' ἄλλως καὶ μηδέποτε κατὰ ταὐτά, ταῦτα δὲ σύνθετα; ἔμοιγε δοκεῖ οὕτως.
ἴωμεν δή, ἔφη, ἐπὶ ταὐτὰ ἐφ' ἅπερ ἐν τῷ ἔμπροσθεν λόγῳ. αὐτὴ ἡ οὐσία ἧς λόγον δίδομεν τοῦ εἶναι καὶ ἐρωτῶντες καὶ ἀποκρινόμενοι, πότερον ὡσαύτως ἀεὶ ἔχει κατὰ ταὐτὰ ἢ ἄλλοτ' ἄλλως; αὐτὸ τὸ ἴσον, αὐτὸ τὸ καλόν, αὐτὸ ἕκαστον ὃ ἔστιν, τὸ ὄν, μή ποτε μεταβολὴν καὶ ἡντινοῦν ἐνδέχεται; ἢ ἀεὶ αὐτῶν ἕκαστον ὃ ἔστι, μονοειδὲς ὂν αὐτὸ καθ' αὑτό, ὡσαύτως κατὰ ταὐτὰ ἔχει καὶ οὐδέποτε οὐδαμῇ οὐδαμῶς ἀλλοίωσιν οὐδεμίαν ἐνδέχεται;
ὡσαύτως, ἔφη, ἀνάγκη, ὁ Κέβης, κατὰ ταὐτὰ ἔχειν, ὦ Σώκρατες.

What is always constant and in the same way, is not this likely to be what is incomposite; but what is at one time in one way, at another in another, and never constant, is not this in turn likely to be composite?
To me, certainly, it seems so.
Let us therefore go, said he, to the same things to which we went in the previous account. This 'being' itself of which we give as an account the 'it *is*' when we ask and answer, is it in the same way always according to the same, or at one time in one way, at another in another? Would the equal itself, the beautiful itself,

each thing-that-is itself, 'what is', ever admit change, even the slightest? Or (is it rather the case that) always, of those, each thing-that-is, being uniform, itself by itself, is in the same way, constant, and never in any way anyhow admits any alteration?

It is in the context of this argument that the notions of ὁρατόν, 'visible' (79a–b, 80c, 81c–d, 83b–c, note 108b; cf. ἀόρατον, 'invisible', 79b, 85e), *versus* νοητόν, 'thinkable' (80b, 81b, 83b; cf. ἀνόητον in the sense of 'not thinkable', 80b), and of σωματοειδές (81b–c, e, 83d, 86a), 'body-like', are introduced.

Finally, the beautiful itself, the good, the big and all the others are introduced at 100b in Socrates' answer to the question of the αἰτία, the 'explanation-by-cause-and-reason', of all coming-to-be and passing-away, a question posed first at 95e10. This eventually leads to the introduction of the terminology first of εἶδος, at 102b, then of μορφή, at 103e, and eventually of ἰδέα, at 104b. From the start, ἰδέα is used in an absolute way. It could thus be 'an appearance', 'a type' or 'a figure'.

Absolute use of ἰδέα is found in pre-Platonic literature as well, albeit in a few restricted contexts. One such context is that of Democritus' philosophy, and we shall now revisit the evidence for the term and the associated concept with the atomist.

6. The world of Democritus

Before reconsidering the term ἰδέα itself in Democritus,[451] we shall consider reports concerning aspects of his atomism. The earliest explicit reports stem from Aristotle, and it is he and Simplicius as his commentator who provide the material that allows to gauge the extent to which Plato in the *Phaedo* may have reacted to the thought of Leucippus and Democritus. The following passages focus on different aspects of the explanation of the world offered by the two atomists:[452]

a. Aristotle, *De generatione et corruptione* 314a21–4 (DK67A9; Taylor 47a):

Δημόκριτος δὲ καὶ Λεύκιππος ἐκ σωμάτων ἀδιαιρέτων τἆλλα συγκεῖσθαί φασι, ταῦτα δ᾽ ἄπειρα καὶ τὸ πλῆθος εἶναι καὶ τὰς μορφάς, αὐτὰ δὲ πρὸς αὐτὰ διαφέρειν τούτοις ἐξ ὧν εἰσὶ καὶ θέσει καὶ τάξει τούτων.

But Democritus and Leucippus say that the other things consist of bodies that are indivisible, and that those are unlimited both in amount and in their forms (τὰς μορφάς), but that the things differ from each other through and by those from which they are and through and by the position and order of those things.

b. Aristotle, *De generatione et corruptione* 315b6–15 (DK67A9; Taylor 42a):

Δημόκριτος δὲ καὶ Λεύκιππος ποιήσαντες τὰ σχήματα τὴν ἀλλοίωσιν καὶ τὴν γένεσιν ἐκ τούτων ποιοῦσι, διακρίσει μὲν καὶ συγκρίσει γένεσιν καὶ φθοράν, τάξει δὲ καὶ θέσει ἀλλοίωσιν. ἐπεὶ δ' ᾤοντο τἀληθὲς ἐν τῷ φαίνεσθαι, ἐναντία δὲ καὶ ἄπειρα τὰ φαινόμενα, τὰ σχήματα ἄπειρα ἐποίησαν...

But Democritus and Leucippus, making the shapes (τὰ σχήματα), made alteration and becoming from those, namely through and by separation and mixture becoming and perishing, but through and by order and position alteration. But because they believed that what is true is in appearance, but that what appears is opposite and infinite, they made the shapes infinite...

c. Aristotle, *De generatione et corruptione* 325a23–34 (DK67A7; Taylor 48a):

Λεύκιππος δ' ἔχειν ᾠήθη λόγους οἵ τινες πρὸς τὴν αἴσθησιν ὁμολογούμενα λέγοντες οὐκ ἀναιρήσουσιν οὔτε γένεσιν οὔτε φθορὰν οὔτε κίνησιν καὶ τὸ πλῆθος τῶν ὄντων. ὁμολογήσας δὲ ταῦτα μὲν τοῖς φαινομένοις, τοῖς δὲ τὸ ἓν κατασκευάζουσιν ὡς οὐκ ἂν κίνησιν οὖσαν ἄνευ κενοῦ τό τε κενὸν μὴ ὄν, καὶ τοῦ ὄντος οὐθὲν μὴ ὄν φησιν εἶναι. τὸ γὰρ κυρίως ὂν παμπλῆρες ὄν· ἀλλ' εἶναι τὸ τοιοῦτον οὐχ ἕν, ἀλλ' ἄπειρα τὸ πλῆθος καὶ ἀόρατα διὰ σμικρότητα τῶν ὄγκων. ταῦτα δ' ἐν τῷ κενῷ φέρεσθαι (κενὸν γὰρ εἶναι), καὶ συνιστάμενα μὲν γένεσιν ποιεῖν, διαλυόμενα δὲ φθοράν. ποιεῖν δὲ καὶ πάσχειν ᾗ τυγχάνουσιν ἁπτόμενα· ταύτῃ γὰρ οὐχ ἓν εἶναι.

But Leucippus believed that he had arguments which – stating things in agreement with perception – would abolish neither coming to be nor perishing, nor movement and the plurality of things that are. But agreeing in that regard with the *phaenomena*, and agreeing with those <people> who posit 'the one' <in assuming> both that movement would not be without the empty, and that the empty is what-is-not, he also says that nothing of what *is* is what-is-not. For what principally *is* is what is full: but <he says> that what is of that sort is not one, but unlimited as regards its amount and invisible because of the smallness of the [or: their] bulks. But <he says> that those things are carried in the empty (for the empty *is*), and coming to stand together they bring about coming-to-be, but dissolving <they bring about> perishing. But they do and have things done to them insofar as they happen to touch: for in that respect they are not one.

d. Aristotle objects to those who posit small indivisible bodies as underlying reality with a sequence of arguments; among them at *De generatione et corruptione* 326a29–35 (Taylor48a):

εἰ μὲν γὰρ μία φύσις ἐστὶν ἁπάντων, τί τὸ χωρίσαν; ἢ διὰ τί οὐ γίνεται ἁψάμενα ἕν, ὥσπερ ὕδωρ ὕδατος ὅταν θίγῃ; οὐδὲν γὰρ διαφέρει τὸ ὕστερον τοῦ προτέρου. εἰ δ' ἕτερα, ποῖα ταῦτα; καὶ δῆλον ὡς ταῦτα θετέον ἀρχὰς καὶ αἰτίας τῶν συμβαινόντων μᾶλλον ἢ τὰ σχήματα.

Indeed, if the nature of all of them is one, what is it that separates? Or why do they not become one when they touch, as water when it touches water? For the earlier [drop or part of water in a given quantity] differs in no way from the former. But if they are different, of what sort are those things? – And it is clear that those things, rather than the shapes, would have to be posited as beginnings and explanations-and-causes-and-reasons of the composites.

e. Aristotle, *Metaphysics* 985b3–22 (DK67A6; Taylor 46a):

οὗτος μὲν οὖν, ὥσπερ λέγομεν, οὕτω τε καὶ τοσαύτας εἴρηκε τὰς ἀρχάς· Λεύκιππος δὲ καὶ ὁ ἑταῖρος αὐτοῦ Δημόκριτος στοιχεῖα μὲν τὸ πλῆρες καὶ τὸ κενὸν εἶναί φασι, λέγοντες τὸ μὲν ὂν τὸ δὲ μὴ ὄν, τούτων δὲ τὸ μὲν πλῆρες καὶ στερεὸν τὸ ὄν, τὸ δὲ κενὸν τὸ μὴ ὄν (διὸ καὶ οὐθὲν μᾶλλον τὸ ὂν τοῦ μὴ ὄντος εἶναί φασιν, ὅτι οὐδὲ τοῦ κενοῦ τὸ σῶμα), αἴτια δὲ τῶν ὄντων ταῦτα ὡς ὕλην. καὶ καθάπερ οἱ ἓν ποιοῦντες τὴν ὑποκειμένην οὐσίαν τἆλλα τοῖς πάθεσιν αὐτῆς γεννῶσι, τὸ μανὸν καὶ τὸ πυκνὸν ἀρχὰς τιθέμενοι τῶν παθημάτων, τὸν αὐτὸν τρόπον καὶ οὗτοι τὰς διαφορὰς αἰτίας τῶν ἄλλων εἶναί φασιν. ταύτας μέντοι τρεῖς εἶναι λέγουσι, σχῆμά τε καὶ τάξιν καὶ θέσιν· διαφέρειν γάρ φασι τὸ ὂν ῥυσμῷ καὶ διαθιγῇ καὶ τροπῇ μόνον· τούτων δὲ ὁ μὲν ῥυσμὸς σχῆμά ἐστιν ἡ δὲ διαθιγὴ τάξις ἡ δὲ τροπὴ θέσις· διαφέρει γὰρ τὸ μὲν Α τοῦ Ν σχήματι τὸ δὲ ΑΝ τοῦ ΝΑ τάξει τὸ δὲ Ζ τοῦ Ν θέσει.

So he (Empedocles), as we say, said that the beginnings were in that way and of that number. But Leucippus and his companion Democritus say that the full and the empty are the elements, calling the one 'what *is*', the other 'what-is-not', but of those on the one hand 'what *is*' <they call> full and solid, on the other 'what-is-not' <they call> empty (therefore also did they say that 'what *is*' is in no way more than 'what-is-not', because body <is in no way more> than the empty <*is*>), but these are cause-and-reason of the things-that-are as matter. And in accordance with those who, making the underlying substance <the> one, letting the other things be born through the affections of that <substance>, positing the rare and the dense as beginnings of the affections, in the same manner these, too, say that the different explanations-and-causes of the other things *are*. And indeed they say that those <different explanations-and-causes> are three, <namely> shape, order and position: for they say that 'what *is*' differs solely in *rhysmos* ('rhythm'), *diathigē* ('being-in-contact') and *tropē* ('turning'). But of those, *rhysmos* is shape, *diathigē* order, and *tropē* position: for A differs from N in shape, AN from NA in order, and Z from N in position.

f. Simplicius, *Commentary on* De Caelo 7.295.1–9 (DK68A37; Taylor 44a):

Δημόκριτος ἡγεῖται τὴν τῶν ἀιδίων φύσιν εἶναι μικρὰς οὐσίας πλῆθος ἀπείρους, ταύταις δὲ τόπον ἄλλον ὑποτίθησιν ἄπειρον τῷ μεγέθει· προσαγορεύει δὲ τὸν μὲν τόπον τοῖσδε τοῖς ὀνόμασι τῷ τε κενῷ καὶ τῷ οὐδενὶ καὶ τῷ ἀπείρῳ, τῶν δὲ οὐσιῶν ἑκάστην τῷ τε δὲν καὶ τῷ ναστῷ καὶ τῷ ὄντι. νομίζει δὲ εἶναι οὕτω μικρὰς τὰς οὐσίας ὥστε ἐκφυγεῖν τὰς ἡμετέρας αἰσθήσεις, ὑπάρχειν δὲ αὐτοῖς παντοίας μορφὰς καὶ σχήματα παντοῖα καὶ κατὰ μέγεθος διαφοράς· ἐκ τούτων οὖν ᾔδει καθάπερ ἐκ στοιχείων γεννᾶν καὶ συγκρίνειν τοὺς ὀφθαλμοφανεῖς καὶ τοὺς αἰσθητοὺς ὄγκους·

Democritus believes that the nature of the eternal things are small substances, infinite in multitude, but he posits for and with them another location, infinite in bigness: but he calls that location by the names of '<the> empty' and '<the> nothing' and '<the> unlimited', but of the substances he calls each by the names of '<the> hing' and '<the> full' and 'what is'. But he believes that <these substances> are so small that they escape our senses and our perception, but that there are for them all sorts of forms and all sorts of shapes and differences as to size: so, in his view, the bulks apparent to the eye and to perception were born and come together from those as from elements.

g. Aristotle, *Metaphysics* 1038b34–1039a14 (cf. DK68A42; Taylor 44b):

ἔκ τε δὴ τούτων θεωροῦσι φανερὸν ὅτι οὐδὲν τῶν καθόλου ὑπαρχόντων οὐσία ἐστί, καὶ ὅτι οὐδὲν σημαίνει τῶν κοινῇ κατηγορουμένων τόδε τι, ἀλλὰ τοιόνδε. εἰ δὲ μή, ἄλλα τε πολλὰ συμβαίνει καὶ ὁ τρίτος ἄνθρωπος. ἔτι δὲ καὶ ὧδε δῆλον. ἀδύνατον γὰρ οὐσίαν ἐξ οὐσιῶν εἶναι ἐνυπαρχουσῶν ὡς ἐντελεχείᾳ· τὰ γὰρ δύο οὕτως ἐντελεχείᾳ οὐδέποτε ἓν ἐντελεχείᾳ, ἀλλ' ἐὰν δυνάμει δύο ᾖ, ἔσται ἕν (οἷον ἡ διπλασία ἐκ δύο ἡμίσεων δυνάμει γε· ἡ γὰρ ἐντελέχεια χωρίζει), ὥστ' εἰ ἡ οὐσία ἕν, οὐκ ἔσται ἐξ οὐσιῶν ἐνυπαρχουσῶν καὶ κατὰ τοῦτον τὸν τρόπον, ὃν λέγει Δημόκριτος ὀρθῶς· ἀδύνατον γὰρ εἶναί φησιν ἐκ δύο ἓν ἢ ἐξ ἑνὸς δύο γενέσθαι· τὰ γὰρ μεγέθη τὰ ἄτομα τὰς οὐσίας ποιεῖ. ὁμοίως τοίνυν δῆλον ὅτι καὶ ἐπ' ἀριθμοῦ ἕξει, εἴπερ ἐστὶν ὁ ἀριθμὸς σύνθεσις μονάδων, ὥσπερ λέγεται ὑπό τινων· ἢ γὰρ οὐχ ἓν ἡ δυὰς ἢ οὐκ ἔστι μονὰς ἐν αὐτῇ ἐντελεχείᾳ.

To those, thus, who consider <the matter> from these <points just mentioned>, it becomes apparent that nothing of the things that are universal is substance, and that nothing of the things commonly predicated denotes a 'this', but <they denote> a 'such'. Otherwise, many other things follow, and also 'the third man'. But further, it is also clear in the following way: for it is impossible that a substance is out of substances which are in it as actuality: for 'the two' in that way in actuality never <is or becomes> one in actuality, but whenever there is two in potentiality, there will be one (as for example the double <line> <is> from two of half <-length> – in potentiality, certainly: indeed, the actuality separates <the two halves as actual halves>), so that if the substance is one, it will not be from substances being in it, and in the way which Democritus states: for he says that it is impossible that from two come to be one or from one two: for he makes the uncuttable quantities the substances. So in an equivalent manner it is clear that it will also obtain for number, if really number is the composition of monads (or: units), as is said by some: for either the dyad will not be one or there *is* no monad in it in actuality.

It is, of course, to be noted that these are paraphrases of Leucippean and Democritean thought, reported by Aristotle and his commentator in the context of Aristotelian exposition. This entails both that elements of the original may have been omitted, others added, inadvertently or deliberately, and emphases changed; and that the language employed need not be that of the author whose position is reported, but may be the language of the reporter and commentator, be it Aristotle or, in turn, his commentator. The reports can nevertheless be used in two ways. Severally or jointly, they may preserve some of the elements of the original without falsifying the intention of Leucippus and Democritus, who in their turn may have had the same or different intentions; and secondly they may on occasion contain an expression or a term that is taken verbatim from their source or sources.

First, as regards elements of thought: Leucippus and Democritus posit indivisible elements which differ in their shapes and forms, are imperceptible and, by and large, without sensible qualities. These elements do not change, nor can they fuse with one another. But through their changing combinations they are the beginnings and causes-and-reasons of the changing and moving things of the perceptible world around us; this is possible because the other constituent of this world is 'the empty' which makes movement of any sort possible.

As regards terminology, on the other hand, we naturally find in the Aristotelian reports much of what is found in Aristotle's description of the world otherwise. It is highly probable, though, that the following terms were actually used by Democritus.

In Passage e., we read: διαφέρειν γάρ φασι τὸ ὂν ῥυσμῷ καὶ διαθιγῇ καὶ τροπῇ μόνον· τούτων δὲ ὁ μὲν ῥυσμὸς σχῆμά ἐστιν ἡ δὲ διαθιγὴ τάξις ἡ δὲ τροπὴ θέσις· διαφέρει γὰρ τὸ μὲν Α τοῦ Ν σχήματι τὸ δὲ ΑΝ τοῦ ΝΑ τάξει τὸ δὲ Ζ τοῦ Ν θέσει, 'for they say that 'what is' differs solely in *rhysmos* ('rhythm'), *diathigē* ('being-in-contact') and *tropē* ('turning'). But of those *rhysmos* is shape, *diathigē* order, and *tropē* position'. The manner in which the three strange words are introduced and 'translated' does not leave room for doubt.

In similar manner, Simplicius in Passage f. tells his readers that Democritus used certain terms for the atoms: προσαγορεύει δὲ τὸν μὲν τόπον τοῖσδε τοῖς ὀνόμασι τῷ τε κενῷ καὶ τῷ οὐδενὶ καὶ τῷ ἀπείρῳ, τῶν δὲ οὐσιῶν ἑκάστην τῷ τε δὲν καὶ τῷ ναστῷ καὶ τῷ ὄντι, 'but of the substances he calls each by the names of 'the hing' and 'the full' and 'what is''.

Like the non-Aristotelian and for the most part non-Attic words ῥυσμός, διαθιγὴ and τροπὴ, the neologism δέν must be part of the atomists' own vocabulary, as there is no conceivable reason why anybody should have invented it for the purpose of reporting his thought.[453] But if δέν, 'hing', is part of the atomists' original terminology, so should be τὸ ναστόν and τὸ ὄν, 'the solid' and 'what is'. The latter term, τὸ ὄν, 'what is', was, of course, not exclusive to atomism, but had been taken over from Parmenides and the Eleatics. But it may be important to note nevertheless that it was, apparently, used in the singular to refer to an atom in the singular.

We can now return to the evidence concerning Democritus' use of the word ἰδέα which had been assembled in Part II, chapter 5, section 4. It must be reiterated that while there cannot be absolute proof, it is generally accepted by modern editors and commentators that ἰδέα was actually *one* of Democritus' terms for his atoms.[454] I quote again the relevant passage from Plutarch, together with Taylor's translation (Plutarch, *Against Colotus* 8.1110F–1111A):[455]

τί γὰρ λέγει Δημόκριτος; οὐσίας ἀπείρους τὸ πλῆθος ἀτόμους τε κἀδιαφόρους, ἔτι δ' ἀποίους καὶ ἀπαθεῖς ἐν τῷ κενῷ φέρεσθαι διεσπαρμένας· ὅταν δὲ πελάσωσιν ἀλλήλαις ἢ συμπέσωσιν ἢ περιπλακῶσι, φαίνεσθαι τῶν ἀθροιζομένων τὸ μὲν ὕδωρ τὸ δὲ πῦρ τὸ δὲ φυτὸν τὸ δ' ἄνθρωπον· εἶναι δὲ πάντα τὰς ἀτόμους ἰδέας ὑπ' αὐτοῦ καλουμένας, ἕτερον δὲ μηδέν· ἐκ μὲν γὰρ τοῦ μὴ ὄντος οὐκ εἶναι γένεσιν, ἐκ δὲ τῶν ὄντων μηδὲν ἂν γενέσθαι τῷ μήτε πάσχειν μήτε μεταβάλλειν τὰς ἀτόμους ὑπὸ στερρότητος· ὅθεν οὔτε χρόαν ἐξ ἀχρώστων οὔτε φύσιν ἢ ψυχὴν ἐξ ἀποίων καὶ <ἀπαθῶν> ὑπάρχειν…

For what does Democritus say? That an infinite number of atomic, undifferentiated substances, incapable of affecting or being affected, travel about, scattered in the void. And whenever they approach one another, these collections appear as water, fire, a plant or a man. Everything consists of the atoms, which he calls 'forms,' and there is nothing else. For there is no coming to be from what is not, and nothing could come to be from what is, since, because of their solidity, the atoms neither are affected nor change. Hence no colour comes into being from colourless things, nor any nature or soul from things which can neither affect nor be affected.

By the time Plutarch is writing, ἰδέα had become a term firmly associated with Plato's philosophy,[456] not least, we can assume, through the criticism of Aristotle, who appropriates for his own philosophy the terms οὐσία, εἶδος and μορφή, but not ἰδέα, which he cites as a Platonic term for a notion of Plato and the Academy which is to be rejected. Moreover, as Aristotle uses the term σχήματα as a word for Democritus' atoms, a term Democritus himself may or may not have employed, there would be no reason for Plutarch to attribute the word ἰδέα to Democritus unless Democritus himself had actually used the term itself, regardless of whether Plutarch had a full text of Democritus or read an intermediate source, to whose usage the same argumentation would apply.

7. Plato's response to Democritus

If this is so, we can now see why Plato would have wanted to introduce the term ἰδέα into the Socratic conversation of the *Phaedo*. Democritus' atoms were called ἰδέαι, 'figures'.[457] They were non-composite, invisible, everlasting, indestructible, the only things that really *are* in addition to what is not, while everything else is appearance (68A37, 57, 135; B9, 11b). This, however, is remarkably reminiscent of *Phaedo* 78b–79a: there, we encounter the notion of 'dispersal', τὸ διασκεδάννυσθαι, the 'composite', συντεθέντι τε καὶ συνθέτῳ ὄντι, the 'incomposite', ἀσύνθετον, 'what is always the same', ἀεὶ κατὰ ταὐτὰ καὶ ὡσαύτως ἔχει, 'change', μεταβολὴν, 'alteration', ἀλλοίωσιν, 'necessity', ἀνάγκη. And at 79a1, right after 78c6–d9, the passage quoted in section 5 above, Socrates continues in contrasting the many things with that itself which is unchanging:

οὐκοῦν τούτων μὲν κἂν ἅψαιο κἂν ἴδοις κἂν ταῖς ἄλλαις αἰσθήσεσιν αἴσθοιο,
τῶν δὲ κατὰ ταὐτὰ ἐχόντων οὐκ ἔστιν ὅτῳ ποτ' ἂν ἄλλῳ ἐπιλάβοιο ἢ τῷ τῆς
διανοίας λογισμῷ, ἀλλ' ἔστιν ἀιδῆ τὰ τοιαῦτα καὶ οὐχ ὁρατά;
παντάπασιν, ἔφη, ἀληθῆ λέγεις.
θῶμεν οὖν βούλει, ἔφη, δύο εἴδη τῶν ὄντων, τὸ μὲν ὁρατόν, τὸ δὲ ἀιδές;
θῶμεν, ἔφη.
καὶ τὸ μὲν ἀιδὲς ἀεὶ κατὰ ταὐτὰ ἔχον, τὸ δὲ ὁρατὸν μηδέποτε κατὰ ταὐτά;
καὶ τοῦτο, ἔφη, θῶμεν.

Then again, you can touch them and see them or otherwise perceive them with your sense, whereas those unchanging objects cannot be apprehended save by the mind's reasoning. Things of that sort are invisible, are they not?
That is perfectly true.
Then shall we say there are two kinds of thing, the visible and the invisible?
Very well.
The invisible being always constant, the visible never?
We may agree to that too.

All of this is, of course, Presocratic in a general sense, and the commentaries point out various affiliations, not least the word μονοειδές, 'uniform', which points to Parmenides. But while this is so, it should be stressed at the same time that everything said about the eternal and immutable here fits Democritus' thought more than any one other known fifth-century system of thought. I do not, of course, suggest that the first half of the *Phaedo* is written exclusively with Democritus in mind. But the use of ἰδέα at 104b–105d seems to indicate that Democritus' system of thought was at least one of the primary targets of Plato's exposition. Plato's ἰδέαι, his 'figures', share with Democritus' that, as the ultimate constituents of the world, they are everlasting, unchangeable, non-composite, indivisible, and also invisible. Plato's 'figures' differ from Democritus' in that they are not the smallest *bodies*, of infinite variety in shape, but that they are altogether incorporeal, a notion probably developed by Plato himself. They are the good, the beautiful, the just, and not full little solids with hooks, nooks and crannies. But each Platonic 'figure' is, like each of Democritus' figures, 'that which *is*', 'what *is*', τὸ ὄν.

If this is so, the Democritus *testimonium* quoted as Passage g. above (p. 237), is of interest in a further respect. Aristotle reports that Democritus commented on the ontological presuppositions of simple arithmetic (*Metaphysics* 1039a7–14):

...ὥστ' εἰ ἡ οὐσία ἕν, οὐκ ἔσται ἐξ οὐσιῶν ἐνυπαρχουσῶν καὶ κατὰ τοῦτον τὸν τρόπον, ὃν λέγει Δημόκριτος ὀρθῶς· ἀδύνατον γὰρ εἶναί φησιν ἐκ δύο ἓν ἢ ἐξ ἑνὸς δύο γενέσθαι· τὰ γὰρ μεγέθη τὰ ἄτομα τὰς οὐσίας ποιεῖ. ὁμοίως τοίνυν δῆλον ὅτι καὶ ἐπ' ἀριθμοῦ ἕξει, εἴπερ ἐστὶν ὁ ἀριθμὸς σύνθεσις μονάδων, ὥσπερ λέγεται ὑπό τινων· ἢ γὰρ οὐχ ἓν ἡ δυὰς ἢ οὐκ ἔστι μονὰς ἐν αὐτῇ ἐντελεχείᾳ.

...so that if the substance is one, it will not be from substances being in it, and in the way which Democritus states: for he says that it is impossible that from two come to be one or from one two: for he makes the uncuttable quantities the substances. So in an equivalent manner it is clear that it will also obtain for number, if really number is the composition of monads (or: units), as is said by some: for either the dyad will not be one or there *is* no monad in it in actuality.

This is remarkably reminiscent of Socrates' puzzling discussion of the addition of 1 + 1, and of how it is that 1 + 1 = 2, at *Phaedo* 96e6–b7, and Socrates' solution to this puzzle at 101b10–c9. This mathematical exercise would have an added poignancy if Plato had intended at *Phaedo* 96e6–b7 already to indicate to the reader that his discussion would, *inter alia*, provide a reasoned response to Democritus. But is this so?

8. Plato and Democritus on explanation, cause and reason[458]

There may indeed be further corroboration for this interpretation of Plato's intention at *Phaedo* 95e–105e. One of the most conspicuous features of the first part of this section of the dialogue is Socrates' account of his early search for an αἰτία concerning coming-to-be and passing-away. In the course of the passage, the words αἰτία and its cognates are used 37 times,[459] and the central issue of causation-and-explanation-and-justification-and-responsibility here has often been connected with the discussion of causation in the *Timaeus*.[460] Plato invites his readers to compare Presocratic explanations of the world with his own, in particular drawing attention to the difference between the system of Anaxagoras, which provided an explanation that introduced νοῦς, 'mind' or 'intelligence'. Anaxagoras is the only one mentioned by name in this section.[461] And because νοῦς occurs in the fragments of Anaxagoras (DK59B11, 12, 13, 14), commentators, having listed other Presocratics for the alternative models here discarded by Socrates, focus on Anaxagoras alone at this point, at most asking to what extent Diogenes of Apollonia may already have fulfilled Socrates' stringent conditions of explanation here.[462] In this, it is generally overlooked that the words αἰτία and αἴτιον are not actually part of Anaxagoras' vocabulary, as far as we know.[463] In fact, although the doxographic tradition, beginning with Plato and Aristotle, abounds with instances of αἰτία and αἴτιον in descriptions of Presocratic explanations of the world, the words do not occur in any of the fragments of the early natural philosophers. The one exception, though, who may have used the term αἰτία not in an ethical, legal or medical, but in a physical context, is again Democritus. As always, it is impossible to be absolutely certain. But there are nine book-titles containing the plural αἰτίαι (Diogenes Laertius 9.45–8) at least one of which, αἰτίαι περὶ ἀκαιρῶν καὶ ἐπικαιρῶν, does form part of one of the Thrasyllan tetralogies. In addition, there is the, admittedly mocking, report by Dionysius of Alexandria (Eusebius, *P.E.* 14.27.4 = DK68B118):

Δημόκριτος γοῦν αὐτός, ὥς φασιν, ἔλεγε 'βούλεσθαι μᾶλλον μίαν εὑρεῖν' αἰτιολογίαν ἢ 'τὴν Περσῶν οἱ βασιλείαν γενέσθαι'· καὶ ταῦτα μάτην καὶ ἀναιτίως αἰτιολογῶν ὡς ἀπὸ κενῆς ἀρχῆς καὶ ὑποθέσεως πλανωμένης ὁρμώμενος καὶ τὴν ῥίζαν καὶ τὴν κοινὴν ἀνάγκην τῆς τῶν ὄντων φύσεως οὐχ ὁρῶν...

Thus Democritus himself, as he says, said that he 'rather wanted to find one' explanation than 'that the kingship of the Persians come to be his': and that he explained randomly and without reason, as starting from an empty necessity and a wandering hypothesis, and not seeing the root and common necessity of the nature of all things...

This passage, full of mocking humour, may just preserve some original terminology. That is clearly the case with ἀνάγκην, κενο-, Leucippus' μάτην; among the few quotations attributed to Leucippus is the following (DK67B2 = Aetius 1.25.4):

οὐδὲν χρῆμα μάτην γίνεται, ἀλλὰ πάντα ἐκ λόγου τε καὶ ὑπ' ἀνάγκης.

Nothing occurs at random, but everything for a reason and by necessity.[464]

It could well extend to πλανωμένη, 'wandering', a poetic word not obviously connected to Presocratic philosophy outside Plato's *Timaeus* 48a, where *necessity* is famously equated with the 'wandering cause', πλανωμένη αἰτία;[465] and it could be evidence of αἰτία itself. If this is true, there are strong reasons to believe that Plato was responding to Democritus at *Phaedo* 97e, i.e. much earlier than is often assumed. This may be confirmed by the collocation, at 97e2, of τὴν αἰτίαν καὶ τὴν ἀνάγκην, 'the cause-and-explanation and the necessity', where mentioning necessity fits the Democritean deterministic system at least as well as Anaxagoras'.[466]

    One may adduce, in addition to these considerations about αἰτία, what Aristotle says about Plato and Democritus at *De generatione et corruptione*

1.2.315a29–35:

Πλάτων μὲν οὖν μόνον περὶ γενέσεως ἐσκέψατο καὶ φθορᾶς, ὅπως ὑπάρχει τοῖς πράγμασι, καὶ περὶ γενέσεως οὐ πάσης ἀλλὰ τῆς τῶν στοιχείων· πῶς δὲ σάρκες ἢ ὀστᾶ ἢ τῶν ἄλλων τι τῶν τοιούτων, οὐδέν· ἔτι οὔτε περὶ ἀλλοιώσεως οὔτε περὶ αὐξήσεως, τίνα τρόπον ὑπάρχουσι τοῖς πράγμασιν. ὅλως δὲ παρὰ τὰ ἐπιπολῆς περὶ οὐδενὸς οὐδεὶς ἐπέστησεν ἔξω Δημοκρίτου.

For Plato only investigated the conditions under which things come-to-be and pass-away; and he discussed not all coming-to-be, but only that of the elements. He asked no questions as to how flesh or bones, or any of the other similar things, come-to-be; nor again did he examine the conditions under which alteration or growth are attributable to things. In general, no one except Democritus has applied himself to any of these matters in a more than superficial way.

(tr. Joachim)

When talking about Plato here, Aristotle may be thinking of the discussion of the 'elements' in the *Timaeus*. But if Democritus, as seems to be implied, really talked about all the things Aristotle says Plato did not, then it may be safe to conclude that Plato had a copy of Democritus in front of him when writing *Phaedo* 95d–99d, where these topics *are* mentioned in a discussion that took its departure from the issue of 'coming-to-be and passing-away'.

This reading of *Phaedo* 95d–99d supports, and in turn receives support from, the suggestion that the term ἰδέα is adopted by Plato for his ultimate constituents of the world from Democritus, who had used it for his own ultimate constituents.[467] It would also strengthen the case for a privileged position of Democritus as the main target of the explanation of the κόσμος through principles which are not only invisible, non-composite, indestructible and ever-lasting, as were the atoms that combined by necessity, but in addition also non-corporeal, just as intelligence, νοῦς, will be non-corporeal in Plato for the first time in Western thought. Plato's interpretation in the *Timaeus* of Democritus' necessity as only an accessory, a συναίτιον,[468] would have been prefigured in the *Phaedo*: despite differences in application of the term in the *Phaedo* and the *Timaeus*,[469] from the outset the target of the criticism would have been the determinism of Democritus.[470]

243

CHAPTER 10

μετέχειν, παρουσία and κοινωνία in Plato's *Phaedo*

1. μετέχειν at *Phaedo* 100b–102d

Identification of Democritus as the probable source for Plato's adoption of the term ἰδέα thus led from 104b–105d back to the context of 95e–100e, Socrates' account of how, when he was younger, he had tried to make sense of the world with the help of the various explanations offered by the natural philosophers. From *Phaedo* 95e onwards, in relating some of the thoughts and attitudes he had held in his earlier years, Socrates describes how, in the course of pursuing his general interest in natural phenomena, he had come across a (or *the*) book by Anaxagoras.[471] In that book, Anaxagoras had submitted that νοῦς, or 'mind', ordering the world, is the cause-and-reason of things' being as they are (97c). Socrates was attracted by that proposition as he hoped that, with this explanation, he would see how everything was ordered for the best, thinking 'that he would no longer yearn for another type of cause-and-reason' (98a2). But he was disappointed and dissatisfied when he discovered how Anaxagoras 'adduced as causes-and-reasons airs and aethers and waters and many other such improbable things' (98c1), without explaining why the things which *are* are good the way they are, and how everything is ordered for the best. Socrates, who is not in possession of this explanation either, then outlines the method of 'hypothesis' he is going to employ in his investigations. This method consists in positing that there *are*, themselves by themselves, the beautiful, the good, the big and all the others (100b). When this is granted, as something that had been agreed on previously, Socrates continues (100c4–8):

…φαίνεται γάρ μοι, εἴ τί ἐστιν ἄλλο καλὸν πλὴν αὐτὸ τὸ καλόν, οὐδὲ δι᾽ ἓν ἄλλο καλὸν εἶναι ἢ διότι μετέχει ἐκείνου τοῦ καλοῦ· καὶ πάντα δὴ οὕτως λέγω. τῇ τοιᾷδε αἰτίᾳ συγχωρεῖς; συγχωρῶ, ἔφη.

…Indeed, it seems to me that, if anything else is beautiful other than the beautiful itself, it is beautiful through nothing else than because it 'has of' that beautiful: and all else accordingly, I say. Do you agree to such a cause-and-reason? I agree, said he.

245

On this and the following pages, forms of μετέχειν abound (100d4–e7, 101b10–c9, 102a11–b3):

…οὐκ ἄλλο τι ποιεῖ αὐτὸ καλὸν ἢ ἡ ἐκείνου τοῦ καλοῦ εἴτε παρουσία εἴτε κοινωνία εἴτε ὅπῃ δὴ καὶ ὅπως προσαγορευομένη· οὐ γὰρ ἔτι τοῦτο διισχυρίζομαι, ἀλλ᾽ ὅτι τῷ καλῷ πάντα τὰ καλὰ καλά. τοῦτο γάρ μοι δοκεῖ ἀσφαλέστατον εἶναι… καὶ μεγέθει ἄρα τὰ μεγάλα μεγάλα καὶ τὰ μείζω μείζω, καὶ σμικρότητι τὰ ἐλάττω ἐλάττω;
ναί.

…

τί δέ; ἑνὶ ἑνὸς προσθέντος τὴν πρόσθεσιν αἰτίαν εἶναι τοῦ δύο γενέσθαι ἢ διασχισθέντος τὴν σχίσιν οὐκ εὐλαβοῖο ἂν λέγειν; καὶ μέγα ἂν βοῴης ὅτι οὐκ οἶσθα ἄλλως πως ἕκαστον γιγνόμενον ἢ <u>μετασχὸν</u> τῆς ἰδίας οὐσίας ἑκάστου οὗ ἂν <u>μετάσχῃ</u>, καὶ ἐν τούτοις οὐκ ἔχεις ἄλλην τινὰ αἰτίαν τοῦ δύο γενέσθαι ἀλλ᾽ ἢ τὴν τῆς δυάδος <u>μετάσχεσιν</u>, καὶ δεῖν τούτου <u>μετασχεῖν</u> τὰ μέλλοντα δύο ἔσεσθαι, καὶ μονάδος ὃ ἂν μέλλῃ ἓν ἔσεσθαι, τὰς δὲ σχίσεις ταύτας καὶ προσθέσεις καὶ τὰς ἄλλας τὰς τοιαύτας κομψείας ἐῴης ἂν χαίρειν, παρεὶς ἀποκρίνασθαι τοῖς σεαυτοῦ σοφωτέροις…

…

PHAEDO: ὡς μὲν ἐγὼ οἶμαι, ἐπεὶ αὐτῷ ταῦτα συνεχωρήθη, καὶ ὡμολογεῖτο εἶναί τι ἕκαστον τῶν εἰδῶν καὶ τούτων τἆλλα <u>μεταλαμβάνοντα</u> αὐτῶν τούτων τὴν ἐπωνυμίαν ἴσχειν, τὸ δὴ μετὰ ταῦτα ἠρώτα…

…nothing else makes it beautiful than, of the beautiful, the presence or community or however and in whatever way it may be addressed: indeed, that latter I do not insist on in addition, but <I do insist> that through the beautiful all things beautiful are beautiful…
And thus through largeness large things large, and larger things larger, and through smallness smaller things smaller?
Yes.

…

What about this: should you not be on your guard and avoid saying that when one is added to one, addition is the cause-and-reason of there coming to be two, or in the case of division the dividing? And say with a loud voice that you do not know with regard to each and everything that it comes to be in any other way than by <u>having of</u> its own being <u>of which it has</u>, and in those matters you do not have any other cause-and-reason of there being two than the <u>having of</u> twoness, and that it is necessary that whatever shall be two <u>has of</u> that, and of unity whatever shall be one, but those dividings and additions and other such elaborate <causes-and-reasons> let go, leaving <them> to those more clever than you to answer <with>…

…

PHAEDO: As I believe, when that was granted to him, and it was agreed that each one of the 'types' *is*, and that, by <u>coming to have of</u> them, the other things acquire the designation of those themselves, after that he asked this…

In investigating the usage of μετέχειν here, wide-ranging conclusions have been drawn for Plato's ontology. First, the contrast of μετέχειν here and ἔχειν at *Phaedo* 103–5 has been explained as indicating a difference between 'participating (in a form)' and 'having (a character)'; next, the fact that Plato here, but not in later dialogues, employs the concept of μετέχειν, has been seen as a 'paradigm-shift': from participation to imitation.[472] But none of this is necesssary.

As we have seen, at *Phaedo* 100b, Socrates announces that he hopes to be able to show that the soul is something immortal if Cebes grants him that 'the beautiful by itself and the good by itself and the large by itself' exist. What is odd in that enumeration is not so much the phrase 'by itself'; as we have seen, that tag is familiar from earlier dialogues, and it was introduced in the *Phaedo* at an early stage.[473] What is odd is the inclusion of 'the large' alongside 'the beautiful' and 'the good'. It is worth noting that in whatever terms Socrates may, in earlier dialogues, have talked about the good or goodness, the beautiful or beauty, the just or justice, the holy or holiness, the moderate or moderation, prudence and temperance, the large had not been one of his concerns.[474] The statement at *Phaedo* 75c–d, in which the equal, the bigger and the smaller and all such things were grouped together with the beautiful itself and the good itself and the just and the holy and all things of which it is said that they *are*, likewise makes for an unusual collection of items in the mouth of Socrates, again partly because the equal, the larger and the smaller are not usually things Socrates talks about, while the beautiful, the good, the just and the holy are. The *Phaedo* is thus from the start a dialogue in which Socrates does unusual things.[475] But these unusual things are embedded in customary conversation on matters concerning the good life and the soul in a way which makes their introduction unobtrusive. So the example discussed in detail at 100c is again that of the beautiful, a topic which we are not surprised to find Socrates discussing.

At 100c2, Socrates proceeds in his explanation. Not only is there a 'beautiful itself': if there is anything else beautiful, it is beautiful because 'it has of that beautiful', μετέχει τοῦ καλοῦ; the use of the verb μετέχειν implies that potentially there are other things, 'the *many* beautiful things', together with which a beautiful thing 'has of' that beautiful which is the beautiful itself. As we have seen,[476] μετέχειν had been used by Plato in connection, not with the beautiful, but with the good, before he composed the *Phaedo*. At *Gorgias* 467e, the 'neither good nor bad' was characterized as ἃ ἐνίοτε μὲν μετέχει τοῦ ἀγαθοῦ, ἐνίοτε δὲ τοῦ κακοῦ, ἐνίοτε δὲ οὐδέτερου, 'that which sometimes shares in the good, sometimes in the bad and sometimes in neither'. It was left open if stones and wood belonged to the last category only, in which case ἐνίοτε would not have a strictly temporal meaning, or if stones 'sometimes had of the good, sometimes of the bad, and sometimes of neither', presumably according to what use was made of them.[477] In the *Phaedo*, the usage of μετέχειν encountered at 100c5 is thus not unprecedented. But it is not only the usage of the earlier dialogues that may be presupposed, Plato had employed μετέχειν and related expression in the *Phaedo* itself.

2. μετέχειν in the *Phaedo*: 57a–100c

Albeit not to the same extent as is the case with the noun εἶδος, Plato has prepared the use of μετέχειν as a philosophical term at 100c from early in the dialogue. A difference between preparation of the reader for the introduction of εἶδος as a technical term in the *Phaedo* and the preparation for the introduction of μετέχειν is the following: As discussed in the chapter on εἶδος in Part II, the noun as noun has different senses, and, as we have seen in the chapter on εἶδος in the *Phaedo*, the sense that becomes relevant at 102b is not common, but part of an already technical vocabulary, belonging to the terminology of a specific philosophical system of thought. By contrast, as discussed in the chapter on μετέχειν in Part I, while the verb μετέχειν has its different applications and certainly occurs in different contexts, the meaning of μετέχειν does not change. The meaning of μετέχειν in common usage and in specialized contexts is the same. The major distinction in application we could discern pertains to the nature of the object shared. And it is just this aspect of the verb to which Plato seems to draw attention in the early part of the dialogue. As in the discussion of μετέχειν in Part I, I shall include here, too, some relevant cases both of μεταλαμβάνειν and of μετεῖναι, and also an instance of μεταδίδωμι.

When, near the beginning of the reported conversation of Socrates' last day, Simmias has challenged Socrates on his verse-making, indicating that his question is prompted partly by a conversation he had previously had with Euenus, Socrates defends himself by invoking a recurring dream; he ends this defence of his peculiar activity with the request that Simmias pass on the answer to Euenus, adding to this that if Euenus is σώφρων[478] he will follow him, Socrates, as quickly as possible. Startled by that, Simmias asks for the meaning of this strange exhortation, and Socrates, before explaining himself, replies with a counter-question (61c6–9):

τί δέ; ἦ δ᾽ ὅς, οὐ φιλόσοφος Εὔηνος;
ἔμοιγε δοκεῖ, ἔφη ὁ Σιμμίας.
ἐθελήσει τοίνυν καὶ Εὔηνος καὶ πᾶς ὅτῳ ἀξίως τούτου τοῦ πράγματος μέτεστιν.

What about it, said he, is Euenus not a philosopher?
He seems so to me, certainly, said Simmias.
Then he will want to; both Euenus and everyone to whom, together with <others of his kind>, there *is* of that thing [i.e. philosophy] in a worthy fashion.

Socrates had introduced the noun φιλοσοφία at 61a3, and declared that his previous interpretation of the dream that told him to 'do music' had been that he should continue to 'do philosophy' as 'being the greatest music'. His rhetorical question now, whether Euenus is a philosopher,[479] is then taken up, generalized and rephrased. Socrates refers to all who are true philosophers as 'everyone to whom, together with <others of his kind>, there *is* of this thing, viz. Philosophy, in a worthy fashion'. This is certainly in tune with the usage of Plato's earlier dialogues, for example the *Protagoras*, where in the myth of Protagoras and its subsequent explication μετέχειν, μετεῖναι and παραγίγνεσθαι were all used to denote the 'sharing in' and 'having of' abilities, and a skill's or ability's 'coming to be with' and 'being with' a person.[480]

At 61c it is thus a skill or ability which is with a person. At *Phaedo* 63c, Socrates is asked, concerning a certain conviction of his and a particular insight into the world, to share this sentiment with his friends before departing (63c8–d3):

τί οὖν, ἔφη ὁ Σιμμίας, ὦ Σώκρατες; αὐτὸς ἔχων τὴν διάνοιαν ταύτην ἐν νῷ ἔχεις ἀπιέναι, ἢ κἂν ἡμῖν μεταδοίης; κοινὸν γὰρ δὴ ἔμοιγε δοκεῖ καὶ ἡμῖν εἶναι ἀγαθὸν τοῦτο, καὶ ἅμα σοι ἡ ἀπολογία ἔσται, ἐὰν ἅπερ λέγεις ἡμᾶς πείσῃς.

What about it, Socrates, said Simmias? Do you have in mind to depart having this insight yourself <and keeping it for yourself>, or would you 'give of it' to us, too? For it certainly seems to me that as something shared it would be (a) good for us, too, *if* you persuade us of what you say.

If Socrates 'gives of' his insight, the others will 'have of' it; if he lets them share, they will share. An insight is something many can participate in (potentially at the same time, to the same extent and in the same respect).

The two most prominent contexts of μετέχειν and its congeners in the *Phaedo* before page 100, however, are 64c–65a and 92e–94b. In the former context, Socrates characterizes the attitude of the philosophical man, who cares for his soul, in contrast with the attitude and the opinions of the many, the non-philosophers, who think that a life without the pleasures of the body is a life not worth living. At 64e and 65a, this is expressed in terms of the philosopher's 'sharing in' things like clothing and care for the body and a concern for such things, as little as possible; the many think that there is nothing sweet and pleasurable, and life is not worth living, unless one 'shares in' those things, and unless one has regard for the pleasures afforded by the body.

The latter context, 92e–94b, is Socrates' rejection and refutation of Simmias' suggestion that the soul is 'of the sort of a harmony'. There are five instances of μετέχειν between 93d and 94a, in the penultimate part of the refutation, which focuses on the possibility of degrees of knowledge, insight or νοῦς, i.e. degrees of virtue or goodness, which, in folk-philosophical parlance, is harmony of or in the soul. On Simmias' model, however, in which the soul itself is a harmony, degrees of virtue could only be achieved by positing 'a harmony of a harmony', a position which is portrayed as nonsensical. The paradox arises because every soul, *qua* soul, is as much a soul as any other soul, but not every soul is as virtuous as any other soul. It may be worth quoting the final lines of this argument, as here indeed μετέχειν refers to the 'having of' degrees of something. This part of the refutation of Simmias' position runs (93d1–94b3):

ἀλλὰ προωμολόγηται, ἔφη, μηδὲν μᾶλλον μηδ' ἧττον ἑτέραν ἑτέρας ψυχὴν ψυχῆς εἶναι· τοῦτο δ' ἔστι τὸ ὁμολόγημα, μηδὲν μᾶλλον μηδ' ἐπὶ πλέον μηδ' ἧττον μηδ' ἐπ' ἔλαττον ἑτέραν ἑτέρας ἁρμονίαν ἁρμονίας εἶναι. ἦ γάρ;
πάνυ γε.
τὴν δέ γε μηδὲν μᾶλλον μηδὲ ἧττον ἁρμονίαν οὖσαν μήτε μᾶλλον μήτε ἧττον ἡρμόσθαι· ἔστιν οὕτως;
ἔστιν.
ἡ δὲ μήτε μᾶλλον μήτε ἧττον ἡρμοσμένη ἔστιν ὅτι πλέον ἢ ἔλαττον ἁρμονίας μετέχει, ἢ τὸ ἴσον;
τὸ ἴσον.
οὐκοῦν ψυχὴ ἐπειδὴ οὐδὲν μᾶλλον οὐδ' ἧττον ἄλλη ἄλλης αὐτὸ τοῦτο, ψυχή, ἐστίν, οὐδὲ δὴ μᾶλλον οὐδὲ ἧττον ἥρμοσται;
οὕτω.
τοῦτο δέ γε πεπονθυῖα οὐδὲν πλέον ἀναρμοστίας οὐδὲ ἁρμονίας μετέχοι ἄν;
οὐ γὰρ οὖν.
τοῦτο δ' αὖ πεπονθυῖα ἆρ' ἄν τι πλέον κακίας ἢ ἀρετῆς μετέχοι ἑτέρα ἑτέρας, εἴπερ ἡ μὲν κακία ἀναρμοστία, ἡ δὲ ἀρετὴ ἁρμονία εἴη;
οὐδὲν πλέον.
μᾶλλον δέ γέ που, ὦ Σιμμία, κατὰ τὸν ὀρθὸν λόγον κακίας οὐδεμία ψυχὴ μεθέξει, εἴπερ ἁρμονία ἐστίν· ἁρμονία γὰρ δήπου παντελῶς αὐτὸ τοῦτο οὖσα, ἁρμονία, ἀναρμοστίας οὔποτ' ἂν μετάσχοι.
οὐ μέντοι.
οὐδέ γε δήπου ψυχή, οὖσα παντελῶς ψυχή, κακίας.
πῶς γὰρ ἔκ γε τῶν προειρημένων;
ἐκ τούτου ἄρα τοῦ λόγου ἡμῖν πᾶσαι ψυχαὶ πάντων ζῴων ὁμοίως ἀγαθαὶ ἔσονται, εἴπερ ὁμοίως ψυχαὶ πεφύκασιν αὐτὸ τοῦτο, ψυχαί, εἶναι.
ἔμοιγε δοκεῖ, ἔφη, ὦ Σώκρατες.

But it's already been agreed that no one soul is more or less a soul than another; and this is the admission that no one attunement is either more or to a greater extent, or less or to a smaller extent, an attunement than another. Isn't that so?
Certainly.
But that which is neither more nor less an attunement has been neither more nor less tuned, is that so?
It is.
But does that which has been neither more nor less tuned participate in

attunement to a greater or a smaller degree, or to an equal degree?
To an equal degree.
But then, given that no one soul is either more or less itself, namely a soul, than another, it hasn't been more or less tuned either?
That is so.
And that being its condition, could any one soul <u>participate</u> to a greater extent than another in badness or goodness, assuming that badness is non-attunement, while goodness is attunement?
It couldn't.
Or rather, surely, following sound reasoning, Simmias, no soul will <u>partici-pate</u> in badness, assuming it is attunement; because naturally an attune-ment, being completely itself, namely an attunement, could never <u>participate</u> in non-attunement.
No indeed.
Nor then, of course, could a soul, being completely a soul, <u>participate</u> in badness.
How could it, in view of what's already been said?
By that argument, then, we find that all souls of all living things will be equally good, assuming that it's the nature of souls to be equally themselves, namely souls.
So it seems to me, Socrates.   (tr. Gallop)[481]

This position is then, of course, rejected. For our purposes what is decisive here is on the one hand that addition of the expressions 'more or less' or 'equal' respectively determines that there are degrees of participation; on the other hand, what is participated in, shared in or 'had of' is 'attunement' or 'harmony' and 'goodness' and 'badness'. While participation in 'goodness' and 'badness' had been encountered in previous contexts, it is impossible to ascertain whether 'sharing in attunement' would have been regarded as in line with common idiom, or whether the reader would at first have been perplexed by the expression. However, as soon as 'goodness' and 'badness' are mentioned, Socrates is in the realm of common language.

We thus see that, before Plato lets Socrates use the term μετέχειν at 100c in connection with what will then soon be referred to as 'the types', the verb and related expressions had been used in the dialogue in non-philosophical and philosophical contexts to denote 'having of' or 'sharing in' of many kinds. But it was used in particular in contexts in which *human beings* 'had of' or 'shared in' things. Among these things, there were material objects, such as food and drink and clothing, everything to do with the body and its needs. μετέχειν was employed to denote the 'having of' life and the soul was said to 'have of attunement'. One further instance of the verb should be noted before we turn to the context of 100c. At 81c, Socrates had, in ironic seriousness, been speaking of ghosts which are souls which in their lives had attached themselves to earthly things and which are now burdened with the heaviness of what they had cared for during their life on earth. He concludes that the shadow images of souls in the vicinity of grave markers are the souls (81d3–4):

> ...αἱ μὴ καθαρῶς ἀπολυθεῖσαι ἀλλὰ τοῦ ὁρατοῦ μετέχουσαι, διὸ καὶ ὁρῶνται.

> ...which, not having been set free in a pure state, but 'having of' the visible, are for that reason also seen.

In the case of 81d, it should be noted that the phrase μετέχειν τοῦ ὁρατοῦ is potentially ambiguous, as it may denote either 'a particular thing's or person's "having of" something particular that is visible' or 'something's "having of" the visible' in the sense of 'something's being the sort of thing that is (by nature) visible'.

3. μετέχειν in the world of Anaxagoras

There is thus indeed, in principle, nothing new in the use of μετέχειν at 100c, either as regards Plato's own usage within the *Phaedo*, or Greek usage elsewhere. But this is not the full story. For there is one Presocratic text not discussed so far which sheds additional light on the use of μετέχειν here in the *Phaedo* (Simplicius *Physica* 164.25 = DK59B6):

> καὶ ὅτε δὲ ἴσαι μοῖραί εἰσι τοῦ τε μεγάλου καὶ τοῦ σμικροῦ πλῆθος, καὶ οὕτως ἂν εἴη ἐν παντὶ πάντα· οὐδὲ χωρὶς ἔστιν εἶναι, ἀλλὰ πάντα παντὸς μοῖραν μετέχει. ὅτε τοὐλάχιστον μὴ ἔστιν εἶναι, οὐκ ἂν δύναιτο χωρισθῆναι, οὐδ' ἂν ἐφ' ἑαυτοῦ γενέσθαι, ἀλλ' ὅπωσπερ ἀρχὴν εἶναι καὶ νῦν πάντα ὁμοῦ. ἐν πᾶσι δὲ πολλὰ ἔνεστι καὶ τῶν ἀποκρινομένων ἴσα πλῆθος ἐν τοῖς μείζοσί τε καὶ ἐλάσσοσι.

> And when there are equal parts of the large and the small, as regards their amount, also in that way everything would be in everything: nor is there being apart, but everything has a part of everything [together with everything else]. When there is nothing which is the smallest, no 'being parted' is possible, nor coming to be by itself, but as it was in the beginning, so now everything is together. And in everything there are many things of those separated off, equal in amount in the bigger and the smaller [things].

It is Anaxagoras who declares that there are equal parts of the large and the small; that there is no being separated; and that coming to be ἐφ' ἑαυτοῦ, 'by itself', is not possible. That is to say, whatever it was Anaxagoras meant, he did speak about 'equal parts', 'large', 'small', things being, or as is the case here, not being 'by themselves'. Because Anaxagoras' κόσμος, his universe, was despite the mention of νοῦς or 'mind' an entirely physical world, anything in it which 'has of' something 'has part of something', μοῖραν μετέχει, because that is the only way in which anything can 'have of' something purely physical.

Thus, when Socrates, at *Phaedo* 100c, after criticism of the shortcomings of Anaxagoras' philosophy, in which Anaxagoras is mentioned by name, says, …φαίνεται γάρ μοι, εἴ τί ἐστιν ἄλλο καλὸν πλὴν αὐτὸ τὸ καλόν, οὐδὲ δι᾽ ἓν ἄλλο καλὸν εἶναι ἢ διότι <u>μετέχει</u> ἐκείνου τοῦ καλοῦ, '…indeed, it seems to me that if anything else is beautiful other than the beautiful itself, that it is beautiful through nothing else than because it 'has of' that beautiful', Plato lets Socrates use Anaxagorean terminology and combine it with Socratic thought concerning the good and the beautiful, as expressed for example in the *Gorgias* and the *Protagoras*, where the notion of 'sharing' did not imply the notion of 'parts'. The *Protagoras* in particular displayed a large number of instances of 'having of', where this 'having of' referred to matters concerning the mind; the phrase μετέχει τοῦ ἀγαθοῦ as such figured in the *Gorgias* (467e). Socrates supplies what he said he missed in Anaxagoras' account: he supplies what is καλὸν καὶ ἀγαθόν, 'beautiful and good', to an account of the world in terms of distinct constituents in which the things as we know them 'have of' other things. Anaxagoras had said (Simplicius *Physica* 164.24 = DK59B12):

τὰ μὲν ἄλλα παντὸς μοῖραν μετέχει, νοῦς δέ ἐστιν ἄπειρον καὶ αὐτοκρατὲς καὶ μέμεικται οὐδενὶ χρήματι, ἀλλὰ μόνος αὐτὸς ἐπ᾽ ἑωυτοῦ ἐστιν. εἰ μὴ γὰρ ἐφ᾽ ἑαυτοῦ ἦν, ἀλλά τεῳ ἐμέμεικτο ἄλλῳ, μετεῖχεν ἂν ἁπάντων χρημάτων, εἰ ἐμέμεικτό τεῳ· ἐν παντὶ γὰρ παντὸς μοῖρα ἔνεστιν, ὥσπερ ἐν τοῖς πρόσθεν μοι λέλεκται· καὶ ἂν ἐκώλυεν αὐτὸν τὰ συμμεμειγμένα, ὥστε μηδενὸς χρήματος κρατεῖν ὁμοίως ὡς καὶ μόνον ἐόντα ἐφ᾽ ἑαυτοῦ.

Now, everything else has a part of everything else, but mind alone is unlimited and self-governed and mixed with nothing, but is alone itself by itself. Indeed, if it were not by itself, but were mixed with something else, it would have of *all* the things, if it were mixed with *anything*: for in everything there is a part of everything, as said by me in what went before; also: what would be mixed with it would prevent mind from governing any [one] thing in the same way it can when being alone by itself.

Anaxagoras had introduced mind and postulated that it was 'itself by itself', but he had not done anything with it; his mind 'is in' everything and governs everything, but at the same time is not mixed with anything; we are told that it is mind who or which governs all, but we are not told why and how; 'large' and 'small', on the other hand, seem to have been on a par with all the other physical things, thin and dense, cold and warm, dark and light, moist and dry (B12);[482] considering all that, it does not become clear in what way, if any, mind is distinct from physical stuff, nor, according to what principles or considerations mind governs and rules. With the introduction by Socrates of the beautiful and the good, and by extension of the large and the equal, as existing by themselves, Anaxagoras' picture is completely subverted, not only modified in one respect, despite adoption of Anaxagorean terminology on a large scale. Introduction of the beautiful and good into the analysis of the world paves the way for what Socrates had claimed an explanation of things in terms of mind should amount to.

4. Rephrasing Anaxagoras: παρουσία and κοινωνία at *Phaedo* 100d

The parallel between 'the beautiful' and matters of the mind is implicitly strengthened by Socrates at 100d, when he says that if there is anything beautiful in this world, nothing else makes it beautiful other than:

> ...ἡ ἐκείνου τοῦ καλοῦ εἴτε παρουσία εἴτε κοινωνία εἴτε ὅπῃ δὴ καὶ ὅπως προσαγορευομένη· οὐ γὰρ ἔτι τοῦτο διισχυρίζομαι, ἀλλ᾽ ὅτι τῷ καλῷ πάντα τὰ καλὰ καλά.

> ...the presence or community of the beautiful, or however and in whatever way it be addressed: indeed, that latter I do not insist on in addition, but [I do insist] that through the beautiful all things beautiful are beautiful.

On the context of this passage, Ross comments: 'In the statement of the ideal theory here, Plato uses certain important terms in connexion with the relation between the Idea and particulars. From the side of the Idea, it is called presence (παρουσία [100d5]), from the side of the particulars participation (κοινωνία, μετάσχεσις, μετάληψις [100d6, 101c5, 102b2]). But Socrates adds that he does not insist on any particular name for the relation, but only on the fact that it is by reason of the Ideas that particulars are what they are, "that by the beautiful all beautiful things are beautiful" [100d7].'[483] This summary by the curate of tradition is good in parts. It does bring out well the aspectual difference between 'presence' and 'participation', as being said from the point of view of the Ideas and from the point of view of the particulars, respectively. But it does not indicate that, in this context, μετέχειν is used first, after Socrates has announced that he will now present his own method after all else has failed. It was, *inter alia*, this introduction of μετέχειν right after the disappointment at reading Anaxagoras that suggested that use of the verb was a direct response to Anaxagoras.

As importantly – a feature shared with many interpretations of this passage – the summary by Ross pays attention only to one aspect of Socrates' assertion 'that he does not insist on any particular name for the relation'.[484] For this assertion immediately prompts a question: 'Why is Socrates telling us about his non-insistence concerning the term with which the relation-ship between the beautiful itself and the many beautiful things should be addressed?' Up to 100c, the reader was not aware of any special name for this relationship. By 100d, the reader has seen that μετέχειν or 'sharing', 'having of', is a word or metaphor that can be used in connection with the relationship between the beautiful itself and a particular beautiful thing; by extension, this will hold for the good itself 'and all the others'. Nothing suggests that Socrates is currently contemplating alternatives, or has previously or elsewhere done so.

That is to say, by letting Socrates assert that he does *not* insist on terminology, Plato draws attention *to* terminology. Plato *does* insist that we, the readers, concern ourselves with terminological issues. By mentioning παρουσία and κοινωνία, Plato – at least potentially – evokes in the reader the contexts in which these terms can be applied, the contexts in which those terms have been applied by him in the dialogues, and the associations which these terms may have. This, then, is one justification for having dealt with the semantics of μετέχειν and παρουσία so extensively in Part I. We shall now turn to some of the contexts in which the alternative terms mentioned by Socrates at *Phaedo* 100d occur.

As discussed above,[485] both the occurrence of the term παρουσία in connection with the beautiful and the good and the grammatical construction with a vaguely instrumental dative occurred at *Gorgias* 497 ff., in a context in which the good life was at stake. Socrates was there talking about the brave and the good as people to whom good or goods were present.[486] Both at *Gorgias* 506c–d and at *Meno* 70a, 'virtue', ἀρετή, is said to be present, or to come to be present, with, by, or to someone, just as beauty, κάλλος, was said to be present in parallel with the παρουσία of the good(s) at *Gorgias* 497e. One reading of *Phaedo* 100d may therefore be that παρουσία τοῦ καλοῦ, 'presence of the beautiful' to beautiful things around us suggests a relation like the one which things (like the good or like virtue) can have to the mind, or the mind to things. What would matter in this analogy is not so much whether Plato or one of his contemporaries could have given a comprehensive, consistent and plausible account of what this relationship between a mind or a man and virtue would entail. What matters is that, at least by the time of *Phaedo* 100d, but as has been suggested in Part I long before that in common Greek parlance, speaking of 'presence of virtue' is part of received idiom; what matters is that this familiar expression can be introduced as uncontroversial. Furthermore, it was precisely in the context of sharing or participation in and presence of goodness and virtues that μετέχειν and παρεῖναι or παρουσία were found side by side in the early dialogues, as in the *Laches*, where virtue is said to be present at 190b and courage is shared in at 193e; in the *Protagoras*, where people are repeatedly said to share in virtue from 322d onwards, and where παραγίγνεσθαι is introduced to refer to the coming-about of the same relationship at 323c; in the *Charmides*, where σωφροσύνη was talked of as coming-to-be in somebody so as to be with somebody (ἐγγίγνεσθαι and παρεῖναι) at 157a, and Charmides is asked whether he shares in moderation (μετέχειν σωφροσύνης) at 158c; and in the *Gorgias*, where the neither-good-nor bad sometimes 'shares in' the good (467e), and where, as has just been reiterated, the good is in various ways said to be 'present to' somebody or something.

Plato thus lets Socrates introduce the noun παρουσία, 'presence', which had been in use *inter alia* in Attic tragedy, where it denoted the presence of a variety of non-corporeal abstract things to a person or to the mind, as a term that was in some contexts in his earlier dialogues correlative with μετέχειν in precisely the way Ross describes: 'what is present is being shared in'. The difference at *Phaedo* 100d is that, whereas in Plato's earlier dialogues this translated into 'what is present to a person is being shared in by that person', this is now extended to cover in addition: 'what is present to a thing [something; anything] is shared in by that thing'. The implicit suggestion is that the relationship denoted by μετέχειν is unproblematic, because it is familiar and within common parlance, and that is to say within what is commonly accepted by all.

At this point a cry rises of 'equivocation'! – Is Plato exploiting without justification the fact that μετέχειν and παρεῖναι are correlative in some contexts so as to prove something in another context in which this correlativity does not hold? No, because Plato does not conclude anything on the basis of the terms used at *Phaedo* 100d. To that extent, one must take Socrates at his word. Plato does not postulate an equivalence, he suggests a possibility. He illustrates one metaphor with another.

The noun παρουσία has thus, in a way, anchored the argument of the *Phaedo* in Plato's own earlier dialogues, and that is to say to some extent in Socrates' world of thought. Next comes the term κοινωνία, offered as another alternative in the description of the relationship referred to as μετέχειν. No story parallel to that of παρουσία can be told, and for that reason there is, in Part I, no chapter devoted to the discussion of the noun κοινωνία and the related verb κοινωνεῖν. But Plato did not choose the word at random. In fact, it had made its appearance on one occasion in the *Gorgias*. It is instructive to read *Gorgias* 507d–508a, together with an excerpt from Dodds' comment on the passage. Socrates has argued his case for restraint as necessary for the virtuous life which is the happy life. He concludes, addressing Callicles (507d6–508a8):

οὗτος ἔμοιγε δοκεῖ ὁ σκοπὸς εἶναι πρὸς ὃν βλέποντα δεῖ ζῆν, καὶ πάντα εἰς τοῦτο τὰ αὑτοῦ συντείνοντα καὶ τὰ τῆς πόλεως, ὅπως δικαιοσύνη <u>παρέσται</u> καὶ σωφροσύνη τῷ μακαρίῳ μέλλοντι ἔσεσθαι, οὕτω πράττειν, οὐκ ἐπιθυμίας ἐῶντα ἀκολάστους εἶναι καὶ ταύτας ἐπιχειροῦντα πληροῦν, ἀνήνυτον κακόν, λῃστοῦ βίον ζῶντα. οὔτε γὰρ ἂν ἄλλῳ ἀνθρώπῳ προσφιλὴς ἂν εἴη ὁ τοιοῦτος οὔτε θεῷ· <u>κοινωνεῖν</u> γὰρ ἀδύνατος, ὅτῳ δὲ μὴ <u>ἔνι κοινωνία</u>, φιλία οὐκ ἂν εἴη. φασὶ δ᾽ οἱ σοφοί, ὦ Καλλίκλεις, καὶ οὐρανὸν καὶ γῆν καὶ θεοὺς καὶ ἀνθρώπους τὴν <u>κοινωνίαν</u> συνέχειν καὶ φιλίαν καὶ κοσμιότητα καὶ σωφροσύνην καὶ δικαιότητα,

καὶ τὸ ὅλον τοῦτο διὰ ταῦτα κόσμον καλοῦσιν, ὦ ἑταῖρε, οὐκ ἀκοσμίαν οὐδὲ
ἀκολασίαν. σὺ δέ μοι δοκεῖς οὐ προσέχειν τὸν νοῦν τούτοις, καὶ ταῦτα σοφὸς
ὤν, ἀλλὰ λέληθέν σε ὅτι ἡ ἰσότης ἡ γεωμετρικὴ καὶ ἐν θεοῖς καὶ ἐν ἀνθρώποις
μέγα δύναται, σὺ δὲ πλεονεξίαν οἴει δεῖν ἀσκεῖν· γεωμετρίας γὰρ ἀμελεῖς.

This seems to me the aim looking at which one must live; and one must direct
all one's powers, and those of one's city, towards this, so that justice will be
present and moderation, to the one who is intent on being happy; and he must
behave in that way, not letting his desires be unrestrained and trying to satisfy
them – an incurable evil – living the life of a criminal. For neither could such
a person <who leads the unrestrained life> be friend to another human being
nor to a god: For he would be incapable of 'having things in common', but 'in
whom there is' not 'community', there will not be friendship. But the wise,
Callicles, say that community and friendship and orderliness and moderation
and justice hold together the sky and the earth and gods and humans, and
this All, which for this reason they call 'order' [κόσμος; 'arrangement'; 'world-
order'], my friend, not 'disorder' or 'unrestraint'. But you seem to me not to
pay attention to these things; and while you are so wise, yet it escapes you that
'geometric equality' has much power both among the gods and among humans;
but you believe one must practice *pleonexia* ['having more'; 'having more than
one's neighbour'; 'greed'; 'accumulation of money, goods and power'], for you
neglect and disregard geometry.

Dodds comments:[487]

[This] is Plato's solution of the νόμος–φύσις controversy (see on 482c4–483c6).
This antithesis is in his view a false one: νόμος is rooted in φύσις; the social
and the natural order are expressions of the same divine law – which reveals
itself as law because it can be stated in mathematical terms. As Aristotle later
put it, ἀκοσμία is παρὰ φύσιν (περὶ φιλοσοφίας fr. 17). This thought too is
further developed in the *Republic*: see especially 500c9 θείῳ δὴ καὶ κοσμίῳ ὅ
γε φιλόσοφος ὁμιλῶν κόσμιός τε καὶ θεῖος εἰς τὸ δυνατὸν ἀνθρώπῳ γίγνεται
['and thus the philosopher, certainly, becomes, to the extent that is possible
for a human being, orderly and divine, having contact with the divine and
orderly'], also *Tim.* 90c–d. Socrates does not, however, claim it as his own;
he appeals in our passage to the authority of οἱ σοφοί (e6), on which the
scholiast remarks σοφοὺς ἐνταῦθα τοὺς Πυθαγορείους φησί, καὶ διαφερόντως
τὸν Ἐμπεδοκλέα ['here he calls "wise"/means by "the wise" the Pythagoreans,
and especially Empedocles']: so also Olympiodorus 166.15. They think of
Empedocles because of the importance in his system of φιλία ['friendship'] as
a cosmic principle; but there is no compelling reason to suppose that Plato had
Empedocles *especially* in mind (the doctrine of "geometrical equality" is not,
so far as we know, Empedoclean). Their identification of the σοφοί with the
Pythagoreans has, however, been generally and rightly accepted:
(a) Plato applies this term to the Pythagoreans in a number of other places (see
on 492d1–493d4).
(b) κοινωνία (sense of community) and φιλία ['friendship'] were important

in the Pythagorean society, not only as an obligation governing the relations of one Pythagorean to another (Iamblichus, *De vita Pythagorica* 237 ff.) but in a much wider sense as a bond between all living things: Sextus Empiricus, *Adversus mathematicos* 9.127 φασὶ μὴ μόνον ἡμῖν πρὸς ἀλλήλους καὶ πρὸς τοὺς θεοὺς εἶναί τινα κοινωνίαν, ἀλλὰ καὶ πρὸς τὰ ἄλογα τῶν ζῴων ['they say that for us there is a community not only with each other and with the gods, but also with "those of the living beings that do not have *logos*"/the animals']: cf. *Meno* 81c9 τῆς φύσεως ἁπάσης συγγενοῦς οὔσης ['all nature being akin'], where Plato is almost certainly quoting Pythagorean doctrine.

(c) The Pythagoreans are said to have been the first actually to call the universe κόσμος (see on a3), and they were certainly the first proponents of the idea of a world-order controlled by mathematical laws (ὅλον οὐρανὸν ἁρμονίαν εἶναι καὶ ἀριθμόν [they say that 'the whole heaven is harmony/attunement and number'], Aristotle, *Metaphysics* 986a2).

(d) The concept of "geometrical proportion" appears first in the Pythagorean mathematician Archytas (fr. 2). And in its political application, though not attested before the *Gorgias*, may well go back to Pythagorean sources (see on 6a).

All of this is important and relevant to an understanding of the *Phaedo*. I shall focus here narrowly on Dodds' second point (b). κοινωνία in the sense of 'community' was a Pythagorean key term in both a socio-political, i.e. ethical, and a cosmic, i.e. physical and ontological context. 'Community' holds between human beings and also between and among everything else in the world. This was a Pythagorean doctrine which, with or without its terminology, is potentially echoed in earlier dialogues at *Meno* 81c and, if that identification is correct, before that, at *Protagoras* 322a, 337b. But regardless of how widespread knowledge of this Pythagorean tenet would have been in educated Greek society, Plato introduces the concept in an unmistakably Pythagorean context in the *Gorgias*. Generally-educated readers of the *Phaedo* would therefore have been familiar with κοινωνία as a Pythagorean concept at least from the *Gorgias*,[488] and Pythagorean readers of the *Phaedo* would have been familiar with the concept anyway.

Thus, when introducing the term κοινωνία at *Phaedo* 100d, Plato was telling the reader that there is yet another analogy for the relation labelled μετέχειν, an analogy with which the reader was likewise already familiar. However, Plato, in the *Phaedo*, had prepared the reader for the introduction of the notion of analogy long before 100d. The one previous instance of the noun κοινωνία in the dialogue is embedded in the context of 64c–66a, a context, as we have seen, that is philosophically significant in other respects, too. At 64c, it was stated that 'death is something'.[489] Death was then defined at 64c5–8:

καὶ εἶναι τοῦτο τὸ τεθνάναι, χωρὶς μὲν ἀπὸ τῆς ψυχῆς ἀπαλλαγὲν αὐτὸ καθ' αὐτὸ τὸ σῶμα γεγονέναι, χωρὶς δὲ τὴν ψυχὴν ἀπὸ τοῦ σώματος ἀπαλλαγεῖσαν αὐτὴν καθ᾽ αὑτὴν εἶναι;

And is not this 'being dead': that the body is separated on its own, away from the soul, itself by itself, and the soul separated on its own, away from the body, 'herself by herself'?

At 64c, one encounters the adverb χωρίς, 'separate', 'apart', and the phrase αὐτὸ καθ᾽ αὑτό, 'itself by itself'; what is here and on the subsequent pages said about body and soul, will later be applied to the things themselves and the many sensible particulars; that cannot be predicted at this stage, but the phrases will have prepared the reader for more explicitly or implicitly Anaxagorean material. Socrates' next statement is to the effect that one must not devote one's attention too much to clothes, jewellery and physical adornments, 'in accordance with there being no great necessity to "have of" them', καθ᾽ ὅσον μὴ πολλὴ ἀνάγκη μετέχειν αὐτῶν (64e1).[490] When that is granted, Socrates characterizes the philosopher as (65a1) ἀπολύων ὅτι μάλιστα τὴν ψυχὴν ἀπὸ τῆς τοῦ σώματος κοινωνίας, 'setting the soul free from community with the body as much as possible'. Subsequently, both κοινωνεῖν and the phrase αὐτὴν καθ᾽ αὑτήν are repeated on the same page (65c–d).

Between 64c and 66a, there are altogether six instances of permutations of the phrase αὐτὸ καθ᾽ αὑτό, 'itself by itself', four instances of the stem κοινο-, expressing 'community' and having in common', and two instances of forms of the verb μετέχειν, 'having of' or 'sharing'. These two instances occur just before and just after the notion of community is introduced with the noun κοινωνία at 65a1. That is to say, Plato has achieved three things at once. First, on the level of the dialogue, Socrates, by using some of the terminology that he will later use for the things themselves, and the sensibles that share in them, in connection with community and separation of body and soul, has paved the way for the notion of the affinity of the soul with the things themselves and the affinity of the human body with the bodily; this will be a crucial point in the final proof of the immortality of the soul of the individual. Secondly, by introducing the notion of 'sharing', Plato has prepared the reader for a discussion of Anaxagorean positions. And thirdly, by introducing the potentially Pythagorean notion of 'community' in a way that suggests proximity in meaning to the notion of sharing, Plato has laid the foundations for the assimilation of the two notions to his own, new philosophy, an important aspect of which is introduced in the same context at 65d–e, with the first occurrence of the term οὐσία. This has been achieved in a way which does not perplex or offend the reader, but which prepares gradually and imperceptibly.

By the time the reader reaches 100d, the use of κοινωνία will implicitly suggest that the relation of the beautiful to a beautiful thing may be parallel to that of soul to body in a way not unlike the Pythagorean community of all things. There is, however, a subtle shift, in that the community of things which Socrates advertises is closely confined to the things Socrates has concerned himself with, 'the beautiful', 'the good', 'the equal', etc. At the same time, Plato lets Socrates present an analysis of the world in which 'the beautiful', 'the good', 'the equal', etc. are 'by themselves'. He thereby corrects Anaxagoras' analysis in which only a mind whose nature and role were not sufficiently specified had this status of being 'by itself'. Use of the word μετέχειν is a similar sort of correction. Anaxagoras was right, Socrates suggests, in analysing the world and reducing what is visible around us to something more fundamental. If, however, one wants to understand the world as made up or constituted of things which 'have of' or 'share in' something else, one would be wrong to say that this sharing is a mutual relation obtaining between all the physical, corporeal constituents. If there is 'sharing', this 'sharing' is not 'having a part of', μέρος or μοῖραν μετέχειν, but it is rather like sharing in courage or excellence, where one person's 'having of' courage does not in any way impinge upon another person's 'having of' courage. Socrates' and Cebes' sharing a cake amounts to their each having a part of that cake; Socrates' and Cebes' sharing in an understanding of the world does not prevent one from knowing what the other knows. Nor does one thing's being beautiful diminish the chances of another's aspiration to the same beauty. But this beauty can also be interpreted as the presence of beauty, a common notion in Attic Greek; or as a community of the beautiful with the many beautiful things, an expression that at least allows for a Pythagorean interpretation.

5. Conclusion

From the point of view of Socrates and his interlocutors, what is at stake at *Phaedo* 100d is the nature of the relation of the ultimate constituents which underlie this world-order to the world of the senses that surrounds us. For if we know the make-up of the universe we will be in a better position to answer questions concerning the nature and the fate of the soul.

Anaxagoras had posited a mixture of small bodies of all sorts, but had introduced in addition something 'itself by itself'. Some of the Anaxagorean examples of those 'seeds', like 'the big' and 'the small', 'the warm' and 'the cold', Plato uses as examples in his discussion. Whatever Plato makes of Anaxagoras' νοῦς or *mind* – and we do not have to decide here if Socrates' criticisms are justified – the notion of something 'itself by itself', introduced into philosophical thought by Parmenides, is one central to Plato's thought, too; so is at least one of the verbs expressing the relation that holds between and among the Anaxagorean 'seeds', and between the 'seeds' and 'mind'. Plato adopts, at least in this part of the *Phaedo*, the term μετέχειν, 'having of', to refer to the relation that holds between the things themselves and the many things that are called by the same name. The term was particularly suitable for Plato's purposes as he had used μετέχειν frequently in his early dialogues to denote the soul's or mind's sharing in some virtue or other, i.e. in non-physical things, and since in the *Phaedo* the soul is in some way likened to those non-corporeal, invisible things which are 'themselves by themselves'. That is to say, because μετέχειν was familiar from both an Anaxagorean and a Socratic context, it could serve as a link and point of departure for an integration of Anaxagorean into Platonic views.[491] At the same time, Plato draws attention to the fact that his philosophical position does not depend on Anaxagorean physics, or even on Anaxagorean terminology. Not only is the kind of 'having of' or 'sharing' which Plato envisages non-corporeal, non-physical sharing in something that is invisible, outside space and time, there are also other metaphors which can be used for the relationship and connection Plato undertakes to establish. One such metaphor is that of the 'presence' of the things that *are* to the things in the world of coming-to-be and passing-away. This term, 'presence', belongs to common Greek idiom in the realm of ethical discussions of the sort Socrates is presented as having in Plato's early dialogues. By using the term 'presence', Plato thus indicates both that the reader has a received and accepted model that can serve as an analogy for what he introduces to the reader from 95d onwards, and at the same time he establishes a connection and makes a claim that Socrates is still working, broadly speaking, in the same field in which he had been working all along: Socrates is still interested in the presence of the good in the world and in himself and his fellow men. On the other hand, Plato offers a second alternative to Anaxagorean terminology when he introduces the term κοινωνία or 'community'. With this term, he addresses readers who adhere to or at least are to some extent familiar with Pythagorean doctrine. 'Community' of all things in the world had been a concept Plato had mentioned in a Pythagorean context in the *Gorgias*. In the first half of the *Phaedo*, Plato had created contexts in which the notions of 'sharing' and 'having in common' were approximated to each other; the examples led the reader to accept that the two notions, the one, 'sharing' or 'having of', familiar from Socratic dialogues, but also, in a different way, from Anaxagoras' philosophy, the other, 'having in common with' and 'community', from the Pythagoreans, could be used interchangeably, or at least in the same context to refer to more or less the same thing(s).

In drawing these strands together at 100c–d, Plato can present his own philosophy as compatible both with what Socrates had said in the early dialogues and with the major systems of Presocratic philosophy. In different ways, Philolaus, Democritus and Anaxagoras had in their philosophical systems captured elements of explanation which Plato could refer to by using the terminology of his predecessors. Using their language, though, need not commit him to specific aspects of their philosophical doctrines. This last point is illustrated particularly well in the case of ἐνεῖναι, the term we shall turn to in the next chapter.

CHAPTER 11

ἐνεῖναι in Plato's *Phaedo*

1. ἐνεῖναι in Anaxagoras

Discussion of μετέχειν and the Anaxagorean context in which Plato found that term leads to a further consideration concerning the development of Socrates' argumentation in the *Phaedo*. Let us revisit some of the fragments of Anaxagoras. Simplicius, our main source, quotes many of the fragments we have more than once. In his commentary on Aristotle's *Physics*, the following three fragments closely follow one another between 164.22 and 165.1 (DK59B11, B12, B6):

ἐν παντὶ παντὸς μοῖρα ἔνεστι πλὴν νοῦ, ἔστιν οἷσι δὲ καὶ νοῦς ἔνι.

In everything there is of everything a share, except of mind, but there are also those \<things\> in which there is also mind.

τὰ μὲν ἄλλα παντὸς μοῖραν μετέχει, νοῦς δέ ἐστιν ἄπειρον καὶ αὐτοκρατὲς καὶ μέμεικται οὐδενὶ χρήματι, ἀλλὰ μόνος αὐτὸς ἐπ' ἑωυτοῦ ἐστιν. εἰ μὴ γὰρ ἐφ' ἑαυτοῦ ἦν, ἀλλά τεωι ἐμέμεικτο ἄλλωι, μετεῖχεν ἂν ἁπάντων χρημάτων, εἰ ἐμέμεικτό τεωι· ἐν παντὶ γὰρ παντὸς μοῖρα ἔνεστιν, ὥσπερ ἐν τοῖς πρόσθεν μοι λέλεκται· καὶ ἂν ἐκώλυεν αὐτὸν τὰ συμμεμειγμένα, ὥστε μηδενὸς χρήματος κρατεῖν ὁμοίως ὡς καὶ μόνον ἐόντα ἐφ' ἑαυτοῦ...
μοῖραι δὲ πολλαὶ πολλῶν εἰσι. παντάπασι δὲ οὐδὲν ἀποκρίνεται οὐδὲ διακρίνεται ἕτερον ἀπὸ τοῦ ἑτέρου πλὴν νοῦ. νοῦς δὲ πᾶς ὅμοιός ἐστι καὶ ὁ μείζων καὶ ὁ ἐλάττων. ἕτερον δὲ οὐδέν ἐστιν ὅμοιον οὐδενί, ἀλλ' ὅτων πλεῖστα ἔνι, ταῦτα ἐνδηλότατα ἓν ἕκαστόν ἐστι καὶ ἦν.

Now as for the other \<things\>, they have a share of everything, but mind is unlimited and self-governing and is mixed with no thing, but alone is itself unto itself. For if it were not unto itself, but mixed with any other \<thing\>, it would have of all things, if it were mixed with any: for in everything there is a share of everything, as was said by me in the foregoing: and the \<things\> mixed with it would have prevented it, so that it would not have ruled any thing in the same way as it \<now\> does, being itself unto itself...
But there are many shares of many things. And altogether nothing is discrete or distinguished one from another except for mind. But all mind is alike, both greater and smaller. But nothing else is alike to anything, but of what there

263

is most in <something ?>, each one individual thing is and was that most clearly.[492]

καὶ ὅτε δὲ ἴσαι μοῖραί εἰσι τοῦ τε μεγάλου καὶ τοῦ σμικροῦ πλῆθος, καὶ οὕτως ἂν εἴη ἐν παντὶ πάντα· οὐδὲ χωρὶς ἔστιν εἶναι, ἀλλὰ πάντα παντὸς μοῖραν μετέχει. ὅτε τοὐλάχιστον μὴ ἔστιν εἶναι, οὐκ ἂν δύναιτο χωρισθῆναι, οὐδ᾽ ἂν ἐφ᾽ ἑαυτοῦ γενέσθαι, ἀλλ᾽ ὅπωσπερ ἀρχὴν εἶναι καὶ νῦν πάντα ὁμοῦ. ἐν πᾶσι δὲ πολλὰ ἔνεστι καὶ τῶν ἀποκρινομένων ἴσα πλῆθος ἐν τοῖς μείζοσί τε καὶ ἐλάσσοσι.

And when there are shares of the big and the small equal in amount, also in that way would there be everything in everything: nor is there 'being separate', but everything has a share of everything. And when there is no 'being the smallest <thing>', it would not be possible to be separated-and-apart, nor to come-to-be unto itself, but just as with respect to its beginning, so also now, everything is together. But in all <things> there are many <things>, and, as regards their number, equal <parts> of what is discrete in the larger and the smaller <things>.[493]

In Anaxagoras, μετέχειν, 'having of', which is μετέχειν μοίραν τινός, 'having a share of something', is said of the things in this world, whatever they are. As already seen, what something has a share of is, anachronistically speaking, corporeal, just as the thing that has a share of something is corporeal. Of the things of which a share can be had, Anaxagoras can also say that 'it is in' that which has a share of it. Fragments B11, B12 and B6 together have half a dozen instances of ἐνεῖναι and εἶναι ἐν. This usage is, of course, also familiar from Fragments B4a and B4b, in which there are altogether another three instances. This language of 'being in', used of the constituents which are ingredients of the other things that 'have a share of' them, befits a material model of the world, in which 'having of' is always 'having a (physical) share of something', and in which 'being in' is thus to be taken literally, that is to say spatially; the share of something is in something else, locally and spatially.[494]

2. ἐνεῖναι in Plato's *Phaedo*

Against this background, it is interesting that Plato avoids any talk of 'being in' between 95e and 102b, the passage in which Socrates deals with earlier natural philosophers, notably Anaxagoras, and introduces his own model of explanation, in which something's 'having of' something else has a certain prominence. Instead of a hypothetical *ἐνουσία, Socrates tentatively speaks of παρουσία at 100d5. This usage proved apposite in the light of Socrates' usage in earlier dialogues, as παρεῖναι, 'being there or by or present', could be said of the virtues and abilities 'of which human beings had', μετέχουσι. In the case of 'having of' or 'sharing in' non-corporeal things like the beautiful, the good and the just, παρουσία and παραγίγνεσθαι is naturally more idiomatic in common Attic than ἐνουσία and ἐνεῖναι, which are in danger of inviting a more literal understanding, which in turn may be suggestive of a material model of explanation.

This interpretation of Plato's usage could perhaps hold its ground, were it not for the sudden introduction of the language of 'being in' at 102b. ἐνεῖναι and εἶναι ἐν then have a function in the final argument for the immortality of the soul from 102b to 106b, a context in which there are over a dozen instances of one or other phrase. The notion of 'being in' forms an essential part of the final argument for the immortality of the soul of the individual.

There are different ways of addressing the introduction of the language of 'being in'. First, it could be seen as a sufficient explanation that, obviously and indeed in a very marked way, 102b forms the start of a new argument. This argument, it has been claimed, introduces the first half of the subtler explanation by Socrates of how and why things are as they are. The subtler explanation is subtler than the simple explanation which says that beautiful things are beautiful through and by the beautiful itself, or through the presence of the beautiful itself, or because they have of the beautiful itself. One of the two additional elements of the subtler explanation, apparently, is a recognition of (the existence of) something in addition to Simmias, supposedly standing for any particular (object, thing or person), and bigness itself, supposedly standing for any Platonic Form (or thing itself): this additional thing is 'Simmias' bigness', which is neither 'bigness itself' nor 'Simmias'. The argument would run: as Plato has just introduced, for the first time explicitly and with an explanation of what he means, Platonic Forms which are eternal and unchanging, a good way of contrasting 'characteristics' or 'qualities' or 'properties' of 'particulars' is: to speak of the Forms as being 'in nature', τὸ ἐν τῇ φύσει, as opposed to the characteristics or properties of particulars which are 'in us', τὸ ἐν ἡμῖν (103b5).[495] If this is so, one can see why Plato would deliberately have withheld any talk of 'being in' prior to 102b: it would have confused an issue on which much depends. It is not the Forms themselves that 'are in' us and in the objects around us: characters which have their names from the Forms 'are in' us and the objects around us. A corollary of this interpretation concerns also usage of μετέχειν and μεταλαμβάνειν as opposed to simple ἔχειν: we and the many things around us 'have of' or 'share in' or 'participate in' the Forms; we do not 'have' the Forms, because Forms do not do or suffer anything; Forms cannot be affected, and, supposedly, if we 'had' a Form it would be thus affected. This explains use of ἔχειν in this sense half a dozen times in this section of the dialogue (102c2, 4, 7; 103b6, e4; 104b4).[496] An additional advantage of an interpretation along those lines is that it goes some way to addressing one of the major concerns raised by Parmenides in the dialogue that bears his name. If it is not the Form that is in the many things, but something other than the Form, there cannot be any question of the Form's having to be divided into parts itself during the process of participation.

If all of that is so, there arises a problem: regardless of the precise ontological status of the Forms in the *Phaedo*, and specifically in this section of the dialogue, 102b–107b, the introduction of Forms in the *Phaedo* is important not only in the context of the dialogue, but also as such: once Forms have been introduced, anybody who is concerned with epistemology or ontology, not only Plato himself, must somehow decide whether the positing of Forms amounts to a good model for an explanation of the world. As this is so, the further distinction between Forms on the one hand and characters or properties on the other, in addition to the many particular things, should therefore likewise be of the highest importance.

But where does Plato come back to this important distinction? One would expect these characters, properties or characteristics to play a prominent part somewhere, be it in the *Symposium*, or if it is judged that the *Symposium* was written simultaneously with or even before the *Phaedo*, so at least in Books 5–7 of the *Republic* or in the *Phaedrus* – wherever Forms are made use of after *Phaedo* 102b–107b, one should hear of particulars, Forms and properties. If Plato's intention at *Phaedo* 102b–107b had been to make claims in parallel with what Aristotle outlines concerning property, genus and accident at *Topics* 1.5.101b35–102b26, one would expect a further discussion of these distinctions at a later stage, quite apart from the question of whether *Topics* 1.5 does or does not presuppose an Aristotelian theory of substance incompatible with the ontology of the *Phaedo*. But Plato does not revisit the distinction which is allegedly introduced here in the *Phaedo*; Socrates does not put forward a similar argument elsewhere. Nor is there any clear link between *Phaedo* 102b–107b and, for example, the earlier discussions of *Meno* 71b and the related *Euthyphro* 11a–b, where the distinction is made between τί ἔστιν,[497] 'what (something) is', and ὁποῖόν τι, 'of what sort (something is)', and where the term πάθος, 'affection', is introduced,[498] a distinction that should be relevant to the present discussion.

3. Socrates' problem at *Phaedo* 102b

I thus propose a different strategy. In order to understand the terminology of the argument that constitutes the final proof of the immortality of the soul, one must first understand the structure of this argument. The structure, however, will become clear not from an analysis starting from the beginning, but from an analysis starting from the end. In outline, it runs thus:

Man need not fear death:

> Because it has been accepted that souls exist before life and that if souls survive death and go to Hades, they will go on from there either back to life or on to better things. (up to 88b8, 95a3)
>
> And soul is immortal and indestructible and, at the death of the man who is mortal, will evade death and go away, and will be and exist in Hades. (106e4–107a1)

> > But the soul is indestructible:
> >
> > > Because it would be silly to think that anything else could escape destruction if that which is immortal, being invisible, could suffer destruction (106d2–4).
> > >
> > > And all would agree that the god and that thing itself which is life and if there is anything else immortal will never perish (106d5–7).
> >
> > And the soul is immortal:
> >
> > > Because there exist the beautiful itself and the good itself and the big itself (100b5–6).
> > >
> > > And a thing is whatever it is by participating or sharing in that itself which really is whatever it is (100b1–102a3).
> > >
> > > And participation in, for example, the big, means that there is 'bigness in us', the bigness we have (102b1–7, 102d5–d9).
> > >
> > > And while we can be big and small, depending on context, the 'bigness in us' will never admit its opposite, smallness (102d5–103a2).
> > >
> > > And because there is a class of things which make whatever they are in have themselves and also necessarily have something else which is an opposite that excludes its opposite (103e2–6, 104b6–104c3, 104e7–106a5).
> > >
> > > > For example, whatever is fire will always be hot and never be cold.
> > > >
> > > > And whatever is snow will always be cold and never be hot.
> > > >
> > > > And if the cold were to approach fire it would either go away or perish (103c9–103e1).
> > > >
> > > > And whatever is three is necessarily also always odd and necessarily never even (103e6–105a1).
> > >
> > > And because soul always brings life to whatever it possesses (105d3–4).
> > >
> > > And because life and death are [mutually exclusive] opposites (105d6–9).

This is not the only interpretation of how the argument is structured, and it is certainly not the only way in which the structure of the argument can be presented. But I shall take this analysis as a point of reference in the hope that it represents fairly the key stages of the final proof. The conclusion, that for which proof and argument are needed, is that 'man need not fear death'. That is Socrates' concern on this day on which he is surrounded by a chorus of inconsolable friends. Everything else is therefore subordinate to the task of removing this fear. Proving the immortality of his, Socrates', soul, is a means to that end.

At this stage, it is useful to look at the ways in which Socrates and his companions in the *Phaedo* had talked about the soul previously. At 67d, philosophers were said by Socrates to be eager to loose (λύειν) the soul from the body and had used the formula, λύσις καὶ χωρισμὸς ψυχῆς ἀπὸ σώματος, 'a loosing and separation of the soul from the body', which could also serve as a definition of death. This could suggest a conjoining of two entities of equal status, something that is also implied in Cebes' objection to Socrates at 88b. At 70c, traditional phraseology and imagery of death and dying are employed when the souls are said 'to be in Hades', ἐν Ἅιδου εἰσὶν αἱ ψυχαί, and 'to be there after having arrived there', ὡς εἰσὶν ἐνθένδε ἀφικόμεναι ἐκεῖ. Similar phrasing is found at 71e and again at 107a, when the final proof is accomplished and Socrates can state that 'the soul is something immortal and indestructible, and our souls really will be in Hades', ψυχὴ ἀθάνατον καὶ ἀνώλεθρον, καὶ τῷ ὄντι ἔσονται ἡμῶν αἱ ψυχαὶ ἐν Ἅιδου. This language which personifies the soul is also found in the context of 73a discussed above, where Cebes uses a phrase potentially connected with mystery religion, saying that recollection is not possible 'if somehow the soul *were* for us before coming to be in this human appearance', εἰ μὴ ἦν που ἡμῖν ἡ ψυχὴ πρὶν ἐν τῷδε τῷ ἀνθρωπίνῳ εἴδει γενέσθαι. This phrase which states that the souls 'are *in* this human appearance' is repeated at 76c, εἶναι ἐν ἀνθρώπου εἴδει. A slightly puzzling image is used at 79e, when Socrates speaks of 'body and soul being in the same', which may be best understood as 'being in the same place': ἐπειδὰν ἐν τῷ αὐτῷ ὦσι ψυχὴ καὶ σῶμα. At last, at 82e, the soul is talked of as 'tied down in the body and glued to it', τὴν ψυχὴν...διαδεδεμένην ἐν τῷ σώματι καὶ προσκεκολλημένην. At 92, this imagery is recalled, when Socrates reminds Cebes that previously the argument from recollection had shown that 'our souls were elsewhere before they were tied down in our body', ἄλλοθι πρότερον ἡμῶν εἶναι τὴν ψυχήν, πρὶν ἐν τῷ σώματι ἐνδεθῆναι.

If proof were needed, it thus appears as if it were part of the common Greek language, and it is certainly part of the usage employed in the discourse on that day, to speak of the soul as 'being *in* the body' while we are alive and 'being *in* Hades' while we are dead. And indeed, the decisive question at the point of proving the immortality of the soul of the individual to the apparent satisfaction of everybody present is this (105c8–10):

ἀποκρίνου δή, ἦ δ' ὅς, ᾧ ἂν τί ἐγγένηται σώματι ζῶν ἔσται;
ᾧ ἂν ψυχή, ἔφη.

Answer then, said he, living will be to whom *what* would come to be in the body?
[i.e.: For somebody to live, *what* is it that must come to be in his body?]
To whom soul would <come to be in the body>, said he.

In the final proof, Socrates has to achieve two things: he has to show that the soul is indeed as close as can be to being immutable and everlasting as are the beautiful itself, the just, the good and all the others. But furthermore, he has to show that, while there are many beautiful things and one other thing, the beautiful itself, many big things and one other thing, bigness itself, many warm things and one other thing, the warm itself, which is manifest in everything warm, but also in every fire – while all this is so, it is not the case that there are many things which are alive and have soul, and *one* life itself and *one* soul itself; because if that were so, Socrates would have shown that life will persist, but he would not have shown that the soul of an individual persists.

Part of the strategy employed by Socrates to prove that there are indeed many individual souls which, each and all of them, continue to exist as individual souls, is to postulate for them the exact opposite of what had been assumed for the items he was primarily interested in, namely the beautiful itself and the just and the good. Far from its being the case that where there are many beautiful things and one thing that is the beautiful itself, and many ensouled things and one thing that is soul itself, Socrates must argue that for all the many big things, there is one bigness itself, but there is also, for each of them, 'their being big', 'the bigness in them' – just as there is, while people are alive, one soul in them. Socrates must then argue that this bigness in them is transitory, because there is nothing to suggest that bigness of any form is either immortal or indestructible: but their soul is not transitory, because it is immortal and indestructible.

Viewed in this way, it becomes apparent that, in order to prove the immortality of the soul of the individual, Socrates had to invent 'bigness in us'. The way Socrates proves individual immortality makes it *necessary* for him to postulate 'bigness in us'. But because Plato does not make use of the concept of 'bigness in us' later, we are entitled to say that the context of the final proof of the immortality of the soul of the individual is also a *sufficient* explanation for the presence of this concept in the *Phaedo*. There *are* no 'immanent characters' or 'immanent forms' or 'properties' besides the many beautiful things and beauty itself in the *Phaedo*.

The language of 'being in' was introduced at 102b *because* the soul is in the body. It could be introduced because it naturally occurred in the vicinity of the language of 'having of' in Anaxagoras and in Diogenes of Apollonia, where those physical things of which something had a share were in the things which had a share of them. The transition from 102b to 105c, on the other hand, was facilitated by the fact that 'being in' and 'coming to be in' were used as technical terms in the Hippocratic corpus, where a disease was regularly said to 'come to be in' a body. This is exactly what Socrates himself says at 105c. Against that, the phrasing that 'something, for example oneness, comes to be in an amount so that the amount comes to be odd', is distinctly contrived and created for the purpose of this argument.

As regards, on the other hand, the distinction pointed to above, between μετέχειν which is used up to 102b and ἔχειν which is used thereafter, it is worth bearing in mind an observation of Aristotle's at *Metaphysics* Δ 23 (1023a8–25):

τὸ ἔχειν λέγεται πολλαχῶς, ἕνα μὲν τρόπον τὸ ἄγειν κατὰ τὴν αὑτοῦ φύσιν ἢ κατὰ τὴν αὑτοῦ ὁρμήν, διὸ λέγεται πυρετός τε ἔχειν τὸν ἄνθρωπον καὶ οἱ τύραννοι τὰς πόλεις καὶ τὴν ἐσθῆτα οἱ ἀμπεχόμενοι· ἕνα δ' ἐν ᾧ ἄν τι ὑπάρχῃ ὡς δεκτικῷ, οἷον ὁ χαλκὸς ἔχει τὸ εἶδος τοῦ ἀνδριάντος καὶ τὴν νόσον τὸ σῶμα· ἕνα δὲ ὡς τὸ περιέχον τὰ περιεχόμενα· ἐν ᾧ γάρ ἐστι περιέχοντι, ἔχεσθαι ὑπὸ τούτου λέγεται, οἷον τὸ ἀγγεῖον ἔχειν τὸ ὑγρόν φαμεν καὶ τὴν πόλιν ἀνθρώπους καὶ τὴν ναῦν ναύτας, οὕτω δὲ καὶ τὸ ὅλον ἔχειν τὰ μέρη. ἔτι τὸ κωλῦον κατὰ τὴν αὑτοῦ ὁρμήν τι κινεῖσθαι ἢ πράττειν ἔχειν λέγεται τοῦτο αὐτό, οἷον καὶ οἱ κίονες τὰ ἐπικείμενα βάρη, καὶ ὡς οἱ ποιηταὶ τὸν Ἄτλαντα ποιοῦσι τὸν οὐρανὸν ἔχειν ὡς συμπεσόντ' ἂν ἐπὶ τὴν γῆν, ὥσπερ καὶ τῶν φυσιολόγων τινές φασιν· τοῦτον δὲ τὸν τρόπον καὶ τὸ συνέχον λέγεται ἃ συνέχει ἔχειν, ὡς διαχωρισθέντα ἂν κατὰ τὴν αὑτοῦ ὁρμήν ἕκαστον. καὶ τὸ ἔν τινι δὲ εἶναι ὁμοτρόπως λέγεται καὶ ἑπομένως τῷ ἔχειν.

'To have' means many things. (1) To treat a thing according to one's own nature or according to one's own impulse, so that fever is said to have a man, and tyrants to have their cities, and people to have the clothes they wear. (2) That in which a thing is present as in something receptive is said to have a thing, e.g. the bronze has the form of the statue, and the body has the disease. (3) As that which contains has that which is contained; for a thing is said to be had by that in which it is contained, e.g. we say that the vessel has the liquid and the city has men and the ship sailors; and so too that the whole has the parts. (4) That which hinders a thing from moving or acting according to its own impulse is said to have it, as pillars have the incumbent weights, and as the poets make Atlas have the heavens, implying that otherwise they would collapse on the earth, as some of the natural philosophers also say. In this way that which holds things together is said to have the things it holds together, since they would otherwise separate, each according to its own impulse. 'Being in something' has similar and corresponding meanings to 'having'. (tr. Ross)[499]

With this, one may compare the discussion of 'being in' at *Physics*

210a14–24:[500]

μετὰ δὲ ταῦτα ληπτέον ποσαχῶς ἄλλο ἐν ἄλλῳ λέγεται. ἕνα μὲν δὴ τρόπον ὡς ὁ δάκτυλος ἐν τῇ χειρὶ καὶ ὅλως τὸ μέρος ἐν τῷ ὅλῳ. ἄλλον δὲ ὡς τὸ ὅλον ἐν τοῖς μέρεσιν· οὐ γάρ ἐστι παρὰ τὰ μέρη τὸ ὅλον. ἄλλον δὲ τρόπον ὡς ὁ ἄνθρωπος ἐν ζῴῳ καὶ ὅλως εἶδος ἐν γένει. ἄλλον δὲ ὡς τὸ γένος ἐν τῷ εἴδει καὶ ὅλως τὸ μέρος τοῦ εἴδους ἐν τῷ λόγῳ. ἔτι ὡς ἡ ὑγίεια ἐν θερμοῖς καὶ ψυχροῖς καὶ ὅλως τὸ εἶδος ἐν τῇ ὕλῃ. ἔτι ὡς ἐν βασιλεῖ τὰ τῶν Ἑλλήνων καὶ ὅλως ἐν τῷ πρώτῳ κινητικῷ. ἔτι ὡς ἐν τῷ ἀγαθῷ καὶ ὅλως ἐν τῷ τέλει· τοῦτο δ' ἐστὶ τὸ οὗ ἕνεκα. πάντων δὲ κυριώτατον τὸ ὡς ἐν ἀγγείῳ καὶ ὅλως ἐν τόπῳ.

Next we must find in how many ways one thing is said to be in another. (1) In one way, as the finger is in the hand, and, generally, the part in the whole. (2) In another, as the whole is in the parts – the whole does not exist apart from the parts. (3) In another, as man is in animal and, generally, species in genus. (4) In another, as the genus is in the species and, generally, the part of the species in the definition. (5) In another, as health is in hot and cold things and, generally, as the form is in the matter. (6) In another, as the affairs of Greece are in the king [of Persia], and, generally, as things are in the first thing productive of change. (7) In another, as a thing is in its good, and, generally, in its end (that is, the that-for-the-sake-of-which). (8) And – most properly of all so called – as a thing is in a vessel, and, generally, in a place.

(tr. Morison, lightly adapted from Hussey)[501]

The collocation of these two texts in this context is useful in more ways than one. There is, as is suggested by the closing statement of *Metaphysics* Δ 23, an overlap in examples of subjects and objects connected by 'to have' and subjects and 'complements' connected by 'to be in'. And while there is no direct parallel in the *Physics* passage, the *Metaphysics* passage conveniently speaks of 'a disease's being in a body'. Most of all, however, for the present purpose, and leaving aside all philosophical intentions which Aristotle may have had in addition to describing and comparing language, his explicit comparison between the usage of 'having' and of 'being in' shows the following: at *Phaedo* 102b–107b, when Plato uses the language and terminology of 'being in', he may naturally move from verbs expressing this notion to 'having', without intending anything of philosophical importance. But this is to say that use of ἔχειν at this place in the *Phaedo* is determined by use of ἐνεῖναι and εἶναι ἐν. And this in turn is to say that use of ἔχειν here need not, in the first place, be determined by use of μετέχειν in the previous section of the dialogue. All this, of course, does not mean that Plato could not have intended a contrast between ἔχειν and μετέχειν as desired by the interpreters: but if he had, he would have marked it, as he does, for example, when he wants to distinguish between διά τι and ἕνεκά του at *Lysis* 218d ff. As in English, 'because of' and 'for the sake of' are in danger of being used interchangeably in colloquial contexts, as is certainly the case with 'wherefore' and 'why'. (Or perhaps one should say: colloquially, 'because of' and 'why' do the work of 'because of' and 'for the sake of' and 'why' and 'wherefore', respectively.) As Plato is aware of the lack of precision of colloquial usage, he takes great care in establishing the distinction. It is thus reasonable to assume that had he intended to establish a philosophically significant distinction between μετέχειν and ἔχειν at 102b–107b, he would have drawn this to the reader's attention, rather than smuggling in an odd ἔχειν in a passage difficult enough in other respects.[502]

Mutatis mutandis, this reading also contributes in a small way to a solution of the problem of εἶδος, μορφή and ἰδέα. The puzzle was: why does Plato introduce εἶδος at 102b for 'Forms', and why does he subsequently use εἶδος and μορφή and ἰδέα, apparently interchangeably for 'character' or 'property', but not μορφή and ἰδέα for 'Form', given that while μορφή is not used after the *Phaedo* at all as a term of Plato's ontology, ἰδέα, as ἰδέα τοῦ ἀγαθοῦ, will come to be used for the greatest and most important of the 'Forms': If the distinction between 'in nature' and 'in us' is to some extent contrived and not necessarily intended to refer to any real distinctions in this context, it is less obvious that one must resolve all the inconsistencies between 102b and 107b, regardless of whether they are real or apparent inconsistencies in the first place. One possible reason for the presence of inconsistencies in *this* part of the dialogue is that Socrates' task to move from rational argument to persuasion is severely hampered by the circumstance that the final argument for the immortality and indestructibility of the soul of the individual will be persuasive only to those who have not followed the previous arguments to their logical conclusions; and Socrates must prevent his immediate audience from discovering that.

To conclude this section on ἐνεῖναι in the *Phaedo*, it may be observed that neither here nor elsewhere[503] is ἐνεῖναι a technical term of Plato's ontology, neither in the strong sense, in which εἶδος and ἰδέα are technical terms here and in subsequent dialogues, nor in the weak sense, in which μετέχειν and παρουσία may, with the necessary qualifications, be called technical terms in the *Phaedo*.

RETROSPECT

At this point, a brief retrospect may be in order. We set out to investigate Plato's philosophical terminology in the *Phaedo*, with a focus on the verbs μετέχειν and ἐνεῖναι and the nouns εἶδος, ἰδέα, μορφή, οὐσία, παρουσία, κοινωνία. In the course of tracing the history of these words in pre-Platonic Greek literature and in Plato's dialogues up to and including the *Phaedo*, two things have become apparent. First, the terms selected have entered Plato's vocabulary from a number of disparate sources; but as far as could be determined, all the sources of immediate relevance to an explanation of the presence of these terms are philosophical in nature. Common language is always in the background; literature and literary stylistics play a role in the semantic development of common as well as technical terms; technical treatises like those of the medical writers have advanced Greek language and thought in general; but the terms that appear as philosophical terms in the *Phaedo* have been adopted by Plato because they were already part of established philosophical terminologies. Even Plato's own coinage, οὐσία, 'what something *is*', has its antecedent in a specific philosophical usage. And παρουσία and παρεῖναι, the two related terms which do not figure in a major way in Presocratic Philosophy, were all the same part of Sophistic vocabulary and had as such been adopted by Socrates in the early dialogues, something that was, of course, also true of μετέχειν in its ethical application.

On the other hand, the terms selected can be said to represent a philosophical terminology of Plato's to varying degrees. μετέχειν, εἶδος, ἰδέα and οὐσία may perhaps lay greater claim to being part of a core terminology of Plato's ontology than the remaining ones. But we have seen that the role of μετέχειν is closely confined. And it has often been observed that the application of εἶδος, and eventually also that of ἰδέα, shift significantly in subsequent dialogues, especially after the *Republic*. The most constant of the terms discussed is the one that is to the greatest extent Plato's own creation, οὐσία, 'what something is'. It is the only term whose development accommodates at each stage what is most central to Plato's view of what the world *is*.

CONCLUSION

Philosophy and language in Plato's *Phaedo*

Central to Plato's *Phaedo* is a new explanation of the world which surrounds us. And central to this explanation is a conviction that what we do is determined by what is good, what is beautiful, what is just, and not by the physical make-up of our bodies, or the physical constituents making up these bodies. This is extended to an explanation of the world as a whole: as is true for us, so also otherwise, what something *is* cannot be explained by having recourse to physical ingredients or constituents. What something is, the οὐσία of a thing, is the central notion in Plato's explanation of the world. Plato developed this concept of οὐσία in response to the notion of ἐστώ which he had encountered in Philolaus. In Philolaus, and one may assume also with other Pythagoreans, 'what something *is*' is seen in oppositions like 'odd' and 'even', 'limit' and 'unlimited', etc. 'There are two types of thing, odd and even, limit and unlimited, etc.' The types, the εἴδη, determine what a thing is. Plato accepts the notion of 'type' as an explanatory factor. Against Philolaus and the Pythagoreans, however, he insists that those types are, on the one hand, not pairs of opposites. Rather, those 'types' are 'the good', 'the beautiful', 'the just', etc., but not 'the bad', etc.[504] On the other hand, whatever the ontological status of the Pythagorean 'types', Plato insists that what determines the world is non-corporeal and immutable, always the same as itself, and accessible not to the senses but to the mind alone. Some of these qualifications, being invisible, always the same, non-composite, etc., Plato also found in the very different, materialist and deterministic explanation of the world offered in the atomistic system of Democritus. One of the names Democritus had given to his atoms was ἰδέαι. Plato adopted the term ἰδέα from Democritus, just as he had adopted the term εἶδος from Philolaus. While the εἶδος of Philolaus had the advantage of having been applied already in the Pythagorean's system to approximately the sort of thing Plato thought offered an explanation of the world, possibly including 'the just' and 'the good', the system of Democritus had the advantage of being more rigorously argued. In particular, Democritus, in explaining the world, employed the concept of 'explanation', αἰτία. This was a huge conceptual advance over all the previous natural philosophies which knew the concept

275

of ἀρχή, 'beginning', but treated whatever was regarded as ἀρχή at once as starting point, as underlying ingredient and, implicitly, as explanatory factor. The atomism of Leucippus and Democritus knew of ingredients *and* explanations. Plato adopted the concept of explanation, and he also adopted one of the terms Democritus had used for his ultimate constituents, ἰδέα. Like Democritus', Plato's ultimate ingredients of the world were always the same, non-composite, invisible and therefore accessible only to thinking: but they were not corporeal: they were 'the good', 'the beautiful', 'the just', etc. Adoption of the term ἰδέα had the additional advantage that ἰδέα was in other contexts synonymous with εἶδος. Having adopted εἶδος as a term for his explanatory 'determining' factors from Philolaus, adoption of ἰδέα allowed Plato a fusion of notions from philosophical systems of disparate provenance. While the 'types' of Philolaus may have been non-corporeal, and while Democritus thought in terms of constituents on the one hand, explanation as something distinct on the other, Democritean atomism was both materialistic and, from Plato's point of view, deterministic: the way in which Leucippus and Democritus employed the notion of 'necessity', ἀνάγκη, meant that they did not offer a true explanation at all. A true explanation is an explanation in terms of what is good. Such an explanation could, in principle, have been provided by Anaxagoras or by Diogenes of Apollonia, who in some respects followed Anaxagoras. Anaxagoras had introduced the notion of νοῦς, 'mind', as setting in motion things in a world in which everything else was mixed, in which there was a part of every-thing *in* everything, and everything had a share in everything, apart from 'mind', which was 'itself unto itself'. Plato, who had adopted the notion of something's being 'itself by itself', αὐτὸ καθ᾽ αὑτό, from Parmenides, found in Anaxagoras' system the equivalent ἐφ᾽ ἑαυτοῦ, side by side with the notion of 'having of' or 'sharing', μετέχειν. But in Plato's system, this 'having of' was not a having by everything of everything; nor was 'mind', by Anaxagoras said to be 'by itself', for Plato a fine material substance, as it had been for Anaxagoras. In Plato's system, what is referred to as 'itself by itself' are the ultimate constituents of the world, the εἴδη or ἰδέαι, which do not change. We and the many things around us 'share' in these ultimate ingredients, but not by having a part of them. Our 'having of' the good, the beautiful, the just, etc., is rather to be seen as in parallel with our 'having of' understanding, excellence and whatever is good and beautiful; one may also think in terms of the 'presence', παρουσία, of the good and the beautiful.[505] However, such terminological matters are ultimately of secondary impor-tance. The words Plato uses disappear behind the ideas.

What we are left with is an entirely new system of explanation of the world. In the *Phaedo*, Plato has taken on board whatever could be used of the conceptual apparatus of the three most powerful systems of explanation on offer in his time. The system of Philolaus perhaps came closest to thinking in non-corporeal terms, but in its boldness was restricted by old-fashioned patterns of thought and potentially hampered by an underlying mysticism.[506] The system of Anaxagoras set mind against the rest of the world and explained the many things in terms of the nature of their ingredients, but remained a thoroughly corporeal and materialist explanation all the same. The system of Democritus, while conceptually the most advanced, was at the same time more explicitly materialist and deterministic than any other. None of these Presocratic systems is untouched by Parmenides, and Plato implicitly acknowledges this Eleatic background, too. By adopting and adapting terminology from his predecessors, Plato remoulds the concepts he encounters and forges them to fit his own explanation, at the beginning of which stands the notion of 'what something *is*'.

If this is accepted as a picture of what Plato was doing, there is an important implication for our reading the dialogues. When we, as modern readers, encounter terms like εἶδος, ἰδέα, μορφή, παρουσία, μετέχειν and ἐνεῖναι, we must not in the first place ask the frequently raised questions:
What is it in the *word* εἶδος that made Plato choose it for his Forms?
What is the significance of the root *u̯id-, behind both εἶδος and ἰδέα, as referring to both 'sight' and 'knowledge'?
What is the precise relation that is expressed by μετέχειν, and to what extent are μετέχειν, παρεῖναι and ἐνεῖναι compatible in the first place?
Do μετέχειν and ἐνεῖναι express rival models and different types of relationships between forms and particulars?
To what extent is the notion of μετέχειν succeeded and superseded by that of ἐνεῖναι?
Was Plato aware of the differences between the ontological or metaphysical models implied by these terms, or was he, on the contrary, misled by his own usage?

Such questions may address important issues. But they are, for all we can tell, *Plato's* questions only to the extent that Plato himself builds on the terms in question, and to the extent he himself lets any conclusions depend on an interpretation (of the implications) of this terminology. But the only point at which one could suspect that this is indeed the case is the *Parmenides*, and that dialogue is best understood as Plato's playful exploration of what would happen if one were to seek for the meaning of for example the *Phaedo* not in what the dialogue does as a whole, but in the meaning and the possible implications of some of the technical terms employed in that dialogue *if* these terms are taken in isolation.

In reading the *Phaedo*, one should rather focus on what Plato has achieved in philosophical terms. At a time in which the most advanced systems of thought operated with models that explained the physical world, generation and corruption, in terms of the combination of its ingredients, Plato, possibly taking his cue from some philosophers in Magna Graecia whose views were, at the time, not necessarily central to speculation in Athens and the rest of Greece, posits that 'what *is*' can only be explained with recourse to a completely different sort of reality. To explain 'what *is*', one must accept that the physical, corporeal world cannot be explained by and through itself. An explanation of the physical, corporeal world can only be achieved with reference to non-corporeal constants. This paradigm-shift had, of course, been prepared by a number of features of some of the systems of the Presocratic philosophers and the Hippocratic writers. But it was Plato who established in the *Phaedo* the contrast between the world of stuff, the 'bodily', τὸ σωματοειδές, and the world of thought. This contrast in approach and in philosophical model is made explicit in the *Sophist* (246a), where the mythical image of generations expresses in allegorical manner the absolute novelty of the new world-view. This paradigm-shift, the explicit positing of something non-corporeal, is so fundamental to any subsequent thought that, by the time of Aristotle's teaching and writing, it had become inconceivable that things could be otherwise, that there should not be stuff and something else. More relevant to a modern discussion is that no modern reader of Plato operates outside the Platonic paradigm of the opposition of corporeal and non-corporeal. For this reason, much of what Plato carefully constructs in the *Phaedo* appears utterly trivial and elementary to many modern interpreters. But what appears most elementary, the beginnings of logical and scientific explanation, was most important at the time. The problems, on the other hand, which are posed by Plato's technical terminology, by the terms εἶδος, ἰδέα, μορφή, μετέχειν and ἐνεῖναι, are of no importance to Plato's thought. The reason these technical terms are employed is that they were technical terms in previous philosophical systems, useful to the extent that they could be stepping stones for those whom Plato addressed. Any author who intends to communicate his thoughts can only ever hope to succeed if, to some degree, he speaks the language of his audience, and a study of Plato's technical terms is useful to the degree to which it sheds light on the shared assumptions against which Plato introduces his radically different view of what *is*.

NOTES

Preface and Introduction

[1] Though our arguments are not the same, I find myself, on *this* point, in agreement with Kahn 1996, 335 f.

[2] Doubtless, this list is not exhaustive, and doubtless it allows for many permutations. But it does contain the major cases which we shall encounter in this investigation.

[3] The Greek word ἐπωνυμία, as used by Plato, can express both the process of 'bestowing a name upon something' and the result, the 'designation', 'appellation' or 'name' which a thing has once it has been named. The now obsolete verb 'bename', which was in active use in the 16th and early 17th centuries, could mean 'to declare solemnly', 'to name' and 'to describe as', and thus captures the various aspects of ἐπωνυμία. With this in mind, one may coin the term 'a benaming' to translate the Greek noun ἐπωνυμία. The prefix ἐπ- had in many respects the same force that the English prefix be- could have until recently; cf. e.g. the Hippocratic treatise *Airs, Waters, and Places*, sec. 13, discussed in Part II, ch. 4, sec. 7, p. 117 below; there, the correlatives ἔφυδρος and ἄνυδρος could be translated as 'be-watered' and 'un-watered' respectively.

[4] The outmoded term 'congener' is used here for the sake of brevity: the other words discussed are almost all etymologically closely related to the terms listed in the text; but in some cases the link is more one of semantics than of etymology.

[5] Among the large number of studies specifically concerned with Plato's vocabulary and terminology, the following deserve particular mention (in chronological order): Ast, F., 1835–8; Campbell, L., 1894; Vailati, G., 1906; Ritter, C., 1910; Taylor, A.E., 1911; Shorey, P., 1911; Gillespie, C.M., 1912; Baldry, H.C., 1937; v. Fritz, K., 1938; Else, G.F., 1938; Brommer, P., 1940; Ross, D., 1951; Diller, H., 1952; Classen, C.J., 1959; Marten, R., 1962; Diller, H., 1964; des Places, É., 1964; Meinhardt, H., 1968; Diller, H., 1971; Sandoz, C., 1972; Fujisawa, N., 1974; Meinhardt, H., 1976; with references to recent literature, the relevant lemmata in Horn, C., and Rapp, C. (eds.) 2002; Motte, A., Rutten, C., Somville, P. (eds.), 2003. Cf. the summary in Kahn, C.H., 1996.

[6] An example is the treatment of the figure of Electra, the daughter of Agamemnon, by the three 5th-century tragedians Aeschylus, Sophocles and Euripides; Aeschylus' *Libation Bearers* is the earliest extant play by any of the three in which Electra makes an appearance; the chronology of Sophocles' and Euripides' Electra plays is a matter of debate; but that does not take away from the usefulness of these texts for a case study of the interaction between one ancient author and one *or more* others; this may serve as a paradigm of how Plato in the 4th century would have read, and how he would have interacted with, works of his predecessors.

[7] Aristotle's early discussions of οὐσία, a philosophical term of Plato's creation, are a case in point.

[8] For some recent discussion, with extensive bibliography, see the chapters by C. Kahn and C.L. Griswold in Annas and Rowe, 2002, 93–144.

⁹ For a recent discussion and arguments for the late date of 424 BC, see Nails 2002, 243–50.

¹⁰ These general remarks may seem excessively vague. But they are not empty, and meant as an indication that my approach to Plato is neither 'unitarian' nor 'developmentalist'/'revisionist'.

¹¹ Usage of the tag αὐτός/αὐτή/αὐτό to single out something and isolate it from its context is itself old and familiar from earlier Greek literature. Cf. e.g. Herodotus 1.214.11–13: ἥ τε δὴ πολλὴ τῆς Περσικῆς στρατιῆς αὐτοῦ ταύτῃ διεφθάρη καὶ δὴ καὶ αὐτὸς Κῦρος τελευτᾷ, βασιλεύσας τὰ πάντα ἑνὸς δέοντα τριήκοντα ἔτεα. 'And thus the largest part of his Persian army perished there, and also Cyrus himself died, having been king for altogether 29 years.' Much of Cyrus' army, which somehow belongs to Cyrus, perished, but so did Cyrus himself. At 1.62.6, Thucydides offers an account of the battle between the Peloponnesians under Aristeus and the Athenians and their allies: καὶ αὐτὸ μὲν τὸ τοῦ Ἀριστέως κέρας καὶ ὅσοι περὶ ἐκεῖνον ἦσαν Κορινθίων τε καὶ τῶν ἄλλων λογάδες ἔτρεψαν τὸ καθ' ἑαυτοὺς καὶ ἐπεξῆλθον διώκοντες ἐπὶ πολύ. 'Both the wing of Aristeus itself and those of the Corinthians and the others who were around him routed those who were opposite them and, pursuing them, went after them for a considerable time.' Here, many of the Peloponnesians are under Aristeus' command, but his own contingent is more closely connected with him than are the nearby contingents of allies, who, however, are also 'around him', περὶ ἐκεῖνον. Thucydides describes a campaign by Pericles in 430 BC. He sends Athenian troops and some allies, army and cavalry, by sea to the Peloponnese; having destroyed a number of other places, they arrive at Prasia in Laconian territory (2.56.6): καὶ τῆς τε γῆς ἔτεμον καὶ αὐτὸ τὸ πόλισμα εἷλον καὶ ἐπόρθησαν. 'And they devastated the land ['partitive genitive'] and took the city itself and destroyed it.' The land belongs to the city; it is destroyed, and so is the city itself. For a relevant example in a Platonic dialogue commonly regarded as pre-dating the *Phaedo*, see *Euthyphro* 5d (*bis*); there, the reflexive pronoun depends, in both cases, on an adjective meaning same or similar, respectively. Otherwise, the usage of the *Phaedo* regarding αὐτό is prepared in the earlier dialogues by the frequently recurring phrase (τὸ) αὐτὸ τοῦτο, often translated 'this very thing/matter', a phrase which is common Attic usage; it can be employed either to approve emphatically or to single out an object under discussion.

¹² For a detailed discussion of these issues, see Herrmann 2004.

¹³ In Greek, τι εἶναι ἴσον means 'something is equal' and 'equal is something'; this, together with a certain fluidity in the use of the definite article with either the subject of the predicate noun in definitional questions and statements, often causes difficulties for translations into languages with fixed word order; Plato shows some awareness of a possible ambiguity for example in the *Theaetetus* in definitions of ἐπιστήμη or 'knowledge'. On *Phaedo* 74a, cf. Rowe 1993, 167.

¹⁴ It seems to me that 64c7 f., χωρὶς δὲ τὴν ψυχὴν ἀπὸ τοῦ σώματος ἀπαλλαγεῖσαν αὐτὴν καθ' αὑτὴν εἶναι, 'and in the soul having been parted from the body, and being by itself' (tr. Hackforth 1955, 44), is an interpolation, added in the light of subsequent pages, especially 67d.

¹⁵ Cf., parallel to the example from the *Protagoras*, also *Gorgias* 496d2, 522e1.

¹⁶ For detailed discussion of the problems inherent in this, cf. Ebert 2004, 210–15.

¹⁷ For discussion of various possibilities, see e.g. Gallop 1975, 121–5.

¹⁸ For discussion in the commentaries, cf. e.g. Wyttenbach 1825, 187; Geddes 1863,

50 f.; Archer-Hind 1883, 80 f.; succinctly Fearenside and Kerin 1897, 98; Williamson 1904, 145; at his befuddled best apodictically Burnet 1911, 56; Hackforth 1955, 69 n. 2; Bluck 1955, 67 n. 3; comprehensive as usual is Gallop 1975, 121–5; Bostock 1986, 78–85; Rowe 1993, 169 f., who stresses rightly that '*Parmenides* 129b αὐτὰ τὰ ὅμοια offers no help with the present passage, since it raises identical problems of interpretation'; in addition, cf. the article by Annette Teffeteller Dale 1987, 'αὐτὰ τὰ ἴσα, *Phaedo* 74c1: a philological perspective', with pertinent bibliography.

[19] The further possibility, proposed by Dale 1987, that the phrase αὐτὰ τὰ ἴσα is not really plural at all, but had retained, even in 5th- and 4th-century Greek, its original (proto-Indo-European) force of a collective or generic (case-*cum*-number), so that it would be not so much a logical as in the first place a linguistic variant to the neuter singular αὐτὸ τὸ ἴσον, can be disregarded. Dale's explanation that 'the relative infrequency of generic/abstract neuter plurals in the Platonic corpus indicates merely that the singular was increasingly becoming the preferred form, owing in part, perhaps, to the progressive reinterpretation of the old mass noun as a true plural and doubtless in part to the ubiquitous 5th-century use of the singular neuter *article* in forming abstract substantives at will from adjectives, participles and verbs' (Dale 1987, 395) can satisfy only in part: if it is true that the collective/generic/abstract force of the old -α forms is still part of the living language in Plato's *Phaedo*, that would explain why the phrase αὐτὰ τὰ ἴσα is permissible, i.e. why there is no need to change the text of the manuscript tradition. This linguistic explanation would not explain why Plato should resort to the 'plural'-phrase after having used 'the singular neuter *article* in forming abstract substantives…from adjectives' at both 65d and 74a. While it is not impossible that Plato used two variants, viz. the plural phrase under discussion and the noun ἰσότης, for the sake of variation, one would assume that his purpose cannot have been to confuse, and that on the other hand, there should be a purpose outweighing the fact that variation in diction at this difficult point in a new argument inevitably introduces at least the potential for confusion.

[20] Forcefully argued by Hoffmann 1923, 1–13 = 1964, 53–64 (my references are to the reprint); cf. esp. 55–7; Hoffmann adduces Proclus, *In Parmenidem* 694 ff., quoted by Diels (Zeno, DK29[19]A15), as not providing information beyond the dialogue *Parmenides*, but adds Proclus 618.30 ff., not mentioned by Diels, as containing information beyond what is reported in Plato's dialogue. This led me to 632.6–15 and 788.29–31 in addition to 619.30–620.1, all discussed in the text below. John Dillon 1987, apparently unaware of Hoffmann, arrives at the same conclusions, both as regards Proclus' Parmenides-commentary as independent evidence for Zeno and as regards the pair 'equal–unequal' as originally Zenonian. Dillon's arguments are set out in section D of his 'General Introduction' (1987, xxxviii–xliii); while he does not there list 632.6–15 among the passages indicating Proclus' having knowledge of Zeno beyond what can be gleaned from Plato's dialogue, he does have a reference to section D of the Introduction in a footnote to the translation of 632.6–15 (1987, 30).

[21] It should be noted that the phrase αὐτὰ τὰ ἴσα occurs a few lines into the argument that runs from 74a9–75d6; other expressions are used in the remainder of the argument side by side with the simple τὸ ἴσον and αὐτὸ τὸ ἴσον; while this may just point to flexibility in expression or lack of a fixed technical terminology, those other phrases, containing the tag ὃ ἔστιν, 'what is', *do* recur, in similar or identical from, in the *Phaedo* and in other dialogues in relevant philosophical contexts.

[22] This is plausible on the assumption that by the time Plato wrote the *Phaedo* the first two paradoxical 'hypotheses' of Zeno's were indeed well known in the select circles that constituted the potential audience and readership of the *Phaedo*. For Zeno's book, cf. also Part I, ch. 1, n. 34 below.

[23] Note that Bostock 1986, 82, suggests that Plato wrote or thought originally:…αὐτὸ τὸ ἴσα…and that this phrase was later adjusted; something like this could be demanded also in the case of a quotation from Zeno's treatise; but that would presuppose that the tag αὐτό in the neuter singular had become a fixed term no longer subject to syntactical modification already at this point in the *Phaedo*. This is not so; rather, because of the *Phaedo*, usage of αὐτό can later develop in that direction.

[24] Solmsen 1971. Solmsen's contribution remains valuable overall even if one does not agree with his judgement in all points of detail. Neither the text of the *Symposium* passage nor all of Solmsen's examples need reproducing here. Cf. also Teloh 1981, esp. 89–91, 233, n. 46, with references to earlier discussions; and Kahn 1996, 340–5.

[25] Solmsen 1971, 67 f.; translations added are mine.

[26] For present purposes it is irrelevant that the actual connections between all concerned are quite different from what they seem at this point.

[27] Cf. also *Lysis* 220c.

[28] For discussion of these fragments see also below, Part III, ch. 10, sec. 3: μετέχειν in the world of Anaxagoras.

[29] See below, Part III, ch. 10, sec. 3: μετέχειν in the world of Anaxagoras.

[30] For discussion of Vancamp 1996, see below, Part III, ch. 7, sec. 4: οὐσία in Plato's *Phaedo*: 78c–d, 92c.

[31] Cases of this sort could be multiplied. For example, *Phaedo* 72a–b, part of the conclusion of the so-called cyclical argument, contains an allusion to Anaximander, prepared by the unusual and unparalleled expression ἰδὲ…οὐδ' ἀδίκως ὡμολογήκαμεν… 'consider…whether we have agreed without justification…', which is followed by the legal verb ἀνταποδιδόναι, 'paying recompense', in the context of coming-to-be and passing away, or generation and destruction; the fragmentary nature of the evidence does not allow us to assess the extent to which Plato's image draws on Anaximander or indeed others in addition; but cf. Stokes 1976, 13, who, however, in making the connection between *Phaedo* 72a–b and Anaximander, considers the possibility that Plato was committed to a similar world-view rather than that he *alludes* to Anaximander without necessarily himself being committed to the argument. The case cannot be done full justice in this context.

[32] For this distinction and a good discussion of pertinent examples, cf. Vailati 1906.

[33] There is a wide-spread view that this concern is misconceived. Kahn 1996, 335, invoking Ross 1951, esp. 13–16, as authority, writes in his interpretation of Plato's Theory of Forms: 'The pre-Platonic usage of these terms [*eidos* and *idea*] has been fully studied, and there is no need to return to the subject here.' Only the results will show whether a fresh investigation is justified.

Chapter 1

[34] From this introduction, together with the summary of the first argument and the subsequent exchange between Socrates and Zeno, we learn something interesting about the structure of the book by Zeno: it was divided into sections, each of which, presumably, started with a proposition which expressed or implied the contradictory of one of

the predicates Parmenides had given to 'being' in the first part of his poem, and that this proposition was followed by a *reductio ad absurdum*. This is in tune with what we learn about Zeno from Diogenes Laertius (8.57, 9.25), namely that Aristotle said that Zeno 'invented dialectic'; if there is any truth in the story, Aristotle may *inter alia* have referred to the structure of Zeno's argument: if A, then B and C; but B and C are contradictory; therefore not A. The text of *Parmenides* 127d, however, suggests that in addition to that, Zeno may actually have called the various propositions he set out to refute ' ὑποθέσεις', which is in itself not implausible; Zeno's paradoxes were treated and solved as 'mathematical' puzzles; and when Socrates introduces his method of ὑπόθεσις explicitly (*Meno* 86e ff.), he illustrates it with a mathematical example. When Parmenides later on refers to Zeno's demonstration, he as well uses both the verb ὑποτίθεσθαι and the noun ὑπόθεσις (135e8 ff.), and his own exercises which make up the rest of the dialogue are referred to as ὑποθέσεις. This could, of course, be the language of Plato, superimposed on the arguments of the Eleatic visitors (so e.g. Robinson 1953, 97), but whether or not Plato in the *Parmenides* reflects original Zenonian usage when he designates propositions whose discussion leads to ἀπορία as ὑποθέσεις, the dialogue helps explain how Zeno could have come to be seen as the inventor of dialectic. (But cf. Barnes 1982, 231–7, esp. 236; and also Schofield 1996, 1634; and see Coxon 1999, 125.) But while Zeno's concept of dialectic differs from that advocated by Socrates in the *Meno* (75d), Parmenides proceeds dialectically in the Socratic sense when he talks to the young man Socrates in Plato's *Parmenides*. The same schema that underlies Zeno's ὑπόθεσις, as well as the ὑποθέσεις of Parmenides in the second half of the dialogue, is also employed by Parmenides in his conversation with Socrates (131a–134e).

[35] In the phrase εἶδός τι ὁμοιότητος, ' ὁμοιότητος' is a so-called genitive of description. (Cf. n. 182 below.) This, and the translation 'type' for εἶδος, is suggested by the *Phaedo*, to which also the subsequent discussion in the *Parmenides* makes frequent reference. In the *Phaedo*, as in the *Parmenides*, the term εἶδος is introduced in connection with 'pairs of opposites': equal and unequal, even and odd, big and small. In each of these cases, one can assume 'two types of things', δύο εἴδη τῶν ὄντων. Regardless of whether the origin of εἶδος as a technical term for a 'type' of thing in this context is Presocratic, Socratic or Platonic, the word is an established part of Plato's philosophical lexicon from the *Meno*, *Euthyphro* and *Phaedo* onwards. For a full discussion of the history of the word εἶδος, see below Part II, ch. 4.

[36] Cf. Aristotle, *Metaph.* A 9.990a33–991b20, and M 4–5, 1078a7–1080a10; typical of 20th-century criticism are e.g. Ryle 1939 and 1966; Vlastos 1954; Scaltsas 1989. An exposition of the opposite view, namely that Parmenides' objections are serious, but that the aporetic nature of the discussion is meant to be a starting point for further investigation into arguments connected with εἴδη, rather than an abandoning of εἴδη altogether, is provided by Allen 1997 ([1]1984).

[37] In addition to μετέχειν and μεταλαμβάνειν, the *Phaedo*, like the *Parmenides*, uses the phrases ἐνεῖναι or 'being in' and χωρὶς εἶναι or 'being separate' in connection with those εἴδη or 'types', as well as the term ἐπωνυμία, 'benaming' or 'designation', and the examples of μέγεθος, κάλλος and δικαιοσύνη, 'bigness', 'beauty' and 'justice', and of μέγα, σμικρὸν and ἴσον, 'big', 'small', and 'equal'; cf. secs. 14–16 below, as well as Part III on Plato's *Phaedo*.

[38] The discussion will largely focus on μετέχειν. In the *Phaedo*, *Symposium* and *Republic*, μεταλαμβάνειν plays a subordinate role only; its usage is always determined

by that of μετέχειν. Whatever type of 'having', 'sharing' or participating is denoted by μετέχειν in a particular context, μεταλαμβάνειν in this context denotes a 'coming to have', 'coming to share' or 'coming to participate', with connotations otherwise identical to those of μετέχειν in the same context; in that, the relation of μετέχειν to μεταλαμβάνειν is parallel to that of εἶναι in its simple and prefixed forms to the respective simple and prefixed forms of γίγνεσθαι.

[39] Since there are differing views on the semantics of μετέχειν, let me quote one which I consider representative in many ways of the majority view; Meinhardt 1968, 16 f.: ' "μετέχειν" selbst ist gegenüber seinen Umschreibungen bereits im weiteren Gebrauch (i.e. if not applied to εἴδη/ἰδέαι) abstrakt und fast ohne Bildgehalt. Es ist ein Compositum aus "ἔχειν–haben, halten" und präverbalem "μετά". Die Konstruktion mit partitivem Genitiv kennt schon das Simplex: etwa Sophokles, *Oed. Rex* 708 f.: "…ἐστί σοι βρότειον οὐδὲν μαντικῆς ἔχον τέχνης – es gibt nichts Sterbliches, das die Seherkunst besitzt." "μετέχω ist ἔχω mit Partitiv…verdeutlicht durch μετά." (Eduard Schwyzer, Griechische Grammatik, 2. Bd., München 1950, S. 103.) "Der Partitiv bezeichnet hier den allgemeinen Bereich der Teilnahme, während ein bestimmter Teil, den jemand erhält, im Akkusativ steht." (Eduard Schwyzer a.a.O.) Das präverbale μετά bringt das Moment der Gemeinssamkeit (Vgl. Eduard Schwyzer a.a.O.S. 482.) ("mit, zusammen") zum Ausdruck. Beides wird für den philosophischen Gebrauch wichtig: Alle Partizipierenden "haben" gemeinsam das Partizipierte, aber "partitiv", einen Teil vom Ganzen, wobei "Teil" hier natürlich qualitativ (= in abgeschwächter Weise) und nicht quantitativ zu verstehen ist. Gleichbedeutend mit "μετέχειν" und "μέθεξις" werden in der vorliegenden Arbeit die von der lateinischen Übersetzung "participatio" gebildeten Vokabeln "partizipieren" und "Partizipation" verwandt, außerdem die deutschen Übersetzungen "teilhaben" und "Teilhabe". (The German equivalents employed by Meinhardt are loan-translations of the Latin words and have as one of their elements the German for 'part', 'Teil'. Cf. also LSJ s.v. μετέχω 'II. In Platonic Philos., *participate in* a universal'; and des Places 1964, 340, s.v. μετέχειν ' "participer" (à) a) en général; b) à une Idée.') It is worth noting that Meinhard insists that the partitive force of the so-called 'partitive genitive' denotes the 'having of a part', but suggests at the same time that 'part' can be used qualitatively as well as quantitatively, in which case qualitative participation amounts to displaying something in a weakened or diminished way. This seems to be less the result of grammatical or linguistic considerations than an attempt to make sense of Plato's Greek on the basis of a preconceived interpretation of Plato's philosophy.

[40] The issue discussed is not specific to any one language, nor does it matter whether μετέχειν is translated 'share' or 'participate' or 'partake'. Indo-European languages other than Greek, like Latin, English or German, start from the notion of 'cutting or dividing something up and distributing it thereafter'. So *participare* is 'to take a part', where *pars* – like Greek μέρος – is originally that which is granted (and received as such), but in historical times simply means 'part' in its modern sense. (Cf. Walde-Hofmann 1965, II, 257–9, s.v. *pars*. Frisk 1973, II, 212, s.v. μέρος.) English 'share' is derived from a root *s-ker- which denotes a cutting. (Cf. Walde-Pokorny 1930, II, 573 ff. Walde-Hofmann 1965, I, 170, s.v. *caro*.) German 'teilen' is a denominative of 'Teil', 'part', and in contemporary German the verb can denote both dividing and sharing. ('Teil' is equivalent to 'deal' in its old sense of 'part'. Its ultimate etymology is uncertain.) In all these languages, the word for 'share' can imply the 'having of a part' if the grammatical object denotes something physical and material which can be divided. That is the case regardless of

the etymological origin of the respective verbs. Conversely, if the grammatical object denotes something immaterial, the notion of divisibility often does not arise or does not apply at all, neither 'quantitatively' nor 'qualitatively' – whatever that latter notion is supposed to signify.

[41] Cf. also the forms of μερίζειν at 131c5–d3.

[42] I use the term 'prefixed verb' as the modern distinction between 'compound words', i.e. those 'consisting of two or more free morphemes', and 'complex words', i.e. those 'containing one free and at least one bound morpheme', does not apply to many prefixed Greek verbs whose first element otherwise functions as a preposition or an adverb. In many cases, for example, it is impossible to determine a distinction between πάρεστι τινί and ἔστι παρά τινι; cf. Schwyzer 1950, II, 423; for μετά in general, 481–7; for pre-verbal μετα-, in particular, 482.

[43] Cf. ch. 2, sec. 1, p. 46 below.

[44] See Frisk 1973, I, 602–4, s.v. ἔχω[1]. A Homeric instance of ἔχειν in the sense of 'hold down, subdue' is *Odyssey* 4.555–8:

υἱὸς Λαέρτεω, Ἰθάκῃ ἔνι οἰκία ναίων·
τὸν δ' ἴδον ἐν νήσῳ θαλερὸν κατὰ δάκρυ χέοντα,
νύμφης ἐν μεγάροισι Καλυψοῦς, ἥ μιν ἀνάγκῃ
ἴσχει· ὁ δ' οὐ δύναται ἣν πατρίδα γαῖαν ἱκέσθαι·

The son of Laertes, living in his home in Ithaca:
but him I saw on an island, shedding a thick tear,
in the palace of the nymph Calypso, who holds him by force;
but he is unable to return to his fatherland.

[45] See Collinge 1985, 47–61; and esp. Plath 1987.

[46] ἔχειν with physical objects as grammatical object *passim*; with non-material habits, states and conditions, bodily and mental, as grammatical object e.g. 1.82, 2.344, 3.412.

[47] Cf. Meillet 1924, 9–13; Buck 1949, 739–49; particularly relevant for the semantic connections and developments of ἔχειν and related words are ch. 11, secs. 11 'HAVE', 12 'OWN, POSSESS', 15 'HOLD', 17 'KEEP, RETAIN'.

[48] As the notion of 'having' is at once so general and so fundamental, it is very difficult to describe or define it adequately. That is not meant to suggest, though, that 'having' is an indefinable relation, merely that the relation expressed is a very general one. While it is not necessary to attempt a precise definition of 'have' in the present context, it is necessary to draw attention to the difficulties in which any attempted definition of the particular relation of 'somebody's having something' would be involved in cases in which 'what is had' is not a physical or material object, for example in such ordinary and every-day cases as 'having a skill'. The particular nature of that 'having' seems to depend to a large extent on the nature of the respective object. The difficulty of defining the verb, though, does not on the whole result in a difficulty in understanding a well-formed sentence containing it, as long as the points of reference of the grammatical subject and object are known.

[49] Cf. Schwyzer 1950, II, 101 ff., on the *genitivus partitivus*. Schwyzer/Debrunner rightly emphasize that, where the genitive 'replaces' nominative, accusative, instrumental, ablative or locative, there is no thought of 'the whole' of what is referred to by the noun in the genitive. I should go further and add that there need, therefore, not be the thought of 'part' either. Of course, when verbs of touching like ἅπτω or ψαύω take the genitive, it is not necessarily wrong to interpret this phenomenon as due to the fact that only

a part is touched. But even with spatio-temporal, physical objects of this sort, where the 'whole' is presumably in the mind of the speaker, the notion of 'part' as such need not likewise be present; compared with the nominative or accusative, this genitive expresses, in a negative way, that the speaker does not specify, either quantitatively or qualitatively, *what* about the object, which itself may be concrete or abstract, is involved: not the whole, but not a specific part either. And since one may argue that the correlatives 'part' and 'whole' cannot be conceived of independently from one another, it may even be misleading to assume that the use of the genitive is motivated by a specific intention to express 'not the whole' of what is referred to by the noun in the genitive. This will be illustrated by the examples discussed below in the text.

[50] Cf. also e.g. *Odyssey* 9.433; 10.264, 323 λάβε γούνων (= 22.310, 342, 365); 19.479–81. Note that the partitive genitive is found with συλλαμβάνω in the active and middle in the 5th and 4th centuries (see LSJ s.v. συλλαμβάνω VI).

[51] Note that the middle form ἔχετο plus genitive, 'he clung to, depended on', is not the object of this discussion.

[52] 'you should assume that' is meant to render the *dativus ethicus* σοι.

[53] Cf. in general Schwyzer 1950, II, 482.

[54] *dativus sociativus*; not a dative of advantage or *dativus commodi*, i.e., Iolaus does not say: 'I shared in very many toils for Hercules' or 'for the sake of Hercules'.

[55] It should be noted that the contention is not that sacrifices and religious festivals, as spatio-temporal events, do not have parts. Rather, one can think of such things as sacrifices and festivals either in terms of their temporal extension and in terms of the elements of which they consist, or one can, complexively, treat them as *one thing*, contrasting, for example, a festival in honour of Athena, as one thing or event, with a festival in honour of Hera, as another thing or event. One may think of these two ways of conceiving of one and the same thing as being parallel to the difference in 'aspect' of Greek tenses, in that the aorist and imperfect tenses, in the indicative and with temporal augment, respectively can refer to one and the same action, event or process in the past complexively as one incident or thing (aorist) or in linear fashion as having duration and, by implication, parts (imperfect); by choosing either the aorist or the imperfect, the speaker of the language decides on the aspect, i.e. on the way in which the action, event or process in question is to be viewed in a given context. In parallel with that distinction, it is here claimed that the speaker in Xenophon's text is not thinking of the duration or of the constitutive elements of the rituals and sacrifices that he claims they share. The precise force of the perfect μετεσχήκαμεν is difficult to determine; it may be something like 'we are such as to share (feasts) with you' or 'we are sharers (of feast) with you'. I am grateful to Antony Hatzistavrou for forcing me to clarify this issue.

[56] Cf. Kühner-Gerth 1898, I, 412 f., on the use of the dative as standing for the 'comitative' with αὐτός.

[57] Another instance of this usage is found in Plato's *Euthydemus*; Socrates asks Clinias (279e6–280a2):

τί δέ; στρατευόμενος μετὰ ποτέρου ἂν ἥδιον τοῦ κινδύνου τε καὶ τῆς τύχης μετέχοις, μετὰ σοφοῦ στρατηγοῦ ἢ μετὰ ἀμαθοῦς; – μετὰ σοφοῦ. – τί δέ; ἀσθενῶν μετὰ ποτέρου ἂν ἡδέως κινδυνεύοις, μετὰ σοφοῦ ἰατροῦ ἢ μετὰ ἀμαθοῦς;– μετὰ σοφοῦ.

What then? Going to war, with which of the two would you rather share danger and fortune, with the wise general or with the ignorant? – With the wise. – What then?

When you are ill, with which one would you rather risk it, with a wise physician or with an ignorant one? – With a wise one.

Apart from the fact that by its position μετὰ ποτέρου can be construed with both στρατευόμενος and μετέχοις, the prepositional phrase μετὰ ποτέρου is here, too, less ambiguous than the bare dative.

⁵⁸ This may be compared with the beginning of Plato's *Euthydemus*. Crito asks Socrates for the names of those with whom Socrates had a conversation the previous day; Socrates replies (271b6–8):

Εὐθύδημος οὗτός ἐστιν, ὦ Κρίτων, ὃν ἐρωτᾷς, ὁ δὲ παρ' ἐμὲ καθήμενος ἐξ ἀριστερᾶς ἀδελφὸς τούτου, Διονυσόδωρος· μετέχει δὲ καὶ οὗτος τῶν λόγων.

This is Euthydemus, Crito, about whom you enquire, but the one who sat next to me on my left was his brother, Dionysodorus: for he as well took part in the conversation.

The difference between this last instance of μετέχειν and the one in the previous Herodotean example is that, in the case of Herodotus, λόγος refers to the content of the statement while, in the *Euthydemus*, Socrates refers to the conversation, the process of talking in which both Socrates' brothers took part; it should also be observed that, in the Platonic text, λόγων is plural; but despite the fact that when Dionysodorus spoke the others were silent and *vice versa*, what Socrates tries to convey is that both brothers were part of the conversation as a whole, listening and talking, as opposed to others who were silent bystanders.

⁵⁹ Text as Treu 1954, 54 f., fr. 58.

⁶⁰ *Pace* Kühner-Gerth 1898, I, 344, who class this example as a case of μετέχειν with the accusative. For the present purpose, however, it is not decisive whether either Xenophon, *Hiero* 2.6 or Herodotus 7.16.3, a slightly different but related case, are instances of μετέχειν with genitive and adverbial complement or with genitive and accusative.

⁶¹ Cf. Xenophon, *Cyropaedia* 7.2.28. In the phrase μετέχειν τὸ ἴσον τῶν ἀγαθῶν τινι, τὸ ἴσον is the direct object in the accusative. It quantifies and makes precise the imprecise, unquantified genitive object τῶν ἀγαθῶν.

⁶² As with the previous example, two different explanations of the syntax are conceivable. Either μοῖραν is taken to be the direct object of μετέχειν, in the accusative because it refers to one concrete, defined physical object, on which an adnominal genitive depends. Or the construction is an extension of μετέχειν with genitive: by way of specification, μοῖραν is added in the accusative. They 'had of the plain: not the smallest part'. It is impossible to know with absolute certainty which of the two is the correct explanation, let alone to say how Herodotus himself would have taken the sentence. The same difficulty obtains at Aeschylus, *Agamemnon* 506 f. The herald, the first of the Greeks returning to Argos to announce the coming of his master, first greets his land: οὐ γὰρ πότ' ηὔχουν τῇδ' ἐν Ἀργείᾳ χθονὶ | θανὼν μεθέξειν φιλτάτου τάφου μέρος. 'For I had never hoped to have, in this Argeian land, of a burial most dear, a share.' At his death he will 'have with <his compatriots> of a burial most dear, his share'. Or will he 'have his part of the dearest burial'? The former may be preferable in the light of *Republic* 465e1 where apparently the same sentiment is expressed: καὶ γέρα δέχονται παρὰ τῆς αὑτῶν πόλεως ζῶντές τε καὶ τελευτήσαντες ταφῆς ἀξίας μετέχουσιν. 'And while they are living, they receive honours from their city, and when they are dead they will "have of" a worthy burial "together with the others".'

In the case of physical objects or perceptible events concerning physical objects, it does not matter greatly which way the syntax of these examples is construed. Given the recession of the free-standing adverbial genitive in the course of the centuries, however, and the comparatively large number of instances of it with this specific construction, it seems to me to be much rather the case that the accusative objects μέρος and μοῖραν are reinforcements of the older construction, in cases where it seemed appropriate, than that the many other cases are instances of elliptical construction.

[63] Modelled on that and therefore not to be counted separately is Isocrates 4.99.

[64] Cf., however, how closely material possessions and what could be non-material rights are linked at Herodotus 4.145: δέεσθαι δὲ οἰκέειν ἅμα τούτοισι μοῖράν τε τιμέων μετέχοντες καὶ τῆς γῆς ἀπολαχόντες. 'They requested that they could live together with them, having a share of their privileges and receiving land.' And cf. also Lysias 31.5, which is syntactically close to Xenophon, *Cyropaedia* 7.2.28 (μετέχειν τὸ ἴσον τῶν ἀγαθῶν τινι); Lysias speaks of the true citizens:

τούτοις μὲν γὰρ μεγάλα τὰ διαφέροντά ἐστιν εὖ τε πράττειν τὴν πόλιν τήνδε καὶ ἀνεπιτηδείως διὰ τὸ ἀναγκαῖον σφίσιν αὐτοῖς ἡγεῖσθαι εἶναι μετέχειν τὸ μέρος τῶν δεινῶν, ὥσπερ καὶ τῶν ἀγαθῶν μετέχουσι.

For there is a great difference for them with regard to the unencumbered well-being of this city, because it is necessary for them themselves to believe that they (must) have their share of afflictions, just as they have <together with us> of the good things.

Here τὸ μέρος can be seen as an addition to an already complete sentence in the same way that τὸ ἴσον, 'to the same extent', is an addition in Xenophon; it may be noted that τὸ μέρος τῶν δεινῶν, 'their share in afflictions', may refer to things like losing one's life: but if one person loses his life and another shares his fate, that does not mean that both lose half their lives: both will lose the same, τὸ ἴσον, when they have τὸ μέρος, their share.

[65] In the same way, the herald at *Agamemnon* 506 does not think of anything but his own burial in his native land, a burial he will have for himself, just as his compatriots, both those who stayed behind and those who have now returned together with him, will have their own burials respectively.

[66] At least: more than one.

[67] Cf. conveniently Nails 2002, 312.

[68] One could construct an argument to the effect that Socrates posits as an entity Courage, and of that Courage he and Laches have the part concerned with deeds, but do not have the part concerned with words. Neither this, however, nor any other such analysis of courage seem to me to be implied in Socrates' position here or anywhere else in the dialogue. Also to be left aside is *Laches* 199c, where Socrates speaks indeed of 'parts of courage'; that, however, is in a different argument artificially contrived to refute Nicias.

[69] Cf. 319e1: Socrates tries to explain to Protagoras why he does not think that ἀρετή, 'excellence', 'goodness' or 'virtue', is διδακτόν, 'teachable' or 'taught'. One of the reasons he provides in support of his position is: ἰδίᾳ ἡμῖν οἱ σοφώτατοι καὶ ἄριστοι τῶν πολιτῶν ταύτην τὴν ἀρετὴν ἣν ἔχουσιν οὐχ οἷοί τε ἄλλοις παραδιδόναι, 'privately, the wisest and best among us are not capable of instilling into others that virtue which they have'. Here as well, the verb governs the accusative. Cf. also *Charmides* 169d–e and 170b6.

[70] Cf., e.g., Wayte 1883, 106. The divine lot consists of a share in σοφία, 'wisdom', or

νοῦς, 'mind'. For the general sentiment cf., e.g., Pindar, *Nemean* 6.1–8.

71   In this case, it would, of course, be sensible to ask for differentiations in wisdom, and it could not be denied that the gods, or at least some gods, have more insight into things than human beings. But this is not the point of Protagoras' story, and it is neither implied nor hinted at. Rather, the emphasis is on what gods and men have in common. Men share the divine predicament in having access to something the other animals do not have access to. In *that* respect gods and men are the same – by 'having of' the same.

72   αἰδῶς is 'awe', 'shame' or 'reverence'. 'Awe' may seem counter-intuitive as a translation of αἰδῶς in this context, especially in view of the subsequent replacement of αἰδῶς with σωφροσύνη. I use the word here as it has appropriate numinous connotations, especially in connection with δίκη in this context; cf. Chantraine 1933, 422 f. For discussion and interpretation of these concepts in the *Protagoras*, see Cairns 1993, 254–60.

73   Cobet's athetizing of δικαιοσύνην would leave αὐτῆς in the next line without antecedent, or would, respectively, require the reader to supply the notion referred to from b2 after having extrapolated it there from ἐν τῇ ἄλλῃ πολιτικῇ ἀρετῇ.

74   Where an individual, looked at in isolation, has a particular art, craft or skill, ἔχειν governs the accusative.

75   Cf. Collinge 1989, 1–13.

76   The aorist μετασχεῖν is complexive. Callicles envisages 'youth as a whole' as one part of life, adulthood as another; he is not thinking of the duration of either period.

77   In that respect, the neither-good-nor-bad at this point in the *Gorgias* differs from the neither-good-nor-bad in the *Lysis* where the phrase is indeed at some point meant to denote things which are neither wholly good nor wholly bad but in-between, partly good and partly not good. There, however, the language of participation is completely absent. Instead, παρουσία, the presence of good, is said to make things good (cf. also *Gorgias* 497e ff.).

Chapter 2

78   I accept the conjecture προσαγορευομένη, proposed by Wyttenbach and adopted by J.C.G. Strachan in the OCT (1995, 158); the confusion in the manuscript tradition will have arisen at an early stage, due to a misinterpretation of *Republic* 4.437e3–6, which was taken to be of relevance in this context; I shall provide a full discussion of that issue elsewhere.

79   I agree with the emendation of *Sophist* 247 as proposed by Campbell 1867, 121. He obelizes παρουσία in the text and has two notes on 247a5 f.: ' – δικαιοσύνης ἕξει καὶ †παρουσίᾳ†] "The possession and presence of justice." See note on *Theaet.* 153b: ἡ δ' ἐν τῇ ψυχῇ ἕξις.' ' – τῶν ἐναντίων] sc. ἕξει καὶ παρουσίᾳ. The plural suggests the conjecture that Plato wrote δικαιοσύνης ἕξει καὶ φρονήσεως.' This is recorded in the apparatus by D.B. Robinson in vol. I of the OCT (1995, 435) as: 'a5 ἢ φρονήσεως add. Cornford: δικαιοσύνης ἕξει καὶ <φρονήσεως> (del. παρουσίᾳ) Campbell' – it is this interpretation of Campbell's note that I think may well give the correct text.

80   These lists are extensive so as to furnish a representative sample. The reader who is interested primarily in the results of this discussion may turn to sec. 4, pp. 54 f.

81   The order in which I have arranged the different uses is not meant to indicate a semantic development and is chosen purely for the sake of convenience.

82   Cf. LSJ s.v. πάρειμι (εἰμί *sum*) I (and IV).

83   Cf. LSJ s.v. πάρειμι (εἰμί *sum*) III.

[84] Cf. LSJ s.v. πάρειμι (εἰμί *sum*) II. 4. I would see this as a category distinct from the following one.

[85] Cf. Brandwood 1976, 715. He asserts in a footnote: 'παρόντι: all instances occur in the phrase ἐν τῷ παρόντι and its variant ἐν τῷ νῦν παρόντι...' Note that *Phaedo* 59a2 is an exception.

[86] One division of this group is the nominal use of παρόντα or παρεόντα, '<things> being present'. The notion of time is present here as well, in that often no distinction is made between 'the circumstances or things present' and 'the present circumstances or things'. Often, the 'things present' are contrasted with ἀπόντα, the 'things absent'. A common exhortation amounts to 'a bird in hand is worth two in the bush', with all its variations. Echoes of that are *Odyssey* 1.140b and Democritus, B191, B224. A reflection of it is also found at e.g. *Gorgias* 493c, where Socrates says about a mythical allegory:

> ...ταῦτ' ἐπιεικῶς μέν ἐστιν ὑπό τι ἄτοπα, δηλοῖ μὴν ὃ ἐγὼ βούλομαί σοι ἐνδειξάμενος, ἐάν πως οἷός τε ὦ, πεῖσαι μεταθέσθαι, ἀντὶ τοῦ ἀπλήστως καὶ ἀκολάστως ἔχοντος βίου τὸν κοσμίως καὶ τοῖς ἀεὶ παροῦσιν ἱκανῶς καὶ ἐξαρκούντως ἔχοντα βίον ἑλέσθαι,
>
> ...this is likely somewhat quaint. But it makes clear how, in showing <this> to you, I want to persuade you to change your ways, if I am at all capable, by choosing instead of an unfillable and unrestrained life a life orderly, sufficient in what is present at any given time, and being in a state of contentment.

Here Socrates tries to persuade Callicles to choose the βίος, the 'life' or 'way of living' (possibly another allusion to the last words of Callicles' introductory speech) which has enough or is content with those things which 'are present' or at one's disposition or at hand at any given time. Cf. also *Gorgias* 499c4: ...καὶ ὡς ἔοικεν ἀνάγκη μοι κατὰ τὸν παλαιὸν λόγον 'τὸ παρὸν εὖ ποιεῖν'..., '...and as it seems it is necessary for me, in accordance with the old saying, "make do with what's there"...' In this text, the thought is labelled as a proverb or standing phrase; cf. Dodds 1959, 317, commentary ad loc.

[87] See ch. 1, sec. 1, p. 24 above. Cf. also Mader 1979–, 837. It is to be noted that *mutatis mutandis* the same is true for the Semitic languages. 'Having' there is also expressed by either 'possessing' as in the possession of e.g. land or 'being to someone'. This is a further indication of how abstract a notion 'having' is in itself.

[88] Cf. Schwyzer 1950, II, 411–32, in particular 411 f., 431 f. Cf. also Meier-Brügger 1991, I, 154–6, with references to further literature.

[89] Cf. Schwyzer 1950, II, 491–8. He says (492): 'Möglicherweise hat auch παρά in einigen Verwendungen eine alte, nicht sekundäre Bedeutung "vor"; die allgemeine Bedeutung von παρά usw, ist jedoch "(unmittelbar) neben, nahe" ... Neben Kasus (Lok., Akk., Abl.) kann jedoch das Bedeutungsmoment der Nähe verblassen; παρά unterstreicht dann als "bei", "zu (- hin)", "von (- her)" lediglich die Bedeutung, die der Kasus an sich hatte.' I would stress that this shift away from expressing 'local closeness' to expressing some sort of more abstract proximity which serves to 'underline the force of the case' is carried by the preverb as well. In that respect, Schwyzer's paragraph on 'παρά as a preverb' (493), is in need of slight modification.

[90] Cf. p. 24 with n. 44 above.

[91] Cf. Schwyzer 1950, II, 64 f.

[92] *Pace* Frisk 1973, I, 34, s.v. αἴδομαι. His assertion, 'Von αἴδομαι, bzw. von einem älteren athematischen Verb stammt αἰδώς f. "Scheu, Ehrfurcht",' is not well founded. Rather than positing an athematic verb of the same root from which the noun is derived,

one should be content with stating that both the thematic verb and the – very old – noun are derived from the same root; cf. also Chantraine 1933, 422 f. Its formulaic occurrence in the *Iliad* as absolute nominative in exclamations or exhortations, i.e. in places where a verbal imperative form could have been used just as well, rather points to the antiquity of the noun; *Iliad* 5.787, 8.228, 13.95, 15.502, 16.422. Cf. Schwyzer 1950, II, 65 f. I would contest his assertion that in the Homeric lines quoted ἐστι is understood or has to be supplied. For the concept of αἰδώς in early Greek thought in general, cf. Cairns 1993.

[93] See sec. 5, on the noun παρουσία, pp. 55 f. below.

[94] The implications of the difference between Mimnermus 8, ...ἀληθείη δὲ παρέστω | σοὶ καὶ ἐμοί, where ἀληθείη is present to the people, and Empedocles 114, ἀληθείη πάρα μύθοις, cannot be discussed here.

[95] Cf. also Empedocles DK31B110:

εἰ γάρ κέν σφ' ἀδινῇσιν ὑπὸ πραπίδεσσιν ἐρείσας

εὐμενέως καθαρῇσιν ἐποπτεύσῃς μελέτῃσιν

ταῦτά τέ σοι μάλα πάντα δι' αἰῶνος παρέσονται,

ἄλλα τε πόλλ' ἀπὸ τῶνδ' ἐκτήσεαι...

Indeed, if, fitting <my teaching> in your steady mind,

you consider it in a well-disposed manner with pure exercizing,

these things will certainly all always be there for you,

and many other things you will gain from them...

It is unfortunate that we do not know if ταῦτα refers to 'Empedocles' teachings' (Diels) or 'the elemental components' (Mansfeld), or to something else again.

[96] e.g. Gorgias, DK82B11, 11.

[97] No particular theory of the mind is implied in or intended with these terms.

[98] There is one instance of παρουσίη in the 4th-century medical treatise *De arte* (9.9).

[99] Sophocles *Electra* 1250 is a different case. The employment of παρουσία there is unusual enough to have created confusion in some of the manuscripts. Nevertheless, I think παρουσία may be the correct reading. Orestes declares that he is aware of Electra's unending suffering from her mother's deed but has mentioned it despite that:

ἔξοιδα καὶ ταῦτ'· ἀλλ' ὅταν παρουσία

φράζῃ, τότ' ἔργων τῶνδε μεμνῆσθαι χρεών.

I know this also, but when the moment

indicates, then is it necessary to remember those deeds.

Here, παρουσία is the present time, the present, which 'indicates it' or 'advises' to think or act in a certain way. This use of the word seems to be unique and confined to this one place.

[100] Cf. LSJ s.v. παραγίγνεσθαι. Since παρεῖναι and παραγίγνεσθαι, like μετέχειν and μεταλαμβάνειν, are otherwise correlatives in pre-Platonic and Platonic philosophical usage, and respectively used to denote state and process, I discuss παραγίγνεσθαι here.

[101] I start quoting at DK II, 358, 8 because of the affinity of the passage with *Phaedo* 60b which was pointed out by Diels.

[102] See sec. 9, pp. 70 f. below.

[103] If τις καὶ δύναμις is 'any power at all', δύναμις παρεγένετο instead of δύναμις ἐγένετο would suggest 'to anybody whomsoever'; for that, it is probably not necessary to change the text by replacing τις with τισι, or supplying τισι elsewhere in the clause.

Cf. also Forbes 1895, 21, with 118, note ad loc.: '...ὅθεν τις καὶ δύναμις παρεγένετο...
These words may also mean, not "whence any power accrued," but "which brought
any considerable force into the field." παραγίγνομαι is very common in Thucydides in
the sense "come into the field," and is never used by him in the sense of προσγίγνομαι,
"accrue." On the other hand παραγίγνομαι is found in the sense of προσγίγνομαι in other
Attic prose authors (see Liddell and Scott): and the use of ὅθεν here (not ᾧ or ἐφ' ὅν)
and the parallel in sense with ἰσχὺν δὲ περιεποιήσαντο ὅμως οὐκ ἐλαχίστην just above
are in favour of the interpretation "power accrued." Stahl proposes to read περιεγένετο,
a slight change which removes all difficulty.'

If or in what sense it is correct to declare that 'other Attic prose authors' use
'παραγίγνομαι in the sense of προσγίγνομαι' is another matter; Thucydides does not. Cf.
also Marchant 1905, 160 f.; and Gomme 1945, I, 126: 'ὅθεν τις καὶ δύναμις παρεγένετο:
ὅθεν shows that the *result* of a war is meant, and we should therefore read περιεγένετο
with Tournier, Stahl, Hude 1908, or τισὶ for τις with Wilamowitz and Hude 1913;
though even with τισὶ we should expect προσεγένετο. Croiset, however, keeping the
MSS. reading, translates: "par suite de laquelle des forces vraiment considérables aient
été mises en ligne"; which is perhaps right.'

[104] Cf. in particular DK I, 435, 1–5. For discussion of the fragment as a whole, see
Huffman 2005, 103–61.

[105] See sec. 9, pp. 70 f. below, on *Gorgias* 506d1. Xenophon, *Memorabilia* 4.2.2, adopts
usage employed by Socrates and others in Plato's dialogues.

[106] John Morgan, without endorsing it, suggested as a possibility that, at Thucydides
1.22, the phrase περὶ τῶν αἰεὶ παρόντων τὰ δέοντα μάλιστ' εἰπεῖν could (also) refer to
'what is always there' rather than (just) to 'what is there at any one time'. If that were
so, the phrase τὰ ἀεὶ παρόντα could be judged uncannily suitable as a way to refer to
Platonic 'forms'; but Plato does not actually speak of the forms in that manner; and
besides, while, on one reading, the forms always *are*, it would be wrong to say that 'they
are always *there*'.

[107] Cf. in particular Snell 1946, esp. 218–23.

[108] The barbarism 'bad(s)' must be excused as a reminder that the adjective is plural
in Greek, and at the same time that the genitive case does not let the reader determine
whether the forms are masculine or neuter in gender.

[109] Cf. also the question of Polus at *Gorgias* 461b4–6: ...ἢ οἴει – ὅτι Γοργίας ᾐσχύνθη
σοι μὴ προσομολογῆσαι τὸν ῥητορικὸν ἄνδρα μὴ οὐχὶ καὶ τὰ δίκαια εἰδέναι καὶ τὰ καλὰ
καὶ τὰ ἀγαθά...; 'Or do you imagine – just because Gorgias was ashamed not to concede
your further point – that the rhetorician knows what is right, honourable and good...?'
(tr. Dodds). Cf. Dodds 1959, 221, for commentary and translation.

[110] *Pace* Irwin 1979, 203. Cf. Dodds 1959, 314. He renders ἀγαθῶν παρουσίᾳ as
'owing to the presence in them of good things'. 'In them' seems to me to be an addition
with the potential to mislead and confuse. Cf. n. 120 below.

[111] See p. 61 above.

[112] Cf. for the topic at large as a stock theme the summary in Sharples 1993, 123, with
references to the main sources and earlier discussions.

[113] All that is said in what Socrates later (329a–b etc.) calls a μακρὸς λόγος, a 'long
speech'; the thoughts discussed by Protagoras and Socrates in Plato's dialogue show an
affinity with what we know of the Sophist otherwise; in a fragment of one of Protagoras'
own writings, referred to as μέγας λόγος, 'big speech', Protagoras expresses a similar

thought (DK80B3): φύσεως καὶ ἀσκήσεως διδασκαλία δεῖται, καὶ ἀπὸ νεότητος δὲ ἀρξάμενος δεῖ μανθάνειν. 'Teaching requires nature and practice and it is necessary to start learning from a young age.'

[114] Cf. *Euthydemus* 286c.

[115] Cf. Herrmann 1995, 101–6.

[116] Gifford 1905, 22, comments: 'ᾧ ἂν παρῇ, a good emendation supplied from Casaubon's unpublished notes by Routh: it indicates the subject to be understood before προσδεῖσθαι, which is left without any subject by the reading ὅταν παρῇ BT Vind. I.'

[117] If the text is sound, it is either the case that the participle παρόντα is, adjectivally in attributive position, qualifying the nominalized ἀγαθά, 'the present goods', or that τὰ παρόντα, 'the things present', are qualified by the adjective ἀγαθά in predicative position: 'the things present, if and when good'.

[118] Irwin 1979, 219, objects to Socrates' argument at *Gorgias* 506c–d: 'Socrates begins with the over-simplified account of the relation between the presence of a good and a person's being good, which he used against Callicles at 497d–e. Here he also claims that the presence of goods produces "goodness" (excellence, virtue; *aretē*; see 457c) in whatever it is present in – an equally implausible claim. The parallel with "When pleasure is present, we have pleasure (enjoyment)" should surely be "When good is present, we are well off (i.e. it is good for us)."...' The objection loses its ground in the light of this statement in the *Euthydemus*. If it is at all correct to say that εἰ ἡμῖν ἀγαθὰ πολλὰ παρείη, εὖ ἂν πράττειν <ἡμᾶς>, and if overall εὖ πράττειν equals εὐδαιμονεῖν, and if εὐδαιμονεῖν and ἀγαθός εἶναι are the same thing, then it is not objectionable to hold with Socrates and Callicles (506c9) that as ἡδὺ δέ ἐστιν τοῦτο οὗ παραγενομένου ἡδόμεθα, so ἀγαθὸν δὲ οὗ παρόντος ἀγαθοί ἐσμεν. The difficulty for both the ancient and the modern reader does not lie with the language or the logic of Socrates' argument, but with a basic disagreement over what is good. From the point of view of Plato's Socrates, it is resolved if the ἀγαθά of the protasis really *are* ἀγαθά.

[119] Cf. also 274d–e.

[120] Cf. Dodds 1959, 314, commentary on 497e: ' "owing to the presence in them of good things". In Callicles' view these "good things" are pleasures (498d3). In later dialogues Plato used παρουσία in a half-technical sense to describe the "presence" of a Form in a particular; but the use of the plural ἀγαθῶν, here and at 498d2, is sufficient to show that the Theory of Forms is not presupposed. We find a similar use of παρεῖναι at *Charmides* 158e7, εἴ σοι πάρεστιν σωφροσύνη, ἔχεις τι περὶ αὐτῆς δοξάζειν, and elsewhere.' Likewise at *Gorgias* 506d1, ἡδὺ δέ ἐστιν τοῦτο οὗ παραγενομένου ἡδόμεθα, ἀγαθὸν δὲ οὗ παρόντος ἀγαθοί ἐσμεν; 'Is not delight the following: when it is there, we are delighted; but good the following: when it is there, we are good?' Dodds comments: 'This sounds like the language of the theory of Forms. But see above on 497e1 and 503e1...' At 503e1 the expression ἀποβλέπων πρός τι, 'looking at something', receives Dodds' attention. Cf. also Vlastos 1973b; Irwin 1979, 202 f. For *Charmides* 157a6, cf. the discussion in ch. 3, sec. 5, pp. 89 f. below.

[121] The same could presumably be said of σωφρονεῖς. Cf. *Protagoras* 332a–e, with comments by Wieland 1982, 138 f. There, however, it is not clear to me whether ὑπὸ σωφροσύνης πράττειν really is in conformity with common Greek usage; but that does not affect Wieland's general point. On transformations of this sort, cf. Lyons 1969.

[122] Cf. sec. 1, p. 46 above.

[123] 'Causal' is here used loosely and meant to have all the connotations of αἴτιον and

αἰτία, i.e. 'cause-*cum*-reason-*cum*-explanation'; see Part III, ch. 9, secs. 7 and 8 below.

[124] Note especially that κάλλος is in the singular and καλούς in the plural.

[125] See sec. 7 above.

[126] Cf. *Gorgias* 486b.

[127] λευκότης must therefore be taken as referring always to the colour, and at no place to the material paint or dye.

[128] Cf. the discussion in sec. 7 above.

[129] See Part III, ch. 10, sec. 4 below.

Chapter 3

[130] Ross 1951, 30, 228; cf. Dodds 1959, 314, cited in n. 110 and quoted in n. 120 above; Vlastos 1973c, 298 f.; Irwin 1979, 203; cf. also Fine 1993, 50 f., 52 with n. 33. For fuller discussion see Part III, ch. 11 below.

[131] As opposed to εἶναι ἐν, which could, as an expression, be thought less specific.

[132] Cf. ch. 2, sec. 1, p. 46 above.

[133] Note, however, Ζεὺς ἄλγε᾽ ἔδωκε in the next line; what is the ontological status of ἄλγεα?

[134] See, e.g., Sophocles, *Electra* 1328.

[135] By the sophist Dionysodorus who exploits a colloquial expression by pretending that language is a logical construct (*Euthydemus* 287c–e).

[136] For ἡδονή as a goddess, cf. Crates 8, 9 Bergck; cf. *Philebus* 12b7–9.

[137] Cf. Kühn and Fleischer 1986, s.vv.

[138] *Protagoras, Meno,* and *Euthyphro* all contain either ἐνεῖναι, or ἐγγίνεσθαι, or at least εἶναι ἐν, in contexts which by some are considered relevant to the 'theory of forms', but at close examination all these occurrences turn out to be of a common nature; they can either be explained on the lines drawn out above, or they are similar to those instances which will now be looked at in detail.

[139] For a detailed discussion of the passage, see ch. 2, secs. 7–9 above.

[140] The text may have been: τί οὖν ὄνομά ἐστιν τῷ ἐν τῷ σώματι ἐκ τῆς τάξεώς τε καὶ τοῦ κόσμου γιγνομένῳ; 'What, then, is the name for that which results from the arrangement and order in the body?' But for our purposes nothing depends on whether γίγνομαι ἐν τινὶ occurs here already, or only in Socrates' next sentence as ἐγγίγνομαι.

[141] The function of the layout is to emphasize that structure.

[142] On *Gorgias* 504d, cf. e.g. Thompson 1905, xx f.: 'This description, if we compare it with those given in the purely Socratic dialogues, the *Laches*, for instance, the *Charmides*, or the *Protagoras*, will be seen to mark an epoch in Plato's mental growth, or, what is the same thing, in the History of Moral Science. Order or Harmony is the germinal idea of the Republic, as it gives unity and coherence to the parts, otherwise ill-connected, of the present dialogue.'

[143] One may compare the passage about the painter in *Republic* 10, starting at 596a and culminating at 598a in Socrates' question (597e10–598a3):

εἰπὲ δέ μοι περὶ τοῦ ζωγράφου τόδε· πότερα ἐκεῖνο αὐτὸ τὸ ἐν τῇ φύσει ἕκαστον δοκεῖ σοι ἐπιχειρεῖν μιμεῖσθαι ἢ τὰ τῶν δημιουργῶν ἔργα;

Tell me about the painter the following: if he seems to you to try to represent that itself <which we have mentioned>, that in nature, or <rather> those works of the craftsmen?

A little later, 598b, Socrates asks if the painter represents what is or what seems to be;

the answer is obvious. But on the one hand it should be noted that this example in *Republic* 10 is not without its own difficulties; on the other, the discussion of 'mimetic' art furnishes a natural context for the art of the painter. It is not unproblematic to adduce '*Republic* 400d–401a where ἡ γραφικὴ τέχνη is listed as a δημηγορία', or 'for painting as a τέχνη...*Ion* 532e–533a' in order to prove that Plato thought otherwise elsewhere, since at the former place Socrates says how things should be but are not, and at the latter he draws a parallel between the visual arts and poetry only to establish a point against Ion; *pace* Murray 1996, 197. At *Phaedrus* 248d, where δημιουργοί are classed below ποιηταί, a possible explanation of the different order is that Socrates refers to those who are commonly called craftsmen, those who just go through a set of motions and rules they have copied from their elders.

[144] Cf. Kühn and Fleischer 1986, s.v. ἀπαλλάσσω.

Chapter 4

[145] Lacey 1986, 78, s.v. 'Form'.

[146] As things stand now, *Iliad* 2.58 marks the earliest occurrence of the noun εἶδος. We do not, of course, know with certainty the relative chronology of composition of the various parts of the *Iliad*; in terms of narrative structure, it is quite possible that this deceptive Dream in Book 2 is rather late. But such considerations do not materially affect the issue at hand.

[147] In any pair or longer sequence of words – nouns, adjectives and verbs alike – the conjunctions τε or καί, 'and', can at their first occurrence be intended either to conjoin strictly separate entities or to add a specification, clarification or explication. There is no *a priori* way of determining whether in a given context the phrase εἶδός τε μέγεθός τε φυήν τ' will mean 'in εἶδος and also in μέγεθος and also in φυή', or rather 'in εἶδος, that is to say in μέγεθος and in φυή'; it should be noted, though, that in a sequence of three or more, rather than two, items, it is less likely that the first of three τε or καί respectively is explicatory or epexegetic.

[148] On the problematic of person, personality and self, which will not be entered into here, cf. Gill 1996.

[149] That does, of course, not imply that the poet had, or could have had, a notion of etymology in any way equivalent to our own.

[150] Other aspects of this passage are discussed in the ch. 6, sec. 1 below.

[151] Here εἶδος ἰδόντες need not be, but may be another case of the poet's showing awareness of an etymological connection.

[152] Cf. Diller 1971, 24.

[153] ἐπὶ εἴδεϊ τῷδε, 'on top of this appearance', could perhaps be rendered a little more freely as 'matching his appearance'.

[154] Cf. e.g. Hölscher 1988, 193 f.

[155] *Pace* e.g. Diller 1971, 24 f. Though it is certainly correct that, when a hero is praised, one of the objects of praise can be his εἶδος, and though most Homeric heroes are both strong and beautiful, the examples discussed above, and perhaps already the counter-examples adduced by Diller himself, should serve as a warning against seeing εἶδος as anything other than the neutral term it is in both *Iliad* and *Odyssey*.

[156] ἔπεστι where one could also expect πάρεστιν.

[157] Probably also at *Iliad* 5.770, despite the wide *hyperbaton*.

[158] The parallel case of εὐώδης, 'good of smell', shows that these early formations could

retain their original meaning regardless of the later more general use of -ειδης and -ωδης as means of forming denominal adjectives.

[159] In this context it is relevant that ἴον first denoted the flower 'violet', and only secondarily the colour. See Frisk 1973, I, 729, s.v. ἴον. Cf. also West 1966, 152 f.

[160] *Pace* Nordheier 1993, col. 281, s.v. μυλοειδής: 'von der Gestalt eines Mühlsteines, groß wie ein M(ühlstein)'.

[161] *Pace* LSJ s.v. μυλοειδής: 'like a mill-stone'; Frisk 1973, II, 268, s.v. μύλη: 'μυλο-ειδής 'wie ein Mühlstein' (Η 270...)'.

[162] *Pace* LSJ s.v. εὐειδής: 'well-shaped, comely'.

[163] Cf. e.g. Nordheier 1991, col. 996, s.v. θεοειδής: 'mit dem Aussehen e. Gottes, göttlich schön'; the latter is, again, interpretation. Since 'mit dem Aussehen eines Gottes' for θεοειδής is a literal translation, while 'von der Gestalt eines Mühlsteines, groß wie ein Mühlstein' for μυλοειδής is not, Nordheier may in the latter case have been influenced in his translation by the scholiast he quotes: 'Σχ sch. D zSt.: στρογγύλῳ, ἢ τραχεῖ.' With θεοειδής in *Iliad* and *Odyssey*, 'looking like a god', cf. later usage at, e.g. *Phaedo* 95c, where ψυχή, 'the soul', is called θεοειδές (τι), 'something godlike'; there 'god*like*' is appropriate, since ψυχή has otherwise been said to be θεῖον and ἀόρατον, 'something godly' and 'something invisible', so that '*looking* like a god' is ruled out as translation for θεοειδής at that point.

[164] See Frisk 1973, I, 27, s.v., with bibliographical references.

[165] Tentatively suggested as a possibility by Beck 1979, col. 898, s.v. ἠεροειδής.

[166] Whether οἶνοψ is always 'looking like wine', or at least sometimes 'like wine as regards his or her or its gaze', 'wine-eyed', is not relevant here.

[167] Cf. Frisk 1973, II, s.v.

[168] Or 'the path of the grey salt*s*', if ἅλς is feminine as a 'collective'; cf. Frisk 1973, II, s.v. πόντος: 'Als urspr. Bed. ist 'ungebahnter, durch Gelände, Wasser usw. führender Weg' anzusetzen; vgl. Benveniste in: Word 10, 256 f.; πόντος ist somit eig. "Fahrwasser" (vgl. ὑγρὰ κέλευθα) mit Beziehung auf eine für ein seefahrendes Volk primäre Funktion des Meeres. Vgl. zu πέλαγος and θάλασσα.' *Pace* Gray 1947, 112.

[169] As stated and amply illustrated by LSJ, s.v., πόντος is 'common from Hom. downwards, exc. in Prose, where it is chiefly used of special seas'. If, not only in Indo-European, but also in early Greek times πόντος was a 'track' or 'way', it would only be natural to add the name of a location when the word is applied to a 'water-way'. In expressions like ὁ Αἰγαῖος πόντος, there is a univocal qualification as to which track is referred to.

[170] The rock of Scylla at *Odyssey* 12.233, can probably be neglected, since the rock with the cave bears the epithet only because it was the epithet of the cave itself at 12.80. But cf. Heubeck and Hoekstra 1989, 171, on *Odyssey* 13.103.

[171] Cf. West 1966, 338, commentary ad loc.: 'cf. *h. Dem.* 275 μέγεθος καὶ εἶδος ἄμειψε...'

[172] Translation by West 1978, 331, commentary ad loc. He continues: 'i.e. let it match it. Tyrt. 10. 9 αἰσχύνει τε γένος κατὰ δ' ἀγλαὸν εἶδος ἐλέγχει; Pind. *O.* 8.19 ἦν δ' ἐσορᾶν καλός, ἔργῳ τ' οὐ κατὰ εἶδος ἐλέγχων. The same dichotomy appears in *Od.* 8.176 f. ὡς καὶ σοὶ εἶδος μὲν ἀριπρεπές...νόον δ' ἀποφώλιός ἐσσι, 17.454 οὐκ ἄρα σοί γ' ἐπὶ εἴδει καὶ φρένες ἦσαν; epitaph of Scipio Barbatus (Dessau, *ILS* I) 3 *quoius fórma uirtutei parisuma fúit.*'

[173] But cf. West 1966, 241, commentary ad loc.

[174] *Pace* West 1993, 96. I am grateful to Anton Powell for this last suggestion.

[175] Or in a transformation equivalent in force, e.g. as an accusative object of a verb like ἔχω.

[176] Cf. also West 1978, 158, commentary ad loc. He suggests punctuating differently, '…ἀθανάτῃς δὲ θεῇς εἰς ὦπα ἔϊσκεν, | παρθενικῆς καλὸν εἶδος ἐπήρατον·…' If I understand his commentary correctly, that would amount to something like: '…that he liken her to immortal goddesses as regards her face, the beautiful lovable appearance of a maiden.' If one accepts that as possible, this would be the first instance of εἶδος where the noun does not refer to 'the appearance of a named individual', person or animal, but as a general term to 'an appearance'. That would not only be unprecedented, but also difficult to explain in the Hesiodic context of language and thought. There are no contemporary or near-contemporary parallels to this usage.

[177] For the sake of readability, I will give West's reconstruction of the text. Cf. Merkelbach and West 1967, 30, apparatus ad loc. They adduce *h. Cer.* 278 (for which see next note) as a parallel for line 74.

[178] The *Hymn to Demeter* describes how the goddess lifts her disguise (275–80): ὣς εἰποῦσα θεὰ μέγεθος καὶ εἶδος ἄμειψε | γῆρας ἀπωσαμένη, περί τ' ἀμφί τε κάλλος ἄητο· | ὀδμὴ δ' ἱμερόεσσα θυηέντων ἀπὸ πέπλων | σκίδνατο, τῆλε δὲ φέγγος ἀπὸ χροὸς ἀθανάτοιο | λάμπε θεᾶς, ξανθαὶ δὲ κόμαι κατενήνοθεν ὤμους, | αὐγῆς δ' ἐπλήσθη πυκινὸς δόμος ἀστεροπῆς ὥς. 'Having said that, the goddess changed her size and guise, pushing away her age, and beauty breathed about and around her. Charming odours are spread from her fragrant *peplos*, far shines splendour from the skin of the immortal goddess, auburn hair lay upon her shoulders, and sparkling brightness filled the house like lightning.'

[179] e.g. Archilochus 196a.7 (West); Tyrtaeus 10.9; Alcman 1.58 (Page); Ibicus 1.5 (quoted above in this section); S166. 26; Simonides 50.4.

[180] *Seven Against Thebes* 507; fr. 393.

[181] Cf. n. 176 above.

[182] The label 'descriptive genitive' has two quite distinct applications in English grammar; throughout this study, it is used as explained here, i.e. as what traditional grammar calls a *genitivus appositivus*. Cf. Kühner-Gerth 1898, I, 264 f., 280 f.; Schwyzer 1950, II, 121 f.; see also nn. 35 above and 232 below.

[183] With Euripides, too, the use of the word as denoting the external, perceptible guise or appearance is predominant. Nine times, εἶδος denotes the guise of a person: *Electra* 1062, *Alcestis* 333, *Hecuba* 269, *Suppliants* 889, *Helen* 263, *Trojan Women* 929, frs. 15. 2; 690; on *Bacchae* 53–4, see ch. 6, sec. 1 below. Once in Euripides, εἶδος it is used of the guise of things: *Io* 585. For discussion of *Iphigeneia in Tauris* 817, see sec. 12 on Thucydides below.

[184] For this and the following sections, I make use of the by no means complete, but on the whole representative, collections of instances of εἶδος in 5th- and 4th-century prose authors compiled by A.E. Taylor in his essay *The Words* εἶδος, ἰδέα *in Pre-Platonic Literature* (Taylor 1911b). Since he quotes most of the passages fairly fully, there is no need to give the same material in full here. Taylor's extensive treatment of εἶδος and ἰδέα in the Hippocratic Corpus in particular (212–48) received immediate discussion and criticism from Shorey 1911; and from Gillespie 1912; cf. more recently Diller 1971. See also sec. 6 on the Hippocratic writings below.

[185] *Pace* Taylor 1911b, 184–6; he is right, though, in emphasizing that εἶδος, here as

elsewhere, does not refer to the complexion or beauty of the face alone. Herodotus 1.8 (2x), 1.196, 1.199, 3.24, 3.61 (2x); Taylor comments: 'The likeness meant is, of course, of physique in general, not merely of features, though this is included.' One could reply: 'The likeness meant is, of course, of look in general, not merely of the appearance of physique or features, though that is included'; 6.61 (3x) here the reason for the 'look's' not being beautiful is δυσμορφία; naturally, the body's shape, μορφή, is one of the factors determining one's look; 6.127, 7.70: there are two different Aethiopian tribes; in comparing the ones in the East with those in the West, Herodotus says: διαλλάσσοντες εἶδος μὲν οὐδὲν τοῖσι ἑτέροισι, φωνὴν δὲ καὶ τρίχωμα μοῦνον, 'they differ in no way from the others in guise, only in voice [=language] and hair'; from that, no more can be inferred than that voice, or language, and hair, or fashion of carrying one's hair, is here not thought of as belonging to one's εἶδος; Taylor's interpretation 'body' is again over-interpretation (cf. 7.56: someone addresses Xerxes who has crossed the Hellespont: ὦ Ζεῦ, τί δὴ ἀνδρὶ εἰδόμενος Πέρσῃ καὶ οὔνομα ἀντὶ Διὸς Ξέρξην θέμενος ἀνάστατον τὴν Ἑλλάδα θέλεις ποιῆσαι...; 'Zeus, why do you liken yourself to a Persian man and assume the name Xerxes instead of Zeus when you want to subdue Greece...?' Here εἰδόμενος refers to "Zeus'" likening himself to a Persian in guise, in external appearance, even if that includes voice – it is set against οὔνομα...θέμενος); 8.105.

[186] Note the occurrence of ἐπωνυμία, 'designation', 'be-naming', in this 'divine' context: the term ἐπωνυμία may have had religious overtones in general, which may be significant when the word occurs in the *Phaedo* in an ontological context; cf. also nn. 3 above and 421 below.

[187] In English, the definite article is one of the devices employed to achieve this pragmatic transformation: 'Mardonius chose those men who had *the looks*, or those he knew to have done something worthy.' This may be said instead of 'Mardonius chose those men who were of *strong* looks, or whom he knew to have done something worthy.'

[188] For Herodotus 2.76, cf. ch. 5, sec. 4 below.

[189] In talking about members of one species, Herodotus does not differentiate whether he refers to many or to all members of that species; but it is clear from the context that the latter must be assumed.

[190] Cf. n. 185.

[191] *Pace* Taylor 1911b, 185 f.

[192] Both κύβοι and ἀστράγαλοι are what we would refer to as 'dice', the ones cubic, the others tetrahedrical; it seems to be implied that the rules of the games played with the respective sets of dice were different.

[193] *Pace* Taylor 1911b, 184. Taylor quotes 'ἐξευρεθῆναι δὴ ὦν τότε καὶ τῶν κύβων...καὶ τῶν ἀλλέων πασέων παιγνίων τὰ εἴδεα (the figures, shapes, of all sorts of toys).' Misreading παιγνίων for παιγνιέων, the genitive plural of the neuter noun παίγνιον, 'plaything' or 'toy', for the genitive plural of the feminine noun παιγνία, 'play, game, pastime', is an easy oversight in any context. Here, the accusative plural τὰς παιγνίας had occurred only a few lines before, and the adjectival genitive plural feminine πασέων makes παιγνίων impossible. παιγνία, on the other hand, cannot anywhere, to my knowledge, mean 'toy'. It is conceivable that reading something like 'then it was that of cubic dice and of tetrahedrical dice and of the spherical ball...' suggested to Taylor that the emphasis of Herodotus' statement lay on the distinction of geometrical figures and shapes, and that Taylor was thus misled to think of the toys rather than the games played

with them. Taylor shares another controvertible assumption with many interpreters and commentators of this passage. They translate as if Herodotus had said καὶ τῶν παιγνιέων τὰ ἄλλα εἴδεα πάντα, which is taken to mean 'all other sorts of games', rather than καὶ τῶν ἀλλέων πασέων παιγνιέων τὰ εἴδεα, 'and of all other games the appearances'. For further discussion of this passage of Herodotus see sec. 10 below.

[194] See sec. 12 on Thucydides, p. 126 below.

[195] On the relative chronology of Thucydides' *History* and various Hippocratic treatises, cf. e.g. Weidauer 1954, and more recently Rechenauer 1991, with bibliography and discussion of pertinent literature.

[196] See sec. 11 below.

[197] On the question of assignment of authorship and date of composition of treatises of the Hippocratic Corpus, cf. the methodological remarks by Lloyd 1975; he begins his survey by saying (171): 'The question of determining the genuine works of Hippocrates, a topic already much discussed by the ancient commentators, still continues to be actively debated, although the disagreements among scholars remain, it seems, almost as wide as ever.' Lloyd lists as 'the most important contributions since 1930' on this question 86 titles. Cf. also P. Potter's opening remarks in the introduction of the Loeb edition of vols. 5 and 6 of Hippocrates (1988, 9.11 f.): 'These volumes contain the most important Hippocratic works on the pathology of internal diseases... About the Treatises' inter-dependencies, authors, and relative dates of composition, nothing can be said with any degree of certainty. There is neither any evidence that would confirm, nor any evidence that would call into doubt, their traditional time of origin about 400 BC.' For the present purpose, only those treatises will be considered which by general consensus can be taken to pre-date Plato's middle period dialogues.

[198] The order of the titles is that in which they occur in Littré's edition, adopted here only for the sake of simplicity.

[199] Jones 1923, 221 ff., n. 2, writes in his introduction to *Breaths*, which he holds to be a 'sophistic essay': '*Breaths* shows a tendency to similes and highly metaphorical language which Plato attributes (*Protagoras* 337C–338A) to Hippias... I do not suggest that Hippias was the author, but I do hold that the book must have been written at a time when the sophistry he represented was a living force...' He seems to imply that with Plato sophistry and public display associated with it had come to a sudden end. For a date of composition of *Breaths* in the 4th century cf. also Blass 1887, 89, adduced by Diller 1952, 393, n. 1. Poschenrieder 1882, 42, 46 ff., adduces passages from Plato's dialogues as parallels to what is said in *Breaths*; but, leaving aside different wording and phraseology, these passages display similarities in content of too general a nature to be conclusive in any way; Poschenrieder's extensive comparison of passages from *Breaths* with Eryxima-chus' remarks in the *Symposium* (60–6), if taken to convey more than the *communis opinio* of the time, suggests a common source for both rather than dependency of one on the other, since each one contains relevant medical material not found in the other. For the view that the relative chronology of *Breaths* and the Platonic dialogues cannot be established with certainty, Jouanna 1990, 81, n. 3 adduces Nelson 1909, 92 f.

[200] *On Ancient Medicine* has received attention in connection with Plato's philosophy for a long time. For a recent discussion concerning its date, cf. Schiefsky 2005, esp. 63 f. Although recent opinion favours a date that would make reception by Plato possible, I do not consider it safe to include the text as evidence for pre-Platonic usage.

[201] On 34 Loeb pages, the term is found in twelve passages, altogether 19 times.

[202] βλαδέα Coray (Kühlewein, Taylor): βραδέα MSS. For all the rarity of the word, βλαδύς, 'soft', seems to fit the context much better. One's choice will, of course, partly be determined by one's preconceptions about εἶδος, since if εἶδος can mean 'body', it is possible to predicate it βραδύ, 'slow'; if, on the other hand, εἶδος still has strong visual connotations, and at the same time is, as here, the 'εἶδος of a person', that would seem more difficult. H. Diller, who in his personal copy of Jones' edition underlines Coray's emendation, has 'βλαδέα' for πλατέα also in the margin of line 3 of the same page, where he wants to read: ῥοικὰ δὲ γίνεται καὶ βλαδέα..., thus suggesting repetition of the same two adjectives in line 20 f. That, to my mind, would give more weight to the phrase θαυμαστὸν οἷον of line 20. The author of *Airs, Waters, and Places* would then say: 'The bodies, σώματα, of the Scythians are crooked and soft, ῥοικὰ καὶ βλαδέα; and the appearance of their girls is so *par excellence*.'

[203] Unless stated otherwise, I give the text and chapter/section numbers of the Loeb editions of the Hippocratic texts by Jones, Withington and Potter.

[204] Cf. also *Airs, Waters, and Places* 19, where in a brief passage εἴδεα occurs three times, twice with a possessive genitive, once as an accusative of respect; εἴδεα is predicated παχέα καὶ σαρκώδεα καὶ ἄναρθρα καὶ ὑγρὰ καὶ ἄτονα, 'fat and fleshy and without joints <showing> and moist and slack'.

[205] Something seems to be wrong with the text. I omit καί.

[206] Note the absolute use of φύσις, *nature*; 'a nature' is a human being of a certain nature, both individually and collectively. For φύσις in Hippocratic writings and beyond, cf. e.g. the recent, very full treatment of the topic by Rechenauer 1991, 112–258, especially 167–74.

[207] Cf. sec. 3 above, with nn. 176 and 181. Cf. also, on a similarly absolute use of φύσις, n. 206 above.

[208] *OED*, s.v. 'Appearance. 14'.

[209] This literal translation is meant to highlight the employment of substantivized neuters in the context of character-depiction in a 5th-century text.

[210] These lines are not quoted since they are not relevant to the point at issue.

[211] Note the repeated un-mediated change of subject.

[212] Jones 1923, 135, if taken literally, seems to construe the sentence in this latter way.

[213] Cf. further in general sec. 9; for ch. 24 of *Airs, Waters, and Places*, cf. also ch. 5, sec. 2 below.

[214] Taylor 1911b, 219, comments: 'The context shows that the meaning is "and the rest pass into a different phase". εἶδος = a distinct stage in an illness marked by special symptoms, a sense derivative from that of "shape", "structure".' Gillespie 1912, 186 f., comments that Taylor does not recognize the advancement of εἶδος 'in the direction of the purely logical meaning of kind or class'. A 'divisory or classificatory suggestion is found in the numerous examples where εἶδος and ἰδέα is conjoined with πολύς, ἄλλος, or ἕτερος, παντοῖος, or παντοδαπός'. One of the examples is 'περὶ ἀέρων 11, I. 53 K. τὰ μὲν (νοσεύματα) ἀποφθίνει, τὰ δὲ λήγει, τὰ δὲ ἄλλα πάντα μεθίσταται ἐς ἕτερον εἶδος καὶ ἑτέρην κατάστασιν. T. "phase," but this is inaccurate: the writer does not think of the disease as persisting in another shape, but as passing into another disease or another form of disease; see περὶ παθῶν 8, vi. 216 L. κρίνεσθαι δὲ ἔστιν ἐν τῆισι νούσοισιν, ὅταν αὔξωνται αἱ νοῦσοι ἢ μαραίνωνται ἢ μεταπίπτωσιν ἐς ἕτερον νόσημα ἢ τελευτῶσιν.' – Jones 1923, 105, translates the sentence of *Airs, Waters, and Places* 11: 'For it is especially

at these times that diseases come to a crisis. Some prove fatal, some come to an end, all others change to another form and another constitution.'

215   W. Temple, *Works* I, 1720, 283, quoted in *OED*, s.v. 'Guise. 5.'

216   Cf. Gillespie 1912, 186 f., quoted n. 214 above.

217   νόσημα seems to be 'someone's being ill' rather than a named disease.

218   Cf. Jones 1923, 141, n. 1, in the *Introduction* to *Epidemics* I: ' "Constitution" is the traditional translation of κατάστασις, climatic conditions of such a marked type as to give a distinguishing character to a period of time. The word is also used of diseases, and so on, to denote a fixed type prevalent at any particular time.'

219   Taking ἐς ἕτερον εἶδος καὶ ἑτέρην κατάστασιν as a sort of ἕν-διὰ-δυοῖν, or hendiadys, 'the diseases turn to a different appearance, and that is to say a different constitution', does not decide the matter either.

220   Up to this point, the translation is taken from Jones 1923.

221   Cf. *Epidemics* 1.1, 12, 16.

222   The author of *Epidemics* uses τρόπος regularly to refer to 'the way' of a disease, i.e. the way in which particular symptoms occur in a particular order, e.g. *Epidemics* 1.1, 2, 3; in 1.10, κακοήθεα τρόπον, an accusative of respect, means 'in a bad way'.

223   δία as a preposition is, to my knowledge, otherwise not at all frequent with the genitive of either εἶδος or τρόπος.

224   A different interpretation of the use of τρόπος in the Hippocratic Corpus is given by Gillespie 1912, 183 f.; its implications cannot be discussed here.

225   The latter part of this translation is taken from Jones 1923.

226   Jones translates: 'The physical characteristics of the consumptives were: skin smooth, whitish, lentil-coloured, reddish; bright eyes; a leucophlegmatic condition; shoulder-blades projecting like wings. Women too so [n. 3: This brief phrase seems to mean that the same characteristics marked consumptive women as consumptive men].'

227   Jones does not seem to take this into account.

228   There are no instances of εἶδος in either *Prognostics* or *On Fractures*.

229   There are, naturally, some cases like those of *Epidemics* discussed above which mark a transitional state; attribution of them to one or the other group will to some extent be arbitrary. 'Guise, appearance' is denoted by εἶδος at *In the Surgery* 3b, 7d; *Instruments of Reduction* 1a–b, 6; *Humours* 1. 'Type' is denoted by εἶδος at *In the Surgery* 3a, 7a–c, 8, 9; *On Joints* 27, 34; *The Sacred Disease* 4, 16 (cf. ch. 5, sec. 1 below); in all probability also at *Humours* 13, on which cf. Gillespie 1912, 189. The one occurrence of εἶδος in περὶ διαίτης ὀξέων, *Regimen in Acute Diseases*, which is sometimes thought early, or even 'by Hippocrates', likewise belongs to that second group. When the author reminds his less knowledgeable colleagues in sec. 43 ὡς χρὴ διαγινώσκειν…ὅσα τε ἡμέων ἡ φύσις καὶ ἡ ἕξις ἑκάστοισιν ἐκτεκνοῖ πάθεα καὶ εἴδεα παντοῖα, that latter phrase is short for καὶ εἴδεα παντοῖα παθέων: 'that it is necessary to understand…which affections our nature and habit engender, and that there are manifold types <of affections>'. Cf. also Gillespie 1912, 186 f.; *pace* Taylor 1911b, 220.

230   'δύο εἴδεα' is a phrase found thrice in *In the Surgery*: 3.3, 7.1, 8.1; its use seems somewhat stereotypical. The treatise may well not be pre-Platonic in the form in which we have it; on the dating of *In the Surgery*, see Withington 1928, xxv, 'General Introduction'.

231   The few other instances of the word in Presocratic philosophical or sophistic texts can all be subsumed under one of the categories discussed above: Gorgias (DK82B22)

contrasts the εἶδος, 'guise', 'appearance', of a woman with her δόξα, here 'reputation' rather than 'judgement' or 'opinion'. With Critias (DK88B48), εἶδος likewise denotes 'guise', external 'appearance'. When Melissus discusses that 'there is only one', ἕν μόνον ἔστιν (DK30B8), he constructs as one of the absurdities which follow from the opposite assumption that while we say that we perceive and comprehend 'rightly' or 'correctly', ὀρθῶς, nevertheless we see again and again that things are one thing and its opposite, whence it follows that we neither see nor recognize what is; that does not agree with the initial assumption. He continues (30B8, 4): φαμένοις γὰρ εἶναι πολλὰ καὶ ἀίδια (?) καὶ εἴδη τε καὶ ἰσχὺν ἔχοντα, πάντα ἑτεροιοῦσθαι ἡμῖν δοκεῖ καὶ μεταπίπτειν ἐκ τοῦ ἑκάστοτε ὁρωμένου. 'Indeed, to us, although we say that there are many everlasting (?) things, having appearances and power, they all seem to alter and change, from that which is being seen at any one time.' Here 'having appearances and power' refers to the posited and assumed objects' having their own, distinct appearance and power or strength; that εἶδος is appearance is partly confirmed by the participle ὁρωμένου, indicating that the evidence adduced is in the sphere of the visible. For Philolaus DK44B5, see the discussion of *Phaedo* 100b ff., Part III, ch. 8 below.

It is appropriate to mention at this point the work of the Centre d'études aristotéliciennes de l'Université de Liège which has consistently contributed to an understanding of the thought of the Stagirite. In 2003, A. Motte, C. Rutten, P. Somville, L. Bauloye, A. Lefka and A. Stevens published an analysis and interpretation of all the instances of the three nouns εἶδος, ἰδέα and μορφή, in the Presocratics, Plato and Aristotle, under the title of *Philosophie de la Forme. Eidos, Idea, Morphè dans la philosophie grecque des origines à Aristote.* This collection of co-ordinated essays by the individual contributors, which presents all the material according to a unified format, supersedes in its completeness all previous studies of the terms in question, with a view to Plato notably Else 1935, Brommer 1940 and Sandoz 1971; but it takes into account a much wider range of modern studies and interpretations than these monographs dedicated to terminological issues (a strange omission is C. Ritter's *Neue Untersuchungen*, especially given that the second volume of his *Platon* [Ritter 1923] has been made use of). Any student of the terminology of Plato's ontology will want to consult *La Philosophie de la Forme*, not only as a list of references, but for the summaries and original interpretations offered by the authors. One may, though, as in the case of Sandoz's study *Les noms grecs de la forme. Étude linguistique*, detect a certain bias in the title already: as may be suspected, given the provenance of the volume and the express aims stated in the introductory pages, the study of the three terms is approached from an Aristotelian point of view; for Aristotle, there may be a strong case for singling out and collocating the three terms εἶδος, ἰδέα and μορφή for joint treatment under the heading of 'form' or 'Form' (at the risk of simplification, there do not seem to me to be significant differences between the authors' usage of 'forme/Forme' and the ways in which English 'form/Form' is employed in anglophone scholarship); as is argued in the text, I believe both that one must exercise great caution regarding what in particular εἶδος and ἰδέα respectively mean at each stage of their semantic development, avoiding the 'reading back' into an earlier context of developments securely attested only for a later stage of semantic development, and that it may well be impossible to arrive at a satisfactorily secure picture by restricting oneself to a study of any one group of texts, even as broad a group as that of the philosophical texts treated in the work of the Centre at Liège. Whether these reservations are borne out, only scrutiny of the individual translations and interpretations will show; and it must be reiterated that there is much to be learned from *Philosophie de la Forme*.

[232] In traditional terminology, a *genitivus possessivus* or an *appositivus* (cf. Kühner-Gerth 1898, I, 264 f., 280 f.; Schwyzer 1950, II, 121 f.; see also n. 182 above). If ἠελίοιο in the phrase ἠελίοιο...ἀγλαὸν εἶδος is interpreted as a descriptive genitive, one could translate 'the bright appearance which is the sun'. A potential line of linguistic development could then be constructed as follows: 'I see the bright sun'; 'I see the sun bright in appearance'; 'I see the sun's bright appearance'; 'I see the bright appearance which is the sun'; a next potential step in that line could be the dropping of the qualification: 'I see a bright appearance'. In that last sentence, the adjective could then be changed, or left out altogether. This hypothetical absolute use of 'appearance' would be similar to what has been encountered in some of the medical writers.

[233] Provided one accepts Diels-Kranz I, 338, *apparatus* ad loc.: 'χροῖα wohl Neutr. Plur. neben χροιά, χρώς wie φλοῖα (Hes. s.v. πίτυρα) neben φλοιά, φλόος' – in accordance with lexicographical tradition, εἴδη καὶ χροῖα could also be 'bodies and skins', or 'bodies and bodies', or 'appearances and appearances' (see LSJ s.vv. εἶδος, χροιά, χρώς).

[234] Not an absolutely compelling argument, as Plato might as well – here as elsewhere – have changed the terminology, if only in this one point; cf., however, for examples: Diels-Kranz III (index) s.v. σχῆμα.

[235] Cf. also discussion of the expression ἐν τῷδε τῷ ἀνθρωπίνῳ εἴδει, 'in this human guise', at *Phaedo* 73a, etc., in Part III, ch. 8, sec. 1 below.

[236] For this way of construing the syntax, cf. Mansfeld 1987, 413: 'Am feindlichsten dem Entstehen und der Mischung und den ausgeprägten Gestalten...sind jene [Teile], die am meisten voneinander verschieden sind, ganz und gar ungewohnt, zusammenzutreten...' A different, but to my mind less satisfactory, solution is proposed by e.g. Diels-Kranz: 'Feindlich dagegen ist am meisten, was am meisten voneinander absteht *in* Ursprung, Mischung und ausgeprägten Gestalten, gänzlich ungewohnt der Verbindung...', an interpretation also adopted by e.g. Barnes 1987, 168 f.: 'But most hostile are the things which differ most from one another | *in* birth and blending and moulded shape, | quite unaccustomed to come together...' (my italics).

[237] Use of εἶδος in this sort of context may be seen as paving the way for the semantic development seen at e.g. Thucydides, 3.82.2.3 and Euripides, *Iphigenia in Tauris* 817; see sec. 12 below.

[238] In this context one is reminded of the report on Empedocles by Diogenes Laertius (8.58 = DK31A1): φησὶ δὲ Σάτυρος ἐν τοῖς βίοις ὅτι καὶ ἰατρὸς ἦν καὶ ῥήτωρ ἄριστος. 'And Satyros in the Lives says that he was a physician as well as an excellent orator.' Schofield (in Kirk, Raven and Schofield 1983, 282), in commenting on 31A1, adduces 31B147 as potential indication of Empedocles' affiliations with the medical profession.

[239] That is to say, leaving aside whether αἷμα was seen as one type of flesh, a question which the grammar of the line leaves open.

[240] Neither suggestion amounts quite to saying: 'From living beings he made dead bodies, changing <them>...' [*pace* Mansfeld 1987, 473]; or: 'From living things he made corpses, changing their forms' [*pace* Barnes 1987, 197].

[241] A different picture is presented in the first substantial chapter by A. Motte in Motte et al. 2003.

[242] Note that, just potentially, that could be said of εἶδος at *Epidemics* 1.20, discussed in sec. 9 above.

²⁴³ For this usage, cf. also the 4th-century poet Timotheus 15 (*Persae*), 136.

²⁴⁴ As elsewhere, brackets indicate that the terms in parentheses are not part of the meaning of the word under consideration but are supplied in the text. The terms in parentheses are given solely to indicate application, i.e. immediate context, of the words discussed and translated.

²⁴⁵ Cf., above, end of sec. 5 on Herodotus 1.94.

²⁴⁶ For this passage cf. in particular Weidauer 1954, 21–31. In an elaborate attempt, Weidauer tries to establish a meaning 'Zustand, Verfassung', which may approximately be rendered 'state (of affairs), constitution (of things)', a meaning Thucydides has allegedly taken from Hippocratic usage. In secs. 6–10 above, I arrived at a different conclusion for the usage of the medical writers; in what follows, I hope to show why Weidauer's position is not tenable for Thucydides either. Rechenauer 1991 does not make his meaning sufficiently clear. He seems to reject Weidauer's further conclusions, but seems to accept his interpretation of Thucydides 3.62. Rechenauer claims (1991, 20 f.): 'Eine weitere methodologische Gemeinsamkeit zwischen Thukydides und der hippokratischen Medizin bildet das semeiotische Verfahren, der Schluß mittels Indizien (τεκμήρια, σημεῖα) auf Verborgenes. Wie der Arzt nach dem Prinzip ὄψις ἀδήλων τὰ φαινόμενα [n. 39] aus den sichtbaren Symptomen die gesamte "Verfassung" (εἶδος) [n. 40] erkennt und, falls möglich, die Krankheitsursache bestimmt, so schließt Thukydides an Hand von Indizien aus der Gegenwart auf die Vergangenheit zurück [n. 41] und erkennt, indem er die geschichtlichen Ereignisse in ihren Wirkungszusammenhängen zurückverfolgt, die tiefere Ursache der Geschehnisverkettung [n. 42].' That is, Rechenauer seems to posit a meaning 'Verfassung', 'constitution (?)' for εἶδος in the Hippocratic corpus and Thucydides at large; that, however, seems to be something different from what Weidauer tries to establish for Thucydides 3.62; Rechenauer's footnote 40 on p. 21 reads: 'Für nicht überzeugend halte ich die Untersuchung Weidauers über den Begriff εἶδος (a.a.O., S. 21–31). Zu der aus den hippokratischen Schriften erschlossenen Bedeutung εἶδος = 'Gesamte Verfassung' findet sich nur eine einzige Parallele in einem nebensächlichen Zusammenhang bei Thukydides (3.62.3).' Be that as it may, neither 'Verfassung' nor 'Gesamte Verfassung', either in the general sense of 'constitution (of a thing)' or in the particular one of 'constitution of a state', seems to me to be justified on the basis of the texts we have. I therefore cannot agree with Hornblower 1991, whose comments on εἶδος and in particular ἰδέα are otherwise more judicious than those of other commentators, when he translates Thucydides 3.62.3, καίτοι σκέψασθε ἐν οἵῳ εἴδει ἑκάτεροι ἡμῶν τοῦτο ἔπραξαν (1991, 455): 'But think how different were the circumstances in which we and they acted.' This suggests εἶδος has, and therefore has acquired, a very general meaning; and that, of course, would require an explanation of how the word came to have that general meaning. But Hornblower continues immediately: 'For εἴδει ('circumstances') here see Weidauer...21 ff.: the word for which see 82. 2n. below, here means almost 'constitution' – in Greek, as in English, a word with medical associations. See my notes on 6.77.2, 8.56.2, and 90.1 (where Andrewes' notes are inadequate; Dover on 6.77.2 is better). In all these passages the notion of a 'political arrangement' is present, most clearly at 8.90; in the other passages it has travelled further, and can almost be rendered 'policy' or 'plan'. It is interesting to find εἴδει used here in a political sense so soon after the closely related word ἰδέα (2n. above) has been used of political motives.' If it can be shown that εἶδος at 3.62.3 does not carry those alleged political connotations, Hornblower's note on 82.2

and on the other passages he adduces, will have to be reconsidered as well; see also the discussion of Thucydides 1.109.1 in ch. 5, sec. 6 below.

[247] It may be worth comparing Gorgias' *Defence of Helen* for the type of argument; in his speech, Gorgias outlines four possible reasons why Helen acted as she did; βία, 'force', plays a prominent part in two of them and is mentioned in connection with the third; if Helen was forced, she is excused; this must be considered a valid argument even if Gorgias' speech as a whole is a παίγνιον. The speech by the Thebans is constructed along the lines of contemporary sophistic technique, as was the speech by the Plataeans beforehand.

[248] Regarding the two faces of τὸ εἶδος τῆς νόσου, the dynamic or processual and the static aspects of the disease, one could render the phrase with the German medical terms 'Krankheitsverlauf' and 'Krankheitsbild' respectively; the latter, however, 'Krankheitsbild', does not capture the purely static, visual aspects alone; 'Bild', like εἶδος, can refer to a whole scene, scenario or setting, either at one moment in time or evolving over a period of time.

[249] I translate 'in the most ways possible' rather than 'in most ways' because Thucydides' point is not that Athenian men are self-sufficient in most, but not in all ways; rather, comparison is made with men from other cities who are not self-sufficient in as many ways as Athenian men are.

[250] εὐτραπέλως encapsulates both 'versatility' and 'seemly behaviour'.

[251] For the sake of easy reference, I provide here in full what has been summarized in the text, together with Warner's translation, 8.89.3:

ἦν δὲ τοῦτο τὸ σχῆμα πολιτικὸν τοῦ λόγου αὐτοῖς, κατ' ἰδίας δὲ φιλοτιμίας οἱ πολλοὶ αὐτῶν τῷ τοιούτῳ προσέκειντο, ἐν ᾧπερ καὶ μάλιστα ὀλιγαρχία ἐκ δημοκρατίας γενομένη ἀπόλλυται· πάντες γὰρ αὐθημερὸν ἀξιοῦσιν οὐχ ὅπως ἴσοι, ἀλλὰ καὶ πολὺ πρῶτος αὐτὸς ἕκαστος εἶναι· ἐκ δὲ δημοκρατίας αἱρέσεως γιγνομένης ῥᾷον τὰ ἀποβαίνοντα ὡς οὐκ ἀπὸ τῶν ὁμοίων ἐλασσούμενός τις φέρει. σαφέστατα δ' αὐτοὺς ἐπῆρε τὰ ἐν τῇ Σάμῳ τοῦ Ἀλκιβιάδου ἰσχυρὰ ὄντα καὶ ὅτι αὐτοῖς οὐκ ἐδόκει μόνιμον τὸ τῆς ὀλιγαρχίας ἔσεσθαι· ἠγωνίζετο οὖν εἷς ἕκαστος αὐτὸς πρῶτος προστάτης τοῦ δήμου γενέσθαι. (90.1) οἱ δὲ τῶν τετρακοσίων μάλιστα ἐναντίοι ὄντες τῷ τοιούτῳ εἴδει καὶ προεστῶτες, Φρύνιχός τε, ὃς καὶ στρατηγήσας ἐν τῇ Σάμῳ τῷ Ἀλκιβιάδῃ τότε διηνέχθη, καὶ Ἀρίσταρχος, ἀνὴρ ἐν τοῖς μάλιστα καὶ ἐκ πλείστου ἐναντίος τῷ δήμῳ, καὶ Πείσανδρος καὶ Ἀντιφῶν καὶ ἄλλοι οἱ δυνατώτατοι, πρότερόν τε, ἐπεὶ τάχιστα κατέστησαν καὶ ἐπειδὴ τὰ ἐν τῇ Σάμῳ σφῶν ἐς δημοκρατίαν ἀπέστη, πρέσβεις τε ἀπέστελλον σφῶν ἐς τὴν Λακεδαίμονα καὶ τὴν ὁμολογίαν προυθυμοῦντο καὶ τὸ ἐν τῇ Ἠετιωνείᾳ καλουμένῃ τεῖχος ἐποιοῦντο, πολλῷ τε μᾶλλον ἔτι, ἐπειδὴ καὶ οἱ ἐκ τῆς Σάμου πρέσβεις σφῶν ἦλθον, ὁρῶντες τούς τε πολλοὺς καὶ σφῶν τοὺς δοκοῦντας πρότερον πιστοὺς εἶναι μεταβαλλομένους.

This, in fact, was mere political propaganda: it was for motives of personal ambition that most of them were following the line that is most disastrous for oligarchies when they take over from democracies. For no sooner is the change made than every single man, not being content with being the equal of others, regards himself as greatly superior to everyone else. In a democracy, on the other hand, someone who fails to get elected to office can always console himself with the thought that there was something not quite fair about it. But what had the most evident effect in urging on the dissident party was the strength of Alcibiades' position in Samos and the fact that they did not believe that the oligarchy would last. Each one of them therefore tried to get in first as leader and champion of the people in general. (90.1) Those among the Four Hundred who were chiefly <u>opposed to the idea of democracy</u> were led by Phrynichus, the man who had quarrelled with Alcibiades when he was in command at Samos, Aristarchus, who had been for a long time a particularly bitter enemy of the democracy, Pisander, Antiphon, and others belonging to the most powerful families. Even before this time – in fact as soon as they came into power and the army at Samos revolted from them and constituted itself a democracy – they sent representatives of their own party to Sparta and did all they could to make peace; and they had also been building the wall in Eetionia. But now, after the return of their representatives from Samos, they became more active than ever, as they saw that not only the people in general but also members of their own party who had previously been regarded as reliable were turning against them.

[252] For the present purpose it does not matter what exactly the connotations of λόγος are at this point, whether it is what they reason or what they say to each other, or what they propose in a speech in public. I do not, however, agree with Warner who seems to take τὸ σχῆμα πολιτικὸν τοῦ λόγου as one phrase and translates it with 'political propaganda'; perhaps he has inferred this alleged meaning from the content of the next clause, which is, to my mind, the beginning of Thucydides' interpretation (as opposed to his professedly objective account of events).

[253] Thucydides' choice of words may be determined by the principle of variation; on the other hand, the whole chapter seems to have a more colloquial ring; in that vein, in the sentence immediately preceding the passage quoted above, 89.2, he states that some of the oligarchs just wanted to get rid of everything they had let themselves in for: ...καὶ ἡδέως ἂν ἀπαλλαγέντας πῃ ἀσφαλῶς τοῦ πράγματος πολλῷ δὴ μᾶλλον ἐπέρρωσαν. '... would have been glad enough to get out of the business, if they could do so safely' (Warner) – a rather loose use of πρᾶγμα. For 'scheme', cf. Hornblower on 3.62.3, who suggests 'plan' as a translation of εἶδος in some contexts.

[254] The only other occurrence of εἶδος in Aristophanes is at *Thesmophoriazusae* 267, where it is said of a man in disguise that 'in appearance', εἶδος, he is a woman.

[255] For the following pages, the reader may wish to consult Roskam 2003 on the *Hippias Minor, Alcibiades* 1, *Apology, Euthyphro, Crito, Hippias Major, Lysis, Charmides* and *Laches*, and Jeanmart 2003 on the *Protagoras, Gorgias* and *Meno*; note that the authors in Motte, Rutten and Sommville 2003 use various impressions of Burnet's Oxford Text throughout.

[256] The verb ἐπονομάζεσθαι, 'naming', seems to occur naturally in this context; it is important to note how the father-son relationship is described in this context, as overtones of this sort of hierarchy may have resonated in the minds or in the subconscious of the reader when the noun ἐπωνυμία, '(be-)naming, is used in the *Phaedo* in connection with things themselves and those particulars which receive their 'benamings' from the things themselves; this connection and these overtones may obtain in addition to what was characterized as a potentially 'divine' or 'religious' background to the noun in n. 43 on the occasion of discussion of Herodotus 2.53 above. Cf. also nn. 3, 37, 186 above and 256 below.

[257] This is not to be taken as a suggestion to read τὸ εἶδος πᾶν καλός. I rather think that given that the whole appearance is contrasted with that of the face, the prefix need not qualify only the adjective to which it is attached. I will not here repeat the argument,

set out at length in the discussion of Homer and other early poetic passages, that there is no need and no justification to take εἶδος to mean 'body' just because the appearance of a person undressed is contrasted with the appearance of his face; that they are looking at Charmides' body, head to toe, is implied by the mention of undressing; one could say it is a matter of pragmatics, not semantics. Nor, of course, does εἶδος mean 'beauty'; *pace* Roskam 2003, 70 f.

²⁵⁸ χείρ can mean 'arm' or 'hand'; the adjective ἄκρος indicates the latter is meant here; Socrates wants to stress that the person is fully clothed.

²⁵⁹ For the *Gorgias*, the edition by Dodds 1959 is used throughout. Dodds (328) translates 503e1 ff. as 'just as all other craftsmen, with an eye to their own function, each of them applies the measures he applies, not at random but selecting them in order to get the thing he is making a particular form,' and has an elaborate note on previous discussions, parallels, and possible implications of the sentence.

²⁶⁰ Here I punctuate differently from Dodds.

²⁶¹ In accordance with Greek idiom, the phrase translated literally as 'just as all the other craftsmen' does not in itself imply that the orator as orator is a craftsman.

²⁶² This is all that can be asserted about this passage. I would therefore disagree with Dodds who declares, loc. cit., after having adduced for comparison *Euthyphro* 6e4, *Cratylus* 389a–c, and *Republic* 596b: 'Nothing, however, requires us to read the full-blown theory of Forms into the *Euthyphro* or the *Gorgias*, though the striking similarity of language in all four passages is suggestive of how Plato may have been led to it.' My point of disagreement, apart from the notion of a 'theory of Forms' itself, is that either Plato had already thought for himself or discussed with his friends what he would say when writing the *Republic*: in that case, the sentence in the *Gorgias* would be an explicit allusion to what Dodds terms 'the full-blown theory of Forms'. Or else, Plato had not yet thought the thoughts he was later to express in writing; in that case, it would indeed be wrong to 'read back the full-blown theory of Forms' into this passage, but so to speak *a fortiori*, because in that case it would be wrong to read any 'theory of Forms' into the *Gorgias*. One cannot allude to something which one has not thought of yet. Perhaps, however, Dodds wants to make this very point when he says that 'the striking similarity of language in all four passages is suggestive of how Plato may have been led to [the full-blown theory of Forms].' In that case my criticism would only regard the ill-chosen 'full-blown'. A different question is what a reader of the *Gorgias*, who had already read the *Republic*, would have thought while reading the passage at hand; but that is not our present concern. With the translation proposed and defended here, contrast Jeanmart 2003, 82 f.

²⁶³ Hamilton 1971 translates 'knowing' and 'believing' which is not wrong altogether, but eliminates the activity and the process which lead to those states, something crucial to the argument; Waterfield 1994 renders the words in his rather free translation of the dialogue as 'I've been taught' and 'I'm convinced' – that will not do, because one can have been taught that the earth is flat and can, subsequently, be convinced of it; the distinction Socrates is aiming at is blurred by this translation.

²⁶⁴ Dodds notes (1959, 206): 'e 1. τε [γε]. This combination is decidedly rare (Denniston, 161). Here γε has little point, and the omission of τε in F suggests that τε and γε were originally alternative variants, which have been conflated in BTW.' That is not necessarily so. In the sentence ἀλλὰ μὴν οἵ τέ γε μεμαθηκότες πεπεισμένοι εἰσὶν καὶ οἱ πεπιστευκότες, Socrates introduces a new thought which contains in some sense

a qualification of what has just been agreed upon; this is expressed most of all by μήν, 'though' or 'yet', which follows the generally contrasting ἀλλά, 'but' or 'however'; since, however, Socrates wants to obtain Gorgias' consent to that further statement as well, he gives it the form of a generally accepted assertion; that is achieved by the particle γε, 'certainly'. In a hypothetical phrase ἀλλὰ μήν γε οἵ τε μεμαθηκότες, there would indeed be an accumulation of three particles at the beginning of a clause; it is, however, perfectly common for an enclitic γε placed after a noun or adjective (here after the article depending on the substantival participle) not only to qualify the word it leans against, but the whole phrase, clause or sentence; and τε as connective must have precedence as a matter of course; a connective correlative to the καί later on in the sentence, however, is to be expected. I should therefore accept the text of BTW.

[265] It is difficult to find an appropriate translation for ἐπιστήμη; 'knowledge, learning, science, craft, profession, understanding' all capture aspects the Greek word had at some time in some dialect (cf. Snell 1924, and Lyons 1969); 'knowledge' is here used for ἐπιστήμη and 'having understood' given as translation of μεμαθηκέναι; it is less important for Socrates' argument to differentiate between ἐπιστήμη and εἰδέναι in the preceding clause; the nominalized infinitive εἰδέναι is there best captured with 'knowledge'; but nothing depends on these choices for the present purpose.

[266] ἔλεγχος and ἐλέγχειν are *voces mediae*, meaning respectively 'proof' or 'refutation' and 'proving' or 'disproving', 'proving right' or 'proving wrong', according to context and circumstances; here, the noun is translated with 'proof' in the first place, since that is what Polus was talking about; the verb, however, must in this context denote 'disproving' or 'proving wrong'.

[267] In this context it does not necessarily matter if any one particular piece of Isocrates was composed before, after, or simultaneously with any one of the dialogues of Plato. Cf., however, Eucken 1983; in a systematic investigation based on content and language, Eucken (cf. in particular the summary 284 f.) is led, if I understand him correctly, to posit more or less the following chronology of selected works of Isocrates and Plato: *Against the Sophists* (390), *Gorgias, Euthydemus, Meno, Phaedo* (?), *Helena* (385), *Symposium, Panegyricus* (380), *Busiris, Republic* (374), *To Nicocles – Nicocles – Euagoras* (371–368/7), *Phaedrus* (c. 370), Isocrates' *Letter to Dionysius* (369/7), *Theaetetus* (367/6), *Politicus, Timaeus, Areopagitus* (354), *Antidosis* (354/3), *Philippus* (346). Without endorsing all the individual arguments for this particular sequence, I accept this chronology in so far as works published after the *Republic* – and to a certain extent that includes Isocrates' *Busiris* which Eucken interprets as written as a reaction to Platonic material related to the *Republic* circulated before its completion – cannot be used as evidence for our purpose of investigating Greek usage potentially influencing Plato while composing his early and middle dialogues. That excludes from consideration *Euagoras* 9, *Antidosis* 74 and 280; nevertheless, those instances could confirm semi-technical use of εἶδος by the rhetorician.

[268] Cf. Eucken 1983, 36–43.

[269] Cf. LSJ, s.v. τέμνειν VI 2 b, VI 3 a; Hippias is still in his extended metaphor of sea-faring vocabulary; therefore this occurrence of the word should be listed under VI 3 a, unless one is of the opinion that the phrase μέσον τεμεῖν, of whatever origin, had become a standing phrase for 'striking a deal, making a compromise, meeting in the middle', before Plato employed it in this passage; in that case, Plato would in accustomed fashion reactivate a metaphor, i.e. make it apparent as metaphor, by setting it into an

extended quasi-allegorical context (for this standard practice of Plato's cf. Classen 1959 and 1960); the phrase as found in this passage, however, is μέσον τι τέμνειν, and the indefinite pronoun seems to me to suggest that Plato lets Hippias indicate that he is coining a metaphor, rather than employing an already existing one.

[270] For a recent, brief discussion of this usage, adducing a number of relevant passages and some pertinent secondary literature, see conveniently Rowe 1995, 4–8: 'Forms, classes, and division.' The *opinio communis* is that, in the *Politicus*, the nouns εἶδος and γένος are synonyms; while I would agree that the two nouns seem to be interchangeable in many or most of their occurrences in Plato's dialogues after the *Republic*, I should argue that that is a necessary but not a sufficient condition for synonymity; I reserve this issue for treatment elsewhere.

[271] For a collection, cf. Ammann 1953. For method and concept of διαίρεσις, or 'division', and a collection of passages in early Platonic dialogues comparable to that at *Laches* 191, cf. Classen 1959, 78–84; cf. also in general Koller 1960.

[272] Here as above, the term 'classification' is used anachronistically as a convenient shorthand; cf., sec. 14 below.

[273] For *Gorgias* 462e5–466a3, see Dodds, op. cit., pp. 224 – 33, especially table and explanation pp. 226 f.

[274] The text of the *Laches* as a whole, and of this and the preceding pages in particular, is not in a good state. On the one hand, there are numerous places in which any two of B, T and W go against the remaining one; and no one manuscript seems to be significantly more trustworthy than the others. On the other hand, there is a fair degree of consensus among editors to athetize two phrases in Laches' statement at 191b4–7; and with the repetition of ἀνδρεῖοί εἰσιν at d6 and d6/7, there arises the question if some or all of the clause καὶ ὅσοι γε πρὸς νόσους καὶ ὅσοι πρὸς πενίας ἢ καὶ πρὸς τὰ πολιτικὰ ἀνδρεῖοί εἰσιν should go as well, especially as it creates an odd imbalance of five types of courage in the face of griefs and fear-inspiring things; my guess is that at least the phrase καὶ ὅσοι πρὸς πενίας ἢ καὶ πρὸς τὰ πολιτικὰ ἀνδρεῖοί εἰσιν is a later addition; but that need not detain us here. What is more relevant is that at 187e7, in a statement of Nicias about Socrates, there is a form γένει which defies explanation and has by common consent been excluded from the text; was it in origin an annotation by the same early reader? In the same vein, it is conceivable that a reader who knew Plato's *Republic* found at this point in the *Laches* the phrase 'people courageous in infantry and cavalry' and was reminded of the φύλακες or 'guardians' of the *Republic*, and for some reason associated this stratum of society with the terminology of τὸ πολεμικὸν εἶδος, 'the warrior-class'.

[275] For a full discussion of *Lysis* 221e7–222a3 and related usage in the *Republic* and elsewhere in Plato's dialogues, and for an assessment of the scholarly controversies connected with the issue, cf. Herrmann 2007, 209–211 and 225–8.

[276] See Onions et al. 1966, s.vv. 'wise'; '-wise'; 'guise'. Cf. Frisk 1973, I, 451–2.

[277] See LSJ s.v. τύπος.

[278] Onions 1973, s.v. 'Type', 5.

[279] As regards its etymology, Latin *forma* may be closely related to μορφή, a word which does indeed denote 'form' or sometimes 'shape'; but this etymology is of secondary importance only, when the actual usage of the English word 'form' is concerned. For the etymology of Latin *forma*, see Walde-Hofmann 1965, II, 530 f., s.v. 'forma'.

[280] Cf. also Gillespie 1912.

Chapter 5

[281] 'Totality', as the original force of *a*-stems was collective/generic; 'in an instant', if the function of the zero-grade of graded roots is just to state the verbal action, as witnessed in the aorist. A comparison of the analyses of ἰδέα by two of the foremost historical linguists of the 20th century teaches how little can be stated for certain at this remote stage of the language. Chantraine 1933, 91: '§ 70. De même que le grec possède un suffixe -ία répondant au masculin -ιος, il existe une finale -εα reposant sans doute sur -εγα à côté de la finale -εος... – ἰδέα "apparence, forme" (ionien-attique) est tiré de l'aoriste ἰδεῖν qui repose sans doute sur une contraction.' By contrast, Hofmann 1950, 70, s.v. εἶδος: 'εἶδος n. Aussehen, Gestalt: aus *ϝeides-....– ἰδέᾱ f. äußere Erscheinung, Gestalt, Anblick (wohl *ϝιδέσᾱ)...' Hofmann's "wohl" signifies, in his own words, an 'uncertain assumption'; I believe Chantraine's 'sans doute' has a similar force. (Given that the first two instances of the word are in Theognis and Pindar, Chantraine's comment 'ionien-attique' may seem in need of justification.) We cannot be ultimately certain about the word's formation, and connotations can only be gleaned from the actual contexts in which the word occurs.

[282] On related grounds, it has seemed on occasion more practical to diverge from a treatment in chronological order.

[283] Text and translation West 1989 and 1993.

[284] Cf. e.g. *Odyssey* 8.164 ff., *Iliad* 3.212 ff., discussed in ch. 4, sec. 1, pp. 97 f. above.

[285] There is a distinct possibility here that regardless of the precise meaning of ἰδέα Theognis felt an etymological connection between εἰδείης in line 125 and ἰδέαι in line 128; cf. n. 151 to ch. 4, sec. 1 above.

[286] For an accusative of respect, cf. the first fragment of Eupolis' *Golden Race*, in which one person accuses another of being κακὸς τὴν ἰδέαν, 'bad of appearance'. A passage in the fables of Aesop (*Fabulae Dosithei*, ed. Hausrath and Hunger, *Corpus fabularum Aesopicarum*, vol. 1.2), telling the tale of a stag discovering its image in the water of a spring, relates (1.3) how it encounters τῇ τοῦ σώματος ἰδέᾳ, 'the appearance of its body', and continues: καὶ μάλιστα μὲν ἐπῄνει τὴν φύσιν τῶν κεράτων ἀνατεταμένων τε εἰς πολὺν ἀέρα καὶ ὡς κόσμος εἴη παντὶ τῷ σώματι. 'And most of all it praised the nature of its antlers both for being stretched out high into the air and for being an adornment for the whole body.' At whatever time this was written, ἰδέα here, as well, does not mean 'body' (a claim often made about εἶδος by those who also state that εἶδος and ἰδέα are synonyms); it may, though, be significant that the aspect of what is referred to by ἰδέα which is praised most of all, the antlers, is distinctive in particular in its figure or shape.

[287] The phrase †ζωρά τε τὰ πρὶν ἄκρητα† of Plutarch's text does not make sense, for ζωρός is something like 'strong, hot', and the five passages contrasting ζωρότερος and ἄκρατος οἶνος in Philumenus *De Venenatis Animalibus* (ed. Wellmann, CMG 10.1.1, ch. 2.3, 4.2, 14.7, 23.4, 37.3), adduced by Kranz, do not prove what Kranz and subsequent editors suppose them to prove: 'rather strong wine' can indeed be opposed to 'unmixed wine'; that does not stop *strong* wine from being the same as *unmixed* wine, as indeed it is from archaic to Hellenistic Greek literature. Cf. Arundel 1962, 109–11. As for the text, in addition to the solution offered there, two possibilities worth considering are: either to read something like ζωρά τε καὶ πρὶν ἄκρητα διαλλάξαντα κελεύθους... 'and what was strong and unmixed before, changing its ways...' – that is to say, a freestanding nominative, picked up by the genitive of line 16; or to read something like αἶψα δὲ θνῆτ' ἐφύοντο· τὰ πρὶν μάθον ἀθάνατ' εἶναι, | ζῷα τε τὰ πρὶν ἄκρητα, 'but forthwith

310

there grew mortal beings: what previously had learnt to be immortal; and living beings: what previously had been unmixed <elements>'.

[288] Neither this emendation, nor the slight difficulty in syntax of this and the following line need detain us here.

[289] LSJ s.v. δέμας: 'living body'.

[290] For a discussion of the syntax, cf. Dover 1968, commentary ad. loc.; and for the sense Sommerstein 1982, note ad. loc. ἰδέας may well be genitive singular and nevertheless refer to each cloud's individual figure, just as ὄμματι in the singular does not imply either that all the clouds had one eye collectively, or else that each cloud was in possession of one eye only.

[291] Cf. in general the discussion of the preceding pages in ch. 4, sec. 7, pp. 118 f. above; note in particular the two occurrences of φύσις in *Airs, Waters, and Places* 24.36–45:

ὅκου γὰρ αἱ μεταβολαί εἰσι πυκνόταται τῶν ὡρέων καὶ πλεῖστον διάφοροι αὐταὶ ἑωυτῇσιν, ἐκεῖ καὶ τὰ εἴδεα καὶ τὰ ἤθεα καὶ τὰς φύσιας εὑρήσεις πλεῖστον διαφερούσας. μέγισται μὲν οὖν εἰσιν αὗται τῆς φύσιος αἱ διαλλαγαί, ἔπειτα δὲ καὶ ἡ χώρη, ἐν ᾗ ἄν τις τρέφηται καὶ τὰ ὕδατα. εὑρήσεις γὰρ ἐπὶ τὸ πλῆθος τῆς χώρης τῇ φύσει ἀκολουθέοντα καὶ τὰ εἴδεα τῶν ἀνθρώπων καὶ τοὺς τρόπους.

Indeed, where the changes of the seasons are most frequent, and <the seasons> most different from one another, there you will also find the appearances and the characters and the natures as differing most widely. These, now, are the greatest differences in nature, then also the land in which someone is reared, and the waters. You will find, indeed, that for the most part the appearances and the ways of the people follow the nature of the land.

[292] It may not be by accident that the rarer, more elevated, and perhaps also more comprehensive word ἰδέα is used only at this point at the end of the treatise, a treatise in which the author frequently talked about the εἶδος or appearance of people, and in which it is not easy to decide if the extension in meaning from 'appearance' to 'type' has already taken place or is approached but is as yet to be realized. Could it therefore be that one should understand: 'Such are the natures and types most opposed to each other: judging from those infer the rest, and you will not go wrong'? A decision cannot be reached for *Airs, Waters, and Places*; for the general semantic development, however, see sec. 5 below.

[293] For chronological matters concerning Xenophanes, it is still worth considering Reinhardt 1916, especially pp. 89–106, 155–8, 221–30. For Anaxagoras' date, see Schofield 1980, 33 (ch. 1, Appendix: Anaxagoras' floruit): 'In the previous section I have implied that the formation of Anaxagoras' thought antedated the rise of the Sophistic movement, and that his book must be dated significantly earlier than the treatise of Diogenes of Apollonia and the oldest treatises in the Hippocratic corpus (I mentioned *On the Sacred Disease* and *On Ancient Medicine* in this respect, but the same goes for *Airs, Waters, and Places* [n. 71]). This is not a controversial opinion. But it is worth while adducing some reasons for putting the date of the composition of his book, as I incline to put it, at roughly 470–460 BC.' Schofield then produces five distinct arguments for this dating. He concludes (35): 'A *floruit* of 470–460 BC fits well enough with what little we can say of the relation between Anaxagoras' thought and that of other fifth-century philosophers. It is late enough for him to have taken profit from the reflection he evidently devoted to Parmenides' work. It is early enough for his book to have antedated, as it probably did, the physical poem of Empedocles [n. 86] and the work of Leucippus.

It leaves the temporal relation of his thought with that of Zeno [n. 87] and Melissus appropriately obscure.' Cf. Sider 2005, 1–12; Sider summarizes (11): '(I) Anaxagoras writes *c.* 470–65, in ignorance of and unknown to Zeno, who writes in this same period. (ii) His book makes its way to Athens, perhaps leading to an invitation from Pericles. (iii) Arrival in Athens 465/4. (iv) His book is read by and influences Aeschylus, Agatharchus, and Empedocles. Later readers include Socrates, Euripides, Democritus, and anyone with a drachma to spare in the book stalls of the Agora, where the work was available from *c.* 450 to 399 (*Apol.* 26de).'

[294] The translation of fr. 4 is a slightly modified version of Schofield's (1980, 101) slightly modified version of the version by Furley 1976, 72.

[295] Cf. the comments by Sider 2005; he translates 'shapes' (92) and comments (96): ' ἰδέας | Vlastos [1950] 32n7…prefers the translation "forms," as in "two ἰδέαι of knowledge" (Democ. B11), but not, as Vlastos thinks, in Hipp. *Nat.Hom.* 2.7 f., 5.15 f. (= 166.16, 176.8 Jouanna), where Jouanna shows that shape, "aspect extérieur," is the more likely meaning. Moreover, Aët. 1.14.4 (A51) τὰ ὁμοιομέρη πολυσχήμονα probably derives from a Theophrastan reading of ἰδέας as "shapes." Nor is this contradicted by Simplicius 44.9 f. κυρίως τῆς ἐναντιότητος ἐν ταῖς ποιότησι θεωρουμένης ἀλλ' οὐκ ἐν τοῖς σχήμασιν, which says only that a seed's shape does not determine its character, as shape does Democritus' atoms.'

[296] For a re-evaluation of the significance of Diogenes of Apollonia, and a sketch of his position in 5th-century philosophy, see Stokes 1971, 238–44. As a provocative starting point still valuable on Diogenes' position within the history and development of 5th-century thought is Theiler 1925; informative on all aspects of Diogenes is the standard edition and commentary by Laks 1983; for a summary of recent debate on Diogenes and the Derveni papyrus see Betegh 2004.

[297] ζῷα are, of course, all 'living beings'.

[298] Cf. Laks 1983, xxxiv f. and xix with n. 2.

[299] See p. 95 above.

[300] p. 155.

[301] See p. 153.

[302] Cf. also Motte 2003, 40.

[303] See Diels-Kranz 1952, II, 99, *apparatus* ad loc. An alternative feminine noun could be οὐσία (cf. Barnes 1982, 344); but this would at best reflect post-Aristotelian usage and could not go back to Democritus himself.

[304] I shall not attempt to translate this lexicon entry. Concerning the evidence for Democritus' employing the word ἰδέα, one could further think of περὶ ἰδεῶν, given as the title of one of Democritus' many books (DK68B6; cf. B5i); the apparatus to B6 has the entry (Diels-Kranz 1951, II, 138): 'Brandis hat erkannt, daß die ἰδέαι sich auf die Formen der Atome beziehen, die in der Schrift περὶ τῶν διαφερόντων ῥυσμῶν dargestellt waren.' But the title has convincingly been emended to περὶ εἰδώλων; see Mansfeld 1987, 648. He groups 68A135, for which he accepts Schneider's emendation of εἴδων to εἰδώλων, together with 68B6, for which he proposes emendation of ἰδεῶν. For the whole question of the meaning of ἰδέα with Democritus cf., however, also Baldry 1937, 141 f., n. 4; Baldry does accept the emendation of ἀτόμους ἰδέας to ἀτόμους ἰδίως in the passage from Plutarch and retains εἰδέων in B167. Of Hesychius, he says that the gloss may just as well refer to, *exempli gratia, Timaeus* 54d f. While I do not agree with Baldry's assertion that εἶδος and ἰδέα are synonyms, or with his suggestion that both

terms or either one of them has developed to mean something like 'quality' (142 ff.), it must be noted that if all emendations changing forms of ἰδέα into something else, but not the one changing εἰδέων to ἰδέων, are accepted, we are left with very little evidence even for the occurrence of the word, let alone its significance or meaning with Democritus. Cf. also the speculations by Motte 2003, 37–48, esp. 38–40. Huffman 2006, 250, suggests that ἰδέα in B167, B6 and A57 means 'shape' and is synonymous with εἶδος as employed by Democritus' 'contemporary' Archytas in DK47B4, where reference is to mathematical shapes. But even if Archytas B4 were genuine, the connection does not seem to me to be obvious.

[305] Cf., in addition to Diels-Kranz, e.g. recently Motte 2003, 38.

[306] Presumably for that reason, v. Fritz does not mention ἰδέα at all in his section on Democritus (1938, 12–38).

[307] Cf. the discussion by v. Fritz 1938, 12–38.

[308] Cf. e.g. Zeller 1920, II, 1058 f., n. 3; and esp. 1063 with n. 3; Taylor 1999, 153, 172; Motte 2003, 40 ff. Cf. also DK68B5i and B6, where περὶ ἰδεῶν is mentioned as a book title ascribed to Democritus. Cf. n. 304.

[309] Cf. e.g. Simplicius *In 'De Caelo'*, 294, 33–295, 24 = Aristotle fr. 208 Rose = DK68A37.

[310] 'Appearance' in an absolute sense would be possible, despite the paradox that the atoms are small beyond perception; that does not stop them from appearing theoretically, even if there is nobody they could appear to.

[311] See pp. 155 f.

[312] See ch. 4, sec. 5, pp. 111 f. above.

[313] Cf. Baldry 1937, 141.

[314] Translation Godley 1926.

[315] I am not absolutely convinced that our knowledge of the usage of Greek pronouns is sufficient to justify the emendation [ἥδε] ἰδέη <αὕτη>. The sense of the clause is unambiguous.

[316] The translation is a very slightly adapted version of that by Godley 1926. He has a note explaining: ' "for the ibis is of two kinds": *Geronticus Calvus* and *Ibis Aethiopica*.'

[317] See ch. 4, sec. 5 above.

[318] A detailed analysis of the semantic development leading from 'appearance' to 'type' is provided in ch. 4, secs. 9–11 and 13 above.

[319] See pp. 136 f.

[320] For the selection of Hippocratic writing considered see ch. 4, sec. 6 above.

[321] See sec. 2, p. 155 above.

[322] Compare in particular *Nature of Man* 2 with Diogenes 64B2 and B5; cf. e.g. Plamböck 1964, 12–16, especially 14, n. 1: 'Die Verwandtschaft mit Gedanken des Anaxagoras und des Diogenes von Apollonia ist natürlich auffällig genug, vgl. etwa Vors. 59B4, 8, 12, 15 und 64B5...'; cf. also Stokes 1971, 238–44, cited n. 296 above. Stokes' view that Diogenes is the first explicitly to name and posit one substance as underlying all fits well with the other features of *Nature of Man* reminiscent of the underrated Presocratic. For a brief recent survey on the date of *The Nature of Man* cf. however also Rechenauer 1991, 175–8; not all his arguments are of equal force.

[323] The interpretations of the significance of the mention of Melissus at this point in the text offered by Jones 1931, 5, n. 1, and by Kühn 1956, 70 (Ch. 3: 'Hypothesis und Wissenschaftssystem von De Natura Hominis'), are not wholly cogent.

[324] For these two passages, and in particular for the meaning of ἰδέα and δύναμις, cf. Plamböck 1954, whose interpretation of chs. 2 and 5 I follow to a large extent.

[325] Though the author does not phrase the thought in such abstract terms.

[326] See p. 178.

[327] For adjectives in -ειδης and their meaning, cf. ch. 4, sec. 2, pp. 100 ff. above.

[328] Cf. the discussion of εἶδος in the preceding passage in Thucydides in ch. 4, sec. 12, pp. 130 ff. above.

[329] This example is discussed, and the others are listed, by Hornblower 1991, 172–4, note on Thucydides 1.109.1; I quote in full, since Hornblower provides an accurate summary and apt criticism of previous views on the matter (Rechenauer 1991 was published simultaneously but does not discuss the word ἰδέα or its uses at all); Hornblower's position serves as a good backdrop against which discussion in the text may be read; he writes:

> πολλαὶ ἰδέαι πολέμων κατέστησαν, 'they experienced the many different forms and fortunes of war'. As the scholiast noted, both notions (forms, fortunes) are probably conveyed by ἰδέαι, lit. 'kinds'. Phrases like this one, often expressed in the words πᾶσα ἰδέα κατέστη, 'there was every form of…', are frequent in Th., esp. with words meaning death (θανάτου, ὀλέθρου). Cp. iii. 81. 5, 83. 1, 98. 3; vii. 29.5; also ii. 19. 1. Th.'s fondness for the locution has not interested commentators, though Classen/Steup do give parallels. It has been studied by K. Weidauer, *Thukydides und die hippokratischen Schriften* (Heidelberg, 1953), 26 f. As he says, the Hippocratic corpus of medical writings uses ἰδέα with the genitive to differentiate particular instances of a general phenomenon, e.g. four kinds of fluid (blood, bile, etc.): τέσσαρες ἰδέαι χόλου, *On Diseases*, iv. 32. Cp. 'all the discharges of bile' to which doctors have given names, ἀποκαθάρσεις χολῆς πᾶσαι, at Th. ii. 49. 3 (though this is really a way of disclaiming excessive technicality; cp. *Thucydides*, 97, 134). Note also ii. 51. 1, in the description of the plague, where we have ἐπὶ πᾶν τὴν ἰδέαν, 'in all its forms', used of the plague itself. These Hippocratic usages are discussed in C.M. Gillespie, 'The Use of Εἶδος and Ἰδέα in Hippocrates', *CQ* 6 (1912), 179 ff., a sensible reply to some needlessly complicated pages of A.E. Taylor, *Varia Socratica*, I (Oxford, 1911). (Note Gillespie, 202. 'in Thucydides, πᾶσα ἰδέα has become so much a formula that it does not matter whether we translate *form, mode* or *kind*'.) Taylor is, however, useful for his collection of all (but see below) relevant passages in Th. and other relevant fifth-century authors. He points out that Th. uses κατέστη only with ἰδέα, not with the closely related word εἶδος. Of κατέστη Taylor claims (189) that it is 'itself a word of medicine' and concludes (190) that 'the repeated conjunction πᾶσα ἰδέα τινος κατέστη points to a borrowing by Thucydides from the language of medicine'. Taylor gives no authority for the claim about κατέστη (nor does Weidauer, quoting Taylor), nor does it seem to be particularly 'medical' (the treatises sometimes use the verb in the special sense 'recover', but that is not relevant here). Perhaps Taylor is thinking of the undoubtedly medical connotations of the related noun κατάστασις, 'constitution' (three instances in one Hippocratic paragraph at *Epidemics*, iii. xvi (Loeb Hippocrates, I. 256)). Even if κατέστη could be shown to be frequent in the Hippocratic writings, it is too common and favourite in Th., as are the other parts of the verb from which it comes, for this to mean much (there are over five pages on καθιστάναι in Bétant's *Lexicon Thucydideum*). Equally, ἰδέα is clearly not a recherché word, though it was perhaps a fashionable one: see

below (it is relevant that Hdt. anticipates Th.'s use of ἰδέα, vi. 119. 2: τριφασίας ἰδέας).

Weidauer (above), discussing ἰδέα and κατέστη, says that Th. and the Hippocratics use some of the same language not because of any borrowing but because they are both fond of tracing divergent phenomena. One can perhaps go a little further than this (though less far than Taylor wanted): if Th.'s language in the present passage sounds semi-technical, or rather – given that the context is warfare, not death or disease – a little pretentious, that is perhaps because such terms as he uses were the small change of philosophical or rhetorical discussion. Cp. Demokritos, DK68B11, 'there are two kinds, ἰδέαι, of knowledge, γνώμη, one genuine, the other bastard [or 'obscure'].' (I do not know why Taylor's section on sophists and Presocratics omits this interesting passage, which is quoted by Sextus Empiricus); and the Hdt. passage cited above. See above, 1. 1n. on ἀξιολογώτατον for the indebtedness of both Th. and the doctors to the language and methods of rhetorical debate.

But what of Th.'s fondness for the *whole phrase* πᾶσα ἰδέα κατέστη or the similar phrase found here, πολλαὶ ἰδέαι κατέστησαν? This seems, despite Taylor, to be an idiosyncrasy of his own.

330 Hornblower translates: 'They tried every means of escape.'

331 Cf. ἐς φύγην ἐτράποντο Herodotus 8.89; cf. τραπόμενοι ἔφευγον Thucydides 3.98.1; cf. also the immediately preceding paragraph in Thucydides 3.11.5: οἱ δὲ λοιποὶ κατὰ τὰ ὄρη ἐς φύγην ὥρμησαν, 'the rest rushed to flight into the mountains'.

332 At Thucydides 6.77.2 and 8.56.2, and at Aristophanes, *Plutus* 316 f. Cf. ch. 4, sec. 11 above.

333 For 3.62, cf. the discussion in ch. 4, sec. 12, pp. 132–5 above. 4.55.2 παρὰ τὴν ὑπάρχουσαν σφῶν ἰδέαν τῆς παρασκευῆς, 'against their accustomed way of fighting'. 6.76.3 τῇ δὲ αὐτῇ ἰδέᾳ ἐκεῖνά τε ἔσχον καὶ τὰ ἐνθάδε νῦν πειρῶνται, 'in the same way they got hold of those, they now also try here'; note the use of the phrase ἐπὶ τοῦτο τὸ εἶδος τρεπομένους ὥστε in 6.77.2 – another case of variation as with 3.62? 7.82.1 ταύτῃ τῇ ἰδέᾳ, 'in that way'; the phrase refers to a way of acting described in the preceding clauses.

334 For a discussion of these passages cf. ch. 4, sec. 12, pp. 136–8 above.

335 For Aristophanes *Plutus* 557–61 ('appearance') and *Clouds* 288 ff. ('figure'), cf. secs. 1, 2, and 3, pp. 152, 154 f., 157–9 above.

336 Dover 1993, commentary ad. loc.

337 In 5th-century oratory the word ἰδέα is rare. At Andocides, *On the Mysteries* 100, 5 and Lysias 2.4.8, ἰδέα denotes a human being's figure, without any connotations of beauty.

338 Ch. 4, sec. 12 above.

339 See sec. 5, p. 166 above.

340 Whether the difficult passage Herodotus 6.119 can be taken as evidence for ἰδέα as 'appearance' or 'figure' in the sense of 'a certain thing' must be left undecided.

341 See sec. 6, pp. 167–9 above.

342 Cf. Plamböck 1954, 15, n. 1.

343 Note that on the one surviving occasion when Democritus distinguishes between 'two types' of something, 68B11, he uses the word ἰδέα. In similar fashion, the author of *The Nature of Man* uses ἰδέα for 'type' in that section of his work in which he otherwise discusses things and their ἰδέα. However, he uses εἶδος for 'type' in the section in which

he otherwise discusses the εἶδος of something. As both εἶδος and ἰδέα could mean 'type', one could conclude that the author's choice of one or other may have been determined simply by earlier use in the same work or section of a work of either noun in any of its senses. It should be noted, though, that in the general sense of 'type', εἶδος and ἰδέα are strictly synonymous; exchanging one term for the other would in no way affect the meaning of the sentences in which the words are employed in the sense of 'type'. This, however, does not allow us to draw any conclusions regarding synonymity of the two words in other applications.

Chapter 6

[344] See Frisk 1973, II, 257 f., s.v. μορφή; and Walde-Hofmann 1965, I, 530 f., s.v. *forma*; cf. Herrmann 2006, 11–13.

[345] e.g. Herodotus 2.76; 2.96; *Airs, Waters, and Places* 14.25; 18,3; 19.3.

[346] See pp. 97–9 for other aspects of this passage.

[347] Rather than: 'god crowns his <deficient bodily> shape with words', as has been suggested.

[348] Even Hölscher 1988, 219, translates 'Schönheit', and builds part of his interpretation, not only of this particular passage, on that notion.

[349] So it is misleading for Mader 1991, col. 424, s.v. εἶδος, to state: 'Austauschwörter: εἶ(δος)...wird aufgenommen von: μορφή ϑ 170, χάρις ϑ 175.'

[350] Paley 1872, 548, ad loc.

[351] *Pace* Diels-Kranz I, 319, who – in translating 'Doch wohlan, schaue auf folgenden Zeugen meiner früheren Worte, falls etwa noch in meinen früheren ein Mangel an ihrer (*der Elemente*) Gestalt geblieben war...' – let μορφή refer to the appearance of the elements rather than to the shape of the words; they probably think of μορφή as somehow synonymous with ἰδέα or εἶδος; cf. also Democritus DK68B141; A57.

[352] Additional information about Empedocles' use of the word, however, can be derived by comparing B21 with B71 (Simplicius *De caelo* 529.28): εἰ δέ τί σοι περὶ τῶνδε λιπόξυλος ἔπλετο πίστις... 'But if, for you, persuasion was incomplete in anything with regard to those things...' In both cases, the four elements are afterwards mentioned as the matter which Empedocles is going to explain. In both cases, he employs the adjective λιπόξυλος, 'incomplete', literally, 'lacking wood'. It would be interesting to know how widespread the use of λιπόξυλος was. The word is not attested in pre-hellenistic Greek apart from these two instances. Its etymology points to the sphere of wood-working crafts as place of origin. If that be so, one would like to know if Empedocles modelled B21 on B71 or the other way around. If λιπόξυλον μορφῇ is earlier than λιπόξυλος πίστις, could μορφή have been applied to the shape of a wooden structure? We know too little about either word.

[353] 'They made up their mind' is the translation suggested by LSJ s.v. γνώμη, III; a literal translation may be 'they laid down, as their insight(s)'. On γνώμη in early Greek literature, cf. Snell 1924, 31–9; on Parmenides' usage in particular, 37 with n. 2. I am not sure, however, if Snell's interpretation of Parmenides' usage as re-evaluation of γνώμη as δόξα is correct in this instance. For mortals, what they posit *is* their cognition and insight; they lay down, as their insight, that 'there are two shapes'; as if they knew. When in B8, 61 other systems of thought are classed under the general term of βροτῶν γνώμη, that is 'what humans call γνώμη' rather than simply 'human opinion' in contrast with 'divine opinion'. Cf. also Lyons 1969, 176 n. 4. It is tempting to take κατέθεντο...γνώμας

as ἔθεντο γνώμην. While the prefix does not present a problem, it perhaps remains difficult to account for the plural of γνώμας. *Pace* e.g. Heitsch 1991, 180: 'In Vers 53 ist γνώμην κατατίθεσθαι [sic!] (vgl. Theogn. 717) zu verstehen wie γνώμην τίθεσθαι: "seine Meinung im Sinne einer Willensäußerung kundtun" (Herodot 3.80.6, 7.82, 8.108.2).' The places adduced all have γνώμην in the singular.

[354] ἐοικός, 'likely', in line 60, is *inter alia* a term of rhetoric. In the absence of facts, one produces arguments 'from what is likely', ἐξ ἐοικότων, in order to achieve persuasion. That fits in well with Parmenides' earlier mention of πίστις ἀληθής in connection with his exposition, and in particular with B8, 38 ff.: … | οὖλον ἀκίνητόν τ' ἔμεναι· τῷ πάντ' ὄνομ' ἔσται | ὅσσα βροτοὶ κατέθεντο πεποιθότες εἶναι ἀληθῆ. '(Being) is whole and unmoved: so that everything will be <mere> name, | <everything> laid down by mortals, persuaded of its being true.' (Here the goddess says explicitly that something which is not true has πίστις, 'power and cause of persuasion'. That is not contradicted by Parmenides' use of the adjective πιστός in B8, 50, for the goddess herself, from her position of universal insight, declares only the one truth as trustworthy, regardless of the persuasiveness of any other view.) At 8.38, the verb employed by Parmenides for 'the laying down' of a name is κατατίθημι, a verb used in legal context in the sense of 'decreeing'; the same verb used in B8, 53: μορφὰς γὰρ κατέθεντο δύο γνώμας ὀνομάζειν, 'they laid down, as their insight(s), to name two shapes'.

[355] Cf. Coxon 1986, 219 f. (with whom, however, I disagree on the 'earliest signification' of the word). Coxon asserts that 'the word μορφή in its earliest use signifies beauty of form, or external form or shape generally, usually as an attribute of a person or of a thing but sometimes, as here, denoting the person or thing itself… P[armenides] uses the word in the plural to refer to a pair of homogeneous, unchanging substances with both sensible and non-sensible characteristics.' The passages adduced by Coxon in support of this usage are Aeschylus *Prometheus Vinctus* 209 f., Sophocles *Electra* 197 f., and Euripides frg. 484.2. Cf. also Taylor 1911b, 252 f., who would translate 'they have made up their minds to give names to two bodies, whereof one should not receive a name'; he supposes that Parmenides' 'reasoning throughout turns on the assumption that if you admit that empty space *is* at all, you must believe that it is a kind of body, as has been well brought out by Professor Burnet.'

[356] For a discussion of μορφή in relation to δέμας in Parmenides, cf. Motte 2003, 23–5.

Chapter 7

[357] Cf. e.g. Thompson 1901, 255–8, in his *Excursus* I, 'οὐσία as a philosophical term in Plato (on [*Meno*] 72B)'; the opening paragraph of this essay reads: 'We have no certain examples of οὐσία in any sense except "wealth", "patrimony" in any writer before Plato. [The fragments of the Pythagorean Philolaus, in which it appears as a philosophical term in the form ἐσσία (cp. *Crat.* 401C), are almost certainly spurious. See Prof. Bywater in *JP*. I pp. 21 f., Archer-Hind on *Phaedo* 61d. For a different view see Zeller *pre-Socr.* I 314 and note: for a summary of the controversy R. & P. §50 c, Ueberweg-Heinze p. 58.]'; v. Fritz 1938, 53: 'An Häufigkeit des Vorkommens den Wörtern überlegen, an philosophischer Bedeutung ihnen kaum nachstehend ist das Wort οὐσία, das in seiner platonischen Verwendung ebenfalls eine Bedeutungsneuschöpfung ist. Dies Wort ist zur Zeit Platons in der attischen Sprache seit langem heimisch, aber *nur* in dieser, wie schon die Bildung zeigt: οὐσίη bei Herodot ist offensichtlich eine Teilionisierung des attischen

Wortes. Das Wort kommt jedoch vor Platon nur in einer ganz speziellen Bedeutung vor: "das Vermögen", "die Habe", "der Besitz". Es ist in dieser Bedeutung abgeleitet von einem ganz speziellen Gebrauch des Verbums εἶναι, in der Konstruktion εἶναι τινί. Es bedeutet ἅ τινι ἔστιν.' Besides Thompson and v. Fritz, the best discussions of the term οὐσία and its history are Hirzel 1913 and Classen 1959a, 158–64; some useful observations in Burnet 1924, 49 f.; Bluck 1961, 221–3; Berger 1961, 1–18; Marten 1962, 7–13. Dixsaut 1991 seems to consider the meaning of the term οὐσία in the *Phaedo* as being self-explanatory, or at least to think that Plato indicates sufficiently by his 'definitions' what is meant by οὐσία; the great virtue of her article is the argument Dixsaut provides for the priority of οὐσία over εἶδος and ἰδέα in the *Phaedo*. Cf. also the summary of a slightly different approach to the subject in Horn and Rapp (eds.) 2002, 320–4, s.v. 'ousia'.

358 v. Fritz 1938, 53.

359 See LSJ s.v. I. Instances of οὐσία in its common, Attic sense in Plato's early dialogues are *Crito* 44e5, 53b2, *Gorgias* 486c1.

360 The syntax of the Greek phrase μου ἐρομένου μελίττης περὶ οὐσίας ὅτι ποτ' ἐστίν is straightforward. On a first reading, however, one may be tempted to pause after the fourth word and understand μου ἐρομένου μελίττης πέρι, with πέρι as a postposition: 'when I asked about a bee'. This type of phrasing is familiar e.g. from *Phaedo* 65d λέγω δὲ περὶ πάντων, <u>οἷον μεγέθους πέρι</u>, ὑγιείας, ἰσχύος, καὶ τῶν ἄλλων ἑνὶ λόγω ἁπάντων τῆς οὐσίας ὃ τυγχάνει ἕκαστον ὄν, 'but I am talking about everything, as for example about size, health, strength, and, in a word, all other things' being, what each happens to be'; for a discussion of this passage see below. The phrase in the *Meno*, however, μου ἐρομένου μελίττης πέρι, could be followed immediately by the indirect question ὅτι ποτ' ἐστίν, 'what it is'; the syntax would be complete without the addition of οὐσίας. That is to say, οὐσίας could be a gloss, added with hindsight on the model of *Euthyphro* 11a and in particular of *Phaedo* 65d. The sense of the *Meno* passage would not be affected; and as a sequence of composition *Gorgias, Meno, Euthyphro, Phaedo* is plausible on independent grounds, these considerations do not make a substantial difference for the history of the semantic development of the term οὐσία either. It is important to note, though, that the very fact that the term οὐσία is strictly redundant in this context in the *Meno* facilitates its introduction with a new, technical, philosophical meaning, as this redundancy excludes any ambiguity or uncertainty concerning the sense of the passage in which the term occurs. The translation given above is meant to reflect these considerations.

361 The Greek phrase τὸ ὅσιον ὅτι ποτ' ἐστίν, τὴν μὲν οὐσίαν suggests on a first reading that τὴν μὲν οὐσίαν, 'the/its being', is in apposition to the preceding τὸ ὅσιον ὅτι ποτ' ἐστίν, 'whatever the pious is' or 'the pious, what it is'; the continuation of the sentence reveals that τὴν μὲν οὐσίαν is in fact direct object of the infinitive at the very end of the clause. The inverted word order of the translation is meant to preserve this syntactical device.

362 There is no literal way of translating πάθος δέ τι περὶ αὐτοῦ λέγειν; 'but to say some suffering about it' makes nonsense; 'to tell me one of its affections/properties/qualities' introduces terminology derived from later, post-Platonic, contexts which may certainly go back to distinctions made here, but ones which are at the same time based on different ontological suppositions; 'something it has happen to it' converts the nominal πάθος δέ τι περὶ αὐτοῦ into a verbal expression but preserves the continuity with the following ὅτι πέπονθε, 'what happens to it'; the perfect in this expression indicates that this 'affection'

is a necessary aspect of 'what the pious is'; Socrates' point here is not that to say 'the pious is god-beloved' fails to answer the question 'what is the pious' on the grounds that the pious would on occasion not actually be god-beloved; the perfect thus indicates that the πάθος in question is, in the terminology of Aristotle's *Topics* 1.5 (102a–b), ἴδιον, not συμβεβηκός, a 'property', not an 'accident': the pious is indeed always already god-beloved – but that is not sufficient for Socrates' purposes.

363 Cf. the excellent discussion of Socrates' etymologizing in Classen 1959a, esp. 1–12, 89–98, 120–37, 151–64.

364 On πάθος see n. 8 above; Bluck 1961, 209–14 discusses in detail the development of the contrast οὐσία – πάθος in Plato.

365 In parallel with *Meno* 72e f. and *Euthyphro* 11a f. above, the syntax of the Greek at *Phaedo* 65d at first suggests that the genitive in καὶ τῶν ἄλλων ἑνὶ λόγῳ ἁπάντων, 'and, in a word, of all the other things', depends on the previous περί of μεγέθους πέρι, 'about size'; the listener or reader is required to adjust his construal of the syntax with the appearance of the term οὐσία. This, in itself, calls attention to that term, as in the two earlier dialogues. The translation is intended to preserve this syntactical device.

366 To render διανοηθῆναι as 'think through' is not wholly satisfactory; it is meant to convey clearly the contrast between the act of the νοῦς or ψυχή, 'mind' or 'soul', denoted by διανοηθῆναι and the act of the body denoted by αἴσθησις, 'sensation'.

367 Emphatic ἔστιν and related forms of the verb are translated '*is*' in what follows; cf. n. 368 below.

368 The adjective ὅμοιος means 'similar', ἴσος 'equal'; the latter is not restricted in its application to what is quantifiable; but the adverb ὁμοίως may be either 'similarly' or 'equally', as the adverb ἴσως means 'perhaps' and cannot normally be used to mean 'equally'.

369 So also Rowe 1993, 177, ad loc.: 'πᾶσα ἡ τοιαύτη οὐσία· lit. 'all being of that sort': οὐσία, a noun originally derived from the verb εἶναι, is here applied collectively to a group of things in virtue of their 'being', i.e. existing (hence 'existents of this sort').'

370 In the present context, these things are the good and the beautiful, and it is of course not arbitrary that this should be so. But ὄντα can be things of any description or status, things like the good and the beautiful or, in the most general way, all the things there are, eternal and transient alike, as e.g. at *Phaedo* 79a6. *Pace* Rowe 1993, 183, ad 78d4. Cf. also the subsequent note.

371 e.g. Euripides, *Andromache* 1068: τὰ ὄντα referring to 'events'; Isaeus 5.9.2, 5.11.12: 'possessions'. Note, though, that in Attic the plural τὰ ὄντα, like the singular τὸ ὄν, could also be a synonym for 'the truth'; e.g. Thucydides 4.108.5, 6.60.2, 7.8.2; Andocides, *De mysteriis* 20.6, 59.2 – but Andocides, *De mysteriis* 138.4: 'possessions'. Cf. the ambiguous use at *Phaedo* 66a3.

372 It is not wholly satisfactory to translate κατὰ ταὐτὰ, 'according to the same', as 'constant'. See Vancamp 1996 for a discussion of the origin and significance of the phrase; but cf. also the interpretation by Ebert 2004, 255 f., which strongly suggests that for Plato himself the context of this phrase was Eleatic.

373 It may be altogether preferable to read here (and at 92d9) αὕτη ἡ οὐσία, 'this being' rather than 'the being itself', letting the demonstrative pick up the last occurrence of the word at 76d–77a.

374 The nominalized neuter participle of the verb 'be', τὸ ἐόν, had been a standard term for 'what is' in Eleatic philosophy since Parmenides (DK28B4.8; 8.32); in Attic, τὸ ὄν

is not common, but where it occurs it denotes 'what really obtained' and is, as such, a synonym of 'the truth' (e.g. Thucydides 3.22.8; Xenophon, *Cyropaedia* 5.4.7, 6.3.7). Plato, writing for an educated Greek, and particularly for an Athenian audience, could have had both usages in mind at *Phaedo* 66a8 and here at 78d4, the first occurrences of the term in his dialogues.

[375] Geddes 1863, 62: 'ἧς λόγον δίδομεν τοῦ εἶναι: *Of which we give this account* (or explanation) *that it absolutely* is. The double genitive depends on λόγον. In 76B, περί is inserted after λόγον διδόναι'. As far as syntax is concerned, this is correct. Archer-Hind 1883, 90, agrees: 'ἧς λόγον δίδομεν τοῦ εἶναι "as whose principle we assign being". λόγον = its definition, notion. τοῦ εἶναι is descriptive genitive after λόγον. Madvig proposes τὸ εἶναι, which Schanz adopts: but MS. authority is entirely against him, and there is no real difficulty in the genitive.' Fearenside and Kerin 1897, 104, offer two alternatives: 'ἧς λόγον δίδομεν τοῦ εἶναι: "of the existence of which we give the proofs", or perhaps better, "the definition whereof we give as BEING". In the first case ἧς depends on εἶναι; in the second, τοῦ εἶναι is epexegetical and might just as well be the accusative, τὸ εἶναι, as Madvig reads.' The grammatical explanation of their second, apparently preferred, alternative explicates the argument of Geddes and Archer-Hind. Williamson 1904, 154, argues along the same lines: 'ἧς λόγον δίδομεν τοῦ εἶναι: this is merely another way of saying οἷς ἐπισφραγιζόμεθα τὸ ὃ ἔστι. (75d): "that essence which we define as *being*". The relation of the two genitives, ἧς and τοῦ εἶναι, to λόγον should be carefully distinguished: ἧς is an objective genitive, the thing "of which" the definition is given; τοῦ εἶναι is the "genitive of definition", describing what the λόγος consists of. Wagner gives a version which is impossible in the context – "of the existence of which we give the proofs".' All of this is correct, and it is obvious that Fearenside and Kerin provided the first of their translations, quoted from Wagner 1870, 131, only as a polite way of rejecting his suggestion.

It was probably the authority of Burnet 1911 which has led subsequent editors astray; he writes, 66: 'ἡ οὐσία ἧς λόγον δίδομεν τοῦ εἶναι, "the reality the being of which we give account of". The hyperbaton of δίδομεν has misled the commentators here. We must take λόγον τοῦ εἶναι together as equivalent to λόγον τῆς οὐσίας or "definition", and as governing the genitive ἧς. For λόγος τῆς οὐσίας cp. *Rep.* 534b3 ἦ καὶ διαλεκτικὸν καλεῖς τὸν λόγον ἑκάστου λαμβάνοντα τῆς οὐσίας; The meaning then is simply "the reality which we define".' Burnet is clearly wrong, not least because his reading presupposes that Plato mixes two idioms, the established λόγον διδόναι with his own alleged coinage λόγος τῆς οὐσίας; at any rate, equating τοῦ εἶναι with τῆς οὐσίας in the way Burnet suggests is stylistically inelegant; in addition, Burnet's literal translation, which is closer to the text, suggests that there is a being of the being or reality which Socrates has just posited; this is in danger of invoking an infinite regress. Burnet's solution, however, is adopted by Bluck 1955 and Hackforth 1955. The difference between the latter two is summarized by Gallop 1975, 138 f.: '78d1–5. The grammar and sense of the words translated "the Being itself, whose being we give an account of" (d1–2) are uncertain. "The Being itself" clearly refers to the domain of Forms... But "giving an account" could mean either "giving a definition" or "giving a proof"; and the use of "being" may be either "incomplete" or "complete"... "Giving an account" of a Form's "being" may therefore mean either "defining its essential nature" or "proving that it exists". Loriaux...defends the existential interpretation.... Similarly Hackforth. For the view adopted here see Bluck and Burnet. The non-existential reading has been preferred, in view of the reference to "asking and answering questions" – cf. 75d2–3. It seems far more natural to associate this with the Socratic quest for definitions than with proofs of the Forms' existence. To "give an account of the being of *F*" is to answer the question "what is *F*?". Questioning and answering of this sort are familiar in Plato's writings, and typical of dialectical inquiry (cf., e.g., *Republic* 538d6–e3), whereas questioning and answering to prove that the Forms exist can hardly be said to occur in the dialogues at all.' Grammatically, this latter view, with its permutations, may not be impossible altogether; whether or not it makes any sense is a different question. I agree with the former reading and its syntactical interpretation both because it seems to me to be the natural way to take the Greek and for the semantic reasons given in the text.

[376] Rowe 1993, 183, ad loc., while otherwise taking a different view of how to interpret this sentence, is correct in stating 'οὐσία is used as at 76d8–9'.

[377] Cf. also Gallop 1975, 230, n. 31, with references.

[378] Up to a point, accentuation is a matter of taste. I follow the OCT, but would find ὅ ἐστι equally acceptable; cf. also Burnyeat 2003, 9.

[379] On balance, this seems to be the correct text.

[380] An unambiguous example, albeit dependent on an expression of ignorance rather than knowledge, is *Meno* 80d1, καὶ νῦν περὶ ἀρετῆς ὃ ἔστιν ἐγὼ μὲν οὐκ οἶδα, 'and now, concerning excellence, what it is, I for one do not know'; it is unambiguous because of the difference in gender, regardless of how one further interprets the indirect interrogative; but for controversy even there, see Bluck 1961, 271 ad loc.

[381] I follow the new OCT with slight change in punctuation.

[382] This highlights the inadequacy of 'what is' as a translation of τὸ ὄν, the nominalized neuter participle of the verb 'be', for which the rendering 'being', however, would give rise to ambiguity with οὐσία.

[383] See in particular DK28B8, 32–8. Cf. Hackforth 1955, 81, n. 2: 'The term μονοειδές recurs at 80B in close conjunction with ἀδιάλυτον, and it is used of the Form of beauty at *Symp.* 211B. It has the same force as πᾶν ὅμοιον which Parmenides asserts of his ἓν ὄν, viz. the denial of internal difference or distinction of unlike parts.' See in particular also Solmsen 1971, esp. 67–70. The arguments by Vancamp 1996 may thus need further revision.

[384] Gallop's translation (1975, 53 f.); Geddes 1863, 123, translates: 'You would loudly protest that you cannot conceive each thing arising in any other way than as it partakes of the particular essence of which it is a partaker,' and comments: 'τῆς ἰδίας οὐσίας = τῆς ἰδέας the universal manifesting itself in, but prior to, the particular, so that the former is an οὐσία (*Seyn*), the latter a γένεσις (*Werden*)'. Hackforth 1955, 135: 'that the only way you know of, by which anything comes to be, is by its participating in the special being in which it does participate'. Rowe 1983, 245: 'you know of no other way in which each thing comes to be except by having come to share in the appropriate essence (οὐσία) of each [thing] in which it comes to share'.

[385] The discerning reader is asked to forgive these barbarisms, which are necessary to convey the fact that the nominalized adjectives in Greek are neuter plural.

[386] Perhaps it should be stated at this point that the absence of the definite article with δύο is not decisive either way, as Plato is here using δύο as generic singular; in that respect, the case of 100e2–3 is different; there, it is indeed the case that the subject of γίγνεται has the definite article, the complement to the predicate does not: τῷ καλῷ τὰ καλὰ γίγνεται καλά, 'through the beautiful the beautifuls come to be beautiful' (if

that is the text). The wider question of the grammar of εἶναι and γίγνεσθαι cannot be discussed here; see Burnyeat 2003, 9, n. 33, who also lists some of the most important contributions to the debate. My own suspicion is that εἶναι in Greek always denotes the 'is' of 'God *is*' or the 'are' of 'the gods *are*'; what is commonly regarded as the auxiliary represents that same verb with a predicative complement: ὁ θεὸς ἀγαθός ἐστιν – 'God *is* (as someone) good, God *is* (as a) good (person).' I am grateful to David B. Robinson for discussion of this issue.

[387] It may be noted that the continuation of that sentence at 101c5–7 is ambiguous in the same way: καὶ δεῖν τούτου μετασχεῖν τὰ μέλλοντα δύο ἔσεσθαι, καὶ μονάδος ὃ ἂν μέλλῃ ἓν ἔσεσθαι: at first one may be inclined to take the phrase τὰ μέλλοντα δύο ἔσεσθαι, 'that which is to be two', as clearly indicating that there is something which is not yet two but will be two, if everything goes according to plan; one would then translate: 'and that it is necessary that whatever is to be two participate in that [the dyad just mentioned], and in the monad whatever is to be one'. But there is no such certainty concerning the prior being of something not yet two (or one, respectively) but about to be two (or one, respectively): at 95b5–6 Socrates warns Cebes of boasting: μή τις ἡμῖν βασκανία περιτρέψῃ τὸν λόγον τὸν μέλλοντα ἔσεσθαι, 'lest some jinx turn around the argument which is about to be'; regardless of whether one translate 'turn around' or 'turn upside down' or 'pervert' or 'cause...to abort', and again 'is about to be' or 'wants to be' or 'intends to be': the argument is not there yet; therefore, in the parallel construction of 101c5–7, Socrates could likewise speak of 'what is to be two' in a case where there is not anything there yet which is something else at present and which will be two in time to come.

[388] Gallop 1993, 52 f.

[389] The (optional) addition of 'whatever it is' is meant to reflect the generic subjunctive with ἄν.

[390] It must be emphasized again, though, that these two words, εἶδος and ἰδέα, have not been introduced yet, and that what Socrates and his audience are thinking of as points of reference of 'each' are the beautiful itself, the equal itself.

[391] Cf. in particular Classen 1959a, 158–60.

[392] Watt 1987, 198.

[393] Thompson 1901, 255–8, omits it altogether, whether by oversight or because he considers usage here 'literal' rather than 'metaphorical'; nor is there discussion in the seminal article by Hirzel 1913. Classen 1959a, 160, only points out that, as in the *Protagoras*, the term οὐσία occurs in the summary of a preceding argument and is followed by a number of illustrative examples. Berger 1961, 28–30, deals with the *Charmides* passage in his section on 'the philosophical being' and places it after his treatment of the *Protagoras* passage; he concludes from the syntactical and philosophical context that οὐσία is what something has as its own being (*zijn*), but he presupposes, for both dialogues, that because of the etymology of the noun any Greek would have connected οὐσία with ὄντα automatically, and that all that needs doing to understand the meaning of οὐσία is to find the requisite sense of ὄντα. This etymological awareness, though, cannot be assumed; contrariwise, the way Plato introduces οὐσία in the *Meno*, *Euthyphro* and *Phaedo* is the clearest indication that no such direct link between noun and verb was felt in everyday usage.

[394] This is not wholly dissimilar to *Symposium* 199c–d, where a similar explanation of directedness is given; δύναμις had been used several times with reference to the specific power of the god, and Socrates will soon use it himself when questioning

Diotima (202e).

[395] Cf. e.g. Herodotus 7.28, τὴν ἐμεωυτοῦ οὐσίην, 'my possession(s)', in which passage it is then explicated what these possessions are.

[396] Taylor's translation (1976, 21).

[397] Taylor's translation (1976, 42).

[398] After 330a4; also 330a6, 7, b1; 331d6; 333a5.

[399] The implications of this cannot be discussed here. It may be noted, however, that when Plato alludes to this passage from the *Protagoras* by letting Socrates put a very similarly phrased question to the guest from Elea at *Sophist* 217a, he uses γένος, 'kind', in place of πρᾶγμα, 'thing'. In the *Protagoras*, the term πρᾶγμα occurs after 330c1 (twice) also 330c4, d4, d5; 331a8; 332a5; 337d4 (with slightly different reference in the mouth of Hippias); after that, with the requisite reference 349b3, 4, c1, and then again 352d3 in a way that combines the specific sense of the philosophical passages with the non-committal usage of 326e8 and 327c7, from where Socrates could have picked up Protagoras' usage in the first place.

[400] For this, see Classen 1959, 158 f.

[401] See LSJ s.v.

[402] Note that this is the only place in Plato at which the noun οὐσία is connected with the verb ὑπόκειμαι. Contrast Aristotle: a TLG word search produces 43 matches with an interval of up to 6 words, of which 6 exhibit direct collocation, 3 of them in the phrase τὴν ὑποκειμένην οὐσίαν. This may just be independent of the *Protagoras* passage; even Aristotle is capable of the occasional philosophical pun.

[403] Hamilton and Jones 2004, 45. Cf. Waterfield 1994, 45: 'all you're doing is calling up a horde of false witnesses against me to support your attempt to dislodge me from my inheritance, the truth'.

[404] Cf., in addition to the notes to the two translations cited, e.g. Dodds 1959, 245 ad loc. and 189 ad 447a3; Classen 1959a. Thompson 1894, 156 ad loc., rightly rejects Stallbaum's suggestion that Plato is playing with a specific philosophical meaning of οὐσία; correct also is Marten 1962, 11.

[405] Classen 1959a, 158 explains in detail how Plato constructs the law-court metaphor, but then continues: 'but the addition τοῦ ἀληθοῦς indicates that οὐσία is not equivalent to τὰ ὄντα in the sense of τὰ χρήματα or ἅ τινί ἐστιν...but is to be understood as πάντα ἃ ἔστιν, i.e. things that exist or are real (or perhaps: 'or that really are')...'

[406] *Pace* Berger, *passim*.

[407] See n. 371.

[408] This view of the *Meno* and *Euthyphro*, which is more specific than a generally 'proleptic' reading that refers everything interesting before the *Republic* to the *Republic*, cannot be defended here, but receives some support in ch. 8, sec. 4, and ch. 9, sec. 4 below.

[409] For the text, this translation and thorough discussion see Huffman 1993, 123–45. The text of Stobaeus as given by Wachsmuth 1884, 188 f. and the text of Philolaus given by Diels-Kranz 1951, 408 f., as DK44B6, differ in significant respects.

[410] For formation of that type see Fraenkel 1925, 46 f., on -εστω in particular 47; cf. also Chantraine 1933, 116–17, on -εστω in particular 117; Schwyzer 1939, vol. I, 478; Frisk 1973, vol. I, 577 s.v.

[411] Chantraine 1933, 117, who mistakenly claims that the simplex, too, is attested for Democritus.

[412] Cf. Buck 1955, 129; *pace* Sedley 2003, 99.

[413] See pp. 214 ff. below.

[414] See Hirzel 1913 *passim* and Classen 1959a, 158–64, quoted in n. 357 above.

[415] I am grateful to Myles Burnyeat for cautioning against unwarranted claims concerning Protagoras.

Chapter 8

[416] This usage is not frequent, and the treatises in which the phrase occurs cannot be dated precisely: *In the Surgery* 3.3, 7.1 and 8.1; *On Joints* 27.4; *Mochlicon* 17.4. See Part II, ch. 4, sec. 10, pp. 125 f., with n. 229.

[417] This 'title' is given to this section of the dialogue by Ebert 2004.

[418] Schleiermacher translates 'nach Art der Arznei', Apelt 'als eine Art Arzenei'.

[419] Ross 1948, I, 128: 'τὰς ἐν ὕλης εἴδει Aristotle does not say that the earlier thinkers recognized the material cause. The ultimate material cause, according to him, is matter entirely unformed, while they, with the exception of Anaximander, only went back to some simple but yet definitely characterized form of matter such as one of the four elements. The causes they recognized were not matter, but only 'of the nature of matter'. For the phrase cf. ἐν μορίου εἴδει *De Caelo* 268b5, ἐν ὀργάνου εἴδει *Pol.* 1253b30; the usage is found several times in Plato. ἐν ὕλης εἴδει is especially common in Aristotle.' It is not clear from this whether Ross thinks that the meaning of the Aristotelian phrase is 'of the nature of matter' on all those occasions. As concerns the assertion that ἐν + genitive + εἴδει is frequent in Plato, apart from the two places in the *Phaedo* and *Republic* 389b, quoted once more at *Republic* 459d, one can perhaps compare *Republic* 544c; otherwise, I have only found *Cratylus* 394d and *Timaeus* 30c4 as further parallels; for *Phaedrus* 249a, see n. 421 below.

[420] On the question of the meaning of αἰτία cf. ch. 9, secs. 7 and 8.

[421] Against this background, we may briefly consider again the case of Cebes. He is the first to introduce the word εἶδος in the phrase ἦν που ἡμῖν ἡ ψυχὴ πρὶν ἐν τῷδε τῷ ἀνθρωπίνῳ εἴδει γενέσθαι. Cebes is young and intelligent, has his own ideas, but seems also to have heard more than others. And Cebes is from Thebes and once speaks in his own dialect (62a8). One is prepared to accept from him rather than from another the unusual expression ἐν τῷδε τῷ ἀνθρωπίνῳ εἴδει γενέσθαι. However, it is not altogether improbable that Cebes may here be using the language of mystery cults; the expression occurs once more in the myth of the soul in the *Phaedrus* (249a8), from where both pagan and Neoplatonist-Christian writers quote it extensively. Cebes knows more about life and death as one would at first expect.

[422] As noted above, most incisive on this aspect of the Pythagorean setting is Ebert 1994 and 2004.

[423] Perhaps the best account of the ontological implications of Philolaus' philosophy as expounded in the extant fragments is Barnes 1982, 378–96.

[424] If Ebert 2001 is correct, Euenus is another individual with at least Pythagorean leanings mentioned by name earlier in the *Phaedo*.

[425] It does not, of course, strictly speaking exclude the possibility that Plato had not read the 'book' of Philolaus, but there is no good reason to assume that he had not. For Philolaus in general, cf. Huffman 1993, and on the 'book' of Philolaus in particular 12–16. Cf. also the chapter 'Archytas and Plato' in Huffman 2005, 33–43.

[426] The vexed question of the 'even-odd' cannot be discussed here; for a recent full

discussion, cf. Huffman 1993, 186–90; but it should be noted that the phrase τρίτον δὲ ἀπ' ἀμφοτέρων μειχθέντων ἀρτιοπέριττον, 'but a third mixed of both of the two: even-odd', is exactly what an ancient reader familiar with the 'even-odd' in Pythagoreanism would have added in the margin on reading that number has two types, and exactly what could have entered the text subsequently as a gloss. The same conclusion is reached by Barnes 1982, 632 n. 23.

[427] See p. 210.

[428] For the role of ἀρχαί in Philolaus, cf. Huffman 1993, 78–92.

[429] It is customary in discussions of the 'table of opposites' to refer to Burkert 1972, 51 f., together with 295 n. 89, and to conclude that the 'table' found in Aristotle thus cannot be used as evidence; but Burkert's aim in discussing the table of opposites is quite specific, and he does not dismiss Aristotle's report as altogether irrelevant to early Pythagoreanism; nor does he ascribe the table in its present form to 4th-century Academics. My claim, on the other hand, is not that *this* Aristotelian table dates back in its entirety to the 5th century, nor that Pythagoreans were the only ones in whose discussions 'opposites' had a role to play. My suggestion is rather that if, as is altogether plausible, opposites played a part in Pythagorean thought, as they did in the 'physics' of others in 5th-century Greece, then the combined evidence of Aristotle *Metaph.* A 5.986a22 ff. and Philolaus B5 may point to a pre-Platonic usage of εἶδος in connection with opposites such as the ones in the 'table of opposites' which includes some pairs of adjectives which also figure prominently in discussions of the *Phaedo*; further, if there was such a use of εἶδος, it is likely that Plato would have been familiar with it, and that he could have exploited it in the same way as he exploited terminological usage elsewhere.

[430] See Introduction, pp. 7–14 above.

[431] It should be stressed that this does, of course, not constitute an absolute proof that Plato took the term εἶδος from the Pythagoreans, or rather specifically from Philolaus: but there are many more contacts between the thought, the examples and the imagery of the *Phaedo* and what little we have of Philolaus than, for example with ch. 19 of *On Ancient Medicine*, which I consider to be quite possibly post-Platonic, as stated above, n. 200, but which has often been adduced as one of the closest parallels and thereby a potential source of Plato's terminology; see e.g. Baldry 1937, 143; Baldry, it should be noted, posits a fourth meaning of 'quality' for εἶδος, which he regards as in all its senses synonymous with ἰδέα. The Hippocratic author of *On Ancient Medicine* writes (15.1–8):

ἀπορέω δ' ἔγωγε, οἱ τὸν λόγον ἐκεῖνον λέγοντες, καὶ ἀπάγοντες ἐκ ταύτης τῆς ὁδοῦ ἐπὶ ὑπόθεσιν τὴν τέχνην, τίνα ποτὲ τρόπον θεραπεύσουσι τοὺς ἀνθρώπους, ὥσπερ ὑποτίθενται. οὐ γάρ ἐστιν αὐτέοισιν, ὡς ἐγὼ οἶμαι, ἐξευρημένον αὐτό τι ἐφ' ἑωυτοῦ θερμὸν, ἢ ψυχρὸν, ἢ ξηρὸν, ἢ ὑγρὸν, μηδενὶ ἄλλῳ εἴδεϊ κοινωνέον, ἀλλ' οἶμαι ἔγωγε ταῦτα πόματα καὶ βρώματα αὐτέοισιν ὑπάρχειν οἷσι πάντες χρεόμεθα. προστιθέασι δὲ τῷ μὲν εἶναι θερμῷ, τῷ δὲ ψυχρῷ, τῷ δὲ ξηρῷ, τῷ δὲ ὑγρῷ.

I am at a loss to understand how those who maintain the other view, and abandon the old method to rest the art on a postulate, treat their patients on the line of their postulate. For they have not discovered, I think, an absolute hot or cold, dry or moist, that participates in no other form. But I think that they have at their disposal the same foods and the same drinks as we all use, and to one they add the attribute of being hot, to another, cold, to another, dry, to another, moist.   (tr. Jones)

First one must note that the author criticizes the theory and method of somebody else;

the concepts he criticizes are tied to the terminology he uses. That is to say, a medical writer must at some stage have used the language of 'itself by itself', the examples of 'hot and cold' and 'dry and moist', and either this author or another must have spoken of 'types' in that connection and of κοινωνεῖν, 'having in common'; in addition, the method of *hypothesis* is mentioned. The former, 'itself by itself' and the examples, are found already in Anaxagoras; but that is not the case with the latter. Without having the date of the treatise, it would not be safe to claim that the author of *On Ancient Medicine* criticized a medical view that had arisen out of an application of the philosophy of the *Phaedo* to medicine. Rather, one is inclined to think of a source that did combine all or most of these terms; and it is not impossible that, at any stage in the 4th century, there were medical theorists and practitioners in some respect applying the same criteria as Philolaus and the Pythagoreans with whom Plato came into contact. It should be noticed that the examples of the hot and the cold and the dry and the moist are the stock examples of medical and physical theory; they are opposites like the opposites of the Pythagoreans; the first pair even appears in the *Phaedo* at a relevant point: but the parallels in terms of examples and in points of content otherwise are much greater between the *Phaedo* and what we know of the Pythagoreans, especially Philolaus, than between the *Phaedo* and *On Ancient Medicine*; that does not, of course, exclude that the terminology of 'types' was more widespread, and that Plato could in consequence have become acquainted with it from more than one context. But if it had been common usage, we would expect to hear about that e.g. from Aristotle; cf. Baldry 1937, 144f. Baldry's further instances (143) of εἶδος and ἰδέα are all cases in which the words mean 'type'; collocation with δύναμις or φύσις suggests just that, that 'type' is contrasted with and supplemented by 'power' or 'nature', rather than that ἰδέα is synonymous with one or other of these terms respectively; the date of the Isocratean examples (144) points, *pace* Baldry, to reception of Plato who by then had written the *Phaedo*, and whose dialogues were in the public domain.

⁴³² Cf. e.g. Ross 1924, I, 146 ff.; cf. also Huffman 1993, 47n1: 'At *EN* 1106b Aristotle says that the Pythagoreans associated what is bad with the unlimited and what is good with the limited. Such a doctrine clearly was held by the Pythagoreans who set out the table of opposites which Aristotle describes at *Metaph.* 986a22 ff., since good is put in the same column with limit and bad in the same column with unlimited. However, Aristotle sharply distinguishes these Pythagoreans from the Pythagoreans he has been discussing previously, who clearly included Philolaus because of the reference to the counter-earth.' (It should be noted that Huffman's note continues: 'Indeed, throughout the fragments of Philolaus, limiters and unlimiteds are presented on completely equal terms and it would appear that Philolaus, at least, saw both as necessary for the world-order to arise and did not consider either category as good or bad.' However, this is irrelevant in the present context, and at any rate, only on one reading of the significance of the table of opposites would other Pythagoreans have done so.) Cf. further Huffman 1993, 225 f.

NB. Without naming individuals, Aristotle at 986a22 ff. undertakes to demonstrate that for (some?) Pythagoreans numbers are (the) 'elements' of things, the στοιχεῖα. There follows the pun with συστοιχία. Adherents of this view of the world did according to Aristotle apparently not think that the world consisted exclusively of numbers; thus, if 987b31 is not a gloss, it need not refer to *these* Pythagoreans, even if Aristotle does not only compare the content but also the form and phrasing of thoughts there.

⁴³³ Perhaps this is the place at which it should be made explicit that whereas looking at

the εἴδη in the *Phaedo* has led to Philolaus and thus to Pythagoreanism, it has not led to Archytas. This may be worth mentioning because Archytas looms large as the friend of Plato who saved his life or, at least, influenced him greatly while in Sicily and southern Italy. Regardless of any personal friendship, and regardless of the undoubted response to Archytas that can be traced in the *Republic*, as regards the term εἶδος or the plural εἴδη which does occur in Archytas DK47B4 (but not B1, where the word belongs to the report by Nicomachus), there does not seem to be a direct line from Archytas to Plato. Archytas Fr. 4, as presented and translated by Huffman 2006, 225, reads:

καὶ δοκεῖ ἁ λογιστικὰ ποτὶ τὰν σοφίαν τῶν μὲν ἀλλᾶν τεχνῶν καὶ πολὺ διαφέρειν, ἀτὰρ καὶ τᾶς γεωμετρικᾶς ἐναργεστέρω πραγματεύεσθαι ἃ θέλει. καὶ ἃ ἐκλείπει αὖ ἁ γεωμετρία, καὶ ἀποδείξιας ἁ λογιστικὰ ἐπιτελεῖ καὶ ὁμῶς, εἰ μὲν εἰδέων τεὰ πραγματεία, καὶ τὰ περὶ τοῖς εἴδεσιν.

Logistic seems to be far superior indeed to the other arts in regard to wisdom and in particular to deal with what it wishes more concretely (clearly) than geometry. Again in those respects in which geometry is deficient, logistic puts demonstrations into effect (completes proofs) and equally, if there is any investigation of shapes, [logistic puts demonstrations into effect (completes proofs)] with respect to what concerns shapes as well.

Huffman's text differs from that proposed by Diels-Kranz only the omission of a posited lacuna. His translation differs considerably. He takes reference of the term εἴδη not to be to 'Prinzipien', as tentatively suggested by Diels-Kranz, but to mathematical shapes. Huffman regards this meaning as common and shared, for example, by Archytas' contemporary Democritus in DK68B167, B6 and A57 (cf. Huffman 2006, 250 f. and 238 f.). As set out in ch. 5, sec. 4, I take Democritus to refer to 'figure(s)' when he employs ἰδέα(ι); there is a large semantic overlap betwen 'figure' and 'shape', so that Huffman might have intended with his translation what I intend with mine; however, Huffman posits that the term εἴδη is used by Archytas in an absolute sense as referring, in a technical way, to 'mathematical shapes', and he claims synonymity for εἶδος and ἰδέα *in that sense*. I cannot follow this identification in the case of these Democritean fragments. If 'shape' will do as a translation in these Democritean fragments, 'shape' has a different application from that posited for Archytas. All one can say is that *if* Archytas B4 is genuine, and *if* Huffman's interpretation (245–52) is correct – as I think it may well be – we have here a context that has not influenced Plato's usage in the *Phaedo*. If Diels-Kranz were right in their tentative suggestion, one might just posit for Archytas reference to what I have posited as 'Pythagorean types'. But Huffman's arguments for a mathematical interpretation are plausible, and the story concerning Plato's adoption of Pythagorean terminology would not be materially affected if Archytas could be enlisted as further evidence for a notion of 'types' prevalent among Pythagoreans.

[434]   Ch. 7, sec. 2, pp. 189 f. above.

[435]   *If* this is so, I would all the same maintain that a wider audience and readership was intended and addressed by Plato from the start.

Chapter 9

[436]   It is not necessary to pursue the issue further in this context as Plato's point of reference at *Phaedo* 103e clearly is Philolaus B5 and as μορφή is not used by Plato as a technical term in a relevant sense elsewhere in his middle period dialogues. There is, however, scope for further investigation into the history of μορφή, in particular with

a view to Aristotle's usage. On this, see especially Barnes 1982, 3/8–96.

⁴³⁷ Cf. Gallop 1975, 200 f.

⁴³⁸ An exception is Gallop 1975, 236, n. 72, who states that Plato does use the three terms interchangeably.

⁴³⁹ This is pointed out e.g. by Gallop 1975, 236 n. 72, but not discussed by Ebert 2004 (see 383 ad loc.), who holds that Plato maintains throughout the distinction of εἶδος as 'Idee' and μορφή/ἰδέα as 'Eigenschaft'; see 372–89 *passim*. Cf. also Wilamowitz 1919, II, 253.

⁴⁴⁰ Cf. 104d2 f.

⁴⁴¹ I quote at this point Gallop 1975, 236 n. 72: 'No clear distinctions seem marked by Plato's usage of εἶδος, ἰδέα, and μορφή. At 104d9, as at 104b9, 104d2, 104d6, and 105d13, ἰδέα appears to be used as a variant for εἶδος as used at 104c7. Bluck (17, n.7) and Hackforth (150, n.1), both with reservations, suggest that εἶδος on the one hand, and ἰδέα and μορφή on the other, may be aligned with 'transcendent' and 'immanent' Forms respectively. But no safe inferences can, in fact, be drawn from the use of any one of these expressions.'

⁴⁴² It could be suggested that Plato introduced the term ἰδέα for reasons of stylistic variation. This consideration, though, must be rejected on the same grounds as considerations of stylistic variation were rejected in discussion of *Phaedo* 74c in the section on Zeno in the Introduction (n. 19): introducing a variant term here, at the very point at which new philosophical distinctions are drawn, with reference to specific philosophical predecessors, would be confusing and counterproductive.

⁴⁴³ Cf. in particular Allen 1970.

⁴⁴⁴ Allen 1970, 26–9.

⁴⁴⁵ Of the modern authorities Allen cites, it is worth quoting in full the note by Burnet 1924, 31, ad *Euthyphro* 5d3:

ἔχον μίαν τινὰ ἰδέαν, possessing a single form or characteristic nature which makes it what it is. The closest parallel is *Meno* 72c6 οὕτω δὴ καὶ περὶ τῶν ἀρετῶν· κἂν εἰ πολλαὶ καὶ παντοδαπαί εἰσιν, ἕν γέ τι εἶδος ταὐτὸν ἅπασαι ἔχουσιν δι' ὃ εἰσὶν ἀρεταί. It is impossible to draw any distinction between εἶδος and ἰδέα, and what is called ἰδέα here is referred to as εἶδος below (6d11). To explain this terminology we must start as usual from mathematics. It seems to me certain that εἶδος was the original word for a geometrical figure, though it was almost entirely superseded by σχῆμα in later days. Now, when we say 'This is a triangle', the predicate 'triangle' has exactly the same meaning, whatever may be the lengths of the sides of the particular triangle which is the subject of the judgement. In the same way, we wish to find a definition of 'holy' which will be identical with itself and contrary to 'unholy' in every judgement into which it enters. That is all we require for the present passage, but we are not entitled to infer that the metaphysical doctrine of 'forms' had not been formulated when this was written. The words εἶδος and ἰδέα would not naturally have been chosen to express a purely logical relation, and the occurrence of παράδειγμα below (6e4) indicates that the developed doctrine is assumed by Socrates. I think Professor Stewart is right in saying (*Plato's Doctrine of Ideas*, p. 17, n. 1) that the terms ἰδέα, εἶδος, and παράδειγμα 'are used here exactly as they are in the later Dialogues'. The view that they are not is only an attempt to bolster up the hypothesis that neither Socrates nor Plato in his earlier writings knew anything about the 'ideas'. (Cf. Gr. Phil. I § 119.)

This is not the place for a full discussion of the word εἶδος, but it may be observed that Aristotle (who generally uses σχῆμα), in discussing the Pythagorean theory of gnomons, adopts the term εἶδος for 'figure' or 'pattern'. Cf. *Phys.* 203a14 ὁτὲ μὲν ἄλλο ἀεὶ γίγνεσθαι τὸ εἶδος, ὁτὲ δὲ ἕν. (See E. Gr. Phil.[3] p.103, n. 2). It is also important to remember that μορφή can be used as a synonym of εἶδος or ἰδέα. Cf. *Phaed.* 103e5.

Burnet's note on *Euthyphro* d11 reads: 'εἶδος…ἰδέα. There is clearly no distinction of meaning here between these two terms, for which see 5d3 n.'

Partly in response to Burnet, Bluck 1961, 224 f., likewise adduced by Allen, writes, ad *Meno* 72c6:

ἕν γέ τι εἶδος. Here we may compare *Euthyphro* 6d: Μέμνησαι οὖν ὅτι οὐ τοῦτό σοι διεκελευόμην, ἕν τι ἢ δύο με διδάξαι τῶν πολλῶν ὁσίων, ἀλλ' ἐκεῖνο αὐτὸ τὸ εἶδος ᾧ πάντα τὰ ὅσια ὅσιά ἐστιν; ἔφησθα γάρ που μιᾷ ἰδέᾳ τά τε ἀνόσια ἀνόσια εἶναι καὶ τὰ ὅσια ὅσια. Neither our present passage nor the *Euthyphro* need imply the *Phaedo* and *Republic* theory of εἴδη παρὰ τὰ πολλά. Cf. Wilamowitz, *Platon*, ii, p. 251. They do not suggest that the ἰδέα (pattern) or εἶδος (form) which is to be used as a standard of reference is ontologically or in any way metaphysically superior to its instances or particulars, or that it has any existence apart from them. It seems to be simply something that they all possess (ἔχουσιν: cf. 75a, τὸ ἐπὶ πᾶσι τούτοις ταὐτόν). In this 'Socratic' sense, as we may call it, the εἶδος will be no more than the 'look' or class-type which any pious act (for example) manifests because of the element of τὸ ὅσιον that it contains. But see Introduction, pp. 46–7.

Burnet (note on *Euthyphro* 5d3) thought that the term εἶδος was borrowed by Socrates (or Plato) from the language of geometry – where it was used, for example, of the 'model' triangle – to do special duty in philosophical contexts. But there is no need to look for the origin of these special uses within so narrow a field, since the word was commonly used (*a*) from Homer onwards to denote the 'appearance' or 'look' of a person or thing, and (*b*) in Herodotus and the Hippocratic writings and elsewhere to mean 'sort' or 'kind'. (Cf. especially A.-J. Festugière, *Hippocrate, L'Ancienne Médecine*, pp. 47–53; also Gillespie, *CQ*, vi (1912), pp. 179–203, and W.H.S. Jones, *Philosophy and Medicine in Ancient Greece*, pp. 79 and 93.) Meaning (*b*) probably arose out of (*a*), since the 'look' of a thing might be taken to show the kind of thing that it is, and gradually εἶδος might come to be thought of as *meaning* a 'kind' or 'sort' (of anything). The 'Socratic' sense will likewise be a development of (*a*), due to the association of 'look' with an idea of 'class' or 'type'. For Plato himself, of course, in his Middle Period, an εἶδος came to be not just a class-type, but itself a substantial 'thing'; it was no longer simply the 'look' of (e.g.) μέγεθος, for it was itself (e.g.) μέγεθος (compare Phaedo 101b with 102b), and as such (for Plato uses abstract nouns and τό with the neuter adjective as though they were interchangeable, cf. 102d-e) identical with τὸ μέγα. Thus (e.g.) τὸ μέγα, which hitherto had been a πρᾶγμα existing in other things (cf. note at b1 above on μελίττης πέρι οὐσίας), now exists apart from phenomena, though of course it still is a 'thing'; and yet as being a sort of pattern it may be called an ἰδέα (e.g. *Rep.* 507b-c) or εἶδος. If this interpretation is correct, whereas for the author of the Socratic dialogues the εἶδος τοῦ ὁσίου would mean something slightly different from τὸ ὅσιον αὐτό, for Plato in his Middle Period the two expressions would mean the same thing. If Socrates used the terms ἰδέαι and εἴδη for the objects of our intellectual apprehension, as he probably did, it would be natural for Plato to retain them, especially as it was in order to justify Socrates' belief in absolute norms that he evolved his new theory; and inasmuch as his ἰδέαι and εἴδη were still to be standards of reference, these terms were still appropriate.

It should be noted that Bluck's distinctions in the last dozen or so lines presuppose that the author of the Socratic dialogues already has the notion of 'the pious/holy itself', as otherwise 'the class-type of the pious/holy' could hardly be believed to be different from or the same as 'the pious/holy itself'. Secondly, Bluck does not seem to adduce any evidence for his assertion that 'Socrates used the terms ἰδέαι and εἴδη', and I do not think that there is any such evidence.

Thirdly, we have seen in Part II, ch. 4 above, how the meaning of εἶδος underwent a multiple development from 'look', 'appearance', to 'type', and then how 'type' had its special application with Philolaus, where the word was applied in a way which Plato could adopt and adapt for his own purposes. In response to Burnet, Bluck, Allen and others of their mould (for all their differences, it seems as if they were at one in their method of reading 'meaning' backwards into earlier texts), it is worth emphasizing again possible distinctions between and among the individual members of a group of terms in English: the terms are 'type', 'sort', 'class' and 'kind'. There are, of course, colloquial and imprecise contexts in which these terms can be used synonymously or at least interchangeably. But as explained above, 'kind', starting from the notion of being related, originally by common descent, in the first place refers to a group. The same is true of 'class', whether or not it goes back to Latin *classis*, 'fleet', whence it was applied to a class of people in society. 'Sort', while going back to Latin *sors*, 'lot', seems to have entered mediaeval Italian, French, Dutch, English and German in the context of commerce, where goods were sorted and sold according to quality; thus, regardless of the meaning of Latin *sors*, English 'sort' is a collective referring in the first place to a 'lot' of items (cloth, paper, etc.) of the same quality. 'Type', on the other hand, from Greek τύπος, etymologically 'blow', meant from early on 'impression' as the result of a blow, and it is that sense which was fertile in the semantic development of the Greek word (well documented in LSJ s.v.) and which lies at the root of French *type* and English 'type'; 'type' is thus in the first place used of a thing with reference to its conspicuous features, in the first place the visible features, but then any features. 'Type' does not, in the first place, refer to a 'group' or 'class' or 'kind'. In that way, as outlined above, the word 'type' is suited to translate εἶδος.

446 Relevant parallels for the phrase ἐκεῖνο αὐτό, in which ἐκεῖνο αὐτό refers to a thing itself in a way similar to *Euthyphro* 6d–e are *Lysis* 220a6–b5 and *Republic* 10.597e10–598a3. The subject of the *Lysis* is τὸ φίλον, a term which, following a tradition among commentators who want to preserve the active and passive connotations of the adjective, I translate as the 'dear-and-friend'; Socrates and Lysis have the following exchange:

οὐκοῦν καὶ περὶ τοῦ φίλου ὁ αὐτὸς λόγος; ὅσα γάρ φαμεν φίλα εἶναι ἡμῖν ἕνεκα φίλου τινὸς ἑτέρου, ῥήματι φαινόμεθα λέγοντες αὐτό· φίλον δὲ τῷ ὄντι κινδυνεύει ἐκεῖνο αὐτὸ εἶναι, εἰς ὃ πᾶσαι αὗται αἱ λεγόμεναι φιλίαι τελευτῶσιν.
κινδυνεύει οὕτως, ἔφη, ἔχειν.
οὐκοῦν τό γε τῷ ὄντι φίλον οὐ φίλου τινὸς ἕνεκα φίλον ἐστίν;
ἀληθῆ.

So does the same argument also obtain concerning the dear-and-friend? For, concerning whatever we say is dear-and-friend to us for the sake of some other thing dear-and-friend to us, we appear as saying this in a manner of speaking only (literally: 'with a word'): but really dear-and-friend seems to be that itself at which all these said friendships arrive as their end-point.

It seems to be so, said he.

Now, that certainly which is really dear-and-friend is not dear-and-friend for the sake of anything dear-and-friend, is it?

True.

While 'that which is really dear-and-friend' is not a Platonic form, it is singled out and distinguished from the many particulars and instances of things dear-and-friend in a similar way to the singling out of the holy as distinct from the many holy things and acts in the *Euthyphro*. At *Republic* 10.597e10, Socrates says:

τὸν μὲν δὴ μιμητὴν ὡμολογήκαμεν. εἰπὲ δέ μοι περὶ τοῦ ζωγράφου τόδε· πότερα ἐκεῖνο αὐτὸ τὸ ἐν τῇ φύσει ἕκαστον δοκεῖ σοι ἐπιχειρεῖν μιμεῖσθαι ἢ τὰ τῶν δημιουργῶν ἔργα;

We have thus agreed on the imitator [or: representer]. But tell me this about the painter: does he seem to you to attempt to represent that itself which is in nature in each case, or the works of the craftsmen?

In the context of *Republic* 10, the many skilled pursuits that result in the production of 'artefacts' are contrasted with the one form that is in nature, the one form made by the divine craftsman. Leaving aside the possible ontological status of the 'things themselves', the usage of ἐκεῖνο αὐτὸ is thus parallel to *Euthyphro* 6d–e. While these are places adduced in support of deleting τὸ εἶδος, one may also turn to the not very frequent instances of the phrase ἐκεῖνο τὸ εἶδος. At *Republic* 454c9, ἐκεῖνο τὸ εἶδος τῆς ἀλλοιώσεώς simply means 'that type of change'. At *Parmenides* 132d5, ἐκεῖνο τὸ εἶδος refers to the εἶδος just mentioned; parallel is *Cratylus* 389b3. Cf. the Aristotelian *Hippias Major*, 289d4, which also contains an un-Platonic use of προσγίγνεσθαι.

Apart from *Phaedo* 103e3, on the other hand, the phrase αὐτὸ τὸ εἶδος only occurs in the *Parmenides* (129a1, 130c2, 132e4, 135a2), where Plato reflects on 'the forms', and once at *Cratylus* 440a9, where the issue is the entirely different one of 'types of cognition'.

There is thus sufficient positive and negative support for regarding τὸ εἶδος as a gloss at *Euthyphro* 6d9–e2, and for reading: μέμνησαι οὖν ὅτι οὐ τοῦτό σοι διεκελευόμην, ἕν τι ἢ δύο με διδάξαι τῶν πολλῶν ὁσίων, ἀλλ' ἐκεῖνο αὐτὸ ᾧ πάντα τὰ ὅσια ὅσιά ἐστιν; ἔφησθα γάρ που μιᾷ ἰδέᾳ τά τε ἀνόσια ἀνόσια εἶναι καὶ τὰ ὅσια ὅσια· ἢ οὐ μνημονεύεις;

[447] So already Burnet 1924, 36 f.: 'The instrumental dative is regularly used of the "form" to express the fact that the universal makes the particulars what they are. If the same predicate can be rightly applied to many things, we must take the sameness strictly.'

[448] Cf. Schwyzer-Debrunner 1950, II, 159–68; here esp. 162.

[449] Translation Gallop 1975.

[450] For a connection of this expression with Socrates' μέθοδος, his 'method', in the *Phaedo* and beyond, see Classen 1960, esp. 33–6.

[451] Cf. Part II, ch. 5, sec. 4: 'ἰδέα in Democritus'.

[452] For general accounts of Leucippus' and Democritus' atomism, cf. Barnes 1982, 342–77; Kirk, Raven and Schofield 1983, 402–33; Taylor 1999; and, succinctly, Schofield 2003, 65–7.

[453] On the coinages of Democritus, cf. the excellent discussions by v. Fritz 1938,

12–38; specifically on δέν as a term of Leucippus, 18 and 24 f. As δέν is a jocular back-formation from μηδέν, 'nothing', by way of 'cutting off' the word μή, 'not', one must do Leucippus justice by rendering δέν as 'hing'.

[454] e.g. Meinhardt 1976, 59; Barnes 1982, 374, 388; Taylor 1999, 172; Motte 2003, 40.

[455] Taylor 1999, 142.

[456] On the Latin side, one may compare Seneca, *Ep.* 65.7: '*figuras...quas Plato ideas appellat, inmortales, inmutabiles, infatigabiles.* Cf. *Ep.* 58.19. See OLD s.v. The Latin Stoic Seneca's testimony is not irrelevant as regards the intellectual climate of the time of Plutarch.

[457] Or: Democritus' ultimate constituent elements were called ἄτομοι ἰδέαι, 'indivisible figures'.

[458] This section is a slightly adapted version of my argument at Herrmann 2005, 53–5.

[459] The literature on 'causes' in the *Phaedo* is vast; among recent discussions, see e.g. Strange 1985; Natali 1997; Sedley 1998; McCabe 2000, 172–5; and Casertano 2003; note Casertano, 33, on the absence of distinctions in application, often claimed to exist, between αἰτία and αἴτιον.

[460] Cf. e.g. Archer-Hind 1888; Sedley 1989; Johansen 2004, 2.

[461] The name of Anaxagoras occurs twice, at 97b and 97d, provided the latter is not a gloss.

[462] Cf. e.g. Theiler 1925, 14; Laks 1983 xix–xxiv, 250–7.

[463] Cf. e.g. Furley 1976, 82, who argues as if αἰτία appeared in the text of Anaxagoras, or as if, while the word is not there, it is obvious that the notion was present to Anaxagoras' mind.

[464] Translation Kirk-Raven-Schofield 1983, 420.

[465] Cf. e.g. Archer-Hind 1888, 167, commentary ad 48a, who discusses Plato's reaction to Democritus in the lemma immediately preceding that on τὸ τῆς πλανωμένης εἶδος αἰτίας.

[466] Cf. also Strange 1985, 26 n. 3; and Casertano 2003, 34 with n. 2, who links not only the notion of 'necessity', but also that of 'randomly' and 'for a reason' (Leucippus DK67B2) to *Timaeus* 28a–c. Note that if the notion of αἰτία has entered Plato's thinking through his reception of Democritus, e.g. the remarks by Natali 1997 on the difference in usage and philosophical concepts between Plato and Aristotle gain a further historical dimension.

[467] The suggestion that Plato adopted the term ἰδέα after having encountered it in Democritus is not new as such. In the penultimate paragraph of the chapter on Democritus in his book *Die vorsokratische Philosophie*, K. Goebel has the following statement about Plato and Democritus (1910, 316): 'Plato und Demokrit stehn allerdings in ihrer Metaphysik einander gerade entgegen, aber in der Ethik haben sie doch vieles gemeinsam. Und den Namen für seine Urbilder mag Plato wohl von Demokrit entlehnt haben. Denn beider εἴδη und ἰδέαι haben das Gemeinsame, dass sie das Seiende sind, das nicht wahrgenommen, sondern nur gedacht werden kann, und dabei ist es doch sonderbar, dass sie etymologisch gerade das bedeuten, das gesehen wird.' This passage raises a number of interesting issues. I shall confine myself to the following.

The circumstance that the etymological root of the term is connected to 'seeing' *may* have been important to Democritus in the sense that a philosophical pun of this sort seems in tune with his use of language elsewhere; for Plato, the etymological connection is not the starting point or the reason for his adopting the term ἰδέα from Democritus; all the same, in the *Republic* in particular, the imagery of mental vision is well developed, and ἰδέα does fit into this imagery; but this is after the term had been adopted for the very different reason that it had been a technical term in Democritus' philosophy. Regarding Plato's adoption of the terms εἶδος and ἰδέα, I thus find myself to that extent in agreement with Kahn 1996, 354–5, that the connection with 'seeing' and 'vision' was not relevant at the outset; my explanation for the usage both of the *Phaedo* and *Republic* and of the earlier dialogues is in other respects very different from Kahn's reconstruction of Plato's intellectual history.

The second point of importance raised in the passage quoted from Goebel 1910 is the claim, occasionally encountered in modern discussions, that Democritus used both terms, ἰδέα *and* εἶδος, to refer to his atoms. Support for this view in fragments and testimonia is slender; the occurrence of εἶδος in a book title, in Hesychius' definition and in *reports about* Democritus are not sufficiently clear or extensive to allow us to decide on the issue. The remarks by Clemens Romanus and especially Plutarch rather suggest that only ἰδέα was used as a term for the atoms, and εἶδος was not used in that way, as it would have been appropriate for these two authors to mention εἶδος, too.

Of course, had Democritus used both ἰδέα and εἶδος as terms for his atoms – a position I think unlikely – my story about the *Phaedo* would change only slightly. Having adopted the term εἶδος from Philolaus or another Pythagorean source as outlined above, Plato could then call his own ultimate constituents εἶδος or ἰδέα, thereby indicating both the shared characteristics and the differences between his own ultimate constituents and those of Democritus; he could do so all the more easily because on that account Democritus, like Philolaus, had used the term εἶδος himself. The overall suggestion that Plato in the *Phaedo* alludes to and draws on several philosophical schools of thought at once would not be affected by that. For *Meno* 73c, I should still argue in terms of Pythagorean, not Pythagorean and Democritean, precedent.

In the context of Plato and Democritus, one may also quote Wilamowitz 1919, II, 252: 'Demokritos nennt seine Atome ἰδέαι; das war Buchtitel, und sie haben ja verschiedene Form. Das kommt von der sinnlichen Erscheinung her, aber da es die Urformen sind, den platonischen Dreiecken des Timaios entsprechend, ist auch hier eine Verwandtschaft. Der Arzt Philistion in Menons Iatrika 20, 25 hat die vier Elemente ἰδέαι genannt, was Demokrits Gebrauche parallel geht.' I agree with Wilamowitz's suggestion concerning Democritus' motivation in adopting the term ἰδέα. Philistion may well be important especially for an interpretation of the *Timaeus*; cf. Taylor 1928, 9, n. 1. But that may not be relevant for the *Phaedo*; and even if one is of the view that chronology allows Plato to have come into contact with Philistion before writing the *Phaedo*, primary reference *in* the *Phaedo* seems to me to be to Democritus. Wilamowitz's further contention that the Hippocratic *Art*, περί τέχνης, antedates Plato seems to me to be untenable; if it did, though, that would not only affect my conclusions concerning the semantic of εἶδος, but also in particular what has been said about οὐσία. The conclusion would then be that either the author of the *Art* had exactly the same intuitions which Plato would then independently have himself, or that Plato simply adopted the terminology which is also found in the *Art*, perhaps making connections with Presocratic philosophy on the basis of similarities in terminology between some Presocratics and the Hippocratic writer; in that case, it would not matter greatly whether Plato drew directly on the *Art*, or whether the *Art* uses existing terminology of a source, written or oral, to which Plato, too, had access.

Zeller 1920, 1058 f., n. 3, cites in addition to Goebel and Wilamowitz also Windelband, *Antike Philosophie*³, p. 125, 6; Zeller himself seems to remain agnostic on the issue, but, following uncritically Aristotelean tradition, posits σχήματα as a further Democritean term for 'atoms'.

⁴⁶⁸ Note that the 'legal pun' in συναίτιον, 'accessory', can be Plato's – there may, but need not have been a legal origin to the Democritean use of the term.

⁴⁶⁹ Cf. recently Johansen 2004, 103–6.

⁴⁷⁰ In fact, it is only the introduction of αἰτία into the speculations of the natural philosophers that allows us to speak of Democritean determinism in the first place. While other Presocratics may well have speculated on the physical components of the world, and on physical change, Democritus introduced the notion of αἰτία, 'cause-*cum*-explanation', into the discussion of physical 'principles', ἀρχαί. He is thus the first western thinker about whom one could even ask whether his system of thought was deterministic. Plato decided that it was, and he argued against it from his early dialogues right to the end, when in *Laws* 10 the question of multiple worlds, un-caring gods, and order and chance, is dealt with again in an ethical-*cum*-political context. Plato's response to Democritus in the *Republic, Sophist, Politicus, Philebus* and the *Laws* cannot be discussed here.

Chapter 10

⁴⁷¹ As regards Plato and Anaxagoras, I find myself in agreement with many of the observations put forward in summary fashion in Furley 1976, 80–3.

⁴⁷² Cf. Fujisawa 1974; Imaizumi 1996; Ebert 2004, esp. 372 f. For detailed study of *methexis* as a philosophical concept in Plato see Fronterotta 2001.

⁴⁷³ Cf. *Lysis* 220c; *Meno* 88c, and especially 100b; *Phaedo* 64c, 65c, 66a, 67a, c, e, 70a, 78d, 79d, 81c, and especially 83b. In terms of content most closely related is, of course, *Phaedo* 74a–75d. For a discussion of the phrase αὐτὸ καθ' αὑτό and related phenomena, cf. Vailati 1906; and see Introduction, pp. 14–19 above.

⁴⁷⁴ As is the case with the use of the term εἶδος, and with the concept of ἀνάμνησις, the triad 'size, health and strength', found at *Phaedo* 65d, is anticipated in the *Meno*, at 72d–e; cumulatively, this confirms that, even if one is not inclined to extrapolate from this one example, the *Meno* at least was written by Plato at a stage at which the ontological considerations reflected in the *Phaedo* had reached an advanced stage, or had already been developed altogether.

⁴⁷⁵ One may add Socrates' exercises in composition (60c–61c).

⁴⁷⁶ See Part I, ch. 1, sec. 8.

⁴⁷⁷ In the *Gorgias*, it is left open what is to be understood by 'the good'. The context is ambiguous.

⁴⁷⁸ Perhaps Plato here lets Socrates use σώφρων in the etymologizing sense of 'of sound mind'.

⁴⁷⁹ On possible implications of that for the character and person of Euenus, see Ebert 2001.

⁴⁸⁰ See Part I, ch. 1, sec. 7.

⁴⁸¹ Gallop 1993, 48 f.

⁴⁸² This, at least, may have been Plato's reading of Anaxagoras. For what Anaxagoras himself might have intended cf. Schofield 1980, esp. chs. 3 and 4.

[483] Ross 1951, 29.

[484] By this I do not mean that the phrase οὐ γὰρ ἔτι τοῦτο διισχυρίζομαι could be taken either as saying that Socrates does not insist on terminological niceties 'in addition' to his innovative ontological suggestion or as saying that once upon a time, he thought terminology was important, but he now does not 'any more/longer' think that this is the case. In theory, ἔτι may have either meaning. But, with most translators, I think that only the sense 'in addition' is intended here. The discussion in the text above is not meant to suggest that, after all, 'any more/longer' should be considered as a possibility.

[485] Part I, ch. 2, secs. 7 and 9.

[486] In addition, παρουσία of the good was a topic of discussion at *Lysis* 217b–218c; but this context may be later than the *Gorgias* and, as some think, even later than the *Phaedo*.

[487] Dodds 1959, 337 f.

[488] Literacy in 4th-century Greece was still the preserve of an elite. It is not outrageous to claim that an educated person who was inclined to read the *Phaedo* would, in all probability, previously have read at least the major Platonic dialogues earlier than the *Phaedo*, regardless of the form of publication, and regardless of the details of life and learning in the Academy.

[489] Cf. Coxon 1999, 27–34.

[490] Here, of course, μετέχειν or 'having of' clothes refers, on one level at least, to 'having some of' the clothes there are in the world, i.e. 'having a physical share', 'a part'; this parallels Anaxagorean usage.

[491] It is useful to bear all this in mind when one turns to the apparent criticism advanced in the *Parmenides*. It has been observed that μετέχειν as a term that denotes participation of a particular in a form is restricted to the *Phaedo*, *Symposium* 211b1–5, *Republic* 472c2 and 476d12 and the *Parmenides*. See in particular the careful study by Fujisawa 1974; in sec. 3 of his article, entitled 'appearance and disappearance of μετέχειν' (40–9), he provides *inter alia* a much needed revised and enhanced version of the table of 'words [Plato] uses from time to time to express the relation between Forms and particulars' compiled by Ross 1951, 228–30; while Fujisawa's article marks a definite advance in an understanding of Plato's usage and terminology, particularly in the *Phaedo* and *Parmenides*, I cannot agree with his general interpretation of the distinction between ἔχειν and μετέχειν as referring to 'having an immanent character' and 'participating in a Form' respectively; all those who assume that there are three things or types of thing, namely, e.g., the beautiful itself, the many beautiful things, and for each beautiful thing an immanent character, 'the beauty in it' or 'its beauty', do not take into account that the reason why there are 'immanent characters' or 'immanent forms' in addition to the many particulars in the final argument for the immortality of the soul in the *Phaedo* is precisely that without them Plato could not conclude this final proof (this is partly recognized by Imaizumi 1996; Imaizumi does, however, not draw the further conclusion that that is the only reason why there are 'immanent forms' in the *Phaedo*).

A couple more reflections on the relation between the *Phaedo* and the *Parmenides* may be in order. In the *Phaedo*, after having done his best to stress the incorporeality of the forms, Socrates introduces Anaxagorean 'spatial' language at the point of transition from his theoretical discussion to the interested proof of the immortality of the soul of the individual: τὸ ἐν ἡμῖν μέγεθος, 'the bigness in us', of *Phaedo* 102d5–6 is reminiscent of the Anaxagorean ἐν παντὶ γὰρ παντὸς μοῖρα ἔνεστιν, 'indeed, in everything there is a share of everything' (DK59B12; on this usage, see further below). If there are apparently 'immanent characters' in the *Parmenides*, that is because the first part of the *Parmenides* represents a critique of a particular reading of the *Phaedo*. Not only is the use of μετέχειν not widespread in the *Symposium* and the *Republic*, the word is absent as a philosophical term from the *Meno, Euthyphro, Phaedrus* and *Timaeus*. (One may wish to exclude *Republic* 472c2 as not concerned with forms, but that would not change the overall picture.) This serves to support the view that it is a particular reading of the *Phaedo* that is under investigation in that part of the *Parmenides*, just as other views of the world are at stake in other parts of the dialogue (cf. especially Coxon 1999, 164 f.). More specifically, it is an Anaxagorean reading of the *Phaedo* which gives rise to many of the confusions introduced in the first part of the *Parmenides*. In the *Phaedo*, Plato had used Anaxagorean language, with which the audience would have been familiar, but had stressed that if one chose to employ that sort of terminology, one should be aware that the constituents of the world which have proper explanatory force are, in contrast with Anaxagoras' analysis, not corporeal. The *Parmenides* demonstrates to what sorts of absurdities one is led when one associates the terminology of, *inter alia*, μετέχειν and μεταλαμβάνειν, in connection with Socratic 'types' or 'forms', with Anaxagorean corporeality. In a final twist in the *Parmenides*, Plato outdoes any 'literal' reading, or, if with Ryle 1939, 134, one regards this interpretation of participation as 'literal' mistaken, perhaps rather any 'Anaxagorean corporealising' reading of the *Phaedo* by alluding to another feature of Anaxagoras' world and transferring it, and its terminology, to an interpretation of what is meant by 'participation in forms': Anaxagoras (DK59B4) had spoken of other worlds besides our own, and in order to show that everything there is the same as here, he had repeatedly used the phrase (ὥσπερ) παρ' ἡμῖν, '(as) with us'; this terminology, too, is now employed by Parmenides in his absurd sophistic conclusion, advanced to test the young Socrates, that there are two worlds, that of us and that of the forms (cf. παρ' ἡμῖν at *Parmenides* 133c9, d2; 134a1, 9, 10, b4, c7, d1, 5, 6, e1, 2); this so-called two-world-theory haunts interpretations of Plato to this day.

To add a further point: when Parmenides treats the verbs μετέχειν and μεταλαμβάνειν as if the only relation they could refer to were that of the 'having of a physical part' of something, a further indication that this part of the argument is 'forced' and unnatural is the construction of μετέχειν and μεταλαμβάνειν with the genitive not only of the things participated in – that is normal usage – but also with the genitive of the word for part (*Parmenides* 131a4, c5,): μέρους μετέχειν, rather than μετέχειν μέρος τινός, is even more unnatural in Greek than the expression 'participating in a part of something' is in English; one either 'shares in something' or 'has a share of something'; one does not 'share in a share of something', unless the intended meaning is that the share itself is in turn subdivided; but this is clearly not the case in the *Parmenides*. However, only if this were the case would Parmenides be justified in proceeding with his criticisms of the young Socrates who is as yet unskilled in this sort of debate.

All of this is, of course, not a Platonic joke. There may well have been those who read the *Phaedo* in such a way, and who would confront Plato with similar objections. In a similar way, *Sophist* 248–9 suggests that there were other readings of the *Phaedo* which Plato felt the need to discuss. Aristotle's criticism of Plato and the Academy suggests that *he* may, at times, have read the *Phaedo* in a similar fashion; and it is uncertain to what extent he was convinced by the arguments presented in the *Parmenides*, and in particular the injunction by Parmenides to unravel the confusions presented in the first part of that dialogue.

Chapter 11

[492] Sider 2005, 128, translates the last sentence of B12: '...but in whatever there are things predominating, these things are, and were, most manifestly each one object.'

[493] Sider 2005, 110, translates the last sentence: 'For many (portions) are present in all things, equal in plentitude, both in the bigger and the smaller things being separated out.'

[494] Both μετέχειν and ἐνεῖναι are also found side by side, and in similar fashion to Anaxagoras, in Diogenes of Apollonia, DK64B5 = Fr. 9 (Laks). Diogenes may well have been implied in the discussion of 'what we think with' at *Phaedo* 96b and, as has been discussed in particular by Theiler 1922 and Laks 1983, Diogenes' νόησις would have been a better candidate than Anaxagoras' νοῦς if Socrates was looking for an intelligence which ordered things for the best. But while Diogenes may thus be implied, as it were as a pupil or follower of or successor to Anaxagoras (in the same way as Democritus, who is likewise not mentioned, was a successor to Anaxagoras?), this does not substantially affect the argument here constructed for Plato's method.

[495] A recent exponent of an interpretation along those lines is Ebert 2004, 372–89, whose section on 102a10–105b4 is entitled: 'Von den Ideen zu den essentiellen Eigenschaften'.

[496] Cf. Fujisawa 1974; Ebert 2004 .

[497] Or: τί ἐστιν. The difference in modern conventions of accentuation does not affect the issue at hand.

[498] For discussion see Bluck 1961, 209–13, commentary ad loc., and cf. footnote 364 on *Euthyphro* 11a–b in ch. 7, sec. 2, p. 319 above.

[499] Ross 1984.

[500] For a discussion of 'being in' in Aristotle, see Morison 2002, ch. 2, 'Being in', 54–80; specifically for a comparison of the two passages quoted in the text, and the relationship between the notions of 'having' and 'being in' in Aristotle, his section 'Having and being in', 76–8.

[501] Morison 2002, 71.

[502] I am grateful to Konrad Herrmann for prompting me to draw attention to the relevance for the *Phaedo* passage of distinctions like the one made explicit in the *Lysis*.

[503] I reserve discussion of *Phaedrus* 237d and *Philebus* 16d for separate treatment.

Conclusion

[504] Cf. Herrmann 2007 for an explication of how Plato develops this issue in the *Republic*; ibid. for use of εἶδος and ἰδέα in the *Republic*.

[505] The notion of 'being in', on the other hand, a notion also found in Anaxagoras and Diogenes, is not used by Plato in this context; when he introduces it into the argument for the immortality of the soul of the individual, this was, as we have seen, done for 'dramatic' purposes, for reasons of the economy of the dialogue as a work of literature; the topic of this dialogue was how Socrates even on his last day was stronger than his friends and prevented them from lamenting by telling them a persuasive story of consolation, based on the immortality of the soul of the individual. Outside this story, the notion of 'being in' does not seem to have a function.

[506] For mysticism in Empedocles and the Pythagorean tradition, see esp. Kingsley 1995. On how the *Phaedo*, including the final myth, is to be assessed against this background,

see e.g. the discussions in Ebert 2004 and, concerning esp. what happens before birth and after death, Herrmann 2004. Plato's own primary concern in the *Phaedo* is not the fate of the soul of the individual after death. The myth can best be understood as part of Socrates' strategy of persuasion within the dialogue, and as Plato's addressing a particular audience of educated readers, not, as has been suggested, necessarily Pythagorean.

BIBLIOGRAPHY

In the text and notes, the following abbreviations have been used:

DK   H. Diels and W. Kranz, *Die Fragmente der Vorsokratiker*, 6th edn, vols. I–III, Berlin, 1951–2.

LSJ   H.G. Liddell, R. Scott, and H.S. Jones, *A Greek-English Lexicon*, 9th edn, Oxford 1940.

OCT   Oxford Classical Texts.

OED   *The Oxford English Dictionary*, Oxford 1933.

OLD   *The Oxford Latin Dictionary*, Oxford 1982.

Adam, J. and Adam, A.M.
   1893   *Platonis* Protagoras, Cambridge.

Allan, D.J.
   1940   'Introduction', in J. Stenzel, *Plato's Method of Dialectic*, vii–xliii.

Allen, R.E. (ed.)
   1965   *Studies in Plato's* Metaphysics, London.
   1997   *Plato's* Parmenides, rev. edn, New Haven and London. 1st edn 1984.

Ammann, A.N.
   1953   -ΙΚΟΣ *bei Platon. Ableitung und Bedeutung mit Materialsammlung*, Freiburg, Switzerland.

Archer-Hind, R.D.
   1883   *The* Phaedo *of Plato*, London.
   1888   *The* Timaeus *of Plato*, London.

Arundel, M.R.
   1962   'Empedocles, fr. 35. 12–15', *CR* 12, 109–11.

Ast, F.
   1835–8   *Lexicon Platonicum*, Leipzig. Repr. Bonn 1956.

Bailey, C.
   1928   *The Greek Atomists and Epicurus*, Oxford.

Baldry, H.C.
   1937   'Plato's "Technical terms"', *CQ* 31, 141–50.

Balme, D.M.
   1962   'ΓΕΝΟΣ and ΕΙΔΟΣ in Aristotle's Biology', *CQ* 12, 81–98.

Barnes, J.
   1982   *The Presocratic Philosophers*, 2nd edn, London. 1st edn 1979.
   1987   *Early Greek Philosophy*, Harmondsworth.

Beck, W.
   1979   'ἠεροειδής', in B. Snell et al. (eds.) *Lexikon des frühgriechischen Epos*, 898.

Berger, H.H.
1961   *Ousia in de dialogen van Plato. Een terminologisch onderzoek*, Leiden.
Betegh, G.
2004   *The Derveni Papyrus. Cosmology, theology and interpretation*, Cambridge.
Blass, F.
1887   *Die attische Beredsamkeit* I, 2nd edn, Leipzig.
Bluck, R.S.
1955   *Plato's* Phaedo, London.
1961   *Plato's* Meno, Cambridge.
Bolotin, D.
1979   *Plato's Dialogue on Friendship. An interpretation of the* Lysis *with a new translation*, New York.
Bordt, M.
1998   *Platon*. Lysis, Göttingen.
Brandwood, L.
1976   *A Word Index to Plato*, Leeds.
Brommer, P.
1940   ΕΙΔΟΣ *et* ΙΔΕΑ. *Étude sémantique et chronologique*, Assen.
Buck, C.D.
1949   *A Dictionary of Selected Synonyms in the Principal Indo-European Languages*, Chicago. Repr. Chicago and London 1988.
1955   *The Greek Dialects*, Chicago.
Burkert, W.
1972   *Lore and Science in Ancient Pythagoreanism*, trans. E. Minar, Cambridge, Mass. German edn Nuremberg 1962.
Burnet, J.
1900–6 *Platonis Opera Omnia*, Oxford.
1911   *Plato's* Phaedo, Oxford.
1924   *Plato's* Euthyphro, Apology of Socrates *and* Crito, Oxford.
Burnyeat, M.F.
2003   'Apology 30b 2–4: Socrates, money, and the grammar of γίγνεσθαι', *JHS* 123, 1–25.
2005   'On the source of Burnet's construal of *Apology* 30b 2–4: a correction', *JHS* 125, 139–42.
Cairns, D.
1993   *Aidōs. The psychology and ethics of honour and shame in ancient Greek literature*, Oxford.
Cairns, D., Herrmann, F.G. and Penner, T. (eds.)
2007   *Pursuing the Good. Ethics and metaphysics in Plato's* Republic, Edinburgh.
Calvo, T. and Brisson, L.
1997   *Interpreting the* Timaeus-Critias, Sankt Augustin.
Campbell, L.
1867   *The* Sophist *and* Politicus *of Plato*, Oxford.
1894   'On Plato's use of language', in B. Jowett and L. Campbell, *Plato's* Republic, vol. II, 165–340.
Chantraine, P.
1933   *La formation des noms en grec ancien*, Paris. Repr. 1979.

Classen, C.J.

1959a   *Sprachliche Deutung als Triebkraft platonischen und sokratischen Philosophierens*, Munich.

1959b   'The study of language among Socrates' contemporaries', *Proceedings of the African Classical Associations* 2, 33–49, German transl. in Classen (ed.) *Sophistik*, Darmstadt, 1976, 215–47.

1960   *Untersuchungen zu Platons Jagdbildern*, Berlin.

Collinge, N.E.

1985   *The Laws of Indo-European*, Amsterdam and Philadelphia.

1989   'Thoughts on the Pragmatics of Ancient Greek', *PCPhS*, 1–13.

Cornford, F.M.

1937   *Plato's Cosmology. The* Timaeus *of Plato translated with a running commentary*, London.

Coxon, A.H.

1986   *The Fragments of Parmenides*, Assen and Maastricht.

1999   *The Philosophy of Forms. An analytical and historical commentary on Plato's* Parmenides, *with an English translation*, Assen.

Crawley, R.

1952   *Thucydides*. The History of the Peloponnesian War, trans. R. Crawley, rev. R. Feetham, Chicago.

Dale, A.T.

1987   'αὐτὰ τὰ ἴσα, *Phaedo* 74c1. A philosophical perspective', *AJP* 108, 384–99.

Devereux, D.T.

1994   'Separation and immanence in Plato's Theory of Forms', *Oxford Studies in Ancient Philosophy* 12, 63–90. Repr. in G. Fine (ed.) *Plato*, 1999, I, 192–214.

Diels, H. and Kranz, W.

1951–2   *Die Fragmente der Vorsokratiker*, 6th edn, vols. I–III, Berlin.

Diller, H.

1952   'Hippokratische Medizin und attische Philosophie', *Hermes* 80, 385–409.

1964   'Ausdrucksformen des methodischen Bewußtseins in den hippokratischen Epidemien', *Archiv für Begriffsgeschichte* 9, 133–50.

1971   'Zum Gebrauch von εἶδος und ἰδέα in vorplatonischer Zeit', in H.H. Euler et al. (eds.) *Medizingeschichte in unserer Zeit*, 23–30.

1975   'Das Selbstverständnis der griechischen Medizin in der Zeit des Hippokrates', in *La collection Hippocratique et son rôle dans l'histoire de la médecine*, Leiden, 77–93.

Dixsaut, M.

1991   'Ousia, eidos et idea dans le Phédon', *Revue Philosophique de la France et de l'Étranger* 116.4, 479–501. Repr. in M. Dixsaut, *Platon et la question de la pensée. Études Platoniciennes*, vol. I, Paris 2000, 71–91.

Dixsaut, M. and Brancacci, A. (eds.)

2002   *Platon. Source des Présocratiques. Exploration*, Paris.

Dodds, E.R.

1959   *Plato. Gorgias*, Oxford.

Dorter, K.

1982   *Plato's* Phaedo: *An interpretation*, Toronto.

Dover, K.J.
1968   *Aristophanes. Clouds*, Oxford.
1993   *Aristophanes. Frogs*, Oxford.

Ebert, T.
1994   *Sokrates als Pythagoreer und die Anamnesis in Platons* Phaidon, Stuttgart.
2001   'Why is Euenus called a philosopher at *Phaedo* 61c?', *CQ* 51, 423–34.
2004   *Platon. Phaidon*, Göttingen.

Else, G.F.
1938   'The terminology of the Ideas', *Harvard Studies in Classical Philology* 20, 17–51.

Ermerins, F.Z.
1859–64   *Hippocratis...reliquiae* I–III, Utrecht.

Eucken, C.
1983   *Isokrates. Seine Positionen in der Auseinandersetzung mit den zeitgenössischen Philosophen*, Berlin and New York.

Euler, H.H. et al. (eds.)
1971   *Medizingeschichte in unserer Zeit*, Stuttgart.

Festugière, A.-J.
1948   *Hippocrate. L'ancienne médecine*, Paris.

Fine, G. (ed.)
1993   *On Ideas*, Oxford.
1999   *Plato*, vols. 1–2, Oxford.

Forbes, W.H.
1895   *Thucydides.* Book I. Part II, Oxford.

Fraenkel, E.
1925   'Zur baltoslavischen Grammatik II.1', *Zeitschrift für vergleichende Sprachforschung auf dem Gebiete der indogermanischen Sprachen*, 53. Band, 1. Heft, Göttingen, 36–47.

Frank, E.
1923   *Plato und die sogenannten Pythagoreer*, Halle (Saale).

Frisk, H.
1973–9   *Griechisches Etymologisches Wörterbuch* I–III, 2nd edn, Heidelberg. 1st edn 1954–73.

Fronterotta, F.
2001   *Methexis. La teoria platonica delle idee e la partecipazione delle cose empiriche*, Rome.

Fujisawa, N.
1974   'ἔχειν, μετέχειν, and idioms of "Paradeigmatism" in Plato's Theory of Forms', *Phronesis* XIX, 30–58.

Furley, D.J.
1976   'Anaxagoras in response to Parmenides', in R.A. Shiner and J. King-Farlow (eds.) *New Essays on Plato and the Pre-Socratics,* 72–85.
1987   *The Greek Cosmologists*, vol. I, Cambridge.

Furley, D.J. and Allen, R.E. (eds.)
1975   *Studies in Presocratic Philosophy*, vol. II, London.

Gadamer, H.G.
1935   'Antike Atomtheorie', *Zeitschrift für die gesamte Naturwissenschaft*, 1, Heft

3, 81–95. Repr. in Gadamer (ed.) *Um die Begriffswelt der Vorsokratiker*, 512–33.

1973 'Die Unsterblichkeitsbeweise in Platos *Phaidon*', in *Wirklichkeit und Reflexion. Festschrift für Walter Schulz*, Pfullingen, 145–61. Repr. in H.-G. Gadamer, *Gesammelte Werke 6. Griechische Philosophie* II, Tübingen 1985, 187–201.

Gadamer, H.G. (ed.)

1968 *Um die Begriffswelt der Vorsokratiker*, Darmstadt.

Gallop, D.

1975 *Plato*. Phaedo, Oxford.

1993 *Plato*. Phaedo. Oxford World's Classics, Oxford.

Gifford, E.H.

1905 *The* Euthydemus *of Plato*, Oxford

Gill, C.

1996 *Personality in Greek Epic, Tragedy and Philosophy. The Self in dialogue*, Oxford.

Gillespie, C.M.

1912 'The use of Εἶδος and Ἰδέα in Hippocrates', *CQ* 6, 179–203.

Godley, A.D.

1926 *Herodotus* I, 2nd edn, Cambridge, Mass.

Goebel, K.

1910 *Die vorsokratische Philosophie*, Bonn.

Gomme, A.W.

1945 *An Historical Commentary on Thucydides* I, Oxford.

Gray, D.H.F.

1947 'Homeric epithets for things', *CQ* 41, 112.

Grube, G.M.A.

1935 *Plato's Thought*, London.

Hackforth, R.

1955 *Plato's* Phaedo, Cambridge.

Hager, M.E.

1962 'Philolaus and the Even-Odd', *CR* XII, 1–2.

Hamilton, W.

1971 *Plato*. Gorgias, Harmondsworth. 1st edn 1960.

Hamilton, W. and Emlyn-Jones, C.

2004 *Plato*. Gorgias, London.

Heinimann, F.

1961 'Eine vorplatonische Theorie der τέχνη', *Museum Helveticum* 18, 105–30.

Heitsch, E.

1991 *Parmenides. Die Fragmente*, 2nd edn, Munich. 1st edn 1974.

Herrmann, F.G.

1995 'Wrestling metaphors in Plato's *Theaetetus*', NIKEPHOROS 8, 77–109.

2003a 'μετέχειν, μεταλαμβάνειν and the problem of participation in Plato's ontology', *Philosophical Inquiry* 25, 19–56.

2003b 'φθόνος in the world of Plato's *Timaeus*', in D. Konstan and N.K. Rutter (eds.) *Envy, Spite and Jealousy*, 53–83.

2004 'Socrates' views on death', in V. Karasmanis (ed.) *Socrates: 2400 years since his death*, 185–99.

2005 'Plato's answer to Democritean determinism', in C. Natali and S. Maso (eds.) *La catena delle cause*, 37–55.

2006a 'εἶδος – Bedeutung und Gebrauch eines Fachausdruckes in Platons Phaidon', *Archiv für Begriffsgeschichte* 48, 7–26.

2006b 'οὐσία – in Plato's *Phaedo*', in Herrmann (ed.) *New Essays on Plato*, 43–73.

2007 'The idea of the good and the other forms in Plato's *Republic*', in D. Cairns, F.G. Herrmann and T. Penner (eds.) *Pursuing the Good*, 202–30.

Herrmann, F.G. (ed.)
2006 *New Essays on Plato. Language and thought in fourth-century Greek philosophy*, Swansea.

Herter, H.
1963 'Die Treffkunst des Arztes in hippokratischer und platonischer Sicht', *Sudhoffs Archiv für Geschichte der Medizin und der Naturwissenschaften* 47, 247–90.

Heubeck, A. and Hoekstra, A.
1989 *A Commentary on Homer's Odyssey* II, Oxford.

Hirzel, R.
1913 'οὐσία', *Philologus* 72, 42–64.

Hoffmann, M.
1996 *Die Entstehung von Ordnung. Zur Bestimmung von Sein, Erkennen und Handeln in der späteren Philosophie Platons*, Stuttgart and Leipzig.

Hofmann, J.B.
1950 *Griechisches etymologisches Wörterbuch*, Munich.

Hölscher, U.
1988 *Die Odyssee*, Munich.

Horn, C. and Rapp, C. (eds.)
2002 *Wörterbuch der antiken Philosophie*, Munich.

Hornblower, S.
1991 *A Commentary on Thucydides*, vol. I, Oxford.

Hornblower, S. and Spawforth, A. (eds.)
1996 *The Oxford Classical Dictionary*, Oxford

Huffman, C.
1993 *Philolaus of Croton. Pythagorean and Presocratic*, Cambridge.

2005 *Archytas of Tarentum. Pythagorean, philosopher and mathematician king*, Cambridge.

Imaizumi, T.
1996 '*Echein, Metechein* and predication in the *Phaedo*', *Journal of Classical Studies* 44. Reference is to the English abstract repr. in *Forty Years of the Journal of Classical Studies*, ed. by the Classical Society of Japan, Tokyo 1998, 368–70.

Impara, P.
1978 *Aspetti Semantici della Filosophia Platonica*, Rome.

Irwin, T.
1979 *Plato. Gorgias*, Oxford.

Jeanmart, G.
2003 '*Protagoras*'; '*Gorgias*'; '*Menon*', in A. Motte, C. Rutten and P. Somville (eds.) *Philosophie de la Forme*, 77–90.

Johansen, T.K.
   2004   *Plato's Natural Philosophy. A study of the Timaeus-Critias*, Cambridge.
Jones, W.H.S.
   1923/1923/1931   *Hippocrates* I, II, IV, Cambridge Mass. and London.
Jouanna, J.
   1990   *Hippocrate. L'ancienne médecine*, Paris.
Jowett, B.
   1970   *The Dialogues of Plato* II, ed. R.M. Hare and D.A. Russell, London.
Jowett, B. and Campbell, L.
   1894   *Plato's* Republic, vol. II, Oxford.
Kahn, C.H.
   1996   *Plato and the Socratic Dialogue*, Cambridge.
Kapp, E.
   c. 1940   'The Theory of Ideas in Plato's earlier dialogues', in Kapp *Ausgewählte Schriften*, 55–150.
   1968   *Ausgewählte Schriften*, Berlin.
Karasmanis, V. (ed.)
   2004   *Socrates: 2400 years since his death*, Delphi and Athens.
Kingsley, P.
   1994   'Review of Huffmann 1993', *CR* XLIV, 294–6.
   1995   *Ancient Philosophy, Mystery and Magic. Empedocles and Pythagorean tradition*, Oxford.
Kirk, G.S., Raven, J.E. and Schofield, M.
   1983   *The Presocratic Philosophers*, 2nd edn, Cambridge.
Koller, H.
   1960   'Die dihäretische Methode', *Glotta* 39, 6–24.
Konstan, D. and Rutter, N.K.
   2003   *Envy, Spite and Jealousy. The rivalrous emotions in Ancient Greece*, Edinburgh.
Kühn, J.H.
   1956   *System- und Methodenprobleme im Corpus Hippocraticum*, Wiesbaden.
Kühn, J.H. and Fleischer, U. (eds.)
   1986, 1989   *Index Hippocraticus* I–II, Göttingen.
Kühner, R. and Gerth, W.
   1898   *Griechische Grammatik* II. *Syntax*, vols. I–II, 3rd edn, Hanover.
Laks, A.
   1983   *Diogène d'Apollonie: la dernière cosmologie présocratique*, Lille.
Lacey, A.R.
   1986   *Dictionary of Philosophy*, 2nd edn, London. 1st edn 1976.
Lamb, W.R.M.
   1925   *Plato.* Lysis, Symposium, Gorgias, Cambridge, Mass.
Lefka, A.
   2003   'Phédon'; 'Banquet', in A. Motte, C. Rutten and P. Somville (eds.) *Philosophie de la Forme*, 91–114.
Leggewie, O.
   1978   *Platon.* Euthyphron, Stuttgart.

Liddell, H.G., Scott, R. and Jones, H.S.

1940   *A Greek-English Lexicon*, 9th edn, Oxford.

Lloyd, G.E.R.

1974   'The Hippocratic question', *CQ* (NS) 68, 171–92.

Löbl, R.

1987   *Demokrits Atomphysik*, Darmstadt.

1989   *Demokrit. Texte zu seiner Philosophie*, Amsterdam and Atlanta.

Long, A.A. (ed.)

1999   *Early Greek Philosophy*, Cambridge.

Luria, S.

1964   *Zur Frage der materialistischen Begründung der Ethik bei Demokrit*, Berlin.

Lyons, J.

1969   *Structural Semantics. An analysis of part of the vocabulary of Plato*, Oxford.

McCabe, M.M.

1994   *Plato's Individuals*, Princeton.

2000   *Plato and his Predecessors*, Cambridge.

McKirahan, R.D.

1994   *Philosophy Before Socrates*, Indianapolis.

Mader, B.

1991   'μορφή', in B. Snell et al. (eds.) *Lexikon des frühgriechischen Epos*, col. 424.

Mansfeld, J.

1987   *Die Vorsokratiker*, Stuttgart.

Marchant, E.C.

1905   *Thucydides* I, London.

Marten, R.

1962   OΥΣΙΑ *im Denken Platons*, Meisenheim am Glan.

Meier-Brügger, M.

1991   *Griechische Sprachwissenschaft* I, Berlin.

Meillet, A.

1924   'Le développement du verbe "avoir"', in ANTΙΔΩΡΟΝ. *Festschrift Jacob Wackernagel*, Göttingen, 9–13.

Meinhardt, H.

1968   *Teilhabe bei Platon*, Freiburg and Munich.

1976   'Idee', in J. Ritter and K. Gründer (eds.) *Historisches Wörterbuch der Philosophie*, 59–60.

Merkelbach, R. and West, M.L.

1967   *Fragmenta Hesiodea*, Oxford.

Mitchell, T.

1832   *Index Graecitatis Platonicae*, Oxford.

Morel, P.-M.

2002   'Le *Timée*, Démocrite et la Nécessité', in M. Dixsaut and A. Brancacci (eds.) *Platon. Source des Présocratiques,* 129–50.

Morison, B.

2002   *On Location. Aristotle's concept of place*, Oxford.

Morrow, G.

1950   'Necessity and persuasion in Plato's *Timaeus*', *Philosophical Review*, 59, 147–64. Repr. in R.E. Allen (ed.) *Studies in Plato's Metaphysics*, 1965, 421–37.

Motte, A.
  2003   *Les Philosophes Préclassiques*, in A. Motte, C. Rutten and P. Somville (eds.) *Philosophie de la Forme*, 19–63.
Motte, A., Rutten, C. and Somville, P. (eds.)
  2003   *Philosophie de la Forme*. Eidos, Idea, Morphé *dans la philosophie grecque des origines à Aristote*, Louvain-la-Neuve.
Nails, D.
  2002   *The People of Plato. A prosopography of Plato and other Socratics*, Indianapolis and Cambridge.
Natali, C.
  2003   'Le cause del *Timeo* e la teoria delle quattro cause', in T. Calvo and L. Brisson (eds.) *Interpreting the* Timaeus-Critias, 207–14.
Natali, C. and Maso, S. (eds.)
  2003   *Plato Physicus. Cosmologia e antropologia nel* Timeo, Amsterdam.
  2005   *La catena delle cause*, Amsterdam.
Natorp, P.
  1893   *Die Ethika des Demokritos. Text und Untersuchungen*, Marburg. Repr. Hildesheim and New York 1970.
Nelson, A.
  1909   *Die hippokratische Schrift* Περὶ φυσῶν. *Text und Studien*, Uppsala.
Nordheier, H.W.
  1991   'θεοειδής'; 'μυλοειδής', in B. Snell et al. (eds.) *Lexikon des frühgriechischen Epos,* II, coll. 281, 996.
Onions, C.T., Friedrichsen, G.W.S. and Burchfield, R.W. (eds.)
  1966   *The Oxford Dictionary of English Etymology*, Oxford.
Onions, C.T. et al. (eds.)
  1973   *The Shorter Oxford English Dictionary*, 3rd edn 1944, reset with revised etymologies and addenda, Oxford.
Paley, F.A.
  1872   *Euripides. With an English commentary*, vol. I, London.
Places, É. des
  1964   *Lexique de la langue philosophique et religieuse de Platon*, Paris.
Plamböck, G.
  1964   *Dynamis im Corpus Hippocraticum*, Wiesbaden.
Plath, R.
  1987   'Hauchdissimilation im Mykenischen', *Münchner Studien zur Sprachwissenschaft* 48, 187–93.
Poschenrieder, F.
  1882   *Die platonischen Dialoge in ihrem Verhältnisse zu den hippokratischen Schriften*, Metten.
Potter, P.
  1988, 1988, 1994, 1995   *Hippocrates* V–VIII, Cambridge Mass. and London.
Rechenauer, G.
  1991   *Thukydides und die hippokratische Medizin*, Hildesheim.
Reinhardt, K.
  1916   *Parmenides und die Geschichte der griechischen Philosophie*, Bonn.

Riddell, J.
1857   *The Apology of Plato, with...a Digest of Platonic Idioms*, Oxford.
Ritter, C.
1910   *Neue Untersuchungen über Platon*, Munich.
Ritter, J. and Gründer, K. (eds.)
1976   *Historisches Wörterbuch der Philosophie*, Band 4, Basel and Stuttgart.
Ritter, J., Gründer, K. and Gabriel, G. (eds.)
1971–2004   *Historisches Wörterbuch der Philosophie*, Basel.
Robinson, D.B.
1986   'Plato's *Lysis*. The structural problem', *ICS* XI, 63–83.
1990   'Homeric φίλος', in E.M. Craik (ed.) *Owls to Athens*, Oxford.
Robinson, R.
1953   *Plato's Earlier Dialectic*, Oxford.
Roskam, G.
2003   '*Hippias mineur, Alcibiade* I, *Apologie, Euthyphron, Criton, Hippias majeur, Lysis, Charmide, Lachès*', in A. Motte, C. Rutten and P. Somville (eds.) *Philosophie de la Forme*, 67–76.
Ross, D.
1924   *Aristotle*. Metaphysics. *A revised text with introduction and commentary*, 2 vols., Oxford. Repr. 1997.
1951   *Plato's Theory of Ideas*, Oxford.
Rowe, C.J.
1993   *Plato*. Phaedo, Cambridge.
1995   *Plato*. Politicus, Warminster.
Ryle, G.
1939   'Plato's *Parmenides*', *Mind* 48, 129–51 and 302–25.
1966   *Plato's Progress*, Cambridge.
Sandoz, C.
1972   *La notion de la forme en Grec ancien*, Fribourg.
Saunders, T.J. (ed.)
1987   *Plato. Early Socratic dialogues*, Harmondsworth.
Scaltsas, T.C.
1989   'The logic of the dilemma of participation and of the Third Man argument', *Apeiron* 22, 67–90.
Schiefsky, M.J.
2005   *Hippocrates* On Ancient Medicine, Leiden.
Schofield, M.
1980   *An Essay on Anaxagoras*, Cambridge.
1996   Article '*Zeno* (1)', in S. Hornblower and A. Spawforth (eds.) *The Oxford Classical Dictionary*, 16–34.
2003   'The Presocratics', in D. Sedley (ed.) *Greek and Roman Philosophy*, 42–72.
Schwyzer, E.
1939, 1950   *Griechische Grammatik* I–II, Munich.
Sedley, D.
1989   'Teleology and Myth in the *Phaedo*', *Proceedings of the Boston Area Colloquium in Ancient Philosophy* 5, 359–83.

1998   'Platonic Causes', *Phronesis* 43, 114–32.

2003   *Plato's* Cratylus, Cambridge.

Sedley, D. (ed.)

2003   *Greek and Roman Philosophy*, Cambridge.

Sharples, R.

1993   *Plato:* Meno, 3rd edn, Warminster. 1st edn 1985.

Shiner, R.A. and King-Farlow, J. (eds.)

1976   *New Essays on Plato and the Pre-Socratics. Canadian Journal of Philosophy, Supplementary Volume* II, Guelph, Ontario.

Shorey, P.

1911   'Review of A.E. Taylor, *Varia Socratica*', *CP* VI, 361–5.

1930, 1935   *Plato.* Republic I/II, Cambridge, Mass.

Sider, D.

2005   *The Fragments of Anaxagoras.* Introduction, text and commentary, 2nd edn, Sankt Augustin.

Smith, R.

1978   'Mass terms, generic expressions, and Plato's Theory of Forms', *Journal for the History of Philosophy* 16, 141–53.

Snell, B.

1924   *Die Ausdrücke für den Begriff des Wissens in der vorplatonischen Philosophie*, Berlin.

1946a   *Die Entdeckung des Geistes*, Hamburg.

1946b   'Die naturwissenschaftliche Begriffsbildung im Griechischen', in Snell 1946a, 217–34. Repr. in H.G. Gadamer (ed.) *Um die Begriffswelt der Vorsokratiker*, 1968, 21–42.

Snell, B. et al. (eds.)

1979–   *Lexikon des frühgriechischen Epos*, Göttingen.

Solmsen, F.

1971   'Parmenides and the description of perfect beauty in Plato's *Symposium*', *AJP* 92, 1, 62–70.

Sommerstein, A.H.

1982   *Aristophanes.* Clouds, Warminster.

Stenzel, J.

1921   'Über den Einfluß der griechischen Sprache auf die philosophische Begriffs-bildung', *Neue Jahrbücher für das klassische Altertum und Pädagogik*, 46, 152 ff. Repr. in Stenzel, *Kleine Schriften zur griechischen Philosophie*, 72–84.

1940   *Plato's Method of Dialectic*, trans. D.J. Allan, Oxford. 2nd German edn, Leipzig and Berlin 1931.

1956   *Kleine Schriften zur griechischen Philosophie*, Darmstadt.

Stokes, M.C.

1971   *One and Many in Presocratic Philosophy*, Washington, D.C. and Cambridge, Mass.

1976   'Anaximander's argument', in R.A. Shiner and J. King-Farlow (eds.) *New Essays on Plato and the Pre-Socratics*, 1–22.

Strange, S.K.

1985   'The double explanation in the *Timaeus*', *Ancient Philosophy* 5, 25–39. Repr. in G. Fine (ed.) *Plato*, 397–415.

Taylor, A.E.

1911a   *Varia Socratica. First Series*, Oxford.

1911b   'The Words εἶδος, ἰδέα in pre-Platonic literature', in Taylor, *Varia Socratica*, 178–267.

1928   *A Commentary on Plato's* Timaeus, Oxford.

Taylor, C.C.W.

1976   *Plato.* Protagoras, Oxford.

1999a   *The Atomists. Leucippus and Democritus. Fragments*, Toronto.

1999b   'The atomists', in A.A. Long (ed.) *Early Greek Philosophy*, 181–204.

Teloh, H.

1981   *The Development of Plato's* Metaphysics, University Park and London.

Theiler, W.

1925   *Zur Geschichte der teleologischen Naturbetrachtung bis auf Aristoteles*, Zurich and Leipzig.

Thompson, E.S.

1901   *The* Meno *of Plato*, London.

Thompson, W.H.

1905   *The* Gorgias *of Plato*, London.

Treu, M.

1954   *Sappho*, Munich.

Vailati, G.

1906   'A study of Platonic terminology', *Mind* 15, 473–85.

Vancamp, B.

1996   'κατὰ ταὐτὰ ἔχειν. Zur Herkunft einer platonischen Redewendung aus dem Bereich der Ideenlehre', *Rheinisches Museum* 139, 352–4.

Vlastos, G.

1954   'The Third Man argument in the Parmenides', *Philosophical Review* 63. Repr. in R.E. Allen (ed.) *Studies in Plato's* Metaphysics, 231–64.

1973a   *Platonic Studies*, Princeton.

1973b   'The individual as object of love in Plato'. Appendix I: 'Is the *Lysis* a vehicle of Platonic doctrine?', in Vlastos, *Platonic Studies*, 35–7.

1973c   'An ambiguity in the *Sophist*', in Vlastos, *Platonic Studies*, 270–322.

v. Fritz, K.

1938   *Philosophie und sprachlicher Ausdruck bei Demokrit, Platon und Aristoteles*. Repr. 1962, Darmstadt.

1943   'νόος and νοεῖν in the Homeric poems', *CP* 38, 79–93.

1945   'νοῦς, νοεῖν and their derivatives in pre-Socratic philosophy (excluding Anaxagoras)', *CP* 40, 223–42.

1946   'νοῦς, νοεῖν and their derivatives in pre-Socratic philosophy (excluding Anaxagoras)', *CP* 41, 12–34.
   (v. Fritz 1943, 1945, 1946 reprinted as v. Fritz 1968.)

1968   'Die Rolle des Nous', German transl. of v. Fritz 1943, 1945, 1946, by P. Wilpert, in H.G. Gadamer (ed.) *Um die Begriffswelt der Vorsokratiker*, 246–363.

Walde, A. and Hofmann, J.B.

1965   *Lateinisches etymologisches Wörterbuch* I–III, Heidelberg.

Walde, A. and Pokorny, J.

1930–2   *Vergleichendes etymologisches Wörterbuch der indogermanischen Sprachen* I–III, Berlin and Leipzig.

Warner, R. (tr.)

1954   *Thucydides. The History of the Peloponnesian War*, trans. R. Warner, London.

Waterfield, R.

1994   *Plato.* Gorgias, Oxford.

Watt, D.

1987   '*Lysis. Charmides*, translated and introduced by D. Watt', in T.J.Saunders (ed.) *Plato. Early Socratic dialogues*, 117–61.

Wayte, W.

1883   *Platonis* Protagoras, 4th edn, Cambridge.

Weidauer, K.

1954   *Thukydides und die Hippokratischen Schriften*, Heidelberg.

West, M.L.

1966   *Hesiod.* Theogony, Oxford.

1978   *Hesiod.* Works and Days, Oxford.

1989   *Iambi et Elegi Graeci* I, 2nd edn, Oxford.

1993   *Greek Lyric Poetry*, Oxford.

Wieland, W.

1982   *Platon und die Formen des Wissens*, Göttingen.

Wilamowitz-Moellendorff, U. von

1919   *Platon*, vols. I–II, Berlin. References to vol. II are to the Dublin/Zurich edn 1969.

Williamson, H.

1904   *The* Phaedo *of Plato*, London.

Withington, E.T.

1928   *Hippocrates* III, Cambridge, Mass. and London.

Zeller, E.

1919–20   *Die Philosophie der Griechen in ihrer geschichtlichen Entwicklung*, vol. I, sixth edn, rev. by W. Nestle, Leipzig. Repr. as 7th edn 1963; 8th edn 2006, Darmstadt.

INDEX LOCORUM

359

7.538d6–e3   321 n.375
8.544c   324 n.419
9.585   199
10.596a   294 n.143
10.596b   307 n.262
10.597e10–598a3   294 n.143,
   330–1 n.446
Sophist
217a   323 n.399
219   199
246a   278
247a5   45, 289 n.79
248–9   336 n.491
Symposium
199c–d   322 n.394
207e, 209b–c   146
210e–211e   14
211a–b   18 f.
211a8, 211a8–b2   14
211b   321 n.383
211b1–5   335 n.491
211b7–d1   14
Theaetetus
153b   289 n.79
155d2–4   xi
160b10   19
Timaeus
28a–c   332 n.466
30c4   324 n.419
48a   242, 332 n.465
54d f.   312 n.304
90c–d   257
Plutarch
Against Colotes
8.1110F–1111A   160 f., 239
De facie quae in orbe lunae apparet
926d   127
Proclus *In Parmenidem*
619.30–620.1, 632.6–15,
   788.29–31   11, 281 n.20
Protagoras
80B3   293 n.113
80B4   154

Sappho
fr. 54   30
Schol. Basilii   160

Seneca
Ep. 58.19, 65.7   332 n.456
Sextus Empiricus
Adversus Mathematicos
7.116 f.   160
9.127   258
9.129   183
Simonides
8.4   50
50.4   297 n.179
Simplicius
In 'De caelo'
7.294, 33–295, 24   313 n.309
7.295.1–9   236–8
7.529.28   316 n.352
Physica
32.11   153
34.28   82, 155
44.9 f.   312 n.295
151.28   156
152.22–153.4   83 f.
155.23   82, 156
159.13   184
164.24   253
164.25   83, 252
300.27   160
327.24   160, 166
Solon
4.9 f.   49
11.6   79
24.1–4   49 f.
Sophocles
Antigone
213–4   80
253 f.   51
Electra
197 f.   317 n.355
368–9   81
948 f.   55 f.
958–62   51 f.
1031 f.   52, 59, 81
1165–9   29
1177   109
1243–4   79
1250   291 n.99
1328   294 n.134

INDEX RERUM

MAR 1 1 2009